Grenada to the Virgin Islands

A cruising guide to the Lesser Antilles

JACQUES PATUELLI

Translated by Stephen Davies and
Elaine Morgan

Imray Laurie Norie and Wilson

THE LESSER ANTILLES

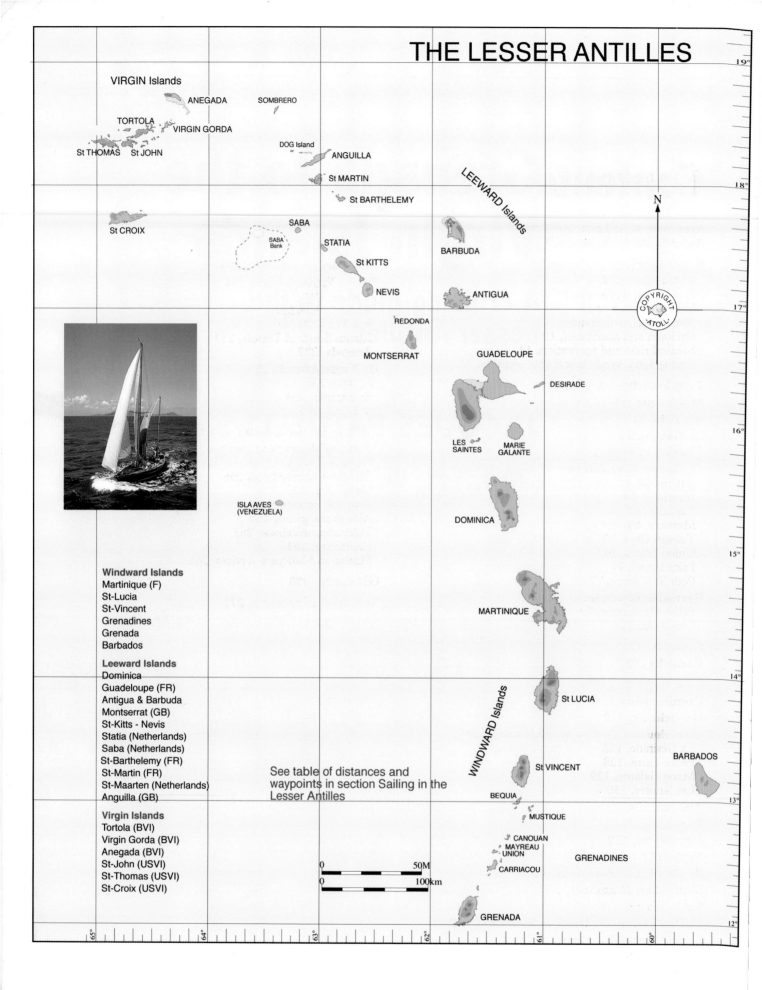

VIRGIN Islands

ANEGADA

SOMBRERO

TORTOLA

VIRGIN GORDA

St THOMAS   St JOHN

DOG Island

ANGUILLA

St MARTIN

St BARTHELEMY

LEEWARD Islands

SABA

St CROIX

SABA
Bank

STATIA

St KITTS

NEVIS

BARBUDA

ANTIGUA

N

REDONDA

MONTSERRAT

GUADELOUPE

DESIRADE

LES
SAINTES

MARIE
GALANTE

ISLA AVES
(VENEZUELA)

DOMINICA

MARTINIQUE

Windward Islands
Martinique (F)
St-Lucia
St-Vincent
Grenadines
Grenada
Barbados

Leeward Islands
Dominica
Guadeloupe (FR)
Antigua & Barbuda
Montserrat (GB)
St-Kitts - Nevis
Statia (Netherlands)
Saba (Netherlands)
St-Barthelemy (FR)
St-Martin (FR)
St-Maarten (Netherlands)
Anguilla (GB)

Virgin Islands
Tortola (BVI)
Virgin Gorda (BVI)
Anegada (BVI)
St-John (USVI)
St-Thomas (USVI)
St-Croix (USVI)

St LUCIA

BARBADOS

See table of distances and
waypoints in section Sailing in the
Lesser Antilles

St VINCENT

BEQUIA

MUSTIQUE

CANOUAN
MAYREAU
UNION

CARRIACOU

GRENADINES

0   50M
0   100km

GRENADA

COPYRIGHT
·ATOLL·

Contents

Published by
Imray Laurie Norie & Wilson Ltd
Wych House, St Ives Cambridgeshire PE27 45BT England
☎ +44(0)1480 462114 *Fax* +44(0)1480 496109
Email ilnw@imray.com www.imray.com

Original published in France as **Guide des Antilles - Croisière et
Tourisme** 2002 by Les Editions Atoll, 631 Avenue Ronsard 83700
Saint-Raphaël, France
☎ 00 33 (0) 4 94 95 40 39 *Fax* 00 33 (0)4 94 95 74 88
Email edition-attoll@wanadoo.fr
www.antilles-guide.com

Design and authorship Jacques Patuelli helped by Marie José Demoulin with
the assistance of Valérie Sangrouber, Céline Hibon

Cartographical design Jacques Patuelli helped by Carole Patuelli, Cyrille
Dubois, Eric Guillemot, Stephan Pouzan

Photographs Jacques Patuelli, Eric Guillemot

Graphics and page make-up Marie José Demoulin, Cyrille Dubois, Jacques
Patuelli

A catalogue record for this book is available from the British Library.

ISBN 0 85288 680 2

CAUTION
While every care has been taken to ensure accuracy, neither the
Publishers nor the Author will hold themselves responsible for errors,
omissions or alterations in this publication. They will at all times be
grateful to receive information which tends to the improvement of the
work.

To improve future editions, you are invited to let the author know your
opinions and observations. Please post, fax or email them to:

Imray Laurie Norie & Wilson Ltd
Wych House, The Broadway, St Ives,
Cambridgeshire PE27 5BT England
☎ +(0)1480 462114
Fax +(0)1480 496109
Email ilnw@imray.com
www.imray.com

Printed in Italy by Eurolitho SpA, Milan

An invitation to the islands

In the Antilles every island offers you a warm welcome. You're tempted by one after another, each more tantalising than the last and never far away – just let yourself be carried along on the magic carpet of the trade winds to live and sail far from the perils of the deep.

Jacques Patuelli

For those able to explore them, the Lesser Antilles – a garden of Eden randomly scattered in a dusting of islands – offer all the beauties of nature. Mountainous islands covered with thick vegetation where fumaroles and waterfalls from the same volcanic heart alternate their dances of fire and water. Coral islands with white sand beaches protected from ocean seas by immense barrier reefs where fish and coral are a dazzling blend of colour. And to perfect and unite this diversity, the same ocean swells crash on every shore and the same trade winds soften the tropical climate.

We could have been satisfied with this varied natural bounty and left the idyllic panorama for its ethnically and linguistically similar indigenous peoples. But after the discovery of the 'West Indies' by Europeans, their spirit of conquest soon destroyed the Amerindians. And then the greed of just a few re-populated the islands with imported labour, mostly Africans reduced to slavery. Today's Antillean population is a result of a varied mix of African peoples, the old European colonists and the later addition of people from Asia: an uncommon racial, cultural and linguistic melting pot. The fortunes of war and peace and the hazards of five centuries of tortured history added yet more to the imbroglio, fragmenting this small archipelago into fourteen states and territories with different legal systems, three national languages and several patois and local tongues.

All this occurs in just forty small, inhabited islands and islets, some minuscule, with a surface area totalling barely 8,000 square kilometres and a population of 1,700,000. All these divisions and differences may have created (and still create) economic and political difficulties, but they also offer an incredible range of possibilities for the visitor.

There is just too much choice, from one island with a fully developed modern infrastructure to another nearby which is almost undiscovered, where the clock of history seems to have been put back half a century. For those who wish to escape from over-organised and overcrowded tourist trails – for, understandably, the Lesser Antilles are attracting more and more admirers – the possibilities are endless. So don't be nostalgic for the Antilles of yesteryear: the islands still have many little-trodden paths and numerous almost deserted inlets for wanderers to discover according to their taste, the means at their disposal and the time they have to spare.

A word of warning, though: to avoid inconvenience and losing time when you arrive, be sure to gather as much information as possible before you set out. Remember that the geographical, political and linguistic variety of the Lesser Antilles doesn't make it easy to get hold of reliable information. To help your trip or cruise be a success, or to choose an island or route, this guide brings together between two covers the maximum amount of information for both sailor and tourist. It will help you learn more about the whole Lesser Antilles archipelago from Grenada to the Virgin Islands.

In the pages that follow you'll find thousands of facts to help you get to the archipelago, stay there, voyage its coasts, explore its inlets, learn more about its history, customs, present-day situation and arrivals procedures. To enhance the prolific descriptions we have added hundreds of photographs showing the charm of the countryside and daily life. There are also aerial views, complemented by numerous plans and charts, which detail both the topography of each island to aid your visit and the coastline to assist your navigation.

So, when the real island hauls over the horizon, you'll be ready to explore and find out more.

Introduction

A short history

The Amerindian Peoples

Arawaks and Caribs

Over the centuries a diverse mixture of people from the South American continent migrated to the Antilles. Several hundred years ago the Arawaks occupied the whole archipelago. A generally peace-loving people, most of their lives were spent growing food, fishing and making pottery. But they also knew how to take a break and would smoke tobacco in the comfort of their hammocks, the most remarkable of all their inventions. This easy-going life was brutally interrupted around the 12th century by fearsome tribes of Caribs (or Kalinas), also from South America.

The new conquerors were redoubtable warriors and cannibals to boot. (The Indian name 'Kalinas', which means ferocious people, has given us, via Spanish, the word cannibal.)

The Caribs cooked the conquered Arawak males in their own pots, but kept the females for their amusement and to keep the art of their pottery alive.

After this warlike interlude, all might have gone on as before in this best of

Caribbean worlds if, in distant Europe, hardy sailors hadn't wished to discover where the ends of the Earth lay and, without knowing anything about it, a Pope hadn't divided it into two parts.

Discovered by Columbus

The sea route to the East Indies was a Portuguese monopoly. They had discovered it not long previously by sailing round the tip of Africa. The Earth had been thought to be round since the time of the famous Greek philosopher Aristotle. So Christopher Columbus, a native of Genoa, proposed to the Spanish monarchs, Isabella of Castile and John of Aragon, that he could reach the fabled 'Spice Route' by going westabout.

On the 12 October 1492 the three ships of the small fleet (the *Pinta*, the *Nina* and the *Santa Maria*) made landfall on an island in the Bahamas, which the locals called Guanahani. In thanks, Columbus baptised it St Salvador (St Saviour). After that Columbus found Cuba and Hispaniola and declared them Spanish territory without any thought for the last Arawaks, fleeing from their Carib enemies, who had found a final refuge there. Spanish colonisation was to set in train their extinction.

Over three successive further voyages (1493, 1498 and 1502), Christopher Columbus discovered almost all the Antilles and named them either as fancy took him or according to the liturgy of the times. But his conviction that he had arrived at the gates of Asia, whether real or simulated, led him falsely to label the islands as a whole the West Indies.

Their second name, the Antilles, was a complete product of the imagination, deriving its origins from the Isle of Antilia, placed at the edges of the ocean by the ancient cartographers.

Conquest and Filibusters

No conquest is philanthropic, and it was the thirst for gold that drove Spanish colonisation. Ignoring the Lesser Antilles, the Spaniards occupied the larger islands where gold at least existed, if not in abundance. Their greed worked against them because by the 16th century the English, French and Dutch had established themselves in the smaller islands in order to intercept the rich treasure fleets on their return voyages to Spain.

This is the origin of the romantic figures of the filibusters whose ships, lying in ambush in the maze of islands, fell upon the Spanish on every occasion that presented itself. If they had a 'letter of marque' from their king, they were privateers and wore their national flags. The rest were pirates, outside the law until captured and hanged. That risk redoubled their legendary ferocity; they were 'beyond faith and law', as their skull and crossbones emblem, the Jolly Roger, bore witness.

A replica of a galleon

Depending on the ups and downs of the alliances and wars which raged in Europe, the French and English royal fleets shared in the pillage. Already weakened by the defeat of its invincible Armada off the English coast, Spain was soon unable to ensure its monopoly over the West Indies and from the 17th century on, it definitively abandoned all its claims on the Lesser Antilles.

The major targets of plunder, gold and treasure from the first days of conquest soon dried up. The filibusters died out of their own accord and the pirates who hadn't been hanged or killed in combat joined them. Nothing was left save the legend of the Brotherhood of the Coast. What followed was the epoch of the colonialists.

Colonisation and slavery

This period in the smaller islands is tied to the establishment of systematic agriculture, particularly of sugar cane. For a while sugar became the 'white gold' of the colonies, as spices had been in their time. The plantations, however, needed enormous quantities of labour but the conquerors had decimated the peaceful Arawaks and the hard labour of the plantations killed off the last few survivors. In the Lesser Antilles efforts were made to meet the shortfall in labour by using indentured labourers, more or less volunteers, who came from Europe under contracts of misery and exploitation. So, as the Spanish had done before them, the English, French and Dutch turned to Africa's reservoir of humanity and the trade in slaves.

This traffic, which the Portuguese began as early as the 15th century, was in contradiction of every consideration of equity and humanity. It offered slave labour for the least cost, and all under the benign gaze of the church and the authorities of the time. It is from that massive transfer by slave ships of the African population (called, as mere cargo, 'ebony') that the ethnic origins of almost all today's Antillean people stem.

What followed over nearly two centuries, particularly between the French and English, was a struggle without quarter over possession of the most fertile islands and over supremacy at sea. It began back in 1626 when, during a short-lived alliance against the Spanish, the two countries peaceably divided the island of St Kitts between them. This first colony was called the Mother of the Lesser Antilles, and it was from there that the colonists moved outwards to all the rest.

From the end of the 17th century until 1815, the struggle was continuous. The rivalry caused an unbelievable turnover in the sovereignty of some of the islands, even the smallest of them. For example, St Lucia changed hands fourteen times before becoming English. It has retained all its French place names and French patois.

Although treaties were made with the fierce Amerindian Caribs from time to time, the real aim was conquest. Despite the odd soldier who got lost and ended up on the roasting spit, firearms ruled. In the end the redoubtable Carib warriors faced inevitable defeat.

Some threw themselves into the sea from cliffs, as at Carib's Leap in Grenada. In St Vincent and Dominica they disappeared into the impenetrable thickets of the interior. The sole remnants, a group of a few hundred, survived on the windward coast of Dominica.

Although punctuated by numerous treaties, the Anglo-French-Dutch land and sea wars (among which was the famous Battle of the Saintes) didn't end until after the Napoleonic Wars. The Treaty of Paris (1814-15) definitively established sovereign claims. France kept Martinique, Guadeloupe and its dependencies, but lost all its other possessions. The British Empire took the lion's share, establishing its authority over the majority of the Lesser Antilles. The Dutch in Sint Maarten, Saba and Statia, and the Danes in the Virgin Is, kept what they started out with. From that point on any change of ownership was a peaceful financial transaction as, for example when France got back St Barthélemy and the Danish sold the Virgin Is to the Americans.

The end of slavery and colonisation

If peace at last reigned in the Lesser Antilles, the problem of slavery nevertheless remained. At bottom the prosperity of the islands was factitious because it depended on the enslavement of that section of the population who hailed from Africa. From the 18th century on numerous slave revolts broke out, though they were always violently suppressed. But over the same period in Europe the Enlightenment had awoken many minds to more humanitarian and egalitarian principles.

The French Revolution put these into effect with the abolition of slavery in 1794, but in 1802 Napoleon Bonaparte re-established it, perhaps influenced by his wife Joséphine, a noblewoman of Martinique Creole extraction. Slavery was re-imposed on the large island of Santo Domingo, resulting in a revolt led by Toussaint Louverture, a black ex-footman who rose to the rank of general. He united black and mixed race slaves and former slaves to expel the French soldiers and colonists from Santo Domingo. Part of the island, under the name of Haiti, became the first free black republic in 1804. But despite that courageous example, slavery continued in the other islands. Appalled, several European thinkers and politicians kept the idea of the abolition of slavery alive. England was the first to make a move, with the Emancipation Act of 1833. Prompted by Victor Schoelcher, France followed in 1848, then the Dutch in 1863.

Deprived of free slave labour, many plantations were in danger of bankruptcy. Importing workers from India was tried, but the pay was not enough given the misery that the work involved. And although the workers were underpaid, they still cost more than slaves. However, thanks to favourable exchange rates, technical developments and agricultural diversification, some estates managed to stay in business until the 20th century.

Despite abolition, the underlying social structure of the European American colonies meant that the majority of the old slaves hardly benefited except as a sub-class within the colonial system. The system lasted until after the Second World War.

The French islands then became 'Overseas Departments'. The small Dutch territories were grouped together in an autonomous federation. The Danes gave up their islands to the Americans. And the British, tired of maintaining the fragile economies of these minute particles of their old colonial empire, got rid of the majority of their islands in the Antilles between the 1960s and the 80s. So ended the period of colonisation. . .

18th-century frigate

The Antilles today

Political status

Politically the Lesser Antilles fall into five principal groups:

The American Virgin Islands

The three main islands of the Virgin Islands archipelago, St Thomas, St Croix and St John together have been made into an Associated US Territory, thereby enjoying a certain level of autonomy.

The independent ex-British islands

These became independent between 1966 and 1983. Scattered from north to south of the island arc, they are: St Kitts & Nevis, Antigua and Barbuda, Dominica, St Lucia, St Vincent, Grenada and Barbados.

The autonomous British islands

Still attached to the British crown, but having considerable autonomy, are: Montserrat, Anguilla and the British Virgin Islands.

The French Islands

Martinique and Guadeloupe, including the far-flung dependencies of the latter, the French part of St Martin and St Barthélémy are all French Overseas Departments and as such enjoy specific regional and customs status.

The Netherlands' islands

Saba, Statia and Sint Maarten (the Dutch part of St Martin) make up the fourth territory of the autonomous colony of the Netherlands Antilles. The three other parts, Aruba, Bonaire and Curaçao, are larger islands close to the north coast of Venezuela.

Economy and tourism

The islands' economic development is partly conditioned by their political status but equally by their geographical location and their attractiveness to tourists.

The American Virgin Islands (US Virgin Is or USVI)

Quite distinct because of their level of urbanisation and high population density, the islands have a modern infrastructure and plenty of natural advantages.

Tourism has been extensively developed, making these small domains an exotic extension of the Florida coast.

The BVI (British Virgin Is)

Right next door to the US Virgins, in the same US dollar area and benefiting from an American clientele, the BVI have enjoyed considerable investment in tourism. It is specially targeted at water-based activities because of the exceptional coastlines, fringed by a multitude of islets.

The French islands

Martinique and Guadeloupe, well placed in the middle of the Antillean arc, benefit from a French Metropolitan led tourism policy, which has dynamically boosted investment in hotels and sea sports.

These incentives, backed by an advantageous tax regime, have even transformed the dependencies of St Martin and St Barthélémy into real little tax havens.

The Netherlands' islands

These islands don't all enjoy the same economic situation. Tiny Statia and Saba, populated by retired folk, have had their tourism development limited by their scant resources and their minute land area. Beaches are few to non-existent, though diving enthusiasts find compensation in superb underwater scenery.

Sint Maarten, the Dutch counterpart to French St Martin, has by contrast vast beaches, an immense lagoon, luxury hotels and casinos. It also has, like its Gallic twin, a very liberal fiscal status. These advantages have driven the development of tourism on a scale that some see as uncontrolled.

The (ex-) British islands

Whether independent or autonomous, each is a special case. In practice, political status has had little bearing on commercial development, the sole point of importance being access to the manna of tourism, whether from Europe or America. In that sense these islands are far from being on an equal footing.

Antigua and St Lucia have the advantage of superb, if very different, coastlines and their plans for hotel development are going ahead full tilt. In much the same fashion St Vincent, if more austere, has the sumptuous Grenadines, emblematic of tropical paradise.

All these islands can hope steadily to improve their present economic situation thanks to tourism.

Aware of this, other islands like St Kitts and Nevis or Anguilla have fallen into step and begun accelerating hitherto evanescent tourism development. The example of nearby St Martin has stimulated them too.

Grenada is a separate case, maybe because it's the most harmoniously balanced thanks to its untamed forests, its cultivation of spices and its stunning beaches. Sadly, successive political problems have undermined its tourism development and, despite current government efforts, a major increase in tourist and cruising yacht numbers has yet to take place.

And what of the forgotten islands...? Montserrat, with its ever peaceful air, a haven of refuge for its faithful English and Canadian devotees, has been sadly devastated by successive hurricanes and then had much of it buried by ash and lava by the violent re-awakening of its volcano.

And Dominica, a wild and primitive island of jungle-green mountains, remains partly virgin and still unexplored.

These islands are still essentially tied to farming, small-scale stock-rearing and the odd old-style artisan. Tourism for them is as yet a passing supplement, often thanks to a neighbouring, more developed island getting overcrowded and a few sailors looking for somewhere less busy to go.

This swift economic review perhaps explains why the income of Antillean people can vary by a factor of four or more and that is what makes for the varying standards and costs of living. It is something the tourist should bear in mind for, if it's true that tourism development brings creature comforts as a corollary, then that necessarily has an influence on prices. The Virgin Islands and the French Antilles are good examples of this.

Antillean children

How to use the guide

The book is in four main parts.

I   Introduction
A quick overview of the archipelago as follows:

A short history of the Lesser Antilles and their modern situation (see above).

Useful information on formalities, travel by air and sea, post and telecommunications, currencies, places to stay and eat, sports and climate.

The natural environment: volcanoes, flora and fauna

Cyclones and hurricanes How to avoid them or protect yourself from them

Medical risks and prevention Tropical diseases, dangerous species, poisoning

Cartography Symbols, abbreviations, geographical layout of the islands, their flags.

II   The islands, in three zones: Windward Islands, Leeward Islands, Virgin Islands

For each island: details of history, tourism, navigation and other useful information.

III   Sailing in the Antilles
Vital general information for sailing in the islands. Includes meteorological conditions, GPS, available charts, radio communications, charter services and cruising routes, listings of marinas and boatyards.

IV   Services Directory
The pages at the end of the book bring together selected tourist and marine services companies classified by island and by type of business, including yachting services and hotels (see classification in Places to stay and eat) and restaurants.

Useful information

Formalities

For a limited stay in the Lesser Antilles as a tourist a current passport is sufficient for anyone coming from the USA or the EU.

Exception Although tourists arriving in the USVI by air or cruise ship do not need visas (though a return ticket is obligatory), those in privately owned pleasure vessels must have obtained a visa from a US Consulate before they arrive (see USVI: Useful Information below)

All international airports have immigration and customs services. For those coming in by sea these services are represented in ports, marinas and the most frequented anchorages.

Note In certain islands local customs and tax laws can affect a boat's length of stay. At the end of a given period of stay (varying between 3 and 6 months depending on the island), import taxes are levied.

Caution Over and above the usual import taxes, some islands (Guadeloupe, Martinique) have additional levies (harbour/sea dues). These affect all goods imported from overseas, including those from metropolitan France or from overseas departments with their own customs regimes.

Drugs There are strict controls against drug-trafficking and use (Virgin Is − No Tolerance).

Animals In most of the islands the temporary import of domestic pets is subject to specific, often complex regulations (a declaration, vaccination certificate, import authority).

Air travel

Long-distance flights The Lesser Antilles are pretty well served. The thirty main islands have ten international, long-haul airports connecting them to Europe and N America plus several services to S America.

Time zones The permanent official local time in the Lesser Antilles is GMT −4. For the majority of EU citizens that means GMT −5 in winter and −6 in summer.

Inter-island flights The islands not served by long-haul airports mostly have small airports or airstrips with regular inter-island services either by local airlines or air taxis.

Services don't always dovetail for making international and inter-island connections. We recommend you check with your airline or travel agent.

Sea communications

Transatlantic services
For lovers of long ocean voyages some ships (container liners and fruit carriers) do take limited numbers of passengers starting from European ports (Le Havre, etc.)

Inter-island services
Inter-island passenger services are well developed. Vessels, some of them high speed, offer regular services between the islands in the same group.

Post and telecommunications

In islands with fully developed infrastructure and services, there are good postal services in all the main towns. The same islands either have service centres (Cable & Wireless, etc.) for telephone and fax services, or phone boxes. The latter are usually card phones: either credit cards, or local phone company cards (France-Télécom in the French islands, Caribbean Phone Card in the independent islands) For mobile phone network coverage see the section on Mobile Phones in the chapter Sailing in the Lesser Antilles.

Currencies

US$ in theVirgin Is (BVI and USVI) EC$ (East Caribbean dollar): the official currency of the ex-British islands with the exception of Barbados (the EC$ is pegged to the US$ at US$1=EC$2.5). The US$ is also accepted with no problem.

B$ (Barbados dollar): the Barbadian currency. The US$ is also accepted.

The euro is the official currency of the French islands. In the dependencies of St Martin and St Barthélémy the US$ is as widely used as the €.

NAF (Antillean florin or guilder): the official currency of the Dutch islands, although the US$ is the more widely used unit.

Places to stay and eat

Accommodation
In the 'tourist' islands the range of places to stay runs from the most luxurious and expensive to the most basic rented rooms. In these islands the prices are pretty much identical to those in Europe and the USA.

In the less developed islands there is the occasional luxury hotel complex and some very basic establishments, but there's little in the mid-range.

Restaurants
Thanks to local produce and external influences, Antillean cuisine is varied (and often spicy), but it is not of uniform quality throughout the islands. American influence is strong in the Virgin Islands as is British in their ex-territories, but in the French islands Antillean cuisine comes fully into its own thanks to its happy marriage with French and Indian cuisines.

Sports

These are numerous but dependent on each island's natural characteristics and the level of development of its facilities.

Land sports Golf is found everywhere and there are a large number of courses. Tennis and horse-riding are similarly ubiquitous. Walkers are well provided for thanks to the footpaths and tracks (called '*traces*' in the French islands) which criss-cross the hills and country parks.

Water sports In this 'sailing paradise' pleasure cruising is the main sea sport, but a rich underwater world has also led to the strong development of diving and diving clubs as well as to marine reserves.

Protected lagoons combined with steady winds have greatly encouraged windsurfing.

Climate

(see also Cyclones and Weather and sea)

Temperature The archipelago falls wholly within the tropics. It follows that temperatures are high (25°C–30°C), with little seasonal variation.

Temperature differences, which can be of the order of 10°C or more, are due mainly either to variation between night and day or to changes in altitude.

The trades The whole zone lies within the zone of the trade winds. The seasonal movements of the trade wind belt also regulate the climate as a whole.

The seasons The seasons vary between the dry season December–April (Lent) and the wet season May–November (Winter).

The latter is typified by more frequent and heavy rain (especially in squalls). The former is typified by established trade winds, characterized by less frequent rain and slightly lower air and sea temperatures.

Rain and the cyclone season The intensity and amount of rain is a function of each island's relief, which generates cloud build-up. Showers are more common on the windward coasts.

The hurricane risk is greatest in the winter, June–November (see Cyclones below).

Sea temperature Given the high and steady air temperature, the sea water temperature stays between 25°C and 28°C and never falls below 20°C even during the winter.

Hummingbirds

The natural environment

Geology

Volcanic and Coralline Massifs

With the exception of Barbados in the east, which is coralline, the archipelago rests on a mountainous ridge in the form of an arc almost 900km long. Geologically, the youngest islands are essentially volcanic, with markedly irregular relief which attains considerable height.

Some of the volcanoes are definitively extinct, others are quiescent (semi-active), marked only by fumaroles and sulphury smoke.

However, some re-activate from time to time and the eruptions can cause significant damage and loss of life, for example, Mont Pelée (Martinique) and la Soufrière (St Vincent) in 1902, la Soufrière (Guadeloupe) in 1976, and more recently la Soufrière of Galway, which has destroyed half of Montserrat.

The older islands, the eroded bases of volcanoes, are now partly topped by limestone formations: for example La Grande Terre near Guadeloupe, Antigua, St Martin, Anguilla, etc.

Flora and Fauna

Because the archipelago is so far from the continent of the Americas, a large part of its flora and fauna has resulted from successive mixing between the islands. The result across the island group is therefore quite homogeneous.

Fauna

The Antillean fauna is relatively poor, especially in mammals. During the colonial period intensive hunting was responsible for the extinction of some species. Today the majority are protected.

Birds are more numerous and characterized by vibrant colours: the colibri or humming bird with its lightning swift flight, the parrots, of which the Sisserou has become Dominica's emblem, the black Great Frigate Birds with the male's scarlet throat, the different heron species and, on the coast, those deft fishermen, the pelicans.

There are several species of batrachians and reptiles, from the frog or giant toad (the Mountain Chicken) of Dominica through numerous lizards to the iguanas.

Snakes are fewer in number but represented in Martinique and St Lucia by a most venomous species, the triangular-headed *fer-de-lance*.

Amongst the mammals you'll find the racoon, now preserved in a Guadeloupe national park, and the agouti, a small rodent. Both are protected but still victims of poaching because their flesh is greatly prized.

The freshwater fauna is very much more rare. The *ouassou* (or *z'habitant*), a river crayfish, is considered a delicacy and is on the way to extinction.

Flora

The most luxuriant islands (Guadeloupe, Dominica, St Vincent, etc.) have the full palette of tropical flora.

Vegetation varies with altitude and rainfall. Because the mountains block rainfall, the vegetation on the windward coasts is usually more abundant than in the dryer climate of the leeward side. The principal zones are: rain forest, dry forest, scrub and thornbush. Tree species are numerous, some having very valuable wood, others good carpentry hardwoods: mahogany, gum tree, acomat, chestnut, etc.

The trees are often entwined with lianas and tree ferns, creating together a great mass of foliage. The coconut palms, once imported for producing nuts, have proliferated and now their fronds line the shores and lowlands.

There are also other species like the breadfruit (imported from Polynesia by Captain Bligh of the *Bounty*), the Traveller's tree, the frangipani with its perfumed flowers, and the flame tree, covered in bright scarlet flowers in summer.

On the shore there are the manchineel trees with their dangerous fruit (see the chapter on medical risks) and the mangrove swamps covered with their thick network of roots.

There are both wild and cultivated flowering plants, most of extraordinary beauty: balisiers (a native heliconium), hibiscus, bougainvillea, anthurium, china rose, etc.

To all of which we must add the major agricultural plants: the banana trees, sugar cane plantations and all the spice trees. You can find the majority of these plants in the many parks and botanical gardens.

Marine flora and fauna

The coral reefs are home to the majority of the species of marine fauna and flora. Made of micro-organisms called polyps, the reefs have been created and have

Opposite top to bottom, left to right
Tropical foliage; Traveller's tree (*Ravenala Madagascariensis*); Balisier; Pride of Barbados (*Caesalpinia pulcherrima*); Allamanda; China rose; Botanical Garden; Palm tree; Banana tree

Botanical Garden

grown over millennia and have come to form barriers protecting the coasts of numerous islands from the ocean swells. It is a fragile ecosystem, readily threatened by pollution. Coral species are very varied both in shape and colour: brain coral, staghorn coral, etc, sometimes covered with sponges and gorgonians (sea fans or fan corals).

The fauna is also very varied: invertebrates, shellfish and above all fish. There are two categories:

Sedentary fish live in and on the coral (parrot fish, trigger fish, trunk fish, globefish, snappers, groupers, moray eels, hogfish, etc.) For the most part these are herbivores.

Pelagic and carnivorous fish cruise along the coasts or temporarily visit the reefs in order to seek their prey: barracuda, the carangidae (jacks and trevallies), sharks, rays, mackerel and wahoo, etc.

Save in exceptional circumstances, these fish offer no direct danger to humans. However, some species are toxic (see section on Fish Poisoning, Ciguatera).

Below Brain coral
Bottom Staghorn coral

Cyclones and hurricanes

Now and then the news shows us the devastating effects of these tropical depressions which, quite understandably, worry everyone who visits the Antilles.

'Cyclone' is the usual term in the French islands and comes from the circular movement of the phenomenon (from the Greek *kuklos*: circle). The technical English term for the phenomenon is Tropical Revolving Storm, more commonly 'hurricane', although strictly the latter technically applies only to cyclones above a certain strength.

This meteorological phenomenon is not restricted to the Caribbean but affects all the world's tropical zones. In SE Asia they are called typhoons.

What is a cyclone?
Classification
Wind strength determines the three-stage classification of cyclones:

- Tropical depression: less than 34kts (63kmh)
- Tropical storm: 34–63kts (117kmh)
- Hurricane: over 63kts

Tropical storms and hurricanes have names which begin each year with the letter A and alternate male and female names.

Hurricanes proper are classified by the five level Saffir and Simpson Scale:

Category 1   64–82kts (153km/h)
Category 2   83–96kts (177km/h)
Category 3   97–113kts (209km/h)
Category 4   114–134kts (248km/h)
Category 5   over 134kts

It is important to remember that whilst all hurricanes have their origins in tropical depressions, not all tropical depressions become hurricanes.

Note Of the 70 areas of tropical circulation that occur annually, less than 10% become hurricanes.

Formation
The following factors are necessary for a cyclonic circulation to form:

- a zone of instability which creates strong convection currents
- a deviating force (the Coriolis effect resulting from the Earth's rotation) which makes the convection currents begin to rotate (in an anti-clockwise direction in the N hemisphere)
- in order for the phenomenon to keep going, energy from warm sea water (minimum 26°C) which allows fierce evaporation from the sea into the atmosphere

These form a cyclone's essential motor.

Note The lower ambient temperatures of

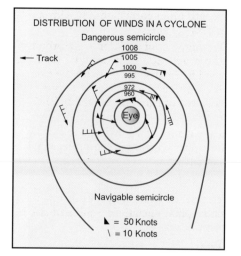

DISTRIBUTION OF WINDS IN A CYCLONE
Dangerous semicircle
1008
1005
1000
995
← Track
972
960
Eye

Navigable semicircle

⬏ = 50 Knots
\ = 10 Knots

Wind patterns in a cyclone

the S Atlantic explain the absence of cyclones in that region.

Season
Sea temperatures reach their maximum at the end of summer (28°–30°) and lead to the maximum occurrence of cyclones in August and September.

That said, the danger period starts at the beginning of summer and lasts until October and, more exceptionally, November (for example Hurricane Lenny from 13–21 November 1999).

Breeding area
In general, cyclones form between 5° and 10°N near the Cape Verde Is. However, some also form near the Antillean arc and even in the Caribbean Sea itself.

The first of these, the 'Cape Verders', have the reputation of being the most violent, their strength having built up during their Atlantic crossing, during which, fortunately, many often weaken and collapse.

Track, speed of advance and extent
The track is in general from E to W in the open ocean before often turning more WNW when approaching the islands.

Cyclones and hurricanes are capricious, so in some cases a track can dip WSW before reverting WNW'ly.

The normal track crosses the Lesser Antilles, heading generally towards the Greater Antilles and the S part of North America.

Those which start life in the Caribbean Sea can follow more erratic tracks either from S–N, or even from W–E as Lenny did in November 1999.

Some experts think that hurricanes lose their energy when they make continental landfall and also that the eye has a tendency to pass between rather than over islands.

The speed of advance of hurricanes is of the order of 8–20kts, an increase in strength often corresponding with a decrease in speed.

The diameter of a cyclonic disturbance is from 600–800 nautical miles (as with David in August 1979), with the eye (the centre of the cyclone and short lived area of light winds) about 10M wide.

At the centre of a hurricane the atmospheric pressure can drop to less than 940Hpa.

Destructive effects

Principal effects: Floods, destructive winds, phenomenal sea state and swell, storm tides.

Floods

Torrential rain causes huge and sudden flash floods, which are the main cause of fatalities amongst the population of a hurricane affected area.

Winds

In the N hemisphere winds are strongest to the right of the hurricane's track, thus generally on the N side (the Dangerous Semicircle), because the speed of the wind is added to the storm's speed of advance. It follows that winds are weaker to the left and generally S side (the Navigable Semicircle).

The wind speed difference between the two sides can exceed 50kts.

This idea is important to grasp in order to anticipate wind strength, depending on whether the eye of the storm will pass N or S of one's position. The same is true for a vessel attempting to head for the navigable semi-circle.

As the eye passes overhead winds generally drop to a relative, if brief, calm before changing direction and resuming with all their preceding force.

It's in the area close to the eye (called the 'eye wall') that the winds are strongest: 100–150kts. Dozens of miles from the centre the winds can still be 50–100kts, reducing proportionally with distance from the centre, above all in the S semi-circle.

Winds can carry along with them parts of houses (corrugated iron roofing sheets), trees, etc., which can cause injury, sometimes fatal.

Swell and sea state

The extreme wind strength and its changing direction can cause phenomenal seas, which are confused and very dangerous.

Making in from E a hurricane is always preceded by an E'ly swell, which turns

steadily W'ly once the centre is past. This is what causes the worst damage since the leeward coasts are seldom adequately protected against such an onslaught.

Storm tides

The lowering of atmospheric pressure is proportional to the proximity of the eye and it can fall to less than 940Hpa at the centre. One result of this is a rise in sea level, which is added to swell effects.

Example: In the hurricane of 1924 in Guadeloupe, the islets in the Rade de Pointe-à-Pitre were covered by a storm tide of some 4m after which the bay partially emptied. This is one of the most dangerous phenomena because it makes the protection offered by any anchorage surrounded by low sea walls or low ground very vulnerable.

Hurricane Frequency

As far as frequency of occurrence is concerned, the most serious hurricanes have been recorded (mainly in Martinique) since the 17th century. The list and the diagram show the main hurricanes (excluding tropical storms), their dates since 1960 and their tracks as they crossed the Lesser Antilles:

10.07.1960: Abby, S of St Lucia

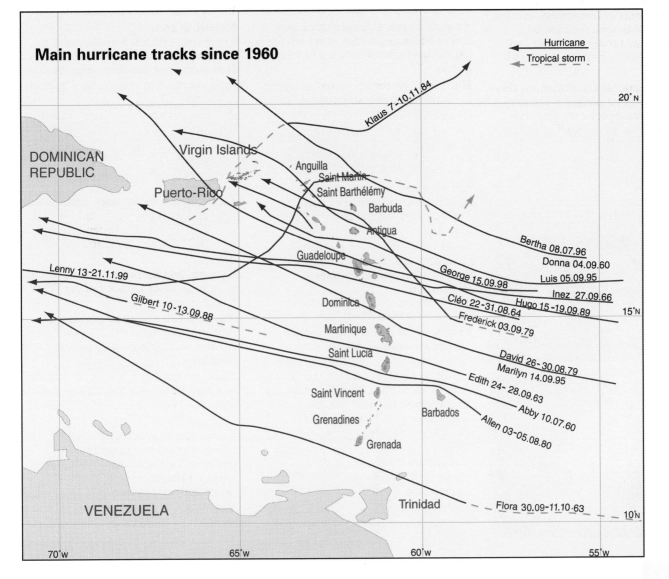

Main hurricane tracks since 1960

LIST OF SMALL CRAFT HURRICANE HOLES

The following classification is the result of research combined with personal opinion. Other opinions may differ.
- • Good shelter, but only relative to how close the cyclone comes
- •• Good shelter, but if the eye gets close its protection could be problematic (swell, storm surge or other various dangers)
- ••• A secure shelter except in exceptional circumstances
- •••• Almost perfect shelter

Islands	Rating	Limiting depth	Observations
St John			
Hurricane Hole	•••	5m	3 reliable hurricane holes but risk of overcrowding
St Thomas			
Benner Bay	••	2–2·3m	Overcrowded – lots of houses
Virgin Gorda			
Gorda Sound	•	5m	Fairly open – significant fetch
Tortola			
Paraquita Bay	••	–1·8m	Limited depths (–1·8m) in pass
St-Martin & St Maarten			
Simpson Bay	••	3–4m	Little shelter from the land significant fetch from large lagoon
Oyster Pond	•••	3m	Difficult access – tight – overcrowded
St-Barth			
Gustavia	•	4m	Unprotected from W swell – quickly overcrowded
Antigua			
English Harbour	•••	3m	Good shelter deep in the mangroves but lots of boats and buildings
Parham Harbour	••	5m	Fairly open – significant fetch
Non Such Bay	•••	2–4m	Expect to access only in good visibility – well sheltered except with significant storm tides
Guadeloupe			
Lagon Bleu	••	2–3m	Tight – overcrowded – poor holding
Rivière Salée	•••	2·5m	Mast must come down if the bridge won't open – well protected but with risk of wreck from storm tide and currents
Martinique			
Windward coast			
Le François	••	2–3m	Open to the wind – many houses
Petite Grenade	•••	2·5m max	Very safe except in significant storm tides, but small
Anse des Roseaux	•••	2–3m	Very safe – difficult access – small
Baie du Tresor (Pte Caravelle)	••	5m	Well sheltered except in significant storm tides, risks overcrowding
Fort de France Bay			
Port Cohé	•••	2–3m	Very well protected but poor holding
Trois Ilets	••	4m	Poorly protected from the wind and big storm tides
South Coast			
Cul-de-Sac du Marin	•••	2–5m	Well protected except in significant storm tide, risks overcrowding
St Lucia			
Rodney Bay Marina	•••	3m	Little protected from the wind and flying corrugated iron roofing, significant risk of storm tide
Marigot Bay	••	4m	Scant security with W swell and significant storm tide – quickly overcrowded and lots of houses
Carriacou			
Tyrell Bay			
1st mangroves	••	3–6m	Too quickly overcrowded
2nd mangroves	•••	1·6m	Total shelter except in significant storm tide. Shallow in the pass
Grenada			
St Georges	•	4m	Too overcrowded – lots of houses Risk from swell and tide
Calivigny Harbour	•••	4m	Good shelter except in significant storm tide
Port Egmont	••••	4m	Total shelter – the best in the whole Lesser Antilles, huge and encircled

05.09.1960: Donna, near St-Barth-St Martin
25.09.1963: Edith, between Martinique and St Lucia
30.09.1963: Flora, to the S of Grenada
24.08.1964: Cleo, over the Leeward Is
27.08.1966: Inez, over Guadeloupe
21.08.1979: David, over Martinique and the Leeward Is
02.09.1979: Frederick, over Antigua and the N islands
04.08.1980: Allen, to the S of St Lucia
08.11.1984: Klaus, over the N islands and the Virgin Is
17.09.1989: Hugo, Leeward Is and the Virgin Is
05–6.09.95: Luis, over Guadeloupe, the N islands and the Virgin Is
14.09.1995: Marilyn, over Guadeloupe, the N islands and the Virgin Is
08.09.1996: Bertha, N islands and Virgin Is
15.09.1998: George, from Antigua to the Virgin Is
15.11.1999: Lenny, from Jamaica to the Leeward Is

What now?

Has the incidence of cyclones and hurricanes increased over the last few years as a result of global warming (such as the El Niño phenomenon)?

It seems that neither the scientists nor their statistics are sufficiently sure to give an unequivocal answer.

However, the existing evidence does not show a decrease but rather the opposite.

Examples and characteristics of selected hurricanes

David One of the most powerful and long lasting (Category 5)
25.08.79 depression forms near the Cape Verde Is
27.08.79 becomes a hurricane
29.08.79 centre passes N of Martinique and hits the S of Dominica

Characteristics (at the storm's strongest):
The cloud mass extended over an area more than 800 nautical miles in diameter.
Central pressure: 932Hpa
Maximum sustained wind (excluding gusts): 140kts

Hugo Extremely violent and devastating (Category 5)
11.09.89 depression forms off Africa
13.09.89 becomes a hurricane when over the Atlantic
16–17.09.89 hits the Leeward Is and then the Virgin Is

Characteristics:
Central pressure: 942Hpa
Speed of advance: 11kts
Maximum sustained wind (excluding gusts): 120–140kts

Luis Very concentrated. Devastated the Leeward Is (Category 4)
29.08.95 depression forms off the Cape

Verde Is
31.08.95 becomes a hurricane when over the Atlantic
05.09.95 crosses the N part of the Antillean arc
Characteristics:
Central pressure: 948Hpa
Speed of advance: 10kts
Maximum sustained wind (excluding gusts): 120–130kts
Lenny Late in the season and with an erratic track (Category 4)
13.11.99 depression forms off Jamaica
13.11.99 becomes a hurricane in the middle of the Caribbean Sea
17–19.11.99 hits the Virgin Is then the N islands. The storm swell devastated the (normally) leeward coasts of the other islands.
21.11.99 collapsed as a tropical storm off Antigua
Characteristics: Track went W–E
Central pressure: 934Hpa
Speed of advance: 12kts but it stopped over the northern islands
Maximum sustained wind speed (excluding gusts): 130kts

Warning signs for approaching hurricanes

These are generally:
(for a normal E–W track a large, long E'ly swell (unless the speed of advance of the hurricane is faster than the wave train)
• a rise in water level
• a drop in the barometer
• cirrus clouds

Forecasts and precautionary measures

Unless you've been able to get away in time before the storm's arrival, you will have to ride it out.

Accordingly, and whether ashore or afloat, you must be as well-informed as possible about the storm's development, its track, its speed of advance and its wind speeds in order best to protect yourself.

The importance of these factors, given the damage that can be done, is evident from the structure of the warning service.

The Miami National Hurricane Center

Above Coaster on the beach at Marigot (Hurricane Luis)
Above left Wrecked sailing boat at St Thomas (Hurricane Marilyn)

(NHC) uses considerable resources to locate and measure cyclones (reconnaissance planes, etc.) including satellite observation. The information gathered is disseminated to all regional weather forecasting services, which then add their own observations.

The No.1 Warning (Approaching Cyclone) is given and the storm's development is broadcast by special bulletins on both local and marine (VHF and SSB) radio; in particular by CROSSAG (Centre Opérationnel de Sauvetage Antilles-Guyane (Antilles-French Guiana Search and Rescue Centre) –VHF 16/SSB 2182kHz) which ensures complete zone cover (see the table of weather stations and local radio in the 'Sailing' section below).

Eventually the No.2 Warning (Storm close to or over the island) is given, then the No.3 (Emergency services call out).

Although the warnings presume some two days during which the phenomenon develops and is tracked, these limits are nonetheless subject to error.

Despite the means available today meteorology is not yet an exact science. *It makes sense to take this into account when making your preparations.*

To monitor information on cyclones, etc. check also these websites:
www.nhc.noaa.gov
www.gobpi.com/weather/storm
www.hurricanehunters.com

Special warning for sailing boats

First and essential rule: Don't be at sea in a cyclone.

Preventive measures
• if possible, plan summer cruises S of 12°N, the zone of least risk (save in exceptional circumstances)–during the hurricane season, monitor weather bulletins regularly

As soon as a warning is given make a choice:
• either head for a better protected shelter or for somewhere far off the predicted track (but this is the most dangerous and possibly fatal choice if the time available is too brief)
• or stay where you are and make preparations to protect yourself and your boat in light of probable risks, what available shelter there is nearby and your surroundings. Look in particular for other boats. Badly moored or anchored and left to themselves, these are the biggest danger because they can badly damage your boat. So, basically, avoid shelters overcrowded with local craft.

Protection against the wind and flying objects
• even a shelter which protects you from the effects of a storm sea won't save you from the wind and all that it blows before it.

Wrecked boat after Hurricane Luis (Simpson Bay Lagoon, St Maarten)

Avoid the riskiest zones (anywhere surrounded by corrugated iron roofing, trees, etc.)

- if you decide to put your boat ashore, don't forget that 100kt winds can blow it over even if it's well tied down!
- remember to take account of windage during your preparations, strip the deck and double or redouble your mooring lines.

Protection against sea and currents
Even if a shelter seems well-protected against a very high swell, the storm tide can make the protection illusory.

In practice the rise in sea level can be 2m or more (3–4m at St Lucia during Hurricane Allen). Waves can roll right over sea walls or low peninsulas.

Swell and tidal effects can also generate outflow effects from one area to another (for example in the Rivière Salée during Hurricane Hugo) causing violent currents of 6–7kts.

These add to the risk of a boat being ripped from its moorings.

Crime
There are people who will aggravate the effects of a natural cataclysm by taking advantage of the general disarray to engage in pillaging and vandalism. It follows that if possible you should avoid leaving your boat too long unattended.

Other preparation
Be prepared with:

- strong additional mooring lines
- food and water sufficient to last through the emergency
- every possible preventive measure against likely problems that can occur when on cyclone watch (mosquitoes, strong smells, isolation, etc.)

Hurricane Shelters

Is there such a thing as a wholly secure shelter against the devastating effects of the close pass of a very powerful hurricane?

Given recent examples (Hugo, Luis, Lenny) nothing is less certain if all possible contributory factors combine such as the effects of the wind, swell and waves, storm tides, currents, environmental dangers (flying objects), other boats, etc.

In short, it's better to hope that you don't have to put any of the shelters in the above table to any test of reliability over and above that noted.

In my opinion, the most trustworthy shelter in the Lesser Antilles seems to be Port Egmont in the S part of Grenada. Unfortunately it lies in one of the lower risk zones at the end of the Antillean arc.

Medical risks and prevention

I. Tropical diseases

Compared to other tropical zones the risks of serious illnesses in the Lesser Antilles are extremely low if one takes basic precautions.

Malaria
No known risk in this zone.

Yellow Fever
No official cases in the Lesser Antilles although they are close to countries at risk.

Dengue Fever
Quite common in the Lesser Antilles. Dengue fever is spread by the same mosquito that spreads yellow fever.

Symptoms Generally like a bad case of influenza: aching joints, fever. The rare, haemorrhagic dengue fever is serious.

Bilharzia
(intestinal variety – schistostomiasis (*S. mansoni*))

An illness caused by a parasite penetrating the skin. The parasite lives in freshwater rivers and brackish ponds etc, polluted as a result of nearby housing (quite common in the poorer islands with ill-maintained, inadequate or non-existent drainage and sewerage).

Symptoms Marked lassitude and stomach pains.

Treatment After relevant tests, treatments by oral medicines are now extremely successful.

Prevention Don't wash or swim (even feet only) in fresh water, which might be polluted.

Hookworm (Larbish)
This is essentially a parasite which is a problem for dogs.

As far as the effects on humans go, the parasite in its pre-adult stage moves around under the skin causing major itching.

Treatment Insecticide ointment or, in a hospital, treatment by topical chilling.

Prevention Don't walk around in bare feet or lie around on beaches contaminated or soiled by animals.

Note beware of other intestinal parasites that can infect you. This happens, as with bilharzia, in a wet environment, but also by eating contaminated fruits and vegetables. The phenomenon is often known as 'la tourista' or Pharaoh's Revenge.

Vaccinations
No vaccinations are obligatory for travel to the Lesser Antilles.

However, as a precaution you can get vaccinated against: tetanus, smallpox, polio, hepatitis A.

II. Attacks and poisoning

There are no land animals dangerous to humans in the Lesser Antilles except in Martinique, where the bite of the viper *fer-de-lance* can be dangerous and even fatal.

Dangerous marine animals
Sharks Species found in coastal waters are generally harmless, in particular the sand shark, nicknamed 'the sleeper', which is the most common.

Accidents are the exception. Two have been recorded in the Virgin Is.

When underwater hunting, avoid attaching the fish you've caught to your belt.

Barracudas Contrary to their reputation and their aggressive demeanour, barracuda don't normally attack divers. On the other hand, if they're wounded, they can bite the underwater hunter who takes them.

In the marine environment there are other more common but less dangerous attacks:

- **jellyfish** tentacles can cause nasty
- stings
- wounds from the spines of **sea urchins**
- burning or stinging **corals** or 'fire corals'

One quickly learns to recognize these 'dangers' by experience. They're no danger to life and limb but are always thoroughly unpleasant!

Poisonous plants
Rare, with the exception of the **Manchineel** tree. This is a very common coastal tree in the Antilles with fruit ranging from green to red looking like small apples (manchineel fruit). They also smell. Eating these fruits causes dangerous interior burns that can be fatal. The sap of the manchineel can also burn the skin.

Fish poisoning
Ciguatera
Although less widespread than in the Pacific Is, in some of the Lesser Antilles there is a genuine risk of significant fish poisoning from ciguatera. There are few informative sources for the tourist or cruising sailor to consult about the dangers of eating poisonous fish.

Definition Ciguatera is a food toxin ingested through eating the infected flesh of certain fish. The toxin is always found in some species of fish but only occasionally in others. This depends on the size of the fish, its habitat and the season when the fish was caught. The fish eats the toxin that in turn contaminates its flesh. The toxin isn't found in only one variant, at least six have been identified, but all fall under the generic label of ciguatera.

IMPORTANT: the toxin is thermostable, which means that cooking does not eliminate it.

The toxins come from the marine micro-organism, *gambierdicsus toxicus*, a microscopic algae. The most usual areas of ciguatera contamination are broken or damaged reefs. Fish that eat the algae store the toxin, which then builds in quantity as it proceeds up the food chain. This explains the greater toxicity of the major predators at the top of the food chain.

Symptoms The incubation period can vary from a few minutes to several hours, but is usually fairly swift. The first symptoms are in general simultaneously neurological and intestinal:

- intestinal: nausea and vomiting
- neurological: feeling queasy, tingling feeling (pins and needles)

Before long these symptoms enter a second, more serious phase:

- intestinal: diarrhoea and powerful abdominal cramps
- neurological: burning sensation or a feeling of electric shock if one touches something cold or water, strong itching sensation (called 'la gratte' or 'the itch'), loss of muscular control and balance
- cardio-vascular: irregularities in heartbeat
- more general symptoms: muscle and joint pains, disorientation, reduced quantity of urine and extreme general lassitude

These symptoms can get worse and one can also see cutaneous symptoms, pruritus, loss of hair and teeth, respiratory paralysis and cardiac arrest leading, if rarely, to death.

Treatment

- corticosteroids (with anti-shock properties) by intra-muscular injection
- anti-histamines
- anti-diarrhoeals
- heart stimulant
- vitamin B
- gastric lavage

These medicines don't pose any particular problems for the user, though with steroids you must guard against overdose.

In mild cases of ciguatera, they may be enough to avoid the necessity for hospitalisation. If hospitalisation is required, the French or American Antilles have more elaborate facilities for treatment although none are absolutely effective in all cases.

Prevention of ciguatera
The only guaranteed prevention is not to eat potentially contaminated fish.

Unfortunately there is no way as yet to detect such fish beforehand. Some believe in tests that seem a bit like sorcery and certainly offer no guarantees. Alternatives:

- offer a bit of the flesh to ants which will avoid it if it's poisonous.
- a piece of pure silver is said to turn black if the fish meat is poisonous.
- give a cat some of the suspect flesh (up to 1/10th of the cat's bodyweight). If 24 hrs later the cat isn't ill, the fish is supposedly OK and edible. This procedure, even more dubious than the others, requires one to have several small cats around to spare.

Even if it's no absolute safeguard, the best prevention always lies in choosing the right sort of fish.

Note In some islands (Guadeloupe), local legislation defines succinctly which fish are poisonous and not to be eaten. Even in a single species toxicity can vary from island to island. Only fishermen have a good idea of how to make a choice. They don't often make a mistake, but even so, sometimes they do. The following selective information is the result of research amongst fishermen and other local people, consultation of hard-to-come-by books and personal experience. The advice appears here with all the usual cautions about following it.

Fishing zones
Some people say the Antilles can be divided into two parts:

- from Dominica to the Virgin Is fish are considered dangerous because they are very toxic.
- S of Dominica all fish are considered edible.

The reality is less black and white:

- It is known that ciguatera is possible S of Dominica and even, for some very hazardous species, as far S as Martinique (barracuda, jacks and pompanos, etc).
- By contrast, further S ciguatera poisoning does seem much rarer at least as far as Grenada, but in the islands near Venezuela ciguatera reappears. The most dangerous area is N of Guadeloupe.

Fishing season
There doesn't seem to be a correlation between season and degree of toxicity. However, some think that risks are greater in the summer.

Fish size
Toxicity is proportional to the weight of the fish. For a given species a larger fish is more likely to be poisonous than a smaller one. In some occasionally poisonous species one additional safeguard is not to eat any specimen weighing over 1kg.

Fish types
Note In order to better recognize the different fish species, it is recommended you get hold of a specialised illustrated guide to fish species such as *Guide to Corals and Fishes* by I & J Greenberg (Seahawk Press).

In the relevant zones one must be aware that there are several levels of risk depending on species. Some are thought dangerous or very dangerous, others of lesser or doubtful risk. Toxicity can also be a function of the zone where the fish are found. The following selection is only based on experience and you are advised, if you have the smallest doubt, not to eat any specimen.

Dangerous fish species
* Photos courtesy of L Parle·Editions PLB

Sphyrenidae
Great Barracuda (*Sphyroena barracuda*)
Barracuda (Becune)

Fundamentally a predator around coral reefs or in inshore waters; one of the most dangerous species.

The most prudent of us don't eat great barracuda caught between Martinique and the Virgin Is, particularly any large specimens.

Carangidae
Jacks are predatory fish, some reaching a good size. Some species have the reputation of being as dangerous as barracuda.

Horse-eye Trevally or **Jack** (*Caranx latus*)
Carangue Gros Yeux (Mayol)

Almaco Jack (*Seriola rivoliana*)
Seriole Limon (Babiane)

Yellow Jack (*Caranx bartholomoei*)
Carangue Jaune

Black Jack (*Caranx lugubris*)
Carangue Noire

Other species are thought less risky although opinions differ:

African Pompano (*Alectis ciliaris*)
Carangue à Plumes

Thought to be risky in some N zones. Fortunately not very common.

Bar Jack (*Caranx ruber*)
Carangue à Pisquettes

Some fishermen and some books hold this fish to be risk free. Others disagree. In any event avoid large specimens.

Serranidae
Groupers are numerous at different depths close inshore. Some species can be highly toxic, particularly:

Yellowfin Grouper (*Mycteroperca venemosa*)
Capitaine Z'Ailes Jaunes (Vieille à Carreaux)

As its Latin name suggests, this fish has been thought poisonous for centuries.

Red Grouper (*Epinephelus morio*)
Vieille Blanche

Thought to be very poisonous, above all in the N islands.

Tiger Grouper (*Mycterperca tigris*)
Vieille Morue (Mérou Tigre)

The cause of numerous poisonings.

Barracuda*

Yellowfin Grouper
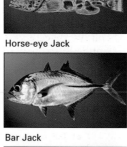

Black Grouper

Tiger Grouper

Red Hind*

Nassau Grouper

Mutton Hamlet

Horse-eye Jack

Almaco Jack

Black Jack*

Yellow Jack

African Pompano*

Bar Jack

Green Moray*

Dog Snapper*

Yellowtail Snapper

Spanish Mackerel*

Wahoo*

Queen Triggerfish*

Yellow Goatfish*

Glass Eye

Big Eye

Hogfish*

Spotted Trunkfish*

Smooth Trunkfish*

Others of the *Serranidae* are thought less risky:

Black Grouper (*Mycterperca bonaci*)
Vieille Noire (Capitaine Noir)

This species can be confused with the Yellowfin Grouper, so avoid it.

Red Hind (*Epinephalus guttatus*)
Grande Gueule Rouge (Couronné Rouge)

Some think this risky, especially large specimens.

Mutton Hamlet (*Alphestes afer*)
Vieille de Rivière (Varech)

Same as the Red Hind.

Nassau Grouper (*Epinephalus striatus*)
Vieille Franche (Vieille Rouge)

Recognizable by the black spot on the upper side of the tail. Thought not to be toxic, although cases of poisoning have been reported in the Virgin Is.

Rock Hind (*Epinephalus adscencionis*)
Grande Gueule Noire (Couronné Noir)

This species is thought not to be poisonous (except in exceptional cases).

Murenidae
Green Moray (*Gymnothorax funebris*)
Murène Verte

Reputedly very poisonous

Note Ciguatera aside, the bite of all moray eels can cause serious infections.

Lutjanidae
Snappers are carniverous fish of coastal waters. Some species offer a significant ciguatera risk.

Dog Snapper (*Lutjanus jocu*)
Pagre Dents de Chine

Schoolmaster (*Lutjanus apodus*)
Pagre Jaune

Other species like:

Yellowtail Snapper
Pagre Queue Jaune

are thought to be edible, provided they have been properly identified.

Species considered risky
Scombridae
The mackerel family are pelagic fish often taken when trolling. In some zones (St Barts, Virgin Is) the species below (especially large specimens) are thought by some to be risky, although others eat them without worrying:

Cero/Painted Mackerel/Spanish Mackerel (*Scomberomorus regalis*)
Thazard Maquereau (Sauteu)

Wahoo (*Acanthocybium solanderi*)
Thazard Bâtard

Kingfish/King Mackerel (*Scomberomorus cavalla*)
Thazard Franc (ou Blanc)

Balistidae (**Triggerfish**)
Queen Triggerfish (*Balistes vetula*)
Balisté Royale (Bourse Blanche)

Some consider the fish in the N islands poisonous. What is certain is that the very rough skin can cause considerable inflammation when handled.

Mullidae (**Goatfish**)
The goatfish is recognizable by its barbels. It lives on sandy bottoms.

Yellow goatfish (*Mulloidichthys martinicus*)
Barbarin Blanc

Identified by a lateral yellow line. Thought risky in some areas, unlike the

Spotted Goatfish (*Pseudupeneus maculatus*)
Barbarin Rouge

Thought to be non-toxic

Labridae (**Wrasses**)
Wrasse and hog fish are found on coral reefs.

Hog Fish (*Lachnolaimus maximus*)
Capitaine (Aigrette)

Thought to be risky in some areas.

Priacanthidae
Commonly called sunfish, jewfish or big eye but there are actually two species:

Big eye (*Priacanthus arenatus*)
Soleil Franc (Juif Rouge)

Possibly poisonous but usually found more than 15m down. Identified by the ventral fins which overlap the anal fin and the uniform red colour.

Glasseye snapper (*Heteropriacanthus cruentatus*)
Soleil Bâtard (Juif Caye)

Reputedly never been found toxic. Living in shallow coral waters, it barely moves and is an easy fish to catch. Identified by the shorter ventral fin and marbled, more or less uniform red colour.

Other, non-ciguatera dangers
Ostraciidae
Spotted trunkfish (*Lactophrys bicordalis*)
Coffre-zingua

Has very toxic glands close to the head which should be removed with care.

Note Tunny, dorados, etc. often taken

trolling are never poisonous. However, if they aren't kept refrigerated or eaten quickly their flesh can putrify and cause serious food poisoning.

Cartography

Warning The chartlets and plans have been drawn for use in conjunction with the information in the guide. They do not replace the need for official charts. This is particularly the case with respect to navigation and where regulations require the presence aboard of official documentation and charts from specific hydrographic services. Although every care has been taken in their creation, the publisher and author take no responsibility for errors or omissions in the chartlets and plans that have crept in despite their care.

Depths and heights are in metres

Scales are in nautical miles (1NM = 1852m), kilometres or metres.

All names of islands and places are taken from local usage and the respective official languages.

All comment and information on the plans is in French for French islands and in English elsewhere.

The conventional symbols for lights and buoys are shown on the charts in conformity with international norms (in English).

Remember The lateral buoyage system in the Antilles accords with IALA Zone B, the system used in the USA (see section on Navigation below).

ABBREVIATIONS USED ON LAND

	Plains/low lying ground
	Medium height hills
	Highest hills
200m	Summits
	Coconut groves
	Mangroves. Mangrove swamps
	Main roads
	Secondary roads
	Unpaved road
	Track
	Main town/Capital
	Secondary town
	Small town. Village
	Groups of buildings, isolated buildings
	Conspicuous house
	Church·chapel
	Fort. Redoubt
	Tower. Mill
	Pylon. Aerial
o	Tourist site – named location
★	Point of interest
	Golf course
oo	Reservoir or water cistern
	National Park boundary
	Frontier
	International airport (long-haul flights)
	Airstrip (inter-island flights)
0 500m	Scale in metres or kilometres

GPS positions and waypoints

(see also *Navigation*)

Lat and long positions on the plans have been established both from official sources and our own successive GPS fixes. Note: Although satellite signals are no longer subject to degrading, GPS precision is not absolute as a result of slight discrepancies in WGS84 and receiver error.

As a result, for safety's sake, the GPS waypoints on the plans are placed well off the coasts and their hazards. All such latitude and longitude and GPS positions are given with the usual disclaimers.

ABBREVIATIONS USED AT SEA

Buoyage

Lateral (Zone B)

Port
Buoy, beacon unlit or lit
Minor marks: buoy, stake

Starboard
Buoy, beacon unlit or lit
Minor marks: buoy, stake

Isolated danger mark

Special marks, zone limits (marine reserves, bathing areas)

Cardinal

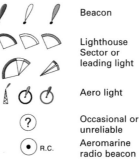

ABBREVIATIONS FOR LIGHTS AND CHARACTERISTICS

Beacon

Lighthouse
Sector or leading light

Aero light

Occasional or unreliable

Aeromarine radio beacon

F	Fixed
Fl	Flashing
Fl(2)	Group flashing
LFl	Long flash
Iso	Isophase
Oc	Occulting
Oc(2)	Group occulting
Q	Quick flashing
VQ	Very Quick
Flashing	
Aero	Aero signal
W	White
R	Red
G	Green
Y	Yellow
O	Orange
18M	Range
True	True bearing

	Mooring buoys
	SPM (large mooring buoy for ships)
	Authorised anchorage limits
	Shallow water <2m
	Shallow water >2m with isolated dangers or danger from swell
	Sea wall or rip-rap
+++	Coral or rocks awash
	Current (1·5kts) each fleche ± 0·5kts
	Recommended route Line of bearing
	Recommended snorkelling/diving
	Submarine cable
	Chain laid along the bottom
Pipe	Submarine pipeline
0 10 M	Scale in nautical miles
	Waypoint (GPS)
	Wreck (showing)
Wk.	Wreck (always immersed)
⚓	Anchorage
	Day or temporary anchorage
	Anchoring forbidden

THE ISLANDS AND THEIR FLAGS

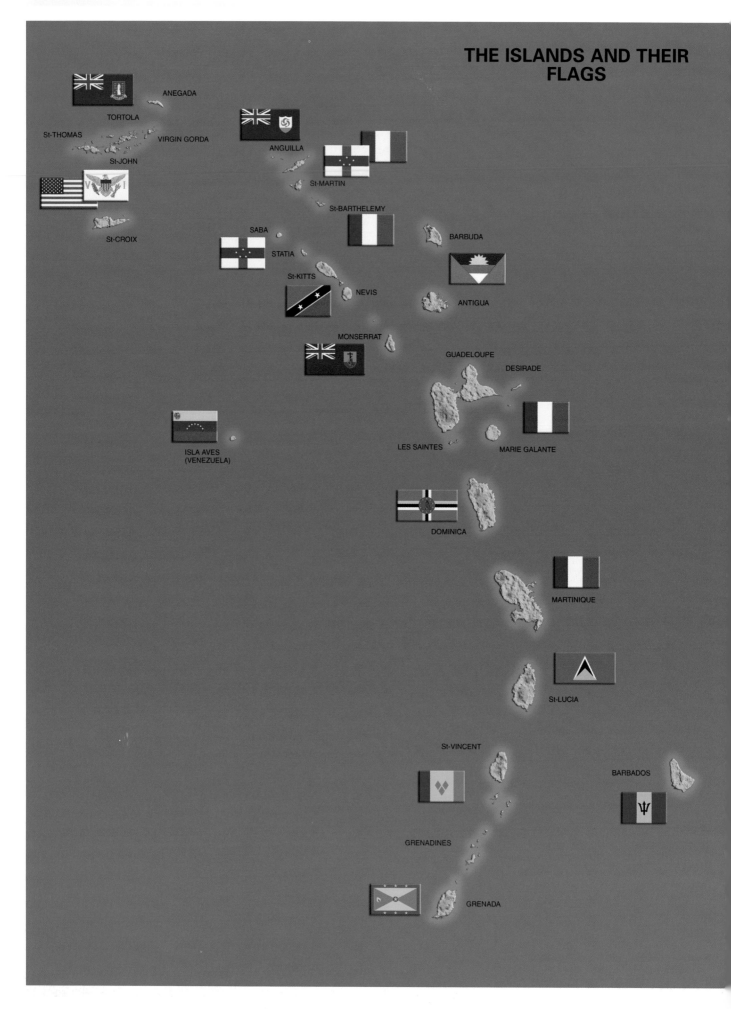

ANEGADA

TORTOLA

St-THOMAS

VIRGIN GORDA

St-JOHN

ANGUILLA

St-MARTIN

St-BARTHELEMY

BARBUDA

SABA

STATIA

St-KITTS

NEVIS

ANTIGUA

MONSERRAT

GUADELOUPE

DESIRADE

ISLA AVES
(VENEZUELA)

LES SAINTES

MARIE GALANTE

DOMINICA

MARTINIQUE

St-LUCIA

St-VINCENT

BARBADOS

GRENADINES

GRENADA

The Windward Islands

Martinique

Land area 1,100 sq km
Highest point: Mont Pelée 1397m
Population 414,000
Main town Fort de France (pop. 120,000)
Language French and Creole spoken by the majority of the population
Currency Euro
Political status French Overseas Department
Distances to other islands St Lucia (Castries)/Le Marin 25M

Top Les Communs (the outhouses), Domaine de la Pagerie, Trois Ilets
Middle Sugar works, Domaine de la Pagerie
Bottom Ruins of the theatre at St Pierre

History

Martinique, for Europeans synonymous with creole, beguine and punch, has a colourful and dramatic past which has influenced the whole Caribbean.

Christopher Columbus discovered the island in 1502, giving it a name almost certainly of Carib origin: Madinina, the Island of Flowers. In June 1635 the Frenchmen Lienard de l'Olive and Duplessis d'Ossonville reached St Christophe, but were quickly put off by those redoubtable allies of the savage Caribs, the *fer-de-lance* snakes. Some months later the rather bolder Belain d'Esnambuc founded Fort St Pierre, beginning a line of excellent governors, amongst them his nephew du Parquet. The latter bought the whole island, which he kept until he died in 1676. After several Dutch and English attempts to conquer Martinique, it was made part of the kingdom of France in 1676, an alliance also due in part to feminine charms. Madame de Maintenon, brought up at Le Prêcheur in the N part of the island, knew very well how to get the king (Louis XIV) interested in so small a territory. Later the Empress Joséphine had to use the same feminine approach with Napoléon Bonaparte.

In 1762 the English conquered the island. By the terms of the Treaty of Paris (1763), France had to sacrifice Canada, 'a few acres of snow', to get back 'the Isle of Flowers'. In the same year Joséphine Tascher de la Pagerie, the future empress, was born. A few

months earlier and she would have been born English!

In 1794, worried by the Revolution, the powerful landowner Dubuc, with some other colonists, helped the English return. Napoléon recovered the island in 1802 in order to re-establish slavery as in Guadeloupe, but lost it again in 1809, the same year in which he repudiated Joséphine. A second Treaty of Paris in 1814 definitively returned Martinique to its first occupants.

Since the end of the 17th century sugar cane cultivation had grown considerably with the regrettable consequence of the importing of African slaves. By the end of the 18th century this practice had completely changed the ethnic composition of Martinique, as with all the sugar islands, such that the vast majority of the population had become of African stock.

St Pierre, the first town and the economic centre, was literally razed in 1902 by the eruption of Mont Pelée. This terrible catastrophe caused 30,000 deaths and utterly changed the economic and social situation of Martinique because the majority of the European population died in the eruption.

Although 7000km from the French capital, the Isle of Flowers became a French department (Département d'Outre Mer (Overseas Department) or DOM)) in 1946. The status gave the island advantages by way of subsidies which, as with Guadeloupe, raised its standard of living appreciably above that of neighbouring islands. All the same, despite these cultural and historical links between France and its American islands, the distance from the capital, the difference in ways of life and customs and the ethnic diversity have often hindered integration with France.

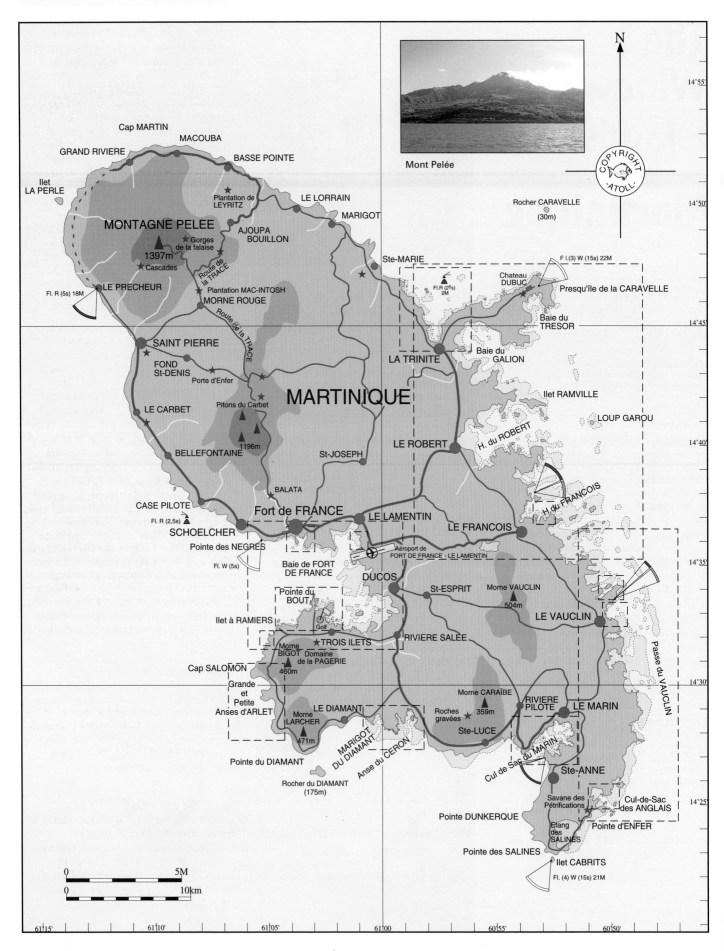

Mont Pelée

N

COPYRIGHT
'ATOLL'

14°55'

14°50'

14°45'

14°40'

14°35'

14°30'

14°25'

Cap MARTIN
MACOUBA
GRAND RIVIERE
BASSE POINTE
Ilet
LA PERLE
Plantation de
LEYRITZ
LE LORRAIN
MARIGOT
MONTAGNE PELEE
AJOUPA
BOUILLON
Gorges
de la falaise
1397m
Route de
la TRACE
Cascades
Ste-MARIE
Fl I.(3) W (15s) 22M
Chateau
DUBUC
Presqu'île de la CARAVELLE
Fl.R (2⁵s)
2M
LE PRECHEUR
Plantation MAC-INTOSH
MORNE ROUGE
Route de la TRACE
Baie du
TRESOR
Fl. R (5s) 18M
SAINT PIERRE
FOND
St-DENIS
Porte d'Enfer
LA TRINITE
Baie du
GALION
Ilet RAMVILLE
MARTINIQUE
LE CARBET
Pitons du Carbet
LOUP GAROU
1196m
LE ROBERT
H. du ROBERT
BELLEFONTAINE
St-JOSEPH
Rocher CARAVELLE
(30m)
BALATA
CASE PILOTE
Fl. R (2,5s)
SCHOELCHER
Fort de FRANCE
LE LAMENTIN
LE FRANCOIS
H. du FRANCOIS
Pointe des NEGRES
Fl. W (5s)
Baie de FORT
DE FRANCE
Aéroport de
FORT DE FRANCE - LE LAMENTIN
Pointe du
BOUT
DUCOS
St-ESPRIT
Morne VAUCLIN
504m
LE VAUCLIN
Ilet à RAMIERS
Golf
Morne
BIGOT
Domaine
de la PAGERIE
TROIS ILETS
RIVIERE SALEE
Cap SALOMON
460m
Passe du VAUCLIN
Grande
et
Petite
Anses d'ARLET
Morne CARAÏBE
RIVIERE
PILOTE
LE MARIN
LE DIAMANT
Roches
gravées
359m
Morne
LARCHER
Ste-LUCE
471m
Cul de Sac du MARIN
Ste-ANNE
MARIGOT
DU DIAMANT
Anse du CERON
Pointe du DIAMANT
Savane des
Pétrifications
Cul-de-Sac
des ANGLAIS
Rocher du DIAMANT
(175m)
Pointe DUNKERQUE
Etang
des
SALINES
Pointe d'ENFER
Pointe des SALINES
Ilet CABRITS
Fl. (4) W (15s) 21M

0   5M
0   10km

61°15'   61°10'   61°05'   61°00'   60°55'   60°50'

The population is densely packed (350 people per sq km), 90% black and mixed race with several thousand Hindus and Syrio-Lebanese. Although proportionally few, thanks to their history and social position the 4000 or so 'Békés' (descendents of old Creole roots) are still influential. There are also several thousand civil servants and private citizens from metropolitan France who have usually lived in the island for several years.

In economic terms Martinique is still largely dependent on agriculture (sugar, bananas and pineapples), although for some years now considerable emphasis has been put on developing tourism both at sea and ashore.

Tourism

Where to stay and what to see

There is a large choice of hotels. The most luxurious are in the bay of Fort de France, mainly round the small marina of Pointe du Bout over which towers the imposing bulk of the Méridien Hotel. In the southern communes the hotels and guesthouses are mostly simpler, often beside lovely beaches lined with coconut palms.

Restaurants use local produce from both market gardens and fishing boats, either Martiniquais or from neighbouring islands.

In the main tourist areas (Fort de France and the leeward coast) restaurant prices are higher than in the small villages in the N of the island and on the windward coast.

In addition to its own natural beauty, on its Atlantic coast Martinique has scores of islets, bays and inlets set within an immense barrier reef. For the most part the green slopes of the mountains end in numerous sandy beaches sprinkled the length of large bays or tucked away in the small ones.

Thanks to its varied relief, the island offers a wonderful range of possibilities for inland travel:

In the mountainous N the thick tropical forest around Mont Pelée and the Pitons du Carbet.

In the centre the low-lying hinterland, covered with plantations, which links Fort de France with the windward coast.

In the S the low hills, flattening out towards the ancient swamps near the Savane des Pétrifications.

An excellent road network serves all of Martinique. Because the terrain becomes less steep and broken towards the centre and S of the island, that's where the network is at its densest, sometimes reaching expressway status and often with heavy traffic.

Fort de France

The town is the base of regional government (Préfecture) and nearly one third of Martinique's population lives within its extensive built-up area. Its lively centre spreads out to the residential quarters in the surrounding hills. The prettiest of the latter, the Quartier de Plateau-Didier has fine examples of colonial houses and a superb panoramic view over the large

Top Yole race
Above Cruise liner dock, Baie des Flamands
Left Cyparis' cell

bay of Fort de France. The nearby Fontaine Didier is a thermal spring with therapeutic properties which has been used for some 150 years. The town of Fort de France has only a few monuments attesting to the various catastrophes to which it has been victim, for example the great fire of 1890. It's best to look round on foot because the central area is quite small and it gets choked with traffic at peak hours . Fort St Louis dominates the bay and houses the museum of pre-Columbian history. Its ramparts lie beside the Place de la Savane which is the heart of the town. The park here, planted with all kinds of flowers and hundred-year-old trees, is where the whole town gathers and strolls around. It is home to the white marble statue of the Martinique-born Empress Joséphine. There are numerous bar-restaurants around its sides and to the W lies the business district. St Louis cathedral, a recent edifice replacing a succession of churches destroyed by earthquakes and fires, lies in the heart of the business district, cheek by jowl with the bubbling and colourfully varied street life. Every day W of the cathedral the central vegetable market fills the morning air with its fruity, spicy smells.

Besides the cathedral the Schoelcher Library is worth a detour for its quaint building in an eclectic architectural style brought back from the Universal Exhibition in Paris in 1889. Opposite the Schoelcher Library the Préfecture is a fine and imposing example of French governmental architecture, inspired as it was by the 17th century. In the Rue de la Liberté on the W side of the Place de la Savane, you'll find the departmental museum, which focuses on the history of the island.

Around the island

N Martinique

For mountain lovers and admirers of luxuriant vegetation the major points of interest are in the N part of the island dominated by 1397m (4584ft) high Mont Pelée.

Schoelcher

Taking the coast road you'll pass through this old fishing village which is named after the French député (member of parliament/representative) who had slavery abolished in 1848. Now a residential extension of Fort de France, it is mainly given over to hotel complexes and a casino.

Case Pilote

Next comes this small fishing village, its church (the oldest in Martinique) and its little port. It was one of the earliest inhabited places in the island and where

Above left St Pierre
cathedral
Above centre Balata
chuch
Above right The golf
course and anchorage at
Trois Ilets
Left Jardin de Balata
(the gardens at Balata)

a Carib chief, who the first French
colonists called Pilote, lived.

Le Carbet

This village lies further N again. It is
where Christopher Columbus came
ashore as did Belain d'Esnambuc later
on. 'Carbet' is the name for the large
square where once upon a time Carib
chiefs and their subjects used to gather.
The nearby Anse Turin is where the
painter Gauguin stayed and discovered
for himself the charms of the tropics
before leaving for the Marquesas in
Polynesia.

Saint Pierre

Today this large village has no more
than 6000 or so inhabitants. On 8 May
1902 almost all of its population died as
a result of the eruption of Mont Pelée.
The only survivor, a prisoner called
Cyparis, owed his life to the thickness of
the walls of his cell. Three parallel

Bottom left Fishing boats, Grand Rivière
Bottom right The beach at Grande Anse d'Arlet

streets now represent the essence of
what's left of the town, which has never
recovered its lost glory and today
survives on fishing and tourism. Small
buildings stand on the foundations of
the remains of the old town. In the
centre of the village the Vulcanological
Museum has an exhibition of relics of
the catastrophe. Some ruins of the old
splendours, such as the theatre (built in
1786 along the lines of the Bordeaux
opera) or the Eglise du Fort bear
witness to the lost grandeur of the old
capital of Martinique, once known as
'Little Paris of the Antilles'.

The other mementos of the catastrophe
are the numerous sunken ships in the
bay, which one can visit either by scuba
diving or in a tourist submarine.

Le Prêcheur

The coast road stops here in this village
of 2000 inhabitants where Françoise
d'Aubigne, the future Madame de
Maintenon and second wife of Louis
XIV, grew up. This may of course
explain the interest shown by the Sun
King for this little island in the West
Indies.

Route de la Trace

Narrow and often vertiginous, this road
follows the old route of the track which,
as early at the 18th century, cut through
the huge rain forest and by-passed the
Pitons du Carbet and the massif of
Mont Pelée before dropping to the wild
N coast. Leaving Fort de France to join
it, don't forget to visit the Balata
Church, a miniature reproduction of
Sacré Coeur de Montmartre and the

nearby Balata Gardens where a wealth
of tropical flora surrounds a fine Creole
house. The road and its many branches
takes us to the very heart of a still
almost untouched Martinique, where
you'll find a succession of shimmering
waterfalls and deep gorges covered in
foliage. The rare villages like Fond St
Denis or Ajoupa Bouillon, full of
flowers, share in this feast of nature.
After Morne Rouge, the centre of this
mountain zone, one reaches Petite
Savane from where, after a long walk, a
steep footpath leads to the top of Mont
Pelée. From Ajoupa Bouillon another
footpath, as much in the river as out,
leads to the Gorges de la Falaise and
their fine waterfalls.

Grand-Rivière

Right in the N of the island surrounded
by deep valleys full of greenery, Grand-
Rivière hangs onto the side of a wild
coastline. This fishing village gives one
the impression of having arrived at the
end of the Martiniquan world, where
the fishing boats drawn up on the shore
add to the local colour. The local
cooking makes this worth the detour.

S Martinique

Trois Ilets, Pointe du Bout

The coast road S of Fort de France Bay
takes you to the pretty village of Trois
Ilets. Close by is the Domaine de La
Pagerie Museum where the future
empress Marie-Joséph-Rose (called
Joséphine) de Beauharnais (née Tasher
de la Pagerie), and first wife of the

Emperor Napoléon Bonaparte, was born in 1763. Overlooking the coast and its three renowned islets a superb golf course has now been created for the clientele of the hotel complex, which covers the whole area of Pointe du Bout.

Anses d'Arlet

Further W, following a succession of small inlets, the coast road reaches Grande and Petite Anses d'Arlet, as well known for their beaches as for their local specialty restaurants, both of which account for the heavy tourist trade.

Le Bourg and Diamond Rock

Thanks to its huge, coconut tree lined beach, this village of 2000 people, one of the island's oldest, now has a fair amount of tourist development in the form of hotel complexes and villas. From the shore you can see Diamond Rock. This small, truncated cone of an islet with its steep cliffs is famous for its role in a heroic episode in the Anglo-French wars at the beginning of the 19th century. Wishing to command the sea approaches to Martinique, in 1804 the English installed some 20 sailors and 4 cannons on the rock, transforming it into an impregnable fortress. For seventeen months it resisted all assaults, meanwhile battering at leisure French ships making in to Fort de France. In consequence the British raised the rock to the status of a naval ship, HMS *Diamond Rock*. According to legend the French only managed to get the better of the English by causing several boats filled with casks of rum to be wrecked on the islet. Dead drunk, the enemy gave up without a fight. (This tale may not be found in English history books.)

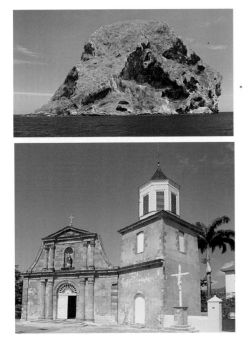

Above Les Fonds Blancs (white sand bottom in shallow water)
Below Diamond Rock
Bottom The church at Marin

Le Bourg du Marin

Tucked into the bottom of its cul-de-sac, this large town of some 6500 people owes most of its economic development to its marina. Today, although business is booming and restaurants are everywhere, the development hasn't completely changed the narrow, twisting streets of the town that, along with its small houses and a church with fine 18th century façade (1766, in the Jesuit style), still retains much of its older charm.

Sainte Anne

The long, well-protected beach has made this elegant village of 3000 inhabitants a holiday resort as much appreciated by tourists as Martiniquais and it is particularly popular at the weekend. Several traditional restaurants line both the main street ending in the Place de l'Eglise and the street level with the shore.

N of the small town the Club Med des Boucaniers (the Buccaneers) has huts set amongst a superb coconut plantation. At the far S end of the island, facing the Atlantic, the Plage des Salines has a superb white sand beach stretching over a kilometre. Nearby and in perfect contrast is the Savane des Pétrifications (Meadow of Petrified Trees) with its air of desolation in which pieces of fossilised wood can sometimes be found.

The Windward coast

This much-indented coast has by and large been spared a heavy tourist influx. From the Baie des Anglais to Presqu'île de Caravelle a plethora of islets is scattered over the coral reefs extending from the long headlands of the coast. Deep in the bays, beaches alternate with small bays full of mangrove swamps. Despite the road with its many byways that joins Le Vauclin to Le Robert, access to the shore isn't always easy. In fact the windward coast remains a vast maritime world which must basically be explored by boat.

Le Vauclin

Apart from its nearby beaches and the fishing port this large village of 7000 people has little of tourist interest. On the perimeter of the old village the new developments have added nothing to the ambience of the place.

Le François

The cottages and concrete buildings of this town of 17,000 line its small streets. Some shops and supermarkets are the hub of the town's activity, along with small restaurants (lolos) with very local menus at very reasonable prices. Thanks to its water sports centre and its small marina Le François is the natural point of departure for visiting the windward coast. The Fonds Blancs (white sand bottom,) and the Baignoire de Joséphine (Josephine's Bath, Ilet Bouchard) are the best known and most frequented spots. Every weekend the Martiniquais, especially the Békés, have a tradition of gathering here to drink ti-punch, up to their waists in the water, their glasses dangling over the sparkling white sandy seabed.

Some of the small islets in the immediate vicinity are inhabited.

Le Robert

Sheltered in the depths of its huge haven, Le Robert has a population of about 18,000. Father Labat, admiring its excellent natural shelter and numerous islets, created the first parish here at the end of the 17th century. The harbour is still the focus of interest in the area since the outskirts of the big town are now rather blighted by a large industrial zone.

Presqu'île de la Caravelle

The landscape and relief of this extended peninsula are full of contrast: steep cliffs battered by ocean waves at the tip, with more sheltered bays and coves on its S coast. A large part of the peninsula has been turned into a natural park the better to preserve its beauties and varied flora. The ruined Château Dubuc, once belonging to a rich and famous family of plantation owners, the Dubuc de Rivery, dominates the Baie du Trésor which was for a long time a pirate lair. At the end of the 18th century legend tells how the young and lovely Aimée Dubuc was kidnapped by Turks, and then became the favourite of Sultan Abdul-Hamid and the mother of the future Mahmud II.

La Trinité

This community of 12,000 is the home of the sub-prefecture of North Martinique and is essentially an agricultural centre focused on banana cultivation, groves of which cover the surrounding hillsides. Very urbanised and developed, La Trinité has little of tourist interest outside its excellent natural harbour.

Sainte Marie

Further N, this large town of 20,000 is an agricultural centre in which sugarcane is the main crop. A small museum commemorates Father Labat's founding of the rum distillery here. As early as the beginning of the 18th century, this famous Dominican, engineer, ethnologist and scientist invented a system of distillation by alembic for the extraction of alcohol from sugar cane. Close to Saint Marie, the St James Distillery and the museum of rum should be visited to learn all about the 'drink of drinks' of the Antilles.

Pilotage

Coast and anchorages

For navigation purposes, the coast can be divided into three sections:

The Leeward coast

From Cape Martin to Diamond Pt, mostly focused on the Baie de Fort de France.

The South coast

From Diamond Pt to Cabrits It, including the natural haven of Cul-de-Sac de Marin.

The Windward coast

Fringed with coral reef as far as the Pointe de la Caravelle, beyond which there is no shelter except la Trinité, to the NE as far as Cape Martin.

Above St Pierre Bay – Mt Pelée
Below Cannons at St Pierre

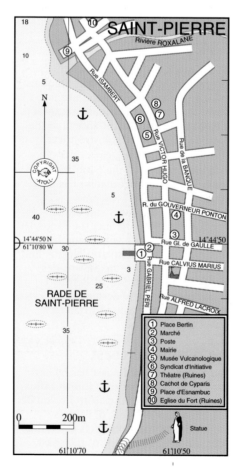

SAINT-PIERRE
Rivière ROXALANE

RADE DE
SAINT-PIERRE

① Place Bertin
② Marché
③ Poste
④ Mairie
⑤ Musée Vulcanologique
⑥ Syndicat d'Initiative
⑦ Théatre (Ruines)
⑧ Cachot de Cyparis
⑨ Place d'Esnambuc
⑩ Eglise du Fort (Ruines)

Statue

I. Leeward coast

Saint Pierre

The bay of St Pierre, dominated by Mont Pelée, is over a mile long N to S. More than a dozen wrecks from the 1902 eruption litter the bottom in depths of 10–50m (see plan). Very often rolly, especially in winter, the anchorage is close to the dock or further N near the Roxane river. The shore is steep-to, quickly dropping off to over 20m. You can also anchor S of the cathedral at the foot of the cliffs on top of which there is a small statue of the Virgin Mary. But note that this is a fishing zone, as you'll see from the boats on the beach, the floats marking the wrecks and the numerous lobster pots all over the anchorage.

Ashore Formalities can be completed at the customs, though their presence can't be relied on. St Pierre itself is not as lively as it once was but even so, there are several small restaurants and shops, a supermarket and a local market for provisioning. There's nothing else by way of yachting services except the possibility of emergency water from the dock and fuel from the gas station.

Le Carbet

Further S the anchorage off Le Carbet, dominated by the pretty bell tower, is off the grey sand beach backed by coconut palms. It is little protected even though it was the spot chosen for landings by the first discoverers

The village and harbour of Case Pilote

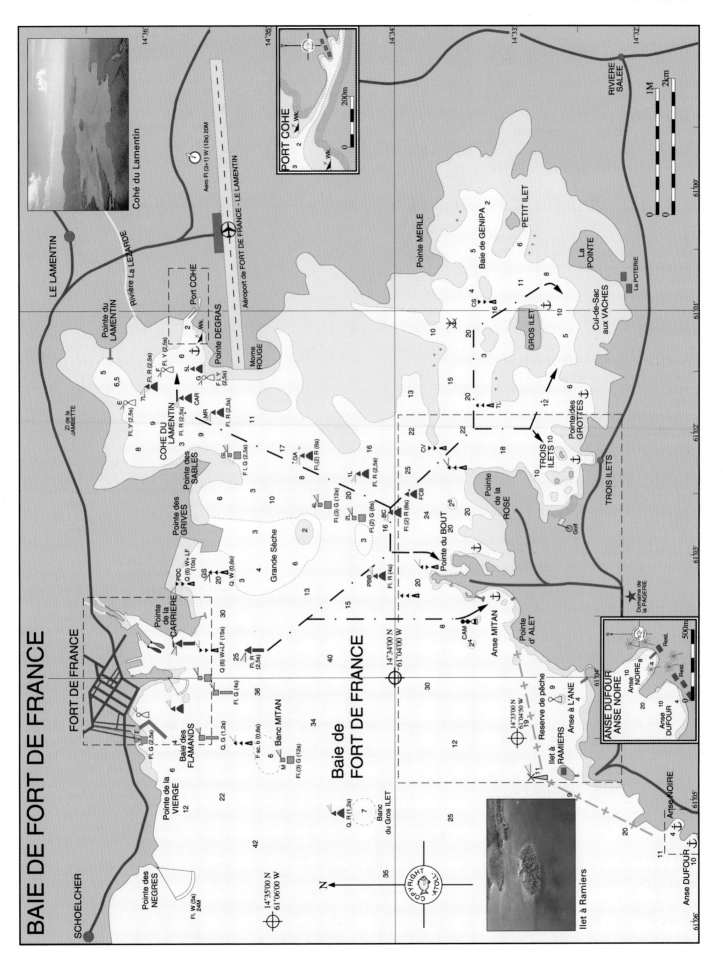

Case Pilote harbour

Columbus (15 June 1502) and
D'Esnambuc.

Caution A few cables S of here, the dock
at l'Ajus has a fish farm around it.
About 2M further S, the tanker jetty
and power station at Bellefontaine are
conspicuous and lit at night.

Case Pilote

The small port of this village, destroyed
by Hurricane David (1979), has been
rebuilt for fishing boats and local
pleasure craft that take up most berths.
Medium sized visiting boats may be
lucky and find a spot alongside the
outer mole.

Caution The dock is fringed by
extensive rip-rap which needs to be
given a wide berth.

For a short stay anchoring outside this
charming fishing village is always
feasible in fair weather provided you
keep clear of the fishing area.

Ashore Small shops are good for minor
provisioning and workshops can cope
with mechanical problems.

Caution 0·5M, 200°T from the mole
there's a fish farm marked by lit buoys.

Fort de France Bay

Along the leeward coast the trades are
irregular and occasionally non-existent.
To find a reliable E'ly you'll need to get
well into Fort de France Bay after
rounding Pointe des Nègres. A few
tacks hard on the wind will bring you
safely to Fort de France even at night.
Once past Pointe des Nègres and its
light, 1M to starboard comes Banc
Mitan buoy marking a 7m shoal only of
concern to large ships. Use Fort Saint-
Louis (lit Fl(4)WRG.15s11-14M) as a
leading mark to enter Baie des
Flamands in the centre of Fort de
France.

Caution At night there are many unlit
vessels in the anchorage.

Fort de France

Baie des Flamands

Fort de France has had a reputation as
a yachting centre for a long time. It was
the meeting place for everyone who

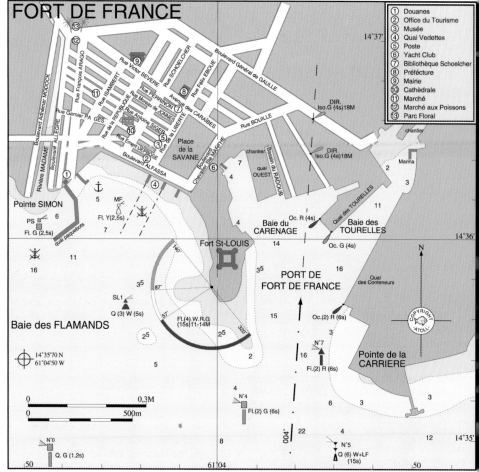

sailed in the Caribbean and one met
legendary figures there, amongst them
those bathing in the glory of a recently
completed circumnavigation come to
Martinique to write the last chapter of
the epic. That's how Fort de France
became one of the cradles of yachting
and chartering. Nowadays things have
changed with chartering a business for
professionals who have all the relevant
certificates and who work for well-
organised companies whose most exotic
dream is the profitability of their
investments. Their fleets, for obvious
reasons of maintenance and efficiency,
are now moored in well run marinas.
That leaves this anchorage, where you
swing round in mad circles, the
closeness of Fort de France being its
main appeal.

The anchorage is limited in the SW by
the new cruise ship jetty and its
manoeuvring area. To the E you must
also leave access for the ferries running
to Pointe du Bout. These limits reduce
space for anchoring in a spot already
very popular with yachts, so after a
short stop you're usually only too eager
to move on. . . The most usual place to
go is on the other side of the bay near
Pointe du Bout where there's a small
marina and the Ponton du Bakoua.
From there it's easy to return when you
wish to visit or reprovision, thanks to
the fast and frequent ferry service.

Ashore Leave and load dinghies at the
dock N of the cruise ship dock.
Immigration is near the terminal at the
root of this dock

As it is a major business centre, Fort de
France has everything you need for
provisioning, offering the widest choice
in all the Antilles. Several shops and
small supermarkets are close to the Baie
des Flamands. For crew wanting to
sample the local cuisine there's plenty of
choice amongst the numerous
restaurants around the sea front and the
Place de la Savane. For maintenance
and chandlery, many specialists and
shops can be found in the general area,
even though a large number of such
concerns have now relocated to the
pleasure vessel centre in the Le Marin
area. Maintenance and repairs can also
be done by the numerous professionals
in the industrial zone of Lamentin on
the road to the airport. On the shore of
Baie des Flamands you'll find both
private and share taxis. The latter criss-
cross the island every which way and
fares are low, with comfort to match.

Port of Fort de France: Baie du Carénage and Baie des Tourelles

After giving Fort Saint Louis (a
Vaubanesque fort) a very wide berth to
port and avoiding the shoal ground S
and SW of the point, you enter the
harbour. The Baie du Carénage is to

port with the docks and premises of the yacht club in the NE corner. There's no room for visitors, though there's a warm welcome for members of foreign clubs wanting to exchange burgees. To starboard lie the West Quay and the Baie des Tourelles where you'll find numerous marine specialists, boatyards and, for very large vessels, the Bassin de Radoub dry dock. A dock for fuel and water can be found at the end of the Baie des Tourelles. The general atmosphere of a busy port area means that you'll only stop here if you're in need of repair or maintenance.

Top Trois Ilets anchorage
Middle left Trou Etienne anchorage
Middle right Bakoua dock
Bottom Pointe du Bout and Anse Mitan

Other anchorages in the Baie de Fort de France

Cohé du Lamentin

Follow the buoyed channel. This is a very sheltered spot, close to the airport, though the water is turbid and the mosquitoes fierce. In the NE the Sailing Club (Neptune Marina) has a small dock. The Lamentin industrial zone is less than 3km from here.

Port Cohé

E of Cohé du Lamentin a small access channel leads to this anchorage in the mangroves. Beware of the wreck N of the entrance. The channel, with 2m in the middle, is marked with a few floating plastic jugs. At the head there's a run down boatyard mostly used by local craft. The creek is only really of much use in a hurricane. However, in such circumstances the crowd of boats

that come to hole-up here make access impossible. That apart, the only interest is in mozzie hunting and the fact that it's a long way from any built-up area!

Pointe des Grives

A basin is being dredged here to make the new l'Etang Z'Abricot marina. The first section, with 400 berths and a boatyard, is expected to be open in 2004/2005 (provisionally).

Gros Ilet and Trois Ilets

Accessed by a buoyed channel, unlit at night, there is excellent shelter behind these islets except in strong NE'lies. The water isn't much clearer than at Cohé du Lamentin, but Trois Ilets village is close by as is the golf course

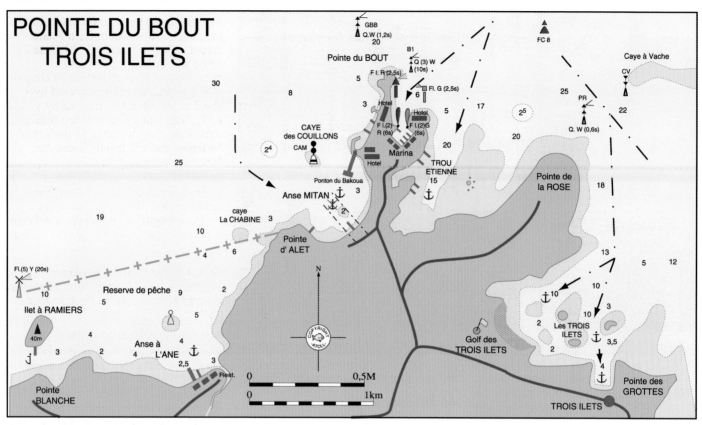

POINTE DU BOUT
TROIS ILETS

and the Domaine de la Pagerie (Joséphine de Beauharnais).

Trou Etienne

Day access as above, but with care given the shoals to the E.

Caution note that closing the shore is very risky (depths <1m) and the anchorage proper is deep (>15m). That said, this is, along with Trois Ilets, the anchorage of choice for boats from Anse Mitan in a W'ly swell.

Anse Mitan

W of Pointe du Bout, this is where Fort de France boat owners keep their boats for holidays and it's pretty crowded, especially at weekends. Things are quieter than in the Baie des Flamands

even if the water isn't always crystal clear. Approach is simple using the building of the imposing Méridien Hotel initially, then the Ponton du Bakoua (VHF 68). But beware of the shoal 300m WSW of the dock, which has 1m of water over it and isn't easy to see, though marked by an unlit buoy.

A bathing zone is marked by yellow buoys 200m off the beach. The anchorage, often rolly, can become very uncomfortable in the occasional W'ly swell. Ashore there are numerous restaurants as well as the facilities of the luxurious Méridien. The big Bakoua dock usually has several berths with fuel and water around its restaurant. Sadly the dock is frequently damaged by hurricanes.

Above Pointe du Bout Marina
Below left Pointe du Bout
Below right Fisherman at Anse à l'Ane

Pointe du Bout Marina

The small marina (VHF 9) tucked into Pointe du Bout is accessed by a beaconed pass. Depths vary from 4 to less than 2m. Night entry is feasible if you give a good berth to Pointe du Bout coming from the W before lining up on the entry lights. Be wary of the narrowness of the channel especially if yours is a larger yacht and so is the one coming the other way. Inside manoeuvring room is equally tight.

Top Anse Noir & Anse Dufour
Above Anse Noir dock
Below Grande and Petite Anses d'Arlet and Cape Salomon

to give a good berth to Caye Chabine pushing out over 200m from Pointe d'Alet. After just under 2·5M Anse à l'Ane will open up, though the anchorage is often disturbed by chop or a N'ly swell. Access is restricted by a shoal of less than 1m, marked by a buoy, which must be rounded before anchoring close to the large dock used by ferries and the fishing boats that liven up the small bay.

Ashore Among the coconut palms, several tourist hotels, restaurants and minimarkets. Along the shorefront a building topped off with pyramidal roofs is very conspicuous.

Ilet à Ramiers

Access to the island is forbidden (military zone) but short term anchoring is possible under its lee close to a small dock.

Anse Noire and Anse Dufour

Twinned together, separated only by a small peninsula, they are nonetheless distinct. Anse Noir has a black sand beach, coconut palms and, near the ferry dock, a small restaurant tucked into greenery. On the Anse Dufour side, called Anse Blanche by some, is a white sand beach with some fishermen's cottages, a snack bar and a grocery. There are several good dive sites in the vicinity used by the local dive clubs. In strong NE'lies, gusts and chop quickly make these anchorages uncomfortable.

Anses d'Arlet

Grande Anse d'Arlet, with its clear water and fine white beach fringed with coconut palms, opens up after you pass

Ashore In addition to day-charterers and dive clubs, the marina has numerous services, supermarket, bank, laundry, bars, restaurants and fashion shops, all with a fairly Mediterranean, deluxe air. Despite the move of lots of marine professionals to Marin, there are still several specialist outfits in the marina's yard. A regular ferry service runs to Fort de France.

L'Anse à l'Ane

To escape from all these overcrowded anchorages, leave Baie de Fort de France and head SW towards Anse à l'Ane and the Ilet à Ramiers, taking care

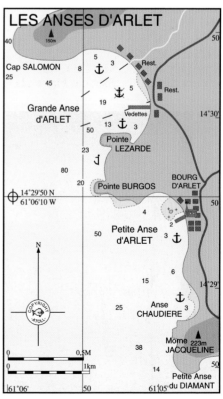

Above Arlet village and Petite Anse d'Arlet
Left Fishermen in Grande Anse d'Arlet
Below right Marigot du Diamant anchorage
Bottom left Marigot du Diamant from the N

Cape Solomon. It's a pleasant anchorage, though crowded at weekends because it is so close to Fort de France. Anchor preferably either in the N or the S of the bay. The central area is by law reserved for fishermen. It's also deep in the middle. It's also important to leave access to the large dock free. On the beach are lots of colourful fishing boats, some cottages and shops but above all several restaurants where day charters drop passengers to drink punch and eat langoustes. Round Pointe Bourgos to find Petite Anse d'Arlet.

Note Be wary of the area of reef N of the dock. You can use the dock more or less in line with the church tower as a leading mark. Anchor S of the dock to go and visit the picturesque village with its nicely laid out sea front.

Ashore you'll find grocery stores and small restaurants with a marked local flavour. In SE'lies this anchorage is very rolly, when the better sheltered Anse Chaudière is to be preferred.

II. South coast

Between Diamond Pt and Sainte Anne

To reach Sainte Anne or Cabrits Islet, you'll be hard on the wind battling a strong current, often of up to 2 knots. Boats with poor windward performance will take longer to make this passage than to reach St Lucia 20M S of Martinique!

Diamond Rock

Heading for Marin you'll pass close to Diamond Rock (*Caution* this dangerous monolith is unlit). Overawed by this 175m high lump of rock, you can only admire the persistence of the English who hauled their cannons to its summit the better to sink French ships.

Marigot du Diamant

The whole S coast here extends seaward in shoal ground, which breaks in moderate seas. To stop (day stops only, in good weather and good visibility) at Marigot du Diamant or Anse Céron, approach with care.

For Marigot du Diamant you must first find Pointe du Marigot, marked by two low white buildings (the luxurious Novotel hotel) and then line up on Morne Cabrits on 027°T. Once clear through the pass (10–20m) give the dangers around Pointe Marigot a good

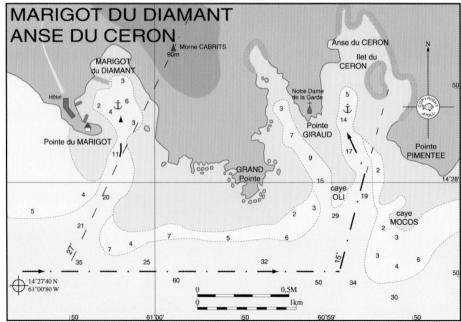

berth. The anchorage close to the small docks of the hotel is partly taken up by some local boats and the shoals pushing out from the shore. In established E'lies the anchorage can be rolly.

Ashore you'll find the hotel-restaurant buildings and a dive club, but nothing specific for yachts. The village of Diamant is about 2km to the west.

Anse du Céron

Access to Anse Céron is made tricky by Caye Oli. The approach line to get past Caye Oli is on 015°T on the right edge of Ilet du Ceron before altering to port to enter the inlet. This deep, remote anchorage is a good one if you tuck well up, though apart from the sense of isolation, there isn't much else going for it.

Sainte Anne

This is one of the loveliest and most popular beaches in Martinique. There's no difficulty coming from the S. But from the N, if you fancy a stiff beat to windward from the Cul-de-Sac de Marin, be careful to round well clear of Banc de la Crique and the other coral outcrops off the Club Med. The Club Med dock is private and you should leave its access clear. Buoys mark the bathing zone off the Club Med and the beach of Sainte Anne. You can also anchor further to the S off the small dock in order to get to the pretty village set either side of the small central square and the charming stone church. Ashore there is provisioning at the shops as well as lots of more or less touristy restaurants.

Cul-de-Sac du Marin

To enter the Cul-de-Sac, your approach is helped by the conspicuous Morne de la Pointe Borgnesse with an aerial on top N of the entrance. Then make sure you identify the first green buoy to port, which should keep you clear of the shoal ground (2–7m) off the Pointe Borgnesse. From there line up on Pointe du Marin (sector light) on

073°T. If you're not experienced a night entry is tricky even though the buoys are lit. Most notably, the light on Pointe du Marin can get lost in the bright lights of the Club Med. Take your entry carefully and watch your course.

Caution Numerous lobster pots around the channel entrance are a major trap for propellers, especially at night.

In the same way, if you're coming from S and your boat draws much water, your main concern will be to avoid the Banc de la Crique (marked by a red buoy) where I've found a shoal with less than 2m over it.

To starboard a second red buoy marks the end of the Banc des Trois Cayes. Then to port a green buoy marks the S tip of the Banc du Singe. After leaving the Pointe du Marin and the Club Med buildings to starboard, head for the inner harbour of the Cul-de-Sac on 050°T for about 0·8M. Next, leave a red buoy to starboard (Pointe Cailloux Shoal) when you'll see to port a green buoy marking the SE end of the Banc Major. Once past it head N leaving to starboard the red buoy off Banc du Milieu. Be careful to give the last a good berth, it extends further N than charted.

Le Marin

From Banc du Milieu there are two possible routes:

- one to the ENE headed for Port du Marin
- the other to the N headed for the Carenantilles Boatyard

The latter is approached by an unlit, buoyed channel dredged to 3m. Haul out facilities and the presence of numerous professional services make this an exceptionally well-equipped boating centre. To reach the Le Marin yacht haven from the Banc du Milieu follow the channel marked more or less by a row of red buoys, which you leave to starboard. To port the Banc de la Douane is marked by two green beacons. S of this route is a huge area full of buoy moorings. The yacht haven (VHF 16/9) has almost 600 berths. A large number of them are taken by charter company fleets, which have been based in this excellent shelter for some years now. Although very recently (though all is relative) the Cul-de-Sac was just a wild and lonely spot used only by local fishermen, now first class management has created what has become the biggest yachting centre in the S Antilles.

Ashore Customs handle formalities and there are all the services of a modern marina around the Capitainerie. The sum total of the yachting business concentrated here, together with the

---

Above right Port du Marin (Le Marin harbour)
Below left St Anne beach
Below centre Ilet Duquesnay at Le Marin
Below right Port du Marin marina pontoons

Grand Cul-de-Sac du Marin from the W

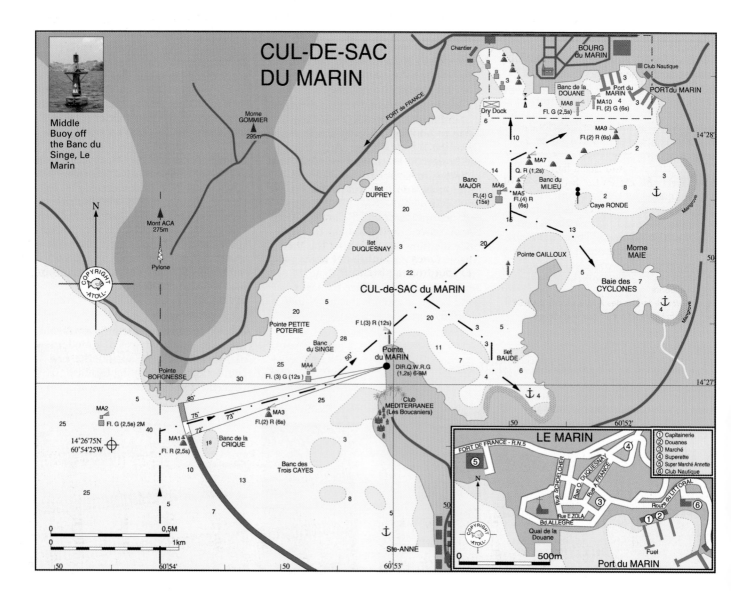

increasing tourist and commercial facilities of Bourg du Marin, have contributed to the transformation of the place. The varied shops, supermarkets and services of the town offer ample provisioning possibilities. And for eating out the crew will find several small restaurants offering different local specialties. Both Lamentin airport and Fort de France are easily reachable in under half an hour by taxi or hire car by an excellent main road.

For those who long for solitude, thanks to the Cul-de-Sac du Marin's size there are still numerous isolated anchorages in the SE part, far from the port's bustle, two of which are well-known hurricane holes. In such an emergency the plethora of charter boats makes for problems of overcrowding, but more normally the deep indents surrounded by mangroves are little visited. The sole danger you'll meet is aggressive mosquitoes.

Ilet Cabrits

From the N as far as Ilet Cabrits the coast is fringed up to 0·5M off by a large reef with only 3–5m of water over it. The barren island has a light (Fl 4 15s 21M) and marks the S extremity of Martinique.

III. Windward coast

From Ilet Cabrits to Point Caravelle

The vast majority of yachts only visit the leeward and S coasts as already described. Doing so reduces Martinique's coast to the bare minimum, which explains why most anchorages on the Caribbean side are overcrowded. However, Martinique does have a unique windward coast, which is the finest in the Lesser Antilles. To reach it, obviously once you're past Ilet Cabrits you have to brave the Atlantic swell (and the often fresh trades), deal with passes and conquer your own fears. But those who have already sailed amongst Brittany's rocks or somewhere similar, who know how to use a hand bearing compass and an echo-sounder, have a powerful auxiliary, the relevant charts and a basic competence, have all that's needed to reach the numerous calm and seldom visited anchorages of the windward coast without much trouble. However, you must always sail in clear weather when the sun is high.

After giving Ilet Cabrits a good berth because of the 2m shoal off its SW side as well as the Table du Diable:

either find and use the Passe du Vauclin in order to be able to sail in the lee of the offshore reefs

or head further N, holding well offshore and to windward of the reefs in order to run back in to use the passes fronting Cul-de-Sac, Frégate, Le François or Le Robert. The Vauclin and François passes as well as that of Le Robert are these days equipped with lit buoyage. All the same, a night passage is out of the question for any but the most experienced. Some leading lines are given below to enable a better run in to the buoys, which aren't always easy to spot from a distance.

Cul-de-Sac des Anglais

If the weather suits, as a first stop one can put into the Cul-de-Sac des Anglais after Pointe Baham. Entry is between Toisroux It and Hardy It.

Note that in a heavy swell entry is very difficult and likewise dangerous.

Orientate yourself with the readily visible reefs S of Hardy It and hold to 300°T before altering for the tiny Aigrettes It, being careful to avoid the reefs extending W of Toisroux It.

Anchorages:

either NE of Aigrettes It in the lee of the reefs, though the 'fond blanc' (white sand bottom) comes up very quickly to less than 2m in the middle.

or further in, in the NW, though the head of Cul-de-Sac is not accessible to boats drawing much water because of a sill across the entrance with only 2m over it.

There are no roads leading here, only a few fishermen and the birds on Hardy It. If you have the time and love isolation, peace and quiet, this is a stop not to be missed.

Route to and Pass of Vauclin

Leaving Cul-de-Sac des Anglais head 025°T for Cap Ferré. Behind Pt Chevalier and Chevalier It a small fishing harbour has a sector light leading through a shallow pass. Once past Cap Ferré head more N'ly to keep well off Pointe Macre which has a large reef extending from it. Once level with Macabou (see Transit 1 diagram: the yellow cliff of the Grand Macabou Quarry in line with the peak of Morne Sulpice 270°T), head 333°T until you

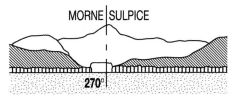

Transit 1:
Gran Macabou quarry on Morne Sulpice 270°T

Top Ilet Cabrits
Below left Cul-de-Sac des Anglais from the ESE
Below right Le Vauclin harbour and village

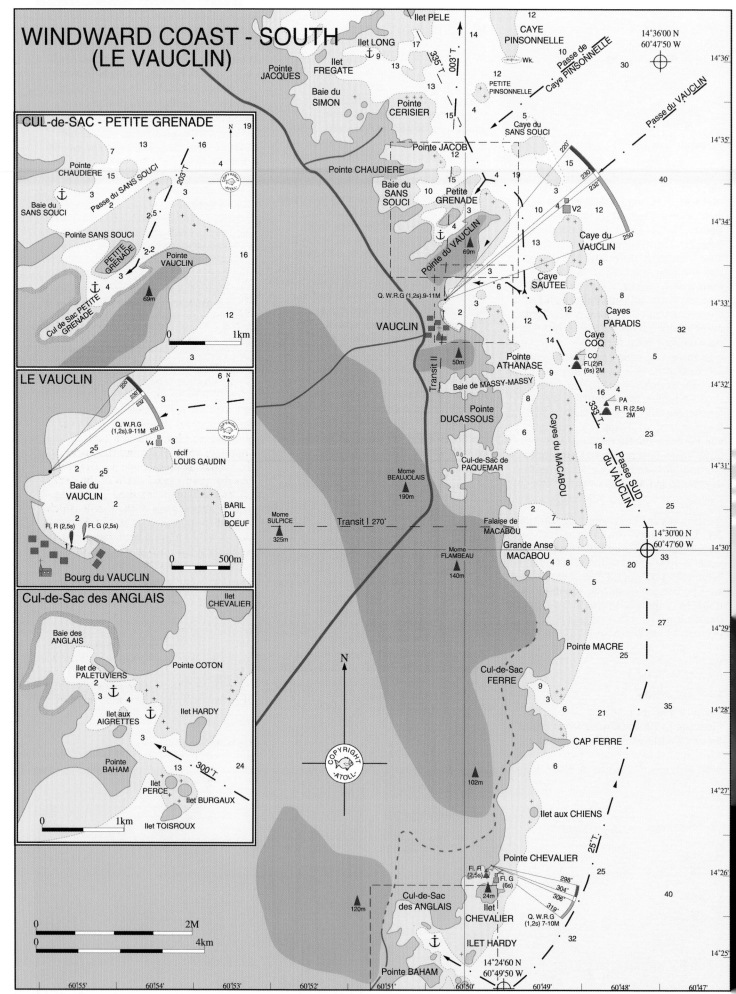

WINDWARD COAST - SOUTH
(LE VAUCLIN)

CUL-de-SAC - PETITE GRENADE

LE VAUCLIN

Cul-de-Sac des ANGLAIS

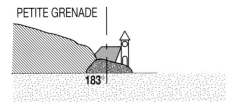

PETITE GRENADE

183°

Transit II 183°T of Petite Grenade on green church roof on W end

identify Pointe du Vauclin. In good visibility you can spot the tiny Pelé It (between Ilet Long and Ilet Thierry) beyond and in line with the tip of Pointe du Vauclin. Following this line Pelé, Bouchard and Thierry Its must always form a continuous line beyond Pointe du Vauclin – if they open up, then you're too far offshore. Leave the first red buoy indicating the S end of Cayes Paradis to starboard. The cayes break visibly in a heavy swell, but to port the Cayes du Macabou are less obvious. Once inside the entrance the swell disappears. Look for the first isolated patch (Caye Coq) marked by the second red buoy, which again you leave to starboard. Watch out to port for another patch, less easy to see, the gap between the two is quite wide at 200–300m. A series of outcrops follows to starboard after which turn W a few degrees to get around Caye Sautée.

Le Vauclin

Access only for boats drawing less than 2m. Come round towards the NW to leave to port the buoys marking Louis Gaudin Reef. The sector light helps local sailors to use the pass between Cayes Sans Souci and du Vauclin at night. The little fishing port has 2m or less because it's often silted up. It's possible to anchor N of the harbour but it is often bouncy. There are several shops in the town for provisions and a few simple restaurants.

Petite Grenade

For a first anchorage I prefer Petite Grenade to Le Vauclin. To reach it, double Pointe du Vauclin giving it a wide berth (the cays are obvious) then head towards the NE tip of Long It.

After about 0·5M you should have the E tip of Petite Grenade bearing 203°T. The passage between islet and coast should then be visible and you'll see the pass through the coral ahead. Depths in the pass come up from 18m to 8m then, between the island and the coast, jump quickly to plus or minus 2·4m depending on tide. Stay in mid-channel. Inside is a calm lagoon, virtually a lake, reputed to be a perfect hurricane hole.

Route towards Le François

Leaving Petite Grenade passage, head 335°T towards Pelé It. After about 1M, on a back-bearing of 183°T, you'll see the green roof of Vauclin church above the W tip of Petite Grenade (see diagram, transit II). Keep on this transit while you steer 003°T. To starboard you'll see Caye Pinsonelle on which there are the remains of a cargo ship that went aground not long back. Once

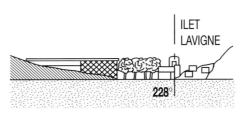

ILET LAVIGNE

228°

Transit IV 228°T town hall tower on S tip of Ilet Lavigne

level with Pelé It, give a wide berth to the coral shoals (3·5m) on which the swell sometimes breaks. 1M further N you'll cross the transit of Ilets Thierry and Aubert to port. Alter to 324°T towards the E tip of Ilet Ramville (transit III).

Before trying this route, you can also make a stop under the islets by leaving them to your N (to starboard) and going to anchor between Long It and Cul-de-Sac Frégate.

Some of the islets are inhabited. On Bouchard (or Oscar) It, an old house has been prettily done up and offers buffet meals.

Passe du François

2M after the islets, if you want to enter Havre du François (Le François Harbour), alter to 228°T with the S tip of Ilet Lavigne in transit with the white bell tower of the town hall (Mairie) of Le François (see diagram, transit IV). In a mile you'll reach the first green buoy, which marks the buoyed entrance channel leading off initially due S between the reefs. After leaving to port the green buoy marking Caye Ronde, you'll reach Havre du François on a course of 250°T. To find the docks of the Centre Nautique and Le François Marina, give a good berth to the reefs off Pointe Bateau (marked by a green buoy), but be wary of the shoals which also lie to starboard on the Le François side. There's an excellent, calm and well-protected open anchorage in the lee of Ilet Lavigne (or Gros Ilet).

Marina du François

The few docks are mostly taken up by ferries and local sailing craft. On the outside to the left there's a fuel and water dock. Depths vary from 2–2·7m depending on the tide. The facilities are a bit rudimentary but berthing fees are reasonable. The marina has a backdrop of greenery fronted by a fine stand of

Top Petite Grenade anchorage
Bottom left Le François harbour and marina from the N
Bottom right Le François marina

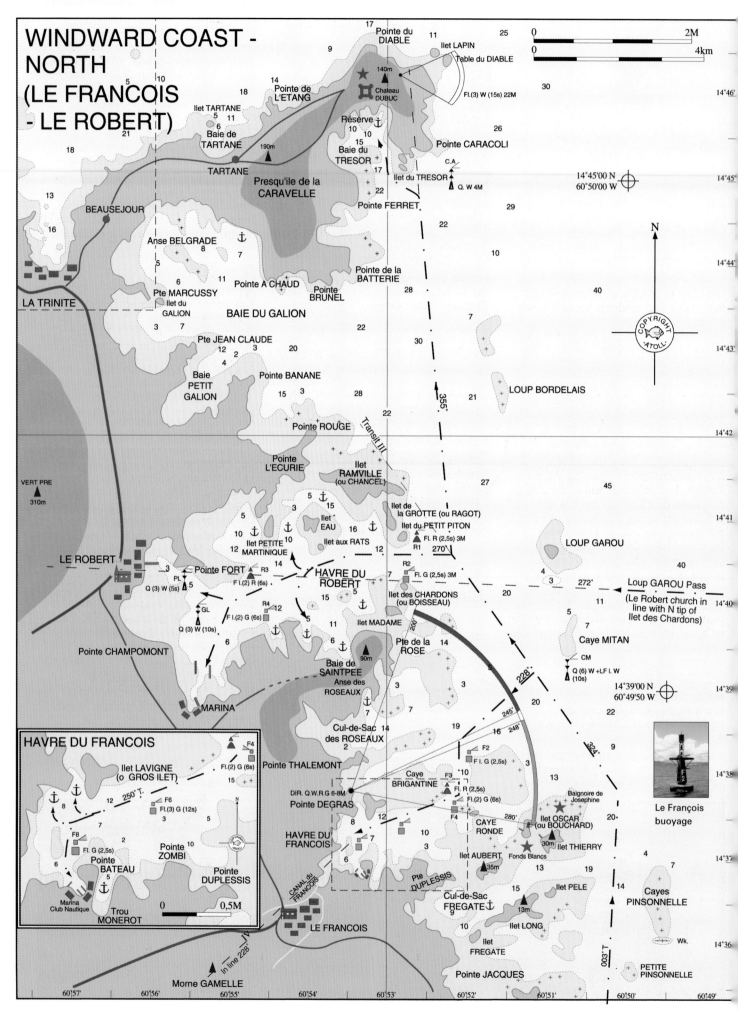

Le François buoyage

coconut palms. You'll usually be made welcome because visitors are few and hospitality and kindness are still a part of the traditional way of life on the windward coast. A passing yachtsman who respects local ways will soon see how swiftly doors are opened and friendly relations established. The locals, especially in Le François, know the maze of islets and cays on this coast like the backs of their hands. So maybe one of them can help you get to know the waters better, as I had the luck to do a long while back, thanks to my Martiniquais friends François Albert Garcin, Joel Ménivier and many others. It follows that Le François is a good base for exploring this coast and even for leaving one's boat. The Centre Nautique has a 24 hour guard and is a good hurricane hole.

Ashore There isn't much apart from a few local craftsmen, a hotel-restaurant and a few simple lolos. But the town is only 1·5km away. It's accessible by taxi or better by your tender, which you can

Top left Marin'erha
Top right Loup Garou islet
Bottom left Baie du Trésor anchorage
Bottom right Château Dubuc on the Presqu'île de la Caravelle

take to the supermarket on the bank of the Rivière des Roses as well as to Le François' other shops.

From Le François to the anchorages of Le Robert harbour

Caution In strong NE winds and swell, it's not advisable to try the Le François pass unless you have a powerful motor.

Cul-de-Sac des Roseaux

Leaving the pass out of Le François, Cul-de-Sac and Anse des Roseaux lie to the W. Make the approach in good visibility and fair weather. The inner part of the Cul-de-Sac is shoal, whereas the Anse (though very tight) has 6–7m.

Havre du Robert (Le Robert Harbour)

To rejoin the route from Vauclin, resume a heading of 324°T on the E tip of the Ilet de Ramville until level with Loup Garou. On the seaward side, this sandy islet with its tuft of greenery surrounded by coral is conspicuous. In fair weather there's a temporary anchorage to be had for small boats in its lee.

Havre du Robert with its buoyed approach opens W of the islet. The first two buoys mark the passage between the shoals round the Ilet de la Grotte and those round Ilet des Chardons. The harbour has a multitude of anchorages.

In the S behind Ilet Madame: the sandy shoals, or 'fond blancs', of the pretty islet are much appreciated by local swimmers.

Further W are three small creeks. Watch out for the coral banks off them and give them a wide berth. In the N there are good anchorages under Ilet de la Grotte, Ilet de Ramville and Petite Martinique. The inner part of Le Robert Harbour is full of coral, as are the waters around Pointe Fort.

Two further buoys mark the shoals SE of Pointe Fort to starboard and N of Pointe Royale to port. For access to the channel towards the town, leave to port the two cardinal buoys showing a line of shoals. All of the buoys are lit, but arriving at night from seaward is not recommended for those without previous experience.

Ashore Several shops and a local market in the town for provisioning. There are no chandleries, but there are some mechanics and skilled workers to help with breakdowns etc. In the S there's

the small Marin' Erha, but it's only for local craft with shoal draft. Inside there are 15–20 berths on the quay with excellent shelter. Ashore, in the premises of the old rum store there are some maintenance and repair services. There's a fuel station too, but at present it's accessible only to boats drawing 1–1·9m depending on tide.

Presqu'île de la Caravelle

La Baie du Trésor

Leaving Le Robert Harbour make a wide detour round Ilet de Ramville and head 335°T towards this bay with its promise of sunken galleons. The sea often rolls in here because there's not much by way of an offshore reef barrier. To your W the Baie du Galion soon opens up but has no really usable shelter. Use the La Caravelle light on 335°T as a mark to begin with when heading into the Baie du Trésor, then leave the coral-girt, barren, black and bare Ilet du Trésor to your E with, to your W, a huge coral reef. The entrance to the pass has 15–20m. Inside the best anchorage is in the NE. Drop a stern

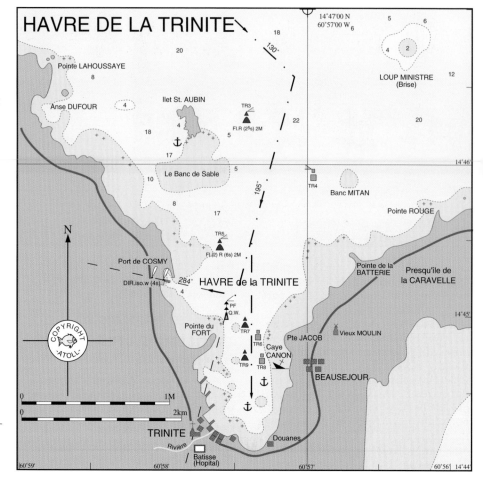

Below Pointe du Vauclin and Petite Grenade from S
Bottom left Baie Sans Souci from E
Bottom right Baie de St Peé, Pointe de la Rose from NW

Top left Ilets Long and Pelé from S

Top right Ilets Thierry and Bouchard (or Oscar) from N

Above Ilet Long and Ilets Thierry and Bouchard (or Oscar) from SE

anchor and take the bow within 2m of the beach to put some lines onto some trees. The usually quiet anchorage is close to the ruins of the Château Dubuc and right in the heart of the nature reserve of Presqu'île de la Caravelle, where some splendid walking is to be had.

Caution To protect the national park only day anchoring is permitted here.

Other passes on the windward coast

There are other routes to the windward coast, particularly when coming from the N:

- come round the reefs of Presqu'île de la Caravelle and head for Le Robert Harbour by leaving the Loup Bordelais Banks to your S
- using the Loup Garou pass and the transit on 272°T given in the SHOM Pilot (Le Robert church in line with the N of the Ilet des Chardons)

Havre de la Trinité (La Trinité Harbour)

Sailing boats don't much visit the port at La Trinité in Martinique's NE. It can be reached from the S around Presqu'île de la Caravelle.

Danger The Loup Ministère is 2·8M W of the Pointe du Diable. Go well N of it before altering course and running in on Ilet Saint Aubin.

The shoals E of Ilet Saint Aubin are marked by a red buoy. Leave the green buoy marking Banc Mitan to port and follow the buoyed channel to the anchorages, either E of the fishery school (white building) or S of a wreck not far from the town.

Caution Keep well away from the shore because of the <1m shallows.

In a N wind the anchorage is not comfortable. To the NW of Pointe Sainte Catherine the jetties of the small fishing port of Cosmy are not accessible

to keel boats. The lit buoyage means a night entry is feasible to those who know the area well.

Ashore The town has a customs post and is useful for those headed directly to Dominica from the windward coast. Otherwise La Trinité is of no real interest to the visiting yachtsman bar a few stores for provisioning, to complete formalities or to tour the local area.

Useful Information for Martinique

AIRLINE CONNECTIONS
Lamentin International Airport
Long-haul flights
Daily to France
Various services to European destinations
Flights to North America, Canada, Haiti
Inter-island services
Daily flights by local companies to Guadeloupe,
St-Martin and the English-speaking islands.

FERRIES
Express inter-island services between
Martinique, Guadeloupe, Dominica and St
Lucia

TELECOMMUNICATIONS
Calling Martinique from abroad: ☎ (0) 596 + six
figure number
Public call boxes: These use France Télécom
cards (Télécartes). French Visa cards (Cartes
Bleues (CB)) with the implanted chip will
always work, cards with only a magnetic data
strip may not.

CLUBS AND ASSOCIATIONS
Yacht Club Martinique, Boulevard Chevalier Ste
Marthe (Carénage), ☎/*Fax* 05 96 70 23 76
Club Nautique du Marin, Bassin Tortue,
☎ 05 96 74 92 48 *Fax* 05 96 74 62 03
CROSSAG: Centre Régional Opérationnel de
Surveillance et de Sauvetage Antilles-Guyane
(French regional coastguard service),
☎ 05 96 73 16 16 *Fax* 05 96 73 57 30
Email CROSS.Fort-de-France@
equipement.gouv.fr
SNSM: Société National de Sauvetage en Mer
(French lifeboat service), ☎ 05 96 26 01 74

TOURIST OFFICES (OFFICES DU TOURISME)
Office du Tourisme: 2, rue E Deproge, Fort de
France, ☎ 05 96 63 79 60 *Fax* 05 96 73 66 93
Email odtm@cgit.com
ARDTM (Martinique Tourism Department), Anse
Gourand Schoelcher, ☎ 05 96 61 61 77
Fax 05 96 61 22 72
Maison du Tourisme Vert, Gîtes Ruraux (Eco-
tourism in local hostels),
9 Boulevard de Gaulle, Fort de France
☎ 05 96 63 18 54 *Fax* 05 96 70 17 61
Gîtes de France, 9 Boulevard de Gaulle, Fort de
France ☎ 05 96 63 74 74 *Fax* 05 96 63 55 92

FESTIVALS/FOLK FESTIVALS
Course des Gommiers (Dugout Races): January
Carnival: March
Commemorative festivals: St Pierre (St Peter):
May
Régates de Juin (June Regattas) at Le Marin:
June
Tour de Martinique des Yoles (Round
Martinique Yole Race): August
Cock fighting: Mongoose and cock fights in
Ducos, Lamentin, Rivière Pilote

PUBLIC HOLIDAYS
New Year's Day (1 January), Easter Sunday,
Easter Monday, Labour Day (1 May), Ascension
Day, Whit Monday, VE Day (8 May), Slavery
Abolition Day (27 May), Bastille Day/National
Day (14 July), Schoelcher Day (21 July),
Assumption (August), Toussaint (All Saints Day,
1 November), Fête des Morts (All Souls Day, 2
November), Armistice Day (11 November),
Christmas Day (25 December)

OFFICE HOURS
Shops: Mon–Fri, 0900–1200, 1500–1800,
Sat 0900–1300
Banks: 0730–1200, 1500–1800, Sat 0730–1300
Government offices: Mon & Fri 0730–1300,
1500–1630
Tues & Thurs 0730–1300

GOLF
Trois Ilets

PLACES TO SEE
Fort de France
Bibliothèque Schoelcher (Schoelcher Library)
Musée 'Gen Lontan' (history of Martinique in
costumes)
La Savane (Public Garden)
St Louis Cathedral: Organs
Fort St Louis: said to be by Vauban.
Precolumbian archaeological museum
St Pierre
Franck A Perret Museum of Vulcanology
Historical museum, Old theatre, Cyparis' cell

Elsewhere
Domaine de la Pagerie: Trois Ilets – Museum
and gardens, Maison de la Canne
Château Dubuc ruins and mini-museum:
Presqu'île Caravelle
Savane des pétrifications, Pointe d'Enfer
(jaspers & petrified wood)
Diamond Rock: Le Diamant
Le Jardin de Balata (Balata Gardens)

Le Sacré-Coeur de Balata (1928)
Route de la Trace
Plantation MacIntosh: Morne Rouge
Pitons du Carbet: for walks and waterfalls
Mont Pelée: for walks and waterfalls
Gorges de la Falaise: Ajoupa-Bouillon, for walks
and butterfly house
Musée Paul Gauguin (Gauguin Museum, Gallery
of History and the Sea): Le Carbet
Plantation de Leyritz: Basse Pointe (1705),
museum of dolls made of plants by Will
Penton
Musée de Rhum St James/de la Banane (Rum
and Banana Museum)
L'Habitation Fonds St Jacques: Ste Marie
Many distilleries to visit throughout the island

ROAD TRANSPORT
Drive on the right
Taxis
Hire car companies in the main towns and at
the airport

FORMALITIES
Arriving by air
Customs and immigration in the airport
Arriving by sea
Fort de France Quai des Paquebots, office hours
0715–1145m and 1330–1615 7 days a week
Le Marin Office hours 0700–1300 7 days a week
St Pierre customs post in the town, variable
hours
La Trinité customs only, variable hours

In theory formalities in Martinique are free.

St Lucia

Area 620 sq km
Highest point Mt Gimie
939m
Population 150,000
Capital Castries (pop. 50,000)
Language English and a French-based
patois
Currency EC$–US$ accepted
Political status Independent state
Distances to other islands Martinique (Le
Marin to Rodney Bay) 22M
St Vincent (Soufrière to Châteaubelair)
34M

History

Discovered during Columbus' fourth voyage in 1502, like Martinique. Until the mid 17th century the Caribs remained masters of the island, resisting every attempt at colonisation. After massacring an English colony in 1639, they finally accepted a treaty with the French in 1660. From around that time conflict between the French and English was incessant and St Lucia changed hands more than fourteen times. Its history was often tied to that of Martinique. St Lucia became French for the last time in 1802 following the Treaty of Amiens. After the Napoleonic Wars in 1814, it became definitively British. Nonetheless, like Dominica the island retained the imprint of the old French presence in many of its place names and in its patois, which is very like creole. After the long period of colonial rule marked by the steady decline in the fortunes of its agriculture following the abolition of slavery, St Lucia became an associated state of the Commonwealth in 1967 and independent on 22 February 1979. The population is predominantly of African origin with some racial intermixing.

Agriculture continues to be the island's economic mainstay despite minor attempts at industrialisation and the oil terminal at Grand Cul-de-Sac. Growing sugar cane has largely been replaced by growing bananas, cocoa, coconuts and citrus fruit. Thanks to the exploitation of the island's natural beauty,

Old cannon, Vigie Cove

continuous expansion of the hotel industry and an international airport, tourism has been expanding rapidly for some years. For all that, the purchasing power of the population remains below that of neighbouring Martinique.

Tourism

Where to stay and what to see

St Lucia's charm lies above all in the spectacular mountains, magnificent beaches and small, unspoiled villages. The best known geological phenomenon, the Deux Pitons, two amazing volcanic sugar loaves, has become the national emblem. In order to protect the lovely landscape's luxuriant vegetation, its birds and reptiles and its underwater world, numerous nature reserves have been created. You may be lucky enough to see the famous St Lucia parrot (*Amazona versicolor*), now a protected species.

Castries

The capital has a population of around 50,000. It has been destroyed by fire several times, most recently in 1948. Founded by the French in the 18th century, the town was named in 1785 after General de Castries, then minister of Louis XVI's navy. For a long time it was the busiest deepwater port in the West Indies. Of the old colonial houses the few remaining are on Brazil Street and around the former Columbus Square, now renamed Derek Walcott Square in honour of the Nobel laureate, who was a native of the island. Nearby is the huge Cathedral of the Immaculate Conception, dating from 1897. The covered market, close to the port, is a colourful, animated scene. Where the port area is being extended, a new shopping mall with luxury outlets is being developed and at Pte Séraphine there's a duty free zone, used by tourist ship passengers.

Cruise liner on the Pointe Séraphine Jetty

Around the island

The steep hills of the island, with their highest point at Mt Gimie, limit the extent of the road network. A circular route, often narrow, serves the S part of the island. Leaving Castries it follows the leeward coast, passing many small inlets (of which Marigot Bay is the loveliest example) and several small fishing villages. La Raye is one of the latter, where you'll see fishing boats and multicoloured nets on the beach. The road takes you to La Soufrière.

La Soufrière

The French also founded this, the island's second town, in 1746. On the steep roads up the hillside there are old houses with original ornate façades, if now rather dilapidated. Not far away towards the Deux Pitons a road leads to the Diamond Botanical Gardens with their waterfalls and then on to Sulphur

Above Fishing boats, La Raye
Below Sulphur Springs, La Soufrière

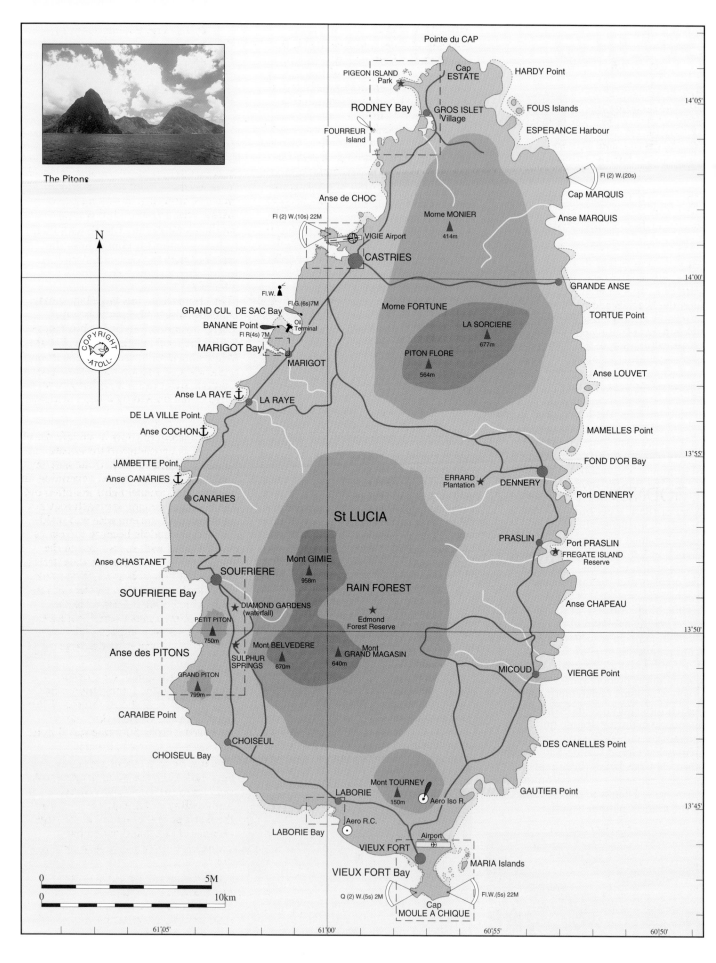

The Pitons

N

COPYRIGHT 'ATOLL'

Pointe du CAP

PIGEON ISLAND Park
Cap ESTATE
HARDY Point
RODNEY Bay
GROS ISLET Village
FOUS Islands
FOURREUR Island
ESPERANCE Harbour

14°05'

Fl (2) W.(20s)
Cap MARQUIS
Anse MARQUIS

Anse de CHOC

Fl (2) W.(10s) 22M
VIGIE Airport
Morne MONIER
414m

CASTRIES

14°00'
GRANDE ANSE

Fl.W.
Fl.G.(6s)7M
GRAND CUL DE SAC Bay
Morne FORTUNE
TORTUE Point
BANANE Point
Oil Terminal
LA SORCIERE
677m
Fl R(4s) 7M
MARIGOT Bay
PITON FLORE
564m
MARIGOT
Anse LOUVET

Anse LA RAYE
LA RAYE

DE LA VILLE Point.
MAMELLES Point
Anse COCHON

13°55'
JAMBETTE Point
FOND D'OR Bay
Anse CANARIES
ERRARD Plantation
DENNERY
CANARIES
Port DENNERY

St LUCIA
PRASLIN
Port PRASLIN
FREGATE ISLAND Reserve

Anse CHASTANET
Mont GIMIE
958m
SOUFRIERE
RAIN FOREST
Anse CHAPEAU
SOUFRIERE Bay
DIAMOND GARDENS (waterfall)
Edmond Forest Reserve
13°50'
PETIT PITON
750m
Mont BELVEDERE
670m
Mont GRAND MAGASIN
640m
Anse des PITONS
SULPHUR SPRINGS
MICOUD
VIERGE Point
GRAND PITON
799m

CARAIBE Point
DES CANELLES Point

CHOISEUL
CHOISEUL Bay

Mont TOURNEY
150m
LABORIE
Aero Iso R.
GAUTIER Point
13°45'
Aero R.C.
LABORIE Bay
Airport
VIEUX FORT
MARIA Islands
VIEUX FORT Bay

0   5M
0   10km
Q (2) W.(5s) 2M
Fl.W.(5s) 22M
Cap MOULE A CHIQUE

61°05'   61°00'   60°55'   60°50'

Springs, where steam jets and fumeroles vent from the ground and water bubbles in natural hot bathing pools.

Vieux Fort – Windward coast

At the extreme S of the island Vieux Fort, the island's second port, is of interest only for the international airport and the beaches and islets at the S end of the windward coast where there's a Club Med. Heading up the Atlantic coast, it becomes wilder and steeper, and one can find several small towns and villages tucked into hillsides covered with banana trees.

Gros Islet Village

Leaving Castries and heading N, the road reaches Rodney Bay where the main tourist attractions of this part of the island are found–Pigeon Islet Park and the picturesque village of Gros Islet. Pigeon Island National Park is a minute island linked to the mainland by an artificial causeway. It offers pleasant walking along its steep paths, which wind in and out of the tropical vegetation. Sleepy Hollow during the week, the quiet fishing village of Gros Islet bursts into life each Friday night. 'Lolos' and other stalls sell barbecued food while tourists mingle with wild local dancers, creating a loud and lively ambiance. S of the village around

---

Above left La Soufrière town and the Deux Pitons

Right Local band

Rodney Bay and the fine sands of Reduit Beach you'll find lots of restaurants, hotel complexes and shops of all sorts.

Pilotage

Coastline and anchorages

St Lucia is a relatively high island and the W coast is often in the wind shadow between the Deux Pitons and Pigeon I. You should be prepared for several miles of motoring. If coming from Martinique boats head directly for Rodney Bay on the W coast.

West coast

Rodney Bay

The approach to this large bay is easy. Anchor close to the sandy isthmus, partly occupied by wooden buildings with blue roofs, joining Pigeon I to the mainland. Don't push too far in towards the coast as there are shallows. There is another anchorage off Reduit Beach, a large beach backed by a hotel complex.

Rodney Bay Marina

Located approximately in the middle of the bay, the entrance to the access channel is hard to spot. Quite narrow, it has 3–3·5m in the centre, depending on silting. The channel lights are often out of order and a night approach requires great care. At the entrance and inside keep to the middle because the banks are cluttered with rocks close to the surface. At present the entrance itself is marked by two lit buoys, which mark the middle of the channel clear of the rocks. Anchoring is allowed in the middle of the inner basin. There are over 200 berths equipped with electricity and water on the large pontoons.

Ashore A large building holds the marina office, the immigration office and several small shops. On the N shore you'll find the Rodney Bay Marine Boatyard with its 50 tonne travel-hoist and several specialist services.

The fuel dock is in front of the boatyard. With the other professional services in the marina or nearby, Rodney Bay is well-equipped. One of the features of the marina is the large number of small and varied bar-restaurants, often lively until the small hours.

Provisioning can be done at the minimarkets and small shops in the marina or in the larger stores on the road towards Castries. Hire cars and taxis are available.

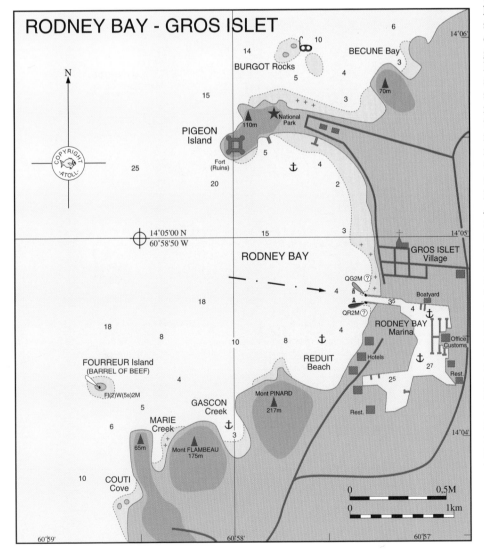

Above Rodney Bay & Gros Ilet

Below Port Castries from the W

Rodney Bay Marina

Rodney Bay Marina arrivals dock

Rodney Bay Marina

Gascon Creek (Trou Gascon)

Fairweather anchorage. To be avoided in a NE swell. The coast is steep-to and rocky. Anchor close off a gorgeous small beach overhung with coconut palms in 3–4m.

Port Castries

After doubling Vigie Pt, entry to this natural harbour presents no difficulties. Note that at night some of the lights are unreliable.

Vigie Cove

Anchoring is OK at the entry to this small inlet in 6–7m, mud. Ashore on each bank are small restaurants frequented by local people. Inside the inlet you'll find the rather careworn pontoons of St Lucia Yacht Services, full of resident boats. Other than fuel available on the jetty, there's not much for passing yachts. By contrast, 100m W of Vigie Cove you'll find the Castries Yacht Center boatyard (VHF Ch 16) with a 35-tonne travel-hoist, several specialist services and a fuel dock.

Square-rigged brig, Vigie Cove

Castries Town

You can anchor N of the commercial dock. Ashore the port immigration service is not accustomed to dealing with yachts. In town the shops, supermarkets and above all the local market offer almost everything you need for provisioning. Apart from that and a quick look round the town, there's not much of interest.

Grand Cul-de-Sac Bay

The whole bay is surrounded by the massive tanks of the oil company and is of no interest except as a very conspicuous landmark even at night when the whole complex is brightly lit.

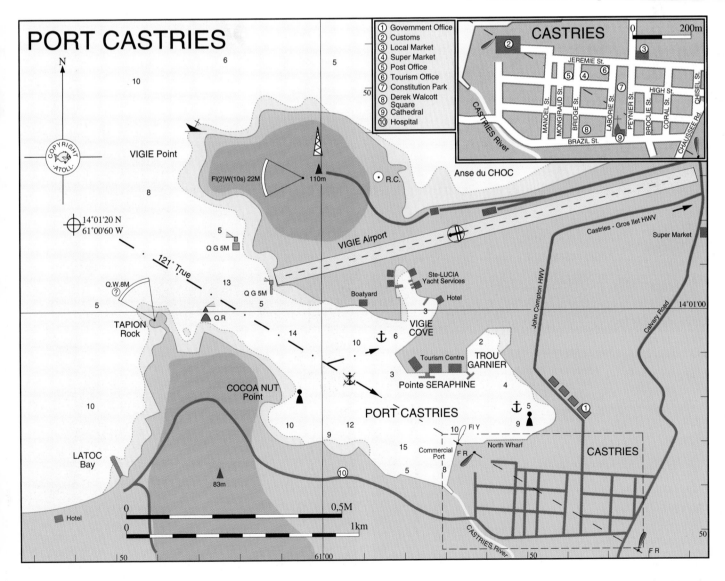

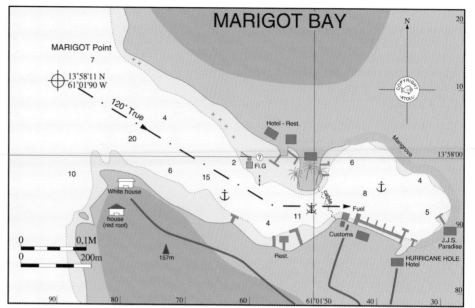

MARIGOT BAY

Above The welcoming committee or 'Boat boys' at Marigot Bay
Below Marigot Bay pass
Below right Marigot Bay
Bottom left Marigot Bay anchorage

Marigot Bay

A picture postcard creek: white sand, coconut trees and mangroves. Its reputation makes it the most visited anchorage in St Lucia. The entry is narrow but easy to spot sailing close inshore thanks to a house with a red roof on the summit of the S entry point.

Inside hold to the centre because the shores are not steep-to. The shoals to port are usually marked by an unlit green buoy. Given how crowded the inner basin often is, some prefer to anchor outside off the small, sandy point in 8–10m. To get into the inner basin, give the sandy point covered with coconut trees a good berth. Anchor in 6–7m, mud, and for those of you wanting to reduce your swinging room (and avoid the expensive moorings offered by the boat boys), you can take a line to the mangroves. The only

downside is the mosquitoes. The pontoons are mostly full of a charter company's boats. However, some berths may be available. You can refuel and water ship.

Ashore Close to the pontoons, there's an office for formalities and a minimarket, though only for stop-gap provisioning. You may get some emergency technical help from the charter outfit.

Around the bay, in addition to an upmarket hotel-restaurant, there are several establishments offering varied menus and live music. The most

popular, tucked away in the mangroves, is certainly J-J's Paradise (VHF 16) owned by Gérard Félix, a charming St Lucian known as J-J. This ex-skipper of luxury charter vessels (including *Vendredi 13*) has now swallowed the hook and set out to introduce cruising sailors and the guests in his luxurious bungalows to his delicious local cooking complemented by French wine. Some evenings around the swimming pool a band warms up the atmosphere with its local rhythms.

South of Marigot

From Marigot to the Deux Pitons (Two Pitons) the entire coast is part of a natural conservation zone regulated by the SMMA. You may not anchor in any protected zone where there are mooring buoys. Fishing is prohibited in some inlets like Roseau Bay just S of Marigot, or to the N of Soufrière Bay. The coast itself is a succession of small cliffs intersected with inlets each with its grey sand beach and its fishing village. The anchorages in the zone are all affected by swell during NE'lies.

Anse La Raye

This is a day anchorage and often rolly, but worth a stop for its typical fishing village and its small colourful cottages. The coast is steep-to except in the N of the bay. There's a dock for getting ashore by tender or, if there's a swell running, you can haul it onto the beach. Ashore there are the boats and the multicoloured nets on the beach and behind them the village of little buildings, cottages, shops and small bar-restaurants. On Friday evenings, as at Gros It, the road livens up for the Friday Night Street Jump. To avoid what can be an uncomfortable anchorage, you can of course come here by taxi from Marigot.

Anse Cochon

About 1M S of Anse de la Raye this inlet, although fairly well tucked away, isn't always protected from the N swell.

Anchor close to the small beach in the N of the bay close to where a hotel complex is under development. There are some buoys available though in principle they are for daytime use only.

Anse Canaries

About 1M S of Anse Cochon, Anse Canaries shelters a small village at the mouth of a river. The coast close-to is fringed with reef. The most protected anchorage is in the N of the bay beneath the cliffs. There are some mooring buoys.

Top left J-J Night
Top right Sunset at Marigot Bay
Above La Raye village and bay
Below left Fishing boat and nets, La Raye
Below right Repairing nets, Soufrière Bay

Anse Chastanet

The shoreline is covered with the 'cottages' of a luxury hotel and a dive club. The bottom drops away steeply and you have to use a mooring buoy.

Soufrière Bay

Give a wide berth to the reef projecting from Grand Caille Point before you alter into this large bay. The best

Above left Soufrière Bay
Above right Cottages and fishing boats, La Soufrière

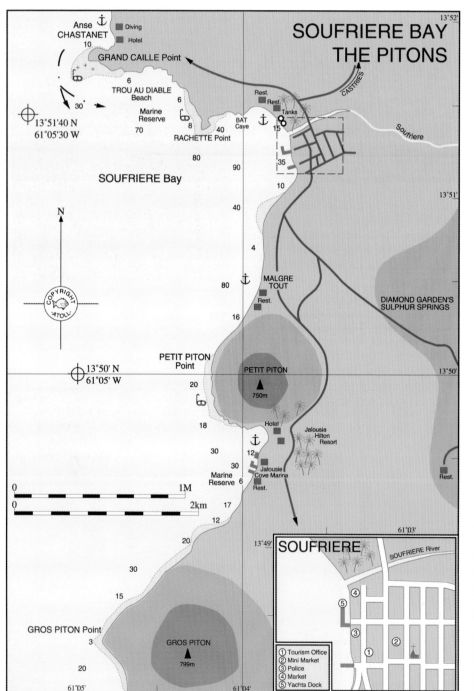

anchorage is in the NE of the bay after Rachette Pt and off two restaurants. Tucked away in the greenery, they're popular with yachtsmen. Avoid anchoring too far to the right where you'll see, under the coconut palms, the boats and cottages of the fishing village. In effect, that area is reserved for local residents.

La Soufrière town

This small typical town is the place to leave from for a visit to Sulphur Springs and Diamond Gardens. N of the town dock a new arrivals dock has been built for yachts and charter boats. The dock is managed by SMMA. You can also fuel and water ship at the town dock if it isn't too busy.

Ashore There are lots of shops and the local market for provisioning. Along the shore and around the square of Church St are several small restaurants that serve local dishes. Close to the dock you'll find the tourist office and the SMMA office where you can get tourist information and information on the marine reserve. There are taxis for visiting the places to see or the restaurants perched on the green hills looking out on the Deux Pitons.

Malgretoute

In the S of Soufrière Bay, this anchorage is often bouncy but has several SMMA mooring buoys. Ashore there are several restaurants at the foot of Petit Piton with menus of local

Beach and anchorage, NE Soufrière Bay

dishes. They also offer various services
for yachts.

The Deux Pitons

The second major 'tourist' anchorage in
the island. Its grey sand beach is fringed
with a superb coconut plantation
forming a vast green and bronze cloak
covering the sides of the valley. The
arrival of a luxury hotel complex, the
Jalousie Plantation, has breached this
wonderful green mantle and it has now
been replaced partly by buildings and
partly by a botanical garden whose
charm is more organised but less wild.
The zone is also part of a marine park
and you must moor on the buoys
provided. Even if you have to pay, this
facility means you can avoid a very iffy
anchorage given the depths and the
intermittent gusts barrelling down
between the two Pitons. An arrivals
dock (fuel and water) is being rebuilt.

Ashore the bar and restaurant of the
hotel are upmarket but open to visitors
who fancy brunch, lunch or dinner in
the lap of luxury. The prices reflect the
venue. The complex includes a fitness
club and all sorts of water sports. Close
to the S of the dock, outside the hotel
compound, there's a small restaurant
serving local food rather better geared
to the average pocket.

SW coast

The majority of cruisers coming from
the N pass this coast by. However, if
you're coming from St Vincent a stop at
Vieux Fort is worthwhile to complete
clearance. The route does require a very
close fetch hardened right in. The SW
coast is open to the swell and offers
hardly any good anchorages other than
Vieux Fort. To reach Vieux Fort you
have to work up against wind and
current.

Laborie Bay

Caution W of Laborie, Balambouche
Rocks lie more than 0·5M offshore.
Laborie is a small fishing village. The
little frequented anchorage is protected
by a barrier reef. The pass is W of the
village in the NNE part of the bay. It
has 3–3·5m, coming up quickly to less
than 3m once inside. It is accessible
only in good conditions and with a lot
of care.

Vieux Fort

Vieux Fort is a banana export outlet
and has kept an authentic local flavour
with its old clapboard houses and its
flotilla of little fishing boats. The
anchorage is either S of the main
banana jetty, or further N near the
small fishing harbour (*Caution* look out
for the shoals off the shore) but being
sure to leave room for shipping to
manoeuvre.

Top The Pitons
Above centre Repairwork with an adze
Above Jalousie Plantation anchorage
Above right Anchorage at Deux Pitons

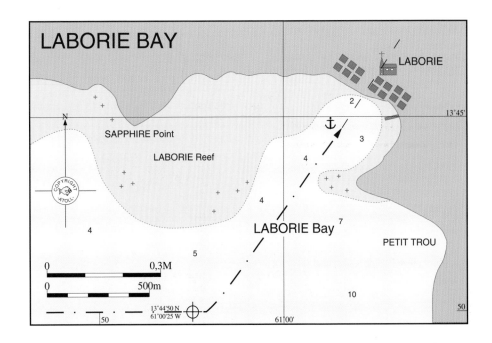

Ashore The customs post is at the root of the jetty but the immigration service is often not manned and you have to go to the airport. There are no specialist boating services. On the other hand there is a good range of market garden produce, fish and other local goods at lower prices than in Castries. It's the same with the restaurants that serve local specialities at very reasonable prices. Close to Vieux Fort, Hewanorra Airport has long-haul international connections.

East coast

The coast is open to the ocean swell and has no reliable anchorages other than some creeks and small fishing boat shelters only accessible to local boats. In very good weather and fine visibility you can anchor temporarily in the lee of Maria I once you've worked upwind and against the swell past Cape du Moule à Chique. There's a Club Med in the bay below Pt Sable along the extensive and very pretty beach.

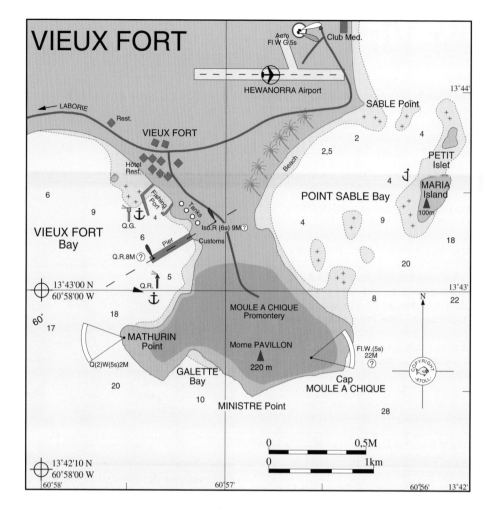

Useful Information for St Lucia

AIRLINE CONNECTIONS
International airport: Hewanorra Airport
Long-haul flights
Regular direct flights to North America and Europe (London, Frankfurt)
National airport: Georges F L Charles
Inter-island services
Daily inter-island flights, air taxi services

FERRIES
Regular inter-island services from Castries to Grenadines, Martinique, Dominica, Guadeloupe

TELECOMMUNICATIONS
Calling St Lucia from abroad: ☎ (1) 758 + seven figure number
Local calls: seven figures only
Public call boxes: Caribbean Phone Cards

TOURIST OFFICES
Tourist Board: Castries, ☎ 758 452 4094
    Fax 758 453 1121 *Email* slutour@candw.lc
St Lucia Philatelic: Castries Post Office

GOLF
St Lucia Golf & Country Club: Cap Estates,
    ☎ 758 450 8523 *Fax* 758 450 8317

FESTIVALS/FOLK FESTIVALS
Carnival: February/March
Jazz Festival: May
Friday Night: Gros Islet and La Raye

PUBLIC HOLIDAYS
Good Friday and Easter Monday, Labour Day (May), Whit Monday, Corpus Christi (19 June), Emancipation Day (1 August), Thanksgiving Day (6 October), National Day (13 December), Christmas Day (25 December), Boxing Day (26 December)

PLACES TO SEE
Fort Charlotte: Castries
Cathedral of the Immaculate Conception
Pointe Séraphine: duty free shopping
Pigeon Island: National Park
La Soufrière: Sulphur Springs, Diamond Falls and Baths: active thermal springs
Morne Coubaril Estate: Ecological Museum
Choiseul: local handicraft centre
Frigate and Maria Islands: Bird and reptile reserves
Forest of Fond St Jacques: walks
Mt Gimie: guided walks

DRIVING
Drive on the left
A licence is obligatory
Hire car companies in the towns and at the airport
Taxis & share taxis (8 people)

REGULATIONS
Underwater hunting is forbidden to non-residents
Sport fishing and diving require a licence and are only authorised via a local club
Trolling when coasting is acceptable

NATURE RESERVES
The reserves have been created to preserve land and sea flora and fauna. Taking anything from the reserves is strictly prohibited and subject to penalty.
National Park: From Marigot to Deux Pitons:

CMMA (Canaries Marine Management Area)
SMMA (Soufrière Marine Management Area)
Mooring buoys: obligatory, to preserve the underwater habitat
Yachts: white buoys with blue band (maximum loa 70')
Dive boats: orange buoys
Fee (EC$30–60 depending on length, for 1–2 days) payable to accredited agents.
SMMA (Soufrière Marine Management Area), VHF 16 ☎ 459 5500/7200 *Fax* 459 7799 *Email* smma@candw.lc or srds@candw.lc for further information, buoy management, supervision of boat-boys if you wish to complain.

FORMALITIES
Arriving by air
Customs and immigration in the airport
Arriving by sea
Rodney Bay Marina on the arrivals dock
Marigot Bay close to the jetties
Castries (little used by yachts) Customs on the cargo boat jetty, immigration in the town
Soufrière Town Dock
Vieux Fort Customs on the banana boat jetty, Immigration officials are either in town or at the airport

Office hours in principle weekdays 0800/0900–1200, 1300–1600/1700
Taxes and fees
Cruising tax and entry permit per boat (by length)
Stays less than 3 days: Simultaneous entry/exit clearance
Overtime charged outside office hours and at weekends

St Vincent

Area 388 sq km
Highest point La Soufrière,
   1205m
Population 112,000
Capital Kingstown (pop. 40,000)
Language English
Currency EC$ (US$ accepted)
Political status Independent state
Distances to other islands: St Lucia
   (Soufrière to Châteaubelair) 34M
Grenada (Halifax to Kingstown) 69M

Above Kingstown
market
Right An arcade in
Kingstown

History

The island was spotted by Christopher Columbus on St Vincent's Day, but he didn't linger. In St Vincent, as in Dominica, the Caribs defended their territory fiercely. Neither English nor French made any serious attempts at colonisation until the middle of 18th century. Finally, in 1763, the English set foot ashore but were soon ousted by the French; however, the island became British again in 1783 under the Treaty of Versailles. Meanwhile a new race of people had emerged: the 'Black Caribs' had resulted from interbreeding between native Caribs and slaves whose ships had been wrecked on the coast. These 'Black Caribs' proved willing to defend their freedom as fiercely as their Amerindian cousins. In 1795 the French sought to make an alliance with them in order to get them to push the English back into the sea, but the colonisers offered stubborn resistance and ended by winning. For the most part the Black Caribs were deported to Honduras. However, those who escaped that fate left a genetic legacy to the people of St Vincent which is still visible in some faces. The French are recalled in many village names and in the names of coastal features.

There's also a tie between this island and distant Tahiti. In his new ship *Providence*, after the mutiny on the *Bounty*, the famous Captain Bligh brought more than five hundred breadfruit trees from Polynesia to St Vincent. The trees' fruit ended up pretty much sustaining the plantation slaves and was soon in cultivation throughout the Antilles.

Another event is more sadly remembered: on 6 May 1902, in the island's north, La Soufrière erupted causing 2,000 deaths. It was a catastrophe but was soon forgotten when two days later Mont Pelée incinerated 30,000 Martiniquais.

Throughout the colonial period and up to the preent day the island has survived on the growing of bananas and through market gardening.

St Vincent became an associated state of the Commonwealth in 1969 and began to develop a tourist industry. The island has no international airport, but does exercise sovereignty over the larger part of the splendid Grenadines.

Two events of importance took place in 1979. La Soufrière suddenly erupted, both causing a more general upset and temporarily dislocating the economy. Then, in October that year, St Vincent attained full independence.

Agriculture remains the most important part of the economy, thanks to the very fertile volcanic soil, and is split between agribusiness and peasant smallholdings.

For all the efforts of the authorities tourism remains relatively lightly developed in St Vincent, unlike in the Grenadines. One reason is that the terrain is precipitous and runs down to a few grey sand beaches. Therefore, apart from a few state-run establishments on the S coast, the island has little by way of a hotel industry or major tourist complexes.

Left Old cannon, Duvernette Island
Right The Police Station
Far right Young Island

Tourism

Where to stay and what to visit

Despite its modest state of tourist development, there are plenty of scenically attractive places worth visiting for their natural wildness, which may sometimes be a bit austere but are always clothed with luxuriant vegetation.

Kingstown

This small town of 40,000 is the island's capital. Most of its business life is focussed on the deepwater port where coasting craft from neighbouring islands and cruise liners berth. Recent work has restored the stone façades and arches of the old colonial buildings, which now house both government offices and bar-restaurants. The Anglican church of St George's (1820) is in the Georgian style and has good stained glass windows. The Romanesque style Catholic cathedral of St Mary (1823) has since been enlarged and supplemented by several styles ranging from Gothic to Baroque. The shops are to be found in the two main roads back from the port, though the most colourful and local feel is to be found in the markets of vegetables and spices, meat and fish on Bay Street. Besides the marvellous view out over the bay to be had from Fort Charlotte, it's worth visiting the botanical gardens (the oldest in the New World) where one can find specimens of the majority of the Caribbean flora.

Things to see on the island

Two coast roads serve the island but curiously they don't link up in the N because the massif of La Soufrière gets in the way. This means that to get from the E side of the island to the W you have to come back through Kingstown. Before reaching the windward coast the road follows the S coast through the small villages of Villa and Calliaqua. From the bay you can see Young I, a mound of greenery under whose frangipanis and flame trees there is a luxury hotel and its cottages. Beyond here you'll come to Mesopotamia Valley, dominated by the nearly 1000m high Grand Bonhomme. A road from

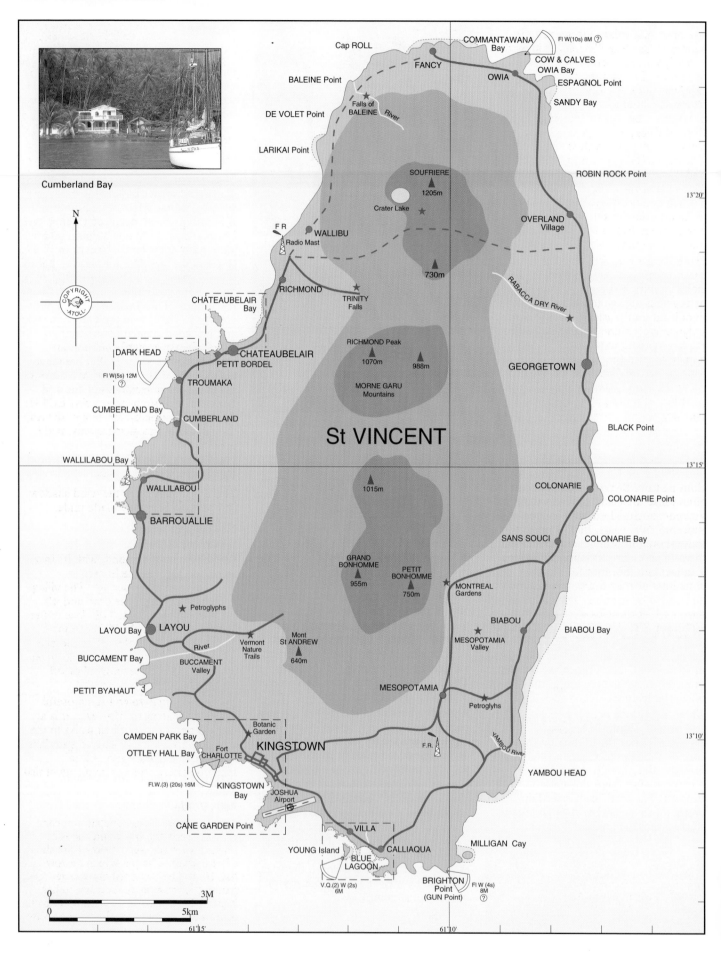

Cumberland Bay

N
COPYRIGHT 'ATOLL'

Cap ROLL

COMMANTAWANA Bay
Fl W(10s) 8M ⑦
COW & CALVES
OWIA Bay

FANCY

BALEINE Point

OWIA

ESPAGNOL Point

DE VOLET Point

Falls of BALEINE

River

SANDY Bay

LARIKAI Point

SOUFRIERE
1205m

ROBIN ROCK Point

13°20'

Crater Lake

F R
Radio Mast

WALLIBU

OVERLAND Village

730m

RICHMOND

RABACCA DRY River

CHATEAUBELAIR Bay

TRINITY Falls

DARK HEAD

CHATEAUBELAIR

RICHMOND Peak
1070m

988m

GEORGETOWN

Fl W(5s) 12M
⑦

PETIT BORDEL

TROUMAKA

MORNE GARU
Mountains

BLACK Point

CUMBERLAND Bay

CUMBERLAND

St VINCENT

13°15'

WALLILABOU Bay

COLONARIE

1015m

COLONARIE Point

WALLILABOU

COLONARIE Bay

BARROUALLIE

SANS SOUCI

GRAND BONHOMME
955m

PETIT BONHOMME
750m

MONTREAL Gardens

BIABOU

Petroglyphs

MESOPOTAMIA Valley

BIABOU Bay

LAYOU Bay

LAYOU

River

Vermont Nature Trails

Mont St ANDREW
640m

BUCCAMENT Bay

BUCCAMENT Valley

MESOPOTAMIA

PETIT BYAHAUT

Petroglyhs

YAMBOU River

Botanic Garden

CAMDEN PARK Bay

F.R.

13°10'

OTTLEY HALL Bay

Fort CHARLOTTE

KINGSTOWN

YAMBOU HEAD

Fl.W.(3) (20s) 16M

KINGSTOWN

KINGSTOWN Bay

JOSHUA Airport

CANE GARDEN Point

VILLA

MILLIGAN Cay

YOUNG Island

CALLIAQUA

BLUE LAGOON

0   3M

V.Q.(2) W (2s) 6M

BRIGHTON Point
(GUN Point)
Fl W (4s) 8M
⑦

0   5km

61°15'

61°10'

Mesopotamia village takes you to the Montreal Gardens. There's a site with petroglyphs and rock carvings not far from here. The windward coast, exposed to the Atlantic swells, is relatively wilder and its grey sand beaches are backed by lots of greenery. Beyond Georgetown (a small village become very much a sleepy hollow following the downturn in the sugar trade) you come to Rabacca Dry River. This relic of the 1902 eruption is the old bed of a huge lava flow. You can get to La Soufrière's crater after a walk of a dozen kilometres or so along a forest track (on a guided visit).

From Kingstown N'wards, the leeward coast has numerous fishing villages along a pretty vertiginous road. The petroglyphs at Layou are the most significant on the island. In Buccament Valley there's a fine walk to be had in the natural park in which there are numerous bird species including the St Vincent parrot. The road ends at Richmond from where trails lead to La Soufrière, Trinity Falls and the Falls of Baleine.

Pilotage

Coastline and anchorages

Coming from St Lucia tidal currents often make the channel across to St Vincent rough. There's no shelter on St Vincent's NW coast. Yachts on this route should in principle head straight to Wallilabou for clearance. St Vincent is in fact better known for the grandeurs of its interior than for its leeward coast,

Welcoming committee, Petit Bordel

which offers only a few rather barren and only moderately sheltered anchorages. The result is that in practice many yachts avoid the coast and head straight to Bequia, or at least as far as Young I after only the briefest of stops for formalities at Kingstown. We might add that the charm of the anchorages isn't helped by the rather pressing attentions of certain 'welcoming committees'. All too often one has to reject their overzealous attentions even when still quite a way outside the anchorage because they come out to intercept you in boats that these days are often motorised. And those that still use oars are as likely to demand a tow. It's best to accept no

offers of services until you're in an anchorage. For it's only there that you have a chance of finding local boat boys offering a more seemly welcome and more reasonable charges (a few EC$ for taking a line ashore). Be sure to develop cautious habits to guard against petty theft.

West and SW coasts

You'll generally be in the wind shadow and passage is usually made under power.

Châteaubelair

Beyond Point Richmond, with its two pylons on top, the anchorage at Châteaubelair will open up. The village dock has nothing to tie onto and it's better to anchor in the NE close to the beach backed by splendid coconut palms. Swell can make the anchorage rolly, indeed very uncomfortable when it's from the N. The snorkelling off Châteaubelair I is very good.

Ashore The small town has no useful commercial services. However, it is a starting point for excellent walks to the slopes of La Soufrière and its waterfalls. A modest restaurant serves local seafood. There seem to be plenty of fish hereabouts.

Petit Bordel

Coming from Châteaubelair you can pass between the coast and the islet making sure you keep clear of the shoal off the latter. The passage is narrow but has 10m. The small fishing village fronting onto a black sand beach has kept its French name, a name promising more than at first view the village seems to offer. . . Depths drop off very quickly, so it's best to anchor and put a line ashore.

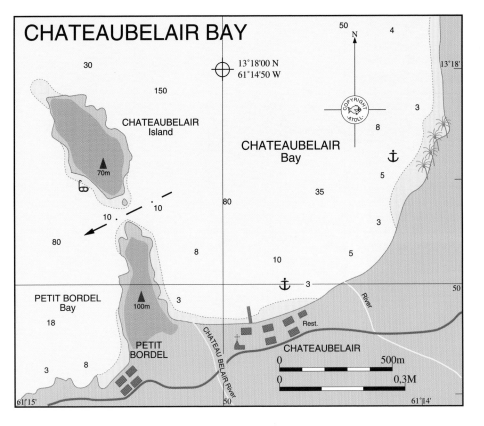

CHATEAUBELAIR BAY

13°18'00 N
61°14'50 W

CHATEAUBELAIR Island

CHATEAUBELAIR Bay

PETIT BORDEL Bay

PETIT BORDEL

CHATEAU BELAIR River

CHATEAUBELAIR

Rest.

River

0   500m

0   0,3M

Troumaka Bay

A day anchorage in the small, little visited bay off the fishing village of Troumaka.

Cumberland Bay

Caution The N point of the bay is steep-to, but there's a reef extending off the SW point. Backing the bay, cut through the middle by a river, there's a large coconut plantation climbing a hill with a village half way up. The anchorage is well sheltered but here too the bottom drops off sharply. Anchor with a line ashore tied round a coconut tree about halfway along the main beach for which you'll pay the usual fee. You'll already have met and been surrounded by the 'welcoming committee' which will have been offering vegetables, fruit, fish, barbecues and other services.

Ashore A few small buildings on the beach house small bars and restaurants with seafood and barbecue menus.

Wallilabou Bay

Immediately S of Cumberland Bay and not to be mistaken for it; to identify it, on the N point look for a rock with a hole in it and on the S point a large radio mast. There are several buildings lost in the trees behind the beach at the bay head. Anchor in 10m about 50m from the beach and put a line ashore round a coconut tree (this will always be done by the welcoming committee) or use a mooring.

Ashore Customs are to the left of the dock. There are two restaurants on the beach. The one to the S, in addition to offering seafood menus, has various services including mooring buoys and has fine printed fabrics for sale. It's also trying to control the boat boys, some of whom, here even more than elsewhere, are often too pushy. A short walk will take you to a fabulous waterfall about 1km from the shore.

Below, from top
Cumberland Bay
Cumberland Bay anchorage
Wallilabou & Barrouallie
Wallilabou anchorage

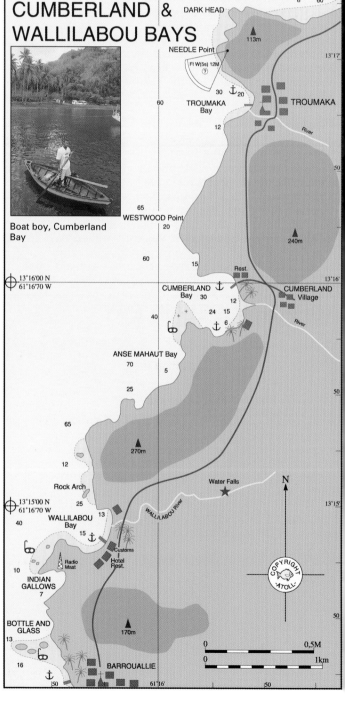

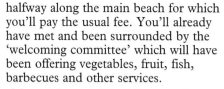

Boat boy, Cumberland Bay

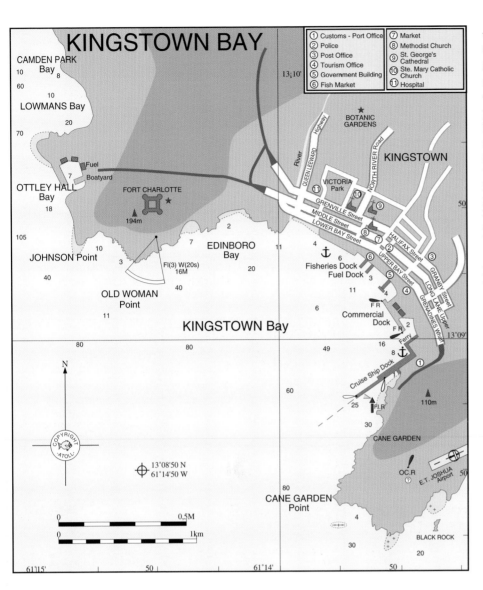

KINGSTOWN BAY

① Customs - Port Office	⑦ Market
② Police	⑧ Methodist Church
③ Post Office	⑨ St. George's Cathedral
④ Tourism Office	⑩ Ste. Mary Catholic Church
⑤ Government Building	
⑥ Fish Market	⑪ Hospital

CAMDEN PARK Bay

LOWMANS Bay

OTTLEY HALL Bay

FORT CHARLOTTE

194m

JOHNSON Point

OLD WOMAN Point

FI(3) W(20s) 16M

EDINBORO Bay

KINGSTOWN Bay

BOTANIC GARDENS

KINGSTOWN

River

Highway

QUEEN LEEWARD

NORTH RIVER Road

VICTORIA Park

GRENVILLE Street

MIDDLE Street

LOWER BAY Street

UPPER BAY Street

HALIFAX Street

GRANBY Street

LONG LANE

GRENADINES Wharf

Upper

Fisheries Dock Fuel Dock

Commercial Dock

F R

Ferry

Cruise Ship Dock

FI.R

CANE GARDEN

OC.R

E.T. JOSHUA Airport

110m

CANE GARDEN Point

BLACK ROCK

N

13°08'50 N 61°14'50 W

0 ———— 0.5M

0 ———— 1km

Barrouallie Bay

Note About 1M S of Wallilabou, W of Barrouallie Bay (pronounced 'Barrelly'), you must pass two islets, Bottle and Glass. The first looks more like a submarine than the bottle suggested by its name. You can anchor behind the reefs off the small village beach.

Ashore A police station, if it's open (it's very unreliable) means there's a chance to do clearance.

Layou Bay

There's a possible day anchorage here off the coconut palm lined beach of the small village. There's a conspicuous hangar. The bottom drops off sharply and a swell can make in.

Petit Byahaut

This small cove in the S of Buccament Bay is quite well protected unless there's a big swell. Anchor close to the beach where there's a small restaurant buried in the trees and some

watersports centres. There's good snorkelling in the N of the bay and good walking in the Buccament Valley.

Ottley Hall

Thanks to the sea wall this small creek has been turned into a marina and boatyard with several berths and a fuel dock. Chop from reflected seas can make mooring alongside very uncomfortable, even dangerous, and the place is effectively just a boatyard for yachts (40 tonne travel-hoist) but also for large ships thanks to its large dry-dock (can handle boats up to 70m loa). You can get fuel and water from the dock on the main jetty (with very good prices for the area). Ashore, other than the haul-out facilities there are few specialist services, though there is a minimarket for provisioning.

Kingstown Bay

The capital and port of entry, Kingstown is also a deepwater port for large cargo ships and cruise liners. A large dock has been built on the SE shore for the latter. The large bay is well protected although the swell often makes itself felt. The best anchorage for yachts, though only short term, is close to the root of the Cruise Ship Dock, near the centre of town and the police and customs offices. At a jetty N of the commercial wharves you can refuel and water ship. If you go ashore, don't leave your boat unattended and be careful how you tie your dinghy up on the dock.

Ashore Customs on the esplanade of the port and the police station in town, near the market. These services are going to be brought together near the Cruise Ship Dock. You may be able to moor near the root of the dock. As far as yachting goes, services are limited to outboard dealers and some shops selling hardware and small chandlery items. On the other hand the local markets and the supermarkets are good for

Below left Ottley Hall from WSW
Below Kingstown Bay from the S

Young Island & Blue Lagoon from the S

provisioning including above all fresh fruit, vegetable and fish. Despite the facilities and the interest of the town itself with its restored old buildings, which might argue for at least a short visit, few yachts stop here. The majority prefer to go to Young I and visit by taxi.

Young Island

Caution Going E be sure to stand clear of Cane Garden Pt off which lies Washing Rock which doesn't show.

Young I anchorage is between the island and the coast (Young I Cut).

There's a strong current, which changes direction with the tide. The middle of the anchorage is taken up with mooring buoys. To anchor you'll have to lie outside, where depths are 10m or more. Using a mooring buoy, for which there's a charge, it's more secure especially if you want to leave the boat and go ashore for a while to visit St Vincent.

Ashore There are two places of interest: On one side Young I with its smart hotel is much in favour with rich honeymooners. Beside the beach there's a shark basin and a swimming pool surrounded by a tropical garden with multicoloured parrots flying about. Staying in the bungalows here is

fabulous and luxurious but hits the pocket book. Even so, you can enjoy the feel of the place by trying one of the umpteen cocktails served by the bar.

On the main island shore, called the Villa Village, you'll find the tourist strip and the most active water sports on the island.

You can water ship at the Aquatic Club.

Ashore there's a tiny square with several shops and a very well-reputed and active dive centre. Running along the shore from there you'll find a line of restaurants and hotels on the edge of a very narrow path right down at water level. The majority have pleasant

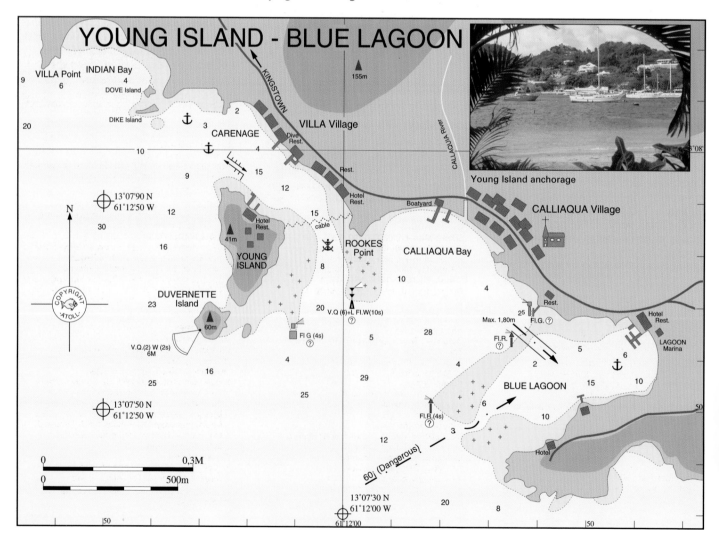

Young Island anchorage

Above left Young Island beach
Above right The Lagoon Marina
Below right Duvernette Island

terraces embellished with greenery and the menus are diverse both in the specialities on offer and the prices. For yachts there are several skilled craftsmen on the road to the village of Calliaqua beyond Rookes Pt. Their skills cover joinery, mechanical, outboard and other problems. The haul-out facilities are only for light displacement motorboats, though apparently a railway slip is planned. Close by, a local boatyard has for some years now been building big GRP catamarans for the day charterers to the Grenadines. You can get a taxi for an excursion round the island, to visit Kingstown and either do your clearance there or in the nearby airport.

Don't forget to visit by dinghy Duvernette Island, S of Young I. After climbing the steps you'll reach a platform with several old cannons in perfect condition and a splendid view.

Blue Lagoon

The pass E of Young I is quite narrow but in theory is marked. It can be used for going to Blue Lagoon, which is the most secure anchorage in St Vincent. However, the main pass in the W is only good for boats drawing less than 1·7–1·8m depending on the tide. The channel is also buoyed. There's another deeper pass to the S of the reef. But it's narrow and twisting and therefore very dangerous when the sea is rough or visibility is poor. The approach is on 060°T. Although I've taken it several times with a boat drawing 2·5m always in optimum conditions of sea state and visibility, I cannot recommend it to the less experienced or anyone who isn't prepared to take risks. Inside there are depths of 10–15m. On the N shore are the facilities of The Lagoon (VHF 68), with several berths on the dock mostly occupied by bareboat companies. If there are berths free, passing yachts are welcomed and can water ship and fuel up.

Ashore The complex includes a hotel-restaurant with a huge terrace and several shops including a grocery. Further W the small dock of another company is dominated by a smart restaurant overlooking the bay. Here too you can refuel and water ship.

Useful Information for St Vincent

AIRLINE CONNECTIONS
Joshua Airport: no long-haul flights
Inter-island services
Daily flights to Martinique, St Lucia and other neighbouring islands. Direct daily flights to St Juan. Inter-island charters and air taxis.

FERRIES
Daily service to Bequia. Regular services to St Lucia, Barbados and the other islands in the Grenadines

TELECOMMUNICATIONS
Calling St Vincent from abroad: ☎ (1) 784 + seven figure number
Local calls: seven figures only
Public call boxes: Caribbean Phone Cards

TOURIST OFFICE/ASSOCIATION
Tourist Office: Bay Street, Kingstown
☎ 457 1502 *Fax* 456 2610
Email tourism@caribsurf.com
Hotel & Tourism Association: Joshua Airport
☎ 458 4379 *Fax* 456 4456
Email svghotels@caribsurf.com

FESTIVALS/FOLK FESTIVALS
Carolling Competition & Nine Mornings Festival: 16–24 December
SVG Blues Festival: January/February
Carnival: (Vincy Mas) June/July

PUBLIC HOLIDAYS
1 January, Discovery & National Heroes Day (22 January), Good Friday and Easter Monday, Labour Day (May), Whit Monday, Caricom Day and Carnival Tuesday (July), August Bank Holiday (1 Monday in August), Independence Day (27 October), Christmas Day (25 December), Boxing Day (26 December)

OFFICE HOURS
Shops: Mon–Fri, 0800–1200, 1300–1600, Saturday 0800–1200
Banks: Mon–Fri, 0800–1200 or 1300, Thursday 1400 or 1500–1700 and at the airport Mon–Fri, 0830–1230, 1530–1730
Government offices: Mon–Fri, 0800–1200, 1300–1615

PLACES TO SEE
Kingstown
Botanical Gardens/Museum (HMS Bounty)
Fort Charlotte
St George's Anglican Cathedral
St Mary's Catholic Cathedral
Young Island
Duvernette Islet (next door)
The island's interior
Trinity Falls
Falls of Baleine
Mesopotamia Valley: Montreal Gardens & Petroglyphs (rock carvings)
La Soufrière volcanic massif
Rabacca Dry River: lava flow
Petroglyphs: near Layou
Black Point Tunnel: (1815, 100m long)

ROAD TRANSPORT
Drive on the left
A licence is obligatory
Hire car companies in Kingstown and the airport
Note some places can only be got to in a 4x4
Taxis (set fares)

REGULATIONS
Underwater hunting is forbidden everywhere on the coast to non-residents
Jet skis are forbidden
Fishing permitted except in conservation areas in the Grenadines (Devil's Table, Bequia; Mustique, E coast of Canouan, Mayreau and Tobago Cays, Palm I and Petit St Vincent)
It is forbidden to buy langoustes out of season (authorised 1/10 to 31/4) with heavy fines for breaking the rules.

FORMALITIES
Arriving by air
Customs and immigration in the airport
Arriving by sea
Wallilabou Office Hours: irregular.
Kingstown Customs close to the quay on the Port Esplanade. Immigration in the Police Station near the market. Both soon to be brought together at Cruise Ship Dock. Office hours: weekdays 0800–1200, 1300–1600 with overtime outside office hours, especially Saturday morning
Taxes and fees
Tax of about EC$10 per person with a supplementary tax for charter boats.
An office for clearance is planned in the Young I area.

The Grenadines

Above left Carriacou–anchorage at Sandy Island
Above right Anchorage at Union
Below Mayreau–Salt Whistle Bay beach and anchorage

Language English and Pidgin
Currency EC$ and US$
Political status In two parts:
Dependencies of St Vincent
 Northern islands from
 Bequia to Petit St Vincent
Dependencies of Grenada
 Petite Martinique and
 Carriacou

History

The history of these islands is intimately tied to the Anglo-French struggle over St Vincent and Grenada both of which, in 1783, became definitively English. The islands were primarily of strategic value because their small land area and lack of water meant they were hard to cultivate. That said, they attracted several families of French and British colonists who made the largest islands fertile using slave labour. After slavery was abolished the islands were left to go back to nature and the population turned to fishing and smallholding. Other than some mixed race people, there's now little trace of the old European presence. For some time the government of St Vincent has been encouraging private (and foreign) initiatives aimed at developing the islands under its authority. The result is a pretty spectacular explosion of tourism and development related to water sports, despite the difficulties of getting labour and materials to islands in the middle of nowhere. Bequia, the closest to St Vincent, and Union, close to the glorious Tobago Cays, are, thanks to their geographical situation and their airports, the two focal points of the N part of the archipelago.

The Grenadan dependencies of Carriacou and Petite Martinique, on the other hand, have stayed relatively untouched by the intense growth in tourism and as a result have a rather more authentic feel, if at the cost of facilities.

Tourism

Where to stay and what to see

A dusting of volcanic islands and confetti of sprinkled sand set in coral, this mini-archipelago lies between St Vincent and Grenada. The Grenadines have been so puffed by tourist brochures as the archetype of a tropical paradise that some of them are now said to be too overcrowded with visiting yachts and charter tourists, a criticism all too valid in high season. Even so, whether discovering them for the first time or revisiting, these small delights have retained so much of their natural beauty that one is inevitably seduced again by their almost mythical charms. Thanks to daily flights by local companies, access to the Grenadines from the larger islands with intercontinental airports is easy. If the size of some of the islands is pretty modest, their number and diversity allow for a great variety of places to stop and routes to take so you can't get bored. Many have hotels and infrastructure offering great comfort and even luxury. The white sand of the beaches and the clear emerald water are certainly considered idyllic. However, to appreciate fully the beauty of Grenadine waters nothing will ever replace exploring them by sea under sail.

Pilotage

Coastline and anchorages

The beauty of the coast and sailing from island to island in armchair comfort (the biggest distance is no more than some 7 miles) can make you lazy and even make you forget your navigational skills. However, you should always be alert because there are many coral reefs, the passes are tricky and the currents are often strong. The regular current runs from W to WNW. However, the tidal current runs E. It isn't a fast set, but it can raise a lively sea in the channels. Don't sail at night because the lights are unreliable. Given how crowded some of the anchorages are, including the prettiest ones, you have to hunt a bit for a quiet spot. Such places are usually surrounded by reefs and therefore require a careful approach in good visibility, avoiding having the sun ahead. Before leaving for the Grenadines you need to know the following:

- fishing and underwater hunting are regulated and mostly forbidden to non-residents. There are protected underwater zones.
- watering ship is not possible in all the islands and water is always expensive
- fuel docks are equally sparse and you must plan ahead thoroughly.
- apart from Bequia, and to a lesser extent Union and Carriacou, repair and maintenance services are not to be relied on.
- provisioning at many of the islands depends on the shops there and the unreliability of their supplies.
- any boat that is wrecked swiftly becomes public property but only to the benefit of certain local 'specialists'.
- even when a boat is in perfect order and afloat, in some places it isn't immune to petty theft (fortunately there are few such anchorages).

However, once you're alert to these potential bothers, provided you take sensible precautions and exercise a minimum of vigilance, you can enjoy peaceful sailing in this micro-paradise for sailors.

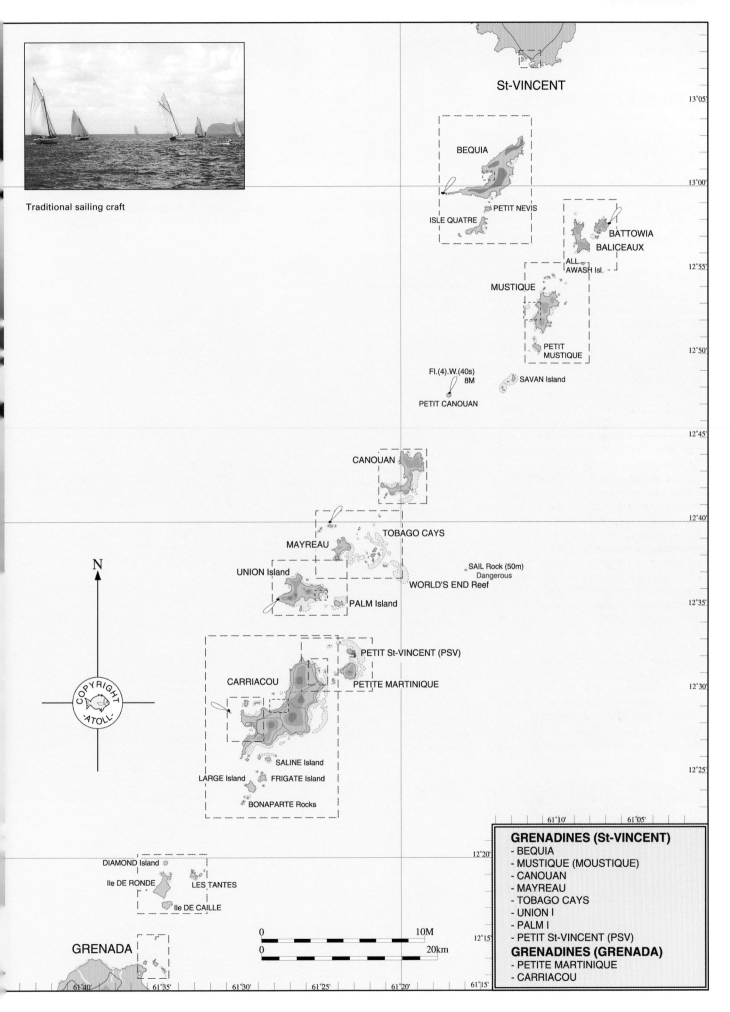

Traditional sailing craft

St-VINCENT

BEQUIA

PETIT NEVIS

ISLE QUATRE

BATTOWIA
BALICEAUX

ALL AWASH Isl.

MUSTIQUE

PETIT MUSTIQUE

Fl.(4).W.(40s)
8M

SAVAN Island

PETIT CANOUAN

CANOUAN

TOBAGO CAYS

MAYREAU

SAIL Rock (50m)
Dangerous

UNION Island

WORLD'S END Reef

PALM Island

N

PETIT St-VINCENT (PSV)

PETITE MARTINIQUE

CARRIACOU

COPYRIGHT
·ATOLL·

SALINE Island

LARGE Island   FRIGATE Island

BONAPARTE Rocks

61°10'   61°05'

GRENADINES (St-VINCENT)
- BEQUIA
- MUSTIQUE (MOUSTIQUE)
- CANOUAN
- MAYREAU
- TOBAGO CAYS
- UNION I
- PALM I
- PETIT St-VINCENT (PSV)

GRENADINES (GRENADA)
- PETITE MARTINIQUE
- CARRIACOU

DIAMOND Island

Ile DE RONDE   LES TANTES

Ile DE CAILLE

GRENADA

0   10M

0   20km

61°40'   61°35'   61°30'   61°25'   61°20'   61°15'

13°05'
13°00'
12°55'
12°50'
12°45'
12°40'
12°35'
12°30'
12°25'
12°20'
12°15'

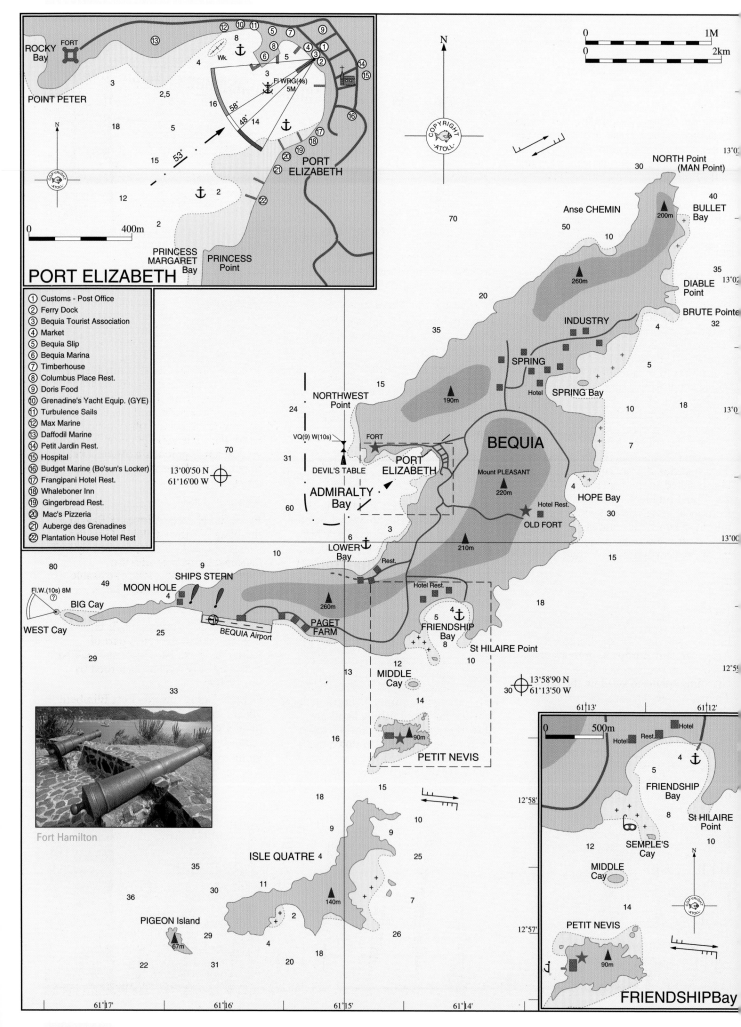

PORT ELIZABETH

① Customs - Post Office
② Ferry Dock
③ Bequia Tourist Association
④ Market
⑤ Bequia Slip
⑥ Bequia Marina
⑦ Timberhouse
⑧ Columbus Place Rest.
⑨ Doris Food
⑩ Grenadine's Yacht Equip. (GYE)
⑪ Turbulence Sails
⑫ Max Marine
⑬ Daffodil Marine
⑭ Petit Jardin Rest.
⑮ Hospital
⑯ Budget Marine (Bo'sun's Locker)
⑰ Frangipani Hotel Rest.
⑱ Whaleboner Inn
⑲ Gingerbread Rest.
⑳ Mac's Pizzeria
㉑ Auberge des Grenadines
㉒ Plantation House Hotel Rest

ROCKY Bay
FORT
POINT PETER
PRINCESS MARGARET Bay
PRINCESS Point
PORT ELIZABETH
Wk.
Fl.WRG(4s) 5M

Fort Hamilton

NORTH Point (MAN Point)
Anse CHEMIN
BULLET Bay
DIABLE Point
BRUTE Pointe
INDUSTRY
SPRING
SPRING Bay
Hotel
BEQUIA
Mount PLEASANT
HOPE Bay
OLD FORT
Hotel Rest.

NORTHWEST Point
VQ(9) W(10s)
13°00'50 N
61°16'00 W
DEVIL'S TABLE
FORT
PORT ELIZABETH
ADMIRALTY Bay
LOWER Bay
Rest.

FRIENDSHIP Bay
St HILAIRE Point
MIDDLE Cay
PETIT NEVIS
Hotel Rest.

FRIENDSHIP Bay
13°58'90 N
61°13'50 W
Hotel
Rest.
FRIENDSHIP Bay
St HILAIRE Point
SEMPLE'S Cay
MIDDLE Cay
PETIT NEVIS

BIG CAY
WEST Cay
Fl.W.(10s) 8M
MOON HOLE
SHIPS STERN
BEQUIA Airport
PAGET FARM

ISLE QUATRE
PIGEON Island

Bequia

(St Vincent Grenadines)

History

18 sq km in area, Bequia (pronounced Bek-way) is the largest of the St Vincent dependencies. Its terrain is volcanic in origin and a ridge of hills runs from one end of the island to the other. The population is about 6000 and is a complicated mixture of mainly black African ex-slaves and old European colonists, mainly Scots and French. To those must be added fishermen from New Bedford (USA) who came in the 19th century to hunt whales and taught the skill to the local fishermen. Whale hunting still takes place at the cost of those rare cetaceans that still pass close to the coast, though the catch is stringently policed by international regulations. Each extremely rare 'event' is announced by a look-out and puts the whole small fishing community into a hubbub. Once aboard their frail skiffs they try to harpoon the whale and bring it back to Petit Nevis Islet in order the better to be able to cut it up and sell it in a general atmosphere of celebration. This traditional practice has naturally also resulted in the fishermen being good boat builders. Although made only from local materials and with their own inherited knowledge and skills, these local craft (or country boats) in no way lack in seaworthiness and toughness.

Tourism

Where to stay and what to see

For several years now the population has been enlarged by the numerous American and European immigrants, often ex-sailors, who have chosen this charming island to swallow the hook. Thanks to the regular tourist traffic, shops have sprung up and hotels and restaurants opened throughout the island, particularly in Port Elizabeth, the principal town in Admiralty Bay. Along its shoreline and in the small streets there are an enormous number of restaurants, from the most modest

Above Port Elizabeth from Fort Hamilton
Below Admiralty Bay, Bequia from the W

'lolo' to the most luxurious.

From the fortified heights of Fort Hamilton you can overlook the entirety of the huge bay which buzzes with the coming and going of ferries, the unloading of the varied cargoes of old coasting craft and the numerous pleasure boats coming to anchor. The activity becomes frenetic when a cruise ship offloads its shipload of passengers at Port Elizabeth, fortunately only for a short visit. If you explore the rest of the island and its shoreline you'll be equally fascinated.

On the E coast, from Friendship Bay though Industry Bay to Spring Bay a rough road runs past lovely beaches backed by huge coconut plantations. Buried here and there in the greenery you'll see hotel-restaurants and villas. On the slopes dominating Hope Bay a small residential hotel, the Old Fort, has been made out of an old French fortlet. In the S the airport, the latest modern amenity, blots the landscape with its ugly mass of concrete. It stops only a short distance from Paget Farm, a small fishing village that, by contrast, seems like a step out of time. Near to the local bars the colourful fishing boats are drawn up on the shore. Inside, some finely etched figures slap down their dominoes between the sips of rum to take away the sharp taste of the salt spray.

Pilotage

Coastline and anchorages

W Coast

Roughly 6M S of St Vincent, Bequia is the first of the Grenadines you'll come to if coming from the N. The channel between St Vincent and Bequia is narrow. Currents are often strong and when the trade wind pipes up it can be very rough. Approaching Bequia you may have to deal with some strong gusts.

Admiralty Bay

From the N enter Admiralty Bay after doubling Northwest Point. Give the shoals of Devil's Table, marked by a W Cardinal buoy, a good berth.
Caution Night entry is not advisable because the lights are unreliable.

Lower Bay & Princess Bay

These anchorages, with their fine beaches, are in the south part of Admiralty Bay. They are less crowded but often very rolly or disturbed by a sharp chop.
Caution Going towards Port Elizabeth and Lower Bay, steer clear of the shoals off Princess Point.

Ashore there are some small restaurants along the shore or up the hill, with a wonderful view.

Above left Beach and coconut plantation on the windward coast
Above right Fishing boat on the windward coast
Below left Friendship Bay anchorage
Below right Friendship Bay from the S

Port Elizabeth

Two anchorage areas are separated by an unbuoyed channel leading to the ferry dock, which must be kept clear:

- to the SE close to the village
- to the north close to Bequia Marina dock.

In the latter there's a wreck with 4m over it, which has already snagged more than one anchor. Although the bay is huge there's not often a lot of room in the SE corner because of the number of boats and moorings. Depths vary from 5m to 12m with only moderate to poor holding. Mooring buoys, for which there's a fee, are often available.

Caution Even if the rules aren't always respected by some, there's a speed limit of 5kts in the anchorage.

Ashore Conveniently for cruising yachts, the offices for clearance and the post office are in the new government block opposite the main ferry dock. It is easy to spot its neo-classical façade that, with its balustraded steps, pompously looks down on the simpler architecture of the surrounding buildings. Thanks to its numerous specialists and well-stocked chandlers, Port Elizabeth is a better

place than any other between St Vincent and Grenada to effect repairs and buy equipment. Beside the dock Bequia Marina and Bequia Slip has a railway slip that can take 50 tonnes and offers other repair services. At the same dock you can also have water and fuel delivered. The majority of services for pleasure vessels listen on VHF 16 or 68. Close to the imposing government building the local fresh produce market (Rasta Market) and several well-stocked small shops or minimarkets are good for provisioning. Other shops sell local artefacts, boat models, etc. To top off the town's attractions there are numerous bars and restaurants. The majority of these are on the S shore and almost all have jetties for dinghies. They all have cosmopolitan managements which match the menus that range from local cuisine through Italian and French dishes. Bar a few modest 'lolos' the restaurants are attractively decorated in garden-like settings. Thanks to the competition between them prices have stayed reasonable.

If you're a bit pressed for time, there are taxis, hire cars and motorcycle hire so you can use your stop here to visit the rest of the island and discover the beaches and other small villages. If they are for the most part pretty unassuming, the restaurants elsewhere on the island are charming and specialize in seafood and local dishes. All together Port

Elizabeth is good place to stop, so much so that some will find themselves tempted to linger.

Moon Hole

Just before you pass the SW point enclosing Admiralty Bay, you'll see a fair sized, cave-like cove cut into the coast. This is Moon Hole. In the 1960s this natural formation inspired the cave dwelling style of housing in the private estate surrounding it. Since then the buildings are only more or less occupied, mostly being used for seasonal lets (visits can be arranged).

South coast

Coming from the N, give the reefs off West Cay a wide berth as you make round to the S coast. Then pass the airport and the small village of Paget Farm until you reach Friendship Bay.

Caution On your way from West Cay you'll have to contend with the wind and current against you, and there are often strong gusts.

Friendship Bay

On entry give St Hilaire Cay a wide berth then anchor to the E of the dock in the NE corner. The anchorage, surrounded by hills, is pleasant and, bar a few fishermen, often deserted, though it's breezy and a swell usually rolls in.

Caution Look out for the shoal ground to the W of the dock and for the bottom, pretty cluttered with this and that, as well as old mooring sinkers.

There are mooring buoys you can use. If you want to go alongside the dock, watch out for the coral off the beach and the surf.

Ashore Friendship Bay Hotel, overlooking the anchorage from its fine natural setting, is patronised by an international clientele of diving enthusiasts. The busy diving clubs here demonstrate the attractiveness of the waters hereabouts. Around the beach the restaurant tucked away in the greenery offers a welcome both to tourists and passing yachtsmen. It's a pleasant spot.

Petit Nevis

This uninhabited islet is just under a mile from Friendship Bay. The anchorage is in its lee off the small dock and the whale catchers' hut.

Caution As you come in watch out for the shoal to port.

Anchor as close as possible to the right of the dock, or drop a stern anchor and then put a line from the bow to the dock.

Top right Building a local boat
Above right Petit Nevis–whaling
Below Petit Nevis and Friendship Bay from the S
Bottom Baliceaux & Battowia from the S

Ashore You'll see the whale catchers' base, with its vats, cauldrons and bits of whalebone. Through the pretty clump of coconut palms to the windward side of the island, there's a fine beach and if you climb the hill opposite the anchorage, there's a marvellous view from the top. If the wind is SE'ly, a swell sometimes makes its way in.

Isle Quatre

Few do it, but you can anchor for a short stop in the centre of the leeward coast in 3–4m. The anchorage is

feasible as long as the sea state doesn't have a big swell rolling down from the N. The island, with its cliffy coast, is part of a protected zone.

Baliceaux and Battowia Islands

These barren and deserted islands are off the standard route for yachts and as a result pretty much only visited by fishermen from Bequia. They are only really viable in settled weather because the anchorages are poorly protected and the currents fierce. Given that wind and current are against you, you'll need several tacks to make it here from Petit Nevis. It's easier to come from Mustique to the S. Anchor in the lee of Baliceaux near where shown on the S end where the fishermen pull their boats up.

Caution Watch out for the shoals around the reefs spreading all across the N part of the anchorage.

To cope with the change of current, use two anchors set at about 45°. With the wind more SE'ly, the swell and currents can make the anchorage untenable. It's also possible to anchor in the bay about 0·5M N, in 3m. In calm seas there's a day anchorage under Battowia's lee behind the cays of Church Cay. The anchorages are far from easy but, for lovers of solitude. . .

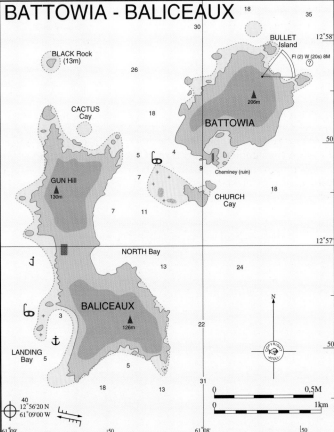

BATTOWIA - BALICEAUX

BLACK ROCK (13m)

BULLET Island
Fl (2) W (20s) 8M

CACTUS Cay

BATTOWIA
206m

Cheminey (ruin)

CHURCH Cay

GUN Hill
130m

NORTH Bay

BALICEAUX
126m

LANDING Bay

12°56'20 N
61°09'00 W

0   0.5M
0   1km

Mustique

(St Vincent Grenadines)

History and tourism

Not long back Mustique's beaches were known only to fishermen. That was until the day when the small, 5 sq km island caught the investment eye of Colin Tennant, a rich entrepreneur, a gentleman and British to boot. Thanks to his aristocratic connections he was able to interest Princess Margaret in his project. She became one of the first buyers of the luxurious houses built in the 1960s. Looking for solitude in the depths of the Caribbean, other rich clients followed suit, including international showbiz and jet-setting celebrities like Mick Jagger, Raquel Welch, David Bowie, etc. Not surprisingly, Mustique quickly acquired its nickname of Billionaires' Island.

Today the Mustique Company, representing all of the proprietors, runs the island's administration.

In the N part of the island there's an old cotton plantation that has been sumptuously turned into a charming five star hotel, the Cotton House. It's one of the Caribbean's most select places (if we judge what counts as select by the size of the bill). Still, its luxury and its standards of service certainly justify the price. Basil's Bar, a restaurant, is on the beach in Britannia Bay (ex-Grand Bay). It's where visitors on their way through can enjoy local langoustes or a barbecue down by the sea. On most evenings the musical ambience adds to the pleasures of dinner. Close to the Cotton House there's a little airstrip at the foot of the hills which ensures that the rich residents can come and go with ease for

Left Treasure Shop
Below Britannia Bay beach
Bottom left Mustique from the S
Bottom right Britannia Bay anchorage

their short stays. Mustique is equally well-known for the shipwreck of the *Antilles*, jewel amongst French cruise ships, in 1971. This superb ship grounded on a shoal as a result of skirting dangerously close to the coast of Mustique. For a long time it decorated the reefs on the N coast, but not long back the rusty hulk slid off its perch and now lies on the bottom.

Mustique is a little jewel box, its beaches and coral superb and now all part of a protected reserve. Although setting foot ashore is likely to empty your wallet, a short stop still has its appeal.

Pilotage

Mustique is the most windward of the inhabited Grenadines, and whether coming from the N (from Bequia) or the S (from Canouan), if the current is strong and sets you W, you'll be hard on the wind and may even have to make a tack or two depending on wind direction. Many sailors don't fancy this and so don't make the effort. On the N coast watch out for the Pillories and the numerous reefs running out two miles and more to seaward. This is where the *Antilles* went on the bricks to become the magnet for divers it now is, although you need to be experienced given the always very strong currents.

Britannia Bay (Grand Bay)

The only sheltered anchorage is in Britannia Bay (ex-Grand Bay).

Caution Half a mile to the west, Montezuma Shoal, a coral reef with only 1m over it, stretches more than 200m N to S. It is marked by a beacon, which is hard to pick out at any distance.

The anchorage in the bay is close to Basil's Bar and has mooring buoys (there's a fee payable to the Mustique Company (VHF 16/68) that manages them). If the buoys are occupied, you can anchor outside the mooring area, though the depths are considerable and there's less shelter from the swell.

Caution According to the regulations governing protection of reserves, especially in Mustique, all anchoring must be clear of any coral.

That means no anchoring in the S of Britannia Bay where, along the shore, there's a fine reef still excellently preserved.

To the right of the mooring area the dock is reserved for the small ferries. The access channel, marked by two buoys, should be left free. The anchorage in Britannia Bay is often rolly, especially when the trades are NE and fresh.

Ashore There are no clearance facilities, for which you must go to the airport. Next to Basil's Bar there are delightful, vibrantly coloured small houses in a neo-Creole style. They are home to several small fashion shops and a bar. For pretty basic provisioning there's a minimarket and a bakery, but best of all a fresh fish market. The last is close to the small fishing village with its coloured boats where the latest landings of fish and langoustes are on offer at the stalls. For a tour round the island, especially to the windward coast with its lonely beaches (Macaroni Beach) there's a hire

company (mini-moke, motor bikes, bikes). Given how small the island is, you could also go on horseback or even by foot. A dive centre does outings to good sites and wrecks around the shores.

Above Basil's Bar on Britannia Bay beach
Left Cotton House

Endeavour Bay

This fine beach is on the edge of the Cotton House Resort. Coming from the N you can make a short stop here to enjoy the surroundings of this prestigious establishment (to which access is restricted to guests). The anchorage is off the dock and usually troubled by swell, so it's no place to linger.

Lagoon Bay

This is S of Britannia Bay and little protected. Still, in fair weather a day anchorage is feasible so you can enjoy the good snorkelling on the coral. To reach it from Britannia Bay give a good berth to Ellis Island, the off-lying coral reef of the S point of Britannia Bay.

Petit Mustique

A good snorkelling spot. In moderate seas and winds, you can day anchor either in the lee of the reefs of Petit Cay or in the first cove on Petit Mustique's NW, or leeward coast.
Caution Beware of Dry Rock, a reef off the SW shore and of the current.

Savan Island

This is another good snorkelling spot. It's easy to get to from Mustique, although sea state and wind strength will dictate where you can anchor for a short stay in the lee of the main islet. The islet is often visited by local fishermen, who have built a few shelters here.

Petit Canouan

Between Canouan and Savan, this barren, utterly isolated, wave-battered and current-swept islet has no shelter. However, in very good weather you can try a dubious and short term anchorage W of the island. The bottom drops off sharply and the currents are often strong. For divers the appeal is that they can find pelagic fish here.

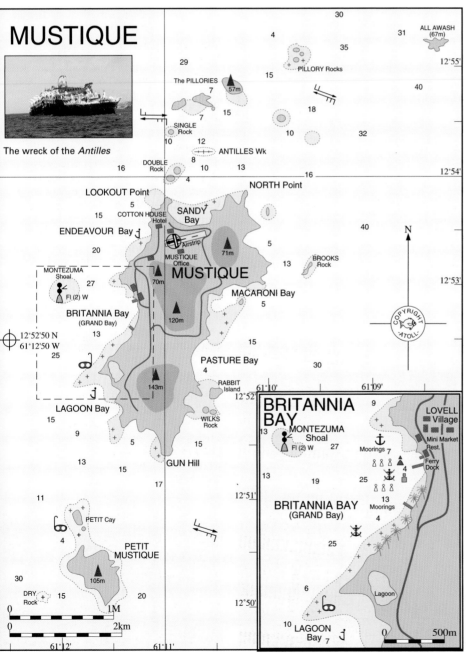

The wreck of the *Antilles*

Canouan
(St Vincent Grenadines)

History and tourism

In the past the island supported just a few inhabitants who survived by fishing and working meagre smallholdings. Most live in Charlestown, an imposing name for a small village tucked into the flank of the hill overlooking Charlestown Bay. This little island of less than 10 sq km is very steeply intersected by hills and valleys but is almost bare. However, the shore has lovely beaches and a reef complex enclosing the whole windward side. As early as the 1970s this was what generated the first tourist ventures, notably a hotel close to the superb South Glossy Beach and the building of a small airstrip on the E side to get clients there. These modest developments didn't much change the fairly wild feel of Canouan, nor much improve the standard of living of the inhabitants. But, during the 90s, a foreign company began to invest heavily and everything changed.

Bulldozers and mechanical diggers ground into action, planing down hills a bit here, cutting away the scrub there and enlarging the airstrip. On the Charlestown Bay side the elegant complex of the Tamarind Beach, with its kitschy neo-Creole architecture, was built along the shore, surrounded by a colourful botanical garden. At Carenage Bay with its wonderful barrier reef, a very upmarket resort with a casino was built, with luxury cottages topping its small hillocks or along the shore of the superb windward coast. To cap it all a landscaped 18-hole golf course (naturally essential), faces the waves rolling in from the ocean. Other projects are in the pipeline including a marina. The present buildings are constantly undergoing facelifts which can lead to one or other of them being intermittently closed.

Until now the Cinderella of the Grenadines, Canouan now seems set on a roll towards the splendours of luxury tourism, no doubt hoping that a rich clientele will appreciate and even make profitable, its air of decorum.

Pilotage

Coming from the N, the approach to the leeward coast has no particular problems.

North coast

Baie Maho (Mahault Bay)

Almost always empty, seen from seaward the bay doesn't appear very inviting. However, a brief stop is usually possible for a small boat in flat calm weather. It's very quiet and has good snorkelling. Anchor in the SE corner as far in as you can get once you're round the reefs off the NE point. It's prudent to use two anchors at 45°.

Caution Coming in from the W give a wide berth to the coral bank and the isolated outcrop N of it about one third of the way across from Jupiter Pt.

Leeward coast

Anse Corbec (Corbec Bay)

A tiny anchorage with room for just one boat. Anchor from the stern and put a line ashore from the bow. Because the inlet is very little protected from the N swell, don't look to using it as more than a day anchorage.

Anse Guyac (L'Ance Guyac)

An excellent and very pleasant anchorage for one or two boats. There's now an off-loading dock for the building work on the island, which has rather spoiled the shore, not to speak of the small coasters regularly disturbing

the peace. Coming in follow the edge of the line of reefs fronting the N part of the bay about 50m off. There are several reef outcrops closer to the coast on the S shore. Strong gusts from all over the place are quite common.

Rameau Bay

From the N, once clear of the shoal ground off Pt Guyac and in the shelter S of the point, there's an anchorage in 7–8m close to the shore.

Caution The bottom drops off very quickly.

The N swell and chop can make life uncomfortable.

Charlestown Bay

Enter the bay on about 150°T using as conspicuous leading marks the large village dock in the S of the bay or the aerial on the hill.

Caution The NE part of the bay has a shoal fringed with reef (visible). The entrance pass is marked by two lit buoys, but a night entry isn't recommended because the lights are unreliable. In an emergency the red aero-light on Glass Pt is a good mark and visible from well out. The preferred anchorage is in the NE, in the bay near the old fisheries building. Mooring buoys (in principle a fee is levied) are available off the dock of the hotel-restaurant. The anchorage gets rolly with a N swell.

Ashore The luxury buildings of the Tamarind take up a large part of the beach. When the place is open, you can enjoy the bar and restaurant, its neo-colonial architecture and glistening new décor buried in the trees, as well as use the dive and snorkelling facilities. A charter company has recently opened a base in the bay. Thanks to the economic growth the village has replaced some of the simple wooden cottages with their corrugated roofs by new concrete buildings. Even so only

Below Tamarind Resort dock and anchorage
Right Charlestown Bay from the N

Canouan, South Glossy Bay from the SW

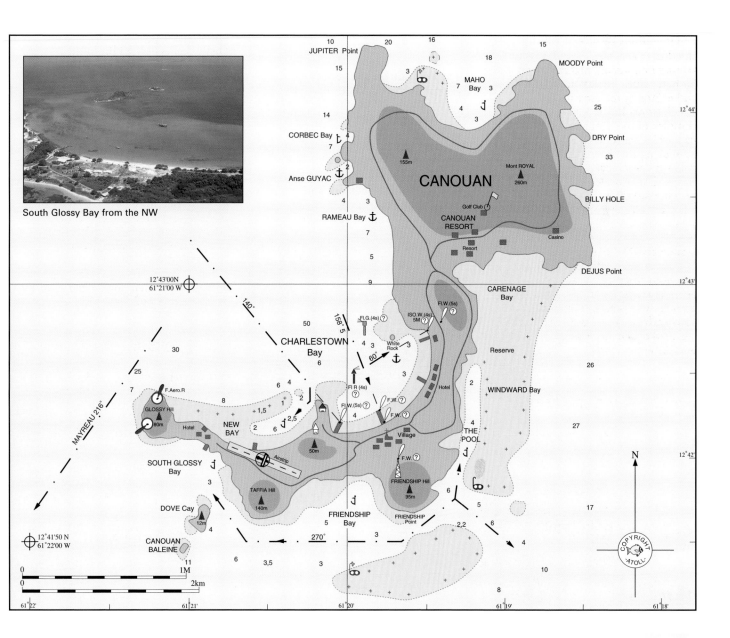

South Glossy Bay from the NW

basic provisions can be bought in the village's few shops (grocery and bakery). There's a gas station W of the ferry dock. In the village or on the hill overlooking it, some small restaurants (a lot simpler than the Tamarind), offer local specialities.

New Bay (Nens Bay)

This is only a temporary stop (limited to shoal drafters). The half-submerged barrier reef offers no protection from N'ly swells. The approach on 140°T requires care and in the pass (2–3m of water) favour the coast. Once inside the 4–6m depths come up quickly to 1m.

South coast

South Glossy Bay

The beach is superb. Unfortunately the anchorage is rolly and, in a strong SE'ly swell, impracticable because the islets of Dove Bay give scant protection. The hotel dock is usable by dinghies unless there's a big reflected sea.

Ashore the Canouan Beach Hotel is the oldest such establishment on the island. It comprises several bungalows and a restaurant, the terrace of which dominates the bay. Yachting visitors are usually made welcome. A dive club operates from the hotel.

Friendship Bay

There is 2·5–3m in the pass between Dove Cay and the coast. Once past the point below Taffia Hill, keep off the shore of Friendship Bay, which is full of reef. A temporary anchorage can be had in the NE corner in the lee of Friendship Hill promontory.

Windward coast

Caution Approaching this coast for a day anchorage should only be done in good visibility, fair weather and with the greatest of care.

The Pool

You must round Friendship Hill promontory. As you do you'll have a barrier reef to starboard which has a large pass in it opening to seaward before you reach the sand islet, which is almost at sea level, at the entrance to The Pool. Either anchor behind the islet or push further into this narrow 'swimming pool' behind the barrier reef and anchor in 3–4m. This wild anchorage is often very windy and choppy because the barrier of the reef is not complete. It's basically a day anchorage for keen snorkellers.

Caution Getting back out and round to the leeward coast is often tricky once

the sun is dropping towards the W because the reefs aren't easy to see. A leading mark of 270°T on the gap between the Dove Cays islets may help.

Above Windward coast, Carenage Bay from the NE
Below Windward coast, looking out from the casino
Bottom Windward coast, Friendship Bay and The Pool from the NE

Caption: Above Mayreau from the NW

Mayreau
(St Vincent Grenadines)

History and things to see

A very small island (less than 3 sq km) with such a big history which was told to me 25 years and more ago by Father Divonne, a Dominican monk, who'd in his time been pastor of the majority Catholic population of Mayreau. That alone is something of an anachronism in a region where Protestantism has all but swept the board. The Catholic faith here comes from the slaves of the old French colonists. The latter were owners of the island by the end of the 18th century and they tried to make the island's meagre resources profitable by using slaves . . . and maltreating them. The result was a wave of successive revolts and their suppression. Once slavery had been abolished the old slave owners and their ex-slaves continued to live on their oceanic pebble, the slaves still dependants of their old masters. Half a century later a primary school teacher from St Vincent avenged his black brothers in his own way. Employed to teach the people, he spent most of his time seducing the daughter of the boss, married her and then locked her away, thereby in one stroke assuring his own succession and seizing control of the island. Despite this the people remained just as poor, although over the years the plentiful resources of the Tobago Cays turned them into capable fishermen.

Nonetheless, in this largely saline area one major problem remained: fresh water. At this point Father Divonne arrived. Good words apart, Father Divonne inspired the people with his example and gave them enough courage to build with their bare hands a large public reservoir on the hillside. The good monk has been retired in Martinique for many years now, his health broken by his work and his hermit's existence. There's still a tiny church on the top of the hill, standing as witness to the dedication of the priest and the faith of this small community. Around the same time the island's owners, descendants of the teacher, authorised the building by a Canadian of a small hotel complex in Salt Whistle Bay. The bungalows of this establishment are well disguised in the vegetation around the sandy crescent of beach, which is visited by the odd passing yacht. For their part, the 200 or so inhabitants maintain their houses on the hillside and the road that leads to them. Some fisherman have discovered culinary talents to the benefit of passing yachtsmen between the occasional visits of cruise ships, which offload their passengers for a quick barbecue on the beach. Recently the owners of the island, in a surprising outburst of generosity, actually gave the land they lived on back to its inhabitants. Obviously such a great change has had major consequences. The superb beaches are now more crowded. The fishermen have replaced their old sails with powerful outboards and the quantity of langoustes moves in inverse relation to their price. But what really matters has survived. To see it, all you have to do is climb about 100m up the hill. There, close to the small church you can take in at a glance the panorama of the huge barrier of the Tobago Cays whose last coral banks almost reach your feet in Windward Bay. In the other direction the crenellated summits of Union hover above the horizon and, when the time is right, turn purple in the shimmering of the setting sun. It's all well worth the effort of climbing the hill.

Above Mayreau from the NW
Below left Father Divonne's church
Below right Barbecue party
Bottom left Fishing under sail
Bottom right Traditional sailing fishing boats

offloading passengers. They promptly occupy the entire beach for several hours with the local vendors of T-shirts and souvenirs as a backdrop.

Once ashore a small and very steep road leads up to the village houses on the side of the hill. Happily, Dennis's Hideway, a bar-restaurant, is half way up for a pit stop. Because of the many passing yachties other small restaurants have now also sprung up in the village offering every kind of seafood specialty. A small grocery store can offer basic provisions and there's a mechanic who can help you out in an emergency.

Pilotage

Coming from the N there are less than 4M between Canouan and Mayreau. Pass E of Dry Shingle (marked by a buoy) off Catholic I.

Mayreau is 100m high and the famous Tobago Cays stretch for several miles eastward from its windward coast.

West coast

Salt Whistle Bay

This is on the N side of Mayreau. To enter it give the N point a good berth to avoid the shoals off it, then head E towards the beach.

The S of the bay is full of coral. Boats drawing less than 2m can get close to the beach and anchor more comfortably. Those with deeper draft must stay further out where in NE winds it's often rolly from the swell. The delights of this fine anchorage mean that it's often crowded in high season and allowing for swinging room, there isn't often much space. There are moorings you can hire. There's a lovely beach on the leeward shore separated from another on the windward shore by a thin isthmus on which the Salt

Whistle Bay Club (VHF 16/68) is buried in the trees.

Ashore The cottages are spread around under the coconut palms, but the most enticing sight is that of the small round stone platforms, topped with a palm leaf hat which shelter each table of the restaurant. In this calm and shady spot you can sample the menu's specialities and have a drink at the bar as you look at your boat through the bronze-trunked palms on the shore.

Saline Bay

This is Mayreau's main anchorage and sometimes a bit rolly.

Note To enter it from the N you must come round the mass of reefs which run out a long way from Grand Col Pt. In theory there's a W cardinal mark on the end of the reef, though it's often replaced with a small marker buoy that's hard to see. N of the reefs off Grand Col Pt there's a submerged wreck with no more than 6–8m of water over it. Anchor S of the docks in 3–4m over sand.

Remember that the bay is regularly visited by cruise liners for beach-barbecues. When that happens the dock is thick with umpteen ship's tenders

Windward coast

Windward Bay

On Mayreau's SE coast there's an anchorage behind a long coral barrier marking the beginning of the Tobago Cays. Once round Monkey Pt, hold off the fringing reef and follow it up into Windward Bay. You need good visibility. In strong winds the anchorage is a bit bouncy. It isn't very popular except with fishermen.

Top left Anchorage and beach at Salt Whistle Bay
Above right High up in the village
Below left Salt Whistle Bay from the NW
Below right Saline Bay

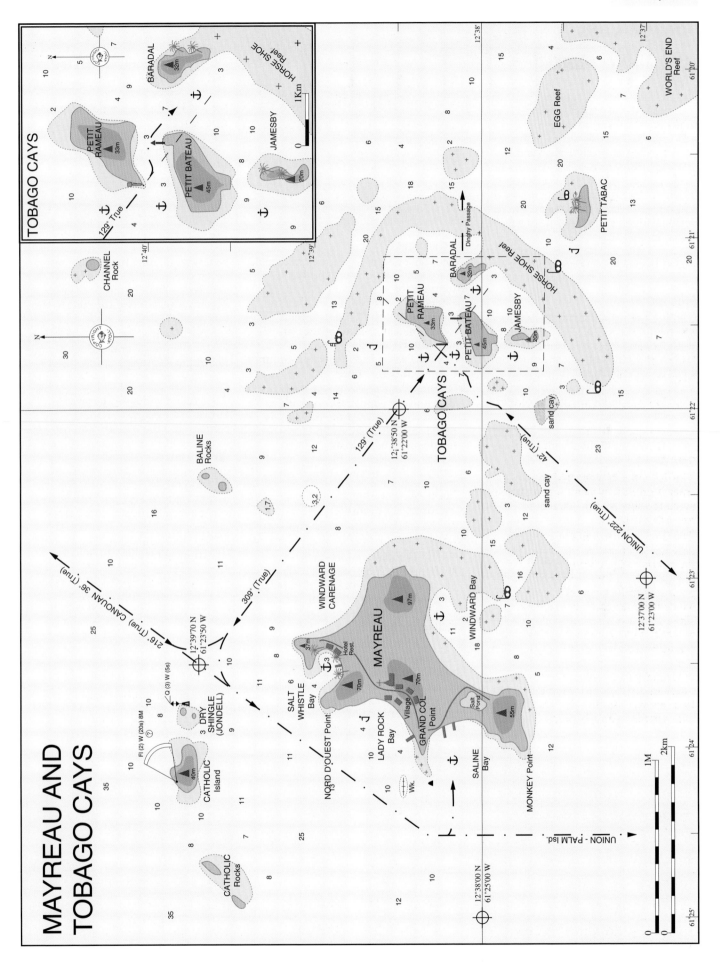

MAYREAU AND TOBAGO CAYS

TOBAGO CAYS

Tobago Cays

(St Vincent Grenadines)

On the chart the Tobago Cays look like five small islands lost in a mass of coral, though accessible through lots of passes and protected to seaward by a huge barrier called Horseshoe Reef and by another further to E called World's End Reef. The Tobago Cays have beautiful beaches, clear water still with lots of fish and well-protected anchorages. These delights are no secret and the downside is that in high season the Cays are saturated with sailing boats. In low season the anchorages are a tad less crowded.

Approaches to the Cays

North Pass Enter between Mayreau and Baline Rocks on 129°T. The line is given by two marks in transit, one on the SW of Petit Rameau, the other on the NE of Petit Bateau. These marks are almost invisible at any distance, but when you're on line the points of the two islands meet.

Caution Follow this route carefully in order to avoid the shoal with less than 1·8m S of Baline Rocks.

South Pass There are actually several passes from the S, most with doglegs or shoal patches. To me the only one that seems relatively easy is the one that goes between the Sand Cays (see chartlet). However, note that these banks never dry, even at low water. To enter from S head for the W side of Petit Rameau on 042°T. Once past SE Sand Cay, you can head for either Jamesby or Petit Rameau. The pass is best tried in good light and when you already know your way round the Cays a bit.

Above Anchorage in the lee of Petit Rameau
Below left Baradal beach
Below right Fishing boats drawn up on the beach, Petit Tabac

Anchorages

Note The Tobago Cays are a protected zone. Don't anchor on the coral. Moorings for which you'll pay are planned in the anchorages which are already mostly cluttered with the mooring blocks of local boats. An anchoring fee to help pay for the National Park is in the pipeline and may be imposed fairly soon.

- between Petit Rameau and Petit Bateau: very popular because it's so picturesque between the beaches on each island. It's rare to find anywhere to anchor in high season.
- behind Petit Rameau: less popular but rather choppy to very choppy with ENE wind
- behind Jamesby: here it's even less popular because the best beach and its coconuts are on Jamesby's windward coast.
- behind Baradal: a more open anchorage looking out to sea. There's not much room in the lee of Baradal because the approach is full of shoals. Lots of boats anchor further S just behind the barrier.

When the trades are strong the anchorage is bouncy because of a sharp chop. From these anchorages you can get into the barrier reef by tender to go snorkelling. You must use the little buoys provided in order to protect the reef.

Here as elsewhere there are omnipresent boat boys offering bread, langoustes or beach barbecues. Don't hand over your garbage to them because, as in Mayreau, they throw the stuff to the four winds!

Caution If you're swimming, watch out for the boat boys' craft, which charge round the anchorage at full speed.

Petit Tabac

To get here you have to leave Horseshoe Reef by the South Pass and come round the barrier. You can anchor in the lee of Petit Tabac, keeping W of the long tongue of sand, though only in daytime, in fair weather when the swell isn't too NE'ly. It isn't very popular except with fishermen whose boats you'll see under the coconut trees.

World's End Reef

It deserves the name. It really is an anchorage at the end of the world, lost in the middle of the Atlantic swells. Those who love wild and lonely anchorages will be pleased with it. You need good visibility and a calm sea though. Leaving Petit Tabac, go S round Egg Reef. Anchor in the lee of the big barrier reef without trying to push in further. This really is a day anchorage so don't leave it too late or you'll have the sun in your eyes when you're trying to get back round Horseshoe Reef to the S.

The Tobago Cays and Horseshoe Reef

Petit Tabac and Horseshoe Reef from the SE

Baradal anchorage

Below left Windwardside beach at Jamesby
Below Petit Bateau, Petit Rameau and Baradal

Sail Rock

A tiny, pyramidal rock lost in the ocean about 5M E of the Tobago Cays. Blasted by the wind, it's only visited by local fishermen. Any bold sailor on passage who happened to bump into it, especially at night, would have found his last mooring.

Union Island
(St Vincent Grenadines)

History and tourism

Union was settled during the 18th and 19th centuries first by English, then Scottish colonists. Just 17sq km, it was both verdant and well tilled. Until the end of the 19th century it boasted up to 5000 inhabitants. Then it was completely abandoned.

Divided between the two villages of Ashton in the SE and Clifton in the E, only a few folk remain, most of them fishermen or smallholders.

The population has grown naturally to 2000 people but nothing much else changed over the years until the end of the 1960s and the arrival in Clifton of a French *béké* from Martinique.

Clifton

André Beaufrand bought a plot of marshy land to the east of Clifton. He drained it and built a small airstrip and then a house-cum-hotel. It was the birth of the Anchorage Yacht Club. With access by air, a good anchorage for charter boats and a hotel and restaurant to provide a welcome, everything was in place to make the Anchorage, only a few miles from the Tobago Cays, a tourist focus in the Grenadines. When André Beaufrand retired, the Anchorage was bought by a genuine Austrian prince, Franz Ulrich Kinsky. This noble scion of the Austro-Hungarian Empire had the happy inspiration of hiring Charlotte Honnart to manage the business. Under her supervision the Anchorage has been reborn. And reborn whilst conserving the charm of its wonderful location, with bungalows on the beach front and its lovely terrace overlooking an aquarium-like basin where turtles and sharks swim by, not forgetting the pontoons where boats cruising the Grenadines tie up. Such dynamism has had its imitators. Beside the Anchorage is Jean Marc Sailly's Bougainvilla, also done up prettily to attract nautical tourists, with a welcoming jetty, restaurant, small shopping centre and technical support services for yachts. Because of this development, with the consequent

Above Anchorage Yacht Club beach
Below right The schooner *Scaramouche*
Bottom Green Island from Clifton

increase in tourist and cruising traffic, the airstrip, previously pinched between sea and hills, has had to be extended into the sea.

Early each morning the anchorage at Clifton is busy as crew members and day charter passengers go aboard their boats. If you're headed for the reefs and beaches of the Tobago Cays, you'll be spoiled for choice. Amongst the boats on offer are the maxi-catamarans of Captain Yannis, who left his native Cyclades many years ago. Or you could choose *Scaramouche*, a large locally constructed schooner, rebuilt authentically by Martin Janet, a Scotsman by birth and Unionian by adoption. In high season two hundred or more people bring the quay to life in a polyglot atmosphere. And on some evenings at sundowners a steel-band helps the rum create an even mellower ambience.

Right next door the small village of Clifton hasn't been left behind by the changes. Thanks to local initiatives shops and small hotels have been started up. Most of these line the main street along the waterfront. As far as places to stay are concerned, for some the local feel of the village hotels is ample compensation for their simplicity.

The restaurants are also charming with seafood menus cooked to local recipes. However, prices, once reasonable, are increasing because of the pressure of tourism.

A small post office, a tourist information office and a bank complete the village's services. Bar the days when the schooners and other coasters arrive from St Vincent with their cargoes which liven up the waterfront atmosphere, not a lot goes on. The only other main activity is the celebration of Sunday services, often in the open air.

Ashton

The second village has been rather left on one side of the tourist development. Sadly, a tourist resort and marina project, which was started then abandoned, has marred the shoreline. The scars of massive terracing and ruined reef flats are all that's left.

Pilotage

Note

1. whether approaching Union's E coast from the S or the N, you should be very wary of the numerous reefs around both the main island and nearby Palm I. Plenty of yachts have ended their days here!
2. returning from the Tobago Cays, a late landfall with the sun ahead dangerously reduces visibility; night arrivals, despite the buoyage (unreliable), aren't recommended for newcomers.

Clifton village and anchorage

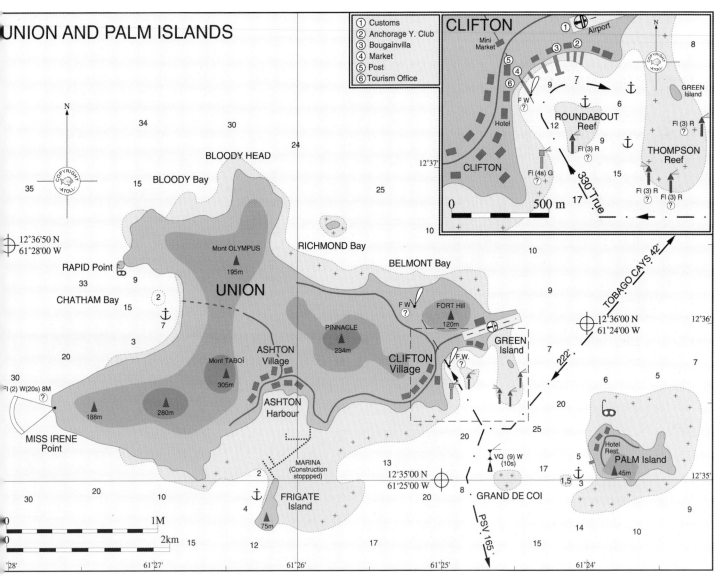

UNION AND PALM ISLANDS

①	Customs
②	Anchorage Y. Club
③	Bougainvilla
④	Market
⑤	Post
⑥	Tourism Office

CLIFTON

Airport

Mini Market

GREEN Island

ROUNDABOUT Reef

THOMPSON Reef

CLIFTON

12°37'

Hotel

Fl (4s) G

Fl (3) R

0   500 m

330° True

N

8

Fl (3) R

Fl (3) R

Fl (3) R

17

15

BLOODY HEAD

BLOODY Bay

34   30   24

35   15   25

RICHMOND Bay

12°36'50 N
61°28'00 W

BELMONT Bay

Mont OLYMPUS
195m

RAPID Point

UNION

33   9

CHATHAM Bay

15   2   7

PINNACLE
234m

FORT Hill
120m

TOBAGO CAYS 42°

12°36'00 N
61°24'00 W

12°36'

3   20

Mont TABOÏ
305m

ASHTON
Village

ASHTON
Harbour

CLIFTON
Village

GREEN
Island

222°

7   7

30

Fl (2) W(20s) 8M

188m   280m

F.W.

20   6   5

MISS IRENE
Point

20   25

Hotel
Rest.

PALM Island
45m

12°35'

13
12°35'00 N
61°25'00 W

VQ (9) W
(10s)

5   17   1.5   3

30   20   10

2

4   FRIGATE
Island
75m

MARINA
(Construction
stoppped)

8   GRAND DE COI

20   14   10   9

0   1M

0   2km

15   12   17   15   PSV 165°

28'   61°27'   61°26'   61°25'   61°24'

75

Clifton anchorage

This anchorage on the windward coast is well protected by a reef barrier. In principle access during daylight is easy because the reef edges and the pass towards the village are marked by beacons. That said, any approach should be made with care and for preference in good visibility in order to spot the reef surrounding the anchorage.

Approach from the NE (Tobago Cays) Steer 222°T on which course you'll see in the distance the hill tops of Carriacou. Once in the offing follow the extensive barrier reef around its S end.

Approach from the S It's best to pass W of the isolated Grand de Coi, normally marked by a beacon, in order to stay clear of the reefs around Palm I.

There are two usable passes into the anchorage at Clifton. The more W'ly one towards the village is buoyed, the other going behind Roundabout Reef is not. If it's your first approach, head for the village jetty on 330°T. Once inside you can either anchor off the Bougainvilla's jetty, off the Anchorage Yacht Club or further to windward in the lee of the barrier reef once you're past Roundabout Reef. The last is less crowded but further from the village. You should think about an anchor watch because the holding is unreliable, especially off the docks. You can take a mooring, though you'll be negotiating with the boat boys who'll often at the same time, and very insistently, suggest you eat in one of the village restaurants. Lock up if you go ashore after dark, it pays to be careful here. Part occupied by some charter boats, the pontoons of the Anchorage (VHF 16/68) and Bougainvilla (VHF 16) have some visitors' berths. You can water ship but fuelling is less certain. Ask at the Bougainvilla office.

Ashore Clearance formalities at the airstrip not far from the Anchorage Yacht Club pontoons. There are only a few local facilities for fixing engines, electrical faults and repairing sails. Some of these, including getting hold of spares and useful information, can also be found at the Bougainvilla. In the patio of the Bougainvilla you'll find various yachting services and small shops (fashion and souvenir shop, grocery and drinks shop, engineering workshop) and the restaurant's terrace opens out on the sea. The Anchorage Yacht Club buildings run out along the small peninsula. In addition to its pleasant bar-restaurant there are travel agents, a laundry, a boutique selling clothing, handicrafts, magazines and stationery as well as pretty bungalows along the beach and under the coconut trees. Minimarkets in the village are good for re-provisioning as is the small local market for essentials, though prices are quite high (as in most of the Grenadines). Fresh produce depends on

Above left Anchorage off the Anchorage Yacht Club
Above right Green Island near Clifton
Below The anchorage and airport at Clifton

local fishermen or the arrival of the schooners from St Vincent.

Frigate Island

Note The E side of the island is fringed with a large coral reef.
You can anchor in the lee of the island close to the terraces of the abandoned marina project. The head of the bay, Ashton Harbour, is full of shoals and access is restricted to local craft and tenders.

Chatham Bay

A large bay in the shelter of Union's lee. The best anchorage is under a small cliff to the NE but if you draw much water you should be wary of a shoal (1·8–2m) hereabouts. Snorkelling and diving are good on the N and S points. Chatham Bay gets a fair amount of breeze including strong gusts, so choose your spot carefully and make sure your anchor has bitten. This is an undeveloped and little visited spot, the main beach of which, at least until recently, had remained fairly untouched except for a small and simple snack-bar.

Palm Island

(St Vincent Grenadines)

Save for its three separated hillocks, at low water this tiny island looks just like a tender to nearby Union I. It's surrounded by a huge coral reef stretching several hundred metres to seaward. Relative to its small size, Palm I not only has the prettiest length of white sand but the biggest reef as well. Only the W coast is accessible, though it's often disturbed by swell and a light chop which you should watch out for when coming to the dock in your tender. It's more sensible to pull the dinghy up on the beach.

Ashore A pretty hotel development has hidden its bungalows under the trees of a splendid coconut plantation. The latter was planted years ago by the Texan circumnavigator John Caldwell. He fell in love with the tiny island, then called Plum I (or Ile Prune in French), rented it for 99 years from the government, gave it the more fitting name of Palm I and built his small resort complex. Since his death a big hotel chain has taken the place over and refurbished it to luxury standards. Close to the dock there's a small complex with the office, some small shops and a pleasant bar restaurant. The latter is open to visitors who can enjoy the terrace, which is on the same level as the wonderful, golden sand beach. On the other hand, the inner part of the island is for hotel guests only unless you have special permission.

Petit St Vincent (PSV)

(St Vincent Grenadines)

This is the last of the St Vincent Grenadines. Coming from the S you cannot, at least in principle, stop in PSV before clearing in at Union, though there seems to be a certain latitude if you only stop briefly. PSV is an attractive little island of two small hills, a huge barrier reef and lovely beaches on the lee coast. To reach the anchorage coming from Union, pass between the two sand islets of Punaise and Morpion–the latter with a conspicuous small thatched umbrella on it. The pass between the two lines up with the W end of Petite Martinique on 163°T. You can make a short stop here to bask on the sand or go for a snorkel over the reef, but watch out for the current.

The centre of the anchorage is shoal and generally one anchors at the N end

close to the hotel jetty. The shoreline is full of shoals. The anchorage, fairly crowded in high season, can be rolly and currents cause yachts to make bizarre pirouettes. The passage between PSV and Petite Martinique is only

From top
Palm Island from the W
Union seen from the beach at Palm Island
Morpion
A beach at Petit St Vincent
PSV from the S

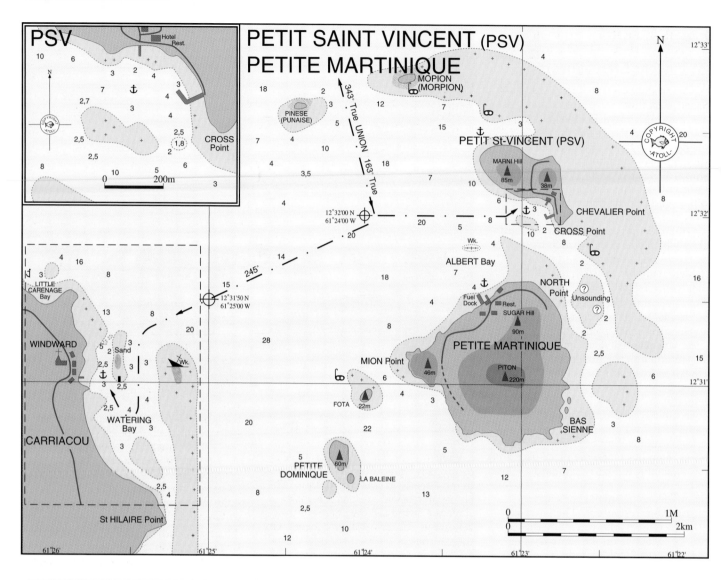

Useful information for the St Vincent Grenadines

AIRLINE CONNECTIONS

The small airstrips mentioned below only offer daily inter-island flights by local lines and air-taxis.

Inter-island flights
Bequia James F. Mitchell Airport
Mustique airstrip, ☎ 784 456 3657
Canouan airstrip
Union airport

FERRIES

Inter-island connections
Bequia Port Elizabeth to St Vincent, Canouan, Mayreau, Union

TELECOMMUNICATIONS

Calling St Vincent from abroad:
☎ (1) 784 + seven figure number
Local call: seven figures only
Public call boxes: Caribbean Phone Cards

TOURIST OFFICE

Bequia Tourist Bureau, Port Elizabeth,
☎ 784 458 3286 *Fax* 784 458 3964
Union Tourist Bureau, Clifton,
☎ 784 458 8350
Oldhegg Turtle Sanctuary, Park Beach, Bequia,
☎ 784 458 3245
Fax 784 457 3322
Email oldhegg@vincysurf.com

FESTIVALS/FOLK FESTIVALS

Bequia local craft regatta: Easter
Union Bougainvilla Cup regatta: Easter

PUBLIC HOLIDAYS

1 January, Discovery & National Heroes Day (22 January), Good Friday and Easter Monday, Labour Day (May), Whit Monday, Caricom Day and Carnival Tuesday (July), August Bank Holiday (1st Monday in August), Independence Day (27 October), Christmas Day (25 December), Boxing Day (26 December)

OFFICE HOURS

Shops: Mon–Fri, 0800–1200, 1300–1600, Saturday 0800–1200
Banks: Mon–Fri, 0800–1200 or 1300, Thursday 1400 or 1500–1700 (and at the airport Mon–Fri, 0830–1230, 1530–1730)
Government offices: Mon–Fri, 0800–1200, 1300–1615

ROAD TRANSPORT

Drive on the left
A licence is obligatory
Hire car companies and taxis in Bequia and Mustique

REGULATIONS

Protected areas: the National Park
Bequia: Devil's Table, Isle Quatre
Mustique
Canouan (E coast)
Mayreau
Tobago Cays
Reefs everywhere

Palm Island
PSV
All fishing is forbidden in these areas
Note throughout the St Vincent Grenadines: underwater hunting forbidden to non-residents.
Trolling for fish is legal.
It is forbidden to buy langoustes out of season (authorised 1/10 to 31/4) with heavy fines for breaking the rules.
All anchoring over or removal of coral is forbidden.
Jet skis forbidden.
NB: all infringements attract heavy fines of approx EC$5000

FORMALITIES

Arriving by air
Customs and immigration in the airport
Arriving by sea
Note formalities are obligatory for all vessels that have not cleared in St Vincent.

Offices at:
Bequia Port Elizabeth opposite the beach
Office hours: weekdays 0900–1800 (overtime after 1600). Saturday morning 0830–1200 (overtime is charged at weekends).
Mustique, Canouan Clearance at airstrips possible
Union: clear at the airport
Office hours: when the airport is operating Customs (Fishing Place): 0830–1800 (variable)
Overtime: outside office hours and at weekends
Fees and taxes: see St Vincent.

navigable by shoal drafters or tenders. A large dock closes off the E end of the beach, but there are no facilities for yachts there. There's a dock in the middle of the beach to help the business of getting ashore.

Ashore Petit St Vincent Resort is still managed by its American founder, Haze Richardson. With its restaurant, bungalows and fashion boutiques it's quite a luxurious place and the prices are top of the range. Cruising folk can enjoy the bar and restaurant with its terrace prettily overlooking the bay and giving a wonderful view as far as Petite Martinique. On some evenings dinner is accompanied by a steel band. If you visit you should make a reservation; access to the bar is otherwise limited (in theory up until 1800hrs). Just be sure not to disturb the peace and quiet of the hotel guests or trespass on the open green spaces around the cottages. On the other hand, the beaches and reefs are open to all.

Petite Martinique
(Grenadan Grenadines)

History and tourism

The island was occupied by the French as early as the 18th century. They came from its big sister, Martinique, and some think this is how it got its name. Others look at its shape, a 200m truncated cone, and recall Mont Pelée, or they say that the *fer-de-lance* snake is found here, as it is in Martinique. The last hypothesis is demonstrably false since the island's shores harbour no venomous snakes or other dangers. On the contrary, its 700 or so inhabitants are amongst the Grenadines' most welcoming. The majority of them are descendants of fishermen and still make their living mainly from the sea. In the past, so folk tales have it, they were also smugglers. They're also still working boat builders; sometimes on the beachfront you'll see the timbers of a hull being built, then swiftly planked up with rough-hewn planks, trimmed with an adze and fitted in the traditional manner. Here in Petite Martinique there's local racing in which well-sailed,

small boats with thoroughbred lines come head to head. Another, more modern and motorised island specialty is a sort of local 'cigarette' with a powerful outboard.

The houses are typically either traditional wooden cottages or more modern small houses, most with two storeys, tucked into the hillside. Other than a few small shops and restaurants, there's not much tourist development. As a result, for the moment Petite Martinique retains an authentic feel like its neighbour Carriacou. A fast ferry connects these two islands and goes on to Grenada.

There's a road, extended here and there by tracks and footpaths. This means you can explore much of the coast and

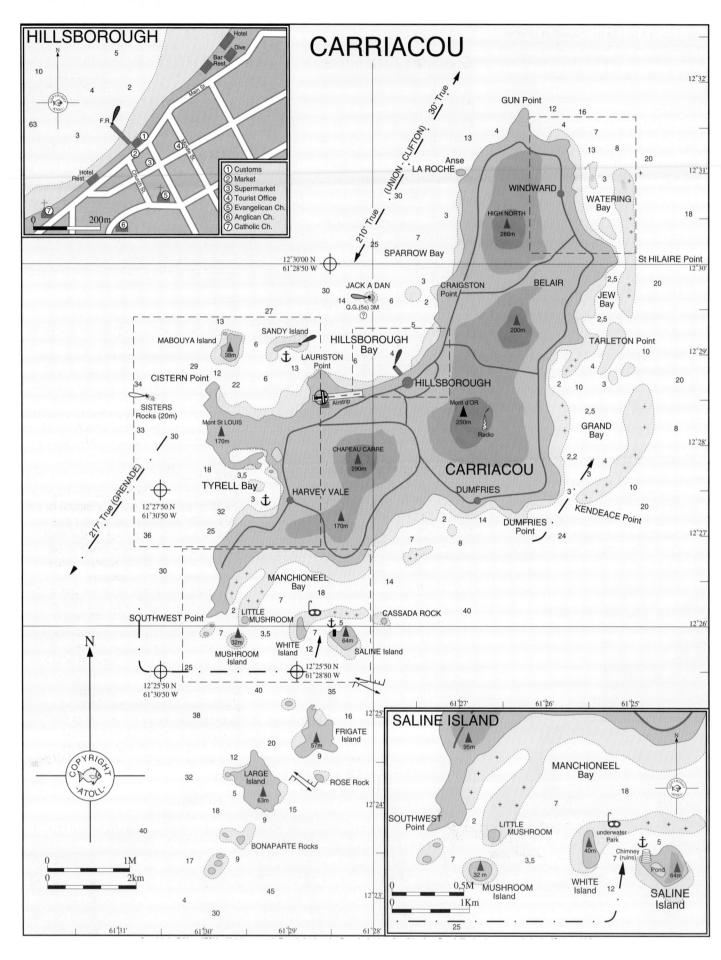

HILLSBOROUGH

N

5

10

4

2

63

3

F.R.

Hôtel
Rest.

Hotel
Dive
Bar
Rest.

Main St.

Middle St.

Church St.

① ② ③ ④ ⑤ ⑥ ⑦

① Customs
② Market
③ Supermarket
④ Tourist Office
⑤ Evangelican Ch.
⑥ Anglican Ch.
⑦ Catholic Ch.

0   200m

CARRIACOU

GUN Point

12   16
4
13   4   7
13   8
20
3
12°32'
12°31'

Anse
LA ROCHE

WINDWARD

WATERING
Bay

St HILAIRE Point
12°30'

HIGH NORTH
286m

3

7

SPARROW Bay

BELAIR

200m

2,5

JEW
Bay

2,5

TARLETON Point
10

12°29'

20

(UNION - CLIFTON)
30° True
210° True

30

25

JACK A DAN

30

14

Q.G.(5s) 3M
⑦

6

CRAIGSTON
Point

5

3
6

HILLSBOROUGH
Bay

4

HILLSBOROUGH

Mont d'OR
250m

Radio

2

10   3

GRAND
Bay

2,5

20

8

12°28'

27

13

MABOUYA Island

38m

SANDY Island

6

13

LAURISTON
Point

6

Airstrip

CISTERN Point

29

12

22

6

34

SISTERS
Rocks (20m)

33

30

Mont St LOUIS
170m

18

3,5

3

CHAPEAU CARRE
290m

CARRIACOU

DUMFRIES

2,2

3

KENDEACE Point

3

10

20

12°27'

217° True (GRENADE)

12°27'50 N
61°30'50 W

TYRELL Bay

32

25

36

HARVEY VALE

170m

14

DUMFRIES
Point

24

30

MANCHIONEEL
Bay

7

18

7

8

N

2   LITTLE
MUSHROOM

7

32m

3,5

WHITE
Island

12

7

5
64m

SALINE Island

CASSADA ROCK

40

14

12°26'

SOUTHWEST Point

MUSHROOM
Island

25

12°25'50 N
61°30'50 W

40

12°25'50 N
61°28'80 W

35

COPYRIGHT
ATOLL

38

16

12°25'

20

FRIGATE
Island
57m

9

61°27'   61°26'   61°25'

SALINE ISLAND

95m

MANCHIONEEL
Bay

N

18

COPYRIGHT
ATOLL

12

LARGE
Island
63m

32

5

ROSE Rock

15

SOUTHWEST
Point

2

LITTLE
MUSHROOM

7

underwater
Park

40m

Chimney
(ruins)

5

Pond

64m

SALINE
Island

18

9

BONAPARTE Rocks

40

17

9

WHITE
Island

7

32 m

3,5

12

0   1M
0   2km

4

45

30

0   0,5M
0   1Km

25

12°24'

12°23'

61°31'   61°30'   61°29'   61°28'

scramble to the island's summit. From the latter there's a wonderful, panoramic view towards Carriacou and the neighbouring islands.

Pilotage

Petite Martinique is part of Grenada and in principle all boats coming from the St Vincent Grenadines should as a preliminary complete clearance in Carriacou. That said, at the moment it seems that the proximity of PSV means some latitude exists for those making short calls between the two islands without formal clearance. Albert Bay anchorage is a little clogged with mooring buoys and local craft but is nonetheless pretty extensive. Be sure to stay clear of the shoal ground off the N coast and the recent wreck, about 500m offshore, of which the superstructure was still recently breaking the surface.

The most important things for cruising boats are the fuel and water facilities (B&C Fuels Co Ltd) at the end of the big jetty. They are among the most reliable and inexpensive in the Grenadines, which is worth noting. Alongside the jetty there is 5–6m. Another jetty a bit further E is reserved for ferries.

Ashore, if you are coming from St Vincent, note there are no facilities for clearance (see Carriacou). Other than a small shop with a few chandlery items and a breakdown service to the W of the jetty, Petite Martinique has very little by way of yacht services.

Petite Dominique (Petite Tobago) & Fota

These two islets SW of Petite Martinique only offer anchorage in very good weather and calm seas, and that's a rarity.

Carriacou
(Grenadan Grenadines)

History

The name comes from the Amerindian 'Karyouacou' and the first colonists were French turtle hunters and fishermen. By the 18th century their successors, still mostly Frenchmen, were cultivating the islands' steeply incised slopes using imported African slaves. Some names of French origin for various bays and headlands have been handed down from that time, as have the ruins of some plantation owners' houses and the towers of the old windmills used by the sugar and cotton plantations. Today's population of around 7000 is mostly descended from the African slaves, with but the slightest admixture from the early European settlers. Carriacou (over 30 sq. km) is the largest (and most populous) of the Grenadines. Running from N to S down the centre of the island is a hill mass with peaks reaching 300m. The majority of the old plantations have been turned into smallholdings and pasture. In addition to these land based natural resources there is commercial fishing and merchant shipping. The latter activity is related to the tradition of smuggling from which the islanders do quite nicely, notably from the trade in alcohol. Their reputation may be a bit exaggerated but it's a notorious fact that in Carriacou it's easier to find a rum dealer than a fuel dock.

Located some 20M N of Grenada, of which it is a dependency, Carriacou has retained considerable cultural autonomy, especially with regard to its religious practices. There are even thought to be voodoo rites of Haitian origin.

Tourism

Where to stay and what to see

Its relative isolation has kept this last outpost of the Grenadines rather off the beaten tourist track for a long time, thereby preserving its particular character. In the past only a few cruising boats knew of its charms and enjoyed its protected anchorages and fine beaches, edged as they are with a screen of small islets and reefs. More recently the anchorages have become a lot more popular with bare boats and charterers. To welcome the tourists, several hotel complexes have sprung up along the coast, as well as many small restaurants, which have proliferated in Hillsborough and above all in Tyrell Bay.

Thanks to its airstrip Carriacou is linked daily to the neighbouring islands and a fast ferry service offers a connection with Petite Martinique and Grenada. As well as the beaches and the coral, the valleys of the interior are worth a visit. This is easy because of the rough but adequate road round the island, and to the bus linking most of the small towns. There are also plenty of taxis and hire cars.

Hillsborough

This small town, tucked on the edge of the W coast, is the island's capital but it only really wakes up on market day or when a cargo boat arrives at the dock. The town has just a few roads lined with cottages or old buildings, some dating from the 18th century. The Carriacou Historical Museum has a collection of Amerindian remains and tools from colonial times. To enjoy a good view out over the bay and islets (amongst them the superb Sandy I), you must climb to the hospital which lies above the town.

Don't miss the two-day fête in Hillsborough on the first weekend in August. It features the big races (the Carriacou Regatta) at which local workboats from Carriacou and its neighbours have a fine old tussle. From

Above left Hillsborough
Left Racing at Carriacou
Below Local traditional boat (Bateau pays) hauled down for careening, Watering Bay

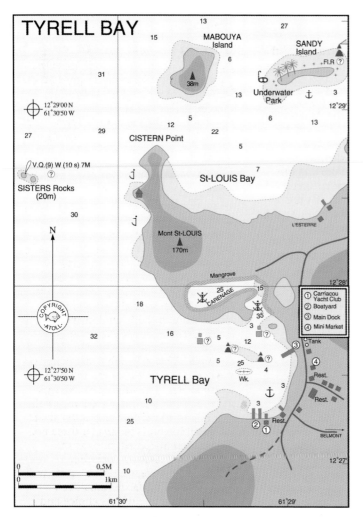

TYRELL BAY

13
27
15
MABOUYA
Island
SANDY
Island
6
Fl.R ?
31
Underwater
Park
12°29'00 N
61°30'50 W
13
3
12°29'
27
29
5
12
6
13
22
CISTERN Point
5
St-LOUIS Bay
7
N
SISTERS Rocks
(20m)
V.Q.(9) W (10 s) 7M
?
30
Mont St-LOUIS
170m
COPYRIGHT
ATOLL
Mangrove
25
CARENAGE
15
12°28'
18
35
① Carriacou
Yacht Club
② Boatyard
③ Main Dock
④ Mini Market
32
16
5
12
Tank
3
④
5
25
4
Rest.
12°27'50 N
61°30'50 W
TYRELL Bay
Wk.
3
10
3
Rest.
25
② Rest.
①
BELMONT
0   0,5M   10
0   1km
12°27'
61°30'
61°29'

Top Sandy Island
Centre Sandy Island beach
Above Saline Island, Cassada Rock, White Island,
from the E

the biggest, gaff-rigged sloops to tiny
'Models', all the crews sail their boats
hard, right up to the end of the regatta
for which they've been training for
months in advance. Here fancy sail-
handling equipment is often replaced by
elbow grease.

At Windward on the windward coast
they still build workboats using the
rough tools and techniques of the past.
On the shores of this anchorage, called
Watering Bay, it's not unusual to see
local fishermen careening their boats,
hauling down their mastheads on tree
trunk deadmen to clean their hulls the
cheapest way.

Pilotage

Coast and anchorages

Carriacou is a dependency of Grenada
and all boats coming from abroad
should clear in at Hillsborough.

West coast

Note Despite the lights on Jack A Dan
and Sandy I (always unreliable), a night
entry is not advisable.

Sparrow Bay

Coming from the N after Anse la
Roche, you'll open up this large bay,
which is poorly protected from N'ly
swell.

Hillsborough Bay

The passage between Jack A Dan islet
and Craigston Pt has a shoal with less
than 1m over it. It's better to go out
round to the W of Jack A Dan before
heading into the anchorage off
Hillsborough's dock. The anchorage, in
3–4m, is often uncomfortable in a N'ly
swell pushed in when the NE trades are
fresh. In the N of the bay the Silver

Tyrell Bay

Beach Resort (VHF 16) has mooring buoys for its clients and a dock for tenders. As well as somewhere to stay and to eat, there are also several other facilities and underwater sports.

Ashore Customs and Immigration are close to the end of the dock. Although the little town with its cottages and small buildings seems a bit simple and dilapidated, you'll find several shops and supermarkets for provisioning, especially where booze is concerned. The local market stalls (opposite the dock) have a good choice of fruit, vegetables and other fresh produce. Nearby there are some restaurants offering local specialties at quite high prices, though still affordable.

Sandy Island

Close to Hillsborough, this is a charming day anchorage, OK even for overnight in fair weather.

Note The island is extended by reef (especially to the SW) and the approach to the S shore is none too obvious. You must anchor some way off. The small sandy island, covered with coconut palms and surrounded by coral, is the archetype of tropical idyll. (It is also a nature reserve and underwater fishing is forbidden.) On the other hand, the swell caused by cyclone Lenny has damaged the reef and the snorkelling is now not that good.

Cistern Pt

There's a tiny creek and a sandy beach just under Cistern Pt. There's a small house on the S point of the inlet's entrance perched on a small promontory. If you fancy a picnic and the swell isn't too large, there's a day anchorage in 3–4m

Note The S point here is surrounded with reef.

Beyond the S point there's another small inlet, but it seems to me less attractive.

The Sisters Rocks

Some 0·75M to the W of Cistern Pt are the two much admired islets called the Sisters. A shoal with 4m over it extends SE from them. It's a fabulous spot for diving and snorkelling, but since there's often a strong current, it's for good weather only.

Tyrell Bay

This is one of the best-sheltered anchorages in the Grenadines. Even when there are a lot of boats, the huge bay never seems crowded. In the ENE part of the bay there's a coral-head. In theory it's marked by buoys but they may not be there.

Note The S of Tyrell Bay is edged with shoals, which push out further than the charts show.

A small sand islet, thrown up by the swell from cyclone Lenny, is visible on the edge of the shoal and near the boatyard dock. You can anchor between the S shore and the village dock in 3–4m. The anchorage is usually very calm because it's protected from all but W winds.

The 'Carenage', a hurricane hole surrounded by mangroves, opens out of the N of Tyrell Bay. In order to protect the mangrove oysters (fishing forbidden), the Carenage is officially closed to boats unless there's a cyclone alert. If you need it, take care at the entrance. There's a shoal with less than 1m over it pushing out in the S part. Access to the inner basin is over a sill (1·5m), which limits it to shoal draft yachts.

At other times you can make a trip into the mangroves in your tender, though keep your speed down or (better) row.

Ashore For a few years now craftsmen have set up shop in Tyrell Bay and now there's a large boatyard to complete the services thanks to its travel-hoist and big area of hard standing. There's also a chandlery (specializing in paints and antifoulings) as well as electrical and mechanical repair services. Next to the boatyard is the small compound of the Carriacou Yacht Club where, at the

Above Hauled ashore at Windward
Below left Watering Bay from N

bottom of the garden, there's a restaurant on the first floor, a few rooms to let and laundry and mail services. Opposite the boatyard there's a barge with a floating workshop where a couple of Frenchmen specialise in sail repair and aluminium and stainless work. Geneviève can also set you and your crew up, thanks to the Shiatsu massage she offers. Taken together these services make Tyrell Bay the most useful service centre in the Grenadines after Bequia. As far as fuel and water are concerned, until the boatyard fuel and water dock has been built (it's planned), there are only dire straits possibilities at the boatyard or the town dock. For provisioning there are several quite well-stocked and popular minimarkets, though as ever the widest choice and best prices are for booze.

The shoreline is now fringed with restaurants, bars, guest houses and even a cyber café. The specialities on their menus are pretty varied and all based mostly on local produce. Prices have gone up a bit given the increased tourist traffic, but they're still quite reasonable. Despite the growth, Tyrell Bay remains one of the prettiest and most charming anchorages in the Grenadines and all the different establishments ensure that come evening the whole place is hopping. It's worth using the good shelter provided by the bay to leave your boat and take a look at the rest of the island by bus, taxi or hire car.

South coast

Saline Island

To reach this small island you must round Southwest Point and its reefs and keep well S of Mushroom I and White I. The Saline I anchorage lies in the N part of the island to the NE of an old limekiln. Don't push too far into the creek because it shoals rapidly. Bahamian moor on two anchors against the change of current, which can run hard at 2–3kts. Though quite well protected, this is a remote anchorage and overnighting isn't really recommended. It is often as deserted as

Saline I itself. That said, the island is private property and has a house (apparently not much used), which leads one to conclude that landing must be confined to below the tideline. The reef barrier which stretches to the N from Cassada Rock to White I is a great dive and snorkelling spot. There are usually plenty of fish and visibility is good.

Note The current can be strong between Saline I and the reef.

Remember that Saline and White Is are nature reserves.

On the coast at the head of Manchioneal Bay you'll see some buildings on the hillside. They're an ex-oceanographic research centre that's been turned into a hotel, the Cassada Bay Resort.

Frigate Island and Large Island

Two deserted islands S of Saline I. The anchorage in the lee of the islands is seldom comfortable because of swell and currents. In fine weather they make a day stop. The little-visited waters are full of fish, but don't stray far from the coast because the currents are very dangerous.

Bonaparte Rocks

Bonaparte Rocks, the southernmost offliers of Carriacou, are inaccessible unless you like taking risks with swell and strong currents.

Windward coast

A large reef barrier lies off the windward coast of Carriacou running from S to N and creating two natural havens protected from the ocean swell. These are Grand Bay in the S separated from Watering Bay in the N by St Hilaire Pt. Despite what some charts show, a keeler can't go from bay to bay because of shoal ground of less than 1·5m.

Watering Bay

One of the last anchorages almost exclusively used by local fishermen, even though a keeler can enter in fair weather with good visibility provided it doesn't draw more than 2·5m. The pass N of the sand bank is only a small boat passage. Only the pass S of the sand bank is navigable. A coaster has grounded on the end of the large barrier reef and the rusting hull makes a good mark. The S end of the sandy islet is often marked by a stake or an old jerry jug. Once you're round it, anchor in the middle of the bay off the village of Windward, though don't get too close to the shallows fronting the shore. Once round it, anchor in mid-bay in front of the village (Windward) being careful not to get too close to the shoal ground

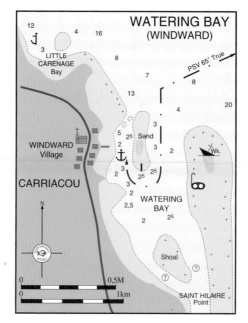

off the shore.

Ashore With its local boat builders and pretty cottages, Windward is a modest fishing village which is still untouched yet welcoming. A few shops and mini markets offer a limited range of goods for provisioning.

Grand Bay

Approachable along the SE coast of Carriacou only in fair weather with good visibility. Once you've doubled Dumfries Pt, steer NE towards Kendeace Pt and the pass will be readily visible. The anchorage in Grand Bay is usually empty, but the chop tends to make it uncomfortable. I've never pushed further N, though according to the locals the best shelter lies up near Tarlton Pt.

Right Les Tantes from NW
Below Diamond Rock & Ile de Rond from NNE

From Carriacou to Grenada

It's about 20M from Grenada to Carriacou. The current through the passage can be very strong, above all the W'ly oceanic current, which sometimes reaches 3kts. When the tide runs against the prevailing ocean current, on the other hand, it kicks up a nasty, irregular sea, especially in the offing of Ile de Ronde. Heading from Carriacou to Grenada you'll normally have a beam wind, sometimes a broad reach. From the other direction you'll be close fetching and may have to put in a tack under Ile de Ronde and another close to Carriacou.

Note there is a 1·5km radius exclusion zone, though it is not enforced, centred over the occasionally active submarine volcano at 12°18'N, 61°38'W. When it is active, the exclusion zone is extended to 5km radius. See also the website www.volcano.si.edu.gvp

Diamond Rock (Kick'-em-Jenny)

This is a 200m tall monolith without a vestige of shelter. Close to the W cliffs there are reefs with depths of 10–15m close to. If the sea is calm and there's not much current, which is pretty rare,

experienced divers can enjoy a fine dive amongst many pelagic fish. In the same area (see note above) is the submarine volcano, which bursts into life now and then, spitting and belching in the depths. For all the gossip and recent underwater eruptions however, there's no new island just about to poke its head above the surface.

Ile de Ronde (Ronde Island)

Bar a few fishermen on the S coast and large numbers of birds, the island is deserted.

Note Coming from the N, reef pushes out a good way from the NW point of the island, so give it a good berth.

The anchorage is close to the beach, but often very rolly as the swell makes round. There are good diving and snorkeling sites in the N part of the island, but only for experienced divers because the conditions are marginal.

Caille Island

No shelter here, but if you've got a fast tender, you can come across from Ile Ronde. The current between the two is often vicious.

Les Tantes

In very good weather there's a usable day anchorage under the lee of the main island. The main attraction of this group of islets and reefs is the underwater world, though the weather and sea state are often too bad for a stop. The fish life is tremendous.

The Sisters

A few tiny islets, or rocks, to the W of Ile de Ronde worth steering well clear of. There's no anchorage to be had.

Useful Information for the Grenadan Grenadines

AIRLINE CONNECTIONS
Airport: Lauriston Airport
Inter-island flights daily inter-island connections by local companies and air taxis

FERRIES
Inter-island connections
Carriacou Hillsborough to Petite Martinique and Grenada.

TELECOMMUNICATIONS
Calling the Grenadan Grenadines from abroad:
☎ (1) 473 + seven figure number
Local call: seven figures only
Public call boxes: Caribbean Phone Cards

TOURIST OFFICE
Carriacou Tourist Office: Hillsborough
☎ 473 443 7948

FESTIVALS/FOLK FESTIVALS
Carnival: February
Local workboat regatta (the Carriacou Regatta): 1st weekend in August

PUBLIC HOLIDAYS
January 1 (New Year's Day), 2 January (Recovery Day), 7 February (Independence Day), Easter Friday to Easter Monday (dates vary), First Monday in May (Labour Day), Whit Monday (date varies), Corpus Christi (date varies), August Holidays (first Monday and Tuesday), Carnival (2nd weekend in August), 25 October (Thanksgiving), 25 December (Christmas), 26 December (Boxing Day)

OFFICE HOURS
Shops: 0800–1200, 1300–1600, half day Saturday
Banks: 0800–1300 or 1400 Mon–Thurs, 0800–1300, 1430–1700 Friday
Govt. Offices: 0800–1145, 1300–1600 Mon–Fri, closed Saturday

TOURIST ATTRACTION
Carriacou Historical Museum: Hillsborough

ROAD TRANSPORT
Drive on the left
A licence is obligatory (see also Grenada)
Hire car companies and taxis in Tyrell Bay and Hillsborough

REGULATIONS
Protected areas: National Park: Sandy, Saline and White Is
All fishing is forbidden
No anchoring in coral
It is forbidden to buy langoustes out of season (authorised 1/10 to 31/4) with heavy fines for breaking the rules.
Note Regulations governing fishing and underwater hunting are being developed. Ask the authorities before you set out.

FORMALITIES
Arriving by air
Customs and immigration in the airport
Arriving by sea
Note formalities are obligatory for all vessels
Offices: at Hillsborough, close to the dock
Office hours: 0800–1145, 1300–1545
Overtime: outside office hours and at weekends (cheaper than Grenada)
Fees and taxes port dues according to boat length, approx EC$50 for a 50 footer. A charge is made per crew according to the crewlist. There's a supplementary tax per passenger for charterers.

Grenada

Area 340 sq km
Highest point Mt St Catherine
840m
Population approx. 100,000
Capital St George's (pop.20,000)
Language English, patois
Currency EC$, US$ accepted
Political status Independent state
Distances to nearby islands Carriacou
17M, Trinidad 80M, Los Testigos (Ven)
85M

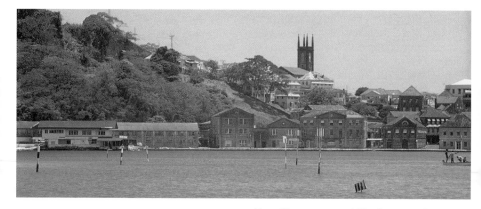

Above The quays round The Carenage, St George's
Below left Old stone and brick building, St George's

History

When the island was discovered by Columbus on his third voyage in 1498, he baptized it Concepcion. Only later did the Spanish sailors give it the name it has today because they likened its green hills to those above Granada in Spain's Andalusia. The English kept the name once they tried colonizing the island in 1609. It was a classic scenario: the Caribs ate some of the invaders and threw the rest back into the sea! Then in 1650 the French arrived from Martinique. They were better informed and bargained for the island with some trinkets and alcohol. Once they'd got over the hangover the Caribs knew they'd been cheated and fought back. The French hung on and, by 1651, had penned the Caribs up on the edge of a high cliff on the N coast. Rather than surrender, the Caribs jumped into the void. Hence the name you'll still find, Morne des Sauteurs (literally Jumpers' Bluff, though locally called Caribs' Leap).

With the Caribs wiped out, the usual scenario resumed. For a century and a half the English fought the French for the lovely, fertile island of Grenada. It took two treaties, of Paris in 1763 and, after a last push by the French, of Versailles in 1783, for the place to become definitively English. Now the only remains of the French are the names of a few villages and headlands, and a few words in the local patois.

Thanks to its volcanic soil Grenada was ripe for agricultural development. With the abolition of slavery and the collapse of the great plantations, numerous old estates were divided between several smallholders. These prospered and, in addition to coconut and banana crops, Grenada also became known as the Spice Island.

After Cyclone Janet caused serious damage in 1955, the island first became an associated state of the Commonwealth in 1967, then an independent member in 1974. The first Prime Minister was Eric Gary who drew in investment capital from far and wide in order to begin a massive programme of tourism and real estate development. However, his authoritarian style, corruption and nepotism led to his overthrow by radicals in 1979. Once in power, their leader, Maurice Bishop, surrounded himself with Cuban advisors, much to the consternation of Ronald Reagan's USA. When the Cubans built the strategically significant Salines Airport, President Reagan had nightmares about Soviet missile emplacements. To add to his apprehension, Maurice Bishop was assassinated and political trouble flared up, perturbing the neighbouring islands and leading the USA to step in. In 1983, after several days of fighting, the US Navy and Marines threw the Cuban 'advisors' back into the sea and replaced the radical politicians with a more conservative regime. Peace prevailed again in Grenada.

The troubles led to a recession from which Grenada's dominant tourism and agricultural sectors (including the famous spices) recovered only slowly. The tourist sector had done well during the 70s with plenty of hotels, villas and marinas appearing on the island, only to be stopped in their tracks by ideological and military conflict combined with bureaucratic red tape. Taken together this put off investors, tourists and cruising boats alike.

But calm has been restored for several years now and the government has busied itself with helping tourism to grow.

Tourism

Where to stay and what to see

As well as having the sobriquet of 'The Spice Island', so evocative of heady tropical scents, to many people Grenada is altogether the archetype of the utterly beautiful island. The volcanically sculpted hills of the island's heart are buried under wonderful greenery full of buzzing tropical life. They tumble down to a shoreline combining intricate inlets and long, lazy beaches fringed with coconut palms. The small but well-maintained road network lets you visit everywhere worth visiting. There's a road round almost the whole coast. The main tourist development is around St George's and the S end of the island, where you'll find many medium and luxury hotels. The restaurants benefit from the island's agricultural riches as well as those of the sea. And the local, often simple, restaurants, unlike those of the big hotels with their classic menus, have spicy and often quite original regional specialities.

St George's (see also Pilotage below)

This small capital with 20,000 inhabitants, tucked away in its natural haven, is one of the most interesting Antillean towns. This is thanks not least to the port itself (The Carenage), with its French Mediterranean style quays and old, painted brick warehouses which have recently been restored. The quays themselves are always lively with the loading and unloading of small local transports which are still called 'schooners' after the old originals. Immediately E of the Carenage's entrance a long jetty welcomes cruise liners. Further S, The Lagoon is the mooring area reserved for yachts.

The town itself is wrapped around the old port in a succession of steep, narrow streets slanting up the surrounding hills. The ancient Sendal Tunnel, built by the French in the 18th century and a pretty

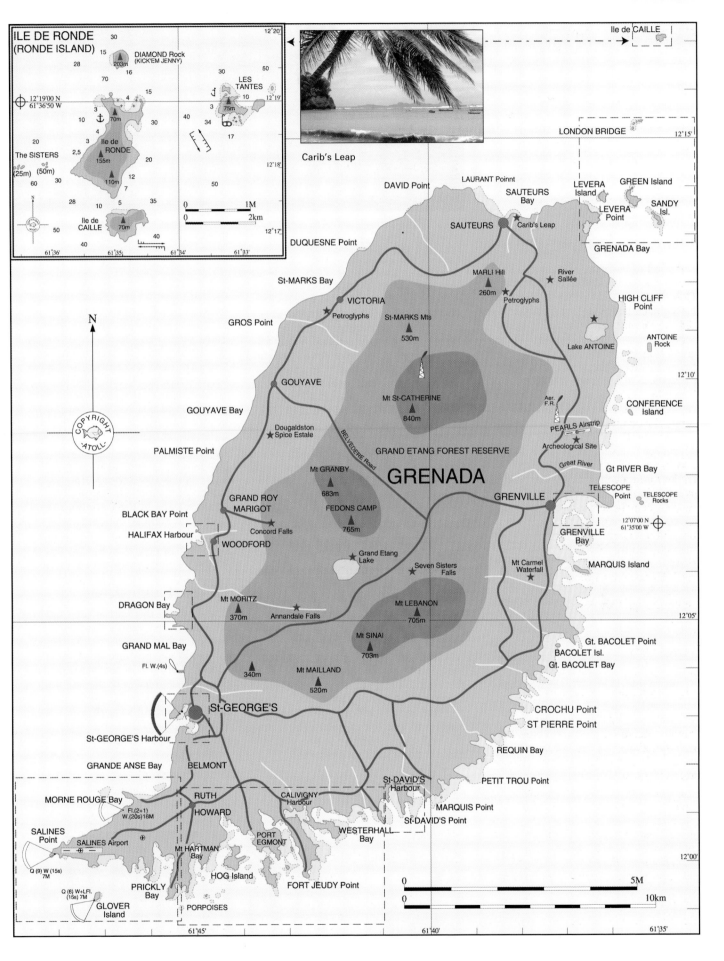

ILE DE RONDE
(RONDE ISLAND)

12°19'00 N
61°36'50 W

DIAMOND Rock
(KICK'EM JENNY)
203m

Ile de
RONDE
155m
110m

The SISTERS
(25m) (50m)

LES
TANTES
75m

Ile de
CAILLE
70m

0   1M
0   2km

Ile de CAILLE

Carib's Leap

LONDON BRIDGE

GREEN Island

LAURANT Poinnt

DAVID Point

SAUTEURS
Bay

LEVERA
Island

SANDY
Isl.

SAUTEURS   Carib's Leap

LEVERA
Point

GRENADA Bay

HIGH CLIFF
Point

River
Sallée

ANTOINE
Rock

MARLI Hill
260m

Petroglyphs

Lake ANTOINE

St-MARKS Bay

VICTORIA

Petroglyphs

St-MARKS Mts
530m

GROS Point

CONFERENCE
Island

GOUYAVE

Mt St-CATHERINE
840m

Aer.
F.R.

PEARLS Airstrip

GOUYAVE Bay

Dougaldston
Spice Estale

GRAND ETANG FOREST RESERVE

Archeological Site

Great River

Gt RIVER BAY

PALMISTE Point

GRENADA

GRAND ROY
MARIGOT

Mt GRANBY
683m

FEDONS CAMP
765m

BELVEDERE Road

GRENVILLE

TELESCOPE
Point

TELESCOPE
Rocks

12°07'00 N
61°35'00 W

BLACK BAY Point

HALIFAX Harbour

WOODFORD

Concord Falls

Grand Etang
Lake

Seven Sisters
Falls

Mt Carmel
Waterfall

GRENVILLE
Bay

MARQUIS Island

DRAGON Bay

Mt MORITZ
370m

Annandale Falls

Mt LEBANON
705m

GRAND MAL Bay

Mt SINAI
703m

Gt. BACOLET Point
BACOLET Isl.
Gt. BACOLET Bay

Fl. W.(4s)

340m

Mt MAILLAND
520m

St-GEORGE'S

CROCHU Point

ST PIERRE Point

St-GEORGE'S Harbour

REQUIN Bay

GRANDE ANSE Bay

BELMONT

St-DAVID'S
Harbour

PETIT TROU Point

MORNE ROUGE Bay

RUTH

HOWARD

CALIVIGNY
Harbour

St-DAVID'S Point

MARQUIS Point

SALINES
Point

SALINES Airport

Mt HARTMAN
Bay

PORT
EGMONT

WESTERHALL
Bay

Fl.(2+1)
W.(20s)18M

Q (9) W (15s)
7M

HOG Island

FORT JEUDY Point

PRICKLY
Bay

Q (6) W+LFl.
(15s) 7M

GLOVER
Island

PORPOISES

N

COPYRIGHT
'ATOLL'

0   5M
0   10km

unusual feature in the Antilles, runs under the hill to link the area round the quays with the W part of the town. There on the Esplanade there's a lively fish market each day and just beyond it the brightly coloured stalls of the fruit and vegetable market. The majority of shops and restaurants line The Carenage on Wharf Road. There are several fine examples of buildings from the colonial period. The national museum in an old 18th century French warehouse, has pre-Columbian specimens and exhibits from the island's past. The old York House, built in 1801, is the Supreme Court these days. The bell tower of the Anglican cathedral of St George dominates the roofs of the town and dates from the 18th century. And further N there's the Catholic cathedral dating from the 19th century. Overlooking the town on its seaward promontory is Fort St George (Fort Royal in French days), which still seems to shelter the small city under its cannons. S of the town you'll find the Botanical Gardens with their stunning variety of local flora and fauna which shouldn't be missed.

Around the island

On the way out of St George's you cross hills red with flame trees. Then suddenly you're in tropical forest, broken here and there by cultivated areas where there are coffee bushes, nutmeg and cinnamon trees. If you go S first you'll follow the seemingly endless Grand Anse, where lots of restaurants have terraces on the white sand beach. All along the coast large tourist complexes, including shopping malls selling local crafts, are mixed with hotels and cottages buried in hibiscus and bougainvillea. Before you get to the international airport at Salines Pt there is the small sandy beach of Morne Rouge sheltered by its rocky headland.

N of St George's, the coast road passes through several villages, which lie between the sea and the jungle. From Concord you can climb up to Concord Falls which cascades into a natural swimming pool of clear water. At the village of Sauteurs you can see the small cliff, the Morne des Sauteurs, where the

Above St George's Harbour from Ross Pt
Below left Ross Pt, St George's Harbour
Below right Grand Anse beach

unhappy Caribs jumped to their deaths. Further E the road reaches Levera Pt where, through the coconuts, you'll see a string of small islets a few cables offshore (Levera, Green and Sandy Is). The windward coast is more rugged and little developed. Half way down is Grenville, the island's second largest settlement, with its colourful fishing fleet sheltered by the barrier reef. The small town, dominated by the belfries of two churches, is rather off the beaten tourist track and retains an authentic Grenadan atmosphere. There's a wonderful choice of inexpensive fish, fruit and vegetables in its market. Close by there's a processing plant for the spices for which the island is famous.

There are two routes back to St George's:

• one follows the much indented S coast past its fjord-like inlets and endless peninsulas, and its innumerable flower bedecked cottages

• alternatively, the inland road passes over the mountains and through the Grand Etang Forest reserve with its rich flora and fauna. In the midst of it all is the Grand Etang Lake in an old crater. Further W the Annandale Falls jet from a crystalline gap 100m above the thick forest into which it tumbles. There are lots of footpaths nearby so you can explore the magnificent forest.

Pilotage

Coast and anchorages

For a long time Grenada was a big pleasure boating centre, but then political problems caused some of the yachties who once chose it as their home port to go elsewhere. Others in the Antilles lost the habit of cruising as far as Grenada and tended to stop in the Grenadines. Today, however, Grenada has all it takes to re-establish its privileged position as a cruising destination: spectacular anchorages, especially in the S, with the best cyclone holes in the Antilles; huge, empty beaches, and a splendidly varied landscape covered with forest. The capital St George's is one of the prettiest ports in the Caribbean thanks to its 18th century buildings, as well as being an all but obligatory stop if you're on your way to Carnival in Trinidad or to the Venezuelan islands.

NE coast and islands

The whole of this part of the coast consists of vast, empty beaches bordered with coconut plantations. Levera Pt extends into three small islands. Very few boats visit because there's little reliable shelter from the Atlantic swell. However, on your way in from Ile Ronde it's worth a detour in stable weather. Once you've got round the London Bridge islets, aim for the W coast of Green I.

Green Island

Note There are several reefs off the W coast. There's a day anchorage in flat

weather on the SW of the island, though depths are 15m. Also note the change of current with the tide.

Levera Island (Sugar Loaf)

Between Grenada and the island the bottom is full of reef but locals use the anchorage here even though the depths are uncertain and the currents strong.

Sandy Island

Here too the W coast has a lot of coral pushing well out both N and S of the island. The S point is low and covered with coconut trees. Anchor towards the N in 3–4m but consider the reversal of current with the change of tide and moor on two anchors. Shelter is fair if the sea isn't too rough, but a swell can work in quickly. Good snorkelling over the coral to the S.

West coast

There's often not much wind so be prepared for several hours' motoring.

Port Halifax

This is the first anchorage if you're coming from the N. It's not so much a port as a sheltered inlet between two forested hills. For preference anchor in the N part in 3–4m, sand. There's less depth in the SE. Beware a power line crossing this part of the bay and reducing air draft to less than 20m. If

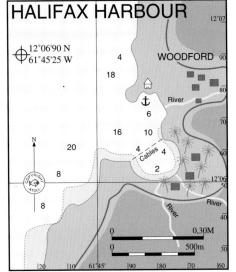

there's an advantage in the anchorage being almost deserted, the downside is that there's a rubbish tip at the head of the bay.

Dragon Bay & Grand Mal Bay

Less than 2M further S Dragon Bay is more open, so less well-sheltered from any N swell. Anchor in the middle of the bay in front of a beach of grey sand edged with coconut trees, keeping clear

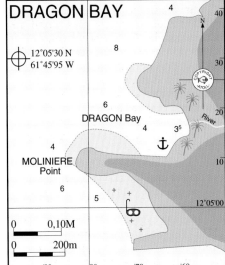

of the shoals on the S shore. S of Molinière Pt, Grand Mal Bay also has a tenable anchorage. Keep clear of the access to the dock and the mooring buoys, which are used by small feeder tankers supplying the depot on the coast. S of the dock there's a prettily placed local restaurant on the shore with a dock for tenders.

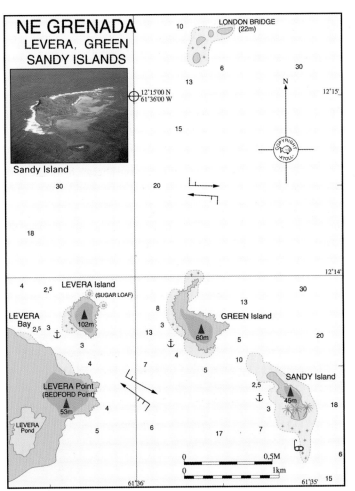

Levera, Green & Sandy Islands from WNW

Dragon Bay & Grand Mal Bay

Port Halifax

St George's Harbour (see also Tourism above)

The N part of the town is obvious from seaward, but to find the entry to the harbour you must head S round Fort George Pt. A night entry is feasible if you remember that the lights are unreliable. By day access is obvious if you look out for the shoals off Ross Pt and on the W side of the entrance to The Lagoon, though this is all beaconed with port hand buoys. Once into the port there are two anchorages, either side of the cruise liner quay (Ship Dock):

- to the NE, The Carenage
- to the SE, The Lagoon

The Carenage

The big basin of the Carenage is mainly for local boats and little used by yachts. Either to anchor or to go alongside you must contact the authorities on VHF 16, but frankly you're not advised to try it.

Note The N part of the Carenage is very shoal. Don't leave either boat or tender unguarded.

Ashore Around The Carenage there are lots of restaurants, amongst which The Nutmeg offers an all-round view of the port. There are equally plenty of fairly well-stocked shops and supermarkets for provisioning. For fresh produce there's nothing better than the local market near the Esplanade (use the Sendal Tunnel), best on Saturday morning.

The Lagoon

This is the favoured yacht anchorage. The entrance runs close past the new Ship Dock and the reef edge N of Ross Pt marked by a lit starboard hand beacon. The channel has 5–9m and is marked by small, unlit starboard hand buoys marking the reef to the S. After a tight dogleg two unlit buoys mark the channel exit, red to starboard and green to port. Two small red buoys on the N shore mark a shoal area. The open anchorage is in the middle of the Lagoon in 5–6m, soft mud, poor holding in places. Here too you need to keep an eye open even if the risks of theft aren't as bad as in The Carenage.

Just to the left as you exit the channel the Grenada Yacht Club (GYC, VHF 16, 06) on the N shore has an arrivals dock and some 30 berths (2-3m), all with water and electricity, and beside it a second pontoon with a fuel dock. With the new arrangements the Grenada Yacht Club is now one of the most secure places to moor in Grenada and has very reasonable rates.

Ashore The office, bar and restaurant of the yacht club overlook the pontoons.

There's always a warm welcome and there are good services (showers, laundry, taxis, etc.) as well as a BBQ party on Friday evenings. The GYC organises local racing during the summer and takes part in the famous sailing week (Grenada Sailing Festival) every January.

Grenada Yacht Services (GYS, VHF 16), recently renamed the Blue Lagoon Real Estate Corp., lies on the W shore, its facilities still steadily going downhill since the days it was one of the major yachting centres in the Antilles. Putting things back in shape has been talked

about for years, but given the investment needed, not much has happened. Meanwhile the pontoons and fittings are pretty ramshackle, though there's still a fuel and water dock.

Ashore Customs and immigration are on the ground floor of the GYS buildings, with the marina office on the first floor. Next door is the bar overlooking the lagoon, which serves as a meeting point for yachties, though given the dilapidation it's lost its old appeal. In the huts ashore and round the lagoon there are a few workshops for basic repairs and the Island Water World

The Carenage and The Lagoon–St George's

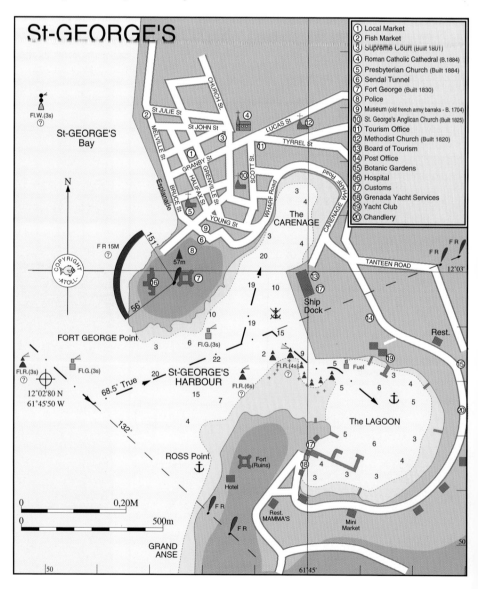

Top Grenada Yacht Club pontoons
Above Wharf in The Carenage

chandlery (a branch of the well-known outfit in St Martin) with a good choice of stock. However, other than the specialists here and a few hardware stores in St George's, there are few specialist services for yachts as compared to what you'll find on the S coast (Prickly Bay, Mt Hartman Bay, etc.), and no boatyard at all. On the road around the lagoon towards St George's there's a fairly well-stocked supermarket and several restaurants. The best known is Mamma's on the lagoon's S shore. The lady who founded the restaurant has been dead for many years, but her family still serves a specialist cuisine as varied as it's original. The only difference is in the prices, which many people now think have become prohibitive given the nature of the establishment and its ageing décor.

Grand Anse Bay

Note When leaving St George's for Grand Anse, keep well clear of the shoals with less than 1·8m over them NW of Ross Pt.

Grand Anse is one of the largest beaches in the Antilles. There are numerous restaurants along the shore as well as hotels and shopping complexes. That said, at present the rules ban anchoring in the middle of the bay. The prohibited area runs from 0·75M S of Ross Pt to about 0·5M before you reach Long Pt. The shore can nonetheless be accessed in a tender once you've anchored near Ross Pt. The first dock on Coconut Beach is where to take the tender to get to one of the many restaurants along the beachfront or, close to the shore, to get to the big shopping centre on the other side of the road if you want to shop.

Note On the way to Pt Salines or returning, be wary of the many shoals around Grand Anse's shores and off Long Pt, especially Long Pt Shoal, 0·5M W of Long Pt opposite Morne Rouge Bay.

Morne Rouge Bay

The bay has a pretty beach, but shoal ground means anchoring well out. There's a pleasant bar-restaurant on the beach and several other places further up the hill above as well as on the beaches S of Morne Rouge Bay.

Below Morne Rouge Bay beach
Bottom left Morne Rouge Bay and Grand Anse
Bottom right True Blue Bay

South coast

The coast is marked by what are almost fjords, which offer the greatest number of more or less untouched anchorages and hurricane holes you'll find anywhere in such a compact area in the Antilles. East of Hartman Creek the majority of the inlets aren't much visited and the estate agent developments (of pretty cottages), where they exist, are excellently blended in.

Recommendations:
• enter the anchorages under power
• some passes are often disturbed by a SE swell and you need good visibility with the sun high in the sky to use them
• look carefully at the charts and plans before you close the shore

If you follow those rubrics, the more W'ly anchorages are easy enough. For those further E beyond Hartman Bay, wait for calmer weather. S of Pt Salines, use the S of Glover I as a back bearing or leading line to avoid shoal ground with less than 5m over it, between Glover I and the main island, that breaks in any heavy swell.

True Blue Bay

This small bay is identifiable by a house with a red roof (conspic) on the W point off which there are reefs and a small islet. Once you're through the fairly narrow entrance, anchor in 3–5m close to the hotel-restaurant dock. The establishment also offers moorings. Further in there's a second dock, managed by a charter boat operator, with a few berths for visitors, at present being upgraded (True Blue Bay Resort & Marina, VHF 16). The mooring buoys are free to yachts that patronize the restaurant. The anchorage (a bit rolly in a SE swell) could quickly become overcrowded with too many boats, though in fact it isn't much visited and therefore remains a pleasant and quiet small haven.

Ashore The restaurant, which has a good reputation and is much visited both by locals and cruisers, has a fine view over the bay. There's a very active dive centre here too.

True Blue Bay, Prickly Bay & Prickly Point

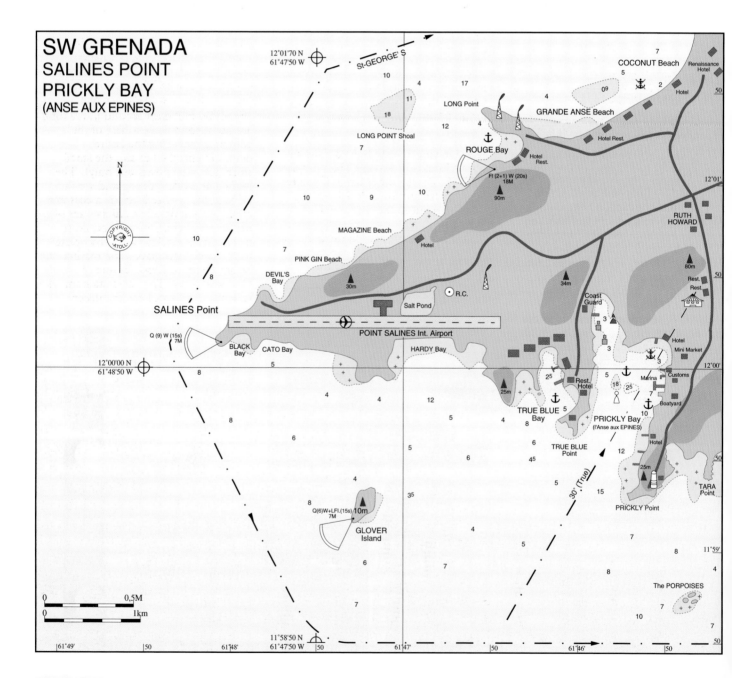

SW GRENADA
SALINES POINT
PRICKLY BAY
(ANSE AUX EPINES)

COCONUT Beach

Renaissance Hotel

12°01'70 N
61°47'50 W

St-GEORGE'S

LONG Point

GRANDE ANSE Beach

LONG POINT Shoal

ROUGE Bay

Hotel Rest.

Hotel Rest.

Fl (2+1) W (20s)
18M
90m

12'01'

N

RUTH HOWARD

MAGAZINE Beach

80m

COPYRIGHT 1ATOLL

PINK GIN Beach

DEVIL'S Bay

30m

Hotel

R.C.

34m

Rest.

Rest.

SALINES Point

Salt Pond

Coast Guard

Hotel

Q (9) W (15s)
7M

BLACK Bay

CATO Bay

POINT SALINES Int. Airport

HARDY BAY

3

3

Mini Market

12°00'00 N
61°48'50 W

25

Rest. Hotel

5

Marina

Customs

18

25

7

Boatyard

12'00'

25m

TRUE BLUE Bay

5

PRICKLY Bay
(l'Anse aux EPINES)

Hotel

TRUE BLUE Point

45

4

GLOVER Island

Q(6)W+LFl.(15s)
7M

10m

25m

30° (True)

15

TARA Point

PRICKLY Point

35

The PORPOISES

0   0.5M
0   1km

61°49'   50   61°48'   50   61°47'   50   61°46'   50   50

11°58'50 N
61°47'50 W

11'59'

Above left Pontoon and restaurant–True Blue Bay
Above Spice Island Marine boatyard
Above right Marina, Mount Hartman Bay
Below Mount Hartman Bay, Tara and Hog Islands from S

Prickly Bay (L'Anse aux Epines)
(pronounced 'Lansopeen')

The most popular anchorage in the S of Grenada and a port of entry. If there's a big swell and you draw much water, avoid the 4m patches extending off True Blue Pt to the SW of the bay.

At the E end of Prickly Pt there's a tower like a lighthouse, though the privately owned building isn't actually one. Enter the bay on 030°T. Ahead of you there's a house with a pyramid shaped roof half way up the hill at the back of the bay. Once around the middle of the inlet, watch out for the shoals to port which are usually buoyed. To starboard there are the docks of the Spice Island Marine Services (VHF 16) near to which it's best to anchor. There's a dock with 30 berths (water, electricity) with a fuel dock on the outer end. You can also anchor off the fine beach in the N, off the Calabash Hotel, though be sure to stay 100m out so you don't violate the rules. In a SE swell the bay can be rolly.

Ashore Customs and immigration offices are on the first floor of a building N of the Spice Island Marine dock. The marina has pleasantly rural surroundings and offers a wide range of services: a small chandlery, a yard (at the head of the bay) with a 35 tonne travel-hoist, several specialist businesses and a bareboat charter company. Above the workshop a minimarket surrounded by several boutiques caters to most provisioning needs. In the evenings cruisers gather at the marina's bar-restaurant 'The Boat Yard', where there's often live music. There are plenty of other well-thought-of haunts and hotel developments around Prickly Bay with good menus ranging from local food, through French cuisine to Chinese. It's easy to hire a car or taxi for an island tour from here.

Mt Hartman Bay

Note Leaving Prickly Bay go right out round Prickly Pt leaving The Porpoises to the S. On the other hand, if you're coming straight from Pt Salines, it's best to go out to the S round The Porpoises (which can be hard to spot) before altering for Mt Hartman Bay on 012°T. On this route you'll leave little Tara It and its shoal ground to starboard. Other than that potential pitfall, it's easy enough to get into Hartman Bay because the marina at the head of the bay has installed an unlit buoyage system.

Note The buoys are generally well-maintained but because they are not official they may sometimes be missing or out of position.

Hartman Bay itself is well protected. Except for the marina buildings and the luxurious Secret Harbour Hotel the shoreline is pretty undeveloped. The best anchorage is E of the marina jetties in 3–4m. Secret Harbour Marina (VHF 16 & 71) has some 50 berths with water and electricity as well as a fuel dock. Some of the berths are permanently taken by the boats of The Moorings charter company. There are also some mooring buoys available for rent.

Ashore the buildings around the marina are home to the huge office of the company managing the entire development, the bar and the small store (for basic provisions only). The marina also offers diving and various other water sports. There is a customs office but immigration officials are often not around, which means you must head over to Prickly Bay to complete formalities. Dominating the marina, the Secret Harbour Resort is one of Grenada's best. The bar-restaurant with its stone arches and elegant décor

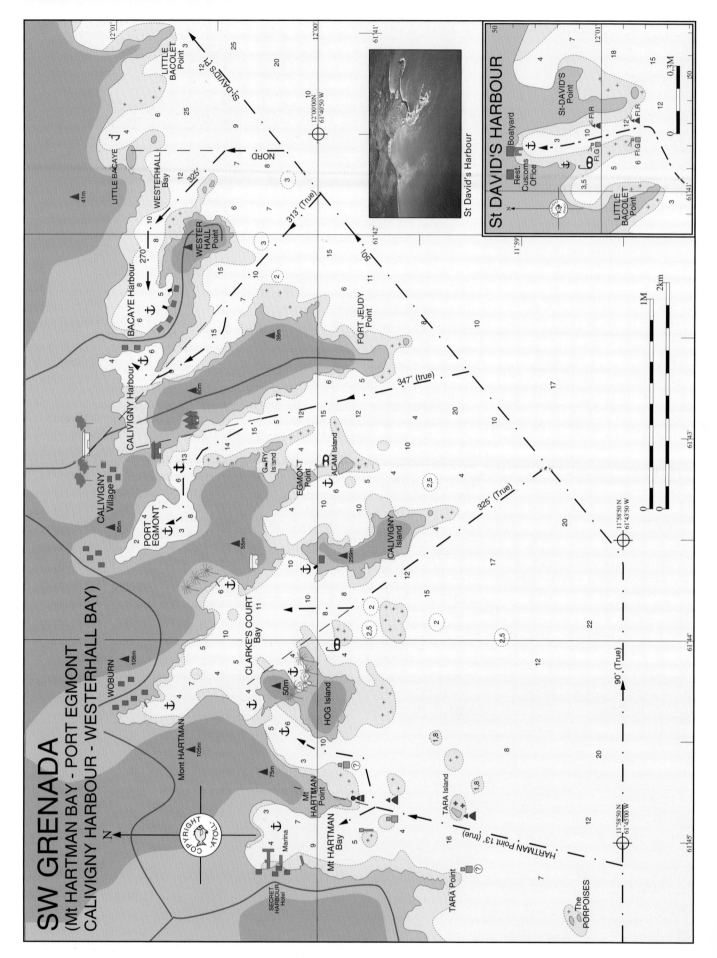

SW GRENADA
(Mt HARTMAN BAY - PORT EGMONT
CALIVIGNY HARBOUR - WESTERHALL BAY)

St DAVID'S HARBOUR

St David's Harbour

Above The swimming pool, Secret Harbour Resort
Above centre Fishing boats, Port Egmont
Above right Port Egmont
Right Port Egmont, Fort Jeudy Pt, Westerhall Pt from S

overlooks the swimming pool and the luxurious hotel cottages wandering up the tree clad slopes. In the evenings the complex often has live music.

Hog Island

W coast anchorage One of the prettiest on Grenada's S coast. Give the large shoal area S of Hog I a good wide berth. Coming from Mt Hartman Bay, once clear of Mt Hartman Pt, head for Hog I by following the buoys (occasionally missing) marking the reefs and cays. The anchorage is in a small inlet on the W side of the island in 3–4m. It's well sheltered but a lot more crowded than it used to be.

E coast anchorage You must go back out to sea because the area S of Hog I is full of reef. You need to make a big loop round the area of shoal (<3m) extending S from the reefs, which breaks in a heavy swell. Once clear S of the shoals S of Hog I, head for the SW point of Calavigny I until the E point of Hog I bears 325°T when you can steer for it. Use the easily visible reefs on the W side of Hog I as a guide. Once you've passed them, alter due N. To port you'll see a small inlet on the E shore of Hog I. The anchorage here is

less frequented than the W side as well as having more cooling breeze.

From either anchorage there's some walking to be had on the island, the only inhabitants being a few cows, the birds and the coconut crabs. There's a fine view from the hill at the N end and a fabulous beach with coconut palms at the S end. BEWARE of the manchineel trees.

Clarke's Court Bay

This large bay opens up N of Hog I and, in the past, cargo ships loading spices and rum used its natural harbour.

Note Beware of the two isolated shoals in the middle of the bay

The best sheltered anchorage is at the head of the bay in 3–4m off the village of Woburn and its dock. The new small

marina, Clarke's Court Bay Marina, (VHF 16/74), has 20 berths and will expand. The boatyard, Island Dreams Yacht Services (VHF 74) does repairs and will arrange yacht-minding and haulout but has no hoist yet.

Ashore The village also has some small shops for basic provisions, as well as some small bar-restaurants serving local specialties. Given the excellent shelter, you can relax, leave your boat and head off to visit the rest of the island.

Calivigny Island

S of Clarke's Court Bay the NW coast of Calavigny I is also well-sheltered. From all the various anchorages you can take the dinghy to get to any of the cays to go snorkelling, though sadly the water clarity isn't always of the best on Grenada's S coast.

Calavigny Harbour anchorage

Calavigny Harbour & Westerhall Bay

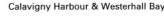

Egmont Harbour (Port Egmont)

The best hurricane hole in the Antilles (see Cyclones section in the Introduction).

Approach From off the W end of Fort Jeudy Pt, steer 347°T towards a house (conspic) with a roof shaped like three pyramids about half way up the hill on the W coast of the Fort Jeudy Pt peninsula. Once Gary I is due W, alter to 337°T, watching out for a large coral patch to port just before the entrance to the first inlet. The entry to Egmont will then open up to port on a roughly E/W alignment. There's about 4·5m in the pass.

Once inside there's a large lagoon surrounded by steep hills, which gives a sense of complete security. You might even feel a bit isolated and lost. The shoreline is entirely composed of mangroves where you'll see a few small fishing skiffs tucked away. Bar a few houses and the village up the valley to the N, for the moment there's not a soul around here. There's talk, however, of development on the SW shore, which happily for the moment seems not to have begun.

Calivigny Harbour (Old Harbour)

With a SE swell access is a bit tricky. The W (Fort Jeudy Pt) and E (Westerhall Pt) sides of the entrance to the bay are fringed with coral, leaving only a fairly narrow channel. Steer 313°T with the sandy point further up the inlet head right ahead. There's also a house well up the hill on the same bearing. Once you're clearly through the narrow entrance, steer in a shallow curve to port (to the W) to clear the reefs on the E shore. You'll then pass a sandy point, planted with coconut trees, which has shoal ground you'll need to round. Once inside, the anchorage is in the NE. Whatever some charts may say the mangroves to the W aren't accessible to keelers because depths are less than 1m. Unlike Egmont Harbour, this is not deserted and there are usually a few boats at anchor. Calivigny Harbour is an excellent haven, though less protected than Port Egmont if a major hurricane occurs. The whole Westerhall peninsula has been developed. The developer, a local landscape artist, has done an excellent job with luxurious villas discreetly tucked away amongst the greenery. Other than a small bar-restaurant and a nearby minimarket, there are no other shops.

Westerhall Bay/Bacaye Harbour

Approach Here too it pays to wait for fair weather and good visibility. The entrance, aligned E/W is quite tight. Give Westerhall Pt and the reefs around it a good offing until you can see, N of you, Little Bacaye islet towards which you steer. On that track you'll open up the entrance to port on a line of approx 325°T, using the easily visible reef to port to line yourself up. Once you've got the villas behind the beach on 270°T, turn towards them on that heading towards the head of the bay. There's an excellent anchorage in the SW of the bay. A small E-tending indent on the S shore near some villas offers perfect shelter for one or two boats.

St David's Harbour

Little Bacaye

E of Bacaye Harbour this small sheltered spot is tucked between the islet's W coast and its reef flats. In fair weather it offers a day anchorage.

Ashore There's just a small hotel-restaurant with cottages serving local specialities.

St David's Harbour

Once upon a time only a few experienced yachtsmen and local fishermen visited the bay, but the quality of its shelter has encouraged a boatyard to set up here.

You can recognize St David's Pt by its head-shaped silhouette as well as the small islet a few dozen metres off. The pass between the E coast and the coral barrier to the W (easily visible at low tide) is now marked by a few buoys. Line up on roughly 350°T. At the head of the bay, off the beach and the boatyard, there's quite a large anchorage, well protected except in a heavy SE swell when the anchorage gets rolly and the entrance dangerous.

Ashore Next to the boatyard office there's a customs and immigration post for completing clearance. There's a simple dock that small boats and tenders can get alongside, and work is in hand for better facilities including a fuel dock. The boatyard (Grenada Marine) has a big, 70-tonne travel-hoist and a large hard standing area. With several craftsmen it offers a range of repair and maintenance services. Island Water World has also set up a branch chandlery. A restaurant (The Galley Restaurant) connected with the boatyard has a pleasant terrace on the shore with plain as well as local dishes on the menu. All up it's an agreeable spot in Grenada's SE countryside for hauling your boat.

Windward coast

Grenville

Grenville, out on the windward coast, is little visited by cruisers. The anchorage, protected by a huge barrier reef, is used primarily by fishing boats. It is also feasible for boats on passage provided there is good visibility, the sea is pretty

Westerhall Pt, Calivigny Harbour, Westerhall Bay from S

Grenville Bay from E

Grenville church

calm and you're used to this sort of landfall. Coming in from seaward the pass runs 291°T on the church tower, the only reliable and easily spotted mark. In practice the official buoyage (partly lit) and leading marks are very unreliable and you should use them with the greatest caution. That the lights may not work well is neither here nor there since any night entry is absolutely impracticable. You'll find the first (lit) red buoy off the shoal ground on the N side of the pass followed, in principle, by a second identical buoy. Then to port a green buoy marks the N end of the Barrel of Beef to port. After that, to get into the anchorage off the town, you must enter a second channel on 350°T marked by one or two (unlit and unreliable) buoys.

Ashore There's a customs post near the dock. The town, the island's second largest is, bar some life around the dock, a pretty sleepy spot. That said, it's full of local colour with fishermen, shops, some small bar-restaurants and a market. The people of Grenville, unused to being visited by yachts, offer a warm welcome. If you stop here you'll be taking a step out of time, off the beaten track. Most yachts give it a wide berth because of the navigational problems of Grenada's windward coast. They visit by land instead, taking in the interior at the same time.

Useful information - Grenada

AIRLINE CONNECTIONS
Point Salines International Airport
☎ 473 444 4101 *Fax* 473 444 4838
International long-haul to USA & Canada, London, Venezuela
Inter-island Daily flights to neighbouring islands.

FERRIES
Regular services to Carriacou and Petite Martinique

TELECOMMUNICATIONS
Calling out of Grenada: USA numbers ☎ 1 + area code & number. Other countries ☎ 011 + country code, area code & number.
Calling Grenada from abroad: ☎ (1) 473 + 44 + 5 digits.
Local call: seven figures.
Public call boxes: Coins and Caribbean phone cards.

TOURIST OFFICE
Tourist Office: Burns Pt, St George's
☎ 473 440 2279 *Fax* 473 440 6637
Email gbt@caribsurf.com

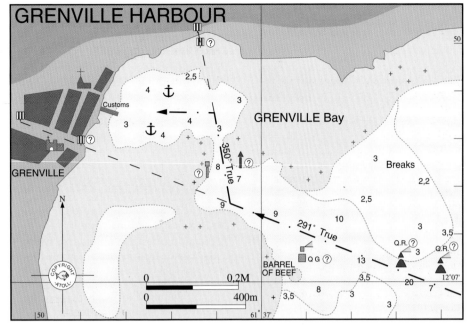

GRENVILLE HARBOUR

CLUBS & ASSOCIATIONS
Philatelic Stamp Collections: Burns Point
☎ 473 440 2526 *Fax* 473 440 4271
Email stamps@travelgrenada.com
Grenada Yacht Club: The Spout Pt, St George's
☎ 473 440 3050 *Fax* 473 440 6826
VHF 16
Grenada Sailing Festival Inc. , The Spout Pt
☎ 473 440 4809 *Fax* 473 440 4811
Marine & Yachting Association, St David's Harbour (Grenada Marine)
☎ 473 443 1667 *Fax* 473 443 1668 (help for cruisers – clearance formalities)

FESTIVALS/FOLK FESTIVALS/SAILING EVENTS
January/February, Grenada Sailing Festival
January/February: True Blue Bay Resort Race
February/March: Carriacou Carnival (see Carriacou, Grenada Grenadines)
March: St Patrick's Day
May: Jazz Festival
June: Grenada Yacht Club Races
July: La Source Yacht Race
August: Rainbow City Festival (Grenville)
August: Carnival
August: Carriacou Regatta (see Carriacou, Grenada Grenadines)
September/October: Grenada Yacht Club races
November: End of Hurricane Season Race

PUBLIC HOLIDAYS
1 January (New Year's Day), 2 January (Recovery Day), 7 February (Independence Day), Easter Friday to Easter Monday (dates vary), First Monday in May (Labour Day), Whit Monday (date varies), Corpus Christi (date varies), August Holidays (first Monday and Tuesday), Carnival (2nd weekend in August), 25 October (Thanksgiving), 25 December (Christmas), 26 December (Boxing Day)

OFFICE HOURS
Shops: 0800–1200, 1300–1600, half day Saturday
Banks: 0800–1300 or 1400 Mon–Thurs, 0800–1300, 1430–1700 Friday
Govt. Offices: 0800–1145, 1300–1600 Mon–Fri, closed Saturday

PLACES TO SEE
St George's
Fort George (1706)
Fort Frederick (Richmond Hill, 1791)
Fort Matthew (1779)
National Museum
Anglican church (18th century)
Botanical Gardens
Elsewhere
Carib's Leap: Sauteurs Bay
Levera: National Park
River Sallee Boiling Spring (near Levera Pt)
Lake Antoine: Windward coast
River Antoine Rum Distillery: the oldest distillery in the Caribbean
Royal Mt Carmel Waterfall: S of Grenville

Seven Sisters Falls (only on foot)
Bay Gardens: Morne Delice, St Pauls
Annandale Falls and Medicinal Plant Garden
Grand Etang Lake
Concord Falls (car access as far as the first cataract)
Dougaldston Spice Estate: a nutmeg factory S of Gouvaye
Petroglyphs (1) S of Victoria, (2) E of Marli Hill
Victoria Waterfalls: St Marks (only on foot)
Sulphur Springs

ROAD TRANSPORT
Drive on the left
A local licence is obligatory but one can be bought for EC$30 if you have an acceptable foreign licence. An international driving licence is valid on its own.
Hire car companies in the main towns and at the airport
Taxis (metered)
Buses cover the whole island, (fares EC$1 around St George's, EC$5 St George's to Grenville.)

REGULATIONS
Fishing and underwater hunting
Note a system of regulation is being planned, be sure to enquire for details.
It is forbidden to buy langoustes out of season (authorised 1/10 to 31/4) with heavy fines for breaking the rules.
Anchoring
Anchoring in coral forbidden
Anchoring prohibited in Grand Anse Bay (see Pilotage).

FORMALITIES
Arriving by air
Customs and immigration in the airport
Arriving by sea
Offices at:
St George's Office at GYS.
Prickly Bay 1st floor, Spice Island Marina
Mt Hartman Bay Marina Office (Immigration service intermittent)
St David's Harbour Grenada Marine, weekdays 0800–1145 & 1300–1545
Grenville opposite the dock (not used to pleasure vessels)
Hours: Weekdays 0800–1145 & 1300–1545
Overtime: outside working hours and weekends (dearer than at Carriacou)
Fees and taxes
Port dues according to boat length. Approx EC$50 up to a 50 footer. Additional tax for charterers with a formula based on a crew list for paying crew.
Taxes paid once only and valid for all of Grenada and its dependencies.

Note in principal if you've cleared in Carriacou, you've cleared into Grenada, but check when you arrive in Grenada.

Barbados

Area 431 sq km
Highest point Mount Hillaby
   340m
Population 260,000
Capital Bridgetown (pop. 110,000)
Language English, Bajan patois
Currency Barbados dollar (Bd$), US$
Political status Independent state (in the
   Commonwealth)
Distances to nearby islands St Vincent
   86M, St Lucia 85M, Martinique 105M

History

Barbados lies some 80M to windward of the chain of the Antilles, so Columbus never came across it on his many voyages. Pedro a Campos and his Portuguese crew were the first to discover it in 1536 when heading for Brazil. Impressed by all the bearded fig trees on the island, they named it 'Isla de los Barbados', the Island of Beards. The name stuck when the first English colonists arrived in 1627, when they founded Jamestown (Holetown). At that time there were apparently no remaining traces of the original pre-Columbian population that had once lived there.

Thanks to its geographical position Barbados was untouched by the Anglo-French wars. The result was that the British influence was continuous for more than three centuries. The effects remain today, for the island is so marked by British traditions and manners that it's nicknamed 'Little England'.

In the 18th century the development of a sugar monoculture made Barbados the biggest English colonial sugar producer. It depended, of course, on the massive import of slaves from Africa who were the ancestors of 95% of today's population. The tiny population of white people is not the remnant of the great sugar estate owning families, but of those condemned for religious or political dissent and deported here from Britain by various governments.

Though these days any discrimination in Barbados has less to do with the colour of your skin than with your wealth and social status.

Independent since 1966, the island's inhabitants think of themselves above all as Barbadians (or Bajans), although they still retain some very British ways, such as 'tea time' in their flower covered cottages, and the uniform of the policemen.

The people are very religious. Although there is a multiplicity of sects, the Anglican church dominates and the island is divided into numerous parishes, each with its church.

Population density is among the world's highest and sugar cane and its by-products still represent one part of the people's economic resources. To this we can add fishing (the Bajans have a fine reputation as sailors) and market gardening. However, in response to the depression in the world sugar market, in order to maintain their standard of living (one of the highest amongst the old British Caribbean colonies) the island has for a while been developing tourism which is now, in addition to offshore banking activities, an important source of revenue.

Tourism

Where to stay and what to see

Barbados holds lots of winning cards as a centre for holiday makers:

- A healthy and sunny climate cooled by the trades, with huge beaches and lots of hotels with welcoming and efficient staff to suit every pocket.

- An international airport with good connections to Europe and North America, and a stop for lots of cruise liners.

- A history which has bequeathed interesting colonial architecture and several archaeological sites.

The larger part of the island is formed by a large, rolling, coralline limestone plateau, either covered with sugar cane plantations or pretty tropical vegetation.

There is a well-maintained, dense network of roads serving the whole island.

The windward coast, battered by massive Atlantic swells and fringed in the S by coral reef, is still quite a wild place. The leeward coast is quieter and has wonderful, long white sand beaches backed by golf courses and cricket pitches, which make it something of the Riviera of the Caribbean.

The many reefs on the coast have lots of good dive sites. The best thought-of are at the N end of Harrison Reefs.

Bridgetown

Bridgetown and its environs are the only really urbanized part of the island and the neatly ordered residential areas give it the feel of a small provincial town in England. Around the Careenage restored buildings ensure an authentic feel to the historical centre. Nelson's Monument keeps watch over Trafalgar Square (renamed National Heroes Square) off which runs Broad Street, an elegant shopping street with duty free shops and fine colonial houses. To the E runs St Michael's Row, leading towards St Michael's Cathedral (17th and 18th centuries). In the N the area full of warehouses around the port is of no interest to tourists.

Around the island

At Needham's Pt, which marks the S end of Carlisle Bay, you'll find fine beaches and plenty of recreational and tourist facilities, including several hotels and the best known yacht clubs in the island. Any visit to Barbados should include a call at some of the fine plantation mansions in the S such as Sam Lord's Castle, as well as the old mills, which are all that's left of the old plantations. The main nature spots are on the windward coast around the middle of the island, mostly all together in the National Park: subterranean caverns and sea caves, the Flower Forest's tropical vegetation, the Wildlife Reserve and, in the S at Bathsheba, the luxuriant variety of the plants in the Andromeda Gardens.

Oistins Bay & Needham Point from SE

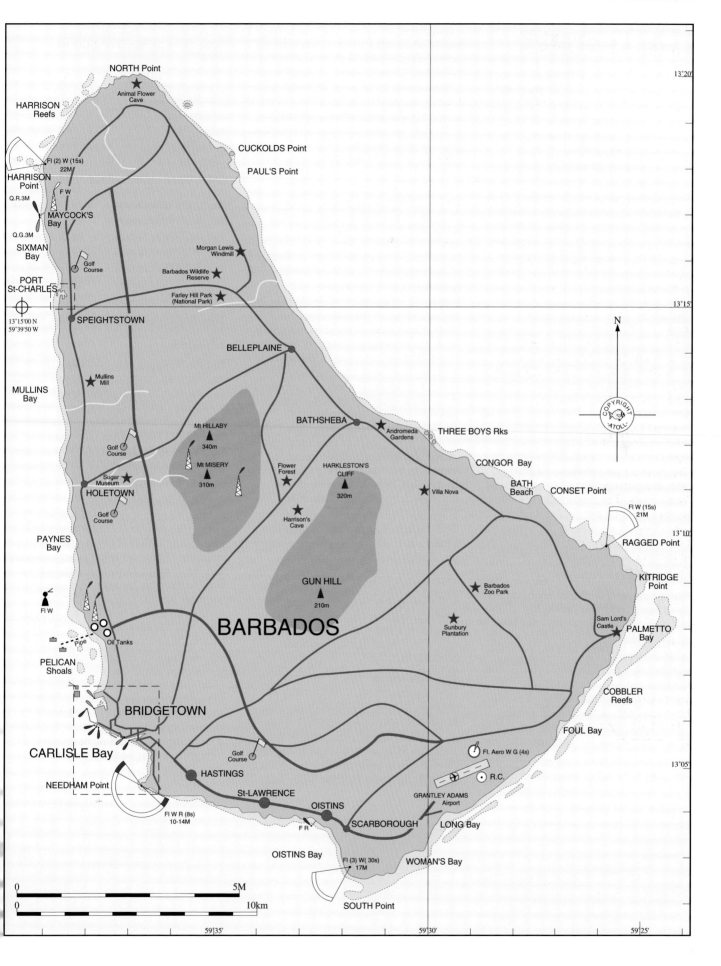

NORTH Point

HARRISON
Reefs

Animal Flower
Cave

CUCKOLDS Point

PAUL'S Point

Fl (2) W (15s)
22M

HARRISON
Point

Q.R.3M

F W

MAYCOCK'S
Bay

Q.G.3M

SIXMAN
Bay

PORT
St-CHARLES

13°15'00 N
59°39'50 W

Golf
Course

Morgan Lewis
Windmill

Barbados Wildlife
Reserve

Farley Hill Park
(National Park)

SPEIGHTSTOWN

BELLEPLAINE

N

MULLINS
Bay

Mullins
Mill

Mt HILLABY
340m

BATHSHEBA

Andromeda
Gardens

THREE BOYS Rks

COPYRIGHT ·ATOLL·

Golf
Course

Mt MISERY
310m

Flower
Forest

HARKLESTON'S
CLIFF
320m

CONGOR Bay

BATH
Beach

CONSET Point

Sugar
Museum

HOLETOWN

Golf
Course

Harrison's
Cave

Villa Nova

Fl W (15s)
21M

13°10'

RAGGED Point

PAYNES
Bay

GUN HILL

210m

BARBADOS

KITRIDGE
Point

Fl W

Oil Tanks

Pipe

PELICAN
Shoals

Barbados
Zoo Park

Sunbury
Plantation

Sam Lord's
Castle

PALMETTO
Bay

COBBLER
Reefs

BRIDGETOWN

FOUL Bay

CARLISLE Bay

Golf
Course

Fl. Aero W G (4s)

13°05'

NEEDHAM Point

HASTINGS

St-LAWRENCE

OISTINS

F R

R.C.

GRANTLEY ADAMS
Airport

Fl W R (8s)
10-14M

SCARBOROUGH

LONG Bay

OISTINS Bay

Fl (3) W(30s)
17M

WOMAN'S Bay

0   5M

0   10km

SOUTH Point

13°20'

13°15'

59°35'   59°30'   59°25'

Barbados and the Atlantic crossing

In years gone by it seems every circumnavigator believed that an Atlantic crossing always made landfall at Barbados. However, these days the new practice, particularly amongst French sailors, is to keep rolling as far as the Antilles to islands such as Martinique and Guadeloupe and, for English speakers, Antigua. After just a few more hours at sea you'll be somewhere better adapted to welcome you with marinas, boatyards and so on. For those who do this, the outpost of Barbados will stay forgotten, unless perhaps they visit as tourists – and by air.

Landfall

Like a billiard table on distant approach, the more rugged features of the Barbados coast become steadily more apparent as you close land. Ragged Pt light, with its 20M range to warn you of the E coast dangers, eases the cares of a night approach.

Note The coast to the SW of Ragged Pt as far as South Pt is fringed by dangerous reefs. There is a light on South Pt. After you've rounded it, you can alter towards Needham Pt with its useful sector light.

Pilotage

Coast and anchorages

West coast

There's no well-sheltered anchorage on this coast except in Carlisle Bay. The whole coast, with the wonderful beaches on which its reputation rests, is usually disturbed by a swell, making a stop of any length thoroughly uncomfortable except in a calm.

Carlisle Bay (Bridgetown)

Head into the bay only after giving Needham Pt and its offlying reefs a clear berth. Anchor in the reserved area in the N of the bay.

The S of the bay off the Yacht Club is reserved for local boats on buoy-moorings. The area is also encumbered by large mooring buoys, shoal ground and wrecks, which are popular sites for local dive outfits. The anchorage can sometimes be rolly and backwash can make landing on the beach tricky. All boats should fly 'Q' and immediately complete formalities. The offices are in Bridgetown Harbour to the N of Carlisle Bay. Some go alongside in the main harbour after contacting port control on VHF Ch 16, or anchor and go by tender.

Refuelling (there's no water) can be done in the Fishing Harbour (to the N of the Careenage) but access to the two pumps is tricky because of the hordes of local boats and the restricted space for manoeuvre.

Ashore The S part of the anchorage is backed by hotels, restaurants and shopping centres. This is where you'll also find the two yacht clubs, of which the well-known Barbados Yacht Club welcomes cruising yachts in its handsome colonial premises (be sure to dress accordingly). It offers some services: information, help with formalities, telecoms, etc. In the N of the bay The Boatyard offers a number of services in its small complex, including moorings, which can be used by cruising boats. Crews often get together in the bar-restaurant here.

There's a haul-out service at Bridgetown Harbour in the 'Shallow Draft' zone. There's a 45 tonne travel lift, and specialist underwater and painting services. The jetty next to the dock is wholly taken up by local boats and charter boats.

Around the zone and in the outskirts of Bridgetown there are several marine specialists, mechanics, sail repair services, etc.

The Careenage

In the centre of town, this is Bridgetown's old harbour. Chock-a-block with all manner of local craft, there's nowhere here that offers a welcome to cruising yachts. It's not as busy as it was now the new commercial port (Bridgetown Harbour) has been

Square-rigged brig

built, but there's still a lot of hustle and bustle and the water is filthy.

Ashore You're right in the heart of the town here, with all its life, shops, bars and restaurants. Provisioning is easy using the numerous shops, supermarkets and the local market.

From Bridgetown to Port St Charles

Before you get to Port St Charles the only two anchorages, in Paynes Bay off Holetown and off Speightstown, are short term only. Even so, because of the strict enforcement of rules on authorized anchorages and the protection of marine parks and reefs, you must find out first what is and isn't allowed.

Port St Charles

In Six Man's Bay a lagoon has been created to offer a sheltered haven. It is part of a luxury residential development and the moorings are reserved for residents. Only the outer port, protected behind a raised earth berm has a very few berths with facilities in 5–6m. Call the port captain beforehand (VHF 16/77). There's a fuel and water dock on the southern jetty to the left (port) once inside the entrance.

Ashore You can complete all formalities in the port office. Depending on how busy they are, the maintenance service for marina residents' boats can help out with breakdowns. There's only a bar and restaurant at the marina, for provisioning you must go to Speightstown at least 2km further S.

Oistins Bay, Carlisle Bay, Bridgetown Point from S

CARLISLE BAY BRIDGETOWN

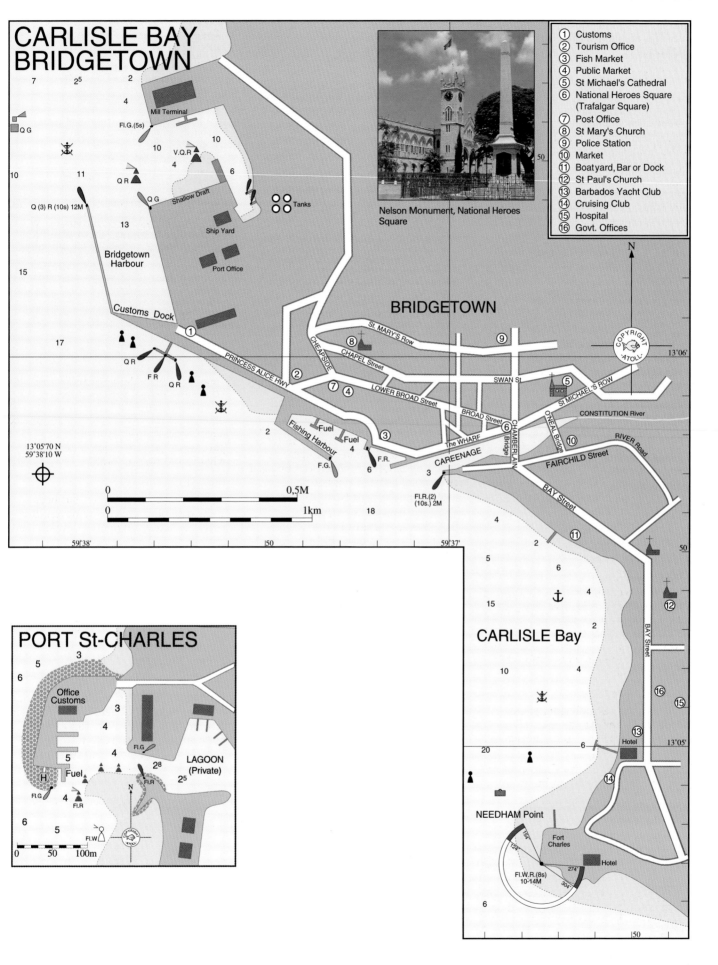

7   2⁵   2

4

Mill Terminal

Fl.G.(5s)

QG

10   10

V.Q.R

QR   4   6

10   11

QG   Shallow Draft

Q (3) R (10s) 12M

13   Tanks

15   Ship Yard

Bridgetown Harbour   Port Office

Customs Dock

17   ①

QR

FR   QR

PRINCESS ALICE HWY

13°05'70 N
59°38'10 W

2   Fishing Harbour   ②

Fuel   Fuel

③

F.G.   4   ②   ③

F.R.   6

3

0   0,5M

0   1km   18

Fl.R.(2)
(10s.) 2M

59°38' |50   59°37'

Legend:
① Customs
② Tourism Office
③ Fish Market
④ Public Market
⑤ St Michael's Cathedral
⑥ National Heroes Square (Trafalgar Square)
⑦ Post Office
⑧ St Mary's Church
⑨ Police Station
⑩ Market
⑪ Boatyard, Bar or Dock
⑫ St Paul's Church
⑬ Barbados Yacht Club
⑭ Cruising Club
⑮ Hospital
⑯ Govt. Offices

Nelson Monument, National Heroes Square

50

N

BRIDGETOWN

St. MARY'S Row
⑧   CHAPEL Street   ⑨

CHEAPSIDE

②   ⑦   ④   LOWER BROAD Street   SWAN St   ⑤
St MICHAEL'S Row

BROAD Street   ⑥

The WHARF   CHAMBERLAIN Bridge   O'NEAL Bridge   CONSTITUTION River

CAREENAGE   ⑩   ⑯   RIVER Road

FAIRCHILD Street

3   BAY Street

COPYRIGHT 'ATOLL'   13°06'

4

2

⑪

5   6

4
15   ⚓   4

CARLISLE Bay

10   4

2

⚓   BAY Street

20   6

NEEDHAM Point

⑫

⑯   ⑮

⑬   Hotel   13°05'

⑭

154°
124°   Fort Charles   274°
Fl.W.R.(8s)   304°   Hotel
10-14M

6

|50

PORT St-CHARLES

5   3

6   Office Customs

3

4

5   Fl.G   LAGOON (Private)

H   Fuel   2⁸
Fl.R   2⁵

Fl.G   4   Fl.R

6

5   Fl.W

0   50   100m   COPYRIGHT 'ATOLL'   N

Useful Information for Barbados

AIRLINE CONNECTIONS
International Airport: Grantly Adams Airport
International long-haul direct flights to Europe (London, Frankfurt, Zurich) and N America (Miami, New York, Toronto)
Inter-island flights daily flights to neighbouring islands

TELECOMMUNICATIONS
Calling from abroad: ☎ (1) 246 + 7 digits
Local call: 7 digits (local calls are free, but 25c from a pay phone)
(Phone cards can be bought)

TOURIST OFFICE/ASSOCIATION
Barbados Tourism Authority, Harbour Rd, Bridgetown
☎ 246 427 2623 *Fax* 246 426 4080
www.barbados.org

ASSOCIATIONS
Barbados Yacht Club, Careenage
☎ 246 427 7318 *Fax* 246 427 7580
Email byc@inaccs.com.bb
Barbados Sailing & Cruising Club, Careenage,
☎ 246 426 4434
Barbados National Trust, Bridgetown
☎ 246 436 9033

FESTIVALS/FOLK FESTIVALS
Numerous regattas throughout the year
Jazz Festival: January
Holetown Festival (a music festival): February
Oistins Fish Festival: Easter
Congaline Carnival: late April
Festival of Gospel Music: May
Crop Over Festival (Sugar Cane Festival): July
Kadooment Day (Carnival): beginning of August

GOLF COURSES
Sandy Lane Golf Club
Royal Westmoreland Golf Club

PUBLIC HOLIDAYS
New Year's Day (1 January), Errol Barrow Day (21 January), Good Friday, Easter Monday, National Heroes Day (28 April), Labour Day (1 May), Whit Monday, Emancipation Day (1 August), Kadooment Day (first Monday in August), Independence Day (30 November), Christmas Day (25 December), Boxing Day (26 December)

OFFICE HOURS
Banks: Mon–Thu 0800–1500, Fri 0800–1300, 1500–1700

PLACES TO SEE
Bridgetown
St Michael's Cathedral (1789 on a 1665 foundation)
National Heroes Square & Nelson's Monument
St Mary's Church (18th century)
Barbados Museum (old military prison)
Elsewhere
Animal Flower Cave: underwater grotto
Andromeda Gardens
Barbados Wildlife Reserve
Barbados Zoo Park
Flower Forest (Orchids) – St Joseph
Harrison's Cave (caves)
Morgan Lewis Windmill (18th century)
The Hutson Sugar Museum – Holetown
Sam Lord's Castle (1820) – S of the island
Sunbury Plantation House (18th Century, St Philip's Museum)
Barbados National Trust: walks

ROAD TRANSPORT
Drive on the left
A licence is obligatory. Visitor Registration Certificate, US$5, Hastings, Holetown or Worthing police stations, international driving licence or not.
Good public transport (buses and minibuses) and taxis
Car hire companies in the town and at the airport

FORMALITIES
Arriving by air Customs and immigration at the airport
Arriving by sea
Offices at:
Bridgetown Harbour (in the S of the commercial port) (VHF 16)
Port St Charles (contact on VHF 16/77)
Office hours: 0600–2200, 7 days a week
Q flag obligatory, be ready for the authorities to come aboard
Fees and taxes Entry/Exit Permit as well as an anchoring fee

Notes
Formalities are complicated – you must complete both entry and exit clearance in the same office.

You must seek authorisation to use any anchorage other than that of your port of entry.

Anchoring only over sand and absolutely forbidden over coral on pain of heavy fines.

Outside the reserves, trolling is permitted.

The Leeward Islands

Dominica

Area 751 sq km
Highest point Morne
  Diablotin, 1445m
Population 80,000
Capital Roseau (pop. 20,000)
Language English, but also a patois with
  French roots
Currency: EC$, US$ accepted
Political status Independent state of the
  Commonwealth
Distances to nearby islands Pt Cachacrou
  (Scott's Head) – Martinique 25M,
  Portsmouth – Les Saintes 20M

History

The mountainous and impenetrable island of Dominica (pronounced Domineeka) was first seen by Columbus on a Sunday in November 1493, hence the name. He passed it by. In the 17th century the French coveted it because it lay neatly between Martinique and Guadeloupe, so they tried to get a foothold. For similar strategic reasons the English made several efforts to turf them out. And just like everywhere else, the result was a century of struggle, although often the combatants joined together to defeat a common foe in the Caribs. For the latter, the island's thick jungle and craggy profile gave them an excellent redoubt from which they could launch harassing raids against the putative colonists. The Caribs' instinct for autonomy was equalled only by their ferocity. So much so that in 1748 both the English and the French were discouraged enough to give up their first efforts at colonisation and wait for better times. The result was that Dominica was pronounced a neutral island belonging to the Caribs.

Fairly soon, however, the struggle began again, and thanks to better tactics the Caribs were pushed back from the coast to the island's interior.

Dominica became English in 1783, though the French hung on until 1805 and weren't finally induced to leave until a substantial indemnity had been paid. A consequence of that long period of French influence can be seen in the numerous place names and a patois, spoken by almost everyone, very close

Above Carib child in the Salibia Reserve
Above right Carib children of mixed parentage
Right Our Lady of Fair Haven Catholic Church,
Roseau
Below A woodcutter
Below right Laundrywomen.

to the creole of Martinique and Guadeloupe. Meanwhile the Caribs, who had been scattered all over the island, were brought together in a single reserve of about 2000 hectares on the windward coast. There are still around 3000 surviving today. However, as a result of intermarriage with the imported slave population, there are only a few hundred Caribs of pure stock left with their yellowish skin, sleek black hair and eyes with an epicanthic fold. They live on the produce of their smallholdings and selling wickerwork to tourists.

In 1967 the island became an associated state of the Commonwealth and gained full independence in 1978. That was followed by significant political upheaval in 1979. Dominica hardly had time to sort itself out after those events before its delicate economy was wiped out by a catastrophe. On 29 August 1979 the devastating Hurricane David hit the island dead on. Helped by international aid Dominica slowly recovered. Cottages have been rebuilt and the forests and fields have repaired themselves.

Although rugged terrain restricts the cultivable area, agriculture is nonetheless the most important sector of the economy. The main crops are citrus fruit, other fruits and cocoa. To

that can be added small-scale crafts (basketwork, wood carving, batik) which survive on a tourist trade that is still quite sparse.

Places to stay are often quite simple with the majority of the bigger ones around Roseau and Portsmouth. In practice the wild and impenetrable hills, a shoreline of a few austere, grey sand beaches and cliffs battered by Atlantic swells have done little to attract more luxurious and upmarket hotel development. Although it's always being planned, the terrain makes the project costly so there's still no international airport and that has kept Dominica off the tour operators' beats with their crowds of tourists. All the same, things are changing with the recent port development at Roseau. Thanks to this, cruise liners regularly call at the new Cruise Ship Dock and offload their large numbers of passengers who promptly book all the island's transport in order to go sightseeing. That said, the invasion is still fairly limited and the lovely and wild island of Dominica is still at the moment spared a little from mass tourism.

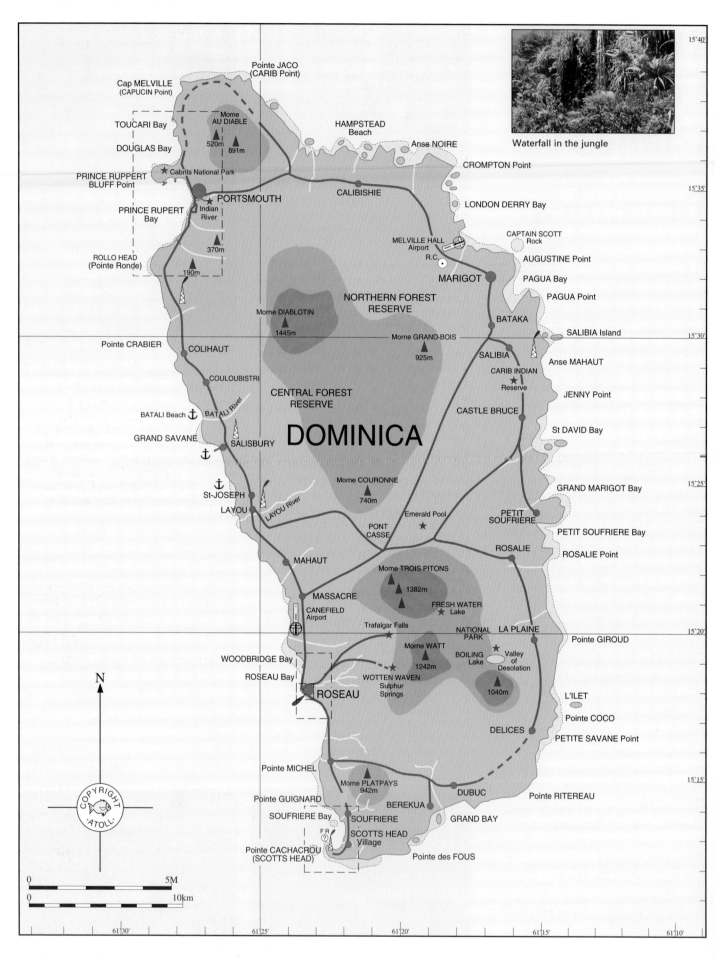

Waterfall in the jungle

Pointe JACO
(CARIB Point)

Cap MELVILLE
(CAPUCIN Point)

TOUCARI Bay

DOUGLAS Bay

Morne
AU DIABLE
520m   891m

HAMPSTEAD
Beach

Anse NOIRE

CROMPTON Point

PRINCE RUPPERT
BLUFF Point

★ Cabrits National Park

PORTSMOUTH

CALIBISHIE

LONDON DERRY Bay

PRINCE RUPPERT
Bay

Indian
River

CAPTAIN SCOTT
Rock

MELVILLE HALL
Airport

ROLLO HEAD
(Pointe Ronde)

370m

R.C.

MARIGOT

AUGUSTINE Point

PAGUA Bay

190m

PAGUA Point

NORTHERN FOREST
RESERVE

BATAKA

Pointe CRABIER

COLIHAUT

Morne DIABLOTIN

1445m

Morne GRAND-BOIS

925m

SALIBIA Island

SALIBIA

Anse MAHAUT

COULOUBISTRI

CARIB INDIAN
★
Reserve

JENNY Point

BATALI Beach ⚓ BATALI River

CENTRAL FOREST
RESERVE

CASTLE BRUCE

St DAVID Bay

GRAND SAVANE

SALISBURY

⚓

DOMINICA

St-JOSEPH

Morne COURONNE

GRAND MARIGOT Bay

LAYOU

LAYOU River

740m

Emerald Pool
★

PETIT
SOUFRIERE

PETIT SOUFRIERE Bay

PONT
CASSE

ROSALIE

MAHAUT

Morne TROIS PITONS

ROSALIE Point

1382m

MASSACRE

FRESH WATER
Lake

CANEFIELD
Airport

Trafalgar Falls

NATIONAL
PARK

LA PLAINE

Pointe GIROUD

WOODBRIDGE Bay

Morne WATT

BOILING
Lake

Valley
★ of
Desolation

ROSEAU Bay

ROSEAU

1242m

WOTTEN WAVEN
Sulphur
Springs

1040m

L'ILET

Pointe COCO

DELICES

PETITE SAVANE Point

Pointe MICHEL

Morne PLATPAYS
942m

DUBUC

Pointe RITEREAU

Pointe GUIGNARD

BEREKUA

SOUFRIERE Bay

SOUFRIERE

GRAND BAY

Pointe CACHACROU
(SCOTTS HEAD)

F R
?

SCOTTS HEAD
Village

Pointe des FOUS

N

COPYRIGHT
·ATOLL·

0   5M

0   10km

15°40'

15°35'

15°30'

15°25'

15°20'

15°15'

61°30'   61°25'   61°20'   61°15'   61°10'

Apart from this link with the international economy, Dominica has to rely on its own resources, so the islanders have a standard of living well below those of its richer neighbours, Martinique and Guadeloupe, which being part of France enjoy generous subsidy.

Tourism

Where to stay and what to see

The fact that Dominica is off the beaten tourist trail is no bad thing in the eyes of real nature lovers. As a result Dominica is valued more for its interior than for its shoreline, being visited primarily by walkers and tourists who seek simplicity. It follows that there are no marinas or ports to speak of, so not many cruising yachts. Dominica, with its craggy, jungle-covered hills full of fumaroles and waterfalls that feed lakes both cool and hot, demands slow exploration on foot. But if you're in a hurry you can capture the essence of the place by car thanks to a road network suitable for all vehicles (although limited and the roads often narrow).

Roseau

The island's small capital is a grid of old, shingled, stone houses mixed in with more brutal, modern and ordinary buildings. Several older buildings are of rather mixed styles, but nonetheless charming with their verandas, balustrading and garlands of motifs looking almost like wooden lacework. Some have now been renovated and painted in lively colours. Also worth a look are the three churches with their very different architectural styles, amongst them the imposing Our Lady of Fair Haven Catholic church. The small shops and workshops give the town quite a bustling air and at the market, most active on Saturdays, the riches of the island's market gardeners are on display. Although the botanical gardens are a bit sparse, they do give a foretaste of the luxuriant flora.

Around the island

From Roseau it's only a short distance on the road for Morne des Trois Pitons before you get to the Trafalgar Falls and other sites in the National Park. After several hours' walk, at 1000m above sea level, you can reach Boiling Lake at the bottom of a big crater. All around the sulphurous gases from it have so wrecked the foliage that people call the area Desolation Valley, a bizarre exception to the generally riotous vegetation all over the rest of the island. From Roseau to Portsmouth the road along the W coast passes through several small villages, over which looms the bulk of the island's highest peak, Morne Diablotin at over 1400m. Deep in the steamy, lush forest you'll see huge gum trees, Dominica's most common tree. Fishermen use it to make their pirogue dug-outs (also known as 'gommiers') from a single trunk. The animal world of the forest is small but includes the large toad called the 'mountain chicken', which is a culinary specialty. Of the rest of the fauna, the best known is the imperial parrot, the 'sisserou' (*Amazona imperialis*) which has become the national emblem.

Portsmouth, the island's second town and the old capital, is situated on the enormous Prince Rupert Bay. It's really just a large village, enlivened by passing yachts and the 4x4's heading out to explore the island interior. Other points of interest are the vine entwined Indian River bordered with huge tree roots, and the marvellous view over Prince Rupert Bay from Fort Shirley.

On the E coast the Carib area is centred on Salibia village S of the village of Marigot. Amongst the impoverished houses of breeze block and corrugated iron, there are still a few buildings on stilts and Carib shanties to be found. Small shops sell the local basketwork, which is worth a look. There are still a few hundred descendants of this Amerindian people, though most here are of mixed ancestry through intermarriage with the local descendants of slaves brought from Africa.

If you head over past Castle Bruce towards Roseau, the road goes through

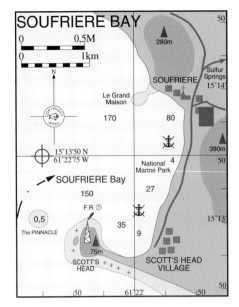

the heart of Dominica, passing close by the natural swimming pools and cascades of Emerald Pool. S of Roseau, again after passing through several villages, the road ends at Soufrière Bay where there are two charming fishing villages, Soufrière and Scotts Head Village, which are on the shore of the marine reserve with superb drop-offs much admired by divers. Indeed diving as a sport is taking off in Dominica thanks to its well-preserved dive sites especially at Soufrière Bay and N of Portsmouth.

Pilotage

Coast and anchorages

Coming from Martinique, you'll make landfall at Scott's Head (Pt Cachacrou).

Note There are unmarked reefs that are hard to see (like The Pinnacle) a bit over 300m WNW of Scott's Head and you must give them a wide berth.

Left House with veranda

Right Scott's Head and Pt Cacherou with Soufrière Bay behind

Above Scott's Head village
Left Soufrière Village church

SW coast

Soufrière Bay and Scotts Head

The whole of the large bay of Scott's Head (Soufrière Bay) as far as Pointe Michel is a National Marine Park. Anchoring by yachts is formally forbidden and the mooring buoys are reserved for local diving club boats. The reserve is actually one of the best underwater sites in Dominica but you must visit under the aegis of a local club.

Along the shore there are two charming villages: Scott's Head in the S with its fishing boats and in the N Soufrière, dominated by the tower of its church. To visit them you'll have to come back by road.

Note W of Soufrière village, the Grand Maison reef, with less than 1m over it, pushes out 200m or so from the shore.

Roseau Bay

The whole bay is quite well protected, but swell can sometimes make the anchorage rolly.

Roseau

The waterfront at Roseau has been developed with a small fishing harbour, a ferry dock and a cruise liner dock. As a general rule yachts only make a brief stop here for formalities or some shopping, because the best overnight anchorage is 1M further SE, off the Anchorage Hotel. Off Roseau itself anchor in 8–12m off the cruise ship dock near the dock of a hotel restaurant built out over the shoreline.

Note The coast here is fringed with a shelf of shoal ground off which the bottom drops sharply to more than 20m. This much reduces the anchoring space, not least because you've also got to leave plenty of swinging room

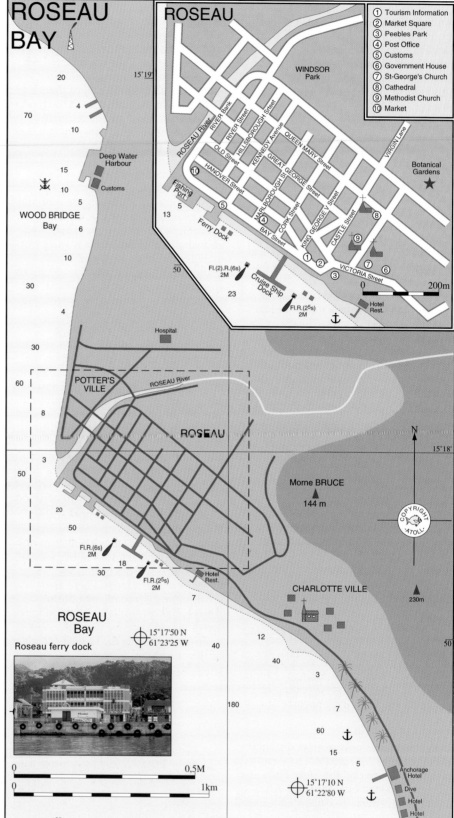

because of gusts, which box the compass.

To get ashore tie your tender to the cruise liner dock piles and climb the big ladders onto the dock. Alternatively, if you prefer, use the restaurant dock, though it's a bit further away.

Ashore Customs are on the ferry dock. If they're not there (during the weekend

for example), there's another office at the Deep Water Harbour about 1M N of Roseau, though it's seldom visited by yachts. If you want to go there by sea, you must ask the port authorities for permission to approach and go alongside (VHF 16).

Other than general hardware stores, there's not much for yachts in Roseau

except the odd skilled mechanic and outboard specialist, and a few small stores with some bits and pieces of chandlery, which might do in emergencies. On the other hand the supermarkets and the local market (Saturdays) are quite good for groceries. There's no fuel or water dock, so you have to jerry jug from a gas station.

In town there are numerous small restaurants with local specialties at reasonable prices. On the waterfront, over the dinghy dock, Fort Young Hotel is one of the island's most upmarket establishments. Built beside an old 18th century fort, it includes a waterfront restaurant and a shopping arcade.

The Anchorage Hotel anchorage

The Anchorage Hotel, run by a Dominican, is a conspicuous large white building. The hotel has a dock for tenders and some moorings. The Anchorage listens out on VHF 16. Their boat watching service allows you to leave your boat for a trip round the island. Given the depths and the possible effects of swell, when you anchor, put a stern line ashore.

Various boat boys will offer their usual services in addition to those of the hotel, but it's better first to contact the hotel reception, or the service agencies next door, which work in collaboration with the hotel.

Ashore, the nicely decorated hotel and restaurant are in a pleasantly green spot. The hotel offers various services: car hire, showers, laundry, telecoms, etc.

Leeward coast

It's often windless on this coast and you'll usually be motoring. N of Roseau the areas around the Deep Water Port and Canefield are mostly warehouses and factories and, apart from the airport at Canefield, are without interest.

From that point on there are several anchorages along the way to Portsmouth, provided you have your Coast Wise Clearance Permit and the sea state doesn't make them too uncomfortable.

Layou

A tiny village between the hill and the Layou River off which you can anchor at some distance from the river mouth. Landslips have partly blocked the riverbed and necessitated some dredging work, the detritus of which lies in piles on the river banks. A trip up the river in the tender has accordingly lost much of its attraction and, in addition, crossing the small bar at the mouth is decidedly tricky.

Note The area around the river mouth is very shoal as is the point just N of the village so you should give both a wide berth.

1M N of Layou, once you're past St Joseph with its conspicuous white church, you can anchor close S of the dock of a small hotel development, the Castaway Beach Hotel.

Note N of the anchorage there's a coral reserve where anchoring is forbidden. Ashore, in a pleasantly rustic ambiance, the restaurant offers seafood specialities. Various services are also available for yachts: island tours, telecommunications and, in an emergency, you may be able to get water and fuel at the dock. At the time of writing all these services were provisionally out of action.

Salisbury

There's a possible short-term anchorage off the dock of this small settlement under Grande Savane Pt.

Ashore there are a few shops, a hotel and a dive club, but no yacht services.

Batali Beach

1·5M N of Salisbury, before you get to the village of Couloubistri, you'll open up Batali Beach. You can anchor here in good weather off the mouth of the Batali River near a restaurant on the beach.

Prince Rupert Bay

Portsmouth

This is Dominica's best anchorage. Either anchor in the NE part of the bay close to the coconut palms and several beachfront restaurants, or further S if you want to be closer to the landing at Portsmouth or to the Indian River. There's another possible anchorage in the S of Prince Rupert Bay off the Coconut Beach Hotel and the Portsmouth Beach Hotel. Both establishments offer a number of services to yachts (showers, laundry, car rental and tours). This is a better anchorage than that in the NE of the bay when the wind is SE, but obviously less sheltered if there's any N swell. It's also closer to the dock and customs post at Glanvillia and the boat boys are fewer and hassle you less.

Top left Roseau market
Top right A leeward coast anchorage north of Roseau,
Above Fort Young Hotel, Roseau
Right The anchorage at Portsmouth

PRINCE RUPERT BAY
(PORTSMOUTH)

N

TOUCARI Village 15°37'

10

TOUCARI
Bay
(Marina Park)

80

30

70m

DOUGLAS Point

3

40

10

DOUGLAS Bay
(Marine Park)

2

15°36'

20

70

6

4

100

8

EAST
CABRIT

Cabrits National
Park

PRINCE
RUPERT
BLUFF
Point

WEST
CABRIT

Fort
SHIRLEY

150m

Rest.

188m

Cruise Ship
Dock

5

4

Rest.

15°35'

Rest.

6

40

17

70

6

Police

PRINCE RUPERT Bay

80

30

5

PORTSMOUTH

INDIAN River

15°34'00 N
61°29'00 W

8

15°34'

GLANVILLIA

5

Customs

3

10

60

35

Dive

PICARD River

4

7

Hotel

65

27

Coconut Beach
Hotel

15°33'

10

LAMOINS River

20

190m

40

47m

0   1M

0   2km

ROLLO HEAD

61°29'   61°28'   61°27'

15°32'

Above, from top
On the beach at Portsmouth
Local regatta at Portsmouth
A cottage at Portsmouth
Coasters driven ashore after a hurricane

The Portsmouth 'welcoming committee' has become a
flotilla of small boats bombarding the cruiser with a barrage
of offers and they're not always good to your topsides. Some
of the boat boys are polite and proper, offering fruit and
vegetables, an Indian River trip and various other services.
But they're mixed with young yahoos from Portsmouth who
are aggressive and occasionally light-fingered. It follows that

Left Indian River, Portsmouth
Above A *pirogue* (locally called a *gommier*)

it's prudent not to leave either your boat or your tender unguarded for long. Fortunately, the official boat boys have been brought together under the aegis of the Indian River Guides Association and can generally be recognized by the badge on their T-shirts. Some listen out on VHF 16. There's an agreed and reasonable tariff for their services. For example, an Indian River visit is US$10–12 a head and, following the new rules, they are advised not to use their outboards once within the river. Trips into this mini-Amazon under oar-power have therefore gained in both authenticity and a sense of peace.

Off some of the restaurants there are small docks for you to moor your tender, though often the surf makes life difficult. Still, you can always beach on the black sand instead.

Ashore In the NE of the bay the traffic of yachts and tourists has led to the building of several small hotels and simple restaurants. They specialize in local dishes and barbecues at reasonable prices. In Portsmouth's main street there are local craft shops, various businesses and minimarkets for shopping. To them you can add the local Saturday market and its fresh produce.

Taxis and 4x4 tours offer trips round the island, but be sure to hire a boat watcher if you leave your boat. Formalities should be completed at the customs post on the commercial dock at Glanvillia, S of Portsmouth. There's a gas station near the commercial dock, which will deliver fuel in cases of real need. In the far N of the bay at Ship Jetty you can leave your tender to visit Cabrits National Park and the partly

restored Fort Shirley. From the heights there's a wonderful view over the bay. It's occasionally possible to water ship here if you're in dire need. The other impressive feature of the shoreline is the large number wrecked coasters, witness to the close passage of successive hurricanes which have thrown them up onto the beach.

Douglas Bay

Beyond Prince Rupert Bluff lies little Douglas Bay, often troubled by the swell. Anchoring here is forbidden because it is a National Park. However the drop-offs along Prince Rupert Point and N of Douglas Pt, called the Toucari Reserve, are often visited by local diving clubs. You can reach them either by bus or taxi.

Useful Information for Dominica

AIRLINE CONNECTIONS
Canefield Airport: Roseau
Melville Hall Airport: secondary airport in the NE of the island
No long-haul flights
Inter-island flights to Guadeloupe, Martinique, St Barts, St Lucia, with other flights to St Thomas and San Juan, Puerto Rico.

FERRIES
Fast ferries to Guadeloupe, Dominica, Martinique & St Lucia

TELECOMMUNICATIONS
Calling from abroad: ☎ (1) 767 + 7 digits
Local call: 7 digits
Public call boxes: Caribbean Phone Card

TOURIST OFFICE/ASSOCIATION
Tourist Office, Valley Rd, Roseau
  ☎ 767 448 2045 *Fax* 767 448 5840
  Email ndctourism@cwdom.dm
Dominica Hotel & Tourism Association, Roseau
  ☎ 767 448 6565 *Fax* 767 448 0299

FESTIVALS/FOLK FESTIVALS
Mas Domnik (Carnival): February
Carnaval (Calypso King): March
Kone Kon-la: local festivity in June
World Creole Music festival: Roseau, October

PUBLIC HOLIDAYS
New Year's Day (1 January), Carnival (February), Good Friday, Easter Monday, first Monday in May, Whit Monday, first Monday in August, Independence Day (3/4 November), Christmas Day (25 December). All shops, restaurants and some government offices are closed on the merchant's holiday on 2nd January; banks and hotels stay open.

OFFICE HOURS
Shops: Mon–Fri, 0800–1300, 1400–1600, Sat, 0800–1300
Banks: Mon–Thurs, 0800–1500, Fri 0800–1700
Government offices: Mon, 0800–1300, 1400–1700, Tues–Fri 0800–1300, 1400–1600

PLACES TO SEE
Botanical Gardens and church: Roseau
In the N:
Cabrits National Park: Fort Shirley & museum
Chaudière Pool: Bense Village
Indian River (Rivière Indienne): Portsmouth
In the E:
Carib Indian Reserve: windward coast
Boli Falls: SE of La Plaine village, access difficult
Sari Sari Falls: above La Plaine village
Victoria Falls
In the S
Sulphur Springs: above Soufrière
In the W
Layou River (Rivière Layou): gorge descent
Trafalgar Falls: NE of Roseau
Centre of the island
Emerald Pool: waterfall and cave
Boiling Lake and Desolation Valley: sulphur springs and boiling mud

Boeri Lake: 900m up
Middleham Falls: in Three Pitons Park

ROAD TRANSPORT
Drive on the left
Local licence obligatory
Hire car services in the towns.
Numerous taxis offering tours round the island.

REGULATIONS
Underwater hunting: forbidden to non-residents. Diving authorised only with local clubs
National Marine Park: Soufrière Bay and Douglas Bay, details on restrictions available from the authorities.

FORMALITIES
Arriving by air
  Customs and immigration at the airport
Arriving by sea
Roseau 2 offices:
Ferry Dock open weekdays 0800–1300, 1400–1600
Deep Water Dock: in the N: not much used by yachts
Portsmouth commercial dock at Glanvillia: open weekdays 0800–1300, 1400–1600
  For a 24hr stay you can enter and clear at the same time.
Overtime: outside office hours and at weekends and holidays
Fees and taxes
To anchor along the coast apply for a 'Coastal Cruising Permit'. A small environmental tax.

GUADELOUPE

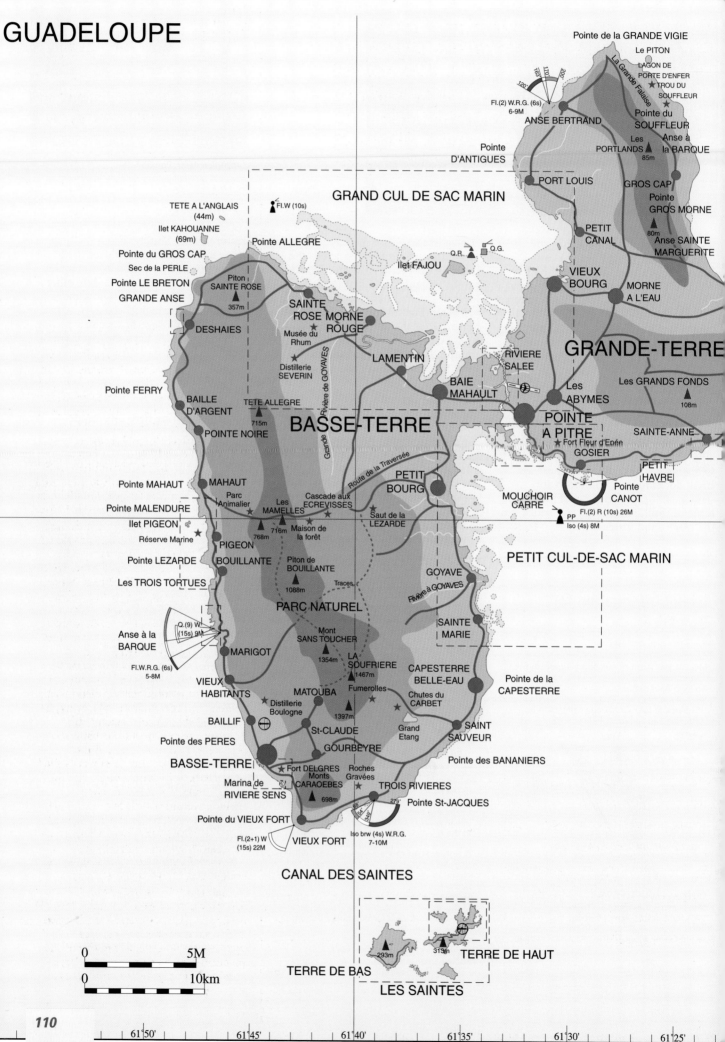

Pointe de la GRANDE VIGIE

Le PITON

LAGON DE
PORTE D'ENFER
★ TROU DU
SOUFFLEUR

Fl.(2) W.R.G. (6s)
6-9M

ANSE BERTRAND

Pointe du
SOUFFLEUR

Les
PORTLANDS ▲
85m

Pointe à
la BARQUE

Pointe
D'ANTIGUES

PORT LOUIS

GROS CAP
Pointe
GROS MORNE

GRAND CUL DE SAC MARIN

PETIT
CANAL

80m

Anse SAINTE
MARGUERITE

TETE A L'ANGLAIS
(44m)

Ilet KAHOUANNE
(69m)

Fl.W (10s)

Q.R.

Q.G.

VIEUX
BOURG

MORNE
A L'EAU

Pointe ALLEGRE

Pointe du GROS CAP

Sec de la PERLE

Ilet FAJOU

Pointe LE BRETON

Piton
SAINTE ROSE

GRANDE ANSE

357m

SAINTE
ROSE MORNE
ROUGE

Musée du
Rhum

GRANDE-TERRE

DESHAIES

RIVIERE
SALEE

Les GRANDS FONDS

LAMENTIN

Distillerie
SEVERIN

Pointe FERRY

BAILLE
D'ARGENT

TETE ALLEGRE

BAIE
MAHAULT

Les
ABYMES

108m

715m

POINTE
A PITRE

SAINTE-ANNE

POINTE NOIRE

BASSE-TERRE

Route de la Traversée

★ Fort Fleur d'Epée
GOSIER

Pointe MAHAUT

MAHAUT

Parc
Animalier

Les
MAMELLES

Cascade aux
ECREVISSES

PETIT
BOURG

PETIT
HAVRE

MOUCHOIR
CARRE

Pointe
CANOT

Pointe MALENDURE

768m

716m

Maison de
la forêt

Saut de la
LEZARDE

Fl.(2) R (10s) 26M
PP
Iso (4s) 8M

Ilet PIGEON

Réserve Marine

PIGEON

PETIT CUL-DE-SAC MARIN

Pointe LEZARDE

BOUILLANTE

Piton de
BOUILLANTE

GOYAVE

Les TROIS TORTUES

1088m

Traces

Rivière à GOYAVES

PARC NATUREL

Q.(9) W
(15s) 9M

Mont
SANS TOUCHER

SAINTE
MARIE

Anse à la
BARQUE

Fl.W.R.G. (6s)
5-8M

MARIGOT

1354m

LA
SOUFRIERE

CAPESTERRE
BELLE-EAU

Pointe de la
CAPESTERRE

VIEUX
HABITANTS

MATOUBA

Fumerolles

1467m

Chutes du
CARBET

BAILLIF

Distillerie
Boulogne

1397m

St-CLAUDE

Grand
Etang

SAINT
SAUVEUR

Pointe des PERES

GOURBEYRE

Pointe des BANANIERS

BASSE-TERRE

★ Fort DELGRES
Monts
CARAOEBES

Roches
Gravées

TROIS RIVIERES

Marina de
RIVIERE SENS

698m

279°

Pointe St-JACQUES

Pointe du VIEUX FORT

Fl.(2+1) W
(15s) 22M

VIEUX FORT

Iso brw (4s) W.R.G.
7-10M

CANAL DES SAINTES

293m

319m

TERRE DE HAUT

TERRE DE BAS

LES SAINTES

0   5M

0   10km

61°50'   61°45'   61°40'   61°35'   61°30'   61°25'

Guadeloupe

Area 1715 sq km
Highest point La Soufrière on
    Basse Terre 1467m
Population 420,000
Main town (Préfecture) Basse Terre (pop.
    14,000), Pointe-à-Pitre (pop. 30,000)
Language French and Créole (spoken by
    most people)
Currency Euro
Political status French overseas
    department (DOM)
Distances to nearby islands Les Saintes,
    Dominica 20M, Antigua 40M

History

The island was occupied by the
Arawaks about two thousand years ago,
and then by the Caribs. The latter
called Guadeloupe (pronounced Gwa-
d'loop) Karukera, which means 'island
of lovely waters'. Columbus discovered
it on 4 November 1493 and named it
after a Spanish monastery, Our Lady of
Guadalupa de Estramadura. It was
colonised in 1635 by Duplessis
d'Ossonville and Lienard d'Olive,
Frenchmen from St Christopher, or St
Kitts as everyone now calls it. Less well
governed than Martinique, Guadeloupe
was taken over by the English in 1759.

The first town founded by the French,
Basse Terre, had meanwhile prospered.
But the English founded a second,
Pointe-à-Pitre, which takes its name
from a Dutchman called Peter, hence
Peter's Point. The Treaty of Paris of
1763 returned Guadeloupe to the
French, only for it to be taken away
again by the English in 1794 and then
immediately recaptured by the
revolutionary commissar of the new
Republic, Victor Hugues. In order to
enforce the revolutionary government's
decrees and the abolition of slavery, he
organised the 'Terror' against the
planters and aristocrats. In 1802,
Napoleon Bonaparte re-instituted
slavery, which was not finally abolished
until 1848. With Bonaparte's rise to
power some of the exiled planters
returned to the island, but
Guadeloupe's Creoles never regained
their former power. That had an effect
on land ownership, whereby the
majority of agricultural holdings were
bought and consolidated by large
companies from metropolitan France.

A department of France since 1946, the
economy of Guadeloupe is tightly tied
to the metropolitan power, most
significantly in terms of the size of the
governmental machine and the large
number of public sector employees it

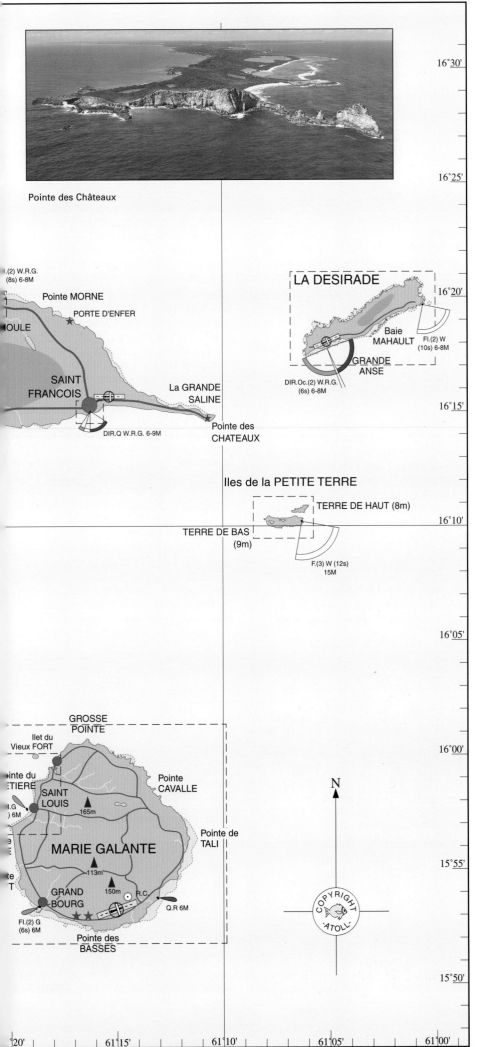

Pointe des Châteaux

has created. Guadeloupe's absorption into France proper as one of the departments sending deputies to the French national assembly has some undoubted economic advantages, but has not resolved all of Guadeloupe's problems. Agriculture (mainly bananas and sugar) is relatively speaking a declining industry, but even so it remains economically important thanks to international demand and farm support policies. That said, after direct subsidies from France, tourism is now the island's economic mainstay.

The population is composed mainly of black or mixed race Guadeloupians. There are still some 20,000 Indians, descendants of 19th century immigrants whose traditions and religion are quite different. A smaller minority is the 'country' or 'native whites', decimated by Victor Hugues, but reinforced subsequently by *békés* from Martinique. There are also some 3000 civil servants and private citizens from mainland France and, finally, some businessmen from Syria and the Lebanon.

Tourism

Where to stay and what to see

Guadeloupe, nicknamed the Emerald Isle, is actually two islands separated by a narrow seawater channel, the Rivière Salée. The ensemble looks rather like a butterfly with its wings spread over the emerald sea under the blue sky. The prosaic geographical truth is one of great contrast. Grande Terre (which means Big Land but in fact is the lower of the two islands) is a large, rolling limestone plateau. Basse Terre (meaning Low Land) is in fact mainly a high, forest-covered, mountainous and volcanic massif. The whole is connected by an excellent and well-maintained road network, which ensures easy access to everywhere worth seeing.

Guadeloupe's varied terrain offers a wide choice of leisure pursuits: the forests and waterfalls of the massif for hill walking, the beaches and lagoons for lounging around or swimming, and to top it all, just a few short tacks away are the miniature delights of the smaller islands, each preserving its own unique character.

There's a huge range of top end hotels in Guadeloupe, mostly in Grande Terre and clustered near the beaches at Gosier and the superb lagoon of St François. On Basse Terre you'll find simpler places and lots of holiday cottages for rent.

The range of restaurants is as varied as everything else. The happy marriage between Antillean specialties, French cuisine and Indian dishes, helped by

Fort Napoléon

easy access to good ingredients, makes Guadeloupe, like Martinique, one of the best places in the Antilles for food.

Around Pointe-à-Pitre, Gosiers and St François restaurants are pretty touristy, though you'll still find good French and local cuisine at affordable prices. In the less visited areas (Grand Terre's windward coast, Grand Cul-de-Sac Marin, and Basse Terre's leeward coast) there are lots of restaurants with local Creole cuisine, in general first class and worth visiting if you make a tour.

Grande Terre

Grande Terre is a limestone island almost entirely given over to farming, its terrain broken into hills and valleys only in the Grands Fonds. Life is focussed on the capital economic and main port, Pointe-à-Pitre. Much of the coast has fine beaches protected by offshore reefs.

Below Pointe des Châteaux, Grande Terre
Bottom left Windsurfing in the lagoon at St François
Bottom right The bay in the Port d'Enfer

Pointe-à-Pitre

Pointe-à-Pitre is a sub-prefecture and has a population of about 30,000. However, if you add in the suburbs and satellite townships, that rises to about 100,000 folk who call themselves 'Pointois' (pronounced Point-wah). Despite the often stifling heat and the noisy traffic jams, which pollute Pointe-à-Pitre, the old town still has some fine places of interest tucked away, their 19th century colonial architecture well worth a visit. The best welcome and the most life can be found around the main street, rue Frébault and the St Antoine market. In the many small shops, which set up stalls on the pavement, you'll find everything there is in the Antilles in the way of fruit, vegetables and spices.

The old port area of the Darse (dock or dockyard) has souvenir sellers who stroll around selling locally made crafts, whilst local fishing boats sell their catch on the quayside. Around the Darse are plenty of shops of all kinds and in the Saint-John-Perse Centre you'll find arcades and restaurants aimed at the passengers off the cruise ships. The Place de la Victoire, which debouches onto the Darse, is one of the town's few tree-lined areas with benches that offer somewhere quiet and cool to sit. The St Peter and St Paul basilica, built in 1847 to replace the church destroyed in 1843 by an earthquake, has an amazing metal reinforcing structure designed to cope with any new quake.

The Saint-John-Perse Museum, which occupies a fine 19th century mansion, offers an example of a typical interior of the epoch in which it was built, as well as housing an exhibition of objects and manuscripts relating to the Nobel Prize for literature. Around the outskirts

there's now a zone of ugly, modern dormitory estates, which add nothing to the town's appeal.

Around Grande Terre island

The S coast road goes through the village of Gosier and its sandy islet (very popular at weekends) which faces many luxury hotels with their groomed beaches. When Pointe-a-Pitre goes to sleep at nightfall, around here things come alive with restaurants and discos. The road carries on through the small town of Sainte Anne where, behind the shelter of the barrier reef, you'll find the Club Méditerranée de la Caravelle and a small fishing harbour. Further E the larger town of St François is also a fishing port, but rather busier. Thanks to the fine lagoon, for a long time now St François has had tourist development on a large scale with a marina, big hotels (including the Méridien), a golf course and an airstrip. Both town and tourist area have lots of restaurants serving local specialties and make an excellent pit stop before heading to Guadeloupe's E'most tip at Pointe des Châteaux, a great spur of steep cliffs jutting into the Atlantic swells.

Le Moule

This small town has slept life away on the windward coast since the time in the 18th century when it was the busiest port in Guadeloupe, with big cargo ships from France loading sugar products here. It makes you wonder at the skill and toughness of those old sailors, once you see the tight little natural harbour sheltering from the Atlantic behind dangerous coral reefs. Heading on N towards the Pointe de la Vigie, the austere windward coast is dotted with wild spots like the impressive Port d'Enfer where waves come roaring in making a noise like hell itself. At Pointe de la Vigie the high limestone plateau stops abruptly in tall cliffs, battered by the Atlantic, overlooking the sea. If you take one of the paths leading to the edge, there's a stunning view. The leeward coast around the Grand Cul-de-Sac Marin is quieter, the Grand Cul-de-Sac Marin itself being a vast park in which underwater flora and fauna are protected in a nature reserve.

Port Louis

This pretty fishing port, like the others facing the huge emerald expanse of the Grand Cul-de-Sac Marin with its scattering of reefs and cays, is still fairly untouched by the tourist onslaught.

Les Grands Fonds

There is a network of country roads that enable you to visit Grande Terre's interior, with its flat, wide green acres of sugar cane and the shady valleys of the Grands Fonds. This essentially agricultural part of the island is still inhabited by some 'Matignon whites', a noble-sounding nickname suggestive of the ancestry of these simple farmers who now mostly scratch a living. Some of their ancestors were indeed disinherited members of noble French families or aristocrats exiled after the 1789 French Revolution. A few surnames, now creolised, are the only echo of that aristocratic past.

Basse Terre

Basse Terre is called 'Guadeloupe proper' by its inhabitants, thus implying, if a bit oddly, that the twin island of Grande Terre is a mere dependency. The outlying foothills of the mountain range (whose higher slopes are heavily forested) are cultivated, being mainly banana plantations. There are numerous footpaths (called *traces* or tracks) running through the National Park, which take you to La Soufrière, the highest point of Guadeloupe, and many other sites such as the Chutes du Carbet (the Carbet Falls, the highest in the Caribbean)

Top left Suspension bridge, Rivière du Carbet
Top right Chute du Carbet (Carbet Falls)
Above left Parc des Roches Gravées, Trois Rivières
Above right Petroglyph (carved rock) in the Park
Below left Racoons in the zoo (Parc Animalier)

Around Basse Terre

Leaving Pointe-à-Pitre in the direction of Basse Terre you'll cross the Rivière Salée, a narrow arm of the sea fringed with mangroves.

Windward coast

Towards the S, the windward coast of Basse Terre is fronted by innumerable coral reefs behind which lie small fishing ports with banana plantations further inshore, places like Petit Bourg, Goyave and Sainte Marie where, as a memorial in a small square witnesses, Columbus landed. From the slopes above, flowing through the forests and fields inland, many rivers run out to the coast. From Saint Saveur a small, steep road leads to Grand Etang and on up to the Chutes du Carbet. The higher of these two falls is only accessible after a two to three hour hike through the forest, but the beauty of the place when you get there makes it worthwhile. Heading on S you'll arrive at Trois Rivières, a small port with a good view of Les Saintes from which there are regular ferry connections. Nearby there are the Roches Gravées, an archaeological park featuring petroglyphs of the Arawak Indians and a gorgeous botanical garden. Leaving Trois Rivières a minor road runs along the black sand beach of Grande Anse through the village of Vieux Fort. Lost at the extreme S tip of the island, this village has a superb view over the Canal des Saintes and as a bonus there is fine embroidery for sale.

Leeward coast

Basse Terre town

As in the 'good old colonial days' the Prefecture here dozes in its bureaucratic torpor. For all the town's long history, the gradual decline of commerce during the 19th century followed by natural disasters like the eruption of La Soufrière in 1976, mean that what life's left is restricted to a few shopping streets around the port. The latter is none too busy either, since most of the refrigerated fruit ships loading bananas use Pointe-à-Pitre. Apart from the government buildings, the town's architectural joys are confined to a few more or less old buildings, some of them rare and lovely colonial houses. The oldest building, Fort Delgrès (once called Fort St Charles) dating from 1643, is at the S entrance to the town. Along the sea front the covered market provides a brightly coloured tableau of produce from local market gardens up in the hills behind the town, grown by the descendants of the Indian immigrants (called the 'Zindiens' in patois). In these foothills of La Soufrière you'll find St Claude, the coolest – and wettest – hill station in Basse Terre. Above St Claude the road leads to the car park at Savane à Mulets from where a footpath leads to the volcano's summit.

Leaving Basse Terre headed N on the coast road, you cross creek after creek of grey sand and find a succession of charming villages like Marigot or Bourg des Vieux Habitants, the name of the latter recalling the site of the first place occupied by the original colonists. There's an interesting Musée du Café (Coffee Museum) to visit here.

Further on fumaroles and geothermal installations signal your arrival in the aptly named settlement of Bouillante (Boiling!). In the Golfe de Malendure, don't forget to visit the 'Réserve Cousteau', a diving area around the Ilets Pigeon, either by diving yourself or going out in a glass-bottomed boat.

From Pointe Mahaut the scenic Route de la Traversée goes inland over the Col des Deux Mamelles and goes straight to Pointe-à-Pitre. The road goes through a nature park, where there's a collection of a vast number of huge trees, lianas and tree ferns where the last surviving species of Guadeloupe's fauna breed.

At the pass itself a view opens up over the whole island right to the limits of Grande Terre. The whole National Park is criss-crossed by numerous tracks which offer a fine variety of walks. If you choose to carry on N from Basse Terre along the leeward coast by the coast road, the next place you'll come to is the charming fishing village of

Rade de Pointe-à-Pitre from S

Deshaies, (pronounced Dez-hay), much enlivened by cruising yachts. A bit further N the coastal sand becomes white again and opens onto the wonderful beach of Grande Anse where you'll again be able to feel the ocean swell.

Running down the SW part of Grand Cul-de-Sac Marin, the road leads back to Pointe-à-Pitre through large villages surrounded by fields of sugar cane. Close to Sainte Rose the Domaine de St Séverin is one of the last distilleries on the island. On the outskirts of Pointe-à-Pitre the small township of Lamentin is an echo of the marine mammal the manatee ('lamantin' in modern French), which once thronged this coast.

Pilotage

Coast and anchorages

The geography of Guadeloupe has dictated the development of the sailing infrastructure. The main economic and tourist centres are on Grande Terre, the coasts of which are quite exposed and, other than the roadstead of the Pointe-à-Pitre, short of natural havens. The latter, at the head of an inlet, is off the main route between Guadeloupe and the islands N and S of it, Antigua and Martinique respectively. That said, the opening of the large Bas du Fort marina in 1978 and the concentration of relevant yachting services in the area was bound to attract both yachtsmen and charter companies. Even so, the marina is relatively remote, stuck at the end of the Petit Cul-de-Sac Marin, egress N being limited by the Rivière Salée.

The restrictions on the latter are:

- depths in general of 2·5–3·5m decreasing, because of a sill in the N part, to 1·7–2m depending on the tide.

- two road bridges which only open once a day very early in the morning.

The passage is marked throughout with lit buoys simplifying pilotage.

Taken together this means that deeper draught boats like large charter boats must either avoid Pointe-à-Pitre altogether or make a round trip Les Saintes–Pointe-à-Pitre–Les Saintes, a 50M detour from the usual N S route between the islands. This state of affairs makes for a straight choice of routes:

- either just cruise down the leeward coast of Basse Terre, bypassing Pointe-à-Pitre

- or weave through the islands of this small archipelago and its various havens, including Pointe-à-Pitre as a stop on your way.

Approaching Pointe-à-Pitre

Petit Cul-de-Sac Marin

Coming from the S you'll pass Pointe Capesterre, then the village of Sainte Marie, avoiding the reefs pushing out a mile from the shore and filling all the NNW part of the Petit Cul-de-Sac, where many boats have ended their days.

The anchorage at Sainte Marie, known as Columbus' landing place, is only a lee behind offlying reefs and little used save by local fishermen. The pass through the reefs is not buoyed and requires experience.

Caution About 3·5M further N watch out for Dupont Reef on which there is what's left of an old wreck, which you leave to port on the way to Pointe-à-Pitre. W of Dupont Reef there's a buoyed channel leading into the small haven of Goyave, sheltered behind its offshore reef. This shallow harbour (1·5–1·8m) is used mainly by local boats and locally based motor boats.

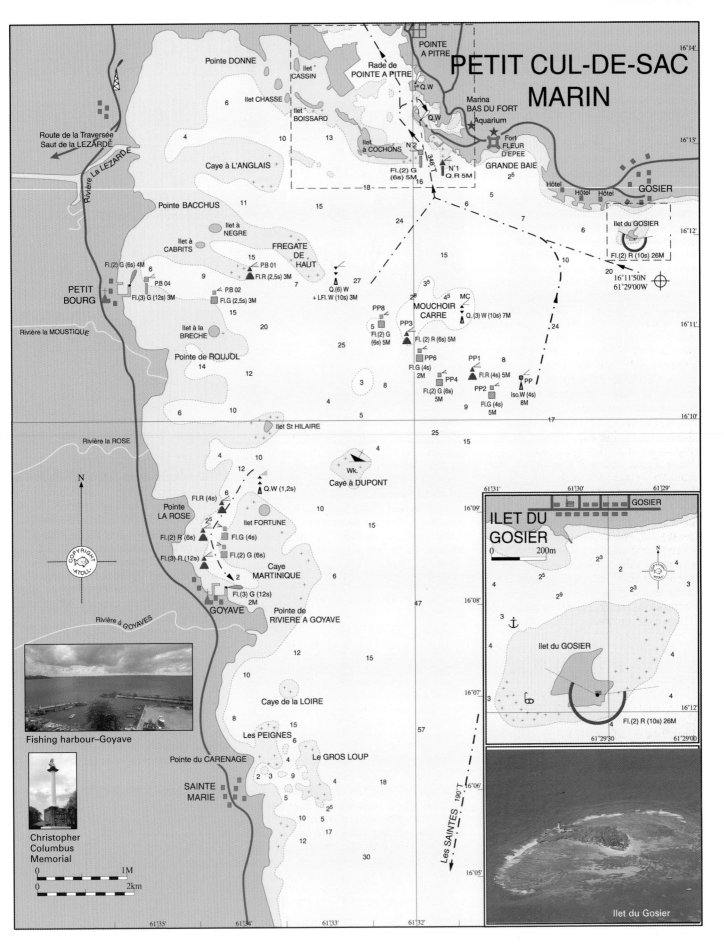

PETIT CUL-DE-SAC MARIN

Pointe DONNE

Ilet CASSIN

Ilet CHASSE

Rade de POINTE A PITRE

POINTE A PITRE

Q.W

Marina BAS DU FORT
Aquarium

Ilet BOISSARD

Route de la Traversée
Saut de la LEZARDE

6

Q.W

Fort FLEUR D'EPEE

Ilet à COCHONS

N'2

348'T

N'1

GRANDE BAIE

Hôtel

GOSIER

Rivière La LEZARDE

4

10

13

Caye à L'ANGLAIS

Fl.(2) G (6s) 5M

Q.R 5M

16

2⁵

Hôtel Hôtel Hôtel

Ilet du GOSIER

Pointe BACCHUS

11

15

18

24

5

6

7

6

Fl.(2) R (10s) 26M

Ilet à NEGRE

15

15

10

20

16°11'50N
61°29'00W

Ilet à CABRITS

FREGATE DE HAUT

Fl.(2) G (6s) 4M

15

P.B 01

Fl.R (2,5s) 3M

27

3⁵

4⁵ MC

24

P.B 04

9

7

Q.(6) W
+ L.Fl. W (10s) 3M

2⁸

MOUCHOIR CARRE

Q. (3) W (10s) 7M

PETIT BOURG

P.B 02

Fl.G (2,5s) 3M

PP8

5

Fl.(2) G (6s) 5M

PP3

Fl.(2) R (6s) 5M

PP1

8

Fl.(3) G (12s) 3M

15

Rivière la MOUSTIQUE

Ilet à la BRECHE

20

PP6

Fl.G (4s) 2M

PP4

Fl.R (4s) 5M

PP

Iso.W (4s) 8M

Pointe de ROUJOL

14

25

Fl.(2) G (6s) 5M

PP2

9

12

3

8

Fl.G (4s) 5M

6

10

4

5

17

16°10'

Ilet St HILAIRE

25

15

Rivière la ROSE

4

10

4

Wk.

4

N

12

Q.W (1,2s)

Caye à DUPONT

16°09'

ILET DU GOSIER

GOSIER

Fl.R (4s)

6

10

2³

2

4

Pointe LA ROSE

2⁵

Ilet FORTUNE

15

2⁵

2³

3

Fl.(2) R (6s)

Fl.G (4s)

0   200m

2⁹

4

Fl.(3) R (12s)

Fl.(2) G (6s)

Caye MARTINIQUE

6

16°08'

3

N

Rivière à GOYAVE

2

Fl.(3) G (12s) 2M

GOYAVE

Pointe de RIVIERE A GOYAVE

47

Ilet du GOSIER

4

16°07'

12

15

4

10

Caye de la LOIRE

Fl.(2) R (10s) 26M

16°12'

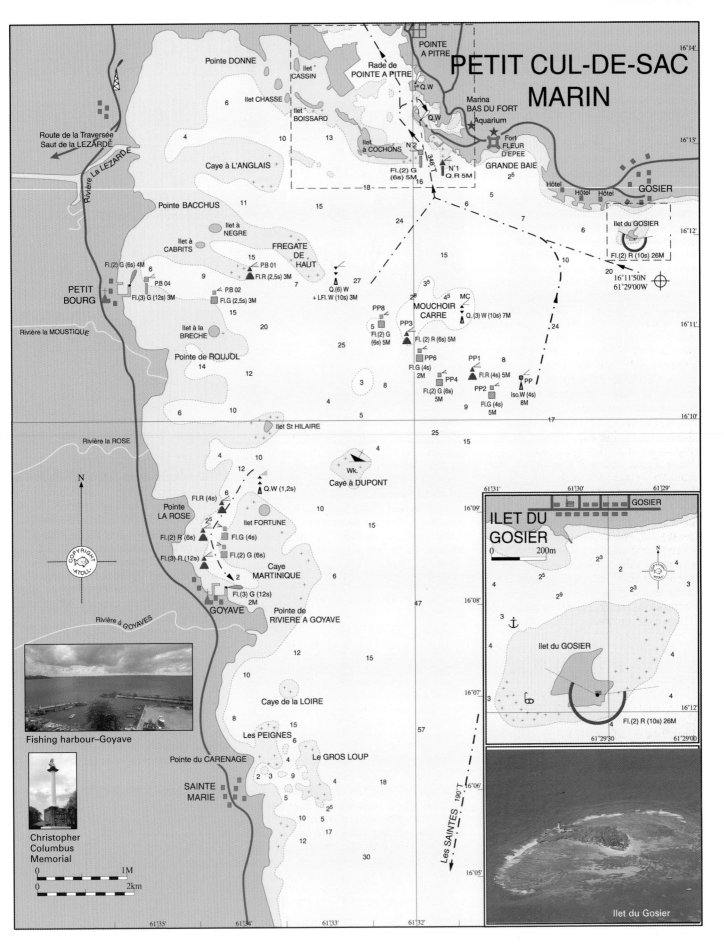
Fishing harbour–Goyave

8

15

57

Les PEIGNES

6

Le GROS LOUP

Pointe du CARENAGE

4

18

SAINTE MARIE

2 3   9

2⁵

190'T

16°06'

Christopher Columbus Memorial

0   1M

0   2km

10

5

17

12

30

16°05'

Ilet du Gosier

Despite the green light on the outer mole end and the lit buoys of the approach channel, only try a night entry if you've been here before. Some local sailing yachts also find quite a well protected anchorage outside the port behind the huge Caye Martinique in depths of 2–2·5m.

Further N, W of Mouchoir Carré two buoys mark the approach to the fishing harbour of Petit Bourg. Here too there are draft limitations restricting access to small craft. The anchorage outside is little protected from swell and chop. Coming to Pointe-à-Pitre from the S, the obvious route is blocked by the Mouchoir Carré, the shoals of which have less than 3m over them and break in a heavy swell. You should turn them on the E side leaving the landfall buoy (PP, Iso.4s8M, RW) to port, followed also to port by the E cardinal (Q(3)10s7M) E of Mouchoir Carré, before heading directly towards the entrance to the channel into the harbour. On this track you will leave Ilet Gosier and its light 1M NE of you.

Pointe-à-Pitre Harbour

For a night entry, the leading lights (348°T) are hard to see, being rather lost among the town lights. The floodlights for the tennis courts on the Presqu'île Monroux, on the other hand, make a good landmark. After following the buoyed, lit channel as far as buoy No.5 (Fl(2)R.25s), a secondary buoyed, lit channel opens up to starboard leading to the Bas du Fort Marina. Be sure to give the shoal ground around Presqu'île Monroux a good offing at the same time staying clear of the reef off Pointe Fouillole marked by a S cardinal (Q(6)+LFl.15s).

Bas du Fort Marina

The Port de Plaisance was created by dredging two basins out of the sand. A natural barrier closes off the S part resulting in a truly artificial lagoon, the Lagon Bleu. There are now over 1000 berths, on 8 pontoons in the N basin and 3 pontoons in the S basin of the Lagon Bleu. The E part of the Lagon

Top Bas du Fort Marina
Above Bas du Fort Marina basin
Below Rade de Pointe-à-Pitre, the Darse and the Carénage

Bleu, with depths of around 2m, is surrounded by villas and also has pontoons partly taken up by charter companies. It is forbidden to anchor in the Lagon Bleu. The capitainerie of the marina (VHF 9/16), customs and immigration and the fuel dock are at the W end of the main quay. The main quay, also the arrivals dock, can take super-yachts of up to 38m loa and 4m draft alongside. The pontoon running N of this quay has the visitors' berths.

Ashore A technical services area ('zone technique'), including both numerous

specialists and a boatyard, lies E and N of the basin. On the road to Pointe-à-Pitre, in the area called the Carénage, there are three other boatyards and other specialists completing Pointe-à-Pitre's services. A host of suppliers of various kinds can also be found on the other side of the harbour in the Jarry Industrial Zone.

This concentration of yachting services, with provisioning in the marina supermarket as well as those at Gosier and Pointe-à-Pitre itself, make Bas du Fort Marina one of the best-equipped stops around for a yacht. On the quay and in elegant small shopping arcades you'll find several shops, a laundry, minimarket, etc. Numerous restaurants offer varied menus and specialties over

RADE DE POINTE A PITRE

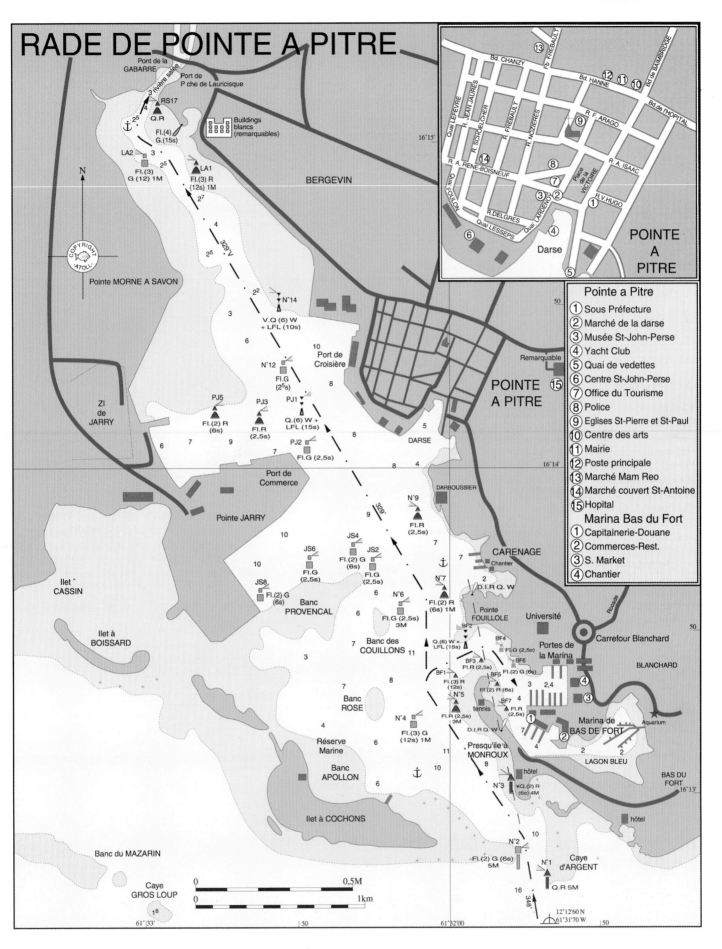

Pont de la GABARRE
Port de P che de Lauricisque
3 rivière salée
RS17
Q.R
Fl.(4) G.(15s)
2⁵
LA2 3
Fl.(3) G (12) 1M 2⁵
LA1
Fl.(3) R (12s) 1M
2⁷
329°V
2⁵ 4

Buildings blancs (remarquables)

BERGEVIN

N

Pointe MORNE A SAVON

ZI de JARRY

3
6
2² N°14
V.Q (6) W + LFL (10s)
10
N°12 Port de Croisière
Fl.G (2⁵s)
8
PJ5 PJ3 PJ1
Fl.(2) R (6s) Fl.R (2,5s) Q.(6) W + LFL (15s)
7 9 PJ2
7 Fl.G (2,5s)
Port de Commerce
8
8 4
DARSE

Pointe JARRY

10 N°9 DARBOUSSIER
9 329° Fl.R (2,5s)
10 JS4
JS6 Fl.(2) G (6s) JS2 CARENAGE
Fl.G (2,5s) Fl.G (2,5s) 7 Chantier
JS8 6 N°7 2 D.I.R Q. W
Fl.(2) G (6s) N°6 Fl.(2) R (6s) 1M Pointe FOUILLOLE
Banc PROVENCAL 6 Fl.G (2,5s) 3M BF2 Université
Banc des COUILLONS 11 Q.(6) W + LFL (15s) BF4 Portes de la Marina
3 BF3 Fl.G (2,5s) BLANCHARD
BF1 Fl.(2) R (6s) BF6
7 8 Fl.(3) R (12s) BF5 Fl.(2) G (6s) 3 2,4
Banc ROSE N°5 Fl.(2) R (6s) Marina de BAS DE FORT
4 N°4 Fl.R (2,5s) 3M tennis Fl.R (2,5s) Aquarium
Fl.(3) G (12s) 1M D.I.R Q W LAGON BLEU
6 Réserve Marine 11 Presqu'île à MONROUX BAS DU FORT
Banc APOLLON 10 8 hôtel
N°3 VQ.(2) R (6s) 4M
Ilet à COCHONS hôtel

Ilet CASSIN
Ilet à BOISSARD

Banc du MAZARIN

Caye GROS LOUP

N°2
Fl.(2) G (6s) 5M N°1 Caye d'ARGENT
16 Q.R 5M
348°

0   0,5M
0   1km

1⁸
61°33' 50 61°32'00 50
16°15'
16°14'
16°13'
12°12'60 N
61°31'70 W

POINTE A PITRE (inset)

Bd. CHANZY
Fb FREBAULT
Bd de BAIMBRIDGE
13
Bd. HANNE
12 11 10
Quai LEFEVRE
R. JEAN JAURES
R. SCHŒLCHER
R. FREBAULT
R. NOZIERES
R. F. ARAGO
Bd. de l'HOPITAL
9
R. A. RENE-BOISNEUF
8
Place de la VICTOIRE
R. A. ISAAC
14 7
R.DELGRES 3 1 R.V.HUGO
Quai LESSEPS Quai LARDENOY
6 4
Darse 5

POINTE A PITRE

POINTE A PITRE Remarquable

15

Pointe a Pitre

1 Sous Préfecture
2 Marché de la darse
3 Musée St-John-Perse
4 Yacht Club
5 Quai de vedettes
6 Centre St-John-Perse
7 Office du Tourisme
8 Police
9 Eglises St-Pierre et St-Paul
10 Centre des arts
11 Mairie
12 Poste principale
13 Marché Mam Reo
14 Marché couvert St-Antoine
15 Hopital

Marina Bas du Fort

1 Capitainerie-Douane
2 Commerces-Rest.
3 S. Market
4 Chantier

50
Carrefour Blanchard
Ricade

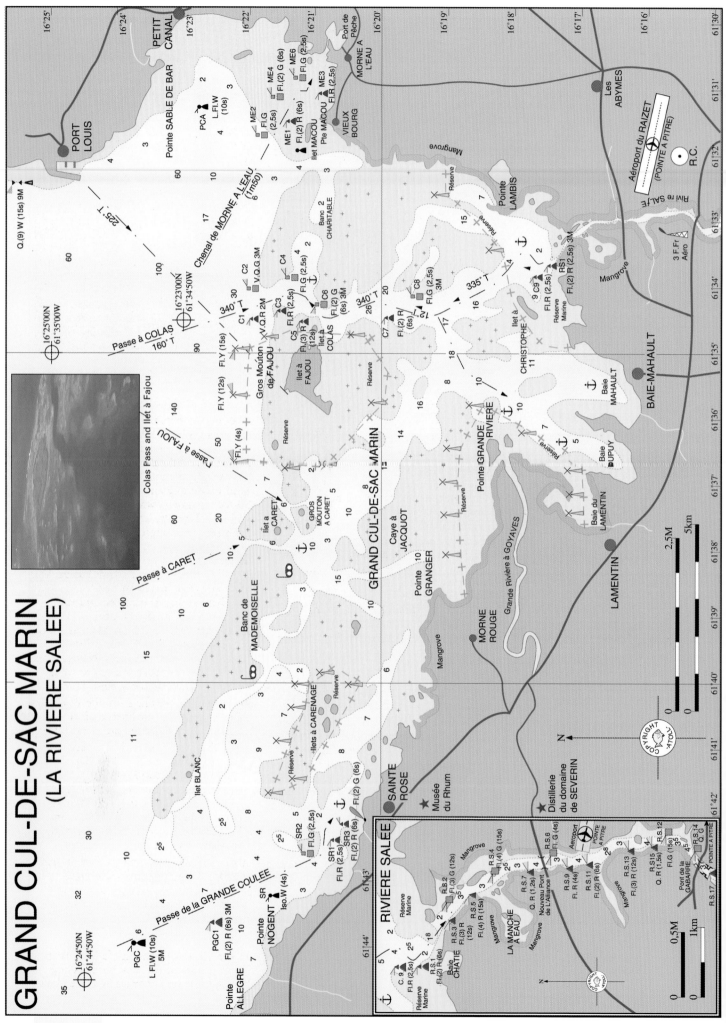

GRAND CUL-DE-SAC MARIN
(LA RIVIERE SALEE)

Colas Pass and Ilet à Fajou

Above La Rivière Salée – Pont de la Gabarre
Right Passe à Caret

the whole price range. Until quite late in the evening they are very busy with yachties and locals, giving the whole area around the marina a great atmosphere. For those who prefer an open anchorage, and no charges, there are three authorised spots in the harbour basin managed by the Port Authority (Port Autonome):

• in the Carénage opposite the big dock
• N of Ilet à Cochons, furthest from everything but with cleaner water. This anchorage is close to the boundary of the Marine Reserve. On the islet there's a simple beach restaurant open at the weekends
• W of the Darse, very close to the town centre and accessible by tender, you can moor in complete security at the Yacht Club.

Ashore Pointe-à-Pitre town has everything you'll need for provisioning, especially in the covered market at the head of the Darse.

Rivière Salée

Note The opening of the Gabarre Bridge (Pont de la Gabarre) controls access to the S end of the Rivière Salée.

This road bridge has now been supplemented by a second bridge (Pont de l'Alliance) just N of the airport which in turn controls access coming from the N. The result is a pattern of alternate openings from Monday to Saturday in high season:

Pont de la Gabarre: 0500
Pont de l'Alliance: 0430–0530

You should be waiting, navigation lights on, N or S of the relevant bridge 15 minutes before it is due to open. The installation of the lit buoys in the Rivière Salée makes passages during these partly dark, very early hours much easier.

Caution The direction of buoyage in Pointe-à-Pitre harbour (Rade de Pointe-à-Pitre) continues as far as the Pont de la Gabarre (red to starboard). Once beyond the bridge (N of it) the

direction changes (green to starboard). Mooring buoys have been installed close to the bridges. Most boats waiting for the bridges moor up for the night nearby in order to avoid moving after dark, especially for the stage from Grand Cul-de-Sac to the Pont de l'Alliance. The S to N passage from Bas de Fort Marina to reach Pont de la Gabarre is the easiest part because of the lit buoyage in the harbour. You should allow half an hour. The course from just outside the marina past Point Morne à Savon to the entry to the narrow channel up to Pont de la Gabarre is 329°T. Be careful as you come to the entrance of the channel because it is narrow, although the shoals are marked by lit buoys. To pass the Pont de la Gabarre, beware of the current that can carry you against the bridge piles, especially if you're in a multihull. Once past the bridge leave the little islet to starboard to stay in the main channel. Depths are >3·5m and don't go below 3m until the Pont de l'Alliance. Once closing Grand Cul-de-Sac the channel shoals here and there to 2·5m. All around there are branches leading off the main channel, getting lost in the mangroves and forming many small islets and enclosed lagoons like the Manche à Eau which you can explore by tender. Leaving the Rivière Salée, the trickiest bit comes as you approach buoy RS1 and between that buoy and the next. The mud bottom is of uncertain depth and, while seldom more than 1·7m, is at best 2m deep depending on tide and whether you've picked the best line. It follows that getting the tide right is important if you draw more than 1·5m. In theory there's a tide gauge close to the Pont de l'Alliance.

Caution There is a speed limit of 5 knots once in the Rivière Salée, though local boats treat it with scant respect.

Grand Cul-de-Sac Marin

Passe à Colas (Colas Pass)

The buoyed channel for going through the Grand Cul-de-Sac and getting to open sea via the Colas Pass is not particularly difficult (see plan). Conversely, coming from seaward you need to identify and approach the first buoys accurately, which requires good visibility. If you're having trouble, you can make your approach via Port Louis then head for the channel entry by lining up the W coast of Ilet Fajou on 225°T. The Caret and Fajou Passes, W of Ilet Fajou, are narrow and unbeaconed but much used by local boats and requiring real local knowledge. There are lots of anchorages in the E part of the Grand Cul-de-Sac in the lee of reefs and islets. Navigate by eyeball and, for those unused to coral waters, in good visibility only.

• on the route leading from the Passe à Colas there's an anchorage off the channel S of C6 starboard hand buoy
• just W of the Rivière Salée, once you're past the reefs off the Ilet Christophe, you will reach the anchorages in Baie Dupuy and Baie Mahaut. These are two good havens close to the villages of Lamentin and Baie Mahaut and to the mouth of the Rivière à Goyave.

It's possible to take your tender up this river for several kilometres, passing through a world where pasture-land alternates with thick, impenetrable Amazonian jungle.

Port Louis

In the NE of Grand Cul-de-Sac, Port Louis is a small and charming fishing harbour but very shoal. There are plans

Port Louis harbour

to dredge it and install a reception dock for yachts. Until these developments take place, if there isn't too much swell you can anchor offshore NW of the sea wall and clear of the shoals along the coast.

Ashore The port with its numerous colourful fishing boats is very Guadeloupian. Elegant lamp-posts line the quays, which are often enlivened by the sale of freshly landed fish. The small settlement also has several charming verandahed buildings. The shops are adequate for provisioning, especially with fresh fish and shellfish from the harbour. Fresh seafood also features in the many and varied local restaurants round the harbour or in town.

Vieux Bourg

Leading E'wards near the N end of the Colas Pass, the Morne à l'Eau channel leads to the small fishing port of Vieux Bourg. It's buoyed and lit but suitable only for shoal drafters (<1.5m) and fishing boats.

Passe de la Grande Coulée (Sainte Rose)

In the far NW of the Grand Cul-de-Sac Marin there's a buoyed passage, the Passe de la Grande Coulée, which leads to Sainte Rose. The approach is easy thanks to the PGC fairway buoy (LFl.10s5M RW). Note that the end of the channel is quite narrow and winding and should be used with care. Anchor close to the last channel buoys. The sides of the channel are very foul.

Ashore Sainte Rose is a simple village not much affected by tourism although real estate development is beginning

given the proximity of Pointe-à-Pitre. There are some excellent local restaurants with fair prices. Re-provisioning can be done in the village shops. There's no buoyed inner channel connecting Sainte Rose with the S of Ilet Fajou, though the locals have their own known short cuts.

Note Several areas are buoyed with yellow buoys marking the limits of marine reserves. Underwater hunting is forbidden. The underwater world is marvellous precisely because it's protected.

From Pointe-à-Pitre to the Pointe des Châteaux

Ilet Gosier

Leaving Pointe-à-Pitre Harbour head E for 3M towards Ilet de Gosier. A large coral reef surrounds the island on all sides and shelters an anchorage with 2–3m over sand, good holding. This is a safe anchorage, suitable for overnight. Although it can be both breezy and a little rolly the surroundings are lovely. During the weekends it's popular with Pointois from the town.

For the most part the island is covered in handsome clumps of greenery set in white sand. At the SE tip the light (Fl(2)R.10s26M) helps a night approach to Pointe-à-Pitre harbour from seaward.

On the coast the village of Gosier, with its round church bell tower, overlooks the anchorage. There's a pontoon for tying up dinghies.

Ashore Stretching along the beach as far as Grande Baie and Fort de Fleur d'Epée are numerous upmarket hotels and restaurants. In the village you'll find several shops and a minimarket for basic provisions.

Petit Havre

Once round Pointe Caraïbe you'll find the small, natural harbour of Petit Havre.

Caution W of the pass an area of sand extraction by dredger has been marked by special purpose buoys, both lit and unlit.

Leave the reef around Ilet du Diamant to port and you'll find entry to the anchorage easy enough. The anchorage is relatively remote because the shore is little developed and it's quite well-sheltered between Le Diamant reefs and the Pointe de la Saline. When the wind is set in the SE it can be very rolly, even untenable.

In the NE part of the bay under Pointe du Petit Havre, shoal water prevents access by keelers but the inlet shelters several fishing boats. There's a small dock there for the fishing boats where they dry and repair their colourful nets.

Ashore There's a huge picnic area, very popular with the locals especially at the weekend, and there's a small lolo on the beach. In the inlet further E (Anse St Jacques) there's another restaurant where they serve a rather more extensive menu of local food on the terrace at beach level. If the weather is fair, you can reach it by tender; otherwise you can go by land.

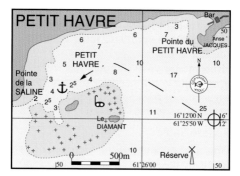

Sainte Anne

The small bay (Baie de la Caravelle), west of the village of Sainte Anne and partly protected by a barrier reef, is occupied by Club Med. You can get into it via a channel marked by Club Med buoys, though the buoyage isn't reliable. There's 3m both in the pass and in the middle of the bay with good holding in the anchorage area though there's not much room given the Club Med water sports and it is really only for medium and small craft. If the wind's SE'ly you'll feel the swell. The beach and coconut palms are superb although wholly taken up by Club Med patrons.

The large bay fronting Sainte Anne itself is sheltered by several reefs, though the W pass into it isn't marked and isn't recommended. It's made dangerous by a 1·5m shoal, Le Baril de

Below left The Grande Coulée Pass & Ste Rose
Below The coast at Gosier

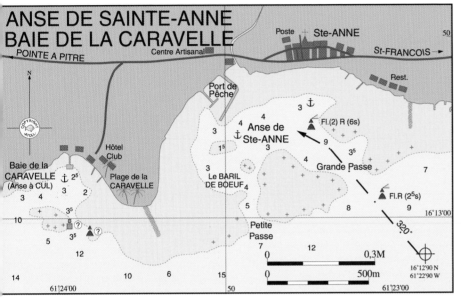

ANSE DE SAINTE-ANNE
BAIE DE LA CARAVELLE
POINTE A PITRE

Town anchorage

A short-term anchorage not generally much visited by yachts. The only reason to be here is because it's close to town and the fishing harbour. The unlit buoyage lets you get close to the dock in 2–3m. Despite the sector leading light, don't try a night entry.

E of the dock you'll see a huge shelter reserved for fishing boats, but it's shallow (<1m). Around the port and in town restaurants offer local specialties and above all seafood.

St François Marina

This marina, near the E extremity of Guadeloupe, is rather off the usual N/S cruising route. That said, from here it's easy to get to Marie Galante and Dominica and even round Pointe des Châteaux for Antigua, a route N'wards that's mostly disregarded. Nevertheless, by taking it you can gain 30M over those who head back round Basse Terre, but you'd better like sailing on a windward coast without any nearby shelter!

Coming from the W keep well S of the barrier reef and cays marked by a S cardinal buoy (Q(6)+LFl.15s3M). Leave this buoy to port before heading NNE towards the buoys marking the entrance to the pass. The line thereafter runs W to E through the first pair of channel markers (lit at night but night entry is absolutely out of the question if you're a newcomer). Access and egress in a strong E swell should also be avoided, especially if you draw >2m.

You can anchor out S of the Méridien Hotel in 2–3m, protected by the reef. In the basin there's generally 2·5m, but in the channel possibly less because of silting.

The marina has been built within a real estate and commercial development managed by the town council. The majority of pontoons are on the N bank (about 120 berths with water and electricity). The quay to the S is for ferries that ply between here and Désirade and the other islands. This is

Boeuf, which is hard to spot. The second, E pass is buoyed but although the buoys are lit, don't try a night entry. Even by day you need good visibility and not too much swell. Heading for the second buoy once you've found the first, and leaving both to starboard, you'll find the bottom varies between 4m and 10m. Anchor in the NE part, although there isn't much room. In the bay's NW there's a small, shallow harbour for fishing boats only. You can also anchor in the S of this small harbour and go ashore by tender.

Ashore The pretty village of Sainte Anne has a nicely laid out sea front with an

area of workshops at the W end. Along the seafront and in the main street there are several shops and minimarkets for provisioning. There are some small restaurants serving local food and seafood at reasonable prices.

From Sainte Anne to St François the coast has few attractions because the numerous reefs force you offshore.

St François

I have split the area into two to avoid confusion, as follows:

- the town anchorage with the fishing harbour
- the lagoon, marina and tourist area

Top Anse de Ste Anne from NW
Below The Club Med beach in Baie de la Caravelle
Right The marina and lagoon at St François from the NW

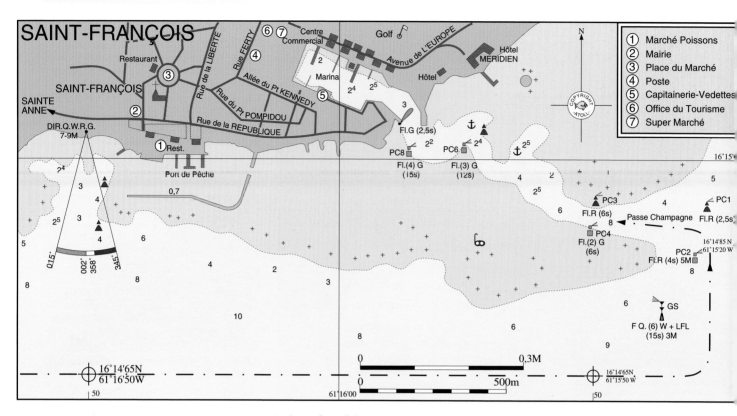

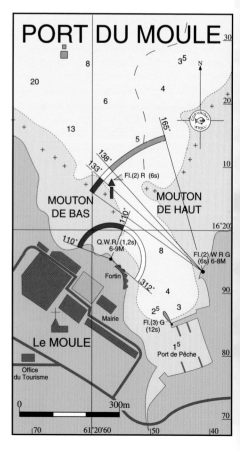

also where the capitainerie is. The fuel dock on the quay here is temporarily out of action because of problems with pollution. That means jerry-jugging from the nearest gas station if you need fuel.

Ashore Other than a few craftsmen working for the fishermen, there are no specialist services for yachts in the St François marina area. You can't complete clearance here either. If you want to clear, you could try to see if the mobile unit ('brigade volante') is at the nearby small airfield. Despite the lack of facilities, rather rough finish, and out of the way location out at the E tip of Guadeloupe, many yachtsmen like St François Marina. It has a welcoming and relaxed atmosphere as well as being pleasantly breezy thanks to the trades. More to the point, the municipality's marina charges are lower than any other on the island.

The marina also has the advantage of being in the middle of an extensive leisure development including a dive club, a golf course, tennis courts and the facilities of the Méridien Hotel. The last fronts a lovely lagoon and, close to the pontoons, there's a shopping centre with lots of restaurants and shops. In the middle of the town, only a few hundred metres away, there are supermarkets and a local market for all the provisions you might need. St François is also the place to catch ferries for Désirade and the other islands in this group and there's good walking out to Pointe des Châteaux and the beaches on the windward coast.

Pointe des Châteaux

Right out at the E end of Grande Terre, Pointe des Châteaux, craggy and battered by the Atlantic, is notable for the cross on its end, although, regrettably, there's no light to mark this E tip of the island.

From Pointe des Châteaux to Pointe de la Vigie

This inhospitable coast isn't much visited by yachts because, bar the harbour at Le Moule, there's no shelter. Worse, access to the latter is tricky and often dangerous if there's a big swell and even then the shelter on offer is only relative.

Le Moule

An old rum and sugar port, Le Moule has the prominent ruins of a fort, parts of which come right down to the waterfront. The port itself is hardly used by any but local boats since it isn't much protected when the trades are brisk. At such times the entrance is dangerous. Despite the sector light, entering at night is foolhardy in the extreme except for local fishermen. If necessity drives you here, and you have fair weather and good visibility, enter the pass on 135°T holding towards the starboard hand buoy. Indeed, you'll find there's often more swell off the port buoy but note that the buoyage isn't always to be relied on. The anchorage off the sea wall of the small, shallow (<1·5m) fishing port is often bouncy

from swell and chop. The town is pretty unspoilt because it's off the main tourist route. The restaurants are inexpensive and full of local colour. There are some shops for provisioning. It is off the beaten track and well worth a visit, but preferably by land!

Le Moule harbour

Trois Rivières harbour

From Pointe-à-Pitre to the Canal des Saintes (Saints Channel)

Leaving Pointe-à-Pitre, follow the coast of Basse Terre as far as Capesterre Point, as described above, until you get to the Saintes Channel.

Canal des Saintes (Saintes Channel) – Trois Rivières

Coming from the E once you have rounded Pointe de la Taste, there is the small harbour of Trois Rivières from where ferries for the Saintes leave. An average sized boat might plan a short stop here, anchoring in the lee of the seawall but being sure to leave clear access to the ferry dock. For a very brief call you may be able to get alongside the dock (if your boat is a shoal drafter) depending on the movement of ferries to and from the Saintes (be sure to enquire before you try).

Ashore Two restaurants can be found either side of the dock and some small shops provide basic provisions. Close to the small settlement there's a noteworthy archaeological site called the Roches Gravées (or petroglyphs).

Basse Terre's leeward coast

Once you're round Pointe de Vieux Fort with its conspicuous light, and level up with the fishing haven of Anse Dupuy where fishing boats and small local craft take shelter, the swell dies away but so does the wind, often

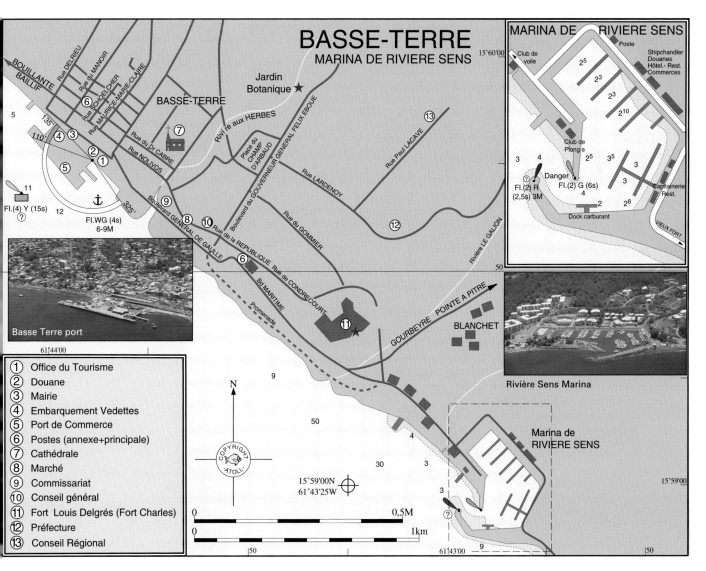

1 Office du Tourisme
2 Douane
3 Mairie
4 Embarquement Vedettes
5 Port de Commerce
6 Postes (annexe+principale)
7 Cathédrale
8 Marché
9 Commissariat
10 Conseil général
11 Fort Louis Delgrés (Fort Charles)
12 Préfecture
13 Conseil Régional

Basse Terre port

Rivière Sens Marina

leaving a flat calm sometimes broken by fierce gusts. Despite the cruising yacht traffic, this coast is noticeable for the almost complete absence of tourist and marina development making it, as a result relatively unspoilt. Thankful for that, one could still wish for a discreet marina here and there to make life easier for yachts on passage between the S and the N of the Lesser Antilles. The building and extension of the Rivière Sens Marina is in fact the only such development undertaken on this coast in some thirty years. Sadly the initiative hasn't been followed up by any more such projects.

Rivière Sens Marina

Before you get to Basse Terre and the famous Fort Delgrès lying at the foot of the imposing massif of the Carib Mountains and the volcano of La Soufrière, you reach Rivière Sens Marina. It's possible to anchor outside, S of the sea wall, but it's inevitably rolly. The entrance has lights either side and the channel between them did have 3–3·5m. However, after Hurricane Lenny (Nov '99) the outer end of the seaward mole was swept away and several large chunks of it fell into the channel reducing depths to 2–2·3m depending on the tide. At the same time the red light on the end of the outer mole was also destroyed and plans both to dredge the channel and replace the light have yet to be acted on. The result is that the entrance is dangerous for deeper draft yachts and for any craft at night.

Once inside there's about 3m off the arrivals dock, but the bottom shoals towards the head of the basin. The marina is small and pretty and has about 350 berths on several pontoons. The first pontoon you come to, in front of the capitainerie, is reserved for visitors (about 30 berths depending on traffic). The fuel dock is also on this pontoon.

Ashore On the quayside near the capitainerie are bar-restaurants and a grocery shop for basic provisions. The small yacht club offers various kinds of help to boats on passage. On the NE of the dock, on the far side of the road, you'll find a shopping centre with a pharmacy, minimarket, car hire agency, bar-restaurant and a small chandlery. To complete formalities, you'll find the customs office here too, though it's manned by a mobile unit, so temporary closures are always possible. On the NW quay you'll find some lively diving and sailing clubs. The Rivière Sens Marina is only 2km from Basse Terre town. You can get there either by road or the pleasant walkway along the shore. This is the place to leave your boat for an exploration of nearby La Soufrière and its surroundings.

Basse Terre

Once a major banana shipment port, there's still a big quay to receive fruit ships in the commercial harbour. However, it isn't very busy since these ships now mainly use Pointe-à-Pitre. There are two small basins inside the main quay N and S, where smaller ships can dock. Ferries to the Les Saintes use the N basin. The commercial harbour isn't much used by yachts because depths are considerable quite close in and you have to veer a lot of cable. More to the point, tying up one's tender on the main docks is none too easy.

Caution Watch out for the unlit mooring buoy for ships about 200m W of the dock.

Ashore A brief stop is fine for visiting Basse Terre, a peaceful, airy town where provisioning is easy thanks to lots of good shops, well-stocked supermarkets and lively vegetable and fish markets. Customs are close to the tourist office near the port. On the other hand there are few services specifically for yachts.

From Basse Terre to Deshaies

Anse à la Barque

6M beyond Basse Terre there's a good, pretty anchorage fringed with coconut palms at Anse à la Barque, in addition Deshaies is the best natural haven on the leeward coast. There's no danger in the approaches and a night entry is made easy by the light on the N point and a second, sector light on the beach; though the usefulness of both depends on whether they're working! There's a dock close to the light at the bay head. The whole area is full of local boats on moorings, so you have to anchor in 7-10m a bit further to seaward.

Caution There are shoals off the two points enclosing the bay and along the shores.

The last problem for this otherwise bucolic and tranquil anchorage is the noise from the traffic along the road running round the shore.

Les Trois Tortues

Half a mile N, on either side of the Pointe des Trois Tortues there are anchorages in two small inlets. The S one, called Petite Anse, is the better sheltered.

Ashore Along the beach the buildings house a hotel, its swimming pool and restaurant. In the N bay there's another restaurant with a pretty terrace over the water with a menu of Creole specialities.

Bouillante

Beyond lies Anse de Bouillante, easily recognized by its plumes of steam, where you can anchor in the large bay. The anchorage is often disturbed by swell and the village is of scant interest, save for a few shops and the local restaurants.

Ilets Pigeon (or Ilets à Goyave)

2M further N, Ilets Pigeon or Goyave are a divers' paradise. They are also a marine reserve (called the Réserve Cousteau) where fishing and underwater hunting are forbidden – so look but don't touch.

Anchoring is forbidden. There are precious few yellow mooring buoys for yachts (if they're not already taken), the other buoys (white and blue) are strictly reserved for dive club boats. The shallowest area, where the fine coral garden is to be found, is 7–8m so for a simple snorkelling outing you'd better have good lungs!

Close to the coast the best anchorage is under the Pointe Malendure NW of the dock for the tripper boats and of the small, rocky headland called Rocher de Malendure. Despite the lee of Pointe Malendure, swell can make this anchorage very rolly and getting off a tender at the dock or on the beach is an acrobatic business.

Ashore Behind the beach edged with coconut palms and as far as the road, the whole area is taken up by buildings housing dive clubs, the tourist office, ticket booths for glass-bottomed boat rides, snack bars and beach restaurants for the numerous tourists who've come to admire the coral.

On the Rocher de Malendure a restaurant terrace offers a marvellous view out over the bay, especially at sunset. S of this headland, the small village of Pigeon has shops for basic provisioning, with more restaurants along the shore. There's no beach on this part of the coast, instead, as a result of Hurricane Lenny, an embankment has been built to protect the road and the buildings from hurricane-generated swell.

Anse à la Barque

ANSE A LA BARQUE LES TROIS TORTUES

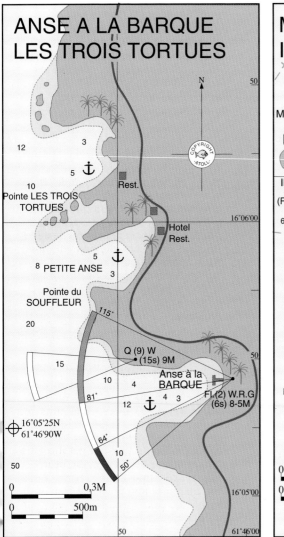

N

50

12

3

5

10

Pointe LES TROIS TORTUES

Rest.

16°06'00

Hotel Rest.

5

8 PETITE ANSE 3

Pointe du SOUFFLEUR

20

115°

Q (9) W (15s) 9M

15

Anse à la BARQUE

10 4

81°

12 4 3

FL (2) W.R.G (6s) 8·5M

64°

16°05'25N 61°46'90W

10

50

50°

50

0 0,3M

0 500m

16°05'00

50

61°46'00

MALENDURE ILET PIGEON

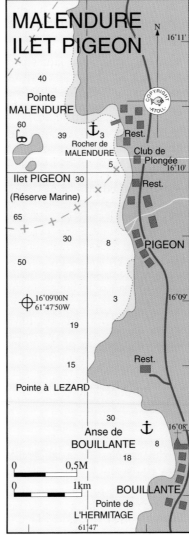

N 16°11'

40

Pointe MALENDURE

60

Rest.

39

Rocher de MALENDURE

Club de Plongée

5

16°10'

Ilet PIGEON 30

Rest.

(Réserve Marine)

65

30

8

PIGEON

50

3

16°09'00N 61°47'50W

16°09'

19

15

Rest.

30

Anse de BOUILLANTE

18

8

16°08'

0 0,5M

0 1km

BOUILLANTE

Pointe à LEZARD

Pointe de L'HERMITAGE

61°47'

16°05'00

extends from Its Pigeon as far as Pointe Mahaut.

For 2M beyond Pointe Mahaut the rocky coast has no real shelter until you get to the village of Pointe Noire and then what's called Baille d'Argent. Here a small fishing port has been built with less than 1·8m. A small yacht could find temporary shelter here in the tiny, rip-rap edged outer port.

Ashore There's a restaurant on the harbour's small esplanade serving Creole specialities and seafood. There are no other services except maybe the possibility of some top-up fuel for which you'll have to talk to the fishermen.

Anse Deshaies

2M beyond Pointe Ferry the best-known anchorage on the coast opens up: Anse Deshaies, protected from the N by Pointe du Gros Morne.

Caution The approach is clear bar a few rocks off the headlands and the fact that the whole area is cluttered with fishermen's net and pot marker buoys.

Anchor towards the head of the bay in 3–5m sand and rock, not far off the small jetty. This anchorage is visited by most boats heading up or down the main N–S route in the Antilles. At the entrance to the Rivière Deshaies, a small harbour for fishing boats and local pleasure boats has been built, but it has no facilities for visiting yachts. You can get some water here and there are mooring buoys you can rent. As far as fuel is concerned, you'll have to jerry-jug from the gas station.

Ashore There's an atmosphere of peaceful calm in a village prettily set around its bell tower and surrounded by coconut palms. Some small shops and grocery stores offer provisioning as well

Pointe Mahaut

Before you get to Pointe Mahaut, there's a lovely beach fringed with coconut palms and fishermen's boats with cottages on the shore, where there's a fair weather anchorage. The drying reefs off the tip of Pointe Mahaut have a good drop-off for diving.

Caution The protected nature reserve

Left Ilet Pigeon & Pointe Malendure
Right Deshaies fishing harbour
Bottom left Anchorages at Trois Tortues and Anse à la Barque
Bottom right Anse de Deshaies

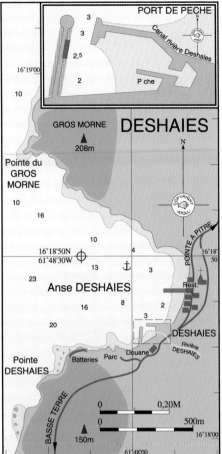

Map labels:
PORT DE PECHE
Canal rivière Deshaies
3
3
2,5
2
P che
16°19'00
10
GROS MORNE
DESHAIES
208m
N
Pointe du
GROS
MORNE
10
16
10
16°18'50N
61°48'30W
13
4
16°18'
50
23
Anse DESHAIES
Rest.
16
8
2
20
3
DESHAIES
DESHAIES
Rivière
Pointe
DESHAIES
Douane
Batteries
Parc
BASSE TERRE
0   0,20M
0   500m
150m   16°18'00
61°48'00

as local produce. There's a very varied choice of places to eat. From the first place you come to, the 'Mouillage, ex-Madame Racine' at the end of the dock, restaurants carry on along the shore and up the village streets. They offer varied menus, mostly of Creole specialities and seafood, again at very fair prices. Given the quality of shelter, you could also use Deshaies as a base for exploring Basse Terre, especially the National Park, because you can hire a car here. S of the village, as you head up the road, you'll find the customs post close to a small park with an old gun battery and a picnic spot. As with Rivière Sens, the officers may not be here if they've been called elsewhere.

Below left A *saintoise*, Bourg des Saintes
Below right Net fishing

N of Deshaies

Once past Gros Morne you'll begin to feel the oceanic swell again, especially in NE winds. This makes anchoring N of Grande Anse often uncomfortable and sometimes out of the question. Watch out for the La Perle sandbank with only 1·8m over it. In favourable weather there's a day anchorage under Kahouanne It with excellent snorkelling, but beware of the currents.

Guadeloupe's nearby dependencies

History and tourism

If it weren't for the islands that surround it, Guadeloupe would lose a significant part of its appeal to tourists. Although they're not far away you get the impression that they are much further, not because of the geographical distance but because of the distinctive way of life each of them retains. If you don't go there while cruising there are regular ferry services (from Pointe-à-Pitre, Basse Terre, St François,) as well as air connections to each of the islands' small airfields. What follows is a short history of each island or island group. After that comes the usual detailed look at the coasts and approaches.

Marie Galante

Columbus discovered the island on 3 November 1493 during his second voyage and it is named after one of his caravels, the *Maria Galanda*. According to the latest archaeological discoveries (pottery), it was occupied by the Amerindians in the second or third century BC, until finally taken over by the Caribs sometime between the 6th and 8th centuries AD. The French set foot on the island as early as the mid 17th century in order to grow sugar cane. Marie Galante became 'the island of sugar' with more than 100 mills. Now only 70 are left, more or less ruins. Even if the majority of the plantations disappeared in the 19th century, this big pancake-shaped island of 160 sq km. between Guadeloupe and Dominica is still basically farmland from which

potent rum is produced. Otherwise the 12,500 inhabitants get their livelihood from fishing, stock rearing and some tourism. There's a good road network either for exploring the interior or following the shoreline. The coast has several geological oddities with evocative names like Gueule Grand Gouffre and Grotte du Trou à Diable, but be warned, some of these places are only accessible with special equipment.

The island's towns, all situated along the coast, are small and simple. In the most important, Grand Bourg in the SW, activities focus round the small port. St Louis on the W coast is a hamlet of painted houses on a superb beach. Vieux Fort, the first colonists' main town, is now just a small fishing village. Here the remains of cottages built 'en gaulettes' (from plaited withies) bear witness to the old building techniques. Facing the Atlantic on the E coast, Capesterre shelters a fine beach behind its barrier reef.

These small settlements have little by way of tourism infrastructure. As a result they have remained mostly unspoilt and the people still offer a warm welcome. Small restaurants and simple *lolos* have a variety of dishes, often spicy, and made from local produce. Don't miss out the distilleries and their introduction to the secrets of rum making, nor on the chance to enjoy the fragrance and powerful kick of their highly alcoholic production – in moderation, naturally. Some of the mills (locally called *sucrotes*) and *habitations* or plantation houses, offer an insight into the ways of the old plantations. The best known, Habitation Murat, has been prettily restored as a museum.

Les Saintes

Discovered by Columbus in 1493 on All Saints Day (1 November), the little archipelago was first called 'Los Santos'. The geographical variety of this small archipelago of less than 15 sq km and made up of two main islands, three smaller ones and several islets, gives it much to boast about. The height of its bluffs and the silhouette presented by its coast offer unforgettable views as well as sheltered inlets and beaches. There are many bike paths and footpaths along

which you might come across an iguana, still to be found here because they are protected.

The natural beauty of Les Saintes is enhanced if you know something of the history of the place; which includes the biggest naval battle ever fought by the French and English in the Caribbean. On 12th April 1782, off the Saintes, Admiral Rodney's fleet defeated the Comte de Grasse's French squadron. This victory is of special significance in that it marks the beginning of the era of British maritime supremacy. The French, who wanted to make an impregnable outpost at the Saintes, in the 19th century built a number of fortifications and batteries, amongst them Fort Joséphine on Ilet Cabrit and Fort Napoléon on Morne à Mire. The latter, dominating Terre de Haut Bay, has been restored and turned into a small museum devoted to the events of the great battle.

The population of 3,000 is split evenly between Terre de Haut and Terre de Bas. These people claim direct descent from the first colonists, supposedly Bretons, who occupied the islands from 1643 on. It's certainly true that inter-marriage has been relatively slight because the poverty of the soil and the resultant small-scale farming meant that there was no need to import slaves. This sense of identity is most marked on Terre de Haut where fishing is still the mainstay and agriculture produces no more than the bare minimum. There are still 100 registered Saintois fishermen who criss-cross Guadeloupe waters in boats called *saintoises*. The result is that in Bourg de Terre de Haut you'll often come across faces which, although well-tanned by sun and salt spray, are reminiscent of Bretons and Normans back in France.

A sartorial peculiarity of the Saintes, now tending to fall out of use, is the

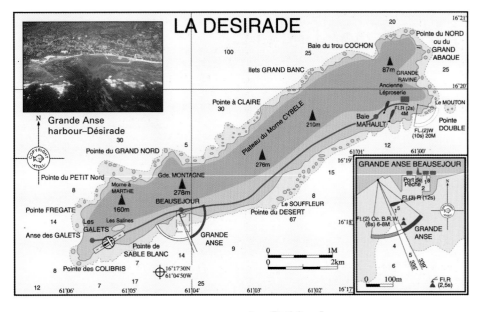

'salako'. This large hat made of plaited plant fibres was originally worn by the colonial maritime infantry of Tonkin and was brought to the Saintes by Annamite soldiery.

In Terre de Bas richer soil meant better farming, hence slave labour and, today, a more mixed population. This slight difference in skin colour between the peoples of the two islands might escape the notice of the passing cruiser. But small though it is, it does seem to affect relations between the two places and their respective ways of life because they are so tiny and so close together.

There's also unequal tourist development, most of the big hotels being on Terre de Haut mainly because it has better, more sheltered beaches. Because of this relatively high-density tourism there are more restaurants and bars on Terre de Haut too. Terre de Bas is less developed and therefore seems a lot more rustic, quieter and unspoilt, which will no doubt make it more appealing to some.

La Désirade

A cliffy tableland, Désirade sits E of Guadeloupe like a forward sentry post. Short of water and desperately hoping for landfall during his second voyage, Columbus named the island Desirada in November 1493. It wasn't a very suitable name for an island destined to have a sad future. From the beginning of the 18th century it became a place of exile for lepers and, a few decades later, for the sons of delinquent families. Some noble family names from France, hardly changed, can still be found amongst the island's surnames. The arid soil was only able to support small-scale cotton farming, and that soon disappeared when slavery was abolished. Thereafter the Désiradiens made their meagre subsistence from market gardening, fishing or, for those who were bold enough, as crew on the merchantmen.

The leprosarium was closed in 1954. Since then the more or less mixed race population of 1700, smallholders and fishermen rubbing along on their 22 sq

Right Iguana
Below Iles de Petite-Terre from NE

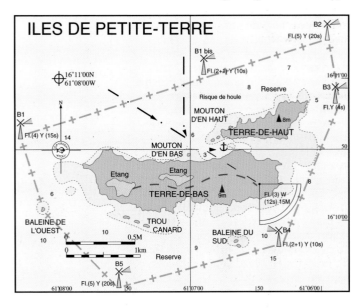

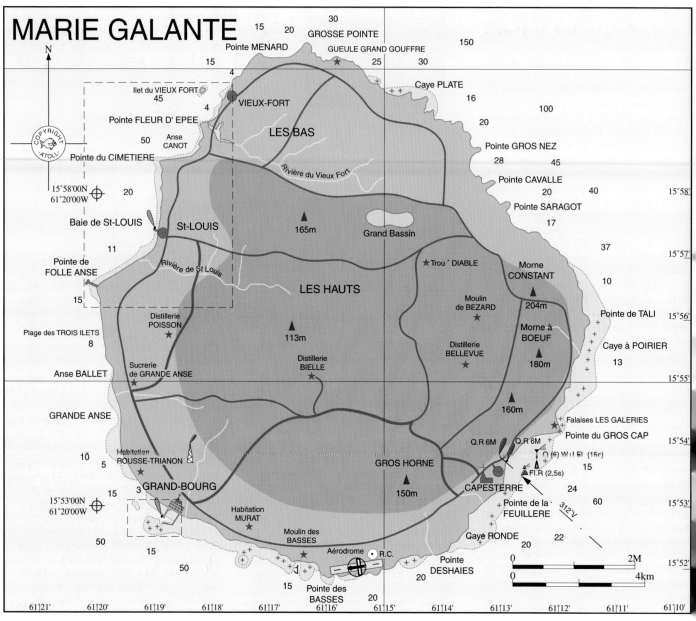

MARIE GALANTE

N

Pointe MENARD · GROSSE POINTE · 15 · 20 · 30
GUEULE GRAND GOUFFRE · 25 · 30 · 150
Ilet du VIEUX FORT · 45 · 15 · Caye PLATE · 16
VIEUX-FORT · 4 · 4 · LES BAS · 20 · 100
Pointe FLEUR D' EPEE · 50 · Anse CANOT · Pointe GROS NEZ · 28 · 45 · 20
Pointe du CIMETIERE · Rivière du Vieux Fort · Pointe CAVALLE · 20 · 40 · 15°58'
15°58'00N 61°20'00W · 20 · Pointe SARAGOT · 17
Baie de St-LOUIS · St-LOUIS · 165m · Grand Bassin · 37 · 15°57'
11 · Trou DIABLE · Morne CONSTANT · 10
Pointe de FOLLE ANSE · Rivière de St Louis · LES HAUTS · Moulin de BEZARD · 204m · Pointe de TALI · 15°56'
15 · Distillerie POISSON · 113m · Morne à BOEUF · Caye à POIRIER · 13
Plage des TROIS ILETS · 8 · Distillerie BELLEVUE · 180m · 15°55'
Anse BALLET · Sucrerie de GRANDE ANSE · Distillerie BIELLE
GRANDE ANSE · 160m · Falaises LES GALERIES · Pointe du GROS CAP · 15°54'
10 · 5 · Habitation ROUSSE-TRIANON · Q.R 6M · Q.R 6M
15 · GROS HORNE · Fl (6) W.L.Fl. (15s) · 15
3 · GRAND-BOURG · 150m · CAPESTERRE · Fl.R (2,5s) · 24
15°53'00N 61°20'00W · Habitation MURAT · Pointe de la FEUILLERE · 312°V · 60 · 15°53'
50 · Moulin des BASSES · Caye RONDE · 20 · 22
15 · Aérodrome · R.C. · Pointe DESHAIES · 20 · 0 · 2M · 15°52'
50 · 0 · 4km
15 · Pointe des BASSES · 20

61°21' · 61°20' · 61°19' · 61°18' · 61°17' · 61°16' · 61°15' · 61°14' · 61°13' · 61°12' · 61°11' · 61°10'

km of limestone pebble, have rarely known better days. From time to time a hurricane, like Hugo in 1989, devastates the island's fragile economy, leaving in its wake just a few shattered cottages. For a while now, attracted by the austere and wild beauty of the wave-beaten cliffs where one can imagine oneself on the prow of a ship, a few tourists have started to arrive. Others are happy with the quiet, sandy beaches like Anse Petite Rivière and Plage du Souffleur. The two main settlements are little more than villages. Grande Anse (or Beauséjour) in the W and Baie Mahault in the E are joined by the island's only road. Places to stay are few and simple with prices to match. The restaurants, simple 'lolos', serve Creole dishes, plain and unpretentious. On top of that you can expect kindness and a warm welcome. Regular small ferries from Désirade's little fishing harbour to St François on Guadeloupe take less than an hour.

Pilotage
Coast and anchorages

La Désirade

Transatlantic sailors making landfall in Guadeloupe often see La Désirade first, picking up its powerful lighthouse if they're in the offing after dark. For all that, few yachts ever visit because the vertiginous shores have no havens and the small harbour at Grande Anse is shallow (<1·5m), offering shelter only to motor boats and ferries. For sailors, therefore, the only choice is to take a ferry from St François and pay a short visit.

Petite Terre
(between La Désirade and Marie Galante)

These two small, all but deserted islands are a protected marine reserve and are difficult for yachts to get to. The anchorage in the pass is accessible from the NW in fair weather but is a death trap in strong NE winds. In effect you're advised not to try it between December and March or whenever there's a big swell. Terre d'en Bas is well known for its light, built in 1835 and one of the oldest in the New World. Lots of Pointois (from Pointe-à-Pitre) come here at weekends by fast ferries. As a result of this popularity, and despite the status as a reserve (marked by special purpose buoys) underwater life has become quite scarce. But on a walk ashore your path may cross those of some fine iguanas.

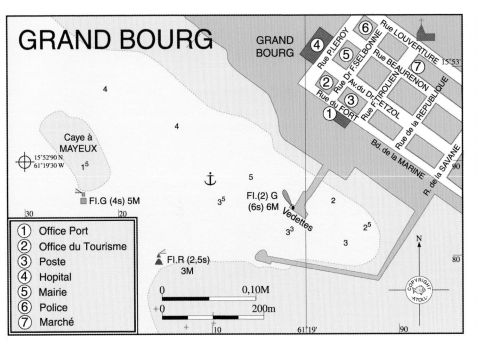

GRAND BOURG

GRAND BOURG

Caye à MAYEUX
15°52'90 N
61°1930 W

Fl.G (4s) 5M

① Office Port
② Office du Tourisme
③ Poste
④ Hopital
⑤ Mairie
⑥ Police
⑦ Marché

Fl.(2) G (6s) 6M
Vedettes

Fl.R (2,5s) 3M

0   0,10M
200m

Marie Galante

An easy approach, but tough sailing in an ESE'ly requiring several long tacks hard on the wind from Pointe-à-Pitre. From St François on the other hand there's no problem. All the anchorages are on the leeward coast, the windward coast being steep-to and wave-dashed.

Anse Canot

In the NW of Marie Galante the best anchorage is in Anse Canot. The anchorage, edged with a fine sandy beach, can be rolly and even untenable if the wind's well set in the NE. There are still plenty of fish around the islet of Vieux Fort, which you can get to in an outboard powered tender in fair weather.

St Louis

Heading S, keep clear of the reefs off Pointe du Cimetière to reach the pretty little fishing village of St Louis. A small light N of the settlement means you can try a night approach but be careful, the approaches are full of fishermen's pots and the depths off the beach, where the fishing boats are drawn up ashore, are limited to shoal drafters. Here too the anchorage can be uncomfortable in NE winds. A big dock has been built for ferries from St Louis to Guadeloupe and the Saintes. Mooring yachts to it is forbidden, though there's a lower platform you can use to get ashore from

Bottom Grand Bourg harbour
Below Port Louis

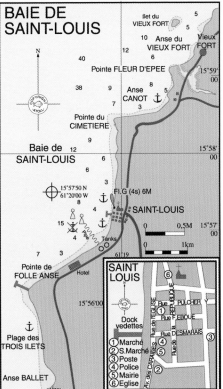

BAIE DE SAINT-LOUIS

Ilet du VIEUX FORT
Anse du VIEUX FORT
Vieux FORT

Pointe FLEUR D'EPEE

Anse CANOT

Pointe du CIMETIERE

Baie de SAINT-LOUIS

15°57'50 N
61°20'00 W

Fl.G (4s) 6M

SAINT-LOUIS

Tanks

Pointe de FOLLE ANSE

Hotel

15°56'00

Plage des TROIS ILETS

Anse BALLET

SAINT LOUIS

Dock vedettes

① Marché
② S.Marché
③ Poste
④ Police
⑤ Mairie
⑥ Eglise

your tender. Don't anchor too far S of the dock. There's a pipeline and several underwater cables there, the former supplying the island's fuel tanks you'll see ashore. They're marked by large yellow buoys.

Ashore There are some small grocery stores and minimarkets, not that well stocked except in rum. There are some restaurants serving local specialties at good prices and a few simple *lolos* where the fairly rough décor is amply compensated for by the warmth of your welcome. Towards Pointe Folle Anse the only fairly upmarket hotel is hidden behind a curtain of plants along the beach. In a NE swell, once you're round the big loading jetty and crane pushing out 200m from Pointe de Folle Anse, it's more comfortable at night off Trois Ilets beach. On the edge of Anse Ballet just to the S, in the cane cutting season the smell from the distillery in Grande Anse is noticeable.

Grand Bourg

Grand Bourg is 3M SE of Trois Ilets, past Pointe Ballet. Two buoys mark the pass, green to port on the SE corner of Caye à Mayeux, red to starboard on the tip of the fringing reef. NW of the harbour wall the shore has been reclaimed as a result of a public works project that's gone nowhere. At present you can anchor on the outside of the port behind the shelter given by the reefs and the seawalls, though the anchorage is none too well protected from any ESE swell, or from the chop and wash of the service vessels connecting with Guadeloupe and the other islands. The anchorage inside the port, in 2–4m, is well protected if space is available.

Note Be sure to leave access to the ferry dock clear.

Ashore Grand Bourg is the island's largest town but small nonetheless. The chessboard pattern streets surround the church and the square with the town hall (Mairie) make quite a picture postcard scene. It's all very friendly and peaceful. There are several shops and minimarkets for full provisioning, not forgetting the vital rum which you can sample on the terrace of the bar overlooking the harbour. Small restaurants serve local dishes and the tourist office will give you kindly and precise directions on where to go and what to see if you hire a car.

Pointe des Basses

There's an anchorage behind the reef on the extreme S tip of Marie Galante, not far from Les Basses village. I've never tried it in a yacht because of the SE swell. The pass is said to be narrow, although some say it's easy enough in

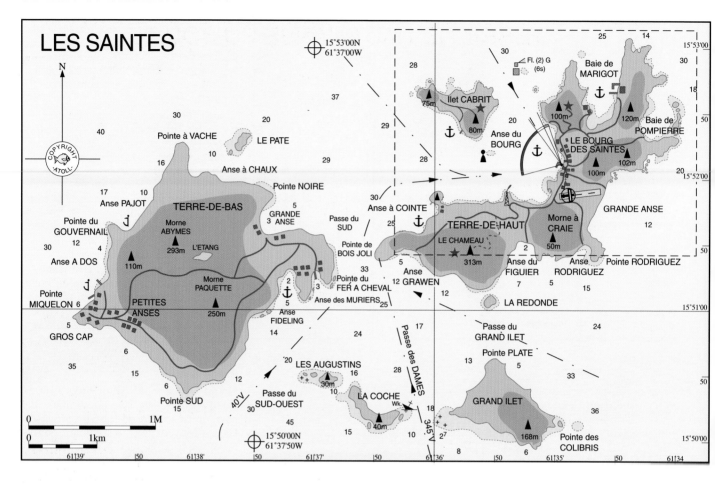

LES SAINTES

15°53'00N
61°37'00W

Fl. (2) G
(6s)

Baie de
MARIGOT

28

30

25   14   15°53'00

30

Ilet CABRIT

75m

80m

Anse du
BOURG

100m

LE BOURG
DES SAINTES

120m   Baie de
POMPIERRE

18

102m

N

30   20

40

Pointe à VACHE   LE PATE

16   10   Anse à CHAUX

Pointe NOIRE

37

29

29   28

20

100m   20   15°52'00

17   10

Anse PAJOT

Pointe du
GOUVERNAIL

30   12   4

Anse A DOS

110m

Pointe
MIQUELON 6

5

GROS CAP

35

6

15

6

TERRE-DE-BAS

Morne
ABYMES

293m   L'ETANG

Morne
PAQUETTE

250m

PETITES
ANSES

5
GRANDE
3 ANSE

Passe du
SUD

Pointe de
BOIS JOLI

33

Pointe du
FER A CHEVAL

2

3

5

Anse des MURIERS 25

Anse
FIDELING

14

24

30   Anse à COINTE

25

TERRE-DE-HAUT

LE CHAMEAU

313m

5   Anse
12 GRAWEN

12

GRANDE ANSE

Morne à
CRAIE

50m

2

Anse du   Anse
FIGUIER   RODRIGUEZ   Pointe RODRIGUEZ

7   5   15

LA REDONDE

12   50

15°51'00

12

'20   LES AUGUSTINS

30m

12   10

16

Passe du
SUD-OUEST

40°V   30

45

15°50'00N
61°37'50W

28

LA COCHE

Wk.

40m

15   10

17

Passe des DAMES

345°V

18

27

8

Passe du
GRAND ILET

Pointe PLATE

13

5

GRAND ILET

168m

6

24   50

33

36

Pointe des
COLIBRIS

15°50'00

0   1M

0   1km

61│39'   │50   61│38'   │50   61│37'   │50   61│36'   │50   61│35'   │50   61│34'

COPYRIGHT
'ATOLL'

calm seas with the sun high in the sky. Inside there's 3–4m. Try it cautiously but only in good weather and if you have a small motorboat.

Capesterre

There is an anchorage on the windward coast here, though it hardly seems worth it given how far off route it is and the risks involved for your boat. I've never tried it, since, looked at from ashore, it seemed restricted to small local craft. There's a leading light for the local fishing boats.

Les Saintes

Sometime or other everyone who sails in the Lesser Antilles fetches up in the Saintes. There are numerous anchorages in the small archipelago, amongst them the superb Saintes Harbour in which Admiral de Grasse's entire fleet anchored. Traditionally the people here have always been fishermen and builders of the famous 'saintoises'. If they've lost their sails these days in favour of powerful outboards, the result is merely that their long narrow hulls flash even faster over the waves. There are excellent dive and snorkelling sites. In good weather the best are off Cabrit

It, on the N of Terre-de-Bas and around the islets to the S.

Terre de Haut

Rade and Bourg des Saintes

Approach the harbour and town in daytime either via the Passe de la Baleine or the Passe de Pain du Sucre. By night it's better to use the Passe de la Baleine with the port hand buoy to guide you because the sector light is often merged with the lights of the town. The Passe du Pain de Sucre is trickier because of a shoal with less than 1m over it a bit over 300m SE of Cabrit Islet.

Caution The unlit isolated danger buoy marking this shoal has often been reported missing although, of course, the reef is still there.

There are several anchorages near Bourg:

- the N'most, in the Anse à Mire in 8–10m, moderate holding, off the docks of the restaurants along the shore.
- in the Anse du Bourg off a conspicuous house shaped like the

Les Saintes archipelago from the NE

House in the style of a ship (Maison du Docteur), Bourg des Saintes

TERRE-DE-HAUT - ANSE DU BOURG

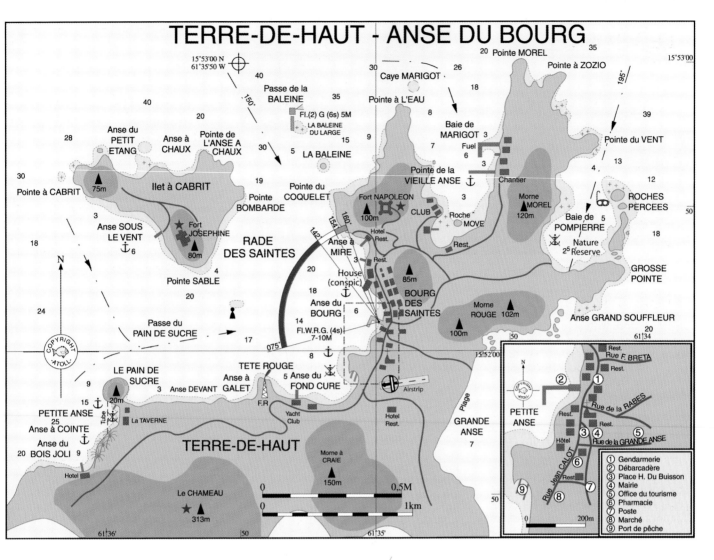

bow of a ship (called the Maison du Docteur) in the same sort of depths and holding.

These two fairly protected anchorages are sometimes a bit rolly and subject to gusts which make yachts swing around a lot. Swinging room needs thinking about in high season when this haven is crowded with boats.

Local boats and big passenger ferries frequently pass at high speed, further diminishing the peace and comfort of these two anchorages.

• further S, NW of the small fishing harbour or in the Anse du Fond du Curé, though the latter is a bit cluttered with lots of moorings.

The town quay is reserved for ferries plying from Trois Rivières, Pointe-à-Pitre and Basse Terre and there's neither fuel nor water to be had there.

There's a chance of finding something at the Yacht Club (VHF 68), which also offers various other helpful services, or you might try at some of the restaurants.

Ashore There are plenty of restaurants and bars where the cruising world gathers, including lots of tourists from the ferries come to admire the pretty village with its painted houses which sparkle like new coins. This daily crowd isn't the only thing to trouble the peace of this pretty town. Despite a local by-law limiting the number of scooters and other local motorbikes, they racket around the small streets at top speed until quite late at night.

Several minimarkets and shops offer most provisions. There's a police station (gendarmerie) opposite the dock but you can't complete clearance because there are no customs. Barring a

Below left Anse à Mire and Anse du Bourg
Below right Anse du Bourg

Petite Anse and the Pain de Sucre from W

hardware store with some chandlery and a sailmaker who lives in Bourg but works in Marigot Bay, there are no specific yachting services (this applies throughout the Saintes, except for emergency fixes).

Ilet à Cabrit

The leeward coast of Ilet à Cabrit, which is inhabited, offers a quieter, more sheltered anchorage if you stay some distance off the dock and the fishermen's shore nets. From there you can visit the island and Fort Joséphine. The fort, now in ruins, was turned into a prison and quarantine hospital for immigrants in 1856 and stayed that way until 1902.

Anses du Pain de Sucre and du Bois Joli

The small bay tucked at the S foot of the Pain de Sucre (a spectacular promontory with basalt pillars) is without doubt the nicest anchorage in the Saintes. That's on condition that it's not too crowded, because it's tight and the bottom drops off quickly to more than 10m.

Caution Make sure you anchor S of the underwater inlet pipe.

There's a dock on the narrow strip of tiny beach from which you can get ashore by tender. Just above, a well known old cruising sailor, Jacques Boone (a writer in his time), has swallowed the hook and established a small guest house and bar here in a stone 'tavern' he built with his own hands. Further S the Anse du Bois Joli is more open to the swell.

Baie du Marigot

The bay is deep, but not well protected in a NE swell and wind.

Note Off Pointe à l'Eau, there's a shoal to avoid, Caye Marigot, which is marked only occasionally.

The most protected anchorage is behind the small breakwater of an old shipyard on an uneven bottom in 2–3m. N of the breakwater there's a fuel dock protected by an L-shaped mole but behind the mole, where there's scant room to manoeuvre, access is limited to shoal drafters under 8m loa. You can fuel up by jerry-jugging.

Ashore The old shipyard has been closed for some years, though the rather overgrown buildings and installations are in the process of being brought back into commission to create haul-out facilities. The local sailmaker's loft is here. Further N there are two small boatyards building small GRP boats and on the opposite shore on the W of the bay another workshop specialising in building 'saintoises'. At the bay head, along the pretty beach, there's a welcoming restaurant serving local Creole specialties and a number of bungalows house a holiday and watersports centre.

Baie de Pompierre

Even in NE winds this bay, E of Baie du Marigot, offers perfect shelter. However, the entrance should be taken carefully and in good visibility. The line is 195°T between two reefs headed for a lovely white sand beach. To the E, the anchorage is protected by a line of rocks, amongst them the famous 'roches percées' (rocks with holes through them). That said, the bay has been classified as a natural park and a Departmental By-law (Arrêté Préfectoral) of 1997 forbids all sailing and anchoring here. All that's left for you is to visit by road from Bourg, admire an exceptional spot and enjoy the marvellous beach shaded by coconuts and Caribbean sea grape (*Coccoloba polygonaceae*).

Anse du Figuier and Anse Grawen

The S part of these inlets offer a day anchorage in settled good weather, but in any E to SE wind the swell rolls in and they are untenable.

Grand Ilet, La Coche, Les Augustins, Les Passes du Sud

There's no safe anchorage amongst these three deserted islets S of the archipelago. The pass from the SW between the Augustins and Terre de Bas is quite wide and without problems. Line yourself up on Pointe du Bois Joli on 040°T. The Passe des Dames between Grand Ilet and Ilet la Coche is a lot narrower. Furthermore, a recent wreck is aground E of La Coche making the pass even narrower and more dangerous. Only use it in flat seas and good visibility.

Terre de Bas

Although a little larger and with as many inhabitants as Terre de Haut, Terre de Bas gets fewer tourists and very few yachts. The people are welcoming, but the bays on the W coast are not well protected and any swell readily makes in.

Anse Fideling

The only overnight anchorage on the E side of the island in 4–5m, sand, though the head of the bay is full of local boats. In a SE'ly a slight swell makes in and there are turbulent gusts. The small village of Grand Anse isn't far away. It's worth strolling over to enjoy the simple but authentic cooking of the small restaurants.

Anse des Mûriers

Less well sheltered than Anse Fideling and in a SE'ly you'll feel the backwash even more. On the E side there's a landing pontoon for ferries linking Terre de Bas with Terre de Haut. You can sometimes get diesel here but don't rely on it.

Anse à Dos (called Des Petites Anses)

Off a small fishing village called Les Petites Anses, the anchorage here is often very rolly. In calm weather it's good for a short halt in order to visit the village with its cottages clinging to the sides of the hills.

Useful Information for Guadeloupe

AIRLINE CONNECTIONS

Pôle Caraïbe International Airport, Le Raizet
☎ 05 90 93 73 73.
International long-haul flights daily to France, other connections to European cities
Flights to N America, Haiti, Venezuela
Local flights, internal and to dependencies
Daily flights by local companies to
Bailiff (Basse Terre), ☎ 05 90 81 15 85
St François
La Désirade, ☎ 05 90 20 05 63
Marie Galante, ☎ 05 90 97 82 21
Les Saintes, ☎ 05 90 99 50 32
Inter-island flights daily to Martinique, Dominica, St Lucia, etc. and to the islands N.

FERRIES

To outlying dependencies Daily
Inter-island Fast ferries from Guadeloupe to Martinique, Dominica, St Lucia

TELECOMMUNICATIONS

Calling from abroad: ☎ (0) 590 + 6 digits
Local call: 10 digits (0590 + 6 digits)
Public call boxes: France Télécom cards (télécartes) or Carte Bleu

RIVIERE SALEE BRIDGE OPENING TIMES

Pont de la Gabarre: 0500
Pont de l'Alliance: 0430–0530
Automatic opening Monday to Saturday morning in high season.
August to November automatic opening Mondays, Wednesdays and Saturdays.
Other days: on demand at the DDE, ☎ 05 90 21 26 50 *Fax* 05 90 21 26 51
Information from the Capitainerie, Bas du Fort Marina.
Note schedule changes possible

CLUBS & ASSOCIATIONS

Comité Guadeloupéen de la Voile (Guadeloupe Sailing Association):
Capitainerie, Bas du Fort Marina
☎ 05 90 90 90 64
Club Nautique de Basse Terre (Basse Terre Yacht Club): Rivière Sens Marina, ☎ 05 90 81 77 61

TOURIST OFFICE

Pointe-à-Pitre 5, Square de la Banque
☎ 05 90 82 09 03 *Fax* 05 90 83 89 22
Email office.tourisme.guadeloupe@wanadoo.fr
www.lesilesdeguadeloupe.com
Basse Terre (Mairie) ☎ 05 90 80 56 40
Marie Galante Grand Bourg
☎ 05 90 97 56 51 *Fax* 05 90 97 56 54
Email info@ot-mariegalante.com

Les Saintes Terre de Haut
☎ 05 90 99 58 60 *Fax* 05 90 99 58 48
Email omt.lessaintes@wanadoo.fr
Gîtes Ruraux de Guadeloupe (Guadeloupe Holiday Cottages): ☎ 05 90 91 64 33 *Fax* 05 90 91 45 40

FESTIVALS/FOLK FESTIVALS

Carnival: end of February, beginning of March
Vaval: Ash Wednesday
Fête Victor Schoelcher: 21st August (commemorating the abolition of slavery)
Fête des Cuisinières (Chefs Festival): beginning of August
Festival de la chanson créole (Créole Song Festival): November
Pitt à coq (cock fighting): Belair

PUBLIC HOLIDAYS

New Year's Day (1 January), Easter Sunday, Easter Monday, Labour Day (1 May), Ascension Day, Whit Monday, VE Day (8 May), Slavery Abolition Day (27 May), Bastille Day/National Day (14th July), Schoelcher Day (21 July), Assumption (August), Toussaint (All Saints Day, 1 November), Fête des Morts (All Souls Day, 2 November), Armistice Day (11 November), Christmas Day (25 December)

OFFICE HOURS

Shops: Mon–Fri, 0900–1200, 1500–1800, Sat 0900–1300
Banks: 0730–1200, 1500–1800, Sat 0730–1300
Government offices:
Mon & Fri 0730–1300, 1500–1630
Tues & Thurs 0730–1300

PLACES TO SEE

Pointe-à- Pitre
Musée Schoelcher (1887)
St Pierre & St Paul Basilica
Musée St-John-Perse
Aquarium: Bas du Fort Marina
Grande Terre
Pointe des Châteaux
Pointe de la Vigie cliffs
Port d'Enfer lagoon
Fort and port of Le Moule
Fort Fleur d'Epée: old fort
Morne à l'Eau: amazing cemetery
Deshaies
Jardin Botanique (Botanical Garden): Once owned by Coluche (a renowned French comedian)
Basse Terre
Ilet Pigeon & the Cousteau Reserve
Le Musée du Rhum (Rum museum): Bellevue Ste Rose
Domaine de Séverin: La Cadet Ste Rose (Reimonenq Distillery)

Shell Museum (Musée de Coquillage): Pte Noire
Caféière Beauséjour (Coffee Plantation): Pte Noire
Coffee Museum: Vieux Habitants
La Soufrière: 1467m and its vents
The Volcano House (La Maison du Volcan)
Les Chutes du Carbet: 3 waterfalls
Le Grand Etang: large lake
Parc des Mamelles: animals threatened with extinction, jungle canopy visit
Saut de la Lézarde (Lizard's Leap Falls)
Cascade aux Ecrevisses (Crayfish Falls)
Maison de la Forêt (Forestry centre): marked trails
Parc animalier (zoo): animals including the local racoon (raton-laveur)
Fort Delgrès (ex-Fort St Charles, 1643)
Distillerie Boulogne (rum distillery): Bailiff
Les Roches Gravées: Trois Rivières, park and gardens with petroglyphs
Allée Dumanoir: palm tree lined road
Les traces (tracks & footpaths): listing from Office National des Forêts (National Forestry Dept)
Les Saintes/Terre de Haut
Fort Napoléon: small museum
Sommet du Chameau: Viewpoint
Ilet Cabrit
Fort Joséphine: ruins
Marie Galante
Habitation Murat: small museum
Gueule Grand Gouffre
Distilleries including Poisson, Bielle, Bellevue
La Désirade
Old leprosarium

ROAD TRANSPORT

Drive on the right
Hire car companies in the towns and at the airport, taxis

FORMALITIES

Arriving by air
Customs and immigration at the airport
Arriving by sea
Pointe-à-Pitre
Capitainerie, Bas du Fort Marina, hours 0800–700, Mon–Sat. Sundays and public holidays: 0800–1200
Commercial harbour, cruise liners and merchant shipping only
Basse Terre
Rivière Sens Marina (mobile unit)
Hours: weekdays 0700–1200, closed weekends.
Port de Basse Terre (commercial harbour), cruise liners and merchant shipping only
Deshaies (mobile unit): Weekdays 0800-1200, closed weekends

All formalities in Guadeloupe are free and obligatory both clearing in and out.

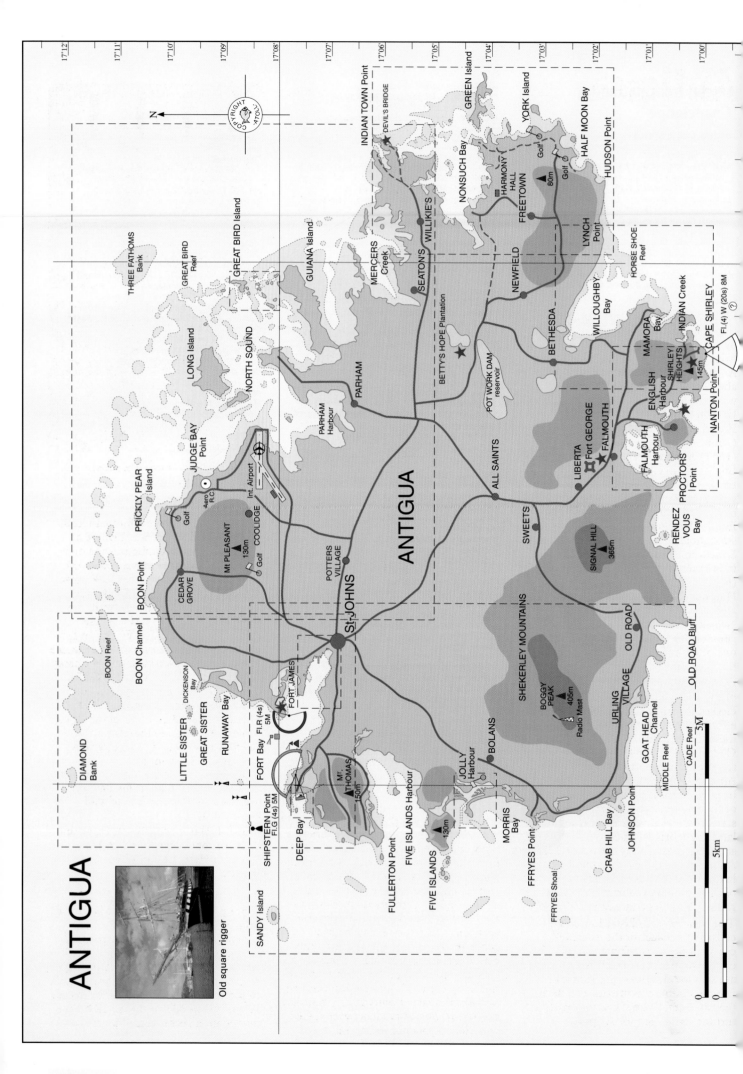

ANTIGUA

Old square rigger

ANTIGUA

DIAMOND Bank

LITTLE SISTER
GREAT SISTER

BOON Reef

DICKENSON Bay

BOON Channel

RUNAWAY Bay

BOON Point

CEDAR GROVE

Golf

JUDGE BAY Point

PRICKLY PEAR Island

THREE FATHOMS Bank

GREAT BIRD Reef

GREAT BIRD Island

GUIANA Island

LONG Island

NORTH SOUND

Aero R.C.

Int. Airport

Mt PLEASANT
130m▲

Golf COOLIDGE

SANDY Island

SHIPSTERN Point
Fl.G (4s) 5M

DEEP Bay

FORT James

Fort Bay Fl.R (4s) 5M

FORT JAMES

Mt. THOMAS
▲150m

St.JOHNS

POTTERS VILLAGE

PARHAM HARBOUR

PARHAM

MERCERS Creek

INDIAN TOWN Point

DEVIL'S BRIDGE

SEATON'S

WILLIKIE'S

NONSUCH Bay

GREEN Island

YORK Island

HALF MOON Bay

Golf

HARMONY HALL

FREETOWN
80m▲

Golf

HUDSON Point

NEWFIELD

LYNCH Point

BETTY'S HOPE Plantation

POT WORK DAM reservoir

ALL SAINTS

BETHESDA

WILLOUGHBY Bay

HORSE SHOE Reef

MAMORA Bay

INDIAN Creek

CAPE SHIRLEY

Fl.(4) W (20s) 8M

NANTON Point

SHIRLEY HEIGHTS
145m▲

ENGLISH Harbour

LIBERTA

Fort GEORGE

FALMOUTH

FALMOUTH Harbour

PROCTORS Point

RENDEZ VOUS Bay

SWEETS

SIGNAL HILL
▲365m

SHEKERLEY MOUNTAINS

BOGGY PEAK
▲405m

Radio Mast

URLING VILLAGE

OLD ROAD

OLD ROAD Bluff

GOAT HEAD Channel

CADE Reef

MIDDLE Reef

CRAB HILL Bay

JOHNSON Point

FFRYES Point

MORRIS Bay
130m▲

FFRYES Shoal

FIVE ISLANDS

FULLERTON Point

FIVE ISLANDS Harbour

JOLLY Harbour

BOLANS

5km

5M

5M

N

COPYRIGHT ATOLL

134

Antigua

Area 280 sq km (excluding
   Barbuda and Redonda)
Highest point Boggy Peak
Population 70,000
Capital Saint John's (pop 25,000)
Language English
Currency EC$, US$ accepted
Political status Independent state
Distances to nearby islands Guadeloupe
   (Deshaies) 40M, Barbuda 25M, St-
   Barthélémy 70M

History

Like lots of other islands Antigua
(pronounced Anteega) was discovered
by Columbus in 1493. It got its name
from the church of Santa Maria la
Antigua in Seville. Immediately
abandoned by the Spanish because it
was waterless, it was occupied by the
English in 1632. It was only ever
French-occupied for one brief year
(1666-7), but after the Treaty of Breda
(1667) Antigua became definitively
English. Three centuries of constant
English presence have made the island a
very British place. Thanks to its natural
havens, of which the best known is
English Harbour, Antigua became the
stronghold of the English Leeward Isles
Squadron. From this den, made
impregnable by numerous fortifications
(for example Fort Berkeley in English
Harbour), the ships of Admiral Rodney,
and from 1784 the great Horatio
Nelson, could easily control the whole
Antilles. Accordingly Antigua became
one of the major British naval assets in
the West Indies.

Despite frequent droughts, by the end
of the 17th century the island was
cleared for sugar cane plantations by the
efforts of the British colonists (amongst
them the well-known Christopher
Codrington in 1684). The plantations
required the import of slaves from
Africa and from that point on the island
became ethnically divided. The decline
of the monoculture and the abolition of
slavery by the British in 1834 led to the
land being broken up into
smallholdings. Today the majority of
Antiguans own their own small plot of
land. Antigua became an associate state
of the Commonwealth in 1967 and
gained full independence in 1981.

The sugar cane industry has now
collapsed because of the extremely
competitive international market. The
only natural resources left to the island
are small-scale cotton growing and
fishing. As these industries also decline,
the small state's fragile economy is
turning to tourism for support.

Tourism

Where to stay and what to see

The reef-girt island has an exceptional
underwater world and the absence of
mountains gives it an admirably dry
climate. Its indented coast has
incomparable beaches that, as the
publicity blurb will tell you, are 365-
strong, 'one for every day of the year'.
Major investment groups, mainly North
American, have built luxurious hotel
complexes around the coast, with
golden-white sand beaches to seaward
and green golf courses inland. But in
Antigua another sport is played on turf:
cricket. It's a national institution to
boot.

The rest of the island's tourist
infrastructure is on a simpler scale with
small cottages for rent, mainly round St
John's. The local restaurants focus on
grills and seafood. Antigua's tourist
jewel, however, has to be yachting,
concentrated around the superb site of
English Harbour with the famous
Antigua Week regatta as its focus.
Finally, there's no doubt that Antigua
benefits from an international airport
linking it to Europe and North America.

English Harbour

Nelson's lair is unquestionably the best-
known spot in Antigua. The port and
dockyard installations (Nelson's
Dockyard), built between 1725 and
1746, were abandoned by the Royal
Navy in 1889. In the 1950s a retired
British naval officer, Captain Nicholson,
was behind the first moves to restore
the place. Since then his pioneering
work has been followed up by the
Nelson's Dockyard National Park. The
result is that today the main buildings,
such as the Admiral's House (now the
museum) the old workshops, the stables
and the officers quarters, have been
restored. The whole represents an
extremely rare example of the historic
architecture of the Lesser Antilles, with
its stone and brick structures topped
with shingles.

You'll see a line of stone pillars, the last
remains of the old dockyard, close to
the Admiral's Inn. This very luxurious
hotel and restaurant has been created
from the elegantly restored 18th century
workshops. Close to the old Admiral's
House, now the home of the museum,
are the equally sumptuous premises of
the Copper Store Hotel. Tourists and
yachtsmen of more modest means
generally frequent the Mainbrace Pub
next door. In the evening the pubs and
bars are often full of the merry noise of
rollicking crew. It's an amazing contrast
to the ambience of quiet luxury you find
in some of the restaurants never sullied
with the polyphonic and metallic
percussion of a steel band.

Top Fort Berkeley – cannon on its carriage
Above Royal Artillery quarters

South of the buildings a footpath leads
to Fort Berkeley (1705-12) where a
single cannon still symbolizes the once
inviolable English Harbour. From this
excellent viewpoint you can look down
on the quays of Nelson's Dockyard
where, in the first weeks of April, the
loveliest cruising and racing yachts
gather for Antigua Race Week. To the
east on the opposite side of the entrance
are the imposing fortifications of Shirley
Heights (Fort Shirley Battery, 1787),
which dominate the sea approaches.
Below them, invisible on the hillside
behind lie the old barracks of the Royal
Artillery. From them there's a
magnificent view and, on a clear day,
you can see Guadeloupe.
At the Sunday evening barbecue party
in the restaurant high in the battery,
there's no shortage of fans of wild
reggae music.

If English Harbour is the centre of this
extensive zone focussed on yachts,
Falmouth Harbour and village next
door are its western annexe.

Around the island

Before you get to the village of Liberta,
about 3-4km outside Falmouth
Harbour, there's a great view over the
whole island from Fort George, which
was built here on its eminence during
the 17th century. Continuing westwards
around the coast, the road runs through
the only green hills in the island before
opening up a succession of huge

Above left Old arsenal, English Harbour
Above right Copper Store Resort garden
Right Half Moon Bay

beaches, each as fine as the next and, with the exception of the tourist and yachting complex of Jolly Harbour, hardly developed.

St John's

The island's capital dates from the 17th century, which makes it one of the oldest commercial ports in the Antilles. The mix of small houses and more modern shopping centres is dominated by the two towers of the imposing Cathedral of St John the Divine, the first parts of which date from 1683. It was rebuilt in stone and completed in 1847, though the interior is entirely done out in pitch pine. There's now a museum in the old Court House (1750), which has collections representative of the island's history. Close to the harbour there's a colourful market on Fridays and Saturdays. On Heritage Quay a duty free zone has been built for the cruise liner trade.

Below left Old dockyard pillars
Below right Nelson's Dockyard – replica of old capstan, presented by HMS *Vernon* in 1974

However, other than tourist activity round the harbour, there's not much life in St John's except on the first Monday in August when Carnival kicks off a week of music and colourful processions.

A mile or so west of St John's on the end of Shipstern Pt there are ruins of Fort Barrington (1780). Fort James, built at the beginning of the 18th century, is in better condition and fortifies the other side of the entrance. Nowadays, a few cannon barrels are all that remain of the extensive artillery batteries that once defended St John's natural harbour. Narrow roads lead from St John's to the small villages in the island's interior, and the coastal road circuit takes you north, to a coast protected by huge barrier reefs, and to the international airport.

In Parham you can visit the interesting small octagonal church of St Peter.

From Parham the road runs out to Crabb's Peninsula with its panoramic view over North Sound. North Sound is a huge area full of small islets protected by an extensive barrier reef. The E'most point of the island is wilder and more intricately rugged as far as Indian Town Pt where you can see the Devil's Bridge, a natural formation.

On southwards the road leads slightly inland, preventing easy access to the prettiest parts of the coast like the little paradise of Green Island, all of which you can only get to by boat. Not far from here is Half Moon Bay which the Antiguans themselves consider the island's best beach.

Luxury hotels dominate the headlands and bays of the coast; one of the most luxurious is the St James Club Hotel tucked away at the head of Mamora Bay.

Pilotage

Coast and anchorages

Innumerable inlets and bays intersect the circumference of the island, however reefs and shoals mean taking care and your navigation must be exact.

South coast

English Harbour

Nelson's hideaway is infamous for an entrance that's hard to spot from seaward. Nothing has changed in that respect and newcomers are often baffled. The famous Pillars of Hercules, better known for their existence than their size, carved by erosion out of the cliffs of Charlotte Pt, are visible enough but really only once you've already found the entrance! Because Cape Shirley light, like the leading lights, is often out of action, a night entry isn't advisable.

Note Reef, usually awash, pushes out up to 100m from the NW side of Charlotte Pt. To be safe hold towards the less hazardous Berkeley Pt.

English and Falmouth Harbours from the SE

Once you're into the channel, you'll find the first anchorage off a beach surrounded by bungalows. Sometimes rolly, but it's airier and for swimming the water's cleaner than further in. Don't forget to anchor clear of the fairway in the NW of the bay. The channel carries on as far as some

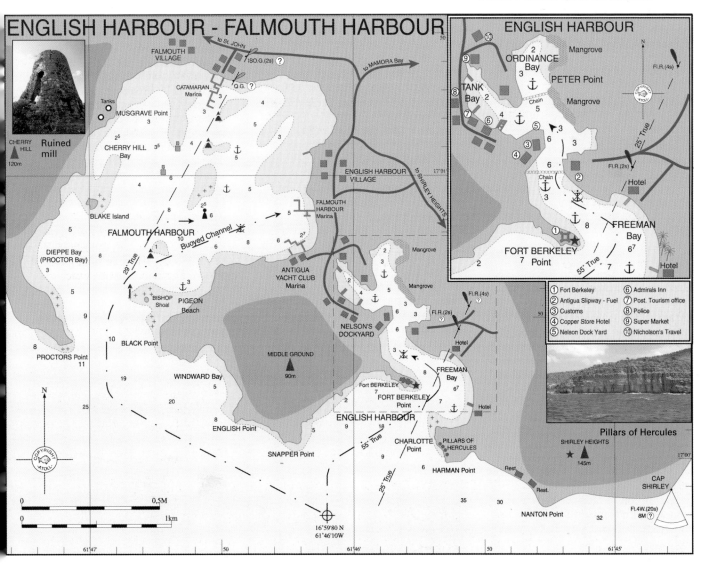

mangroves to make the excellent hurricane hole of English Harbour. You can anchor N or S of Nelson's Dockyard on a mud bottom which is quite poor holding.

Note Watch out for old mooring chains on the bottom that are traps for anchors (see plan).

In high season the anchorages are usually very crowded. Nelson's Dockyard quays have full facilities (water and electricity) for any up to the very largest yachts. If you intend to go stern-to here, drop your hook as far as possible towards the opposite shore to find the best holding.

Note There are also regulations limiting the speed of all vessels in English Harbour to a maximum of 4kts, with heavy fines for non-compliance.

Ashore Customs, immigration and the port authorities are on the quayside. The whole English Harbour–Falmouth Harbour zone shares a large variety of yacht services. They have an excellent reputation and usually listen out for their clientele on VHF 68, though in high season and during Antigua Week they are less reliably available. On the far shore, opposite the Arsenal, Antigua Slipway has good haul out facilities, lots of specialist services and a well-stocked chandlery. To round off this concentration of facilities there's a pontoon with some 20 berths (water and electricity) and a dedicated water and fuel dock. Close by is a restaurant

with a pretty terrace and a friendly atmosphere to welcome visiting yachtsmen.

There are several brokerage and chartering agencies, amongst them the well-known Nicholson Yacht Charters. The founder of the last, Rodney Nicholson was the founding father of chartering here over 40 years ago and made English Harbour the main centre of the business in the Antilles.

You can provision here using the minimarket on the road out of English Harbours (though to find a big supermarket you'll need to take a taxi or hire car to St John's). Around the quays and all the way over to Falmouth Harbour as far as the top of Shirley Heights you'll also find lots of bars, pubs, pizzerias and restaurants from the simplest to the classiest and to suit all pockets. In the evenings, especially during Antigua Week, you can join all

the other yacht crew in enjoying the life of this major centre of international yachting.

Falmouth Harbour

Heading W from English Harbour you are immediately in the offing of Falmouth Harbour, though some of this otherwise huge bay is blocked by shoals. Bishop Shoal on the E side of the entrance is easily enough seen since the swell usually breaks on the windward side. It's usually marked by a buoy or a stake to be left to starboard. Don't try a night entry because the leading lights, two greens on 029°T, aren't reliable. The leading line takes you, via a channel amongst partly buoyed shoals, to the Catamaran Hotel Marina. The pontoons of the Catamaran Club Marina (VHF 16 and 68) have 40 berths with 3m depth, mostly reserved for large yachts. The usual services are available, including water and fuel.

Ashore The hotel complex includes shops, among them a small chandlery and a pleasant bar-restaurant with a terrace. There are useful technical services close by.

You can also hold N around Bishop

Above Carlisle Bay beach
Right Johnson Point & Goat Head Channel from W

Shoal before heading more E to the pontoons of the Antigua Yacht Club and the Falmouth Harbour Marina (VHF 68). Anchor leaving clear access to the pontoons. The Antigua Yacht Club pontoons have been enlarged to accommodate super-yachts (60 berths for draughts 3–5m). There is a fuel dock. The complex as a whole includes restaurants, small shops and various services.

Falmouth Harbour itself is well sheltered, though water clarity isn't that good, especially in the E. Falmouth Harbour is divided from English Harbour by an isthmus just 200m wide so you can get from one to the other on foot in a few minutes.

Goat Head Channel

It's best to take this passage between Middle Reef and Antigua itself only in clear weather when the sun is high in the sky.

Coming from Old Road Bluff, steer 292°T using the left end of Johnson Pt as a lead. After 2M alter to port to 280°T using as a back-marker the white hotel on the Curtain Bluff headland slightly open to the left of a notch in the outline of Old Road Bluff (see sketch).

Note If you come from seaward Cades Reef and Middle Reef, although exposed at low water, are often hard to see. Be sure of your navigation and give the reefs plenty of room. In calm weather with appropriate care you can enjoy good snorkelling between Cades and Middle Reefs (a marine reserve) coming in from the W. Anchor between the two reefs, though be careful not to anchor on or over coral.

Carlisle Bay

This rarely visited anchorage, with coral all round its shores, is at the E end of Goat Head Channel. In an ESE wind it can be very rolly and uncomfortable overnight. There's a private club on the beach.

Morris Bay

Even less sheltered from residual swell than Carlisle Bay, the shores of Morris Bay are also very shoal. On Curtain Bluff overlooking the bay the Curtain

Bluff Hotel is amongst Antigua's most select. On the beach there's a rather simpler hotel with the roofs of its restaurant beneath the palms on the beach.

West coast

Between Johnson Pt and Five Islands

It's shallow (5–6m) for 1.5M or so off the shore on this stretch of coast and

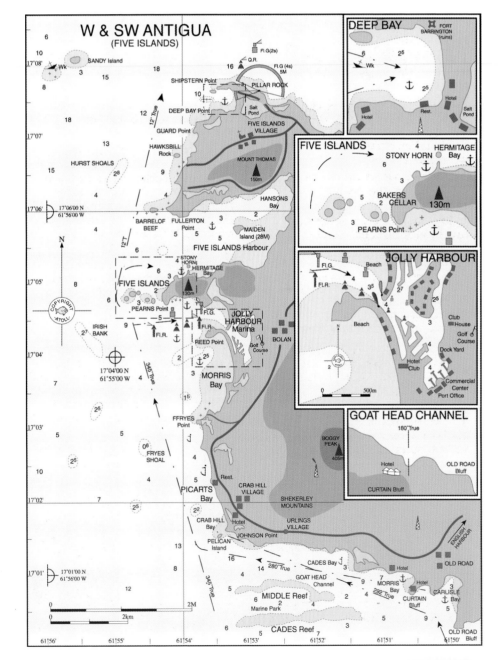

you should watch out carefully for the many shoals, which are hard to see. Making this passage requires exact navigation, especially if you draw >2m. Once you've given Johnson I and little Pelican I a wide berth, head for the westmost islet of Five Islands on 345°T. This should keep you in at least 4-6m.

Crabb Hill Bay & Picart's Bay

You can close the coast to anchor off the superb beach in Crabb Hill Bay (S of Picart's Bay) in front of a restaurant. Or you can anchor further N under Fryes Pt, off another pretty beach overlooked by a bungalow development. Swell can often make both anchorages uncomfortable, especially overnight.

Morris Bay

Further N this huge bay is called by the same name as the small inlet on the S coast dealt with above. The long and lovely beach is not much visited, but the anchorage is often rolly, especially in any sort of SE wind. The many shoals prevent one getting very close to shore.

Jolly Harbour

This is a huge lakeside complex, enclosing a very large, excellently protected, all-weather marina. The 200 hectare basin has been dredged out of the old Salt Pond. A buoyed channel (in theory dredged to 4m) makes for easy access from the W by closing the first, easily visible, lit starboard mark. You can anchor out, preferably S of the channel. Inside, artificial islands dotted with multicoloured buildings have created a canal labyrinth in which every plot has its own pontoon. Towards the SE end of the lagoon, in depths of 4m, you'll find the marina with its 150 berths, fuel dock and boatyard.

Note Anchoring in Jolly Harbour is prohibited

Ashore Customs and immigration are here so you can clear in and out. The port office (VHF 16) is on the upper floor of the small shopping centre in which there are several shops and restaurants including a post office.

There's a dive centre operating around the nearby reefs. For services you'll find the marina has both a boatyard with a good range of services and several independent specialists. Visiting yachts will find here most of what they might need for maintenance or to cope with breakdowns.

Above Five Islands Harbour from W
Right Jolly Harbour channel beacon
Below Stony Horn beach
Bottom left Jolly Harbour Marina pontoons
Bottom right Jolly Harbour Estate

Around the large basin the lakeside real estate development has a swimming pool, tennis courts and an 18 hole golf course. The luxury development is nicely landscaped, but its sheer size and the out-of-the-way location make it all a bit impersonal.

Five Islands Harbour

The large Five Islands Harbour Bay isn't much visited. Most of the head of the bay beyond Maiden Island is pretty shallow, the water is quite murky and the mosquitoes are aggressive. You can anchor W of Maiden I, being careful of the reef patches. The island is a bird sanctuary and landing is forbidden. In the SW are two other fine anchorages either side of the small headland of Stony Horn. To the W, anchor off a small, pretty beach or in Harmony Bay to the E. In a N swell both can be uncomfortable.

From Barrel of Beef to St John's

Once past Barrel of Beef, if you're heading straight for Boon Channel, steer 012°T to clear all the offlying dangers like Warrington Bank W of St

St John's Harbour from W

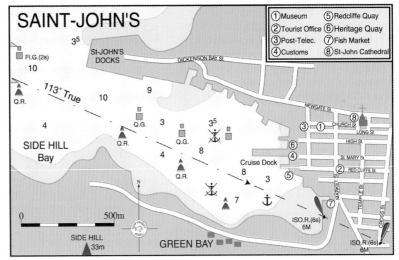

John's Harbour. Further offshore you'll see Sandy I. Alternatively hold to the coast to head for Deep Bay and St John's past Hawks Bill Rock and its distinctive Falcon's Head.

Deep Bay

This pretty anchorage off a sandy beach is well sheltered, though it can be slightly rolly if the NE wind is well set in.

Note A wreck with less than 1m over the superstructure blocks the middle of the bay, be sure to give it a wide berth N or S. Its ends are marked by two buoys.

A luxury hotel complex between the shore and the lagoon beyond means the bay has lost some of its old charms, even though the buildings aren't very obvious from the anchorage. It has several restaurants and tourist shops. The wreck of the cargo ship *Andes*, which sank at the beginning of the 19th century, makes a great shallow water dive. There's a fine view over St John's Bay from the ruins of Fort Barrington that dominate Deep Bay from the top of Shipstern Pt.

Saint John's Harbour

St John's is a commercial harbour and the capital of Antigua and until recently wasn't much frequented by yachts. However, thanks to the development of Redcliffe Quay for yachts, it's now easier to visit St John's and its historic quarter, as well as provisioning at the many shops.

A wide, dredged and buoyed channel makes entry easy. You can anchor S of Redcliffe Quay, but there's an absolute prohibition against anchoring in the channel or in the manoeuvring basin close to Cruise Dock

Note Dredging work for the development of the Fish Market Dock SE of Redcliffe Quay has made depths here uncertain. One effect is that access to the fuel dock on the S dock is limited to shoal drafters.

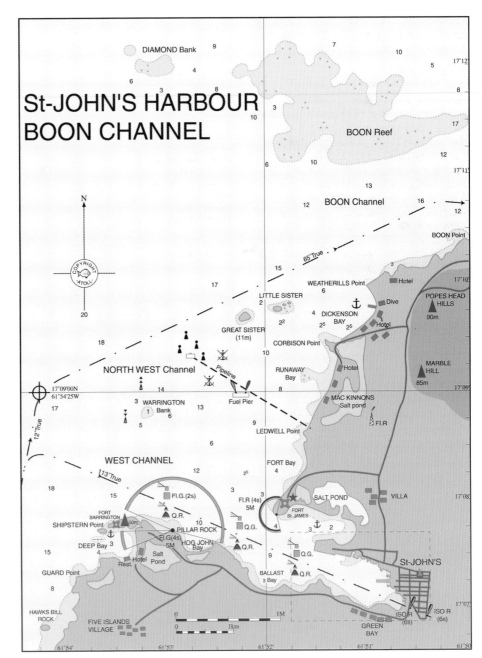

Mooring at Redcliffe Quay should be arranged with the St John's Yacht Club or with Joe's café on the quayside (VHF 16). That said, there are no berths equipped with standard supply posts (water and electricity). Water supply in any case is unreliable.

Ashore There are two customs and immigration offices. The main one is close to the main commercial dock in the N of the harbour. The second, sometimes closed, is close to Heritage Quay.

Redcliffe Quay, St John's Harbour

Fringing Redcliffe Quay the colourful small houses have a village air, with their small squares and narrow alleys within which you'll find several small shops, bars and restaurants. Around here, the centre of St John's, you'll find the liveliest and the most interesting part of town, worth a stop for a visit to the old quarter and its monuments. Several restaurants offer local specialties at good prices. For provisioning there's a good local market (especially on Friday and Saturday) as well as lots of shops and supermarkets. As far as yachting services go, they're limited to a few mechanics and outboard specialists.

Great Sister and Dickenson Bay

Once past Warrington Bank with its two cardinal buoys, you'll see the black mooring buoys marking the end of the oil pipeline. Round the latter and head 065°T. You leave Great Sister to starboard, keeping well to seaward, because the shoal ground extends a good way.

Note It is possible to pass between Little Sister and Antigua only if you are shoal draft, the actual depths being often less than 2m. As a result, in order to reach the anchorage off the beach at Dickenson Bay, you need to go N round Little Sister before anchoring preferably in the N of the bay off the hotel dock. The anchorage can be rolly if the swell is N.

The beach along the coast as far as Runaway Bay has several hotels and restaurants on it. Ashore at about the midpoint of the bay but a little inland, there's a small shopping centre for essentials.

North coast

Boon Channel to Prickly Pear Island

Coming from the SW, in order to find the anchorages off Long Island on Antigua's NE shore, you should use Boon Channel between the offshore reefs and Antigua. From off the Sisters, staying about 0·5M offshore, hold on 065°T past Weatherills Pt until NW of

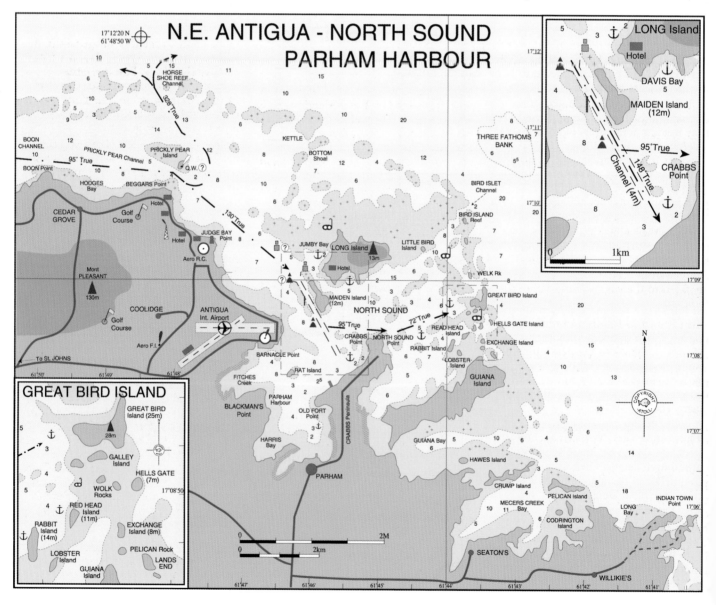

Above North Sound & Guiana Island from E
Right Great Bird Island anchorage

Boon Pt when Prickly Pear should bear about 095°. Alter to that course using the S point of the islet as a mark.

Note To avoid getting snared by the huge complex of reefs WNW of Prickly Pear Island don't stray N of this route. The passage between Prickly Pear Island and the coast of Antigua needs to be eyeballed favouring the Prickly Pear Island side.

Horse Shoe Reef Channel

N of Prickly Pear Island there are several more or less feasible passes leading seaward through the outcrops of coral E of Boon Reef. The least tricky is called Horse Shoe Reef Channel and runs 328°T once you've steered to a point about quarter of a mile E of Prickly Pear Island. Using this pass to leave for Barbuda is easy enough in good weather with good visibility provided you're careful. On the other hand, approaching the N coast of Antigua from seaward by this passage is confined to the very experienced or the foolhardy.

Long Island to Maiden Island

Once past Prickly Pear Island alter towards the N tip of Maiden I on 130°T. After about 1.5M take the rather sketchily buoyed channel along the Maiden Island shore on about 148°T towards Crabbs Peninsula.

Note The few buoys are often either out of position or missing altogether. Make sure you stay in mid-channel and watch your course keeping.

Before taking the channel it is possible to anchor in Jumby Bay on the W coast of Long Island. There's a hotel and bungalow development on the island. There's also an anchorage on the S of Long Island close to the coast of uninhabited Maiden Island.

North Sound

North Sound is a large open expanse of water protected by Long Island in the N and a large barrier reef in the E. There are lots of anchorages, though navigating in North Sound has to take account of the many coral outcrops and banks. The anchorages are often deserted and invite one to stay and stay, but you need to have thought of this beforehand with respect to provisioning. As a result of Crabbs Marina closing down (replaced by a small industrial zone), there's only the village of Parham, which can't offer more than emergency supplies.

The loveliest and best protected anchorages are in the lee of Great Bird Island and the necklace of islands running off to the S of it. To get there from just S of Maiden Island, steer 095°T to leave North Sound Pt to starboard. Once off North Sound Pt alter to 072°T for the W end of Great Bird Island. If you hold to that route, you should avoid the shoal ground N and S of it. The pass to seaward just N of Great Bird Island is narrow, twisting and fairly shallow and is really only sensible as a boat channel for tenders heading off to explore the reef. NE of Little Bird Island there's another pass, Bird Islet Channel of which the same is true.

Note The area around Great Bird Island where several species of bird breed is now part of the Antigua National Park

(sea and land) and is subject to the usual sorts of rules and regulations of such protected places. Further S, Guiana Island is also a reserve and in principle you shouldn't go ashore. S of Guiana Island there are several anchorages accessible from seaward in Guiana Bay and Mercer's Creek. However, given how difficult they are to reach, I've never tried any of them.

Parham Harbour

Once upon a time this village was quite a busy port though these days it's fallen completely asleep. You can either anchor off the dock or under Old Fort Pt (or Umbrella Pt) in 3m. You have to anchor well off because there's very little depth closer in.

Ashore There are a few shops and the local market for essentials. There's also a simple bar-restaurant. At present that's all the town has to offer.

East coast

Nonsuch Bay

A large bay open to the sea but entirely protected by a large barrier reef and by Green Island. Along with North Sound it is the best anchoring area in Antigua. It can be reached either from N whether from Long Island or Barbuda, or from S coming from English Harbour. (The latter is the best way round to take things.) A conspicuous sea mark to the north of Half Moon Bay on the top of Friads Head is a white house with what looks like a small bell tower. Hold well E of York Island before altering to 320°T using the right hand end of Conk Pt as a leading mark. The coast here is dominated by the Mill Reef Yacht Club development with its many fine houses. Be sure to give the large offlying coral banks S of Green Island a clear berth.

Green Island

On the S coast of Green Island there are anchorages in the two small inlets except when there is a well-developed SE wind.

Above Anchorage at Rickett Harbour, Green Island
Above right Nonsuch Bay & Green Island from SE

Tenpound Bay, the further E, is the narrowest and most exposed in a SE wind

Rickett Bay (Rickett Harbour) isn't much bigger but is better protected.

The creeks can't hold more than two or three boats given the coral that makes them very tight. On the beach there are picnicking sites built for and reserved for Mill Reef Yacht Club, which leases the island. A better protected anchorage is in Nonsuch Harbour proper under the lee of the NW coast of Green Island off a pretty little beach. The whole area is pretty crowded in high season. To reach it you take the pass between Conk Point and Green I, with the usual care.

From Conk Pt to Ayres Creek

Nanny Island

The anchorage SE of this islet is little protected from chop when the trades are fresh, and shoal ground prevents penetrating further in. You also have to stay away from the E side of Conk Pt, the private property of Mill Reef Yacht Club where visiting yachts are not welcome.

Brown's Bay

This small inlet is quite well protected. As a mark you can use the small hill through the trees in transit with the mill of Harmony Hall. Anchor in 2–3m staying N of the dock because the shoreline is poorly defined.

Ashore On the hill is the Harmony Hall restaurant (managed by Italians, with Italian specialties) in a gorgeous setting. It's built around the tower of an old windmill and surrounded by greenery. From the upper platform of the old mill there's a fantastic panorama over the

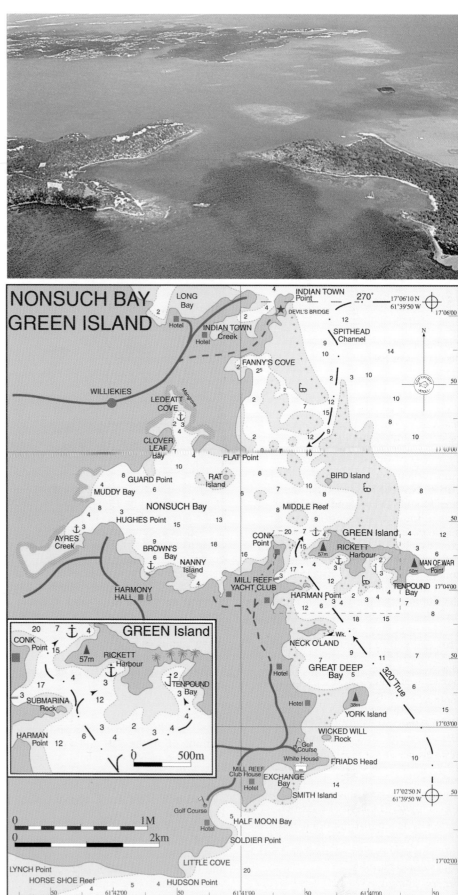

whole of Nonsuch Bay. In Harmony Hall you'll also find some exhibitions of local art and crafts.

Top Brown's Bay
Above Harmony Hall

Ayres Creek

This long inlet surrounded by mangroves is a perfect retreat if you like being on your own.

Clover Leaf Bay/Ledeatt Cove

An excellent hurricane hole in the N part of Nonsuch Bay. To get there be sure to go S of the large coral bank on which Rat Island lies. As its name suggests, this small bay is shaped like a clover or trefoil leaf, each of the three tiny creeks being fringed with mangroves. The N and E parts, the best protected, have 2-3m depths. A hotel development in the W part is at present on hold.

Spithead Channel

N of the small islet of Bird Island there is a N/S trending pass through the barrier reef called Spithead Channel. To leave to seaward using it, be sure to give a clear berth to the reefs W and N of Bird Island.

Below Beach on Green Island, Nonsuch Bay
Below right Marmora Bay and St James Club pontoons

Note The pass is quite deep but should only be used in good weather and very good visibility. Coming in from seaward is very tricky and dangerous in any other than calm and clear weather because there are no obvious landmarks to orientate yourself by, Indian Town Pt being lost in the shoreline.

From Green Island to English Harbour

Willoughby Bay

This large bay with its entrance mostly closed by coral opens up just past Hudson Pt. The pass is in the middle of the bay and trends 309°T. You should

hold to the right in Horse Shoe Channel because the left of the pass (SW side off Isaac Pt) is full of reef with depths less than shown on the charts. Entering the bay in a SE swell isn't recommended. Visit only in fair weather and good visibility. Anchor NW of Horse Shoe Channel at which point you're a good way from anywhere and there's not much to see except the reef.

Mamora Bay

A well-protected lagoon. The whole E side of the entry channel has reef extending off it. There's a buoyed channel on 320°T to be used in calm weather and with great caution if you draw much water because there's only

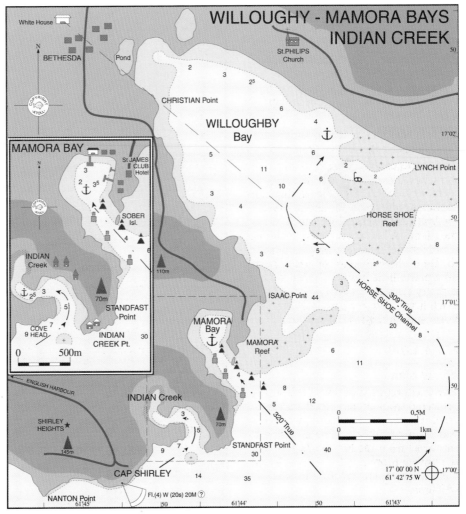

2·8–3m in the pass. The very chic St James Yacht Club Hotel has built bungalows on the E point and the NE side of the bay around a fine beach with attendant coconut palms. The marina has some 30 berths with water, electricity and a fuel dock. For the most part in season the berths are all taken by a very 'select' clientele of big motor yachts.

Ashore You'll find water sports, hotel accommodation, a casino, several restaurants and shops in an idyllic setting, all aimed at tourists and yachtsmen, preferably rich ones.

Indian Creek

A small hurricane hole limited to small to medium sized boats. The shallow water towards the mangrove-ringed head of the creek puts a limit on draught.

Note Right outside the entrance in the middle of the direct course in there's an awash reef. It's best to leave it to starboard (pass W of it). On Indian Creek Pt there's a conspicuous house to serve as a mark on your approach.

Redonda

Although only 9M from Montserrat, this massive, steep-sided boulder of about 2 sq km and some 300m high is actually a dependency of Antigua 25M away. For such a small islet it has quite a history. Around 1865 someone

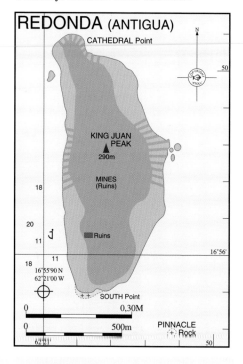

discovered a deposit of phosphates which brought dozens of miners. Curiously in the same year an Irishman, orginally from Montserrat, annexed the tiny place that no other state had yet claimed. Fifteen years later he crowned his only son King of Redonda. This almost mythical kingdom is kept alive today thanks to a brotherhood which, when the first king died, continued to elect a successor from amongst its members. The effectively imaginary existence of this puppet empire in no way prevented the continued exploitation of the phosphates by a mining company, which abandoned the works at the beginning of the 20th century. Since then Redonda has again become empty, peopled only by birds flying over the mine's ruins. It's all of relative interest, and only for boats on passage which seldom if ever stop because there's no sheltered anchorage. However, in fair weather one can seize the opportunity to put a lunch hook down in the island's lee. Anchor in 6-8m very close to the shore, being on your guard against possible currents. It's a wild spot, dominated by the island's rocky bulk, but the anchorage is surrounded by good fishing because it isn't much visited.

Useful Information for Antigua

AIRLINE CONNECTIONS
International airport: VC Bird Airport,
☎ 268 462 3147
Long-haul flights direct connections to Europe (London, Frankfurt, Zurich) and North America (Miami, New York, Toronto).
Inter-island flights daily flights to neighbouring islands

FERRIES
Connections with other islands by ferries and cargo vessels, particularly to Montserrat.

TELECOMMUNICATIONS
Calling Antigua from abroad: ☎ (1)268 + 7 digits
Local call: 7 digits
Note some numbers are only callable from within the area (i.e. no international connection)
Public call boxes: Caribbean Phone Card

ASSOCIATIONS
Antigua Yacht Club: Falmouth Harbour ☎/*Fax* 268 460 1799
Antigua Sailing Week: ☎ 268 462 8872 *Fax* 268 462 8873
Email aswinfo@sailingweek.com
Organisers of Antigua Sailing Week (Race Week): www.sailingweek.com

TOURIST OFFICE
Tourist Office: St John's
☎ 268 462 0029 *Fax* 268 462 2483
Email deptourism@candw.ag
National Parks Authority: Nelson's Dockyard
☎ 268 460 1379/1053 *Fax* 268 460 1516
Email natpark@candw.ag

FESTIVALS/FOLK FESTIVALS/REGATTAS
Red Stripe Regatta (Jolly Harbour): February
Classic Regatta: 2nd half of April
Carnival: beginning of August

Antigua Sailing Week: end of April/beginning of May
Jolly Harbour Regatta: September

PUBLIC HOLIDAYS
New Year's Day (1 January), Good Friday, Easter Monday, Labour Day (1st Mon in May), Whit Monday, Queen's Birthday (2nd Sat in June), Caricom Day (beginning July, everything closes), Carnival (1st Mon and Tues in August), Independence Day (1 Nov), Christmas Day (25 December), Boxing Day (26 December)

OFFICE HOURS
Shops: Mon–Wed & Fri 0800–1200, 1400–1600, Thurs & Sat 0800–1200
Banks: Mon–Thurs 0800–1400, Fri 0800–1200, 1400–1600

GOLF
Numerous courses around the island

PLACES TO SEE
English Harbour/Falmouth Harbour
Fort Berkeley
Shirley Heights Fort (1787)
Admiral's House (Maritime Museum)
Great George Fort (1669)
St John's and environs
Court House: (1747) Museum of Antigua and Barbuda
Fort Barrington: Goat Hill (1779) ruins
Fort St James: (1796) restored (10 cannons)
Cathedral of St John the Divine (1638) Anglican church rebuilt in the 18th century
Megaliths: Green Castle Hill S of St Johns
Elswhere
Fig Tree Drive: picturesque road across the island
Parham Harbour: St Peter's Church (1711 rebuilt 1840), architect Thomas Weeks
Devil's Bridge, Indian Town: natural, wave cut arch on the windward coast (also called Blowers' Hole)
Mill Reef/Half Moon Bay: pre-Columbian remains
Betty's Hope: (1674 - old Codrington family plantation)

Harmony Hall: (1842) craft centre
St Philip's Church: (1830) on the way to Harmony Hall on N shore of Willoughby Bay

ROAD TRANSPORT
Drive on the left
Local licence obligatory
Hire car companies in the main towns and at the airport
Taxis: be sure to agree on the fare

REGULATIONS
Underwater hunting forbidden to non-residents
Land and marine reserves: ask about regulations at the tourist offices
Speed limits of 4kts in Falmouth and English Harbours, fines for infraction

FORMALITIES
Arriving by air customs and immigration at the airport
Arriving by sea
English Harbour Nelson's Dockyard, hours 0800-1600, 7 days a week
St John's Heritage Quay – not much used by yachts: hours variable
Jolly Harbour 0800-1600, 7 days a week, call VHF 16
Overtime charged outside office hours except at English Harbour
Fees and taxes
Entry tax and Cruising Permit: by length
Crew levy: by individual
Anchoring fee (for upkeep of the area): Falmouth and English Harbours
The total of the fees payable is cumulative and quite complicated, though the total is always reasonable enough. For example, a 40 footer with 4 crew staying for a week will pay around EC$100 (US$40) to EC$150 (US$60) depending on the season

ACCESS TO BARBUDA
In principle, before heading for Barbuda from Antigua every boat must get authorisation from the authorities in Antigua. Check before you go.

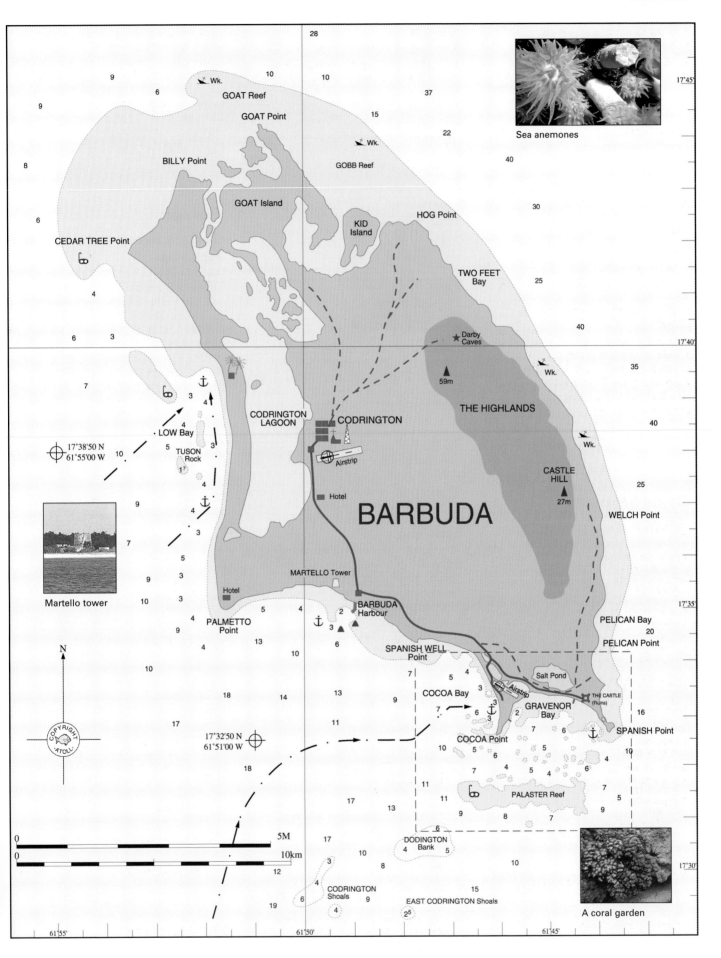

Sea anemones

9

10   10

6   GOAT Reef   37

9   GOAT Point

15

8   BILLY Point   Wk.

22

6   GOAT Island   40

HOG Point   30

KID
Island   TWO FEET
Bay   25

6   3   CEDAR TREE Point   40   17°40'

Darby
Caves

4   Wk.   35

7   59m

3   4   THE HIGHLANDS   40

5   CODRINGTON   CODRINGTON

LOW BAY   TUSON
Rock   LAGOON   Airstrip   CASTLE
HILL   WELCH Point

4   27m   25

Hotel

9   17°38'50 N
61°55'00 W
10   BARBUDA

7

9   3   MARTELLO Tower

10   3   PELICAN Bay   20

Hotel   BARBUDA   PELICAN Point   17°35'

5   4   2   Harbour

4   PALMETTO   SPANISH WELL
Point

9   13   6   Point

4   Salt Pond

10   10   7   3   4   THE CASTLE
(Ruins)   16

18   14   13   9   COCOA Bay   Airstrip   GRAVENOR
Bay   SPANISH Point

17   11   7   6   2   10

17°32'50 N
61°51'00 W   10   3   GRAVENOR
3   COCOA Point   6   7   6

18   11   7   4   4

17   13   11   9   PALASTER Reef   7   5

8   7   9

0   5M

0   10km   17   6   DODINGTON
Bank

3   10   5   10   17°30'

12   8

4

6   CODRINGTON
Shoals   9   EAST CODRINGTON Shoals

19   4   2   5

N

Martello tower

COPYRIGHT
ATOLL

A coral garden

61°55'   61°50'   61°45'

Barbuda

Area 160sq km
Highest point The Highlands
  on the E coast at 60m
Population about 1500
Capital Codrington
Language English
Currency EC$
Political status Dependency of Antigua
Distances to nearby islands
Antigua 25M, St-Barthélémy 60M

Above Anchorage in
the N of Low Bay
Left Codrington church
Bottom left Cocoa
Point
Bottom right Spanish
Point anchorage

History

Barbuda was discovered by Columbus
in 1493 and became English in the 17th
century. It was leased to the Codrington
family in 1685 in principle to farm it,
though in fact they used it as a slave
park from which slaves were delivered
for re-sale to other islands. The lease
was ended in the 19th century and all
that's left of the family presence is the
name of the village where almost the
whole population lives. Barbuda was
always a dependency of Antigua and
with independence became part of the
new state. One of the sole benefits of its
attachment to Antigua as a dependency
is the presence of public services such as
police and customs in the island.

The population depends mainly on
fishing (especially langouste), farming
and salt ponds. Until now the
Barbudans seem to have managed to
preserve their simple way of life, relying
mainly on the island's natural resources.
Accordingly, the various projects by
foreign businesses aimed at intensively
developing the island's tourism potential
have all been put a stop to by the
island's own people.

Tourism

Where to stay and what to see

Barbuda is a low, flat island of some
160sq km set on a large coral platform.
The highest point (The Highlands) is
60m above sea level. Its shore, almost
free of buildings, is ringed with an
infinity of sandy beaches protected by
coral reef.

Codrington

Lying E of the lagoon, the island's only
settlement houses almost the whole
population. It's made up of small
cottages surrounded by little gardens
clustered round the tiny church. This
scene of simplicity exudes a peaceful air
and seems at times to lie outside time.

Business is confined to one or two
shops and a minimarket with slender
stocks, to which you can add the two
'restaurants' with their rustic furnishings
and basic local menus. Close by the
town there's a mini airstrip connecting

the island to Antigua. The more
luxurious hotels are in the S of the
island at Palmetto Pt and Cocoa Pt on
the edge of endless white sand beaches.
Various showbiz celebrities do come to
these very exclusive places from time to
time, but they don't emerge to join in
life elsewhere on the island. One of the
hotels even has a private airstrip for air
taxis.

There are a few driveable roads running
N/S and to The Highlands in which you
can see the deep chasm of the Derby
Sink Cave.

A large part of the W of the island is
taken up by a huge, mangrove-fringed
lagoon which is an ornithological
reserve mainly sheltering an important
black frigate bird colony (a guided visit
is possible). Barbuda has also got a
reputation as a hunting venue thanks to
the introduction of animals such as wild
pigs and fallow deer, left here by the
early colonists. The coral reef encircling
the island is a huge underwater park. In
it you'll find a stunning variety of
underwater flora as well as every species
of fish and crustacean, amongst them
the langoustes (local lobsters) for which
the island is famous. This concentration
of natural underwater riches, to which
you must add the many wrecks around
the shores, has made Barbuda one of
the best-known dive sites amongst
scuba enthusiasts.

Pilotage

Coast and anchorages
Approaches

The island is about 25M N of Antigua,
off the usual route towards St Martin
and the Virgin Islands. As a result it
isn't often visited. You must plan your
arrival to be in daylight and ideally in
good visibility. The island is low and
hard to spot from seaward. It is
surrounded by reef and shoals,
particularly the Codrington Shoals that
push out a long way from the S coast.
These shoals (3–4m) sometimes break
in a heavy swell. The best possible
approach is from the SW, thereby
avoiding the reefs and shoals of Palaster
Reef. In the N you should spot
Palmetto Pt and the ruins of the
Martello tower a bit further E. Make
your approach in the afternoon if you
can with the sun behind you, and head
towards the beach between Spanish
Well Point and Cocoa Point, using the
complex of hotel buildings as a lead.

South Coast

Cocoa Point

The N part of the bay is full of coral
outcrops, so anchor towards the S
keeping clear of the shoals around
Cocoa Pt itself. Don't anchor too close
to the beach of the Cocoa Point Lodge,
it is reserved for the water sports of the
clientele and doesn't welcome visitors.
Further N there's now another high
ticket hotel complex, though its
restaurant and facilities are open to
cruisers – but obviously, given the
prices, preferably the well-heeled.

Top Gravenor Bay and Spanish Point
Above Cocoa Point from S

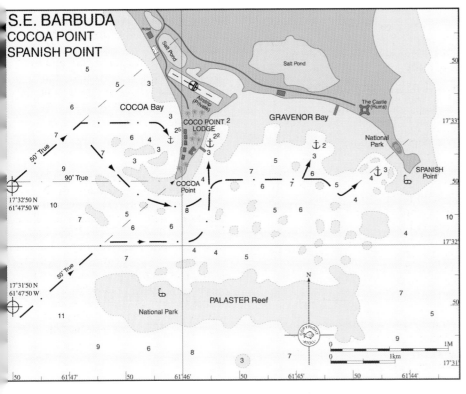

S.E. BARBUDA
COCOA POINT
SPANISH POINT

Gravenor Bay and Spanish Point

In good visibility and with a careful lookout, give the reefs around the S and W of Cocoa Pt a very good berth to get to Gravenor Bay. Several indentations split up the masses of coral which otherwise block access to the coast, and they make quite well-protected natural havens except when there's a SE swell. The most isolated of these spots is

under the lee of Spanish Pt to the S of the ruins of an old fort, protected from the Atlantic swell by the point and the reefs off it.

Note The approaches to all these anchorages must be made by eyeball in good visibility with a sharp lookout for the umpteens of bommies.

If the weather allows it, you'll be able to

stay long enough to explore the marvellous underwater world of Palaster Reef. The whole area is now classifed as a Nature Park.

West Coast

Barbuda (Boat) Harbour

This small and precarious haven, close E of the Martello tower, an old defensive work, serves small coasters and barges. You can identify it by the large sandhills on the shore and there are usually two starboard hand buoys (red here) showing the channel through the reefs on 030°T. Although it's given as a port of entry, there aren't usually any staff here. To clear you need to go to Codrington. It follows that the harbour is of no interest to cruisers.

Palmetto Point/Low Bay

On the S side of Palmetto Pt you'll see a hotel-restaurant behind the superb beach. Once around the long sand spit off Palmetto Pt you'll see the endless beach of Low Bay: more than 10km of almost deserted golden sand.

Note For boats drawing much water, the shallowest water with only 2·5–3m lies off the NW of Palmetto Pt. A thin isthmus of sand separates the sea from the lagoon and at the narrowest point (see plan) you can without much difficulty lift a light tender across into the lagoon to get to Codrington. The middle and the N of the bay are full of isolated reef patches. You can get round the first, Tuson Rock, by passing between it and the shore in order to anchor a bit further N, close to a small building beneath a topknot of palms. The anchorage is calm except in a N swell. In this immensity of sand that seems almost awash, just a few boats are testimony to the presence of humanity. It's a rare enough experience, even in the Antilles.

Useful Information for Barbuda

AIRLINE/SEA CONNECTIONS
Codrington airstrip: connections with Antigua by a local airline and by air taxi
Ferry services to St John's and English Harbour.

TELECOMMUNICATIONS
Calling from abroad: t (1) 268 + 7 digits
Local call: 7 digits

TOURIST OFFICE/ASSOCIATION
See Antigua

ROAD TRANSPORT
Taxis (drive on the left)

REGULATIONS
Land and sea reserve, all underwater hunting forbidden to non-residents

FORMALITIES (see also Antigua)
In Codrington: Police and customs in the village. In principle you can clear in and out here. Find out if you need a cruising permit.

Montserrat

Area 106sq km
Highest point Chances Peak
913m
Population about 12,000;
after the eruption around
4000
Capital Plymouth
Language English
Currency EC$
Political status British dependent territory
Distances to nearby islands Guadeloupe
(Deshaies) 32M, Nevis 30M

Note Montserrat's volcano (Galway's Soufrière) resumed activity in 1995 after being extinct for a long time. The first eruptions in 1995 required the evacuation of the S of the island and Plymouth, the capital. From April 1996 the build-up of andesite lava created a large dome which, collapsing in several stages, caused pyroclastic flows. These successive outflows and discharges, which are still going on, were interspersed by explosive eruptions of which some (as in August 1997) throw tons of ash up to 10,000m in the air. The events have claimed several lives and devastated the island's whole southern part, burying Plymouth and its surrounding settlements as far as the airport. Protected by the massif of Central Hill, only the N of the island has been spared. The part of the population from the afflicted zone that hasn't left the island has taken refuge in the N. An Exclusion Zone has been instituted, covering the whole S of the island up to two nautical miles off the shores, to which access is forbidden. Montserrat Volcano Observatory is following how Galway's Soufrière is evolving so as to keep the population informed and to issue timely alerts.

History

The island was discovered by Columbus in 1493. It reminded him of the countryside around the Catalan monastery of Montserrat, so he named the island after it. From 1632 the island became the refuge of Irish Catholics suffering from English persecution during Cromwell's time. Given its strategic position, it was one of the centres of the struggles between the French and the English during the 18th century. It became definitively British following the Treaty of Versailles in 1783. As with Antigua, the brief French interludes have left no trace, quite unlike the island's Irish past, which is echoed in some of the local surnames of today's descendants of African slaves, as well as in some traditions like the celebration of St Patrick's Day. Some people fancy that, just as Catholicism has survived here, there's a trace of an Irish accent too.

These days, although Montserrat is still a British colony, the island has a certain autonomy in that the Governor chooses a Chief Minister from a legislative council elected by universal suffrage.

The island's volcanic soil is very fertile; in the middle of the 17th century the development of farming was encouraged, particularly the growing of sugar cane. With the abolition of slavery cane growing rapidly declined. With a diversification into cotton growing, fishing and market gardening, the island these days is all but self-sufficient.

As far as tourism is concerned Montserrat's green hills led to it being called the 'Emerald Isle'. The tranquil and cool ambience of the countryside attracted many British and Canadians to the island. However, those first flowers of a tourist trade were brutally nipped in the bud by a succession of fearsome hurricanes. Then, to deliver the *coup de grâce*, Galway's Soufrière erupted, burying the entire S of the island (see above). All the island's everyday life and government shifted entirely to the small settlements in the N of the island, principally Salem and St Peter's. Now that the land in the S, always the most fertile, is lost, agriculture has all but collapsed. The cataclysm caused almost half the population to emigrate to neighbouring islands, leaving less than 4000 people behind.

Tourism

Where to stay and what to see

The small airstrip of Blackburne (William H Bramble) is now closed. The island can be reached by ferry from Antigua, or by helicopter. The loveliest places in the S have been destroyed, which means the Bamboo Forest and the Great Alp Falls are no more. All the same, the N part of Montserrat has some beautiful spots, with the possibility of good walking through the tropical greenery. Along the road to Salem, the lovely green site of Runaway Ghaut is a splendid place to picnic. There's a mineral water spring here. According to the legend, which you'll

Above Cottage at St Peter's
Below Galway's Soufrière & the ruins of Plymouth

hear from the local guide, if you drink from it you'll certainly come back to Montserrat.

Except during periods of eruption alert, tours are organised to the 'Day Time Entry Zone'. From the heights of Garibaldi Hill you can see the huge volcano that still belches out jets of steam from its jagged dome. On its S side you'll see what looks like the aftermath of an atomic bomb explosion running down to the sea, from which the calcined ruins of Plymouth poke out of the ashes. It's a desolate sight for those who knew the little town with its coloured old colonial houses.

In the N of the island a few simple hotel-restaurants are still open and others have reopened after moving up from the S.

In the N the coast has several fine beaches of black sand, Rendezvous Bay being the only one with white sand. The seabed here, volcanic in origin, has several fine dive sites. To these meagre attractions the Montserratians add their own warm welcome to the infrequent tourists who arrive, and, subject for the moment to the power of nature, they try to survive as best they may.

Pilotage

Coast and anchorages

Montserrat always had the reputation of having few protected anchorages. The eruption has reduced what there was still further.

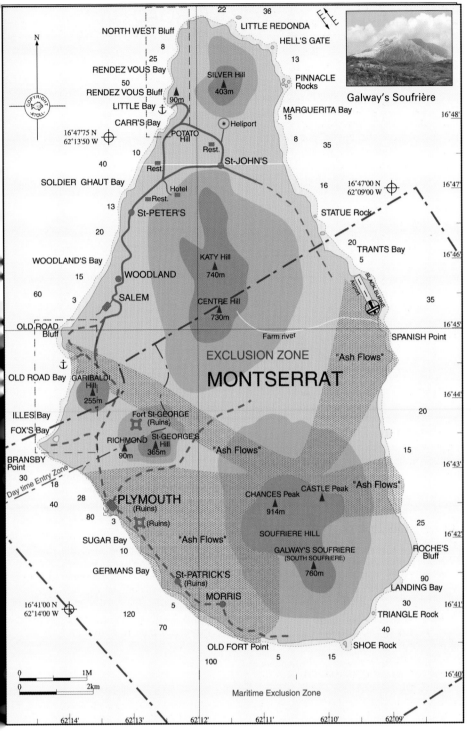

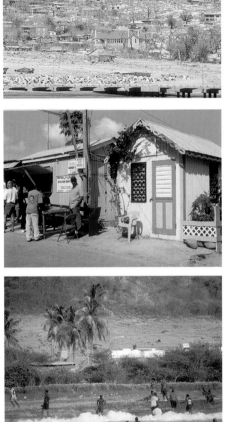

Above, from top
The ruins of Plymouth
A bar and shop at Little Bay
Swimming at Little Bay

Note The approaches to the S of the island and Plymouth are prohibited. The Exclusion Zone extends out to 2M from the coast

Little Bay

This haven is the port of entry for Montserrat and hence an obligatory first stop. The authorities listen out on VHF 16. The harbour facilities are limited to a dock for ferries to ensure connections to Antigua and for coasters to transport the island's freight. If the wind and swell swing to the NE it can become rolly and uncomfortable. The best anchorage is S of the dock in 3–4m,

being sure to leave manoeuvring room off the dock. The shoreline is not entirely obvious, so be cautious.

Ashore In the small port zone you'll find the port office, the police and customs with whom you can complete formalities.

Note Use clearance to find out about the accessibility of the anchorage at Old Road Bay. Although it is outside the Exclusion Zone, it is often off limits as a result of frequent alerts. On the road out of the port and beside it there are some huts and small painted cottages housing simple bars with a very local atmosphere. There are also small

souvenir shops but nothing for provisioning. To find the first grocery stores you have to head for the small settlements of St John or St Peter's. The only supermarket is several kilometres away in Salem. Numerous taxis are available for making the trip (about EC$40 to Salem) or to take you round the part of the island open to tourists. It's also possible to hire a car. The few hotels and restaurants are spread on the hills in the neighbourhood of, or on the roads leading to St Peter's and St John.

Rendezvous Bay

In good weather you can anchor off the island's only white sand beach. In any well-established wind swell makes the bay untenable. You can also get to the beach by coming along the footpath from Little Bay. It's a deserted spot bar a single house overlooking the shore.

Old Road Bay

Protected by the point at Old Road Bluff, this anchorage is generally the least uncomfortable when there's a N swell. The whole S part of the shore has

Anchorage off Rendezvous Bluff

been buried in the ash flow that destroyed the old golf course. The hotel buildings a bit further N have for the time being escaped.

Note The volcano's outpourings have pushed the beach seawards and markedly reduced depths close to shore. The small dock is only accessible by tender. Just now the area is still menaced by the volcano and everything is closed down.

Useful Information for Montserrat

AIRLINE/SEA CONNECTIONS
Blackburne Heliport:
  Service to Antigua (Wednesdays excepted)
Ferry service from Little Bay to Antigua
  (Sundays excepted)

TELECOMMUNICATIONS
Calling from abroad: ☎ 664 + 7 digits
Local call: 7 digits

TOURIST OFFICE
Tourist Office, Olveston
  ☎ 664 491 2230 *Fax* 664 491 7430
  www.visitmontserrat.com

PUBLIC HOLIDAYS
New Year's day (1 January), St Patrick's Day (17 March), Good Friday, Easter Monday, Labour Day (1st Monday in May), Whit Monday (7th Monday after Easter), 1st Monday in August, Christmas Day (25 December), Boxing Day (26 December), Festival Day (31 December)

OFFICE HOURS
Shops: Mon, Tues, Thurs, Fri, 0800–1600.
  Wed & Sat 0800–1200
Government Offices: Mon–Fri, 0800–1600

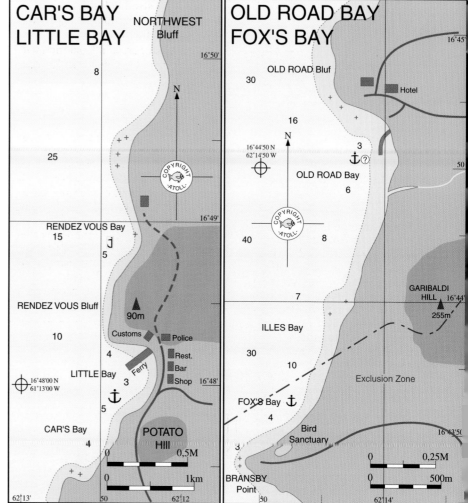

SAFETY INFORMATION
Montserrat Volcano Observatory:
  ☎ 664 491 5647 *Fax* 664 491 2423
  Email mvo@mvomrat.com
  www.mvo.ms
Note In case of eruptions, the situation in the S of the island affects visits there.

To get information:
Volcano Observatory (see above)
Tourist Office ☎ 664 491 2230
Radio Montserrat, 88·3/91·1/95·5 FM
See also the radio station website
  www.mratgov.com/newsradio.htm and that of the local newspaper, (The Montserrat Reporter) www.montserratreporter.org

FORMALITIES
Little Bay
VHF 16
  Hours: 0800–1600 Monday to Friday
  Overtime: out of hours, weekends (approx EC$100)
Fees and taxes
Port dues EC$35-40.

For visits of less than 24hrs, entry and exit clearance is done simultaneously.

Below left Little Bay from the SE
Below right Rendezvous Bay & Northwest Bluff

Nevis

Area 90sq km.
Highest point Nevis Peak
  985m
Population 10,000
Capital Charlestown
  (population 2000)
Language English
Currency EC$–US$ accepted
Political status Independent state with St
  Kitt's
Distances to nearby islands
  Montserrat 30M, St Kitts 2M

History

Called Oualie by the Amerindians,
Nevis has a history closely tied to that
of St Kitts. In 1493 Columbus called
the island Las Nieves (the snowy ones),
because of the clouds, looking like snow
peaks, that often crown Nevis Peak. As
early as 1628 several dozen English
colonists from St Kitts founded
Jamestown on the N coast. The
settlement was destroyed in an
earthquake in 1680 and disappeared
under the sea. Charlestown was built
instead under the guns of Fort Charles.
Thereafter, unlike St Kitts and despite
French attacks, Nevis remained British.
In the 18th century it became a
prosperous island covered with
plantations and fine houses, so much so
that it became known as the Queen of
the Caribbean. The island has had its
famous figures too. On 11th March
1787 Horatio Nelson married the young
island widow Frances Herbert Nisbet.
And on 11th January 1757 one of the
future fathers of the USA, Alexander
Hamilton, was born in Charlestown.

At the time Nevis was renowned as far
away as Europe for its hot sulphur
springs, thought to be good for the
health. A spa hotel was founded as early
as 1778. From this period of plenty
little survives save a few old houses and
the traces of rich plantations in the
countryside.

Then Nevis went to sleep, with the last
sugar plantation being closed in 1930,
and these days there are only
smallholdings run by simple farmers.
The economic decline has only partly
been compensated for by tourism and

Cannons at Fort Charles

the island has steadily lost its
population, their number falling from
14,000 to 10,000 in ten years.
Nevis has been part of a federation with
St Kitts since independence in 1983.

Tourism

Where to stay and what to see

The peacefulness of Nevis, allied to its
tranquil countryside, has attracted
people from Britain and North America
for many years now, above all rich
retirees. Old plantation mansions have
been restored and turned into charming
hotels amidst the greenery, and new
luxury hotels have been built along the
leeward coast. The 90sq km of land is
dominated by the ancient volcanic cone
of Nevis Peak, the island's only
mountain. Its slopes run in sweet green
curves down to the sea giving Nevis its

round, almost regular shape. The shore
has fine sandy beaches fringed with
coconut palms, several amongst them
still nearly empty of people.

Charlestown

The island's capital, which was partly
destroyed by fire in 1873, has a
population of less than 2000, which
gives it a sleepy, even happy-go-lucky
atmosphere. The red-roofed, partly
restored wooden houses with stone bases
share the streets with even simpler
cottages. The only parts of town with
much life are around the port and on
Main St, which runs through the
charming, shady little Memorial Square.
On Main St there are several banks and
travel agents as well as small shops,
some of which sell local crafts. In the
grocery stores and minimarkets the
variety is mainly of rum and other
alcohol. For fresh produce, the Public

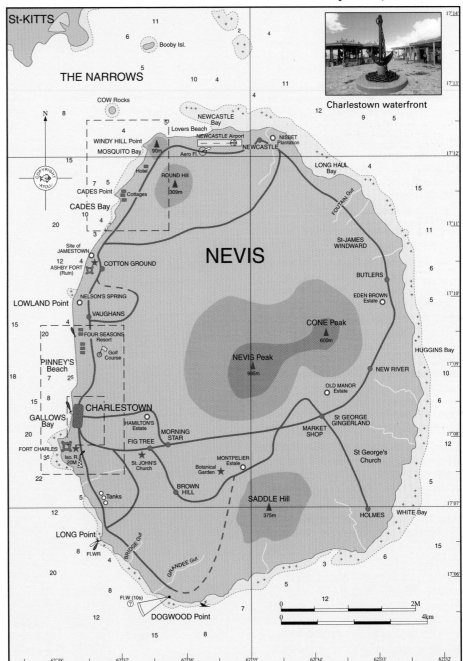

Charlestown waterfront

Above Nevis and The Narrows from S
Right Pinney's Beach and Gallows Bay from NW

Market is where you'll find all the island's market garden produce as well as fresh fish. For stamp collectors the Nevis Philatelic Bureau has fine specimens of rare and other stamps. The churches and government buildings are good examples of colonial architecture; in particular look at the Methodist Church on Chapel Street, with its quite severe, gothic arched porch, which was built by recently liberated ex-slaves in 1844, and the smaller and simpler St Paul's Anglican church. At the other end of town the Bath House is no longer in business despite several attempts to get it back in working order. The basins of the old hot baths are now empty. Of Fort Charles, built in the 17th century to defend the town approaches, only overgrown walls and a few old cannons on the edge of the sea remain.

Around the island

Heading N the road runs along the seemingly endless Pinney's Beach. Half way up it you'll find the huge and luxurious Four Seasons Resort with its superbly landscaped golf course. Further on you'll pass close to Nelson's Springs where, according to legend, Nelson watered ship during his many stops here before going off to fight in American waters. Then come the ruins of Ashby Fort, below which are the now submerged ruins of the old capital of Jamestown.

In the extreme N of the island you'll find Newcastle airport beside the village of the same name, with its pottery studio. Close by, the fine Nisbet Beach is fringed with a large coconut palm grove.

The coast road ringing the island runs on through old plantations, some of which have been turned into cottage resorts.

In the middle of the island, on the SW slopes of Nevis Peak you'll cross Nelson's path as you go through the village of Fig Tree where the Admiral and his bride Frances Nisbet were married. Further S is the Montpelier

Plantation where the couple briefly lived. Close to both is the Morning Star Estate where there's a collection of Nelson's documents and personal effects, which an American Nelson

enthusiast put together. The other notable figure in Nevis' past, Alexander Hamilton, lived for his first five years in a fine Georgian house on the edge of Charlestown, which is now a museum.

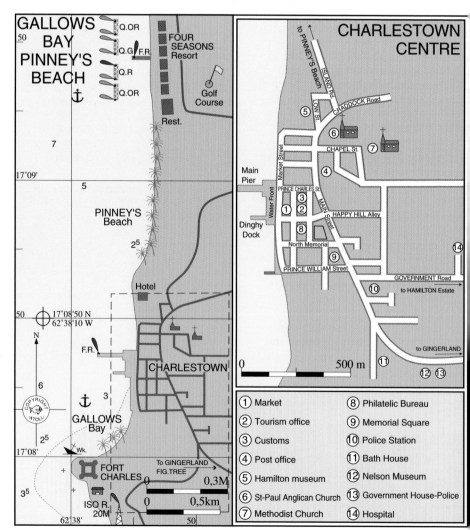

① Market	⑧ Philatelic Bureau
② Tourism office	⑨ Memorial Square
③ Customs	⑩ Police Station
④ Post office	⑪ Bath House
⑤ Hamilton museum	⑫ Nelson Museum
⑥ St-Paul Anglican Church	⑬ Government House-Police
⑦ Methodist Church	⑭ Hospital

Pilotage

Coast and anchorages

Like its neighbours, thanks to its mountain Nevis is easy to pick up on approach. Coming from the S round Dogwood Pt and hold a good distance off the shore towards Long Pt. There you'll see the new deepwater harbour installation on its reclamation. Bar the presence of the authorities for clearance, there's nothing for yachts in this area dominated by tanks and warehouses. In principle the dock is lit at night.

Note Approaching Fort Charles Pt keep a good 0·5M off. There are shoals <2m pushing further out than shown on the chart.

Gallows Bay (Charlestown)

Once round Fort Charles Pt you're in Charlestown or Gallows Bay. The air warning lights on the radio mast on Fort Charles Pt are very obvious at night. The best anchorage, sometimes a bit rolly, is on your starboard hand between the dock and the ruins of the fort on sand in 2.5-4m. The Charlestown waterfront has a recently built concrete dock for small coasters and ferries and another smaller one for tenders. It's possible to have fuel and water delivered to the dock (large amounts only) if you get authorisation to come alongside from the authorities first (VHF 16)

Ashore The Waterfront esplanade is lovely, with pretty kiosk-like shelters and several brightly painted small buildings housing restaurants and a shopping centre. Customs are close to the dock and the police a bit further E. Other than a few mechanics to cope with breakdowns, there are no specialized yacht services in Nevis.

The shops and minimarkets are fine for essentials, as is the produce market (especially on Saturday morning). There are small restaurants in more or less restored old houses, which have local dishes at good prices. You can hire cars or taxis if you want to use the chance to make a tour of the island.

Dr Walwyn Plaza

Useful Information for Nevis

AIRLINE CONNECTIONS
Newcastle Airport ☎ 869 469 9543
No international long-haul flights
Inter-island services: Daily flights to neighbouring islands (Antigua, St-Martin, St Croix) and to San Juan

FERRIES
Regular daily services between St Kitts and Nevis

TELECOMMUNICATIONS
Calling from abroad: ☎ (1) 869 + 7 digits
 Local call: 7 digits
 Public call boxes: Skantel cards

TOURIST OFFICE
Tourist Office: Main Street, Charlestown
 ☎ 869 469 1042 *Fax* 869 469 1066
 Email nevtour@caribsurf.com
Nevis Philatelic Bureau: ☎ 869 469 5535
 Fax 869 469 0617
 Email philbur@caribsurf.com

FESTIVALS/FOLK FESTIVALS
Culturama: end of July/beginning of August
Carnival: end of December (Christmas Sport)

PUBLIC HOLIDAYS
New Year's Day (1 January), Carnival/Las' Lap (2 January), Good Friday, Easter Monday, May Day (1st Mon in May), Whit Monday, Queen's Birthday (June), August Monday/Emancipation Day (beginning of August), National Heroes Day (16 September), Independence Day (19 September), Christmas Day (25 December), Boxing Day (26 December)

OFFICE HOURS
Post Office: Mon–Wed & Fri 0800–1500, Thurs 0800–1100, Sat 0800–1200

PLACES TO SEE
Fort Charles (1690)
Hot Baths: old hot springs (1778)
Ashby Fort
Nelson Museum
Hamilton House (Museum of Nevis)
Botanical Garden

ROAD TRANSPORT
Drive on the left; licence obligatory
Taxis, hire cars available in Charlestown and at the airport

FORMALITIES
Arriving by air customs and immigration at the airport
Arriving by sea
Charlestown customs near dock, immigration on Independence Square. Hours: 0800–1200 weekdays
Long Point Port hours 0800–1600 weekdays, Saturday 0800–1000 (overtime charged)
Fees and taxes
Each boat is taxed and pays an entry fee, a port due and a small tax per crew member. For some anchorages a Cruising Permit is required.
Formalities and payments are common to St Kitts and Nevis
To go on to St Kitts you must get authorisation first.

Pinney's Beach

After checking in at Charlestown, most boats go and anchor about 1M further N off this long, lovely beach, usually near the Four Seasons dock. In a N swell the anchorage can be uncomfortable.

Note You must keep clear of the four beach-preserving breakwaters built by the hotel a cable or so either side of 17° 09'·5N about 100m off the beach. In principle they're lit at night. The hotel dock is reserved for hotel boats and hotel clientele.

Ashore You'll find the luxurious facilities of the Four Seasons Hotel. Some restaurants are to be found at both S and N ends of the beach.

Cades Bay (Tamarind Bay)

This little bay N of Pinney's Beach is sheltered by Cades Pt. Part of the shoreline is encumbered with shoals and there are several local boats on moorings, so there's not much room to

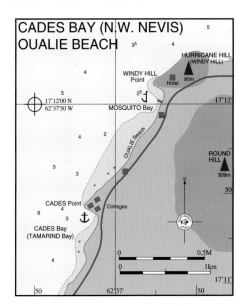

CADES BAY (N.W. NEVIS)
OUALIE BEACH

tuck in. If there's a N swell things quickly get uncomfortable. Along the shore and in the neighbourhood are several hotels, cottages and bar-restaurants that welcome passing yachts as well as tourists. Further N there's no real shelter to be had. You can always get to pretty Oualie Beach by a short walk from Cades Bay. On your way you'll discover that from up on Cades Pt there's a good panoramic view over both bays. In Oualie Beach there's a hotel with its cottages and a dive and water sports centre. The best dive sites in Nevis are on the N coast and in good weather on the drying reefs and islets of The Narrows. That said, you should always watch out for the currents, which can sometimes be very strong.

St Kitts
(St Christopher)

Area 168sq km
Highest point Mount Liamuiga (pronounced Lee-a-mee-ga) (Mount Misery) 1150m
Population 6000
Capital Basseterre
Language English
Currency EC$ (US$ accepted)
Political status Independent state (with Nevis)
Distances to nearby islands St Eustatius (Statia) 7M, St-Barthélémy 30M

History

In giving his own name to this small island, Christopher Columbus could never have known that it would become the 'Mother Island' of the Lesser Antilles from which all the British and French colonists left to conquer the other islands. The first English colonists, led by Thomas Warner, arrived in 1624. Several months later the French followed them, led by the famous Norman Belain d'Esnambuc. The two groups allied in order to combat first the Caribs and then the Spanish who, in 1629, pushed them all off the island and burned their houses. Some went on to found the buccaneer lair of Tortuga, others returned. The two colonial groups got organised and divided the island between them. The far N and the S (including the town of Basseterre) went to the French; all the rest went to the British. You can roughly trace the old division in the names of many places.

The land was fertile, indeed the Caribs had called it Liamuiga or Fertile Island. Tobacco, cotton and then sugar plantations all rapidly prospered. It was during this period, led above all by the French, that the conquest of the other islands of the Caribbean began. D'Esnambuc took Martinique, where he died in 1638. Chevalier Lienard de l'Olive and le Sieur Duplessis d'Ossonville occupied Guadeloupe. The famous Captain General Philippe de Lonvilliers de Poincy pushed as far as the Virgins where he captured St Croix, but he returned to St Kitts to build himself a castle, where he died in 1660. This ostentatious dwelling was once held to be the 'marvel of the islands', which didn't stop it being destroyed by an earthquake in 1685.

Following the Treaty of Utrecht on 31 March 1713, Louis XIV ceded the French part of the island to England. However, 6000 Frenchmen under the command of the Marquis de Bouille came back in 1782 and took the 'Gibraltar of the West Indies', Brimstone Hill Fortress, by storm. They held on for a year until the French fleet was defeated in the Battle of the Saints. The Treaty of Paris in 1783 made the island definitively British.

During colonial times St Kitts, Nevis and Anguilla were administered together by the Colonial Office. The

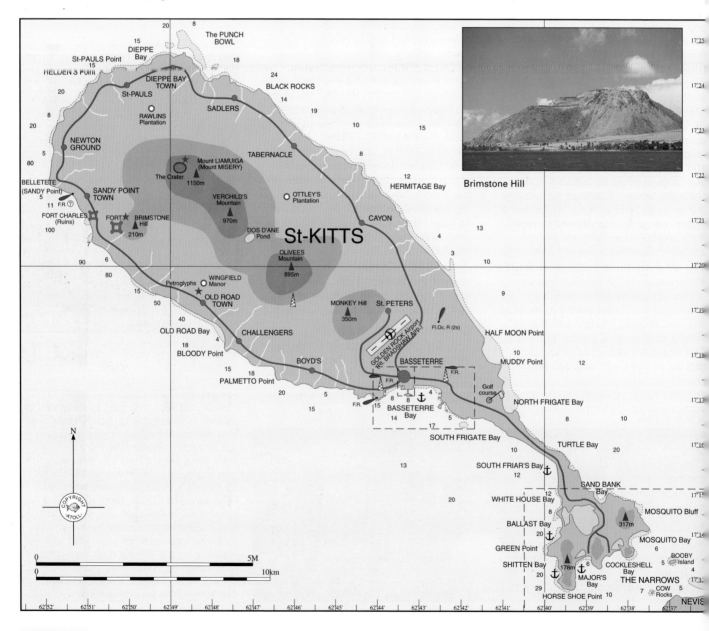

Brimstone Hill

group was then made an associated state of the Commonwealth on 27 February 1967. Distant Anguilla was not happy to become what it felt to be a colony of an old colony, so seceded and has since then not been part of St Kitts (see Anguilla). In September 1983 the Federation of St Kitts and Nevis became an independent state of the Commonwealth. Economically, and despite the growth of tourism, St Kitts relies mainly on agriculture, particularly sugar cane production, which occupies most of the cultivated land. All of the sugar cane grown on the island is treated in the single processing plant in Basseterre, which is worth a visit. That said, to ease the problem of a declining agricultural sector, for some years now the government has actively encouraged the development of tourism. Mute testimony to that emphasis are the recently completed and projected hotels and other attractions which cover the gamut from super luxury to simple cottages. Some of these are charming old restored houses in the middle of old and lovely green plantation scenery. In the same spirit, in Basseterre itself the waterfront has been developed to provide docking for both cruise liners and yachts.

Tourism

Where to stay and what to see

The island's interior is dominated by two volcanic massifs and by the vegetation covering them, which varies as you ascend the slopes. The highest summits are pastureland. Lower down the slopes you'll see tropical forest. Below 300m the natural forest has mostly gone and fields take its place. Like the forested hills, the salt lake dominated peninsula forming the S appendage of St Kitts is virtually uninhabited.

Basseterre

Built by the French in the 18th century, the capital, which has the same name as Guadeloupe's, has been frequently ravaged by hurricanes and earthquakes, though the fire of 1867 that destroyed virtually all the old French buildings stands out. Rebuilt in the late 19th century to the geometric pattern common at the time in the Antilles, the town's pastel-hued houses, surrounded by balustraded verandas, give it a very British charm. The heart of the town is partly made up of a quaint, small, octagonal square called The Circus, in the middle of which is the Victorian Thomas Berkeley Memorial clock tower. Around are numerous bar-restaurants some of which have marvellous terraces overlooking the square. If you head off down Bank Street, you'll reach Independence Square enclosed by colonial style buildings. The Catholic Church of the Immaculate Conception and its two towers sits not far from the Anglican St George's Church. The latter, built in the 17th century, has been destroyed several times. Its present appearance with a massive brown tower dates from the end of the 19th century.

On the colourful stalls of the Public Market, on Bay Road west of the port, you'll find all sorts of market garden produce and fresh fish.

On the new sea front, which is still being finished off, luxury shops have been grouped in big shopping arcades for the new cruise liner tourist trade.

Top St Kitts from NW
Right Thomas Berkeley Memorial, The Circus, Basseterre
Below Independence Square, Basseterre

Around the island

Main Road, the single road around almost the whole of the island, runs west towards Bloody Point where, in the 17th century, 2000 Carib Indians were massacred for trying to resist the colonists. Close by, Wingfield Manor is built on an old Carib site where there are still some rock carvings. A bit off the road you'll also find the old plantation mansion of Romney Manor, these days home to the Caribelle Batik Factory.

On Brimstone Hill, there's a grey stone fort from which there's a stunning view over the sea and the neighbouring islands. It was in this massive fort that the decisive battle took place between the English and the French over possession of the island during the American War of Independence in 1782. Today the site is a National Park and Brimstone Hill Fortress houses a museum dealing with the history of St Kitts. Further N past some beaches the road reaches the windward coast and

the site of Black Rocks, where lava flows have suddenly solidified as they reached the sea. From Black Rocks walkers can climb Mt Liamuiga (Mt Misery as it used to be called), which takes several hours. The interior of the mountain's crater is now filled with tropical rain forest and populated with rainbow-hued birds and, on Monkey Hill a bit further S, monkeys. The vervets or green

Above The Narrows and Nevis from NW
Below The S of St Kitts and The Narrows

monkeys, which were introduced by the French in the 17th century, are one of the island's curiosities. From Basseterre along the narrow neck of land that extends the island south eastwards there are concentrations of tourist development, the main one around Frigate Bay.

Pilotage

Coast and anchorages

St Kitts is separated from Nevis by a strait less than 2M wide called The Narrows. In its S part St Kitts extends in a peninsula around which you'll find the island's best anchorages with lovely white sand beaches.

The Narrows

Yachts who don't know this area don't much use The Narrows because it has some awkward shoals and the islets of Bobby Island (38m) and Cow Rocks (2m). In addition the current can be very strong. Coming from N, to find the easiest route hold Bobby Island on 198°T until about 0·5M N of it roughly due E of Mosquito Bluff, then leave Bobby Island to port and head to pass S of Nag's Head (Horse Shoe Pt).

Anchorages S of Basseterre

Cockleshell Bay

This is not the best anchorage in The Narrows because quite lively in fresh trades. The W part is somewhat shoal (1·5–2·5m). Anchor in the lee of the small headland in the E part in 3–5m.
Ashore You can get to the fine beach of Turtle Bay by following the track around the salt pond. In Turtle Bay there's a restaurant and water sports centre.

Major's Bay

This is more comfortable than Cockleshell Bay, though it is often empty. That said, it can also be rolly if the wind is ESE. Best to anchor well into the bay under the E point.

Shitten Bay

Once round Nags Head (Horse Shoe Pt) Shitten Bay opens up. It's a small, quiet inlet, which although quite well sheltered isn't much frequented.

Ballast Bay

N of Green Pt the large, open reach of Ballast Bay with its beach is one of the best anchorages in St Kitts. Anchor S of the low headland of Guana Pt.

Note Bommies and offliers push at least 100m W of Guana Pt. Coming over the small hills, gusts can sometimes be violent.

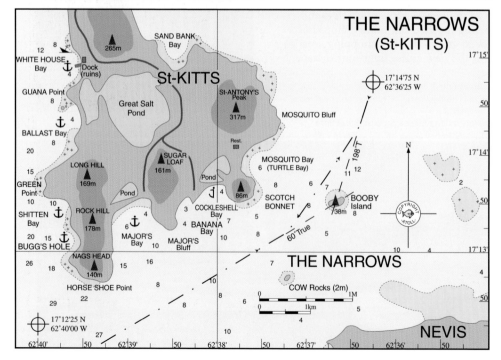

White House Bay

N of Guana Pt White House Bay is also a good anchorage. Though not as commodious as Ballast Bay it's often less windy. Anchor in 4m close to the ruins of an old dock.

Friar's/Frigate Bay

Swell can make anchorage in this large, open bay uncomfortable. Its large beach is the island's most touristy and around the shores are several hotels, a golf course, a casino and water sports centres as well as several restaurants.

Above Basseterre Bay and Frigate Bay
Below left Port Zante Office, Basseterre
Below right Port Zante Marina

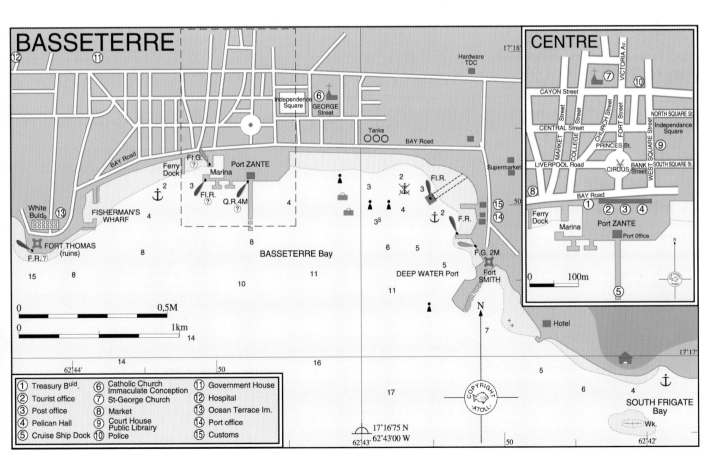

BASSETERRE

CENTRE

①	Treasury Buid.	⑥	Catholic Church Immaculate Conception	⑪	Government House
②	Tourist office	⑦	St-George Church	⑫	Hospital
③	Post office	⑧	Market	⑬	Ocean Terrace Im.
④	Pelican Hall	⑨	Court House Public Librairy	⑭	Port office
⑤	Cruise Ship Dock	⑩	Police	⑮	Customs

NW St Kitts with Mt Liamuiga (Mt Misery) and Brimstone Hill

Basseterre Bay

Swell can also make this uncomfortable. However, it is an unavoidable stop for clearance and if you want to visit the island. In a SE swell the best spot is close to the Deep Water Port provided you leave access to the dock free.

The Basseterre sea front has been developed with a huge esplanade where a long cruise ship dock reaches the shore with, on one side, a small marina. The work has often been delayed by hurricane damage. The last, Hurricane Lenny in November 1999, destroyed the dock and part of the marina. The whole area is called Port Zante. You can take on fuel and water here at the marina where there are about 30 equipped berths. In a swell a violent reflected sea can penetrate and rattle round this small shelter.

Ashore On the bit of the esplanade facing the sea there's an imposing building in a neo-classical style housing the port office, customs and immigration. If there's no one there, there's another set of offices at the Deep Water Dock. Behind this building you'll find Pelican Hall in a large neo-colonial building with its many luxury shops.

Thanks to the shops and the market Basseterre is a good provisioning stop. The larger supermarkets are on the way to the commercial port, as is a very large hardware and general store for any emergency. When you stop here, don't forget to enjoy a wander round the streets and visit the charming bar-restaurants. The new marina allows you to leave your boat safely to hire a car and tour the island.

N of Basseterre

The leeward coast beyond Basseterre to the W has no real shelter. As you sail along the coast you'll see lots of stone chimneys, remains of old sugar works, until you reach dominant, fortified Brimstone Hill.

The NW coast has no shelter to speak of but does have interesting dive sites much visited by local clubs.

Useful Information for St Kitts

AIRLINE CONNECTIONS
Robert L Bradshaw International Airport (Golden Rock Airport) ☎ 869 465 8472
International long-haul flights Several times a week to New York
Inter-island flights Daily flights to neighbouring islands (Antigua, St Maarten) and San Juan

FERRIES
Regular daily service to/from Nevis

TELECOMMUNICATIONS
Calling from abroad: ☎ (1) 869 + 7 digits
Local call: 7 digits
Public call boxes: Skantel cards

TOURIST OFFICE
Tourist Office, Pelican Mall, Basseterre
☎ 869 465 4040 *Fax* 869 465 8794
Email tourinfo@caribsurf.com

FESTIVALS/FOLK FESTIVALS
Music Festival: July
The Caribbean Offshore Race (St Maarten–St Kitts–St Maarten): last full moon in May/first full moon in June
Food Festival: November
Carnival (Christmas Sports): end of December

PUBLIC HOLIDAYS
New Year's Day (1 January), Carnival/Las' Lap (2 January), Good Friday, Easter Monday, May Day (1st Mon in May), Whit Monday, Queen's Birthday (June), August Monday/Emancipation Day (beginning August), National Heroes Day (16 September), Independence Day (19 September), Christmas Day (25 December), Boxing Day (26 December)

PLACES TO SEE
The Circus & Berkeley Memorial: centre of Basseterre
Independence Square
St George's Anglican Church (1856-69)
Brimstone Hill Fortress: Museum
Wingfield Manor: old plantation and petroglyphs
Romney Manor: Caribelle Batik Factory
Mt Liamuiga (Mt Misery): walks

GOLF
Royal St Kitts Golf Club: Frigate Bay
☎ 869 465 8339 Fax 869 465 4463 (18 holes)

ROAD TRANSPORT
Drive on the left – local licence required (costs EC$50)
Hire car companies at Basseterre and the airport
Taxis

FORMALITIES
Arriving by air at the airport
Arriving by sea – 2 offices:
Basseterre Port Zante, in the Port Office (see plan)
Deep Water Port (see plan), VHF 16
Hours: weekdays 0600–1900
Saturdays 0600–0900, Sundays 1500–1700
Overtime: out of office hours, weekends and public holidays
Fees and taxes
Boat levy, Cruising and entry permit, port dues (according to boat length) plus a small tax per person.
St Kitts & Nevis have a common system of formalities
To go on to Nevis you must get authorisation first.

Statia
(Sint Eustatius)

Area 21sq km
Highest point Mazinga (The Quill) 600m
Population 2000
Capital Oranjestad
Language Dutch (official), English (everyday)
Currency Dutch Antilles Florin (Guilder), US$
Political status Constituent part of the self-governing Dutch Netherlands Antilles Federation
Distances to nearby islands St Kitts 7M, Saba 14M

Top Fort Oranje battery and Gallows Bay
Above left Entrance to Fort Oranje
Above right Oranje Baaï from Fort Oranje

History

Statia (pronounced Stay-sha) was discovered in 1493 by Columbus. From 1630 on the English and French occupied the island in turns before it was colonised by Dutch Jews. It was they who built Fort Oranje. In 1713, when the fighting between French and English was settled by the Treaty of Utrecht, the Dutch got definitive possession. As a free port Statia was one of the most active in the Caribbean, especially during the US War of Independence. The wealth of its inhabitants, who numbered nearly 8000 in the 18th century, gave it the sobriquet 'Rock of Gold'. On 16 November 1776, Oranjestad's Fort Oranje became the first place in the world to fire a salute to the new flag of an American ship, the *Andrew Doria*. In 1781 Admiral Rodney revenged himself on what he took to be an insult to England by pillaging the island. It was the beginning of a decline and today there's scarcely a trace of that boom time, save Fort Oranje and a few ruined warehouses on the shore. The resident population has collapsed to a mere 1500 or so, most of them retirees. An administrator and a local council attend to the island's own affairs and otherwise

Below left Ruins of the Synagogue
Below right The old Anglican church and cemetery

Statia is part of Sint Maarten. A few farms and the beginnings of a tourist industry just about keep Statia awake.

Tourism

Where to stay and what to see

Statia's 20sq km of gentle green slopes culminate in the steep extinct volcano of The Quill (also called Mazinga) in the island's S. The hilltops are forested and the central plain is given over to farming. The steep terrain and volcanic origin of the island mean there are only a few beaches of grey sand. The hotels are generally small, with a clientele mainly of dive enthusiasts, for the island's underwater world is kept well preserved by the National Park and that's why dive centres have sprung up in Oranjestad.

Oranjestad

The only settlement in the island, Oranjestad is divided into Upper and Lower Towns. The former is built on the cliff top. The latter lies on the shore, its older buildings mostly ruins because of the ravages of the sea and hurricanes. That said, some of them, now renovated, are testimony to the attractive architecture of these former warehouses. A steep, narrow road, the Old Slave Road joins the two. It dates from the 18th century when it was used for slave traffic. Dominating the bay, the best preserved monument is Fort Oranje. It has been restored down to the last detail, which gives it rather the air of a film set. From the commanding heights once used to defend the town, the fort now looks out over a marvellous view covering the whole of Statia's leeward coast. Other contemporary buildings are witness to the lost wealth and to the past of the island.

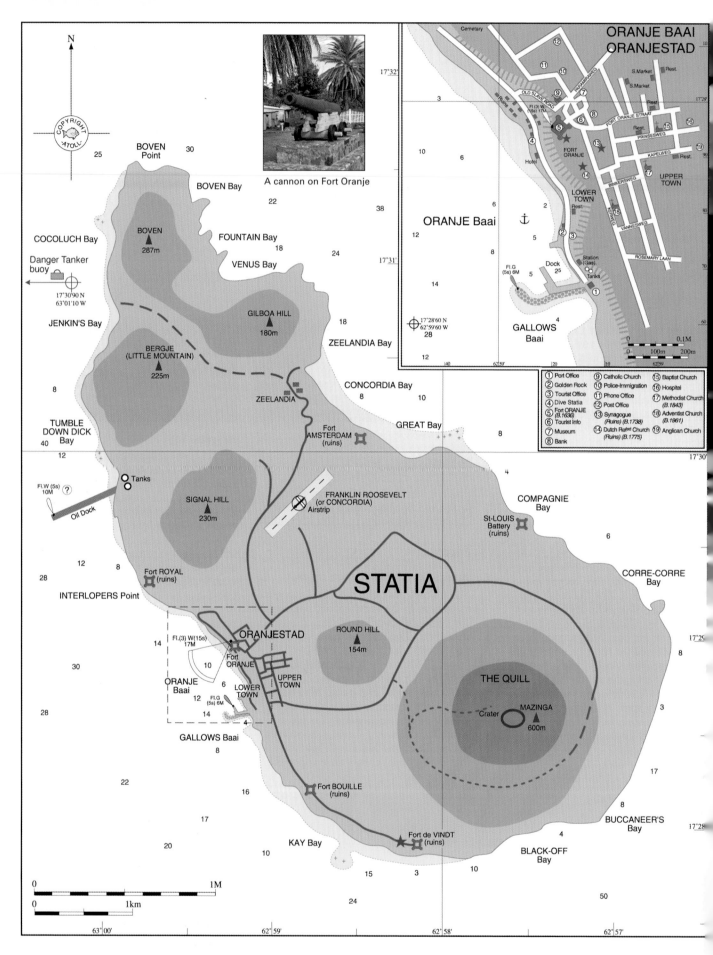

Above left Cottage with veranda
Above right Cottage with verandah

The ruins of the Honen Dalim Synagogue, built in 1739 and being restored, are witness to the great importance of the Jewish community to the growth of St Eustatius.

Close by you'll see the old bell tower and the last remains of the old Dutch Reformed Church, built in 1775. Other old houses, like the Simon Doncker House, now a museum, or the Government Guesthouse, are also fine examples of the architecture of this ostentatious time. Most of the town consists of pretty little houses with verandas. The town proper comprises just a few roads of small houses and shops. It's all clean, quite pretty and very quiet – even if a little too much to the taste of a sleepwalker.

Around the island

The road network amounts to access to Oranjestad, the airport and the foothills of The Quill. But although it's small, Statia still has places to go. At the far S end are the remains of Fort de Windt, which in the 18th century played an important role in the struggle for regional supremacy, as do other remnants of outposts and batteries around the coast. The climb up The Quill, the 600m high extinct volcano, brings you to the crater rim, 300m in diameter. From it you can see all of Statia and look out towards the nearby islands.

Pilotage

Coast and anchorages

A channel about 7M wide separates St Kitts and Statia.
Note Coming from the S, give a good

berth to False Shoal pushing out more than 800m from Kay Bay. Thereafter the coast as far as Oranjestad is low cliffs.

Oranje Baai (Oranjestad)

This is the island's only anchorage. A recently built quay and breakwater form a harbour for local boats and offloading cargo.
Note At night the lights on the breakwater and on Fort Oranje are very unreliable.

Anchor N of the harbour works to get some protection from the normal SE swell. On the other hand, in the heavy N swell that occasionally makes, this can be a dangerous spot. The alternative is to anchor S of the breakwater. Some mooring buoys have been laid for visiting boats.

Ashore The immigration office and the port office (VHF 16/14) are at the root of the dock. It's possible to organise water at the small dock through a dive centre, though it's a tedious business and you need to find out how to set things up beforehand. You can jerry-jug fuel from the gas station on the waterfront nearby.

Other than the dive centres and two or three hotel-restaurants, there's no other business in Lower Town. Upper Town, on the other hand, only a hundred metres or so uphill by the Old Slave Road, has quite well-stocked minimarkets and small shops for essentials. There's virtually nothing in the way of chandlery or specialised yachting services. There are just the local mechanics and the dive outfits for emergency fixes.

For all its small size, Oranjestad has quite a variety of restaurants offering menus ranging from local cuisine to Chinese food. There are other possibilities in the outskirts as well as in places like Zeelandia in the NE. Given the island's small area, a short stop will be enough to visit the town and make a tour of the island by hire car or taxi.

Note About 1M N of Gallows Bay there's a huge oil dock pushing out several hundred metres to seaward. Opposite Jenkins Bay, but about 1M to seaward, the other danger is an SPLM, in theory lit at night.

Useful Information for Statia

AIRLINE CONNECTIONS
President Franklin D Roosevelt Airport,
☎ 599 31 82357
No international long-haul flights
Inter-island flights Daily Winair flights to Sint
   Maarten and Saba

TELECOMMUNICATIONS
Calling from abroad: ☎ 599 31 + 5 digits
Local call: 5 digits
Public call boxes: Caribbean Phone Card

TOURIST OFFICE
Oranjestad, ☎/Fax 599 31 82433
   St Eustatius National Park:
   ☎ 599 31 82884 Fax 599 31 82913
   Email fpsxe2@sintmaarten.net

FESTIVALS/FOLKLORE
Carnival: end July /beginning August
Statia/America Day: 16th November, celebrates
   Statia's first recognition of the flag of the
   USA

PUBLIC HOLIDAYS
New Year's Day (1 January), Good Friday, Easter
Sunday, Easter Monday, Queensday (30 April),
Labour Day (1 May), Ascension Day, Statia Day
(16 November), Christmas Day (25 December),
Boxing Day (26 December).

OFFICE HOURS
Shops: Mon–Sat 0800–1800/1900
Banks: Mon–Fri 0730/0830–1530/1600
   depending on the bank
Post Office: Mon–Fri 0730–1600

PLACES TO SEE
Fort Oranje (1629) (restored)
Honen Dalim Synagogue (ruins)
Simon Doncker House (18th century), Museum
Fort de Windt (18th century)
Fort Amsterdam or Concordia
Anglican church (ruins)
The Quill: climb the volcano

ROAD TRANSPORT
Drive on the right
Local licence obligatory
Hire car agencies in hotels and at the airport
Taxis: fixed fares

REGULATIONS
All of Statia's coast is a marine park
Underwater hunting and taking of stock is
   forbidden
Diving only with local clubs.
Ask the St Eustatius National Park authorities
   for details

FORMALITIES
Arriving by air at the airport
Arriving by sea Oranjestad, Lower Town Dock.
   Hours: 0800–1600 7 days a week, weekends
   0800–1200
Fees and taxes Entry fee: approx US$15
   (according to length)
Marine Park tax: approx US$10 (according to
   length)
Statia is a free port, there are no customs.

The oil dock at Tumbledown Dick Bay

Above Oranjestad from the Old Slave Road to the harbour   *Below* Statia from the SE

Below Fort Bay, Saba

Below Saba from SW

Below Windwardside, Saba

Below The Bottom, Saba

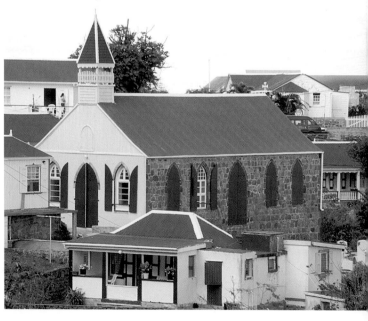

Saba

Area 13sq km
Highest point Mt Scenery, 887m
Population 1100
Capital The Bottom
Language Dutch (official), English (everyday)
Currency Dutch Antilles Florin (Guilder), US$
Political status Constituent part of the self-governing Dutch Netherlands Antilles Federation
Distances to nearby islands Statia 14M, Saint Martin 24M

Saba Bank
Note 6M SW of Saba, Saba Bank is a large area of potentially hazardous shoal ground, especially in a heavy swell. There are depths less than 6m. Keep clear.

History

Around 1640, Dutch fishermen were already using Saba (pronounced Say-bah) as their base for fishing the huge Saba Bank. So fertile was what is now the valley of The Bottom that some of these early visitors were tempted to settle. The pioneers chipped out The Ladder, the vertiginous, 800-step stairway up from the landing on the W coast. It's only today's perspective that leads one to be surprised at finding people living on this steep-sloped, 5000 years extinct volcano; in the past, the

absence of good anchorages and the difficult landing were the best guarantees against being attacked. Who was going to risk ships and men to conquer a rugged rock? So although Saba may have changed hands a few times in various treaties, the inhabitants were always the same and over the centuries the island remained cut off from the larger world.

In 1943, with the same stubborn decisiveness, a steep road was built towards Fort Bay on the S coast. Here coasters could be off-loaded, if at the mercy of the whims of the swell. It was only in 1972 that a breakwater was built to create a small port accessible to coasters.

The first air link was established in 1964 when a daring pilot from St Barts,

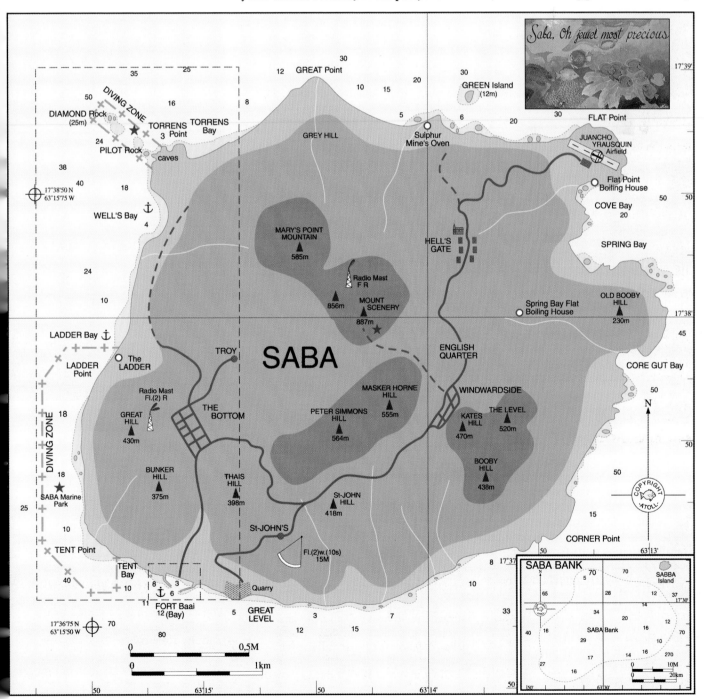

WINDWARDSIDE

① Post Office
② Restaurant / Bar
③ Church Of St-Paul
④ Tourist Office
⑤ Mini Market
⑥ Anglican Church
⑦ Saba Museum
⑧ Captain's Quarters Restaurant
⑨ Bank

Rémy de Haenan, landed on the island's only fairly flat spot, a solidified lava flow forming a small headland in the N of the island. After that bold feat a proper airstrip was built, though one restricted to highly skilled pilots and passengers who like thrills and spills.

The island's population is stuck at around 1000 people, by origin half African and half European and, as far as one can see, living happily together as Sabans. As in Statia, many of them are retired folk or women, the active male population mostly having left the island for work, although most return to their home to die.

The residents still farm in a small way, work a gravel quarry on the S coast, and warmly welcome tourists, who are bemused by this rock with no coconut palm lined beaches, though they find a friendly welcome. The women make lace. The men paint and repaint their houses. The government does the rest.

Saba has the same political status as Statia and Sint Maarten, with an administrator and a local council dealing with local problems.

Tourism

Where to stay and what to see

There's no beach at all around the steep shores of this island. Instead they plunge down into the sea falling in superb drop-offs. In consequence Saba has become well-known as a place to go diving because of the wonderful beauty of its underwater flora and fauna. The coast has been classified as a marine reserve since 1987 under the watchful eye of the Saba Marine Park. The local dive centres organise frequent trips to good dive sites.

The Bottom

Coming out of Fort Bay up a steep, even vertiginous, road you reach the island's mini-capital, The Bottom, with its less than 500 inhabitants. Contrary to legend, the name has nothing to do with the old crater where it's buried, but instead to the English corruption of the Dutch 'botte', meaning bowl. In the town centre you'll see along the minute streets small, multicoloured doll's houses with little fenced gardens, each bright as a new pin amidst its blooming, Dutch style flower garden. Some souvenir shops, the administrator's small mansion and the police HQ are all also in the same Lilliputian style. Visiting Saba is worth the effort.

You can keep going on the road up the side of the mountain, with its red lava banks, to reach other, even smaller villages like Windwardside. This is the liveliest place, where you'll find most of the small hotels and restaurants that welcome tourists and dive parties. All these establishments are small and simple, often pretty and all with a wonderful view.

The route rolls on to the small settlement of Hell's Gate, the terraced buildings and gardens of which hang over the small airport that clings to the edge of the island between the mountain and the sea. If you're a walker, don't leave the island without climbing Mt Scenery, the summit of a volcanic cone thrusting out of the sea.

Pilotage

Coast and anchorages

Except in very hazy weather the distinctive volcanic cone of Saba is easy to pick up from miles away. The coast of Saba is steep-to and free of all dangers except Diamond Rock and Green I off Torrens Pt. Saba has no well sheltered anchorages and everywhere can become untenable in heavy swell from an adverse direction. The Saba Marine Park has created three authorized anchoring zones (see plan): Fort Bay, Ladder Bay and Well's Bay. Two other

Right The Tourist Office
Below left (top) Small garden and gazebo in Windwardside
Below left (bottom) Typical house, The Bottom

Below Diamond Rock, Torrens Point & Well's Bay
Bottom The Ladder & the Old Customs House

sites are reserved for diving, in the SW of the island and around Diamond Rock at the NW tip. The whole area of these zones is equipped with mooring buoys for pleasure craft or dive boats (see plan of Well's Bay).

Fort Bay

Note Coming from the NW give a large berth to the dive area pushing out WSW from the coast.

The small haven is protected by the main 80m long wall in the SE, lit at night by streetlights.

Caution The breakwater is often battered by passing cyclones, so look out for large

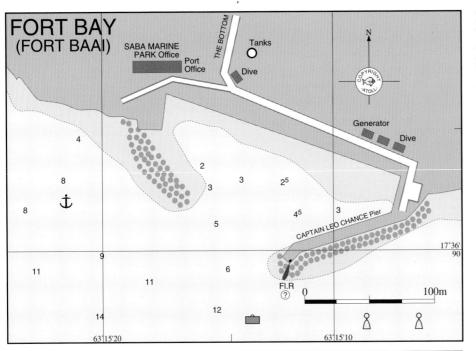

FORT BAY (FORT BAAI)

If you're like the majority, don't forget the other ways of getting here, by ferry or aeroplane from Sint Maarten. Many prefer these more comfortable and less chancy ways to visit so as to enjoy, for a short while, the peculiar charm of this small volcanic island.

Useful Information for Saba

AIRLINE CONNECTIONS
Juancho E Yrausquin Airport:
☎ 599 41 62222
No international long-haul connections
Inter-island services Daily links with Sint Maarten and Statia

FERRY CONNECTIONS
Regular ferries to/from Philipsburg and Simpson Bay (Sint Maarten)

TELECOMMUNICATIONS
Calling from abroad: ☎ 6 599 41 + 5 digits
Local call: 7 digits
Public call boxes: cardphones

TOURIST OFFICE
Windwardside: ☎ 599 41 62231 *Fax* 599 41 62350
Email iluvsaba@unspoiledqueen.com
www.turq.com/saba

FESTIVALS/FOLKLORE
Carnival: end of July
Saba Days: first weekend in December (donkey races)

PUBLIC HOLIDAYS
New Year's Day (1 January), Good Friday, Easter Monday, Queen's Coronation Day (30 April), Labour Day (1 May), Ascension Day (always a Thursday), Saba Days (beginning December – see Festivals above), Christmas Day (25 December), Boxing Day (26 December)

OFFICE HOURS
Shops: Mon–Sat 0900–1200, 1400–1800
Banks: Mon–Fri 0830–1500/1530
Post Office (Windwardside): 0800–1200, 1300–1700

PLACES TO SEE
The Bottom
The Ladder & Old Customs House
Museum: Windwardside
Mt Scenery 8/7m: waymarked footpath

ROAD TRANSPORT
Drive on the right
Hire car companies and taxis in The Bottom and Windwardside

REGULATIONS
Saba Marine Park – VHF 16 ☎ 599 41 63295
Fax 599 41 63435
Email snmp@unspoiledqueen.com
info@sabapark.org
Saba's coastline is a marine reserve
Underwater hunting is forbidden. Diving only with local clubs. Enquire from the authorities at Saba Marine Park HQ

FORMALITIES
Arriving by air Immigration at the airport
Arriving by sea VHF 16/11
Fort Bay (on the 1st floor beside the Saba Marine Park office)
Office hours: 7 days a week 0800–1700, no overtime
Fees and taxes
Entry tax: US$5-20 depending on loa
US$3 tax per person per week
Marine Park fee: for park maintenance according to boat length
Simultaneous entry/exit procedures

---

below surface boulders off the ends of the wall.

Inside, the space is small, the whole NW part being taken up by local boats. The SE Quay is the only place you can get alongside because the rest are all edged with shallows. However, the fast turnaround of ferries and dive boats means it's usually busy. If you need to go alongside, arrange beforehand with the port office (VHF 16/11). Chop and slop make lying alongside difficult. In the worst conditions you'll need to hold yourself off using an anchor.

If the wind is well set, especially from the SE, anchoring off the port can be very uncomfortable, and anyway the depths drop off very quickly. If the mooring buoys are free, you can use them.

Ashore The port office (for clearance) and the Saba Marine Park office are next to each other. You can jerry jug fuel and water from the gas station. But in Fort Bay itself there are no shops other than two dive centre offices. One of the latter has a mechanical workshop. In fair weather you can leave your boat and head for The Bottom or Windwardside in a taxi both for a visit and to lay in supplies from a supermarket.

Ladder Bay and Well's Bay

The first anchoring area is at the foot of The Ladder, dominated by the Old Customs House. For the fit, the staircase goes to The Bottom. The second area at Well's Bay is slightly protected by Torrens Pt and the reefs around Diamond Rock nearby. Anchor in 5-8m clear of all coral, or use a mooring buoy. From both areas access by fast tender to dive sites both N and S is easy. The anchorages are generally

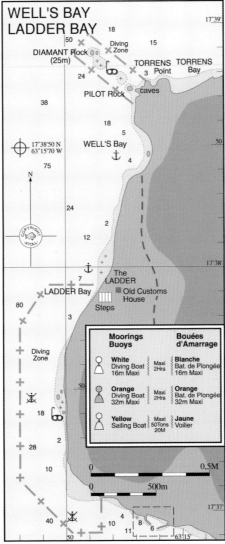

WELL'S BAY LADDER BAY

better protected than Fort Bay, but nonetheless are untenable in any swell from the N.

The lack of calm anchorages means yachts seldom make the detour to Saba.

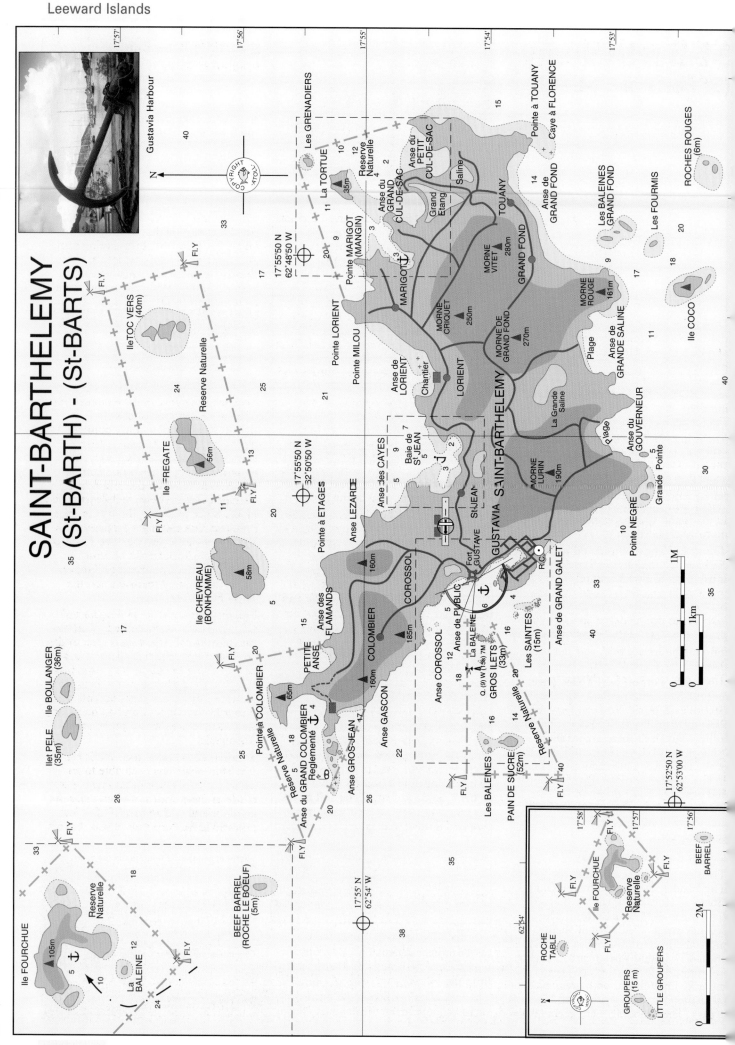

SAINT-BARTHELEMY (St-BARTH) - (St-BARTS)

Gustavia Harbour

St-Barthélémy
(St Barts or St-Barth)

Area 24sq km
Highest point Morne du
  Vitet, 280m
Population 6800
Main town Gustavia
Language French and a half-Norman,
  half-creole patois
Currency Euro, US$ accepted
Political status Canton of the department
  of Guadeloupe, but a free port
Distances to nearby islands
  St-Martin 11M, St Kitts 30M, Barbuda
  60M, Antigua 70M

Left Rade de Gustavia
from Fort Gustave
Right Fine sailing stock

History

During his second voyage Columbus did the only Spanish favour to this dry and hilly island. He gave it the name of his brother Bartolomeo, in French Barthélémy, but it is popularly known as St Barts or St-Barth. Around 1685 a hundred or so peasants from western France took over St Barts, which until then everyone had ignored. By a century later their numbers had swollen to 600, who worked themselves into the ground to cultivate such a barren spot. And despite the best efforts of the British who developed a sudden interest in the island's strategic value, they clung on to what they had.

Then in 1784 the ungrateful king Louis XVI ceded the island and its 600 inhabitants to Sweden in return for a vague right to have a French trading base in Gothenburg. The Swedes didn't lose on the deal because, in order to profit from the Anglo-French wars, they made Gustavia (named after the Swedish King Gustav III) a free port.

The result was that Caribbean trade could tranship through a port sheltered from the fighting elsewhere. It made the Swedes a fine profit, even if St Barts' inhabitants never saw a sou. But the wars ended and a century later the Swedish governor thought his small island with its 600 poor peasants scratching a living on its slopes was all too much. So in 1877 France agreed to

buy the place for 80,000 francs, thereby undoing Louis XVI's mistake. She took back into her bosom her peasants, who were still as Norman as they had been the day they were abandoned. There had been no intermarriage because, as slaves of their own small pittance, they hadn't had the wherewithal to import any African replacements. Gustavia stayed a free port, however, and some of the St Barts, following the Swedish example, tried commercial ventures and even smuggling. The result was a fine fleet of schooners and a good stock of seamen. Or at least that was the case until 1950 when a terrible hurricane destroyed a large number of the boats and, ten years later, another hurricane did for the rest. That was the end of St Barts' fleet and the only riches left to exploit were its natural beauty.

But 30 years ago the island had almost no road or hotel infrastructure. So to give a kick-start to tourist development, the St Barts elected as their mayor Rémy de Haenan, a Dutchman by origin. Sailor, pilot, always pushing at the edges of the legally permissible and often head-to-head with the authorities in Guadeloupe, of which St Barts is a dependency, this modern adventurer had the first roads built. Then, thanks to his flying skills, he opened up the first airstrip in the hills to connect St Barts with the other islands.

With tourism up and running land prices began climbing and happy landowners were rubbing their hands. The growth kept rolling even after 1977 when the mayor lost his position and retired to his fine hotel, the Eden Rock, in the Baie de St Jean. Later still he left the island to carry on his travels by air, despite his advanced age.

The result of the economic development was that the population, only a few hundred souls sharing some 20 surnames in 1960, rapidly increased. Even so, it remained largely white because immigrants were mainly from metropolitan France with a few from North America. That makes St Barts unique in the Antilles.

Tourism

Where to stay and what to see

Such a strong pace of development has often gone hand in hand with unrestrained property development. To check the sprawl of concrete from threatening such a lovely place, the authorities have insisted on planning regulations based on the principle of 'single houses on large, well-landscaped plots'. Since following the rule is pricey, it follows that owning a property in St Barts is not for everyone. The result is that the small island has become something of a Caribbean St Tropez, favoured by rich Americans and the European jet set.

St Barts is more or less bilingual and US clients are much desired. That has naturally had its effect on prices, to the point that even the rich clientele has begin finding the place 'very expensive'. Happily, for a while now the increasing numbers of shops and restaurants has meant lively competition and hence at least some places where prices are reasonable.

So when all is said and done, St Barts' tourist invasion has been able to go ahead without much damaging the way of life of these scions of Normandy. As an old friend said to me, 'If life's less peaceful in St Barts than it was, I can't

St-Barthélémy from S

Right The Swedish belfry
Far right Wickerwork at Corossol
Below The Select Bar, Gustavia

say I'm any the less happy.' In sum, St Barts clings onto its quiet calm and lack of crime. So much so indeed that compared to St Martin, its night life is almost monastic. No casinos and very few night clubs. But also, of course, few muggings or petty crime.

Gustavia

The capital of St-Barthélémy has been a free port since the 18th century and has

a rich history of adventuring and smuggling. Around its rectangular harbour there's a chessboard pattern of streets full of small, red-roofed houses. The whole is colourful and well-maintained, marrying different Creole architectural styles, although here and there are older buildings in a more severe Nordic style. For tourists, above all for Americans, Gustavia is very much France's shop window with lots of shops selling the most famous French brand names that are, best of all, duty free. On the narrow area round the quays you'll be spoiled for choice over bars, restaurants and menus. The Select, founded by Marius Stakelborough whose ancestors were Swedish, is the bar favoured by yachtsmen. Of the three forts which once defended the harbour, only Fort Gustave and Fort Oscar still stand on the edges of the town.

Around the island

Over all the island is little developed, especially on the SE coast. A good number of the luxurious homes, as well as the small cottages, fit well into the landscape, often being buried in the greenery. The biggest concentration of hotels and restaurants is around Gustavia, the Baie de St Jean and the bays of Grand and Petit Cul-de-Sac.

There are good roads which switchback over the island allowing you to reach the many small inlets, each with its individual appeal and most with nice white beaches. Amongst the prettiest are the Anses du Gouverneur and Grand Saline in the S and the Baie de St Jean, the Anses de Grand and Petit Cul-de-Sac in the N.

Outside Gustavia the island's other settlements are only little villages made up of a few pretty painted cottages untouched by tourism. So they still retain much of the way of life of yesterday, such as the rare old ladies of St Barts who still wear the traditional Breton or Norman headdress, the *calèche* or bonnet that's called 'Quichenotte', and which you'd see not long back in Lorient or Corossol. Although very close to Gustavia,

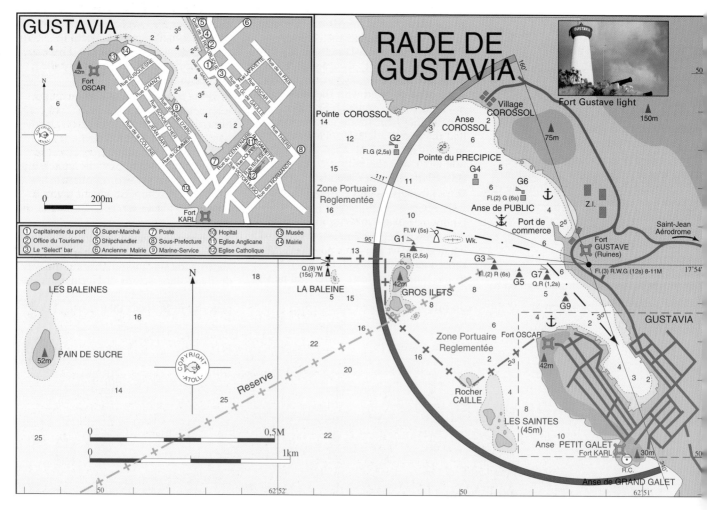

Above NW St Barts, Rade de Gustavia and the Baie de St Jean
Right Shipchandler du Port Franc (the chandlery)

Corossol, tucked into the back of its bay, seems miles away from tourism. All it has is a quiet trade in shellfish, celebrated by a small museum, and a small but skilful production of wickerwork. Corossol also has some fishermen but because of the hardship of the work and the seductions of working in tourism, few young folk are taking it up. Ciguatera means some of the fish are toxic (as in many of these more northerly islands) and the care needed to sort out the catch doesn't help profitability.

Pilotage

Coast and anchorages

St Barts is small, but the deeply indented coastline has lots of anchorages. However, any approach should only be made after you've had a very careful look at the charts because the approaches from all directions are encumbered with reefs and islets. To preserve the underwater environment, since 1996 several sites have been classified as natural marine reserves and access is regulated. In theory they're marked by lit yellow 'special' buoys.

Below left Gustavia Harbour
Below right Rade de Gustavia, Anse de Corossol and Gros Ilets

Southwest Coast

Rade de Gustavia

It's possible to make a night approach, but you have to come in from the west to pick up the Gustavia sector light leading to the buoyed channel. The hazardous Sec de la Baleine (300m W of Gros Ilets) is buoyed (W cardinal).

Danger in addition to lots of anchored yachts, the approaches to Gustavia have several unlit buoys.

Gustavia Harbour is known to offer all-weather shelter although objectively speaking it's too open to the NW if there's a hurricane about, as witnessed by the swell damage done by recent cyclones. If the old schooner fleet has disappeared, cruising yachts have more than compensated and there's been considerable development of the port. In order to leave the old port clear for yachts, a commercial harbour has been built in the Anse Public. That's where you'll find the fuel dock. The designated port zone now covers the whole of the Rade de Gustavia (see plan). Anchoring is regulated and a fee levied. The best-protected area, hence the most popular, is under Pt Oscar, where the water is clear but yachts swing around crazily. The anchorage is rolly in a SE swell.

In the old harbour the Quai de Gaulle has been extended by the new Quai de la République to give about 60 stern-to berths in 3–5m. The result is that

Gustavia is a port of call both for large and lovely luxury yachts and transatlantic racers. When you anchor do so on a long scope, dropping most the way across to the far side and slightly upwind since gusts barrel down along the line of the harbour.

Note Given the swell that makes onto the dock, make sure you hold the stern a good distance off the wall. There are also buoy moorings in the SE part of the basin.

Ashore Complete formalities with the capitainerie (Port Office, VHF 16). The office also has plenty of information about the island including anchoring regulations, natural reserves, weather forecasts, etc. Opposite the capitainerie, the Bureau de Tourisme (Tourist Office) has all the information you'll need on what to see in St Barts and the services it provides.

For cruising yachts the big local chandlery has a good stock including fishing tackle. It also offers various

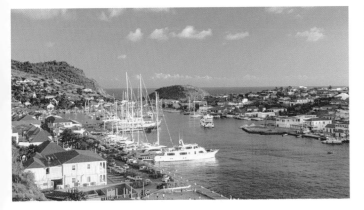

Above left Anse de Grand Colombier from E
Above right Beach in the Grand Cul-de-Sac

specialist services. A few workmen complete what's on offer for boat maintenance. On the other hand, there are no haul-out facilities bar a small railway slip (see Anse de Lorient) for small shoal draft vessels. Most haul-out is done in St Martin.

A stop in Gustavia is a good opportunity to enjoy the facilities for tourists and the duty free shopping as well as the restaurants around the charming little harbour. Provisioning is a breeze thanks to supermarkets, the local market and the wine merchants selling French wines.

Anse Public and Anse de Corossol

Immediately NW of Gustavia, Anse Public is almost entirely filled with the commercial port and its swinging area. There's a small area in the N where you can anchor, but the swell usually makes in. In the W part of Anse de Corossol there's shoal ground with only 2–3·5m over it. There are usually a dozen or so fishing boats moored whose owners tend to head out very early in the morning and their wash really bounces you about.

Anse du Grand Colombier

Caution Coming from S, give a wide berth to Ile de la Pointe, which is fringed by shoal ground. Anse du Grand Colombier is a lovely spot, calm in E winds and seldom very busy. The reefs on the S shore offer good snorkelling. It's classed as a nature reserve and anchoring is forbidden. Mooring buoys have been installed.

North coast

From Pointe Colombier to Baie Saint-Jean the bays are all open to the sea and in fresh ENE tradewinds the sea can be quite rough. The three islets of Chevreau (Bonhomme), Frégate and Toc Vers offer no shelter and are anyway in the marine reserve so anchoring is forbidden.

Baie de St Jean

A fair-weather anchorage when the visibility is also good, and a no-no if the wind is in the NNE. The Eden Rock Hotel on its small headland in the middle of the bay is conspicuous and makes a good leading mark. Head towards the coconut palms on the beach

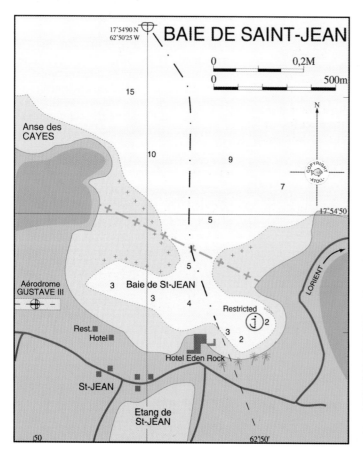

Below Baie de St Jean
Bottom Baie de St Jean and the Anse de Lorient

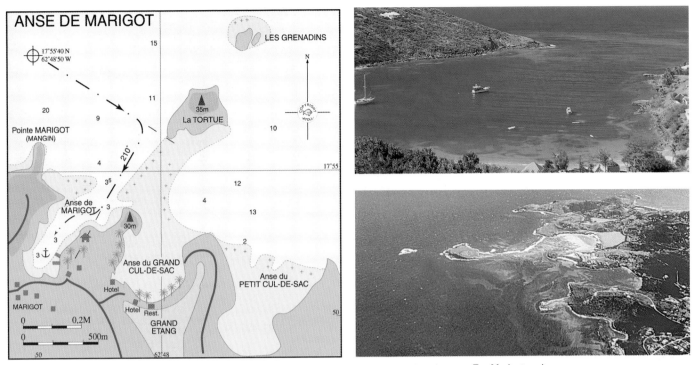

ANSE DE MARIGOT

17°55'40 N
62°48'50 W

LES GRENADINS

Pointe MARIGOT
(MANGIN)

La TORTUE
35m

N

Anse de
MARIGOT

30m

Anse du GRAND
CUL-DE-SAC

Anse du
PETIT CUL-DE-SAC

Hotel

MARIGOT

Hotel   Rest.

GRAND
ETANG

0   0.2M

0   500m

Top Marigot anchorage
Above Anse de Marigot, Anse du Grand & Anse du Petit Cul-de-Sac

on roughly 160°T between the big reef off the W point and the shoal ground to the E. Close to the beach the bottom comes up to less than 2m very quickly.

Note A municipal by-law (*arrêté municipal*) prohibits anchoring in boats with cabins within a line drawn between the E and W points. That means you have to anchor out, which is untenable in any ENE swell.

Ashore There's a superb beach backed by restaurants and hotels, amongst the best of which is the entirely refurbished Eden Rock.

Anse de Lorient

For shoal draft boats only, this precarious haven is accessible by a narrow pass that genuinely needs local knowledge. Ashore there's a small boatyard for small, light displacement vessels and a stainless steel fabrication workshop.

Anse de Marigot

You can take a chance in fair weather and first class visibility. The E shore of the bay can be recognised by a few small white cottages with pyramidal roofs. Align yourself on these on about 210°T then, once through the pass, alter course to the SW to get to the anchorage. It's well sheltered unless there's a heavy NE swell.

Ashore There are a few shops in the nearby small village of Marigot.

Anses du Grand and Petit Cul-de-Sac

With their shores fringed with sand and ringed with coconut palms these are amongst the loveliest parts of St Barts' coast. But the scant depth and the reefs that fill the two large bays effectively make them off limits to cruising keelboats. These pretty idyllic spots are accordingly more or less reserved for the water sports of the clients of the fine hotels on the shore.

Ile Fourchue

The barren Ile Fourchue, privately owned, lies about 3M W of St Barts. It's within one of the marine reserves. On the S coast there's an excellent, well-sheltered anchorage for E winds.

Caution Entering the inlet note that off the S entrance La Baleine Reef (awash) extends a good 100m to seaward from the shore.

The anchorage is quite comfortable, though in squalls the wind can reverse direction, so don't anchor close to the beach.

Danger Heading on W and towards St Martin, you should look out for the Groupers Rocks and Roche Taillé (Hewn or Cut Rock, mistranslated as Table Rock on some charts).

Ile Fourchue

Useful Information for St-Barthélémy

AIRLINE CONNECTIONS
Gustave III Airport: St Jean ☎ 05 90 27 65 41
No international long-haul flights
Inter-island flights daily to Guadeloupe, St-Martin and neighbouring islands. Several weekly flights to St Thomas and Puerto Rico.

FERRY CONNECTIONS
Daily connections and charters to St Maarten & St-Martin. Day charters to Anguilla, St-Martin and Saba.

TELECOMMUNICATIONS
Calling from abroad: ☎ +33 590 + 6 digits
Local call: 05 90 + 6 digits
Public call boxes: France Télécom cards or Carte Bleu

TOURIST OFFICE/CLUB
Quai General de Gaulle, Gustavia,
☎ 05 90 27 87 27 *Fax* 05 90 27 74 47
Email odtsb@wanadoo.fr
www.st.barths.com
Yacht Club de St-Barth ☎/*Fax* 05 90 27 70 41
Organises many races

FESTIVALS/FOLKLORE
Carnival: Feb/March
St-Barth Regatta: February

Gourmet Festival: April
St-Barth Festival of Caribbean Cinema: Last weekend in April
Regattas and races: Transat 2 GR (Lorient: St Barts) in May every other year organised by St-Barth Yacht Club.
Festival of Gustavia: 20th August, fishing contests, parties and dancing
St-Barthélémy's Day: 24th August, blessing of boats, regattas, fireworks, public ball
Feast of St Louis: 25th August in Corossol, fishing festival, games, party and fireworks
International Art Exhibition: December

PUBLIC HOLIDAYS
As Guadeloupe

OFFICE HOURS
Shops: Mon & Tues, Thurs & Fri 0800–1200, 1430–1700, Wed & Sat 0800–1200
Banks: Mon–Fri 0800–1300, 1430–1700 (may vary according to bank), Sat (Crédit Agricole only) 0800–1300
Post Office: Mon & Tues, Thurs & Fri 0800–1500, Wed & Sat 0800–1200 in Gustavia, different hours in St Jean & Lorient.

PLACES TO SEE
Round the island by car
Wall House: Municipal Museum, Gustavia
Swedish bell tower: Gustavia
Le Brigantin: Swedish house, Gustavia

Inter Ocean Museum, Corossol: museum of shells and shellfish

ROAD TRANSPORT
Drive on the right
Hire car companies in Gustavia and at the airport
Taxis

REGULATIONS
Various marine parks have been created in which regulations apply governing anchoring, small craft use and underwater activities.
Enquiries: ☎ 05 90 27 88 18
Fax 05 90 27 52 79
Email resnatbarth@wanadoo.fr

FORMALITIES
There are no customs in St Barts, it is a duty free zone.
Arriving by air immigration at the airport
Arriving by sea Immigration at the capitainerie (Port Office), Gustavia.
Hours: weekdays & Saturdays 0730–1230, 1430–1730, Sundays (in high season) 0800–1200
Hours out of season: weekdays 0730–1230 & 1430–1730, closed Sundays
Fees and taxes A small local tax for anchoring in the anchoring area outside the harbour.
Speed limit within port limits
Exit clearance obligatory

Saint-Martin/Sint Maarten

The island is split between France and the Netherlands, which makes it the smallest area in the world divided into two countries' dependencies. Although the border is almost entirely theoretical and without frontier posts, there are distinctions: each part is of a different nationality, has a different administrative system and also manages its sea space differently. Accordingly, it makes sense to treat the two here as separate places.

History

The island was discovered by Columbus on 11th November 1493, St-Martin's Day. St-Martin was occupied by the Spanish until 1644, in which year it was conquered by Dutch forces commanded by the Governor of Curaçao, Petrus Stuyvesant, and French forces from St Christopher. Four years later in 1648 the island was split into two. Legend has it that the border was drawn following a walking race between a Dutchman heading S and a Frenchman heading N from Oyster Pond. Despite the rugged terrain the Frenchman covered more distance than the Dutchman, giving France 3/5ths of the 90sq km island. The shrewd Dutch, however, got the salt ponds of the S. Since then the division has never been questioned, and, other than during some English incursions in the 18th century (finally ending in 1816), the two flags have peacefully fluttered in the same breeze for over three centuries.

Economically, salt from the salt ponds was the major business of the Dutch for a long time. Despite the dry climate and arid soils, until the abolition of slavery, which abruptly put an end to them, there were also prosperous sugar cane plantations. Despite a venture into cotton growing and continuing exports of salt, the island's economy underwent a steady decline. That lasted until the 1960s when, especially in the Dutch half where the international airport was built, the tourism business started to grow.

Below Duty free shopping
Bottom The Franco-Dutch border

Saint-Martin

Area 55sq km
Highest point Pic Paradis 425m
Population 30,000
Sub-prefecture Marigot
Language French (official), English (everyday)
Currency Euro (official), Euro and US$ (everyday)
Political status Free port and canton of the French department of Guadeloupe
Distances to nearby islands Anguilla 6M

Saint Martin today

Marigot is the sub-prefecture of the two cantons of St-Martin and St-Barth, both part of the department of Guadeloupe 250km away to the E! However, unlike the other French island dependencies, St-Martin doesn't actually have very strong or deep French roots because most of the French colonists left when slavery was abolished. They were replaced by Anglo-Saxon planters and a few Swedes who rented their old estates. The slaves, now free, had to assume a surname and often took that of their new employers. At the same time they adopted the English language, in the process partly turning it into a pidgin. When agriculture took a definitive downturn, the St Martinois emigrated to the USA. Then later on tourism to the island from N America took off and the Anglo-Saxon bent of the island increased. In consequence,

ST MARTIN AND SINT MAARTEN

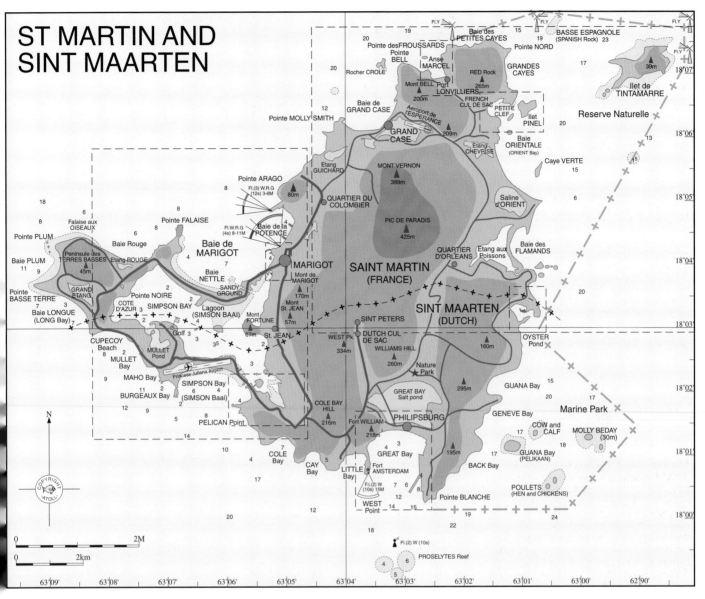

although St-Martin is French, names and language are mostly English. The population these days is 75% black or mixed race Caribbean and 25% whites, mostly from mainland France. Much as with Dutch St Maarten, the French part of the island has turned decisively towards developing the tourist infrastructure along American lines. Local taxation (or its absence) has encouraged housing and hotel developments, often in very kitsch styles, to spring up all over the place. The local council, mostly run by successive generations of the island's most influential family, the Flemings, has encouraged this spectacular trend. What has resulted is that French St-Martin, although often frustrated to the limit by administrative decisions made by the prefecture in Guadeloupe, has finally caught up with the Dutch half in the intensive race to tourism development. Its free port status, which has eased the way to the inflow of capital and to its profitable employment, has for a good number of

years now attracted the world of offshore finance. The French authorities back in Paris often speak of rethinking St-Martin's particular fiscal status. But at present nothing is being done to risk fracturing the dynamics of the island's economy, resting as they do on recreational real estate development and tourism.

Over the last few years the numerous residential and hotel developments have occasioned the arrival of more or less clandestine immigrant workers, mostly Haitians and Dominicans. The result has all but doubled the resident population in 20 years. It follows that St-Martin has to keep growing economically to avoid the risk of a rise in unemployment and, as a likely consequence, delinquency.

For better or worse, then, the 'French Side' continues to be the nearest shop window to the USA for luxury goods with the 'Made in France' label, though that doesn't entirely compensate for the absence of casinos (gambling of that sort being officially illegal in St-Martin).

Tourism

Where to stay and what to see

The French part of St-Martin is the larger in area. Its highest point (and the highest point of the whole island) is the 425m Pic de Paradis, covered with scrub. The coast has the island's best beaches, which are St-Martin's trump card since, given the dry climate, the vegetation isn't much to write home about.

There are innumerable hotel developments, mostly on the coast. Some of them are extremely luxurious aiming for rich American and European clients.

Marigot

The main town of the French part and a sub-prefecture, Marigot's free port status has led to it having lots of fashionable shops selling luxury goods. Recent development of the relatively deep water Port Galisbay facilities on the N of the town means that small cruise liners can now call and offload streams of passengers to quarry the shops in the town's grid-pattern streets around the marina of Port la Royale. That said, the choice of duty free goods like audio-visual and photographic equipment, as well as the number of shops selling them, is not as great as in Philipsburg in the Dutch part. Even so, prices appear attractive provided buyers remember what they may have to pay in duty when they reach the customs control in their home country – or the risk of being caught if they don't. The majority of the restaurants in the town centre or further out concentrate on French cuisine, only the simpler establishments offering Creole specialties.

Beside the sea there's a fine esplanade running past the quays where small craft moor. Every Wednesday and Saturday there's a market for local and neighbouring island farmers' and fishermen's produce, though the bulk of stalls concentrate on clothing and knick-knacks.

Fort St Louis (Fort Marigot), built in the 18th century, dominates the town from a small hill. There's a superb view out over the bay from its ruins.

Around the island

The road out of town to the N passes through the Quartier du Colombier with its many flower gardens. A small road leads from Colombier to Pic de Paradis, which, once you reach it, gives a panoramic view over the whole island and as far as Anguilla in the W and St Barts in the E.

On northwards you'll reach the village of Grand Case with lots of restaurants and colourful houses lining an extensive beach. This is the place to come for the best variety of seafood dishes cooked in the local way. Close by is the small airport of Espérance serving neighbouring islands.

At the island's north end there's a big development in the Anse Marcel, which includes the marina of Port Lonvilliers.

Top Marigot market on the esplanade
Above Pointe Basse Terre
Below Marigot Bay and The Lagoon

There's a road from there to Baie Orientale with its immense beach and small offshore islets all partly protected by barrier reefs. On to the S, once past the Quartier d'Orléans, you can get to the extreme SE of the French part of the island at Oyster Pond (L'Etang aux Huitres). Tucked away in this old mangrove swamp there are now several hotel developments, Captain Oliver's Resort being the best known.

You head W along a thin strip of land between the lagoon and the sea to get back to Marigot whence you can head for the Terres Basses Peninsula. The name's a bit misleading since it's modestly hilly and covered with vegetation, among which you'll spot some of the island's prize real estate. If you keep on along the road you cross the border into the Dutch part and reach the Princess Juliana International Airport.

Pilotage

Coast and anchorages

The majority of the anchorages on the French coast of the island are on the leeward coast and quite well sheltered. The downside is that the wind can rapidly change direction and there are occasional small, but awkward surges

NW coast

Baie Longue and Baie Rouge

The Terres Basses peninsula ends in the W at Pointe Basse Terre and in the N at Pointe Plum. Give both a good wide berth, especially at night, because neither is lit. Either side of Pointe Basse Terre you'll find fine beaches, both of which are still pretty deserted:

- to the S, Baie Longue backed by the Samanna, one of the island's most luxurious hotels.
- to the N, Baie Rouge, generally a better anchorage especially in an ESE swell.

Baie de Marigot

The approaches to the large bay are clear and there is a sector light for a night approach.

Caution There's a large mooring buoy in the NW of the bay that at the moment isn't lit.

The usual anchorage is in the SE of the bay in 3m. A swell can sometimes make it rolly.

Caution The S part of the bay near Sandy Ground (the entry channel to the lagoon) has shoal patches with less than 2m over them.

Off the point with the fort on it a new, 300m long quay has been built, lengthening the ferry jetty, which will shelter a new marina with some 200 berths. The latter is still being finished, will be called the Marina Front de Mer and will be managed by Sensamar. The town docks have also been tidied up and you can leave your tender there provided it's clear of the ferry dock. Further N in the N of the Baie de la

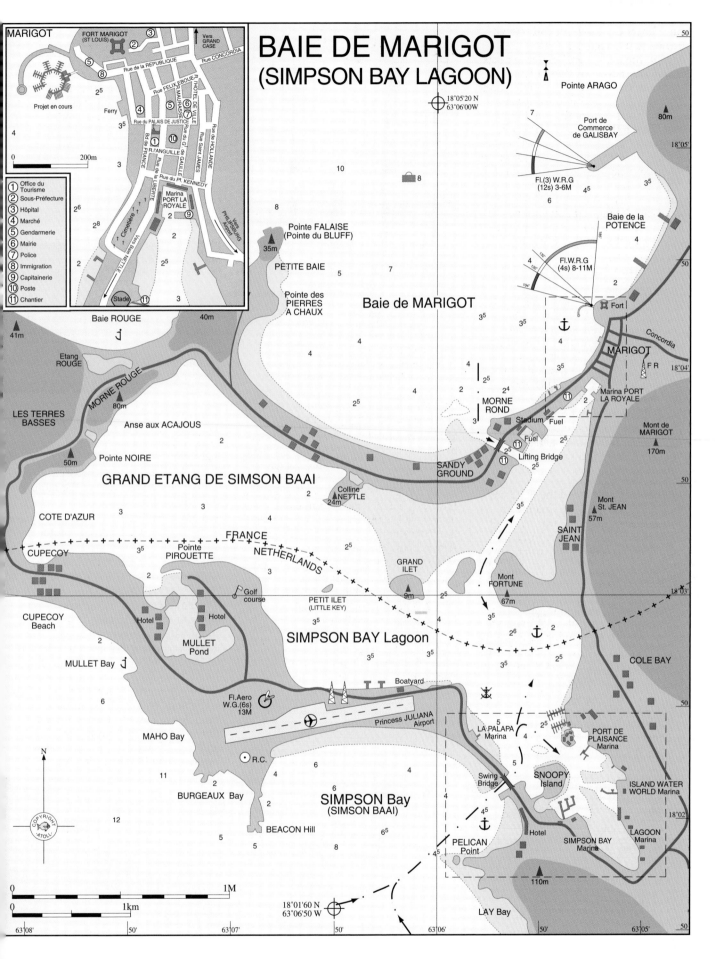

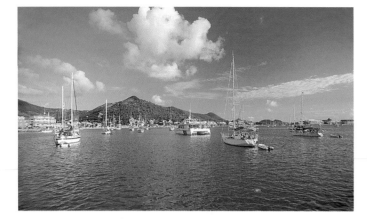

Potence the new Port de Galisbay is for commercial traffic only, though yachts may be able to get fuel delivered there.

Ashore The offices for immigration clearance are next to the ferry dock. Along the town quay there's a wide, smart new esplanade on which the market is held. The busiest and liveliest streets of the town all end at this vast open area (see Port la Royale).

The Lagoon and Sandy Ground

The channel leading from the sea to the lagoon is closed by a lifting bridge. Opening is several times a day depending on the season. The access channel to the bridge is in theory dredged to 2·5m but drift sand can reduce the depth.

Caution Watch out for the shoals W of the entrance to the channel and to the N close by its exit on the lagoon side. Once inside there's a channel heading N to the marina of Port la Royale. Another has been dredged out S'wards so you can get to the Dutch side and the navigable parts of Simpson Bay.

The unlit buoys which used to mark the two channels have for now disappeared and depths vary depending on the location and extent of silting. Towards Port Royale there's seldom 2m and often less. Heading towards the Dutch side it varies between 2·5 and 3m. It follows that you should proceed carefully.

Numerous boats are anchored throughout the year between Sandy Ground and Port la Royale over a more or less trustworthy bottom cluttered with old wrecks, all of which rather

obstruct access to the marina.

Ashore Almost the whole W shore of the lagoon between Sandy Ground and the marina is now filled with boatyards, workshops and two fuel docks. One of the yards, Time Out, has also organised some pontoons with 15 berths (water and electricity) with 2–3m. The haul-out facilities are usually medium and heavy lift cranes. In the general area roundabout as well as on the opposite shore you'll also find lots of specialist services as well as two chandleries.

Port la Royale

Given its small size and awkward access via a shallow channel, the marina is only home to small and medium sized craft on its 80 berths.

Ashore The capitainerie (marina office) (VHF 16) is on the end of the S dock and has the showers, phones and a weather forecast. On the same jetty you'll find a few charter company offices and all sorts of brokerages. Right in the heart of town the marina is surrounded by restaurants and shops, so it's full of life, though such an urban setting may soon pall for lovers of the wide open spaces.

Marigot

On the bustling streets there's a plethora of shops and restaurants as well as lots of supermarkets and grocery stores, so provisioning is a breeze. If you add together the yachting infrastructure, the lagoon's technical services and the wide-ranging stock of the town's many shops, a stop in Marigot is worth considering as far as boat maintenance

Top left Marigot anchorage
Top right Marigot Bay and The Lagoon from SW
Above Port la Royale quayside

and provisioning are concerned in French St-Martin.

Baie de Grand Case

Caution Coming from the S, give a very wide berth to Molly Smith Pt. In addition to the shoal ground off the point, look out also for the isolated shoal with 1.5m over it a few hundred metres further N.

The anchorage off the beach is very pleasant and not usually too crowded though it can be rolly when the trades are settled in the NE. A small dock can be used by tenders, the other is reserved for service boats.

Ashore Grand Case is the second largest settlement on the island and is built on the edge of an old salt pond. The town's houses are mostly small, pretty and well looked-after cottages. Tourist business has caused a big growth in the number of restaurants along the main

Below left Port la Royale
Below right Port Lonvilliers from SE

Grand Case Bay, village and airport from W

street and you've a wide choice. Lots of cruisers prefer the anchorage here to the one in Marigot because it's quieter and the restaurants are better value. There are enough minimarkets and small shops for essentials and Espérance airport is less than 1km away.

Anse Marcel

Coming from the S leave Rocher Crole to starboard. Going between the rock and the coast isn't a good idea if you're sailing because of the current and the chances of getting into irons when you tack. Once into the bay, go north around the islet known locally as Rocher de l'Anse Marcel because a coral bank connects it to the main island shore.

Anse Marcel is well sheltered except in northerly swells. Anchor close to the beach, well clear of the bathing zone marked by yellow buoys. The shore is wholly taken up by hotel cottages which don't add a lot to the bay's appeal.

Port Lonvilliers

On the E side of the bay a narrow channel leads to the marina of Port Lonvilliers (VHF 16). There's 3m if you keep to the middle of the channel. Once inside there's not much room to manoeuvre, although some berths can accommodate large yachts. There are at present about 100 berths all with water and electricity and excellently sheltered. There is a fuel dock. The capitainerie is

Right Ilet Pinel & Orient Bay
Below Anse Marcel from NW
Below right Green Cay & Orient Bay

charmingly set overlooking the pontoons.

Ashore The marina is in the middle of a large residential development that includes a luxury Méridien hotel. The development in general is in a pastiche Creole style, classy but kitsch. The hotel and its restaurants, like the marina, are as expensive as you'd expect. The whole area is private and restricted to hotel guests and marina clientele. That obviously entails that the area is well-guarded and patrolled, with the result that this yachting-cum-tourist complex feels a touch like a concentration camp. Other than a fairly well-stocked chandlery, there are no other permanent technical services on site. They come regularly from Marigot or from the Dutch side to maintain or fix a breakdown for the charter boats or visiting yachts. In the shopping centre there's a dive centre, a small supermarket, a hire car company and some shops and restaurants. Next to the marina there is also another luxury

Privilège hotel whose sports complex with gym and tennis courts is on the small hill overlooking the marina.

Windward coast

To protect the best marine sites on this coast, a marine reserve has now been set up. From the N tip of the island as far as Oyster Pond it includes the Ile de Tintamarre (see plan).

Once the haunt only of the experienced, yachts are now visiting this coast more and more. That said, it's still worth being cautious in your approach to the anchorages by avoiding poor visibility or when there's a heavy swell running.

Caution Coming from Anse Marcel watch out for the Basse Espagnole, a shoal about 1M ENE of North Point (Pointe Nord), which is hard to see. To avoid it, once you've altered SE and have North Point abeam, keep heading for about 1M towards the S end of Tintamarre Island.

Tintamarre

Still in the French part, this is a small, uninhabited, privately owned island about 1·5M NE of Saint Martin. The best anchorage is in the bay on the SW of the island close to the point with a sandbank off it. There's a fine beach, though the anchorage can be rolly in either NE or SE winds.

The sea bottom round about is pretty with several good spots for a dive or a snorkel. There's the wreck of a small tug sloping between 10m and 15m down close to the island's NW end.

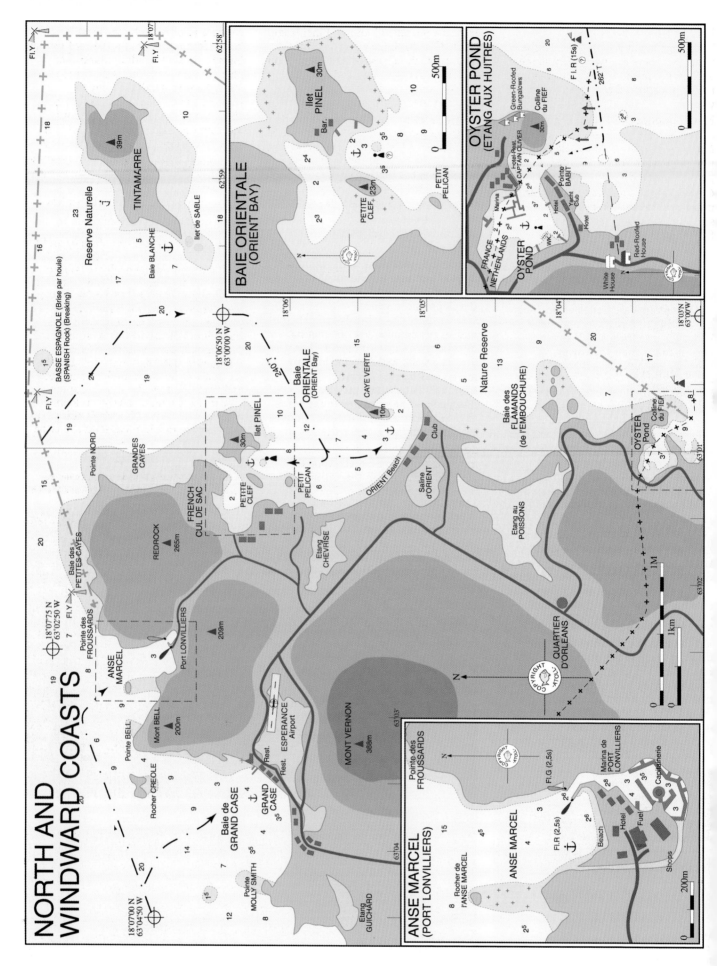

NORTH AND WINDWARD COASTS

BAIE ORIENTALE (ORIENT BAY)

OYSTER POND (ETANG AUX HUITRES)

ANSE MARCEL (PORT LONVILLIERS)

Baie Orientale (Orient Bay)

This large bay is mostly open to the wind, but there are two partly sheltered anchorages in the lee of islets and coral reefs for a short, day stop in quiet weather.

North anchorage is between Ilet Pinel and Petite Clef in 2–4m. You can get into it by keeping S round Ilet Pinel until you can head for the steep-to E point of Petite Clef.

Caution There's a shoal right in the middle of the anchorage, which is sometimes buoyed. You can't push further in if you're a keeler because

there's a <1·5m sill joining Pinel It and Petite Clef It. Since a few small snack bars in shacks appeared in Pinel It along with all sorts of water sports, the fine beaches round about have lost their charm, especially in high season.

South anchorage This is in the lee of Green Island or Green Cay (Ile Verte). Come round Green I to the N and keep going until you're in 2–3m off its S end. It's rolly in brisk NE winds. On Orient Beach, which is huge, there are several restaurants, a bungalow village and some shops.

Baie des Flamands (Flemish Bay)

This is for those with local knowledge only. The narrow pass through the middle of the coral barrier isn't feasible for keelers.

Oyster Pond (L'Etang aux Huitres)

In everyone's view Oyster Pond has an iffy entrance, and even more so when there's a swell running. Luckily the manager of Captain Oliver's Marina (VHF 16/67) has put in some buoys. They're a bit swell-battered from time to time, but useful enough.

The entrance is S of Fief Hill (Colline du Fief) which you can spot coming from the N by some green roofed bungalows. From off the entrance you must take a rough line of 262°T

running in on a white house with, beside it, another with a red roof on the hillside ahead as leading marks (see plan). Keeping on the same course, leave the first (landfall) buoy to starboard and once past it, follow the channel indicated by the red buoys marking the edge of the reef S of Fief Hill. After about 200m turn sharply N onto about 340°T towards the entrance to Oyster Pond.

Despite the new, lit landfall buoy a night entry would be high risk unless you know the way in perfectly.

It's a long time since my old friend Alain Le Henaff (on *Gros Bonda*) and I were alone in this little hurricane hole having found our own way in. But in the 1980s another sailor (and an ex-big restaurant owner in Paris) criss-crossing the islands and well-informed by yachting pilots found his way in here and fell under its spell. It was no passing infatuation because Oliver Lange very quickly bought this bit of the coast so he could build a fine hotel and restaurant on the shore, Captain Oliver's. It's a name always welcome to a yachtsman's ear. The whole thing had to be done quickly because, if the coast

Below, from top
Oyster Pond, Baie des Flamands and Orient Bay
Oyster Pond anchorage & Captain Oliver's Marina

was French, the sea was Dutch – the border follows the shoreline. On the Dutch shore, by contrast, marine leisure development is encouraged rather than, as with the French, snarled up in red tape.

Today the extensive pontoons have nearly 150 excellent berths with water and electricity as well as a fuel dock. You can also anchor in the bay if you look out for the sand banks, though there's in fact very little room.

In addition to Captain Oliver's, this fortunate spot has also attracted bareboat charter companies which has led to the recent increase in the extent of the pontoons.

Ashore Whether yachties or clients cosily settled in Captain Oliver's 4-star paradise, visitors to Oyster Pond are a cosmopolitan bunch making for a lively atmosphere round the marina where, on some evenings in the season, things are hopping in the Dinghy Dock Bar.

There are no specialists on site for repairs and maintenance, though Captain Oliver's or the charter companies' staffs can usually help out over minor problems. If it's serious, specialists from Philipsburg can get here easily except during the busiest part of high season.

On the dock is the marina office, some shops, a minimarket with a chandlery shelf as well as the various charter company offices. You also can't miss Captain Oliver's luxury development, its lovely bungalows around the pool and the restaurant with its terrace lapped by the lagoon. It's also a bit of a giggle to cross a frontier every time you go to the bar for a drink.

Captain Oliver's bar

Useful Information for Saint-Martin

AIRLINE CONNECTIONS
Espérance Airport: Grand Case
☎ 05 90 87 53 03 *Fax* 05 90 87 09 71
International long-haul – no flights, see Sint Maarten
Inter-island daily flights by local companies

FERRY CONNECTIONS
See also Sint Maarten. There are ferries from Marigot to Anguilla (Blowing Pt)

TELECOMMUNICATIONS
Calling from abroad: ☎ +33 590 + 6 digits
Calling the Dutch side: 00 599 + 7 digits
Local call: 0590 + 6 digits
Public call boxes: France Télécom or Carte Bleu

TOURIST OFFICE
Marigot: Rue du Morne Rond,
☎ 05 90 87 57 21 *Fax* 05 90 87 56 43
Email sxmto@wanadoo.fr
www.st-martin.org

CLUBS/ASSOCIATIONS
Yacht Club International de Marigot (co-organises Heineken Regatta and organises regular races locally)

FESTIVALS/FOLKLORE
Carnival: February, Mon and Tues 40 days before Easter
Schoelcher Day (Grand Case): July
Races: see Sint Maarten

PUBLIC HOLIDAYS
See Useful Information for Guadaloupe

OFFICE HOURS
Shops: 0900–1200/1300, 1400/1500–1900
Banks: Mon–Thurs 0830–1530, Fri 0830–1630

PLACES TO SEE
Fort St Louis (Fort Marigot) (1789)
Shellman Museum: Concordia Marigot
Butterfly Farm (La Ferme aux Papillons), Galion Beach
Quartier Orléans (the French quarter with pretty cottages in amongst greenery)
Pic Paradis (either walking or by car)

ROAD TRANSPORT
Drive on the right
Hire car companies in main towns and at the airport:

SANDY GROUND BRIDGE OPENING HOURS
Bridge operator: ☎ 05 90 29 04 75, VHF 16
Capitainerie, Port la Royale:
☎ 05 90 87 20 43
Hours: Weekdays (Jun–Nov): 0900, 1400, 1730
Weekdays (Nov–Jun), Sundays and holidays: 0900, 1730
Secondary channel to Simpson Lagoon

FORMALITIES
No customs because Saint-Martin is a duty free zone
Arriving by air immigration at the airport
Arriving by sea to the left on the ferry quay at Marigot
Hours: weekdays and Saturdays 0800–1200, 1400–1800. Overtime of US$20 charged outside these hours.

Sint Maarten

Area 35sq km
Highest point West Peak 334m
Population 32,000
Main town Philipsburg
Language Dutch (official), English (everyday)
Currency Netherlands Antilles Florin (Guilder) (official), US$ (normal)
Political status Free port and constituent part of the self-governing Dutch Netherlands Antilles Federation
Distances to nearby islands Philipsburg – St Barts 11M

Sint Maarten today

Since 1919 Sint Maarten has been the seat of the governor of what are called, the Dutch Windward Islands (Sint Maarten, Saba and Statia). They are at present formally joined to three other territories in the Dutch Leeward Islands, N of Venezuela (Aruba, Bonaire and Curaçao). Together the four territories form the self-governing Dutch Netherlands Antilles Federation whose Governor-General and legislative assembly are in Curaçao.

However, following a recent referendum, Sint Maarten's population has expressed a wish to secede from this confederation. Its future status within the Dutch community has yet to be decided.

If in the past the Sint Maarten economy depended on sugar cane and salt ponds, these days it's all radically changed and the duty free, tax free zone is nicknamed the Little Hong Kong of the Antilles. Real estate development is going full tilt and reclamation in the lagoon and levelling of the hills is helping Philipsburg grow. The sole object of all the hotel construction is to attract tourists, preferably American. The dollar rules, with the result that the florin (or 'guilder') is largely an administrative fiction. In just the same way few speak Dutch because everyday life is conducted in English (if often mixed with the *papiamento* of Curaçao). On official maps all the names of places and bays, etc. are in Dutch, though in

Philipsburg ferry arrivals dock

Courthouse, Philipsburg

fact the tendency is more and more to call them by anglicised versions.

Tourism

Where to stay and what to see

All there is to the Dutch side are vast hotel developments along the SW coast and the shore of the lagoon, lots of them with night clubs and casinos. There's also an international airport, the Princess Juliana Airport, built on a low-lying isthmus between the sea and the lagoon. All intercontinental air traffic comes through it and therefore to the Dutch side, although both sides of the island contributed money to have it built. Other than the beaches and the lagoon there's not much to see, tourists being principally attracted by the duty free shopping in the many shops in Philipsburg.

Philipsburg

Founded in 1733, the town is built on a thin strip of land between the Great Salt Pond and Groot Baai and consists of small buildings mostly lining Back Street and Front Street, the two main streets with most of the business premises. Further back and to the E around Great Salt Pond there's a new quarter with big modern buildings where you'll find the banks and the government offices.

There's a very nice sandy beach on Philipsburg's sea front (Front Street) with, on its E side, the ferry dock. Close to the dock small and lively Walthey Square is surrounded by lots of shops, bars and restaurants. On its farther side you'll see the Old Courthouse with its campanile and bell turret, a charming bit of period architecture. In Front Street and Back Street there are lots of restaurants with a wide variety of menus from Chinese through Indonesian.

On the seaward end of the E side of the bay there's a vast new jetty where cruise liners dock. Every day in the season, the cruise ships offload their hordes of passengers to invade the narrow streets

and the duty-free shops. But before night falls, these day-trippers clamber back aboard their floating palaces and the streets are all at once deserted. All that are left are the night birds aiming to end their evening in the casinos or nightclubs around the lagoon. If Sint Maarten isn't Las Vegas, it's certainly one of the Lesser Antilles whose night life is pretty lively and cosmopolitan.

Around the island

The road out of Philipsburg towards the N, Dutch Cul-de-Sac and Sint Peters runs largely through residential quarters. There's another road heading W up Cole Bay Hill from where there's a superb panorama of Simpson Bay Lagoon and the sea, from where it runs down to run along the lagoon and its succession of marinas, hotels and villa developments before it reaches the airport and the French side. Eastwards a small road reaches Oyster Pond and the windward coast. The numerous Dutch forts are now mostly ruins though the most impressive remains are those of Fort Amsterdam to the W of Philipsburg.

Great Bay and the Cruise Dock

Pilotage

Coast and anchorages

Coming from St Barts it's quite normal to stop over in the Dutch side in Groot Baai before heading on for Marigot and the French side. On the S coast the anchorages can be uncomfortable in SE winds. Occasionally, especially in summer, the wind can go WSW for a while. You also need to be aware of a sort of local mini-surge wave that can put poorly anchored boats on the beach. The relatively hilly E part of Sint Maarten is readily visible when you're on your way in from St-Barth. Once round the islets on the E (Molly Beday and Hen and Chickens) aim for Pointe Blanche. This whole coastal area is now part of the Nature Foundation of Sint Maarten Reserve. If you're coming from S watch out for the shoal ground of Proselyte Reef, 0.75M S of Witte Kaap (White Cape). It has only 4m over it and is hazardous in a heavy swell. It's marked with an isolated danger mark.

Sint Maarten, Groot Baai & Simpson Bay from S

You can make a night approach using the light on Fort Amsterdam.

Groot Baai (Great Bay)

Philipsburg

Once round Witte Kaap (White Point), you enter Groot Baai. To starboard the new cruise liner dock pushes a long way out.

Caution There are mooring dolphins and mooring buoys to watch out for. At night lit buoys and lights on the jetty ends mark the limits of the jetty.

At the root of the Cruise Dock there's a large esplanade which is being turned into a commercial harbour. Once you've got around this area, you can head roughly N into the bay holding for preference to the line of the channel to the ferry dock. You should be in depths of 2·8–4m. In theory the channel is marked by some buoys.

The anchorage area is either to the E or the W of the ferry channel. In a SE swell the whole S facing bay can get uncomfortable, especially in the W. In the N of the bay you'll find the two Great Bay marinas:

Bobby's Marina (VHF 16) has some 30 berths with water and electricity. There's a fuel dock at its seaward end. Depths are 2·5m at the outward end shoaling to 1·5m near the dinghy dock. Most of the berths are occupied by resident boats.

Just S of Bobby's are the pontoons of **Great Bay Marina**, a small number of which have been put out of action as a result of the big works going on to construct the new commercial harbour. This huge flat reclaimed area has now pushed as far as the old southern breakwater of the small marina. All the same, there are a few berths for visiting boats.

To complete the port works in Great Bay there's a big project under way. There's a mega-marina on the drawing board which embraces the whole area now occupied by Bobby's and Great Bay Marina. It'll be protected by two

enormous breakwaters and closed by a floating pontoon. The haven is designed to accommodate the largest yachts.

Ashore The office for clearance is at the Commercial Dock. Bobby's has lots of specialist workers on tap and a branch of one of the islands main chandleries is here too. There are also shops, a grocery and the much frequented

Seafood Galley restaurant and bar. Bobby's Boatyard has the monopoly on lifting heavy yachts here on the Dutch side. However, the relatively small space available in Philipsburg has led the yard to shift some of its hard standing operations to a second yard in the lagoon, near the airport. Bobby's also has a great variety of repair and

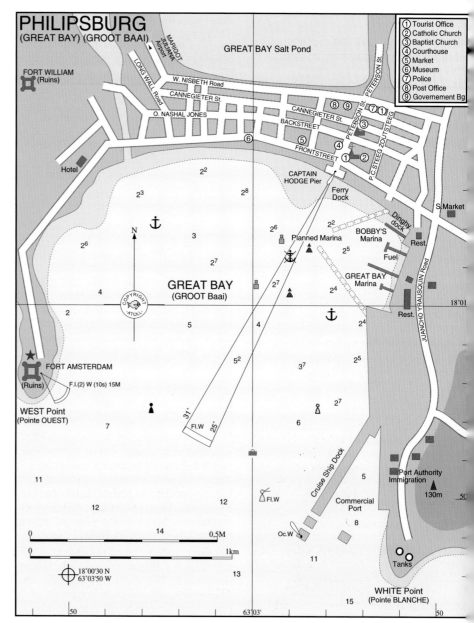

Above Great Bay, Philipsburg
Above right Philipsburg beach
Right Simpson Lagoon from SW

maintenance services available.

Great Bay Marina office is in the same building as Chesterfield's bar and restaurant on the quayside. Nearby are several yachting services as well as a minimarket.

For provisioning the best choice is offered by the Philipsburg supermarkets, especially the two or three really big ones on the edge of town. Other than the practical reasons for coming to the town, there's also pleasure to be had wandering the streets, mingling with the tourists on the hunt for duty free bargains, or, if more or less exotic food takes your fancy, sampling the town's restaurants.

Simpson Bay

Caution Give Pelican Pt a wide berth to clear the reef off its SE side.

You can anchor in 3-4m in the NE of the bay to starboard of the lagoon access channel. It's usually calm unless the SE wind has set in.

Note Don't anchor in the lagoon access channel.

Ashore On the E side, there's the Pelican Resort, a luxury hotel-casino with a shopping mall, tennis courts, swimming pool and restaurant. It's for the well-to-do only! To the W of the lifting bridge, there's a new bulding which houses another immigration office.

Simpson Bay Lagoon

Known as a hurricane hole, the Dutch part of the lagoon gets better equipped to welcome yachts each year that passes. That said, as Luis and Lenny showed in 1995 and 1999, boats in the lagoon are in no way guaranteed immunity from damage because the fetch across the lagoon is large.

Access to the lagoon is under a lifting road bridge opening 3 times a day. The channel is dredged to 3·5–4m. Level with the bridge the channel is about 11m wide. Other than a few shoals, particularly two N of Snoopy Island,

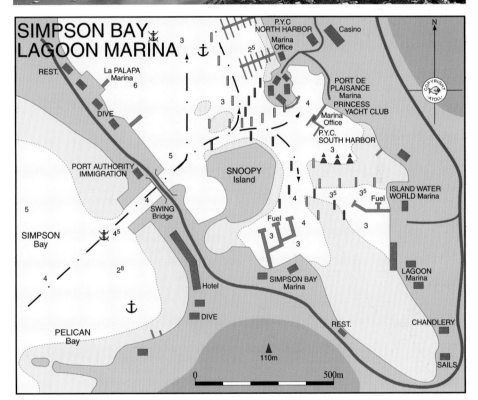

most of the large lagoon is navigable with 2·5 to 3·5m. On the other hand the French part in the NE often has depths below 2m. You can anchor anywhere in the lagoon except in line with the airport runway or in any of the marine access channels. You should note that in the W of the lagoon the anchorage can become uncomfortable in fresh trades given the fetch across the whole width of this large area of water. The bottom is sand and

mud and no dream spot if clear water's what you're looking for.

NE of the bridge there's a buoyed channel around Snoopy I leading to the main marinas. The SE shores of the lagoon are now taken up by several areas in which you'll find marinas and various technical services.

- on the E shore the services are clustered round the island's oldest chandlery: Island Water World (VHF

Left Simpson Lagoon from NW
Above Mullet Bay from NW

16/74): A dredged, buoyed channel (>3m) leads to its pontoons. It has around 50 berths with water and electricity and a fuel dock. A crane can haul out small and medium sized boats. In addition Island Water World has a very large and excellent chandlery with everything you'll need for repairs and maintenance.

- further S another recently dredged 2·5–3m channel leads to the Lagoon Marina complex: It's actually just an arrivals dock, but close by are lots of specialist services as well as the island's other chandlery, Budget Marine.
- N of Island Water World is the huge complex of the Princess Yacht Club (once called the Port de Plaisance) which has extended its facilities and now has several pontoons in two blocks. N of its small peninsula is North Harbor and S, South Harbor. Access to both is beaconed. The entire development has some 80 luxuriously equipped berths in 3–4m. One of the pontoons has a fuel dock on the end.

Ashore The hotel and residential complex has the entire gamut of services and distractions to perfect its image: casino, shopping mall, fitness centre, tennis courts, swimming pool and several restaurants. The ensemble is aimed at clients as refined as they're moneyed.

On the W shore, S and N of the lifting bridge respectively, are two other facilities.

- Simpson Bay Yacht Club Marina has tucked its pontoons in the shelter of Snoopy Island S of the bridge. To get there you have to go round the E side of the island using the beaconed channel. The pontoons have more than 100 berths and a fuel dock in 3·5m.

Ashore Close to the jetties you'll find the office, several shops and restaurants. Several technical services and a branch of Budget Marine are also nearby.

- La Palapa Marina N of the bridge is a dock parallel with the shore built to accommodate maxi yachts with some 20 berths and a fuel dock.

Ashore On the dock or the other side of the road are several bars and restaurants and several technical services. There's a small supermarket for basic supplies.

Useful Information for Sint Maarten

AIRLINE CONNECTIONS
International Airport: Philipsburg, Princess Juliana Airport ☎ 599 54 54211 *Fax* 599 54 53578
International long-haul flights direct to Europe, N America and San Juan (Puerto Rico)
Inter-island daily services to most islands in the Caribbean

FERRY CONNECTIONS
Services to St Barts and Saba and day-trips to Saba and St Barts

TELECOMMUNICATIONS
Calling from abroad: ☎ 599 54 + 5 digits
Local call: 7 digits
To call the French side: 00 590 + 6 digits
Public call boxes: TEL-EM phone cards and credit cards

TOURIST OFFICE/YACHT CLUB
Tourist office Vineyard Bldg, 1st fl. 23 Walter Nisbeth Rd, Philipsburg ☎ 599 54 22337
Fax 599 54 22734,
Email info@st-maarten.com
www.st-maarten.com
Sint Maarten Yacht Club,
☎/Fax 599 54 42075
Email secretary@smyc.com

FESTIVALS/FOLKLORE
Heineken Regatta: first full weekend in March organised by the Sint Maarten YC
Carnival: 2nd fortnight in April
Guavaberry Regatta (to St Kitts & Nevis): last full moon in May or first full moon in June
Anguilla Race: November
St-Martin's Day Regatta: November 11
Statia Race: January

Further N between the lagoon and the airport you'll find Bobby's Boatyard's new yard and hard standing. All of the facilities and the number of specialist yacht services here in the Dutch end of the lagoon make Sint Maarten one of the best equipped spots for yachting in the Lesser Antilles.

Further W still is Mullet Pond, a small, shallow lagoon, though you can only anchor off its entrance. Tourists and their watersports from the Mullet Bay Resort make it a lively spot. Further W still the anchorages become uncomfortable when the trades are fresh because of the considerable fetch. And all along the narrow isthmus separating the lagoon from the sea, it's wall-to-wall hotels and restaurants.

PUBLIC HOLIDAYS
New Year's Day (1 January), Carnival Monday (April – Carnival actually lasts 3 weeks), Good Friday, Easter Monday, Queen's Coronation Day (30 April), Labour Day (1 May), Ascension Day (always a Thursday), St Maarten Day (11 November), Christmas Day (25 December), Boxing Day (26 December)

OFFICE HOURS
Shops: 0800–1200, 1400–1800

PLACES TO SEE
St Maarten Museum: Museum Arcade, 7 Front St, Philipsburg
St Maarten Zoo: Madam Estate, Arch Rd, Philipsburg (island flora and fauna)
Fort Hill, Fort Amsterdam (1631) & Old Spanish Fort: ruins

ROAD TRANSPORT
Drive on the right
Your own national driving licence required.
Hire car companies in Philipsburg and at the airport
Taxis

BRIDGE OPENING
St Maarten Port Authority,
☎ 599 54 24979 VHF 12
Weekdays 0600, 0900, 1100, 1730
Sundays: twice daily

FORMALITIES
No customs
Arriving by air immigration at the airport
Arriving by sea
Philipsburg Commercial Port for Immigration and Port Authority
Hours: weekdays 0800–1200, 1300–1600, weekends 0900–1200
Simpson Bay SW side of entrance channel for Immigration and Port Authority (may not always be there)
Hours: 7 days a week 0700–1800
Fees and taxes small immigration fee

Anguilla

Area 90sq km
Highest point Crocus Hill, 60m
Population 7000
Capital The Valley
Language English
Currency EC$
Political status British Dependent Territory
Distances to nearby islands St-Martin (Marigot) 6M, Virgin Gorda 75M

History

Out at the archipelago's northern extremity, Anguilla is the last of the Leewards before you reach the Virgins. When they discovered it the Spanish called it Anguilla ('the eel') because of its long flat shape. The original Amerindian inhabitants had called it Malliouhana. The English were the first colonists and arrived in the 17th century. They tried, without much success, to grow tobacco and sugar cane on its meagre soil. The English stayed in control throughout the colonial period despite the nearby presence of the French in St-Martin and their attempts at conquest in 1745 and 1796. The first was swiftly repelled, but during the second the British holed up in the fort on Sandy Hill until they had repulsed the enemy and were again wholly masters of their island.

The island's dry climate prevented any major plantation development. And in the 19th century the place was parcelled out to the newly emancipated slaves and a few poor white settlers who had intermarried and from them today's population is descended.

Because of the English dominance, Protestantism in all its forms – Anglican, Methodist, 7th Day Adventists and so on – is the main religion. There are even a few Rastafarians, and it's interesting to remember that their movement (its name taken from the Negus Ras Tafari Haile Selassie of Ethiopia) holds that the Ethiopians, not the Jews, are the true descendants of King Solomon.

Below left and centre Wallblake Plantation
Far right Cottage in The Valley

Sombrero

Thirty miles NW of Anguilla, Sombrero I is part of St Kitts and Nevis, though in fact it's only really visited by Anguillan fishermen. It's a flat island less than 1M long and uninhabited. There are some ruins of some shacks and the remains of a small railway, all that's left of an old mine. Yachts seldom approach Sombrero unless at the end of a NNE tack beating up from the Virgins.
Caution At night, if the light isn't working, the island is a serious hazard.

Anguillans are fiercely loyal to their island even if they're exiles who, given the poverty of their homeland, have gone to work elsewhere. Indeed some have made their fortunes in the States or even Britain. And like all Anguillans, even those who have stayed at home in poverty, they share in their island's rich past of master sailors and builders of graceful schooners. It's from this background the islanders get their proud and fiercely independent character.

When the British decided to decolonise, the technocrats of the Colonial Office decided to go for a tidy solution and lumped Anguilla in with St Kitts and Nevis, making St Kitts, the largest island, the seat of government. Becoming a colony of an old colony wasn't quite what the Anguillans fancied. So they revolted and declared their island free and independent. There was a vain attempt by St Kitts to reconquer, but their weak soldiery was swiftly pushed back into the sea. Britain stirred from its slumber and in 1969 sent a gunboat and some assault troops. Luckily there were neither fighting nor casualties. Following UN intervention, in 1971 Anguilla became an Autonomous Crown Colony and then, in 1980, a British Dependent Territory. These days there is a constitution, an elected assembly and an island government. A governor represents the crown and looks after foreign affairs and the administration of justice. All those fiery events are now in the past and the Anguillans have returned to their fishing, thanks to the island's rich waters, its main natural resource. You can add to that a few herds of goats and the exploitation of the salt pond at Sandy Ground.

Tourism

Where to stay and what to see

Fishing, goats and salt were the economic mainstay, until the 1980s, when the first moves towards developing a tourist industry were made. The wonderful beaches and lovely small neighbouring islets surrounded by coral reef were attraction enough but in addition the government has created several well protected marine reserves to preserve the rich submarine flora and fauna.

Since then big tourist money has moved in and several hotels have been built. Some of them are truly five star with prices to match. There are also now several small restaurants on the coast and the islets owned not only by locals, but by Europeans and Americans. They offer a wide range of seafood menus with pride of place given to the famous langoustes. No matter whose restaurant it is, you can be sure of a warm welcome, though their popularity with tourists and day charterers from St-Martin means that prices are high. That said, compared to St-Martin, come nightfall there's little going on. No discos. No casinos. The Anguillans don't want to lose their souls. . .

Around the island

If the coastline is superb, the bare, flat interior has little going for it. A road runs the length of the island with tracks leading off it to the beaches and many small villages, the small population being very well spread out. Wallblake Airport, which is very simple, has only inter-island flights.

Close by, The Valley, a very symbolic micro-capital, has a few scattered houses on their small plots, a few simple shops and one or two government offices including the Tourist Office. Otherwise there's only Wallblake Plantation House, built in stone in 1787, which has an exhibition of the island's history. For religious services there are two churches, of which one, the neo-gothic confection of St Gerard's Catholic Church, has an amazing façade of stones. The Fountain cave is one of the few natural sites to visit provided it's open (it is being done up). The cave is

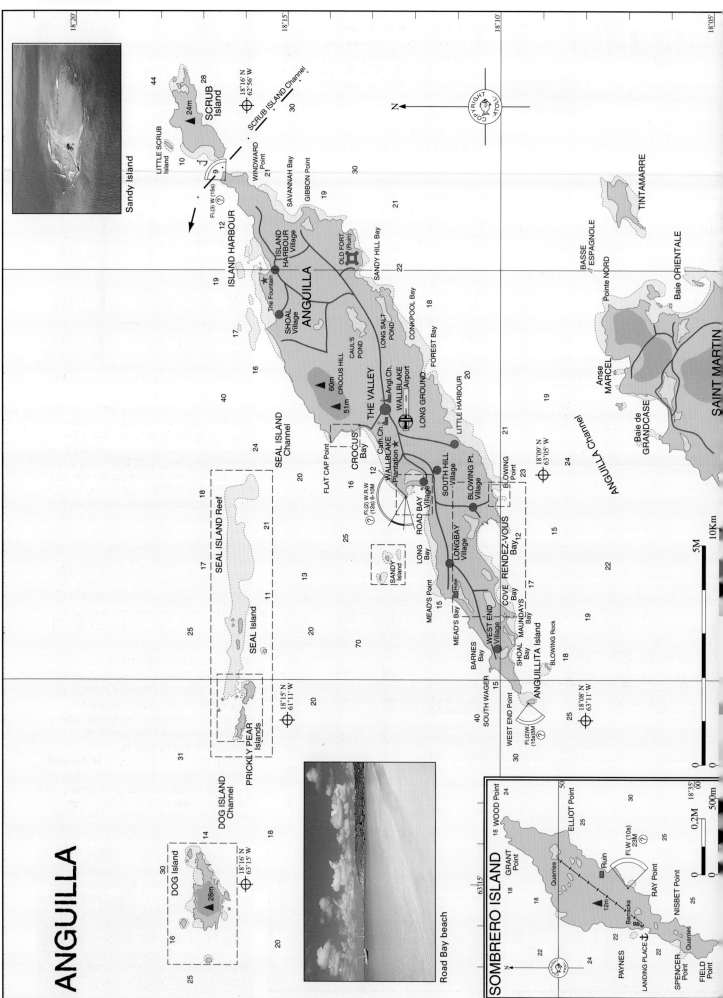

St Gerard's Roman Catholic Church

the island's sole spring and was an important pre-Columbian religious site, to which some petroglyphs and a stalagmite sculpted into the form of Jacahu, an Amerindian deity, bear witness.

Pilotage

Coast and anchorages

Scarcely 6M separates Marigot Bay and the E coast of Anguilla. The channel is rarely rough unless there's a strong NE wind. Stretched out ahead of you is all of Anguilla, though the largely featureless coast has scarcely any landmarks to help you identify the inlets. The S point is marked by Anguillita I, which is very unreliably lit, just like the very few other Anguillan

lights, thanks to the difficulty and costs of maintenance. It follows that making landfall at night is out of the question, especially from the W given the mass of reefs and islets NW of Anguilla.

East coast

Barely in the lee of St-Martin, Anguilla's E coast has very few permitted anchorages.

Blowing Point Harbour

This is the port of entry for the ferries from St-Martin. Given how tight it is and the number of local boats using it, it's not popular with yachts. That said, it is a harbour and is accessible to small yachts so you can do your clearance here if you want. Identify Shaddick Pt and avoid the shoal ground extending some 300m SW of it to find the entrance to the pass into Blowing Point Hrbr.

Caution A long sand bank runs out from the shore about 100m W of the line of the pass.

The entrance is aligned about 003°T and has a leading line. However, both the leading marks and the two buoys marking the pass may be missing.

Rendezvous Bay & Cove Bay

Rendezvous Bay is large and well sheltered and anchoring is forbidden.

Anguillita & the SW point of Anguilla

SE Point Blowing Harbour and Rendezvous Bay

Note The management of the Rendezvous Hotel, one of the island's oldest, is quick to help enforce these rules. If you want to anchor you can in the smaller opening of Cove Bay a bit further W between two coral reefs. It's usually fairly full of local boats, but it's quite well protected unless the swell's from the ESE.

West coast

Coming from the east before you can get to this coast you have to pass Blowing Rock and round Anguillita I.

Caution The pass between Anguillita I and the main island shore isn't feasible for keelers.

Barnes Bay & Mead's Bay

Two bays with fine sandy beaches that are fairly open to NE swells. They are pleasant day anchorages in good weather. There are a few hotels ashore. The Malliouhana Hotel, with its imposing half oriental, half Mediterranean architecture, is the most luxurious and overlooks Mead's Bay. If you're a cruiser with deep pockets you'll enjoy the restaurants and its luxury shops.

Road Bay

There are no difficulties in the approaches to this huge bay provided you steer clear of the shoal ground on its NE shore. Note that the light on Road Pt rarely works, so a night approach is out. The big dock in the SE of the bay is for small coasters and local boats and the approaches should be left clear. In the NE there's a small dock for dinghies to use. The anchorage is large

Rendezvous Bay, Cove Bay, Maunday's Bay & Anguillita

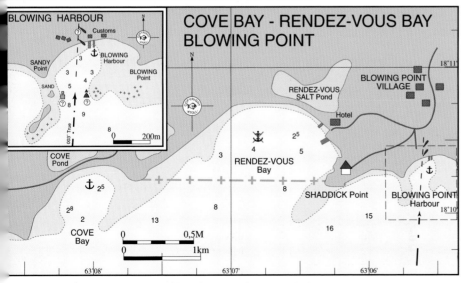

Top left Road Bay from NW
Top right Road Bay beach and anchorage
Above left Crocus Bay from NW
Above right Crocus Bay anchorage

and very pleasant, the shoreline fringed with a lovely sandy beach. If there's much of a N swell a strong slop can make in.

Ashore The building with customs and the police is at the end of the small dock in the NE used by tenders. The regulations governing anchoring and fees are quite complicated. Make sure you've found out about them before you arrive. Other than a small chandlery and a workshop for outboards, there's not much for yachts. There are shops and minimarkets for provisioning with essentials. For greater variety the large supermarkets are in The Valley, easy to get to by taxi given the short distance between Road Bay and the little capital.

The major interest in Road Bay apart from its fine sandy beach is the number and variety of the restaurants along the shore. Some have various services for cruisers (water, taxis, etc).

Crocus Bay & Little Bay

N of Road Bay, these anchorages aren't as busy. The best sheltered from swell is Little Bay, but anchoring is strictly forbidden. You must use a buoy (white) if one is free. N of Little Bay as far as Flatcap Pt there's a fine reddish ochre cliff sculpted and hollowed by wind and waves, worth a visit in the tender or by snorkelling. Otherwise anchor S of Pelican Pt in Crocus Bay off the sandy beach.

Note Watch out for the reefs on the N and S of the anchorage

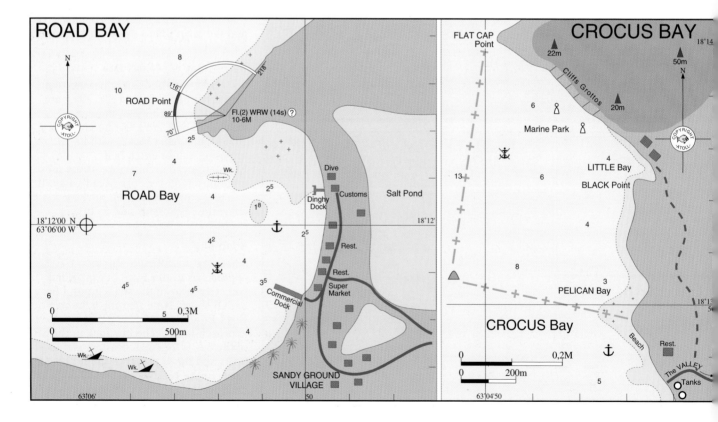

Left Fisherman, Crocus Bay
Right Sandy Island & Coral Island
Below Island Harbour
Below right Scilly Cay, Island Harbour

Ashore is Roy's Restaurant, one of the W coast's oldest.

Sandy Island

The big coconut trees of this islet about 1M from Road Bay were flattened by the last cyclone. There are young trees pushing up to replace them, but it'll be a few years yet before this small patch of sand surrounded by coral has any shade. The only authorised anchorage is W of Sandy I. In theory it's marked by buoys, and in the anchoring zone there are supposedly yellow mooring buoys, but they're often carried away by the sea. Use your tender to get to the islet

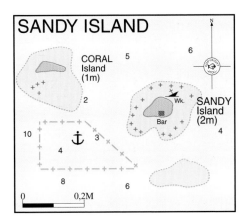

SANDY ISLAND

through a small pass in the S of the coral reef around the island. There's a small shack ashore with a simple snack bar and on the N coast there's a wreck from the last hurricane.

NE coast

Upper Shoal Bay and Island Harbour

The coast is fringed with both reef and offshore patches, some of them extensive. There is a passage between the coastal reef and the offliers with 5–12m in it, though it's not very wide. S of the passage Upper Shoal bay has only 1·8m so is for shoal drafters only and is usually only used by local boats.

Island Harbour is a bit further E. You can either head on along the narrow pass, or avoid most of the reefs by going N of them, in which case the line of approach is 115°T. Once off the bay, to get to the anchorage off the village eyeball in between reefs on both sides on approx. 170°T using the village houses, amongst them a modern white house, as a leading mark. Depths are between 4m and 7m, but watch out for the occasional shoal with less than 2m over it. Basically this place is for experienced hands in small yachts only in good weather and good visibility. Otherwise steer clear. Island Harbour Village is a typical fishing village, which

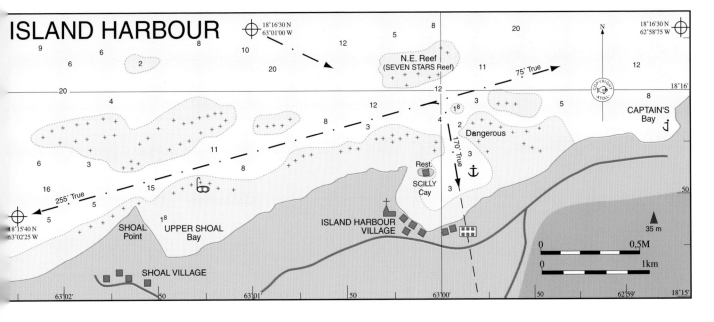

ISLAND HARBOUR

stirs at dawn when the fishermen go out. The village's small restaurants, including the charming one on Scilly Cay, are great for seafood and especially langoustes, the specialty of the local menu. Further E is Captain's Bay, a gorgeous bay, but the NE swell usually stops you staying for long.

Scrub Island

There's a fair weather day anchorage here, but if there's swell from the NE give it a miss. If you draw less than 2m you can anchor between the two coral reefs. There's a wonderful beach and good snorkelling among the reefs. The island is uninhabited and mostly covered with thorns. To the E the pass between Scrub I and Anguilla is easy to get back round to the E coast and St-Martin, though watch out for the current and for a pretty lively sea if the trades are fresh.

Seal Island and Prickly Pear Islands

This collection of islands and the huge reef on which they sit has lots of good spots, but the only permitted anchorage is SW of Prickly Pear East. The holding is bad, but mooring buoys have been laid, at least in principle. If you want to visit anywhere else, you'll have to get there in your tender. The bay on the N side of Prickly Pear East is accessible by tender through the pass between Prickly Pears E and W. There's a pretty, coral fringed blue lagoon with a white sand bottom and beach, but it's pretty busy with day trippers. They and the visiting yachts crowd the bar-restaurant ashore where seafood and grills are served non-stop.

There are lots of snorkelling sites on the Sandy Island reef. The best sheltered spots are near Seal Island and Prickly Pear North.

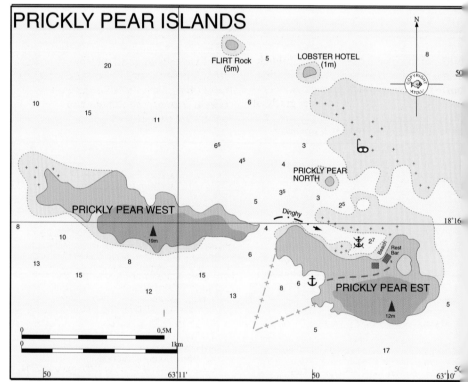

Top Scrub Island & Windward Point from SW
Above Prickly Pear West and Prickly Pear East
Below left Scrub Island beach

Dog Island

10M from Anguilla, this is the last stop before the Virgins or for a brief stop in fair weather. The 3km long island is deserted and a sanctuary for frigate

PRICKLY PEAR ISLANDS

SEAL ISLAND REEF - PRICKLY PEAR ISLANDS

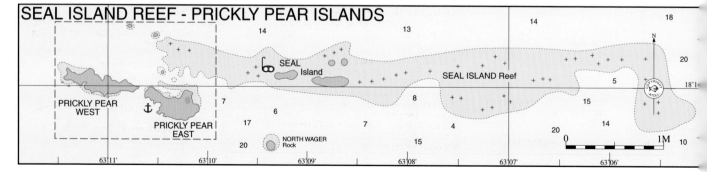

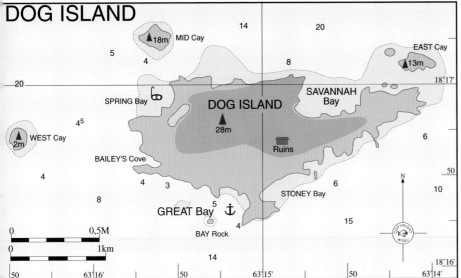

DOG ISLAND

(chart labels:) MID Cay 18m · 14 · 20 · EAST Cay 13m · 5 · 4 · 8 · 18°17' · 20 · SPRING Bay · DOG ISLAND 28m · SAVANNAH Bay · WEST Cay 2m · 4⁵ · Ruins · 6 · BAILEY'S Cove · 4 · 3 · 6 · 50 · 8 · STONEY Bay · 10 · GREAT Bay 5 · BAY Rock 4 · 15 · 0 0,5M · 0 1km · 14 · 18°16' · 50 · 63°16' · 50 · 63°15' · 50 · 63°14'

Top left Dog Island from NW
Top right Prickly Pear beach
Above Great Bay anchorage, Dog Island

Note Stay clear of Bay Rock in the S of Great Bay. There's a lot of fine coral around the island, but rough seas usually make snorkelling problematic.

birds which breed here. On the hillock in the middle there's a ruined building buried in thorny bush and an old landing strip on the W coast is gradually being overrun by scrub. There isn't a good anchorage anywhere, and you need well set-in good weather to make a stop. The only authorised anchorage, in Great Bay, with its fabulous empty beach, is poorly protected and untenable in a SE swell.

Useful Information for Anguilla

AIRLINE CONNECTIONS
Wallblake Airport: The Valley,
☎ 264 497 2514
No international long-haul flights
Inter-island flights daily to St Maarten, St Thomas and other neighbouring islands and to Puerto Rico.

FERRY CONNECTIONS
Daily service between Blowing Point and Marigot (St-Martin)

TELECOMMUNICATIONS
Calling from abroad: ☎ (1) 264 497 + 4 digits
Local call: 7 digits
Public call boxes: Caribbean Phone Card

TOURIST OFFICE
The Valley ☎ 264 497 2759
  Fax 264 497 2710
  Email atbtour@anguillanet.com
  www.anguilla-vacation.com
Department of Fisheries: The Valley,
  ☎ 264 498 2871 *Fax* 264 497 8657
  Email dfmr@anguillanet.com

CLUBS/ASSOCIATIONS
Anguilla Yacht Club, Sandy Ground, Anguilla, VHF 16 ☎ 264 497 2671 *Fax* 264 497 2901

FESTIVALS/FOLKLORE
Carnival & Boat races: Friday before the first Monday in August

Moonsplash Music Festival: 3 days in March
Anguilla Day (Independence): end of May
Anguilla International Arts Festival: every other odd year (www.artsfestival.ai)

PUBLIC HOLIDAYS
New Year's Day (1 January), Good Friday, Easter Monday, Labour Day (May), Whit Monday, Anguilla Day (end of May), Queen's Birthday (early June), August Monday (1st Monday in August), August Thursday (1st Thursday in August), Constitution Day (1st Friday in August), Separation Day (19 December), Christmas Day (25 December), Boxing Day (26 December)

OFFICE HOURS
Government Offices: Mon–Fri 0800–1600
Post Office: Mon–Fri 0800–1530
Shops: Mon–Sat 0800–1700/1800 (some to 2100 and some on Sundays)
Banks: Mon–Thurs 0800–1500, Fri 0800–1700
Gas stations: The Valley, Mon–Sat 0700–2100, Sun 0900–1300, Blowing Point, Mon–Sun 0700–2400

PLACES TO SEE
Wallblake Historic House (1787)
Anguilla National Museum, The Valley
Heritage Collection Museum, South Hill Plaza: local household artefacts
The Fountain National Park: Cave & pre-Columbian site
Crocus Hill Prison: old prison and island's highest point
St Gerard's Roman Catholic Church

ROAD TRANSPORT
Drive on the left. Local licence compulsory, US$10 for a 3 month licence on production of your national licence.
Hire car companies and taxis (regulated fares) in The Valley and at the airport

REGULATIONS
Underwater Reserves: hunting and any take of catch, shells or coral forbidden to non-residents. Jet skis forbidden.
Regulated anchoring/mooring areas, fees for buoys from EC$35-60 a night

FORMALITIES
Arriving by air customs and immigration at the airport
Arriving by sea
Blowing Point Harbour, near the ferry dock
Hours: 0700–2000. Not usually used by yachts
Road Bay by the dinghy dock.
Hours: Daily 7 days a week, 0830–1200/ 1300–1600
Overtime for outside hours and holidays. You can simultaneously clear in and out for stays of less than 24hrs.
Fees and taxes
Cruising permit (obligatory for anchorages other than Road Bay)
EC$100 a day for vessels <20 tonnes
EC$5 Immigration tax per person
EC$30-60 Additional port dues for vessels >20 tonnes
The cumulative burden of these fees is quite heavy.

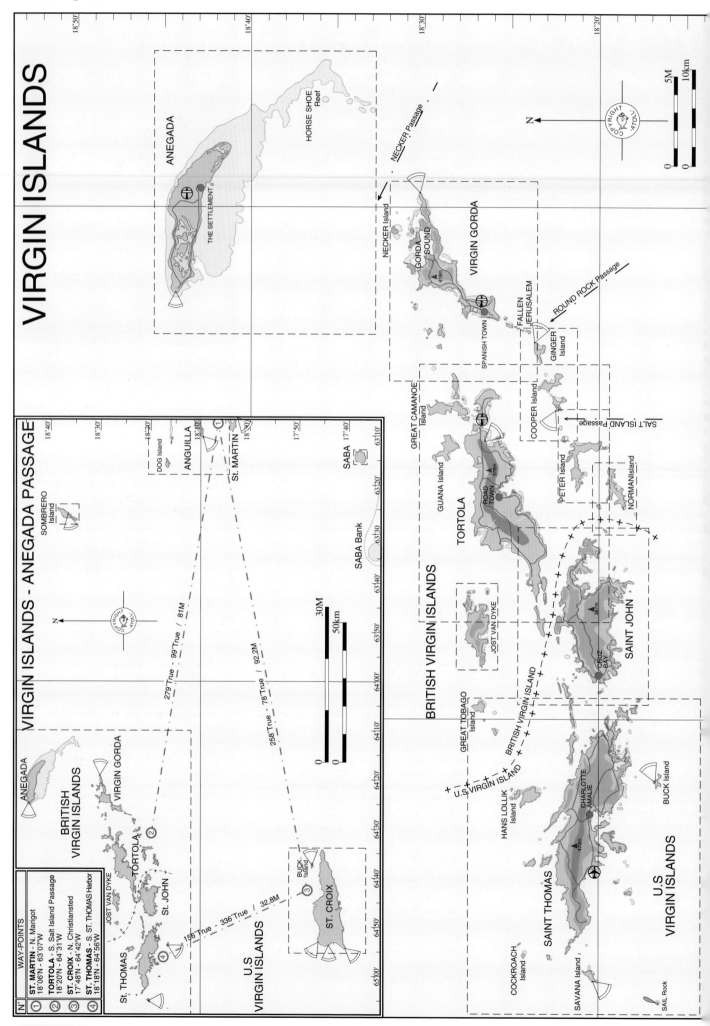

VIRGIN ISLANDS

VIRGIN ISLANDS - ANEGADA PASSAGE

The Virgin Islands

History

Columbus was enchanted by this archipelago in 1493, so much so that he gave the entirety a single name, 'The Eleven Thousand Virgins', thereby commemorating the 11,000 companions of St Ursula who were martyred in the 5th century by the Huns. The islands were at the time only inhabited by Amerindian tribes and, for all their beauty, the Spanish passed them by, since they were a great deal more interested in conquering the gold rich territories of South America. What they'd missed was that their choice would in the end work against their own best interests.

In order to find fair winds for their voyage to Spain, the Spanish treasure fleets, heavily laden with the fruit of their pillage of the New World, had to pass the Virgins. Naturally the islands became a haunt of the filibusters, mostly English but with a few Dutchmen and French buccaneers. Hidden in the maze of islands, they would launch themselves on the heavily laden Spanish ships and, their piracy done, would disappear back into the maze to await then next bonanza. John Hawkins and Francis Drake were amongst the best known of the filibusters who used this means of filling their holds and their pockets.

The whole morally questionable business was obviously very lucrative and the English, who established themselves as early as 1620, never again left the eastern part of the islands (Tortola, Virgin Gorda and Anegada) which they formally annexed at the end of the 17th century. That was the birth of the British Virgin Islands (BVI), today an autonomous Crown Colony.

The three other islands in the W and SW, St Croix, St John and St Thomas, were successively Dutch, British, Danish and French as the fortunes of war ebbed and flowed. It was only at the beginning of the 19th century that they became definitively Danish, then the Danes ceded them to the USA in 1917. So finally these three islands became the US Virgin Islands, an associated but not incorporated US territory.

Economically, in the past most of the islands depended on the monocultures of sugar and cotton. But as everywhere else in the Caribbean, with the abolition of slavery and the disappearance of free subject labour, the plantations went rapidly downhill. The majority went out of business or, especially in the BVI, shifted to simpler market gardening. Since then the rapid growth of tourism, especially the water sports based variety, has brought new prosperity and allowed most of the population to achieve a standard of living close to that of the developed world.

Tourism

These islands may fall geographically within the Lesser Antilles, but many think of them as a distinct group because they're a lot closer to Puerto Rico and hence the USA. For if there's one thing that's distinctive of the Virgins as a whole, it's the American influence. That's most obvious if you look at tourist numbers which are overwhelmingly American, at the type and management of the hotels and marine sector, and above all the ubiquity of the US$. Business as a whole is, as a result, closely tied to the North American market.

But for all the commercial and geographical linkages, the two parts of the Virgins have quite different political statuses and each is unique in its own way. Basically this comes down to the relative extent of urbanization and population density. The BVI are much less densely populated, for example. But there's also a difference in the way of life of the local people. So we'll look at the islands in two parts: the BVI, then the USVI.

Pilotage

The Anegada Passage

It's about 75M from Anguilla to Virgin Gorda across the Anegada Passage. There's usually a W-flowing current of about 0·5kt, often more. The sea is usually quite rough in fresh trade winds. It's no problem getting to the Virgins because you've a following wind; heading the other way is tougher. Some head off on starboard tack towards Sombrero I, others take port tack towards Saba. If the wind is against you and the current is running quite strongly, you'll have to sail twice the rhumb line distance to get to St-Martin. It's not a good idea to make landfall in the Virgins at night because there are few lights in the BVI and they're not that reliable. If you're in any doubt it's better to alter slightly south to make St Thomas and the good lights on its S coast.

Caution Anegada or Horseshoe Reef covers almost the entire NE approaches to Virgin Gorda and is the biggest boat cemetery in the Lesser Antilles. Give it a good, wide berth.

Navigating in the Virgin Islands

In some parts, the waters between the forty or so tightly clustered islands of the group (the number excludes insignificant islets) are almost like lakes. Only two of the islands lie at some distance from the group as a whole, Anegada, 10-15M N and St Croix, its opposite number, about 30M to the S. Winds are usually pretty steady and there are lots of anchorages close to each other across stretches of protected water. That alone explains why the islands have seen such a growth in yachting.

Navigation and buoyage

Day navigation is hardly a problem, at least provided you're sensible. Night sailing, on the other hand, is especially not a good idea in the BVI where lights and buoys are unreliable. In the USVI, even if sailing at night still isn't the wisest course, at least the lights are both more numerous and more reliable because better maintained.

Buoy moorings

Mooring buoys in lieu of anchoring are now fairly ubiquitous in order to protect the seabed. The National Park systems in both BVI and USVI, as well as private companies, have laid buoys (usually fee paying) in the most popular anchorages and in protected marine areas (see Useful Information for the BVI and USVI).

Tides

They're hard to reckon because they are both diurnal and semi-diurnal depending on the season and where you are. Luckily tidal range is slight, generally being less than 0.3m.

Current

Within the island chain there is little current. However, it can be strong between two islands and especially in The Narrows between Tortola and St John where it can run up to 3kts W.

Note

Formalities The authorities in both the BVI and USVI are very strict with respect to clearance formalities both clearing in and out of their respective territories. You must equally note that every foreigner entering the USVI on a pleasure vessel must already have a visa from an American consulate (see the section on How to Use this Guide in the Introduction)

Hurricane risk Statistics confirm that more than half the hurricanes crossing the Antillean chain during the hurricane season (June to November–see the section on Cyclones in the Introduction) cross a smaller or larger segment of the Virgin Island archipelago. The damage wrought is often significant, especially on the more urbanised islands and those with a considerable yachting infrastructure. That said, after each devastating passage by a hurricane, the damage is swiftly repaired in order to ensure that the Virgin Islands keep the main source of their revenue – tourism – rolling in.

British Virgin Islands

The Baths anchorage, Virgin Gorda

History

Declared a British possession in 1672, in 1773 the BVI was given a constitution by the British government, giving it some degree of self-governance. The BVI are today still a British colony with the British colonial form of government that began life in the West Indies nearly four centuries ago. That said, in its modern form with the Chief Minister and the Legislative Council elected by popular suffrage, the result is effective governmental autonomy.

These days the old plantations of sugar and cotton have disappeared. All that's left are smaller estates and smallholdings of market gardens for local needs, plus some small scale stock-rearing. Almost all the population are descendents of the slaves imported in the 17th and 18th century to work the sugar and cotton plantations and freed in the 19th.

Although the BVI has a small land area (about 150sq km in total), the population is still proportionately small with only 12,000 people spread amongst the islands. The result is a quieter, more easygoing atmosphere than in the USVI, especially on relatively crowded St Thomas.

The authorities, although anxious to boost tourism for economic reasons, are aware that unduly free access to the islands by foreigners is likely to lead to increased levels of criminal and anti-social behaviour. As a result the peace and stability, as well as the traditional and family orientated values of the BVI population, are well protected – at least for now – but without too much frustrating the growth of tourism which continues to expand with luxury hotels, marinas, charter fleets and so forth. The whole lot has been financed mostly by money from abroad attracted by the BVI's mild tax regime. Part of that economic liberalism can also be seen in the number of mega-yachts which sport the BVI flag, a flag of convenience for a fee. And even if that fee isn't exactly small, it is still a fraction of what mega-yacht owners would have to pay elsewhere and helps the local economy.

Tourism

Where to stay and what to see

Whether you're visiting the BVI by criss-crossing the waters in a yacht or by staying in a luxury hotel, everything that goes on here is sea-orientated. There are four main islands, a dozen less important and lots of small islets. The biggest is Tortola, which with Virgin Gorda and Jost van Dyke are all pretty hilly, in marked contrast to the flat coralline platform of Anegada that seems almost awash. Although the climate is generally dry, there is some useful rainfall. However, even on the bits of hillside that are best watered, the vegetation is pretty meagre. The old plantations cleared most of the original forest, so what's left is mostly thorny scrub. But what matters for the islands isn't the scrubby interior; it's the stunning coastline with its scatter of offshore islets and its creek-indented shores. The other islands extending miles to the S of Tortola form an almost uninterrupted chain, enclosing an inner sea protected from the ocean swells called the Sir Francis Drake Channel. Each island merits a visit to enjoy its beaches and inlets, or even its secrets such as that of Norman Island where, it's said, there's treasure buried deep in

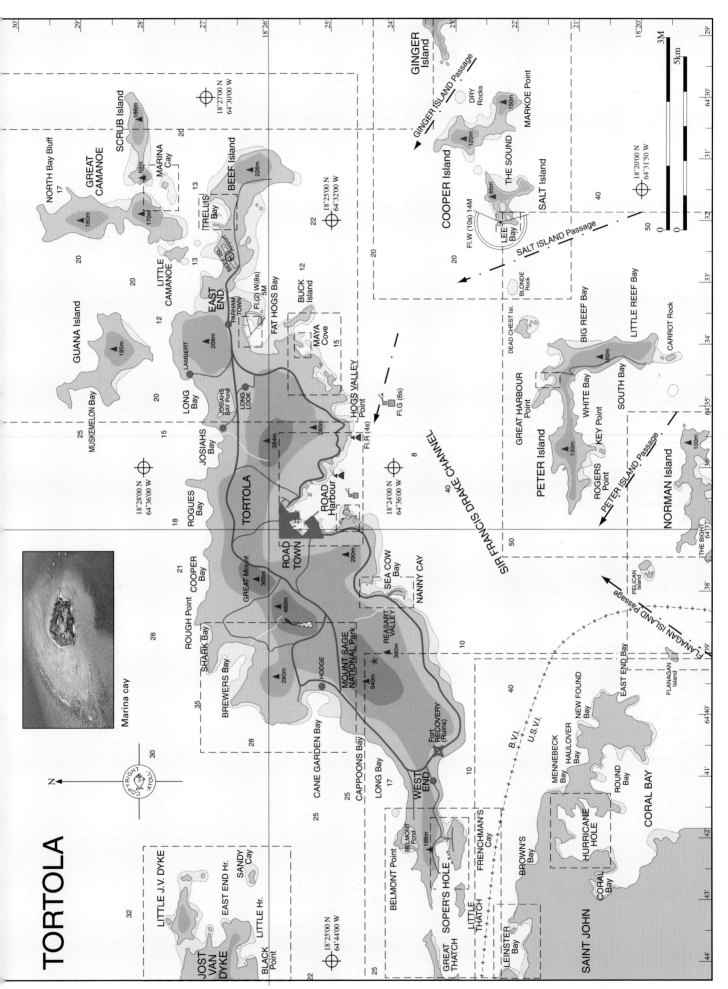

TORTOLA

JOST VAN DYKE

LITTLE J.V. DYKE

EAST END Hr.

SANDY Cay

LITTLE Hr.

BLACK Point

32

30

N

COPYRIGHT ATOLL

18°25'00 N
64°44'00 W

22

25

Marina cay

28

30

GREAT CAMANOE

NORTH Bay Bluff
17

186m

SCRUB Island

68m

MARINA Cay

160m

170m

20

LITTLE CAMANOE

13

13

2d

18°27'00 N
64°30'00 W

BEEF Island

228m

TRELLIS Bay

EAST END

BEEF ISL. Airport

PARHAM TOWN

Fl.(2) W(8s) 5M

FAT HOGS Bay

BUCK Island

12

22

18°25'00 N
64°32'00 W

20

GUANA Island

185m

MUSKEMELON Bay

20

20

25

18°28'00 N
64°36'00 W

15

18

LAMBERT 268m

LONG Bay

JOSIAHS BAY Pond

LONG LOOK

JOSIAHS Bay

384m

260m

MAYA Cove

15

HOGS VALLEY

HOGS Point

Fl.R (4s)

Fl.G (6s)

12

ROGUES Bay

TORTOLA

ROAD Harbour

ROAD TOWN

18°24'00 N
64°36'00 W

8

SIR FRANCIS DRAKE CHANNEL

40

50

GINGER Island

GINGER ISLAND Passage

COOPER Island

120m

DRY Rocks

MARKOE Point

150m

THE SOUND

85m

SALT Island

LEE Bay

Fl.W (10s) 14M

SALT ISLAND Passage

18°20'00 N
64°31'50 W

40

50

3M

5km

BLONDE Rock

DEAD CHEST Isl.

GREAT HARBOUR Point

130m

PETER Island

ROGERS Point

KEY Point

PETER ISLAND Passage

BIG REEF Bay

160m

WHITE Bay

SOUTH Bay

LITTLE REEF Bay

CARROT Rock

100m

NORMAN Island

THE BIGHT

64°33'

64°34'

64°35'

64°36'

64°37'

PELICAN Island

FLANAGAN ISLAND Passage

FLANAGAN Island

EAST END Bay

NEW FOUND Bay

HAULOVER Bay

MENNEBECK Bay

ROUND Bay

BROWN'S Bay

CORAL Bay

HURRICANE HOLE

LEINSTER Bay

SAINT JOHN

CORAL BAY

18°21'

18°22'

U.S.V.I.

B.V.I.

10

40

10

50

20

ROUGH Point

COOPER Bay

21

35

SHARK Bay

GREAT Mount 365m

480m

290m

HODGE

MOUNT SAGE NATIONAL Park

540m

290m

380m

REASART VALLEY

SEA COW Bay

NANNY CAY

10

BREWERS Bay

28

CANE GARDEN Bay

LONG Bay

17

CAPPOONS Bay

WEST END

Fort RECOVERY (Ruins)

25

BELMONT Point

186m

SOPER'S HOLE

FRENCHMAN'S Cay

LITTLE THATCH

GREAT THATCH

18°25'00 N
64°40'00 W

Tortola

Area 60sq km
Highest point Mt Sage
543m
Population about 10,000
Capital Road Town
Language English
Currency US$
Political status Self-governing British
Crown Colony
Distances to nearby islands Anegada 25M
(from Road Town)

Above Road Town
Right Swimming pool in the greenery, Road Town

some caves.

Tourism

Where to stay and what to see

Tortola is the biggest and the busiest
island in the BVI. Its coast is much
indented and with the islands that go
with it, the choice of anchorages is
huge. A crest of steep, but not very
high, hills runs from E to W along the
length of the island. The airport (Beef
Island Airport) is the hub for the BVI
and has been built on a short, flat bit of
land on its eponymous island at the east
tip of Tortola. The runway has just
been lengthened, but it's not expected
that it will be able to handle jumbo jets.

Road Town

Most of Tortola's life takes place
around the capital, Road Town, which
lies at the head of Road Harbour's
spacious bay. The settlement of small,
brilliantly coloured houses is focussed
on the main street, which runs along
the shore and connects the marina of
Fort Burt on one side with the
concentration of yacht business at
Wickham's Cay N of the town. It's here
that you'll find most of the shops and
restaurants. A wide level bit of ground
next door to Wickham's Cay has been
recently developed for government
offices and a big dock for cruise liners.
Almost every day another cruise ship

Below left The Baths, Virgin Gorda
Below right Trellis Bay Beach, Tortola

comes in and disgorges its passengers
onto the small town's streets.

Around the island

There's a road that runs along the S
coast headed for the village of West
End. Several restaurants can be found
on the lovely beaches of Long Bay and
Cane Garden and around Soper's Hole
with its marina. Dominating the S of the
island is Mt Sage, now a National Park,
which includes vestiges of the island's
original rain forest. There are footpaths
for walkers leading to the summit, from
where there's a marvellous view out over
Sir Francis Drake Channel and the
islands. Headed E from Road Town the
road leads to the airport via lots of small
bays and inlets many of which are
fringed with mangroves. A road bridge
connects Tortola with the airport on
Beef Island.

Pilotage

Coast and anchorages

Road Harbour

This is the main port of entry for the
BVI. Road Harbour and the shores
immediately around it form the single
largest concentration of marinas in the
Lesser Antilles. The approaches and
entry are clear as far as Hog's Valley Pt
coming from the E. You can get your
bearings using the tanks of the Shell
depot on the W shore of Fish Bay. From
there head between the Scotch Bank

buoy, and the buoy at the tip of Burt
Point marking Lark Bank.
Caution Some of the lights on the buoys
may not be working.
Coming from the SW, stay clear of
Denmark Bank, which is dangerous for
deep draft keelers in a heavy swell.

Prospect Reef Marina

On the S side of Burt Point, this
minuscule marina is part of a hotel and
real estate development. The access
channel has been blasted through the
coastal reef and has only 1·7m which
any swell can reduce even more. Not
only that but the channel is narrow and
once past the breakwater you have to
turn about 90° to port to get into the
main basin.
Note Given all the difficulty the marina
is not accessible to large keelboats.
What's more, the marina doesn't
welcome visiting yachts since it's
basically reserved for small boats and
motorboats for fishing and diving.
Ashore The shops are spread along the
quays with a restaurant and bar and a
dive centre. A bit further on around a
small lake are the luxury buildings of
the Prospect Reef resort, nicely
landscaped in charming gardens with a
restaurant, swimming pools and tennis
courts. The ensemble is very upmarket
with prices to match.

Fort Burt Marina

Note Make a wide circuit to the N to get
round the shoals pushing a good 200m
out from Burt Point. From there the
access channel is, in theory, buoyed as
far as the anchorage zone in front of

Road Town & Wickham's Cay from S

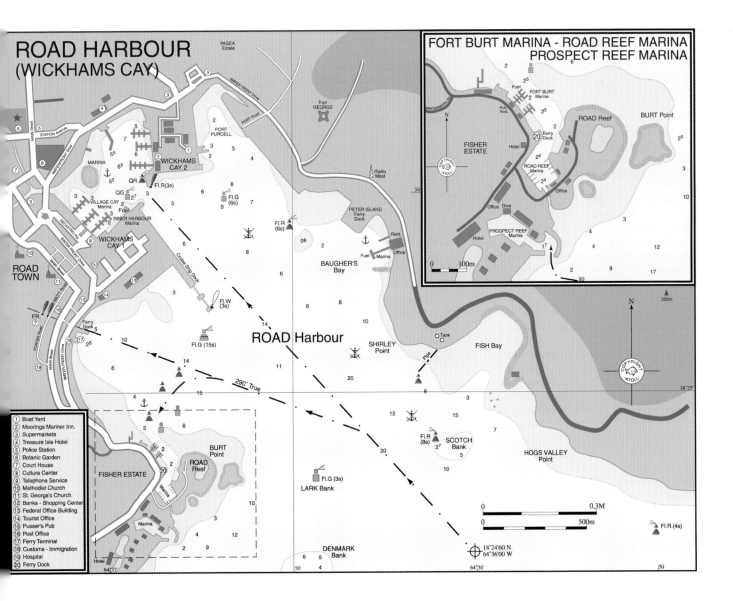

ROAD HARBOUR
(WICKHAMS CAY)

ROAD Harbour

290° True

ROAD TOWN

FISHER ESTATE

BAUGHER'S Bay

SHIRLEY Point

FISH BAY

SCOTCH Bank

HOGS VALLEY Point

LARK Bank

DENMARK Bank

BURT Point

ROAD Reef

18°24'60 N
64°36'00 W

0   0,3M

0   500m

1. Boat Yard
2. Moorings Mariner Inn.
3. Supermarkets
4. Treasure Isle Hotel
5. Police Station
6. Botanic Garden
7. Court House
8. Cultura Center
9. Telephone Service
10. Methodist Church
11. St. George's Church
12. Banks - Shopping Center
13. Federal Office Building
14. Tourist Office
15. Pusser's Pub
16. Post Office
17. Ferry Terminal
18. Customs - Immigration
19. Hospital
20. Ferry Dock

FORT BURT MARINA - ROAD REEF MARINA
PROSPECT REEF MARINA

FISHER ESTATE

FORT BURT Marina

ROAD Reef

BURT Point

ROAD REEF Marina

PROSPECT REEF Marina

0   100m

Above Prospect Reef, Road Reef and Fort Burt Marinas

Below right Wickham's Cay & Road Harbour from NE

Fort Burt Marina. There's often a chop and it's usually quite crowded.

The marina (VHF 12) has 2–2·5m off the pontoons, all with water and electricity. There's a fuel dock on the outer dock.

Ashore There's a well-stocked chandlery and a sailmaker nearby. The Rite-Way supermarket is good for provisioning. On the right, with a dinghy dock, the Pub Paradise terrace is the usual yachtie hang-out. On some evenings when there's a disco, the place is hopping.

Road Reef Marina

This marina is in the old, once mangrove-lined Careening Cove, and you get to it down a narrow, buoyed channel with at most 2–2·5m. You need to be careful in your approach by holding to a line just off the ends the ferry jetties on the west shore. Tortola Marine Management (TMM) looks after the marina (VHF 12). There's not much manoeuvring room to get into a berth (all with water and electricity). Check before you enter to find out whether there's a berth since most are occupied with TMM charter yachts. There's no fuel dock because if there's a spill, it won't flush away and there's an obvious adverse environmental impact.

Ashore There's a sailmaker, an electronics expert and TMM's own service staff can offer help with maintenance. Nearby there are some small shops and a minimarket.

Road Town

The anchorage off the ferry dock is poorly sheltered and uncomfortable. Its only advantage is that it's close to Immigration and customs for clearance and to the town centre. Going alongside the dock is not advisable because of the heavy slop and chop. In practice most yachts prefer to anchor a bit further S off Fort Burt Marina and head across in the dinghy.

Wickham's Cay

This wholly developed inner lagoon has several marinas. It is in the NW of the bay. To get there, leave the cruise liner dock and its long extension jetty to port. At night there's a light marking the E breakwater of the narrow entrance. Depths within are 3–4m. Anchoring is tolerated close to the small, mangrove covered islet, but there's very little room and the area has lots of mooring buoys.

Wickham's Cay I

There are two marinas in this SW part of Wickham's Harbour:

Village Cay Marina (VHF 16) This is the most popular with visiting yachts. There are berths for over 100 yachts up to the biggest (<25m loa) in 2–3m. All berths have water and electricity. For fuel see Inner Harbour Marina (next entry).

Ashore Village Cay Marina is usefully placed off a commercial and residential development. Most of the professionals are found on the other, E side in Wickham's Cay II, but this is the side that has the widest choice of shops, bars and restaurants both along the harbour wall and in the streets around about. The majority serve seafood, others a broadly European cuisine and prices cover the gamut. Various shops, a chandlery and a big Rite Way supermarket make up the rest of this lively spot.

Inner Harbour Marina (VHF 16) Right next door to Village Cay Marina on the S wall, this marina has 20 berths with water and electricity, but there's only 2·1m, maybe less. The majority of the berths are taken by the boats of the charter company that also manages the marina. There's a fuel dock at an angle on the end of the quay, but watch out, just E of this dock depths come up to less than 2m.

Ashore Beside the fuel dock is the marina office and above it a restaurant.

Wickham's Cay II

The E part of the lagoon has two separate outfits:

The Moorings/Mariner Inn Marina (VHF 12) The berths of the three pontoons are almost all taken up by the Moorings company's charter boats. The fuel dock is on the middle pontoon. Several berths are available for visiting boats to berth and provision, but do check with the office in advance.

Ashore The Mariner Inn has its rooms and restaurant on the quayside. The complex includes a few small shops and a dive centre. Close by there's a pretty well-stocked minimarket that the charterers of the bareboats use for provisioning.

Treasure Island Dock (Footloose Dock) On the N shore this pontoon off the Treasure Island Hotel has several berths usually taken by a charter company affiliated to The Moorings (Footloose Sailing Charters).

Ashore On the large flat area of Wickham's Cay II you'll find the boatyard of Tortola Yacht Services

that's been here for ages. It has a big travel-hoist and a well-stocked chandlery. Around and about are a dozen and more yacht repair and fabrication specialists, making the whole a really useful boatyard. You'll see Cay Electronics, the same outfit you'll find in Antigua. Taken altogether, what's here in Wickham's Cay II makes Road Harbour a good place for repairs and maintenance. With St Thomas, it's the biggest concentration of skilled services and stockists you'll find in the Virgins.

To add interest to a stop here, provisioning is also easy given the supermarkets and other shops in the area.

Port Purcell

This is the main cargo vessel dock and not used by yachts at all with the exception of the very largest mega-yachts.

Baugher's Bay

Baugher's Bay is in Road Harbour on the E shore. The N shoreline is full of shoal and a red buoy shows the general limits of the coral. The head of the bay has the big jetty of which the N side is reserved for the ferries to Peter Island.

Baugher's Bay Marina

Close by on the S of the big quay is the dock of Baugher's Bay Marina, protected behind a small rocky breakwater. There are some 30 berths with water and electricity with 3–4m and there's a fuel dock at the end of the pontoon. A few berths are usually available for visitors.

Ashore On the ground floor of the building you'll find the marina office with, on the first floor, a restaurant and bar overlooking the water. There's a small railway slip for light displacement craft.

Below Baugher's Bay
Below left (top) Nanny Cay Marina pontoons
Below left (bottom) Nanny Cay Marina from ESE

Other Anchorages on Tortola

West of Road Harbour
Nanny Cay Marina (Hannah Bay)

This marina that's been built in what was called Hannah Bay is less than 2M W of Burt Pt. A pass has been blasted through the fringing reef off the point of Nanny Cay to create an entry channel. Coming from the E come wide out round the coral off the point to the S before running in on approx. 307°T, lining up on a white house with a red roof. On the point to starboard there's a restaurant on piles, which is also conspicuous. The channel (buoyed red and green) aligns on 320°T and has about 3m.

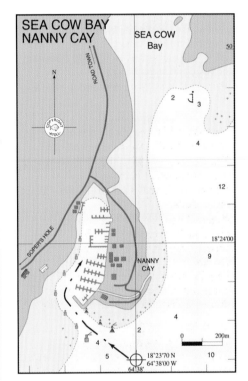

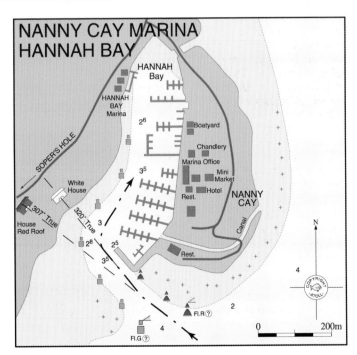

Caution The outer buoys are charted as lit, but they may be out of service so arriving towards dark or at night is not advisable. Call the marina office (VHF 16).

Inside the W shore is shoal, the limits of which are shown by a line of buoys. From the E shore several large pontoons extend that have some 200 berths all with water and electricity. The arrivals dock is the first to starboard.

In the far N of the bay, also on the E shore, you'll find the boatyard and a fuel dock. On the W shore the new docks and cottage development of Hannah Bay Marina are now complete. There are about 20 berths, most occupied by residents.

Ashore The Nanny Cay Marina office is near the middle of the E shore on the 1st floor of a neo-Creole style building surrounded by greenery.

Note There are no facilities for clearance at Nanny Cay.

Opposite the pontoons there's a restaurant and bar that's the usual yachtie rendezvous. There's a small shopping centre with a minimarket, chandlery, and various small shops. At the other end there's a hotel and a restaurant to complete this sea-orientated complex in its green and landscaped setting. Despite all the business going on, the ambience still has a certain calm except, maybe, during the season when races are held, when it's difficult to find a berth in any case. The whole N part of the complex is set aside for the boatyard with its travel-hoist and good range of services.

Soper's Hole/West End

This anchorage at the SW end of Tortola is very well sheltered. Called Soper's Hole on the charts, the locals usually call it West End, both the name of this area of Tortola and of the settlement near Soper's Hole. Approach either via Thatch Island Cut or between Frenchman's Cay and Little Thatch, neither presents any problem because the coasts are steep-to. Most of the bay has considerable depths. Yachts usually anchor in the ENE corner, but given the depths it makes sense to take one of the paying buoys (depending on availability). In the N there's a jetty reserved for the ferries for Virgin Gorda, St Thomas and St John. Customs and Immigration offices are in the offices at the ferry dock for clearance.

Note The access channel to the jetty is buoyed with lit buoys and should be left clear.

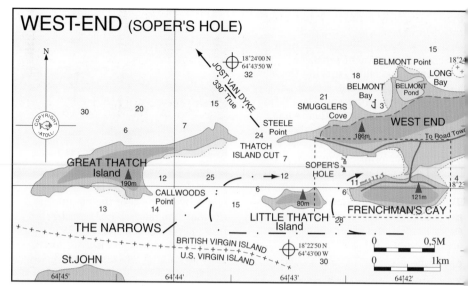

WEST-END (SOPER'S HOLE)

Soper's Hole Wharf and Marina

On the W shore of Frenchman's Cay you'll see the pontoons of this marina (VHF 16) with some 30 berths with water and electricity as well as a fuel dock.

Ashore The small complex on the quay has several shops, a minimarket and a dive centre. The general atmosphere of the Creole style cottages is given an extra boost in tone by the balustraded

Top Soper's Hole Marina
Above Soper's Hole from NW
Left Frenchman's Cay

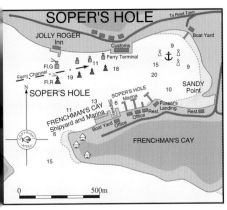

Right Soper's Hole Marina
Far right Cane Garden Bay

decorum of Pusser's Landing, with its terraced restaurant overlooking the marina. It's a lively enough spot without upsetting the ambience, so you can sit, relax and appreciate the pleasing purlieus.

Frenchman's Cay Marina & Shipyard

This boatyard (VHF 16) is on the same shore as the above. It has a 40 tonne travel-hoist and a railway slip that can

Below, from top to bottom
Frenchman's Cay Shipyard & Marina
Marina Office, Soper's Hole
Jolly Roger Inn

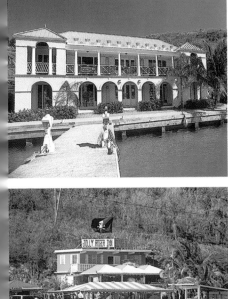

handle 200 tonnes capable of hauling very large yachts. It has a wide range of services for repair and maintenance. Additional to the boatyard a large quay has several berths for very large yachts.

At the farthest E end of Soper's Hole there's a rather more bucolic pontoon in front of the repair and maintenance workshops.

You can take your dinghy through the pretty channel, surrounded by mangroves, that joins the E end of Soper's Hole to the sea. There's a small restaurant and bar at the far end with a local menu. There's another restaurant on the N side of Soper's Hole that draws attention to itself with its Jolly Roger flag–the same flag that long ago served as the ensign for pirates.

NW coast

Cane Garden Bay

This is an excellent anchorage S of Dubois Pt off a pretty, coconut tree lined beach. It's also pretty crowded with charter boats and tourists.

Caution To get into the bay hold towards the N shore. On the S shore a large tongue of coral pushes out N–NW from the coast for about 400m.

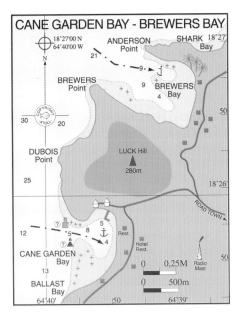

The pass is usually buoyed with two buoys. Anchor in the centre of the bay in 4-5m or use one of the mooring buoys (paying). The anchorage is often encumbered by boats and moorings. In addition pretty frequent gusts of wind barrel between the hills. There's a small dock for tenders.

Ashore There are several bar-restaurants along the beach that have live music on some evenings, though the menus and prices are for the tourists. There's a small grocery store for this and that.

Brewers Bay

Identifiable by the fine black rocks of Anderson Point, this is a more isolated anchorage and prettier than Cane Garden Bay. That said, it's worse protected in ENE winds and the entrance is trickier. You need good visibility to be able to spot the extensive coral reefs pushing out from each shore.

Caution Submarine cables running in along the centre of the bay restrict anchoring to the N part.

Tucked between the shoals on the N shore and the reef in the middle, it's a tight spot. You'll find 8–10m and fair holding. This is a day anchorage if the weather suits. There's good snorkelling.

East coast

The N coast of Tortola is beautiful but exposed, so there are no viable anchorages. The E coast, on the other hand, has plenty of shelter thanks to the cluster of islets just offshore.

Little Bay

This is a little visited but pretty little nick on the Tortola coast opposite Guana Island. It's rolly in a NE swell, especially in winter.

Guana Island

This is a private island and takes its name from a rock on the NW point, which looks like an iguana's head. Going ashore is forbidden.

Guana Island

Above W coast of Guana Island from SSE
Above right Trellis Bay & Bellamy Cay from N
Right Colourful local boats, Trellis Bay
Far right Marina Cay beach
Below right Marina Cay & Beef Island

There are two possible anchorage sites:
- In White Bay in the N. This is the most sheltered with a good beach; the N part is full of coral.
- Under Monkey Pt in the S under the shelter of some small cliffs, though you'll find it's more exposed to swell from the N.

Lee Bay, Great Camanoe

This is the only anchorage on the leeward side of Great Camanoe and sometimes rolly in a NE swell. The pebble beach isn't very attractive. The wind can gust strongly through the pass between the two hills. Nearby are the remains of an 18th century plantation.

Pass between Great and Little Camanoe

This is for fair weather and the experienced only and mainly for the pleasure of doing it. Hold towards the Great Camanoe shore, which has fewer offliers apart from the small reef pushing out at about the midway point, above which there's a white villa. Start on about 150°T before the turn, then alter to 165°T for the exit.

Caution The NE point of Little Camanoe has a large reef off it. Strong currents are possible between the islands.

Pass between Beef Island and Tortola

This is NOT possible for a sailing boat. There's less than 1m and there's a fixed bridge with scant air draft.

Long Bay

Not an anchorage with much appeal except that it's close to the airport.

Pass between Beef Island and Little Camanoe

Try this only with care and in good visibility. Coming from the W head for Trellis bay, leaving the coral pushing

out from the S of Little Camanoe to starboard. Next leave to starboard a shoal that lies about 0·25M off Conch Bay that's usually buoyed. Give the S end of Great Camanoe a good berth to avoid the coastal reef that's hard to see. Then alter course either for Trellis Bay or Marina Cay.

Trellis Bay, Beef Island

This is an excellent anchorage, but always very busy. Bellamy Cay splits the anchorage into two parts.

Caution Entering into the W part of the bay, watch out for the reef extending at least 200m N of Conch Shell Pt. It's usually buoyed.

There's not much depth around Bellamy Cay, and its S point extends in a shoal with less than 1m over it.

Coming in from the E give Sprat Pt and the reefs round Cow Rocks a good

berth, there's usually a buoy marking the outer end. You can either anchor E of Bellamy Cay or S of it. There are also buoys available.

Note It's forbidden to anchor W of the islet because of work on enlarging the airport which now runs out to Conch Shell Pt.

Ashore All of Bellamy Cay is The Last Resort restaurant. For many years its English owner, Tony, was part of what gave this spot its name amongst yachties. But it seems as if this splendid jazz-player has for the time being had to give up his musical evenings. On the Tortola shore there's a splendid, semi-circular beach. There are usually several colourful traditional boats drawn up as well as a very active windsurfing centre. A hotel, a restaurant and bar, a small grocery shop and an art and craft shop–Aragorn's Studio– are the only

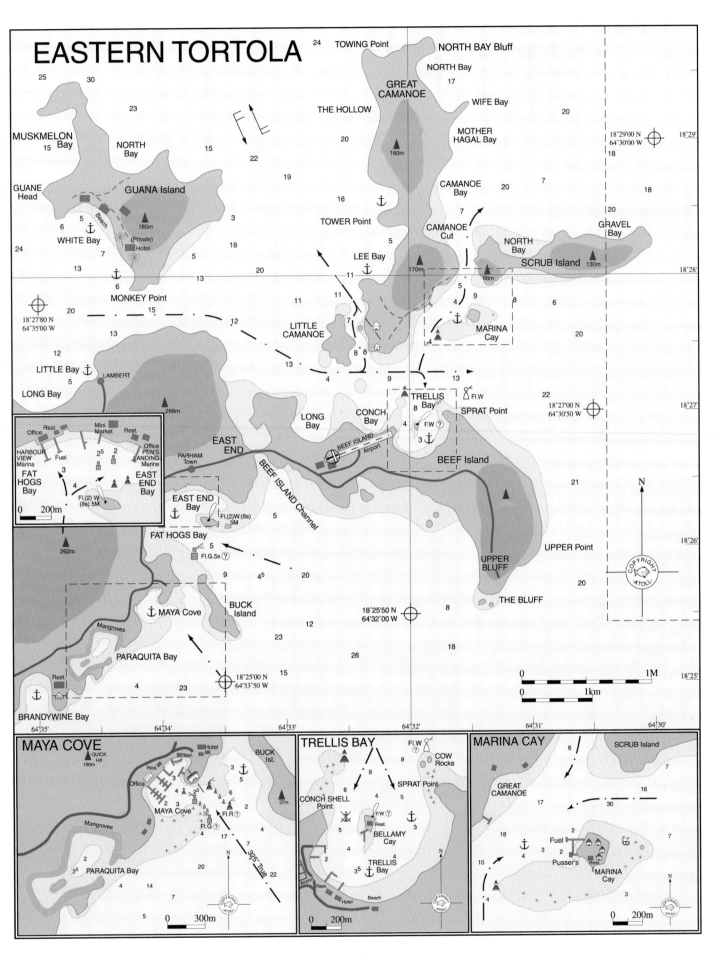

EASTERN TORTOLA

24   TOWING Point   NORTH BAY Bluff

NORTH BAY

25   30   GREAT   17

CAMANOE

23   THE HOLLOW   WIFE Bay   20

MUSKMELON   NORTH   15   20   MOTHER
15 Bay   Bay   160m   HAGAL Bay   18°29'00 N   18°29'
                64°30'00 W

19   CAMANOE   18
GUANE   GUANA Island   16   Bay   20   7   GRAVEL
Head   TOWER Point   7   20   Bay
6   5   185m   CAMANOE   NORTH   SCRUB Island   130m   18
   WHITE Bay   (Private)   Cut   Bay
24   7   Hotel   LEE Bay   170m   5   68m   6   18°28'
13   13   20   11   4   9   8
6   MONKEY Point   11   7   MARINA   20
20   15   12   LITTLE   4   Cay
18°27'80 N   13   CAMANOE   7   8 8 8
64°35'00 W   13   13
12   LITTLE Bay   4   9   13
5   LAMBERT   TRELLIS   Fl.W   22
LONG Bay   LONG   CONCH   8 Bay   18°27'00 N   18°27'
    268m   Bay   Bay   4   F.W   SPRAT Point   64°30'50 W
                3

FAT HOGS BAY (inset)

Office   Rest.   Mini   Rest.
      Market
HARBOUR   Office
VIEW   Fuel   PEN'S
Marina   2 5   2   LANDING
FAT   Marine
HOGS   3   EAST
Bay   4   END
     Fl.(2) W   Bay
     (8s) 5M
0   200m

262m

EAST   BEEF ISLAND   BEEF Island
END   PARHAM   Airport
     Town   21
EAST END   BEEF ISLAND Channel
Bay   Fl.(2)W.(8s)   5   UPPER Point   18°26'
    5M
FAT HOGS Bay   5   UPPER
    Fl.G.5s   BLUFF
    9   4 5   20   20   THE BLUFF
    4 5   8
MAYA Cove   BUCK   18°25'50 N
   Island   12   64°32'00 W
Mangroves   23   18
PARAQUITA Bay   26
    4   23   15   0   1M   18°25'
Rest.   18°25'00 N
BRANDYWINE Bay   64°33'50 W   0   1km
64°35'   64°34'   64°33'   64°32'   64°31'   64°30'

MAYA COVE

QUICK   Hotel   Rest.   BUCK
Hill   Rest.   Isl.
190m   Office   3   3   5
    4   2 5   6   37m
   MAYA COVE   Fl.R
Mangroves   Fl.G   17   7   4
    2 5   PARAQUITA Bay   20   22
    4   14   7
    5
0   300m

TRELLIS BAY

Fl.W
       8   COW
      9   Rocks
CONCH SHELL   SPRAT Point
Point   4   3
   F.W   3
   5   Rest.
    BELLAMY
    Cay
    4   TRELLIS
Airport   3 5   Bay
Rest.   Hotel   Beach
0   200m

MARINA CAY

      6   SCRUB Island
GREAT   16
CAMANOE   17   30
     18   Fuel   7
10   4   3   2   Pusser's   MARINA
    4   Rest.   Cay   3
0   200m

other points of interest in this charming spot still as yet little affected by rampant tourism, the only downside being the noise of the airport.

Marina Cay

The pretty little island with its hotel and restaurant can be spotted from a good way off thanks to the bright red roofs of its bungalows.

Caution The islet is surrounded by extensive reef from NW through SW, in the SW over 300m off the islet shore. The seaward end is usually marked by a red buoy.

In good visibility come in from either NW or SW giving a good berth to the coral. The anchorage is much frequented by charter yachts. Some use the hotel's mooring buoys. Anchor in 8–10m.

Ashore There's a ferry dock for ferries plying from Trellis Bay. The office of Marina Cay (VHF 16) offers several services including fuel, showers and dive centre. Next to the dock the Pusser's Landing Store shop, carefully done in Creole style, in no way mars the beauty of the place. The restaurant terrace hangs over a lovely beach running out into the coral. By the menu (mostly BBQ and seafood) there's a history of the place, which was built by an American couple after the Second World War.

SE coast

You can get to these anchorages easily, either from Road Harbour or by coming round the E end of Beef Island.

Fat Hog's Bay/East End Bay

Once upon a time this was a centre for building the lovely local boats, but not any longer. You enter by leaving to starboard the edge of the reefs pushing out from the S of East End Bay (beaconed) and the large reef flat joining Buck Island to the W side of Fat Hog's Bay (buoyed).

Right Hodge Creek Marina pontoon, Maya Cove
Far right Fat Hog's Bay anchorage
Below left Fat Hog's Bay & East End Bay from SE
Below right Maya Cove from E

Caution the marks and their lights are unreliable

Fat Hog's Bay is not that good a shelter for keelers, especially if there's a SE swell. The shoal ground filling the E of the bay, called East End, stops you pushing far enough in to get shelter from the reef. Lots of moored boats also reduce the available space even more, so you have to anchor too far towards the open part of the bay. If you're prepared to pay for a buoy, on the other hand, you can get into more sheltered water. There are two areas of the bay, E and W shores, where you'll find a welcome:

- Harbour View Marina has two pontoons with some 15 berths with water and electricity and a fuel dock on the end.

Ashore is the management office of Tradewind, a chandlery and a dive club. On the 1st floor of the building there's a restaurant with a fine view out over the whole bay.

- the ex-Sea Breeze pontoons. At present, since the charter company left, these are pretty much out of commission.

- Penn's Landing Marina (VHF 16)

Right at the E end of the bay, the approach is marked by two buoys. The dock has a dozen berths with water and electricity. These are the best sheltered berths in the whole bay, but draught is limited to 2m or less.

Ashore is the office that manages the pontoons and the mooring buoys with a restaurant beside it. In the immediate surroundings and out along the coast road you'll find fairly close by two or three other restaurants and some small shops, one of which is a minimarket.

Maya Cove (Hodges Creek)

Coming to Maya Cove from the E you must give a good wide berth to the S of Buck Island, the end of the dangers S of which is none too obvious. You must then make sure you've identified the pass.

In good visibility, line yourself up on approx. 325°T on the conspic pink house with its red roof on the point forming the N side of the bay's entrance.

Heading in on this course you'll see the first buoys marking the pass. Although these are lit, they aren't reliably so and the problematic approach means a night entry is out. After about 200m the channel makes a sharp 90° turn to port before entering the natural lagoon formed by the large protecting reef.

Caution In the SW and the N there's less depth and you need to hold as much to the middle as you can consonant with leaving access to the pontoons clear. The space for anchoring is much reduced by the number of boats on paying moorings. Most of the latter belong to charter companies, whose boats also take up most of the berths in Hodge Creek Marina (VHF 16). On the end of the dock there's a fuel berth.

Ashore The marina is managed by Sunsail-Stardust. Just beside their office is a restaurant and bar with a small, pleasant swimming pool overlooking the docks. The menu features both local and Mediterranean food. Still on the dock, you'll see a dive club and close by a well-stocked minimarket. You can book taxis or hire cars through the office.

In the N part there's another restaurant right down on the water. It serves local food in a simple setting. A small road runs one way to the main road and the other to a charming hotel with a fine swimming pool, that dominates Maya Cove. All up the marina is well-equipped and a pleasant place to be, for all that it's usually full.

Paraquita Bay

S of Maya Cove, about half way to Brandywine Bay, there's a haven completely surrounded by mangroves and, according to the locals, an excellent hurricane hole. The entrance is in the middle of the E coast of the large bay within, but has depths of less than 2m (±1·8m) which restricts it to small keelers or multihulls.

Brandywine Bay

Lying between Maya Cove and Road Harbour, this bay offers a secure and pretty overnight anchorage in fair weather with the wind not too SE. The two shores are fringed with coral and you need good visibility to identify the pass between the two areas of reef. On the tip of the N point right at sea level you'll spot as a conspicuous mark a house in typical neo-colonial style. The best anchorage is in the NE part of the bay in 2-3m opposite a condo development of small buildings on the shore. There's a small dock for dinghies belonging to a restaurant that has buoys its clients can use for mooring.

Ashore A short path leads up the hillside to the Brandywine Restaurant which overlooks the Sir Francis Drake Channel. Italian food is the specialty and the views wonderful. If the weather suits, it's worth a stop.

Below, top to bottom
Brandywine
Brandywine Bay from SE

Virgin Gorda

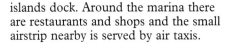

Area 30sq km
Highest point Virgin Gorda Peak 410m
Population About 1100
Main town Spanish Town
Language English
Currency US$
Political status Part of BVI
Distances to nearby islands Anguilla 75M, Tortola 5M

Tourism

Where to stay and what to see

It was the American Lawrence Rockefeller who started the tourist development in Virgin Gorda when he built the luxurious Little Dix Bay Hotel in the 1960s. The island's superb lure is its beaches and lagoons. In the N of the island it's fairly hilly whereas in the S it's quite flat by comparison. In the past it was in the S that the sugar cane plantations flourished, these days replaced by market gardens and real estate development. In the uncultivated parts the ground cover is mostly cacti and succulents, making inland Virgin Gorda look a bit like Central America.

Spanish Town

The settlement has only a few grid-pattern streets and simple shops. The tourist and water sports areas are further N around St Thomas Harbour where the ferries from neighbouring

Below The Baths–granite, emerald swimming pools and white sand
Bottom The Baths anchorage

islands dock. Around the marina there are restaurants and shops and the small airstrip nearby is served by air taxis.

Around the island

There's a road running from N to S of the island connecting with a few driveable tracks.

In the S, close to Coppermine Pt, you can see the remains of an old 16th century mine once exploited by the Spanish. All the way from N to S the wild and more rugged windward coast is unprotected from the Atlantic swells. As a result it's pretty untouched by tourist development. It's on the leeward coast that you'll find one of the finest natural sites, The Baths. It's a vast heaping up of granite boulders forming a natural maze within which you'll find small emerald pools with white sand bottoms. It's a busy spot and the smart move is to visit as close to first light as you can manage, before the day's sea-borne and land-borne crowds start to arrive.
In the island's N all of the hill country has also been placed within a National Park and offer walkers fine viewpoints from the hilltops at over 400m. Walking the footpaths, in addition to the goats, you should come across some fine iguanas, a protected species here.
To get to the N coast the road system doesn't offer much choice and only partly serves the huge Gorda Sound area. A goodly part of the watersports and hotel developments here are therefore only accessible by sea, either by boat or ferry.

Pilotage

Coast and anchorages

Yachtsmen probably like Virgin Gorda more than any of the other islands in the archipelago. If sometimes the W coast anchorages are a bit uncomfortable because of swell, Gorda Sound's vast reaches, which take up all of the N coast, offer a splendid variety of anchorages protected by its islets and reefs.

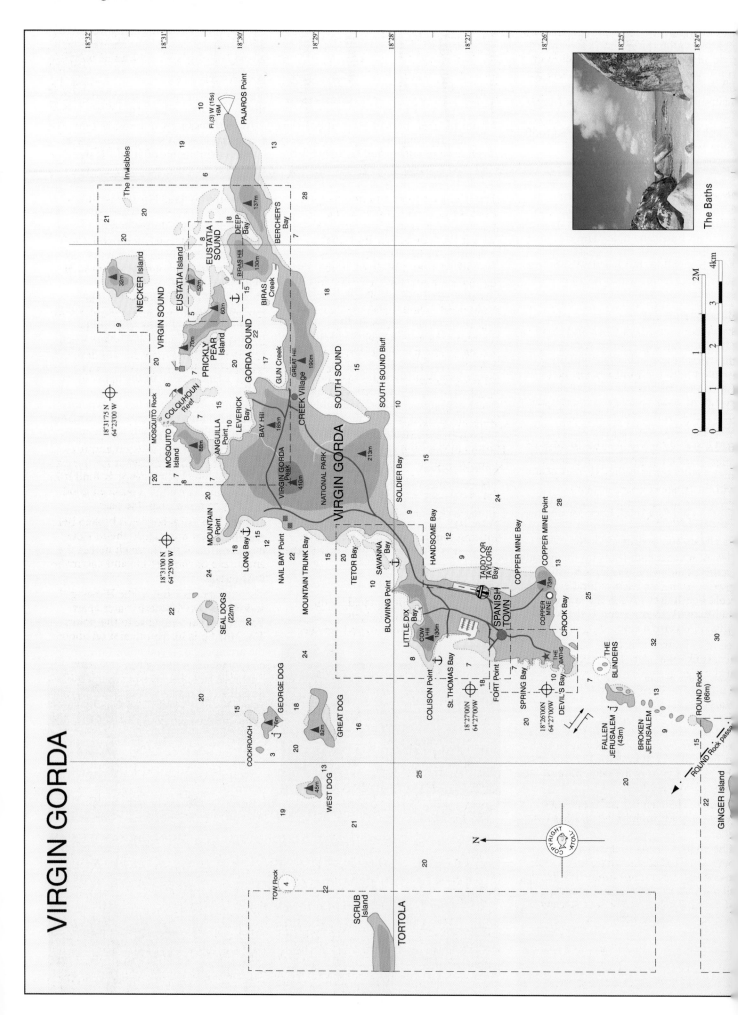

VIRGIN GORDA

The Baths

TORTOLA

SCRUB Island

TOW Rock
4

22

19

21

WEST DOG
45m
13

COCKROACH
3

GEORGE DOG
76m

GREAT DOG
82m

25

20

20

18

20

15

16

24

SEAL DOGS
(22m)

18

22

20

24

24

MOUNTAIN
Point

LONG Bay
15

NAIL BAY Point

MOUNTAIN TRUNK Bay

18

22

15

TETOR Bay

20

SAVANNA
Bay

BLOWING Point

10

MOSQUITO
Island
88m

ANGUILLA
Point
10

LEVERICK
Bay

BAY Hill
185m

VIRGIN GORDA
Peak
410m

NATIONAL PARK

213m

SOLDIER Bay

9

7

8

7

8

COLQUHOUN
Reef

MOSQUITO Rock

PRICKLY
PEAR
Island
70m

15

GORDA SOUND

GUN Creek

GREAT Hill
190m

CREEK Village

SOUTH SOUND

SOUTH SOUND Bluff

10

15

9

HANDSOME Bay

12

LITTLE DIX
Bay

COW
Hill
130m

8

COLISON Point

St. THOMAS Bay

FORT Point

SPRING Bay

DEVIL'S Bay

FALLEN
JERUSALEM
(43m)

BROKEN
JERUSALEM

ROUND Rock passage

GINGER Island

SPANISH
TOWN

COPPER
MINE

THE
BATHS

7

7

10

THE
BLINDERS

ROUND Rock
(66m)

32

13

9

15

30

20

22

COPPER MINE Bay

COPPER MINE Point
73m

TADDY OR
TAYLORS
Bay

CROOK Bay

25

13

28

24

N

NECKER Island
32m

9

20

The Invisibles

21

20

20

VIRGIN SOUND

EUSTATIA Island
52m

5

60m

EUSTATIA
SOUND

BIRAS Hill
130m

15

BIRAS
Creek

DEEP
Bay

8

137m

BERCHER'S
Bay

7

28

PAJAROS Point

Fl (3) W (15s)
16M

10

6

19

13

18

17

22

20

15

VIRGIN GORDA

18°31'75 N
64°23'00 W

18°31'00 N
64°25'00 W

18°27'00N
64°27'00W

18°26'00N
64°27'00W

0   1   2   3   4km

2M

Above left The Baths from the W
Above right Virgin Gorda Yacht Harbour

West coast

The Baths

This anchorage lies in the far S of the W coast and is often made rolly by swell.

Caution Keep clear of the reefs around the N and S points of the bay and the isolated hazard off the S entrance to Little Trunk Bay.

Off the bay the bottom falls off quickly to more than 10m, but there are mooring buoys for you to use. The Baths are easily spotted thanks to the huge granite boulders that create the site. Take your dinghy into the beach with its fringe of coconut palms.

Caution Beware of the surf that can capsize a small boat

St Thomas Bay (Virgin Gorda Yacht Harbour)

Caution Coming from the N be sure to give Colison Pt a wide berth, there are reefs awash up to 100m off the coast, in theory marked by a buoy.

In good weather you can anchor in the lee of Colison Pt provided you leave the access channel clear for ferries to dock at the pier in the NE corner of the bay.

To reach the Virgin Gorda Yacht Harbour Marina (VHF 16/11) follow the dredged channel through the barrier reef that comes from the bay's S point most of the way across the bay. Come in from due W aiming for the first of the buoys marking the beginning of the buoyed channel.

Caution The channel isn't very wide (especially for multihulls) and has two doglegs.

The channel leads to the marina between two breakwaters (3m). Once inside three pontoons house 120 berths, all with water and electricity in depths of 3-5m. The fuel dock is to starboard beside the marina office.

Ashore The customs and immigration office for clearance is now at the end of the town dock (Little Dix Jetty). You can get there by tender from the anchorage, or from the marina by a footpath of a few hundred metres. The marina is attractively integrated in a garden setting and excellently maintained. There's a shopping centre with minimarkets, various shops, a dive centre, banks and several restaurants and bars. The menus are pretty varied even if you're not exactly getting great value for money – a point that applies equally well to the cost of stores. By way of compensation, the busy atmosphere all this gives is stimulating without destroying the generally relaxed feeling of this quality location or the warmth of your welcome.

On the S side of the marina you'll find the boatyard with a 70 tonne travel lift, its many specialist services and a chandlery. If you choose to stop here, you can tour the island by taxi or hire car, or if you're leaving, get easily to the airstrip.

Little Dix Bay

This small bay is dominated by the Little Dix Bay Hotel with its conspicuous, pyramid roofed cottages and main building. The bay is almost closed by a barrier reef. The only opening is in the W. Inside the anchorage is extremely tight and not recommended for sailing boats of any great size. It's completely out for all if there's a NE swell running.

There's 3m in the pass and inside, though the bottom comes up quickly to less than 2m as you get close to the dock and the whole E end of the bay is full of reef. Other than the wonderful buffet in the hotel, the bay doesn't have much going for it, so it's a day anchorage at best.

Savannah Bay, Pond Bay & Tetor Bay

There's a long barrier reef protecting these anchorages to seaward and it's sufficiently clear of the coast for there to be fair temporary anchorage behind it in settled, quiet weather. You need good visibility to go through the pass.

Caution The coral barrier is broken here and there and only partly shelters the bay from the N swell, which makes the anchorage uncomfortable and can make it dangerous.

The entrance is close to the Blowing Pt end of the bay. It's clear water apart from a few patches close to the point. The best tip is for you to aim on about

Right top Little Dix Bay from S
Right bottom St Thomas Bay & Virgin Gorda Yacht Harbour

209

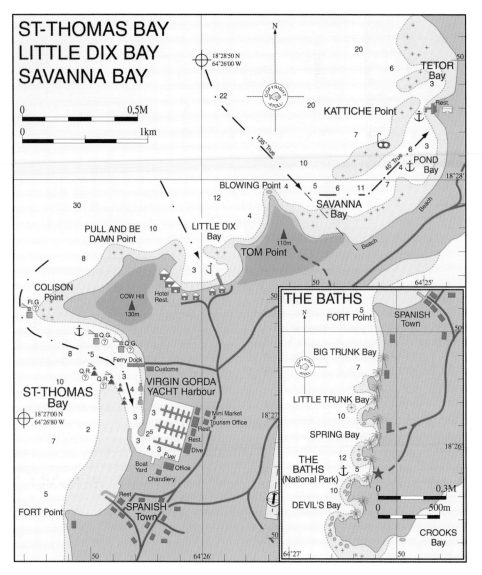

ST-THOMAS BAY
LITTLE DIX BAY
SAVANNA BAY

135°T for a small rocky headland on the W end of the beach. When you've got Blowing Pt on 270°T, alter steadily till you're headed roughly E. You'll have the barrier reef to port and the big reefs off the beach to starboard. There

Below left Savanna Bay and Blowing Point from Kattiche Point
Below right Savanna and Pond Bays from SW

are big openings in the reef off the beach. You can keep nosing in with the greatest care until you're in 3-4m, sand. The anchorage is often empty and has a splendid beach.

It's possible to push on more to the NE into Pond Bay by heading on about 045°T towards the Kattiche Pt headland with a conspic building on top. The best anchorage hereabouts is

just below the point, but holding well clear of the shoal ground off the dinghy dock of Giorgio's Restaurant. For a sailing boat it's advisable not to push too far to the N. For all that there is a winding passage through, the area isn't perfectly surveyed. You can use your tender to go for a snorkel over the coral. Ashore Giorgio's Table Restaurant is tucked into the foot of the cliff and has a menu of local and Italian dishes. The décor is elegant with a fine view over the bay – and prices to match. On the top of the headland an upmarket real estate development has hung its villas and their swimming pools between the sea and the sky. The view is terrific, especially when the sun's at the right angle and brings out the palette of blues of the lagoon below.

Long Bay

Under the lee of Mountain Pt, Long Bay anchorage is quite well protected unless there is a N swell, which will either make it uncomfortable or untenable. You need to push in as far as you can to the NE of the anchorage where the coast is steep-to, leaving S of you an isolated house on an almost deserted beach lined with a few coconut palms. The shore is fringed with coral. If you've time in hand, there's snorkelling off Mountain Pt.

Small Islands West of Virgin Gorda

West, George and Great Dogs

The three Dog Islets – West Dog, George Dog and Great Dog – are halfway between Virgin Gorda and Scrub Island off Tortola. There are no good anchorages on Great Dog and West Dog unless it's flat calm. George Dog is better sheltered and you can get a lunch hook down in its lee in a light trade. The islets are in the National Park and mooring buoys have been installed at West Dog and Great Dog. There's good snorkelling.

Above left Colquhoun Reef Passage (Gorda Sound)
Above right Leverick Bay & Gun Creek

Gorda Sound (North Sound)

This huge bay and its surroundings are, despite the hordes of charter yachts, still somewhere you can find almost deserted anchorages.

There are two entrances into Gorda Sound:

The pass between Virgin Gorda and Mosquito Island, for shoal drafters

only since the least depth is 1.7m or less. Only go through under power and hold to the middle of the pass from W to E until you're past Anguilla Pt. At that point alter more SE to avoid the <1m shoal ground off the S point of Mosquito Island.

- The pass N of Mosquito Island and Colquhoun Reef. This is the only way under sail and for boats that draw

much water. Give a wide berth to Mosquito Rock, then head for Vixen Pt on the S side of Prickly Pear Island on 135°T. Once you're past the N part of Colquhoun Reef, alter in a curve more to the S. The pass is in fact buoyed, but the lights on the buoys are too unreliable for a safe night entry.

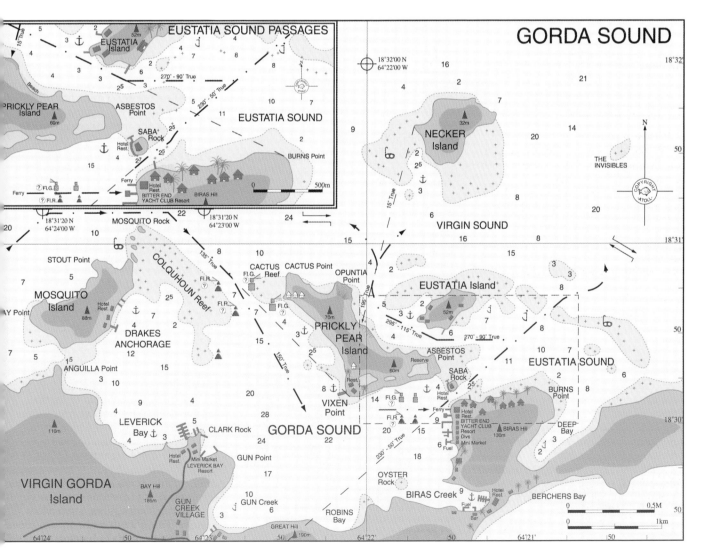

Above Gorda Sound from SE
Right Leverick Bay & Marina Lighthouse

Drake's Anchorage

- The first anchorage between Colquhoun Reef and Mosquito Island off the Drake's Anchorage Hotel can be choppy and uncomfortable in fresh ESE winds. There are mooring buoys available, managed by Drake's Anchorage Hotel

Ashore The cottages and restaurant of the establishment are on the beach and cater primarily for a well-heeled clientele, though provided they reserve (VHF 16) yachties are welcome too. Mosquito Island itself is private and you can't roam the interior.

- The second anchorage closer to Colquhoun Reef is better protected provided you nose in carefully to get close to the first offlying coral heads. From this anchorage there is good access to the reef to look at the marine life (as yet not too badly preserved).

Leverick Bay

W of Clark Rock the Leverick Bay Resort complex has a 60m long dock with some 20 berths (water and electricity) and a fuel dock on the end. There are also moorings for rent. You can anchor nearby keeping clear of the buoy mooring area, or you can use the latter, which belong to the hotel. The anchorage is a bit crowded and in a fresh trade there's a fair amount of slop and chop.

Ashore There's a residential complex around the hotel with some shops, a pretty well-stocked minimarket and a dive centre on the dock. On the ground floor of the main building you'll find a Pusser's Landing 'store' with beside it The Lighthouse grill and restaurant that has, on its first floor, a fine terrace which overlooks the bay. The name of the restaurant comes from the miniature lighthouse you'll see beside the swimming pool open to all the hotel's clients. With its neo-colonial architecture and general ambience,

Leverick Bay Resort is a well set-up and pleasant spot. The staff offer a friendly welcome and the prices are fair enough given where you are.

Gun Creek

The village fishing boats from Creek Village use the head of the creek as their haven, but it's only reachable by tender. Anchor in 4m close to the E shore. In NE winds the anchorage can be disturbed by chop. It's also a bit noisy with the regular traffic of boats and ferries from the village.

Ashore Once you've reached the dock in your tender, the small village is about 100m away. The shops are all right for essentials and there's a simple hotel-restaurant.

Biras Creek

Caution Oyster Rock and its reef about 200m off the Virgin Gorda shore lies between Gun Creek and Biras Creek.

Biras Creek is an excellent all-weather haven, though the mosquitoes are plentiful. The anchorage is separated from the sea only by a thin, but quite high-ridged isthmus. The Biras Creek Resort (VHF 16) is on the crest of the small ridge looking down one side to the Atlantic swells and the other to the mirror calm of the mangrove fringed inlet. The hotel has installed a small marina with a dozen berths (water and electricity) in 3m with a fuel dock on the S shore. Otherwise you can anchor or take one of the paying moorings. Ashore the luxurious bungalows are spread around lovely landscaped gardens. From the restaurant there's a fabulously panoramic view. If you dine

there in the evening, you'll need to dress accordingly – that means polo shirt and long trousers for men.

The Bitter End

The anchorage off the Bitter End Yacht Club is probably the most popular hereabouts for cruisers and charterers alike. The approach is clear, though almost the whole area off the restaurant is full of moorings. To anchor you'll have to lie to the W of Saba Rock. In high season the boats there are also pretty numerous and the trades can raise an uncomfortable chop for smaller yachts. It follows that off The Bitter End is no dream anchorage for those who crave solitude!

There's a beaconed channel you must keep clear that marks the approach to the marina pontoons and dock for the ferry from Tortola.

The pontoons of the Bitter End Yacht Club (VHF 16) have some 20 berths with water and electricity in 4–5m. You can water ship and fuel up here and a small crane can lift out small craft of slight displacement.

Ashore A pontoon encircling an aquarium basin means you can land close to the bar and restaurant. Built in the habitual neo-colonial style, the terrace is pleasantly set at beach level with a pretty luxurious décor inside. From around 1700 the bar is pretty busy. And if at lunch the cold buffet is served in a relaxed atmosphere, come dinner time, as the ambience segues to soft light and sweet music, things get more formal with guests attired to match.

Above left Saba Rock &
The Bitter End Resort
Above right Biras Creek
Marina
Far left Saba Rock
Resort
Left The garden at
Bitter End
Below left Bitter End
Resort
Below right Bitter End
Marina

The cuisine is international and elegantly presented and prices are in harmony with the general status of the place. Completing the picture of sybaris is a hotel with its cottages in lovely landscaped grounds in the trees or around the beach with a superb swimming pool. There's a small shopping centre concentrating mostly on tourist knick-knackery, with a minimarket for essentials. A wide range of water sports are catered for, including underwater exploration organised by Kilbrides' Scuba Dive, one of the oldest dive outfits in the Virgins.

Saba Rock

Lying between Prickly Pear I and the Bitter End, the islet of Saba Rock was turned into a resort by the well-known diving instructor Burt Kilbrides. Since then the Saba Rock Resort (VHF 16) has been completely renovated and has a bar and restaurant, a fashion shop and several rooms all clinging to the surface of the small rock. A jetty serves the ferry traffic to which you can also tie your dinghy to go for a sundowner or have dinner in the restaurant.

Caution There is no passage between Saba Rock and Prickly Pear Island, the channel is full of coral.

Prickly Pear Island

The island is part of the Nature Reserve. There are two possible anchorages in Prickly Pear's lee:

• in the NW S of Cactus Reef there's an isolated anchorage which isn't much visited and is sheltered from the wind by some small cliffs.

Pirates

• under Vixen Point staying clear of the coral which runs out a fair way off the W end of the point. There are mooring buoys laid and a small dock for going ashore in the tender. Ashore there's a very pleasant restaurant right down on the lovely beach that encircles Vixen Point. The place isn't very luxurious, but there's a jolly mural that recalls how the island was once a pirate lair.

Pass to Eustatia Sound between Saba Rock & Virgin Gorda

Not many yachts use this pass even though it's OK for drafts up to 2.5m. That said, you need good visibility and someone aloft or at least on the pulpit spotting. Begin by holding to the Virgin Gorda side, which is clear, on a course

of approx. 050°T. Leave the reefs around Saba Rock to port. To starboard you'll see the shoal ground pushing out from the small dock on the coast round the corner from The Bitter End.

Caution Once past the small dock alter to port slightly to avoid a long tongue of reef pushing out from the Virgin Gorda shore, whilst keeping a wary eye to port on the rest of the reefs E of Saba Rock.

Once you're past all these dangers, return to 050°T to get into Eustatia Sound. On your way back, be careful not to have the sun ahead of you. Use as a leading mark on about 230°T Great Hill, the summit E of Creek Village.

Eustatia Sound

This large stretch of water is protected from the Atlantic by a long coral barrier. The sea is usually calm although a lively Trade will raise a brisk chop. There's an anchorage in the long inlet of Deep Bay to the SW, though the sea can be quite lively. An alternative is to find shelter in the lee of the big reef a bit behind the main barrier. The anchorages are all seldom used. The barrier reef has excellent snorkelling.

Pass through the Eustatia Sound barrier reef

Caution Don't even think about this except in quiet weather, calm seas and excellent visibility!

If you hold Saba Rock on a back bearing of 230°T as far as the barrier reef, you'll find the main opening to seaward. Once you've eyeballed your way mostly through, alter more to the E in order to avoid the deeper reef patches N of the exit, which are dangerous if there's a swell (being only 3m or so down). Once out and clear you can begin altering for Necker Island.

Pass between Eustatia Island and Prickly Pear Island

This is another pass that not many boats use although it can take yachts with drafts up to 3m. Coming from Necker Island leave the reefs NW of Eustatia Island clear to port and hold to a course of about 195°T using a small cliffy headland about midway down

Top Eustatia Island & Prickly Pear Island from NE
Above Eustatia & Gorda Sound from NE

Prickly Pear Island as your leading mark. You should stay in depths of 4–5m. When you're about 200m from Prickly Pear Island, turn to port onto about 115°T, which should have your bow lining up with Burns Pt, NE of Biras Hill on Virgin Gorda. Once you've got Eustatia Island's E coast in transit with the end of the dock pushing out from the island's SE tip, alter to port again to about 090°T between two reefs to get into Eustatia Sound. There's an anchorage in the pass, the best spot being off the W side of Eustatia Island.

Necker Island

This is a private island owned by Sir Richard Branson, the Virgin everything chap. It's completely surrounded by coral except for a narrow pass in the S. The anchorage is accessible, but you must have good visibility. It can be choppy when the wind is fresh and it isn't much visited. You get into it from the S by using the W point of Necker Island as a leading mark on about 355°T. There's a conspicuous house more or less ahead. Keep pushing in carefully, eyeballing the bommies to avoid them. Anchor S of the island in around 3m. There's good snorkelling everywhere on the reef.

Jost van Dyke

Area 10sq km
Highest point Maljohhny Hill 325m
Population 150
Main village Great Harbour
Language English
Currency US$
Political status Part of BVI
Distances to nearby islands Tortola 3M

History and tourism

This relatively steep and hilly island is just 3M NW from West End, Tortola. Its name comes from a Dutch pirate, and from the end of the 16th to the early 17th century Dutch planters were the main inhabitants. Then it was settled by the English, amongst them a Quaker community. It was from that stock that, for English speakers interested in history's by-ways, John Coakley Lettsom (often mis-spelled Lettsome) was born on Little Jost Van Dyke in 1744. He was educated in England and made a fortune as a London doctor earning up to £12,000 a year; in modern money that's several million! He was a noted philanthropist – some say he founded the British or London Medical Society, though Roy Porter's magisterial *The Greatest Benefit to Mankind* makes no mention of it. In his day he was at least as well known as a social climber, caricatured by contemporaries as 'Dr Wriggle'.

History then took a back step here until the years of Prohibition in America, when the island had a reputation as a smuggler's haven.

Today there are fewer than 200 inhabitants, though every one of them is fiercely proud of their island. However, that has been no impediment to tourism becoming the main money earner. Each day dozens of yachts, boats and day charters offload tourists who pack every bar and restaurant around until late. Given the intense traffic, you can clear into the BVI in Great Harbour where there's an immigration post.

Other than the little villages and the odd isolated house, Jost Van Dyke is pretty undeveloped and the road system comes down to a short, narrow road and a few tracks and paths. An E to W walk allows you to ramble over the hilltops and look at the wonderful, panoramic views over the whole of Jost Van Dyke and its neighbours.

Pilotage

Coast and anchorages
White Bay

This is a small anchorage in the SW of the island, though you need good visibility because a coral barrier closes the entrance. There are three passes through it, the centre one being the widest usually buoyed with two buoys each side. On the beach the White Bay Sandcastle Restaurant is half buried in the trees. There are two white leading marks on the restaurant: front square and back triangle, giving the line of the pass (356°T), though the trees tend to get in the way of the back mark. Once inside the anchorage (3m) is tight, but the beach superb. If the wind's SE it can be uncomfortable.

Great Harbour

This is the island's only village and a port of entry to the BVI. Approach on 350°T leaving the ferry channel marks to port. Shoal ground extends from both E and W shores as well as the head of the bay. That means anchoring in the middle about 200m from the dock. You'll be in 8-10m or more and paying mooring buoys have now been laid, further reducing anchoring space, the bay usually being pretty crowded in high season.

Ashore The customs office is opposite the dock. The village has a few houses around a small church, two or three shops, one of them a minimarket for essentials, a small hotel and several bar-restaurants along the lovely beach. The best known and the oldest is Foxy's Bar. Foxy, the owner, is known as the man who organises the famous Wooden Boat Regatta and the orchestrator of the liveliest parties on the island. Often in the evenings the partying at Foxy's, liberally lubricated with punch and accompanied by music in a pulsating atmosphere, goes on late into the night.

Above Manchineel trees on Great Harbour beach
Below Great Harbour & White Bay from SE

Little Harbour (Garner Bay)

Shoal ground extends all round the bay. The fairway is in theory marked by two buoys. Inside depths are 8–10m. Part of the bay is taken up with (paying) moorings. The best sheltered anchorage is in the NE. Little Harbour is often less crowded than Great Harbour.
Ashore, on the east shore is Abby's restaurant (VHF 16) that has a dock for tenders. Abby's also manages some of the paying moorings and sells some groceries. On the opposite shore, in the shelter of a tiny bay, are two charming restaurants, Harry's Place and Sidney's Peace and Love. Both have terraces on the beach and serve seafood.

Eastend Harbour

Despite being called a harbour this bay is poorly sheltered from any E swell.

Little Jost Van Dyke

There are two possible anchorages:

- At the SW of the island to the N of Long Bay: the S point of Little Jost van Dyke gives sufficient protection for a day stop if the swell isn't too much SE'ly. The pass between Little Jost van Dyke and Jost van Dyke is obstructed by awash reefs and by the breaking swell, though the latter makes this a wild and lovely spot.

- to the E of the island behind Green Cay and Sandy Spit: these anchorages are better sheltered than the preceding one except in a strong SE'ly swell. That said, you shouldn't in general plan on overnighting. Keep clear of the islets which have coral outcrops off them. Sandy Spit is a very picture postcard spot with its pretty sandy beach and the coconut palm topknot. If the weather's calm enough, there's good snorkelling to be had on all the reefs around.

Top left White Bay from S
Top right White Bay anchorage and beach
Above left Little Harbour from SW
Above right Little Harbour

Sandy Cay

The scene is just like Sandy Spit though the anchorage under the islet's lee is often both more rolly from swell and more crowded. Anchor in 5–6m on sand a good way off the beach. The islet belongs to the Rockefeller Foundation and is mostly covered with scrub and trees. There are a few footpaths for a short stroll. In good weather there's good snorkelling over the coral on the windward side.

Tobago Island

Two miles W of Jost Van Dyke there's a fair, settled weather day anchorage in the bay on the leeward side of Tobago Island. Good snorkelling on the reefs in the NW.

Caution Watch the current.

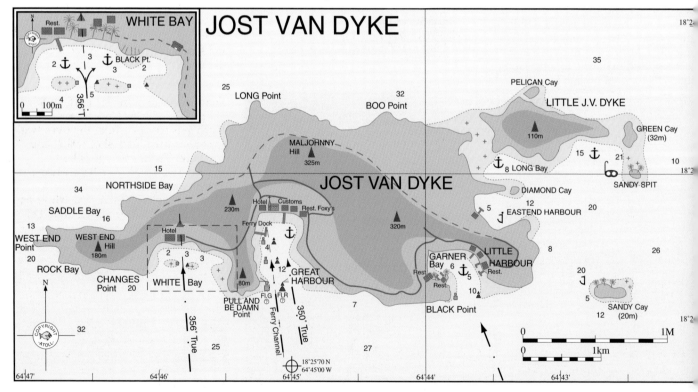

Above left Beach at Foxy's, Grand Harbour

Above right Fordable passage between Jost Van Dyke and Little Jost Van Dyke

Below, from top
Eastend Harbour, Little Jost Van Dyke, from S
E of Little Jost Van Dyke with Green Cay and Sandy Spit
Sandy Cay and E of Little Jost Van Dyke

Islands South of Tortola

From Virgin Gorda to St John

These are the islands, in a line S of Tortola, which form the major protection against the ocean swell for Sir Francis Drake Channel. They are part of the BVI as far as Norman Island. Other than fishermen, a few bar-restaurants and a hotel on Peter Island, they are uninhabited.

Fallen Jerusalem

This small, barren island S of Virgin Gorda owes its name to the imaginations of those who compared its barren rocks to the ruins of Jerusalem after its destruction by the Romans. Under the lee of the island there's a fair-weather day anchorage.

Caution Coming from the E don't pass between Round Rocks and the reefs of Brocken Jerusalem because the pass is full of nasties. In good weather you can explore the underwater world of The Blinders.

Caution Currents round here can be very strong.

Ginger Island

There's no sheltered anchorage around this desolated and uninhabited island, just the lighthouse. Coming from seaward passage between Round Rock and Ginger Island is deep and clear of all danger.

Cooper Island

The anchorage in the lee of the NW of Cooper Island is in Manchioneel Bay, which gets its name from the trees (with poisonous fruit) several of which line the shore. The anchorage is best protected in the N. The S part towards Cistern Pt has more reef in it. A N swell can quickly make the whole bay uncomfortable or even untenable. Off

Above Fallen Jerusalem

217

Above left Manchioneel Bay beach
Above right Salt Island Pond
Left Cooper Island from SW, with NE point of Salt Island

Cooper Island Beach Club (VHF 16) there are moorings you can use (pay at the Beach Club), though they limit the available space for anchoring. The weedy bottom is poor holding.

Ashore There's a fine beach backed by a coconut plantation under the trees of which you'll find the restaurant and the bungalows of the Cooper Island Beach Club with, beside it, a dive centre. There's also a possible day anchorage in Haulover Bay a bit further S. The snorkelling off Cistern Pt is good.

Caution Between Ginger and Cooper Islands there's a dangerous reef in the middle of Ginger Island Passage called Dry Rocks.

Salt Island

The island takes its name from the small salt ponds which were in production for hundreds of years. The anchorage in Salt Island Bay is often uncomfortable as a result of the swell and is only really a day stop except in settled weather. Anchor on poor holding in 5–6m off the dock.

Ashore Some small, more or less dilapidated houses are no longer occupied, except now and then by fishermen. Quite often the place is deserted and has a generally rather sad feeling, albeit peaceful, like all abandoned places. Inland the stagnant waters of the salt pond reflect the tops of some coconut trees.

There's another day anchorage in Lee Bay, often very bouncy, which is used to take a tender to dive or snorkel over the wreck of RMS *Rhone*. This British mail steamer was overwhelmed in a tremendous hurricane on 29 October 1867. You can see the fore part of the wreck in 10/15m in line with the SW point of Lee Bay. The second part, lying deeper, is about 50m to the NW. It's best to dive in the morning because in the afternoon the current is usually a lot stronger.

Caution The wreck site is a protected zone and you must have authorisation to dive on it.

There's a light on the W end of Salt Island.

Caution In the middle of Salt Island Passage, Blonde Rock with only 2·5m over it is unmarked and hazardous in any swell.

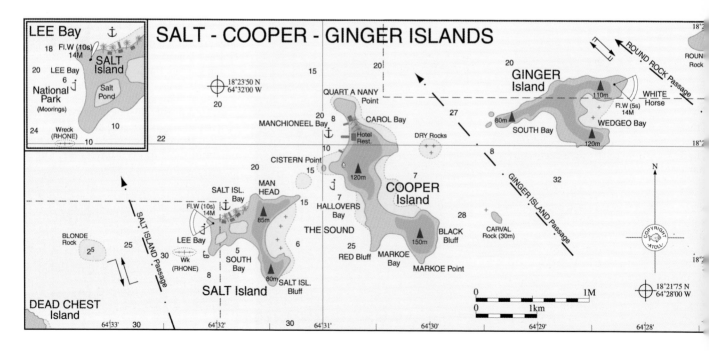

SALT - COOPER - GINGER ISLANDS

Norwegians, which explains the style. Since then a new company has bought it and now manages it. The hotel and restaurant (with swimming pool) is in the super luxury class with a clientele who can afford that sort of thing. There's another restaurant for lunch, on the fabulous Deadman Bay beach. The whole complex is impeccably groomed. There's a regular ferry run to Tortola.

Deadman Bay

Anchor in the E part of the bay off the fine sand beach in 4m, clear of the reefs that push out from Cabey Pt. Any swell from the NE will come in and make the anchorage very rolly. In theory the beach is for the hotel guests. That said,

electricity). Some mooring buoys (paying) are also available further into the inlet.

Ashore You'll find the Dock Master's office (VHF 16) and the showers. The small railway slip and the workshop are, exceptions allowed for, for the resort's boats only. The Peter Island Resort and Yacht Harbour was originally built by

op Salt Island from SW
bove centre Salt Island beach and anchorage
bove Shacks on Salt Island

Top right Peter Island Yacht Harbour, Sprat Bay, from SW
Right Peter Island from W
Below Peter Island and Deadman Bay from E

Peter Island

This is the largest island of the group etween Virgin Gorda and St John. There are three good anchorages and a narina.

Peter Island Harbour, Sprat Bay

Night entry is possible because the dock s lit by several dock lights. Keep to the niddle of the entrance on a course of bout 145°T in 4m depth keeping clear f the shoals pushing NW off Sprat Bay t on your port hand. The 'T' shaped ock has 2·5–3m off it on its N side and here's a fuel dock at the outer end. There are 20 berths for yachts (water &

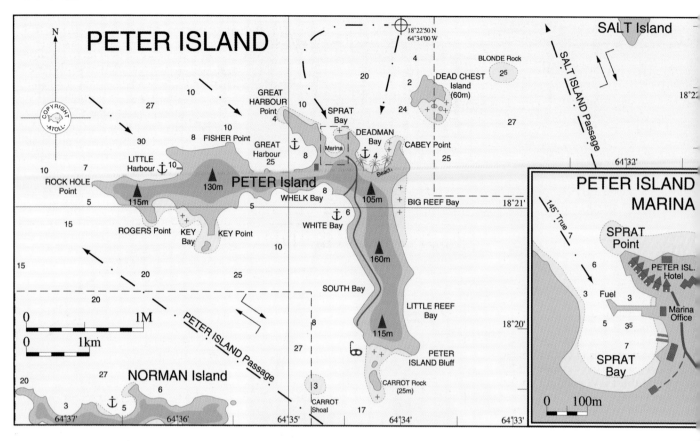

from this or any of the other anchorages you can set off on walks in the interior of the island giving you wonderful views from the hilltops.

Great Harbour

The depths here drop to over 20m. The fishermen's activities stop you getting closer than 200m to the SE shore. They also get seriously cross if you try. The best spot is in the NE in 7–8m. A narrow isthmus separates this bay from Sprat Bay.

Little Harbour

This is a well sheltered bay but quite small, with room for only 6 or 7 boats at most. Given the problem of swinging room, use two anchors. It's a peaceful spot but the fairly unattractive beach is backed by private land.

White Bay

In fair weather there's is a day anchorage S of the island. Good snorkelling near Carrot Rock.

Norman Island

N of Norman Island, if the weather suits, stop off at Pelican Island and The Indians, both National Park territory, for the excellent snorkelling (be wary of the current).

Norman Island is best known for its caves and buried treasure. According to some, Robert Louis Stevenson had learned of the discovery of this treasure through an old letter of his grandfather, and that inspired him to write *Treasure*

Above Little Harbour, Peter Island, from E
Above right Bungalow, Peter Island Resort
Right Peter Island Yacht Harbour

Island. Others talk of an old family with French origins who found Spanish doubloons in a cave around 1900. Whatever the truth really is, why not keep the legend going anyway?

The Bight

This is a huge bay in the W coast of Norman Island and has lots of well-sheltered anchorages.

Caution To get in be careful to steer clear of Treasure Pt surrounded by several reefs.

The best anchorage is in the NE in 8–9m clear of the mooring buoys. Gusts can sometimes come barrelling in from the steep hills round the bay. The

William Thornton II (VHF 16) is an old topsail schooner which is anchored here, offering a welcome to passing boats.

Ashore Billy Bones Beach Bar and Grill (VHF 16) is on the beach and at the moment is the island's only establishment. It manages most of the moorings. If you fancy it, take the quite steep footpath, to find, up on the tops, wonderful panoramic view.

The Caves and Privateer Bay

This area is part of the National Park and anchoring is forbidden. If you've got a permit, there are National Park mooring buoys you can use. You can also day anchor further S in Privateer Bay and reach the caves in your tender. Given the size of the diggings, the treasure, if there was any, must have been pretty small. It's best to visit by snorkelling (best in the afternoon for good light given that the caves open to the W) and admire the beauty of the seabed, especially in the third cave.

Benures Bay

This is quite well protected and often has fewer boats than The Bight. Anchor under the small headland in the NE part on sand.

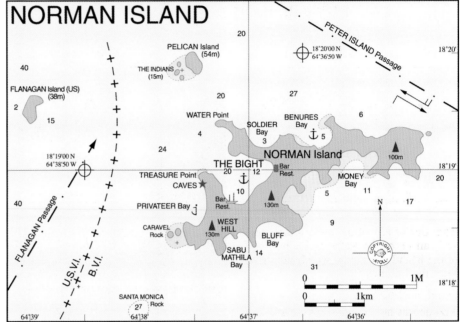

Top Norman Island from SW
Above The Bight from E
Left The Caves

Anegada

Area 35sq km
Highest point 10m
Population 350
Main settlement The Settlement
Language English
Currency US$
Political status Part of BVI
Distances to nearby islands Virgin Gorda 13M

History and Tourism

This flat island sits on an immense coral barrier, which is its main interest. This is an aquatic universe in miniature and since the island was first settled, has been the focus of the island's fishermen. Their ancestors are passed off as pirates and later notorious wreckers whose victims litter the long coral bank which stretches miles S of the island and, because it's just awash, is a death trap to ships at sea. But these days it's that mélange of wrecks, fish and living coral which entices divers.

Thanks to the productive fishing there are several restaurants, particularly in the N of the island, to welcome the tourists and sailors who arrive every day. The only settlement is appropriately called The Settlement and is just a simple fishing village and interesting only as that. Much of the island is taken up with mangrove-fringed lagoons (Flamingo Pond, etc.) bustling with bird life. There are some driveable roads serving the various inhabited areas. Close to The Settlement there's a small airstrip for the tourist trade.

Pilotage

Coast and anchorages

Anegada has much in common with Barbuda and like it and every other similar, flat coral island, your approach to such dangerous shores should only be made in daylight and good visibility. You should also be sure to study your charts carefully before you set out and then navigate carefully so you know without mistake exactly where you've made landfall.

Setting Point

This is the most accessible and the most popular anchorage. It's opposite the Anegada Reef Hotel between Pomato and Setting Points. Begin your approach by heading for the dock off Setting Pt on 060°T. The channel is marked by port and starboard buoys. There's 3m or so in the channel and the outer part of the anchorage, but this decreases to <2m near the docks. Keeping on going up the channel to the NW of the bay, you'll find the best

Top Setting Point anchorage from SW
Above Beach and anchorage W of Setting Point

sheltered part of the anchorage. There are several paying buoy moorings that make the anchoring area quite small.

Ashore Around the bay from Setting Pt to near Pomato Pt there are several hotel-restaurants on the beach, the Anegada Reef Hotel amongst them. Most of the establishments monitor VHF 16. All are relatively small and simple and have pretty terraces opening onto the beach. They are regularly invaded by swarms of day trippers and cruising sailors to whom they offer seafood menus, the waters of Anegada still teeming with fish and lobster. Those establishments aside, there are few small knick-knack shops, and for provisioning what you see is what you'll get – which is true for water and fuel

too. From the anchorage you can call a taxi or hire a car for touring the island, the ponds and The Settlement.

Raffling Point

Keeping headed up the channel you must make a large detour to the W to get round the coral reef off Pomato Point. Between the latter and Raffling Pt there's a long sandy beach. It is almost deserted and is one of the loveliest and wildest you can get to by boat in the Virgins. The best anchorage is N of Pomato Pt where a nick in the shoals lets you get a bit closer to the beach. If you go by tender to the S of Raffling Pt you can have some great snorkelling on the barrier reef.

Ashore A little way back from the shore and hidden in the vegetation is a restaurant serving local specialties.

Setting Point from SW

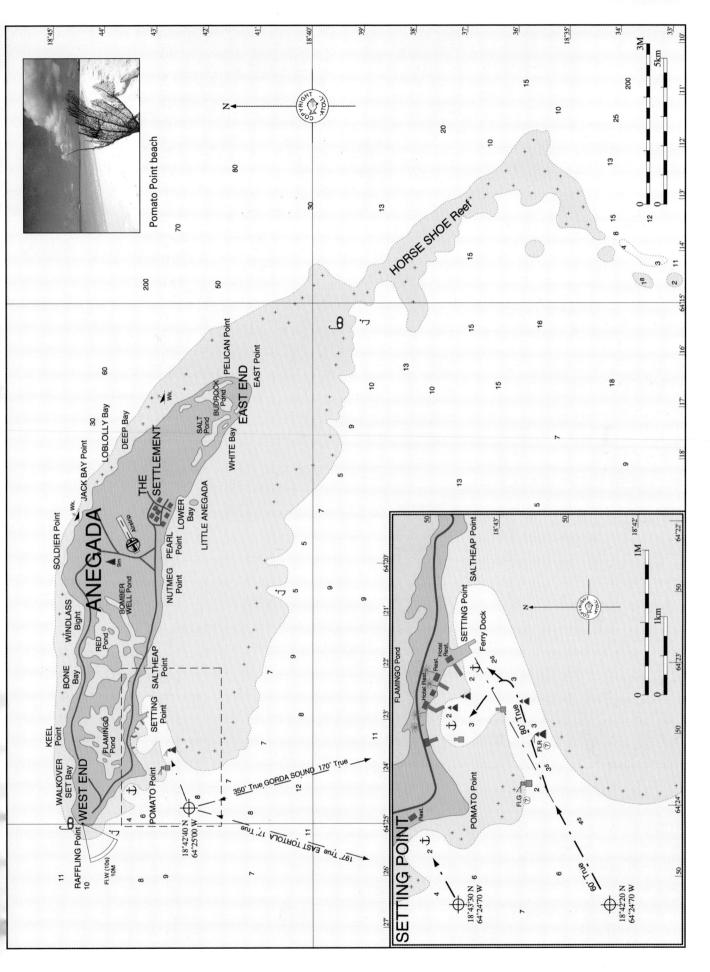

Pomato Point beach

ANEGADA

HORSE SHOE Reef

WEST END

EAST END

THE SETTLEMENT

LITTLE ANEGADA

KEEL Point

WALKOVER SET Bay

SOLDIER Point

WINDLASS Bight

BONE Bay

JACK BAY Point

LOBLOLLY Bay

DEEP Bay

RAFFLING Point

FLAMINGO Pond

RED Pond

BOMBER WELL Pond

Airstrip

NUTMEG Point

PEARL Point

LOWER Bay

SALT Pond

BUDROCK Pond

WHITE Bay

PELICAN Point

EAST Point

POMATO Point

SALTHEAP Point

SETTING Point

9m

Wk.

Wk.

Wk.

Fl.W (10s) 10M

350' True GORDA SOUND 170' True

197' True EAST TORTOLA 17' True

18°42'40 N
64°25'00 W

SETTING POINT

FLAMINGO Pond

POMATO Point

SETTING Point

SALTHEAP Point

Ferry Dock

Hotel Rest.
Rest.

Rest. Hotel Rest.

Rest.

Fl.R

Fl.G

80' True

60' True

18°43'30 N 64°24'70 W

18°42'20 N 64°24'70 W

1M

1km

3M

5km

Above Pomato Point beach and anchorage
Right Anegada Reef Hotel beach, Setting Point

Other anchorages

You can anchor elsewhere in the lee of Anegada, for example either close to Little Anegada and The Settlement or W of Horseshoe Reef. But approach to any such hostile anchorages buried amongst the bommies needs to be closed in fair weather, good visibility with a lookout aloft and the greatest of care. Everyone must work out his or her own technique, always remembering that what you've got yourself into, you must be able to leave. Those who delight in old wrecks and snorkelling will find it difficult to tear themselves away from the pleasures of Anegada's underwater world. Restrictions in this area may have been enforced recently and it is best to check before going there.

Useful Information for the British Virgin Islands

AIRLINE CONNECTIONS
There are no international long-haul flights to the BVI
Tortola
Beef Island Airport
Inter-island services daily to San Juan (Puerto Rico), Sint Maarten, St Thomas, Antigua, Trinidad, and almost all the other Lesser Antilles
Virgin Gorda
The Valley Airport (airstrip)
Inter-island services daily services to Tortola, San Juan (Puerto Rico), St Thomas
Anegada
Air taxis

FERRY CONNECTIONS
Regular ferry connections within the BVI and between the BVI and USVI.

TELECOMMUNICATIONS
Calling from abroad: ☎ (1) 284 + 7 digits
Local call: 7 digits
Public call boxes: Caribbean Phone Card

TOURIST OFFICES/ASSOCIATIONS
Tourist Offices:
Tortola: Akara Building, Road Town
☎ 284 494 3134 *Fax* 284 494 3866
Email bvitourb@surfbvi.com
You can also check the online events guide at www.bviwelcome.com or the online edition of the Limin' Times, www.limin-times.com
Virgin Gorda: Virgin Gorda Yacht Harbour
☎ 284 485 5181
Royal BVI Yacht Club, Road Reef Marina, Tortola, ☎ 284 494 3286 *Fax* 284 494 6117
Email rbviyc@surfbvi.com – organises the annual Spring Regatta Cup

FESTIVALS/FOLKLORE
Tortola
Spring Regatta: first weekend in April
Carnival and BVI Summer Festival: end July/beginning August
L'Interline Regatta: September/October
Virgin Gorda
Virgin Gorda Easter Festival: April
Jost Van Dyke/Norman Island/Anegada
New Year's Day
Valentine's Day: Feb 14th
Foxy's Dance Marathon: February 1st April
Foxy's Wooden Boat Regatta: May
Anegada Race: August

William Thornton's & Virgin Cup: October
Hallowe'en: 31st October

PUBLIC HOLIDAYS
1 January (New Year's Day), Commonwealth Day (2nd Mon in March), Good Friday, Easter Monday, Whit Monday (May), Queen's Birthday (2nd Monday in June), Territory Day (1 July), Festival (beginning of August), St Ursula's Day (21 October), Prince Charles' Birthday (14 November), Christmas Day (25 December), Boxing Day (26 December)

OFFICE HOURS
Shops: 0900–1700 Mon–Fri
Banks: 0900–1400 Mon–Fri (Barclays until 1600, Chase Manhatten until 1700 & Sats 0900–1200)
Govt. Offices: 0830–1630 Mon–Fri

PLACES TO SEE
Tortola
JR O'Neal Botanic Garden: reconstitution of a tropical forest
Fort Recovery (1648): guided tour
North Shore Shell Museum: Carrot Bay
Sage Mountain National Park: walking
Virgin Gorda
The Baths: Natural rock formation
Coppermine Pt: ruins of 16th century coppermine
Gorda Peak National Park: walking
Anegada
Flamingo Pond: birdlife
Norman/Treasure/Salt Islands
RMS *Rhone*: wreck (Salt Island)
The Caves: Treasure Point
The Indians: snorkelling

ROAD TRANSPORT
Drive on the left
Local licence required, BVI licence US$10 on production of valid driving licence from home country (Police HQ or hire car company)
Hire car companies in Tortola, Virgin Gorda and Anegada
Taxis

REGULATIONS
Protection of the underwater world
Forbidden
Destruction or taking of submarine flora
Fishing or underwater hunting by non-residents (without a permit) and total proscription in protected sites
Anchoring or jet skiing within National Marine Parks
Note break these rules and heavy fines are levied and your boat may be confiscated
General advice: don't anchor on coral bottoms

Buoy moorings
In most anchorages managed by various companies including Moor Seacure Ltd (☎ 284 949 4488 *Fax* 284 494 2513), these are US$15–20 per night and are labelled with instructions where to pay.
Buoys at protected sites
Norman Island & Pelican Island
The Indians, Peter Island and Dead Chest Island
Salt, Cooper, Ginger and Guana Islands
West, Great Dog and Cockroach Islands
Virgin Gorda

Red/orange: day mooring (max 90 mins)
White: for diving
Yellow: professional/commercial boats only
Blue: tenders only

Mooring permit obligatory (Marine Conservation Permit) and buoys to be paid for when used.
Further information
BVI Immigration ☎ 284 494 3701
BVI National Parks Trust ☎ 284 494 3904/2069
Fax 284 494 6383
Email bvinpt@caribsurf.com

FORMALITIES
Arriving by air
Customs and Immigration at the airports
Arriving by sea
In the BVI (unlike in the USVI) EU nationals do not need a visa but a valid passport is obligatory, US citizens and Canadians may get away with birth or citizenship certificates or a voter's registration.
Tortola
Government Dock, Road Harbour
Soper's Hole Ferry Dock, West End
Virgin Gorda
Virgin Gorda Yacht Harbour (at the end of the ferry dock N of the Marina)
Hours (in general): weekdays 0830–1630, Sats 0830–1230
Jost Van Dyke
Great Harbour
Hours: 7 days a week 0830–1300 & 1400–1700
For a short stay. Entry and exit processed simultaneously.
Fees and taxes (for a medium sized vessel) (*Note* these may change):
Tax by day by person: US$2–4 depending on boat and season
Port tax and boat tax: <40 tonnes approx. US$10
Charterers must pay for a licence
Overtime paid outside working hours, at weekends and public holidays.

The BVI have a zero-tolerance policy on all drugs.

US Virgin Islands

The American Virgins (USVI), once Danish, were bought by the USA in 1917 for strategic reasons, mainly as a Caribbean base and to cover the approaches to the Panama Canal. The USVI are self-governing and attached to the USA but not integrated as part of the union, although there is a voting delegate from the USVI in the US House of Representatives. Hence USVI nationals resident in the USVI, although they are US citizens, cannot vote for the US President or for members of either of the US Houses of Congress. The territory includes three main islands and a multitude of islets. St John and St Thomas lie close together, but St Croix is 35M to the S of St John. Each has a different history and has developed in a different way: St John is still in an almost untouched natural state and part of it is a National Park; St Thomas is modern and touristy; and St Croix is still living in its colonial past.

bove from top Cruz Bay beach, St John; St Thomas Harbor roads; Old stillery, St Croix

Above from top Francis Bay anchorage and beach, St John; Great St James Island anchorage, St Thomas; Windmill, St Croix

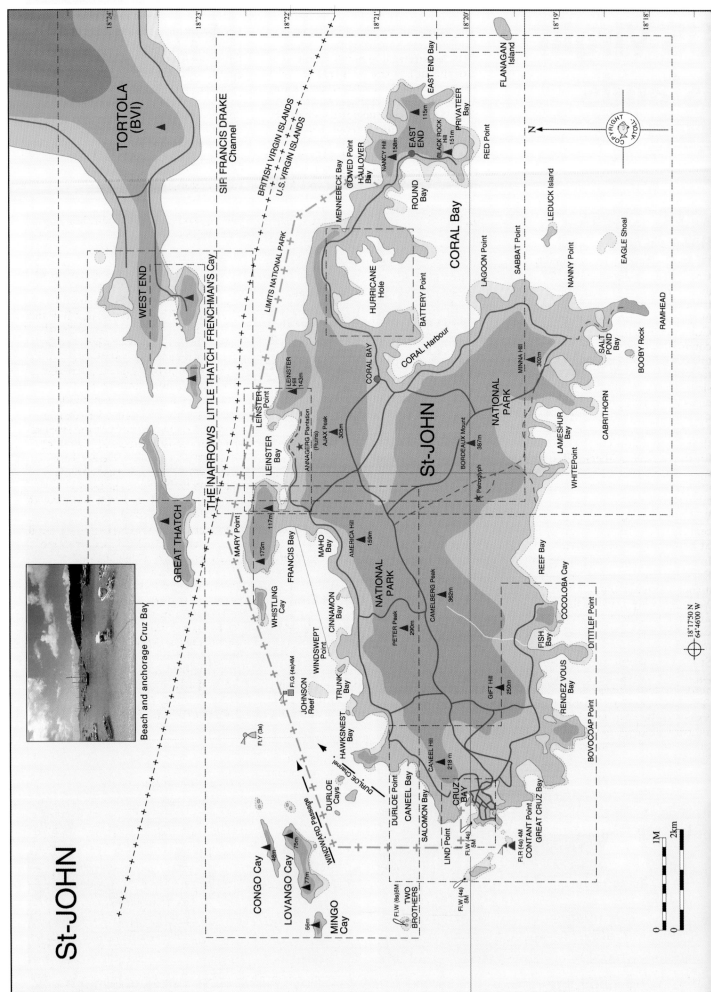

St-JOHN

Beach and anchorage Cruz Bay

St John

Area 52sq km
Highest point Bordeaux Mt 387m
Population 3000
Main town Cruz Bay
Language English
Currency US$
Political status Part of the USVI Unincorporated Territory and a free port
Distances to nearby islands St Thomas (Red Hook) 3M, St Croix 35M, Tortola (West End) 2M

History

Discovered and given its name by Christopher Columbus in 1493 and after a long period uninhabited apart from a few pirates, St John was annexed by the Danes from St Thomas in 1717. Colonists from a number of different countries settled and ran sugar cane and tobacco plantations using slaves and treating them brutally. In 1733 the slaves revolted and chased their erstwhile masters from the island. The colonists appealed to the French in Martinique to help them punish the slave revolt and the French sent a frigate and 200 soldiers. What followed was a bloody and pitiless repression involving the massacre of many of the rebel slaves.

With the end of slavery in the early 19th century, the plantations collapsed and St John returned to its natural state.

In 1954 the island was bought by LS Rockefeller who gave it to the nation so it could be made into a National Park. Mr Rockefeller's side of the deal was that he could build a luxury hotel in Caneel Bay reserved for only the most well-to-do.

St John has few people living on it, but big ferries arrive daily debouching hordes of tourists avid to see this 'Tropical Paradise'. Most of the residents obviously live from the tourist industry although some still work some smallholdings or work as traditional fishermen.

Tourism

Where to stay and what to see

Looking at St John from seaward you can only admire Mr Rockefeller and his friends' initiative in preserving this beauty (and who cares whether it was philanthropic, commercial or both?). Ecologists talk of it as the 'Pearl of the Virgins'. There's been no large scale brutal real estate development to destroy the fantastic tropical vegetation or make its shores ugly. And because it's mountainous, St John has a balanced climate that gives it enough annual rainfall to keep it green.

The National Park, which covers three quarters of the island, also includes most of the coast and within its boundaries hunting and fishing are forbidden.

On top of all that, there's no airport. A few small seaplanes guarantee more or less regular connections with St Thomas and St Croix. But most must get to the island by sea, mainly by ferry from Red Hook (St Thomas), and some of us by private or chartered yacht.

Cruz Bay

This small village consists mostly of small, brightly painted houses and cottages. Some are also tiny fashion and souvenir shops for tourists. Other, larger buildings are for a few government and tourist organization offices. Some of the sea frontage has been developed and has an elegant shopping mall, the Wharfside Village, which includes several shops, bar-restaurants and the terrace of the 'pub' overlooking the bay.

Further NE another very luxurious arcade has been built in the middle of a landscaped plot full of trees. It's called Mongoose Junction and has several luxury shops and arts and crafts outlets as well as a very elegant restaurant. Close by on the N dock you can visit the National Park office for information about things to see and do and for the park regulations.

Cruz Bay is where all the walkers leave from, as do most of the waymarked paths around St John. There are several

St John's National Park

hire car companies who also hire out 4x4's/SUVs.

Around the island

North Shore Road runs along many of the lovely beaches on the N and W coasts as well as past the delightful Underwater Trail in the Trunk Bay area of the marine section of the National Park. The majority of the beaches are fringed with coconut palms only interrupted by occasional houses and sometimes a hotel like the luxury Caneel Bay Resort N of Cruz Bay.

The NE of the island has a track that reaches Leinster Bay where the ruins of the 18th century Annaberg Plantation overlook the bay. The 'Center Line' runs down the middle of the whole island passing the highest point, Bordeaux Mount, and going on through Coral Bay to East End.

The shores of the huge reaches of Coral Bay are very little developed, with the exception of the village of Coral Harbor, and much of them is untouched and lost in the mangroves. Because the roads and tracks are fewer and rougher, or reduced to footpaths criss-crossing the hills, the S of the island is less accessible and so is the best preserved. If you want to visit this area it makes sense to take a guide. On the footpaths around Bordeaux Mount above Reef Bay you can see a few Arawak petroglyphs buried in the forest.

Below Cruz Bay, St John, from W

Pilotage

Coast and anchorages

The coast of St John is much indented and hence offers plenty of well-sheltered anchorages and hurricane holes. Coming from Tortola sailors usually run down The Narrows, the quickest way to reach Cruz Bay, the port of entry. Once you've passed Whistling Cay to port, head towards the gaggle of buoys marking the N side of Johnson Reefs, leaving them to port.

Caution Coming from W or S past the Two Brother Islets and Stevens Cay, be careful of the large area of reef surrounding them.

Thereafter you have two possible routes:

- by the Durloe Channel
- N of Rata Cay through Windward Passage

All of the islets are steep-to and conspicuous.

Cruz Bay from S

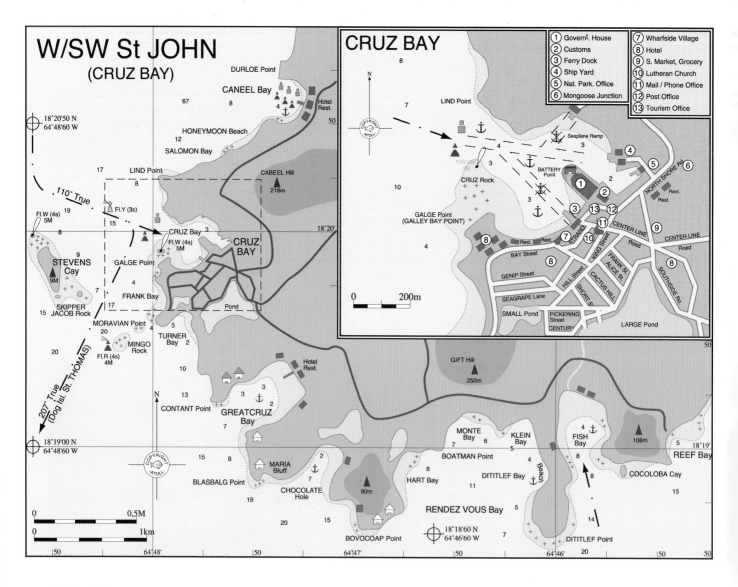

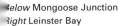
Cruz Bay beach and anchorage

West coast

Cruz Bay

There's a landfall buoy a good way off Lind Pt. On your approach hold to the N side of the entrance to Cruz Bay, the S is blocked by reef. There's a lit beacon marking the reefs pushing out from Galge (or Galley Bay) Pt. Once into the Bay there are two buoyed channels. The N channel is taken by barges and seaplanes after they've landed. The S channel is for ferries. The anchorage is in a narrow triangle between the two channels. You can also anchor S of the ferry channel, though it's very tight because the bottom comes up quickly. In high season it's often so crowded you have to anchor outside S of Lind Pt or S of the reef.

Ashore Immigration is on the N shore of the Battery Pt peninsula with a dock usually taken up by service craft. Opposite the small Caneel Bay Shipyard has its premises with a travel-hoist, some repair facilities and a fuel dock. It's not always working and when it is, is usually busy with local boats. The village with its shops and the two shopping arcades of Wharfside Village and Mongoose Junction offer a wide choice for provisioning and souvenir buying. Numerous restaurants of every category offer a wide choice of food over the whole price range. All of them, despite all the competition, are undeniably touristy

The beach is pretty with a pleasant air, provided the tourists aren't swarming.

The downside is that the anchorage is crowded and bounced about by ferry wash, none of which suggests leaving your boat unattended for long, if at all, to visit the island. As a result of recent rules, drawing your tender up on the beach is forbidden and you must make it fast to the dock.

Caneel Bay

A bit over 1M N of Lind Pt, Caneel Bay is dominated by its luxury resort hotel. There's a small, buoyed channel to the dock reserved for the hotel boats. Be sure to leave it clear as well as keeping clear of the buoyed swimming zone off the beach.

Ashore There's a restaurant and a souvenir shop prettily tricked out in an old 18th century plantation house. The bar and lunch buffet are open to the public. In the evening for dinner it's all very sober and couth but not exactly lively, the guests being either rich retirees or honeymooners who, for differing reasons, go to bed early. Prices are in line with the general atmosphere.

North coast

This is more popular than the S coast even though some of the anchorages are uncomfortable in a NE swell. Some of the beaches are only accessible by sea and there are some private properties along the shore. Any line of yellow buoys designates a reserved bathing area or other watersport activity and anchoring is forbidden.

Hawknest Bay

Conspicuous is a big statue of Christ of the Caribbean on the point of Perkins Cay. It shows the site of the old Denis Bay Plantation. Hawknest (some charts have Hawksnest) Bay Beach is pretty but completely covered with on and below surface water sports for tourists, and there's a buoyed area where anchoring is forbidden. The anchorage is uncomfortable in a NE swell and is often only tenable for a day visit.

Trunk Bay

Another lovely beach and just as touristy with a marked 'Underwater Trail' you can follow snorkelling. There's also a good walk to the small hill above the bay with a panoramic view. As with Hawknest Bay, if there's a NE swell the anchorage is uncomfortable.

Johnson Reef

A large, half-mile long reef stretching N of Trunk Bay and very dangerous although to N and S marked by several buoys, some lit. The passage between Johnson Reef and the coast is clear.

Cinnamon Bay

This is always uncomfortable in a NE swell and is where the National Park Camp Ground is ashore.

Maho Bay

It's a good anchorage and a pretty beach, though the beach is partly private. There are several free mooring buoys available. The restaurant on the campsite ashore is open to the public.

Francis Bay

This is the best anchorage on the N coast because it's the most protected even in winter when the trades are fresh. There's the usual line of buoys marking off the bathing zone the full length of the very long beach. When you anchor make sure your hook has bitten because the bottom drops off quickly to over 20m, though here too mooring buoys have been laid. The National Park Service limits stays here to 14 days for environmental reasons.

Below Mongoose Junction
Right Leinster Bay

Caneel Bay, Hawknest Bay and N coast of St John from W

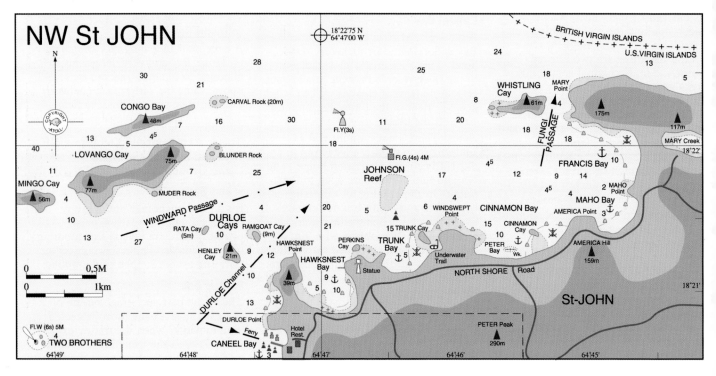

Fungi Passage
Though narrow, this pass is perfectly practicable, but use your motor if the wind is northerly. The shoreline is steep-to except the W end of Whistling Cay. Once past Mary Pt and heading E into The Narrows you'll find that you've normally got wind and current against you.

Leinster Bay/Watermelon Bay
Watermelon Bay is the E extension to Leinster Bay. It's a good anchorage with a sand bottom or you can take a mooring. This is a good place for a visit to the Annaberg plantation ruins nearby.

South coast

From Cruz Bay to Coral Bay
SW of Cruz Bay you must pass Steven Cay on its W side unless it is quiet weather and good visibility in which case you can eyeball the pass between the cay and the coast. Follow the pass by heading for the S of Dog Island (St

Great Cruz Bay from SW

Thomas) on 203°T. The reefs N of Steven Cay are marked by a beacon and the end of Mingo Rock by a red buoy.
Caution The line of reef SW from Moravian Pt runs for over 400m.

Great Cruz Bay
Once round Contant Pt you'll open up Great Cruz Bay. The NE part of the head of the bay has been dredged and there's now about 4-5m. In the E of the bay the bottom comes up very quickly to less than 2m. The wide bay is pleasantly breezy but very crowded with local boats on buoys or anchored. The shore is mostly taken up by a hotel. The dock is only for the service ferries and the hotel's own boats.

Chocolate Hole

In the NE the bottom comes up to less than 2m. It's a well-protected anchorage but I've found that when the wind's SE it's rolly. Another downside is that because the head of the bay is crowded with local boats, you have to anchor quite close to the entrance. The shore and its small beach are little developed.

Keeping going E you round Bovocoap Pt with a remarkable house cantilevered out over space, with beside it several cottages equally airily perched.

Rendezvous Bay

This bay isn't much visited because you can't get to it by road. It's wide open to the S and if there's a SE swell the best shelter is either in the NE in Klein Bay or Dittlif Bay.

These anchorages are almost deserted and the shore with its pebble beach has no buildings at all.

Fish Bay

Another remote anchorage but the bay is a bit open to the SE and that makes it

Fish Bay and Rendezvous Bay

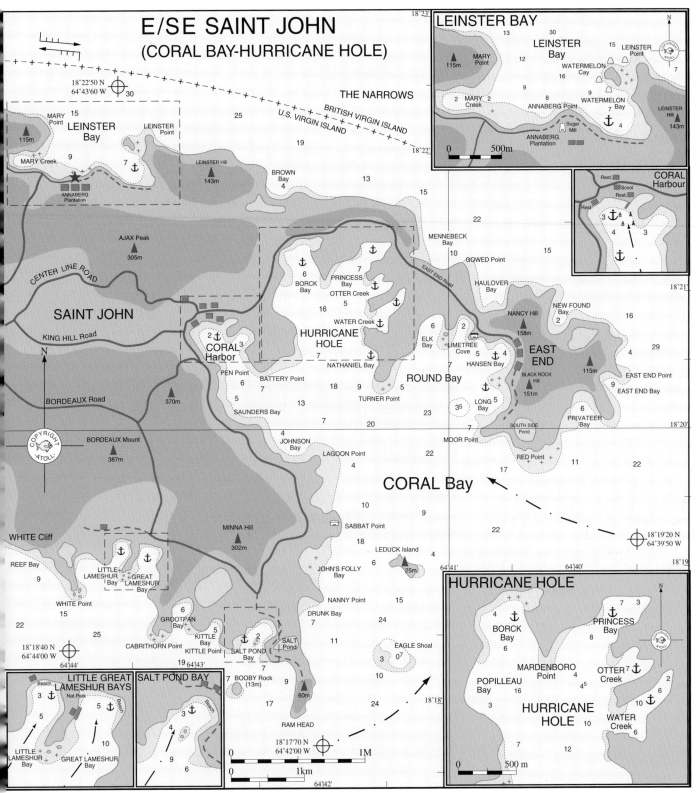

Above left Grootpan, Little & Great Lameshur Bays
Above right Coral Harbor from NW

iffy in a SE swell. The sides of the entrance have coral pushing out a good way and at the head of the bay, where there's a little beach and a few houses, it's pretty shallow (<3m).

Reef bay

This is wide open to the S and anyway anchoring is forbidden. The white cliffs of White Cliff are conspicuous.

Lameshur Bays

There are two parts to this bay (hence the plural name):

Little Lameshur Bay This is the W part and is well sheltered unless the wind is S. You can't anchor but in theory there are moorings available. At the head of the bay the small sandy beach is fringed with thorny scrub and there's no development bar a few picnic sites.

Caution Leaving eastwards note that the point is extensively fringed by shoal.

Great Lameshur Bay Once round the reef girt point, you'll reach the second anchorage. On the W shore there's a building with a small dock exclusive to the National Park Service. An environmental study and research centre is based here. There's 5–7m but here too anchoring is forbidden and there are mooring buoys available. The small beach on the E side is as deserted as the previous one. Leaving to the E give Cabrithorn Pt and its fringing reef a wide berth

Salt Pond Bay

One of the loveliest remote anchorages of the coast, but not easy to get into. Try it only in good visibility on a NNE heading. Keep well clear of Kittle Pt and its extensive reef. The pass is between the W shore and the large patch of reef in the middle of the bay. The bottom comes up to 3m before dropping back to 4–5m in the anchorage. However, anchoring is forbidden and you must use one of the mooring buoys provided. In the NE a pretty beach has some picnic places. The only houses visible are scattered on the little hillocks round about.

Booby Rock

You can pass this isolated rock on either side. In calm weather there's good snorkelling if you come by tender.

Caution The current is strong.

Below Coral Bay from SE
Bottom Coral Bay from SW

Coral Bay

Once you're past Ram Head you approach Coral Bay.

Caution Less than 1M NE of Ram Head Eagle Shoal extends for more than 500m and has less than 1m over it. Pass W of Eagle Shoal holding towards the coast of St John, or give it a large berth in going E out round it. Once clear you'll come to Sabbat Point, easily spotted because of a white building on its tip.

There are three anchoring areas in Coral Bay: Coral Harbor, Hurricane Hole and Round Bay.

Coral Harbor

In the days of the sugar cane industry this was the main port for St John because it was directly accessible from the open sea by sail. Some ruins of old buildings are mute witnesses to those prosperous old days.

Caution Give Lagoon Pt a wide berth to clear the reefs off it.

In the lee of Lagoon Pt Johnson Bay has a reasonable small anchorage in 3–4m, though it's full of local boats and fairly choppy in NE winds.

To keep on for Coral Harbor, stay on about 330°T.

Caution Several buoys mark an approach channel to the small dock on the NE shore that you must leave clear.

The whole anchorage, although pretty big, is full of local boats and private moorings. If you can, anchor in the NW in 3–4m, mud.

Caution The shoreline in general is both very shoal and cluttered with wrecks, especially in the NE. If the trades are from the SE, they raise a fair chop.

Ashore The village is on the N shore, set back a little, and only consists of a few rather unattractive buildings. On the W and NW shores there are two or three restaurants and bars serving local food. Though it's all a bit relative, the E shore is where the action is. There's a restaurant and bar here that has a welcoming atmosphere and is the home of the local yacht club. Next door in a large shack is the only boat or yachting service in the area offering mechanical and other repair services. Other than a cyber café, a small souvenir shop and a small grocery store in the village, Coral Harbor has no other shops. Taken together the settlement is pretty bucolic, not to say dilapidated. But for all that, Coral Bay is a free haven and throughout the year shelters a heteroclite fleet of all the yachties who sail in the Virgins and elsewhere

Hurricane Hole

Not every anchorage in the bay is a hurricane hole, that would be too much to expect. Mosquitoes, on the other hand, are everywhere.

Caution Some of the headlands have shoal ground off them.

Borck's Creek This is open to the S and a SE swell can make it uncomfortable.

Princess Bay This is an excellent shelter and even up to the standards of a good hurricane hole if you can push into the mangroves.

Otter Creek A very good shelter surrounded by rocks and thorny scrub, that's as calm as a lake.

Water Creek A wonderful hurricane hole both pushed in amongst the mangroves and also in the small tuck in the SE corner that's a perfect haven for 2 or 3 boats.

Caution The N point extends in a tongue of sand.

Nathaniel Bay This is the most open and least protected bay, but in normal weather the airiest. Anchor in 5–6m about 50m from the small beach.

Top Round Bay from S
Centre Princess Bay, Otter & Water Creeks, Round Bay from W
Above Otter Creek anchorage
Right Anchorage and beach at Coral Harbor

Round Bay

To get into this bay from S, give Red Point & Moon Points a wide berth because they've shoal ground off them.

Caution There's a shoal with only 3m over it in the middle of Round Bay and if there's a swell running deeper draft yachts could rap it.

There are two anchorages:

- in the N towards Limetree Cove & Elk Bay
- NE of Moon Point, though it's a bit cluttered by several moorings.

Note There are several houses on the shore of Hansen Bay, but there are no shops.

Useful Information for St John

AIR AND SEA CONNECTIONS
Inter-island seaplane service irregular
Daily ferries to/from St Thomas, Charlotte Amalie and the BVI

TELECOMMUNICATIONS
Calling from abroad:☎ (1) 340 + 7 digits
Local call: 7 digits
Public call boxes: Caribbean Phone Card

TOURIST OFFICE
Cruz Bay Visitors' Bureau ☎ 340 776 6450 (see also www.usvitourism.com or www.usvichamber.com). The bureau is the starting point for guided hikes.

CLUBS/ASSOCIATIONS
St John Yacht Club – organises the Island Hopper Race, January
Coral Bay Yacht Club, c/o Skinny Legs (☎ 340 779 4982), Coral Bay – organises sailing courses and the Thanksgiving Day Regatta, end of November

FESTIVALS/FOLKLORE
Cruz Bay: an event every last Saturday of the month
Carnival: week of 4th July

PLACES TO SEE
Annaberg Sugar Mill: Ruins in Leinster Bay
Battery Pt: Fortifications (1735) and small museum
Enighed Estate Manor (1700): museum and pre-Columbian artefacts
Underwater Trail: Trunk Bay, a snorkelling circuit

PUBLIC HOLIDAYS
New Year's Day (1 January), Three Kings Day (6 January), Martin Luther King Day (15 January), President's Day (19 February), Holy Thursday, Good Friday, Easter Monday, Transfer Day (31 March), Memorial Day (28 May), Organic Act Day (18 June), Emancipation Day (3 July), Independence Day (4 July), Hurricane Supplication Day (23 July), Labour Day (beginning September), Puerto Rico/Virgin Islands Friendship Day (mid-October), Hurricane Thanksgiving Day (mid-October), Liberty Day (1 November), Veterans' Day (11 November), Thanksgiving Day (mid-November), Christmas Day (25 December)

OFFICE HOURS
Government Offices: Mon–Thurs 0900–1700
Banks: Mon–Fri 0830–1500

ROAD TRANSPORT
Drive on the left
Local licence required – available from hire car companies on production of your licence.
Hire car companies and taxi services in Cruz Bay
Dollar Buses: island tours

REGULATIONS
National Park
Over the majority of its land area and coast St John is a National Park.

Forbidden
Fishing, hunting, taking or destroying any submarine flora or fauna
Anchoring or jet skiing in any National Marine Park protected zone.
Note any offence incurs a fine

MOORING BUOYS
These have been installed by the USVI National Park especially in protected zones such as: St John: Reef Bay, Lameshur Bays, Salt Pond Bay, Ram Head, Leinster Bay, Whistling Cay, Maho Bay, Hawknest Bay, Lind Point.
Stays are limited to two weeks a year in these zones.
Buoy coding
White: for day or overnight use.
White (marked 'DAY'): day use only
Yellow: one hour only
Orange: for diving on certain sites, make sure you enquire.
Blue: commercial permit holders ONLY.
Note Use is restricted to boats LESS THAN 16·8m (55') loa
Use is forbidden in adverse weather
The National Park Service disclaims all responsibility for defective moorings
Information from: National park Service, Cruz Bay ☎ 340 776 6201

FORMALITIES
Arriving by sea
Cruz Bay: Battery Pt Dock (The Creek)
Hours: 7 days a week 0700–1200, 1300–1800
Fees and taxes Formalities free (you may have to pay for the forms)
Overtime: Sundays and public holidays
Note for related information see also St Thomas

St Thomas

Area 83sq km
Highest point Crown Mountain 470m
Population 48,000
Capital Charlotte Amalie (pop. 15,000)
Language English
Currency US$
Political status Part of USVI Unincorporated Territory and a tax-free zone
Distances to nearby islands St John (Cruz Bay) 3M, St Croix 35M

History

The Danes occupied St Thomas around 1672 and quickly annexed St John's too. They were, however, a minority in the population, which had a majority of English, Dutch and French protestant (Huguenot) settlers. Despite a few sugar plantations, agriculture wasn't the only economic activity. In 1691 The Danish West Indies Company founded Charlotte Amalie (named after the Danish queen), which soon became one of the principal entrepots in the Caribbean. Traders, slave dealers and pirates from every country came to do business or to sell their booty. The port, open to everyone, was also a neutral zone and those at each other's throats beyond port limits had to respect the rules and 'leave their sword in the cloak room'. St Thomas thus had a golden age, witness to which are the old warehouses and fortifications around Charlotte Amalie.

But with the end of almost a century of warfare in 1815, St Thomas entered a long decline. The population steadily fell despite the occasional group of immigrants like the two to three thousand French (most from St-Barthélémy) who arrived in the 19th century.

From 1868 the Danes wanted to be rid of their Caribbean possessions (St Thomas, St John and St Croix) and offered to sell them to the Americans. The latter finally accepted in 1917, during the First World War, primarily to have forward strategic cover for the Panama Canal. They paid Denmark the then considerable sum of US$25 million.

St Thomas soon replaced St Croix as the centre of government for the USVI. The Governor, who has been elected by the USVI population since 1970, is in charge of the executive branch. The legislative branch of government (the Senate with 15 members) is popularly elected and sits in Charlotte Amalie.

St Thomas has had an expanding tourist trade ever since 1950. Each year more than 1 million tourists arrive, attracted by the territory's tax-free status and by the wonderful beaches.

They come by sea but also, thanks to the international airport, by long-haul flights as well. It has to be said, however, that the development has by no means had a salutary effect on the island's previously peaceful way of life. There has been a conspicuous increase in criminal activity, notably theft and muggings. And there has unquestionably been an increase in drug taking and drug-related crime. To remedy the situation the authorities have made a tough stand, with strict regulations governing immigration and seeking to eradicate drugs.

Tourism

Where to stay and what to see

The island, created by volcanic activity, has a long, mountainous spine running up to the high point of 470m and then dropping more gently to the flatter parts in the E. Thanks to their forested hills and the fact that they are less developed, the W and NW of the island are still quite unspoiled and wild. On the other hand the E and SE of the island from Charlotte Amalie to Red Hook are much built up with houses and hotels that have invaded almost all the lovely beaches.

There's a well-maintained road network serving most of the coast as well as the

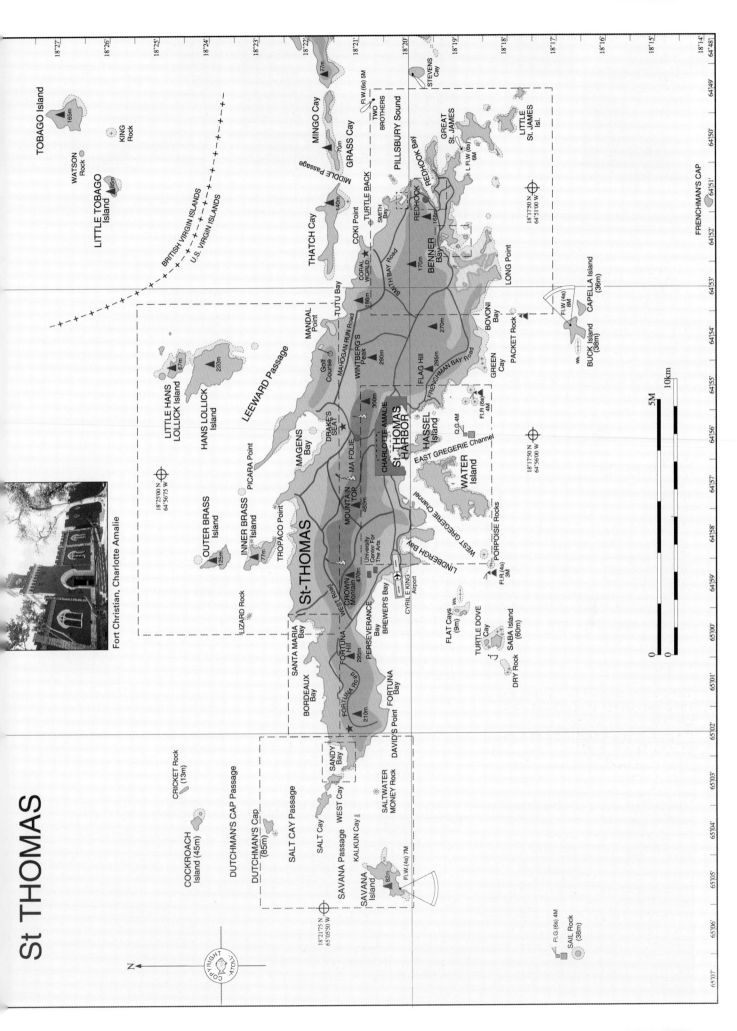

Fort Christian, Charlotte Amalie

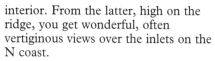

Left Fort Christian
Right Main Street, Charlotte Amalie
Far right Legislature Building,

interior. From the latter, high on the ridge, you get wonderful, often vertiginous views over the inlets on the N coast.

Note Unlike in continental USA, in the USVI you drive on the left. This is occasionally forgotten by some of the American tourists, which can lead to some alarming surprises on blind corners!

Charlotte Amalie

The capital of the USVI lies on the shores of a natural, deepwater harbour protected by two islands. In it cruise liners regularly call to offload their cargoes of tourists, who climb back aboard a while later festooned with cameras and jewellery bought in the duty-free shops on Main St, which runs along the sea front.

The 17th-century Fort Christian lies to the E of the waterfront. It's been in turn a prison, a church, the Governor's Residence and is now home to a small museum of pre-Columbian artefacts. Small, Danish style, brightly painted houses climb the hillsides around the town centre. A very long flight of several hundred steps lined with flowers leads to the upper town as far as Frederik Lutheran Church (1666) with its fine stone façade. Charlotte Amalie has some fine old buildings such as Government House, the Governor's residence. Government House also contains some paintings by Camille Pissarro who was a St Thomas native.

Great St James & Sapphire Marina from E

Crown House, an old private mansion, still has fine 18th century furniture and fittings. And also of architectural interest there's the synagogue.

In the French quarter of Mafolie on the heights overlooking the town and in Frenchtown (or Cha-Cha-Town) in the west of St Thomas Harbor, you will find the descendants of those French immigrants from long ago, the Huguenots, and of those who later fled St-Barthélémy. Some of the road names are still French and some of the inhabitants from St Barts still keep contact with the island of their distant origins.

Around the island

The two islands opposite Charlotte Amalie have two quite different characters. Water Island is home to luxury hotels. Hassel Island is still little developed and is a nature reserve. There are a few private houses, but they're nicely landscaped in its botanical park where you can also see the remains of 18th century Danish fortifications. Oh, and some iguanas too.

The road from Charlotte Amalie to the east leads to the east end of the island before turning back west along the N of the island winding past a succession of fine, white sand beaches. At Coki Pt there's an underwater observatory, Coral World, where you can watch the rays and sharks weaving their complex ballet. Next comes Magens Bay, the fine beach of which is sheltered by a long arm of land reaching out into the sea. From the heights of Mafolie to the top of Crown Mountain there are several small roads criss-crossing the

hilly western part of the island. From the edges of the roads you get marvellous panoramic views over the inlets and islets on the N coast or, looking S, over the grand extent of St Thomas Harbor.

Pilotage

Coast and anchorages

The best anchorages and places for boats to get things fixed are on the S coast. The wilder N coast and the nearby islets offer some infrequently visited anchorages which are affected by the NE swell, especially when the trades are blowing freshly in winter.

Caution St Thomas is surrounded by islets at varying distances distant from the coast. At night, given that most are unlit, they are a danger to beware of. On the other hand, thanks to the fine drop-offs around it, St Thomas is now a major dive centre with many local clubs and dive centres. The only limits on you reaching many of the best sites are sea state and the often strong currents.

East coast

St Thomas is separated from St John by narrow Pillsbury Sound. In the N of the latter there are five islands in a line running W to E (Thatch Cay, etc.), though none offer any real shelter given their orientation. There's also no navigable passage between them except between Grass Cay and Thatch Cay. In the middle of Pillsbury Sound you'll find the Two Brothers reefs which are readily visible. The S of them is lit and there are clear passages either side.

American Yacht Harbour,
Red Hook

Red Hook Bay

This is one of the rare havens on this coast. An E wind can raise a bit of a chop in the anchorage, though the ferries plying in and out are as bad or worse. The channel to the ferry dock is buoyed and should be left clear. Most yachts anchor in the S part towards Muller Bay or, if there's room, close to the dock on the shore.

In the bay on the N shore the American Yacht Harbor Marina (VHF 16/68) has five docks with a fuel dock on the

second dock. There are nearly 100 berths all with water and electricity, most taken by game fishing boats and charter yachts. Opposite the American Yacht Harbor are the docks of Vessup Point Marina with some 30 berths with water and electricity.

Ashore The majority of shops and businesses are on the American Yacht Harbor shore. The marina office is in the middle of a group of neo-Creole design buildings of some charm. There are several yacht services – repair and

maintenance, charter companies and a chandlery – either in the group of buildings or further towards the head of the bay. On the far side of the road there's a supermarket and several shops so provisioning is a breeze. There are also some restaurants and bars around the dock or on the terrace overlooking the area with another on the other side at Vessup's.

In addition to the shops and services Red Hook has the advantage of being close to St John by regular ferry services. However, you can't turn up here directly from a non-American island because there are no clearance facilities.

Sapphire Beach Marina

N of Red Hook below Cabes Pt a marina has been built along with a tourist real estate development. To get to it you must avoid the reefs round Shark Island. It's perfectly sheltered but the entrance is narrow. There are 60 berths with water and electricity all with 2–3m. There is also a fuel dock.

Ashore The office is on the NW of the basin. If you need work done you can

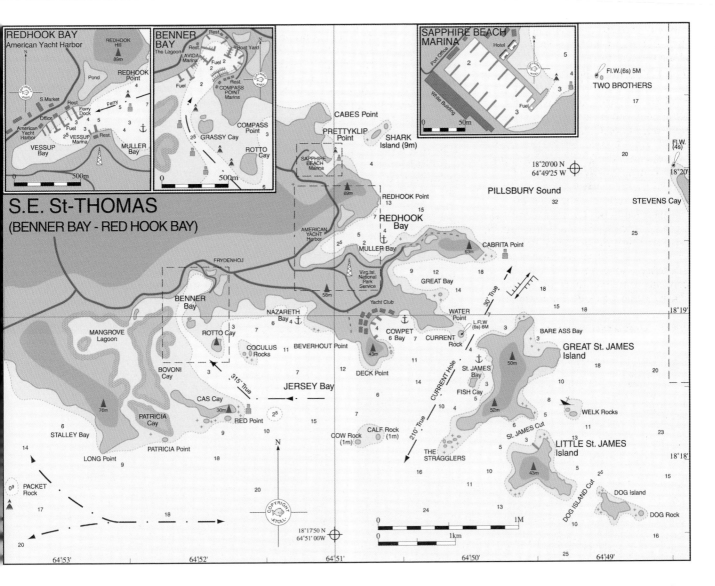

Left Sapphire Beach Marina from N
Right Sapphire Beach Marina
Below right Current Rock

get people from Red Hook. There's a hotel complex with conspic red roofs, restaurants and shops on the large area of flat land behind the pretty beach. Given that most of the berths are taken by residents or charter yachts, this isn't likely to attract many visiting yachts.

South coast

To reach the S coast of St Thomas you should take the Current Cut passage, which has Current Rock (lit) in the middle.

Caution Take the E pass because the W is for shoal drafters only.

St James Bay (Christmas Cove)

There are two anchorages, one S of Fish Cay, the other N.

Caution The passage between Gt St James I and Fish Cay has reef patches. These are well-sheltered anchorages – except against ferry wash – and pleasant too, but very popular. Good snorkelling on the S tip of Gt St James and at Little St James about 0·5M S.

Caution When snorkelling, watch the current.

Little St James

There's a day anchorage on the S side of Little St James. It's seldom visited but uncomfortable in a SE wind.

Cowpet Bay

This is the home of the St Thomas Yacht Club and much of the bay is full of moorings for members' yachts. The anchorage is often bouncy from wash and chop.

Jersey Bay/Nazareth Bay

Once past Deck Pt, leaving Cow and Calf Rocks to port, you'll open up the large expanse of Jersey Bay. You can anchor up in Nazareth Bay in the N, which isn't often crowded, though in a SE it's usually rolly. Watch out for the reefs along the shoreline.

Below Benner Bay & Jersey Bay from W
Bottom left Fish Cay anchorage, Great St James
Bottom right Great & Little St James from N

Above left Great St James, Current Hole & Cowpet Bay from E

Above right Benner Bay (The Lagoon) from E

Right Compass Point Marina (The Lagoon)

Benner Bay (The Lagoon)

Caution You must be sure where you are on your approach by identifying Cas Cay and Bovoni Cay on the W of the channel and Rotto Cay and Grassy Cay on the E.

There are lots of anchored boats around these cays. The access to this perfect hurricane hole of a haven has been dredged to around 2.4m, but you shouldn't count on more than 2.1m at most and in some places once inside, no more than 2m. The buoyed channel begins NW of Rotto Cay. Once inside, the large lagoon is focussed on two main areas:

- in the SE, Compass Point Marina. The docks – round 80 berths – are almost all taken by resident boats and the fleets of several charter companies, so there are few berths for visitors.

Ashore Charter companies, repair specialists, a dive club and a few typical local restaurants can be found in the small, lightly built shacks.

- on the N and W shores, several docks are spread along the coast and managed by different companies:

in the W, Fish Hawk Marina with a fuel dock and Tropical Marina.

in the N, La Vida Marina with a fuel dock.

All of these docks are really accessible only to shoal drafters and are in any case mostly full of residents' boats.

Ashore On the little esplanade of La Vida Marina there is a small restaurant and bar with, next door, a couple of mechanics.

On the coastal road nearby, East End Boat Dry and its boat park, a dive shop, two outboard and inflatable tender agencies complete the services on offer.

The NE shore is taken up with docks and buildings of the huge Independent Boatyard yard with several specialist services available (mechanics, joiners, etc.). It has haul-out facilities (travel-hoist and crane). Nearby you'll find workshops and a chandlery that's well-equipped with stuff for maintenance.

For all its security as an anchorage and its numerous yacht services, Benner Bay is a long way from any town and even if you find the minimarket and a few quite lively restaurants, there really isn't much to make it worthwhile for a boat paying a short visit. That's no mentioning the fact that free berths are rare and there are limits on how much water yours can draw.

St Thomas Harbor

Once you've doubled Long Pt, stay clear of Packet Rock shoal, marked by a red buoy and then further W again leave to starboard the red buoy marking the shoals of Channel Rock and The Triangle off the coast. Immediately NW you'll see the large white building of the Frenchman's Reef resort on Muhlenfels Pt, which helps identify the buoyed channel into St Thomas Harbor. This huge bay offers good shelter for the large cruise liners, but it's often a bit lively for yachts. Nor, because of the town, is the sea very clean. Once inside the bay you'll find various anchoring areas.

Paquereau Bay

You can anchor N of Frenchman's Reef Resort dock, whence you can get access to the hotel's shopping centre. The anchorage is a bit outside St Thomas and as a result the sea is cleaner.

Long Bay/Safehaven Marina

This is one of the most popular anchorages in the Antilles. There's a veritable fleet of boats anchored or on moorings off the marina (VHF 16/68). Keep NE of the buoys marking the manoeuvring area for the cruise liners coming alongside West Indian Dock. The marina has 200 berths on several pontoons, all with water and electricity.

St Thomas Harbour from S

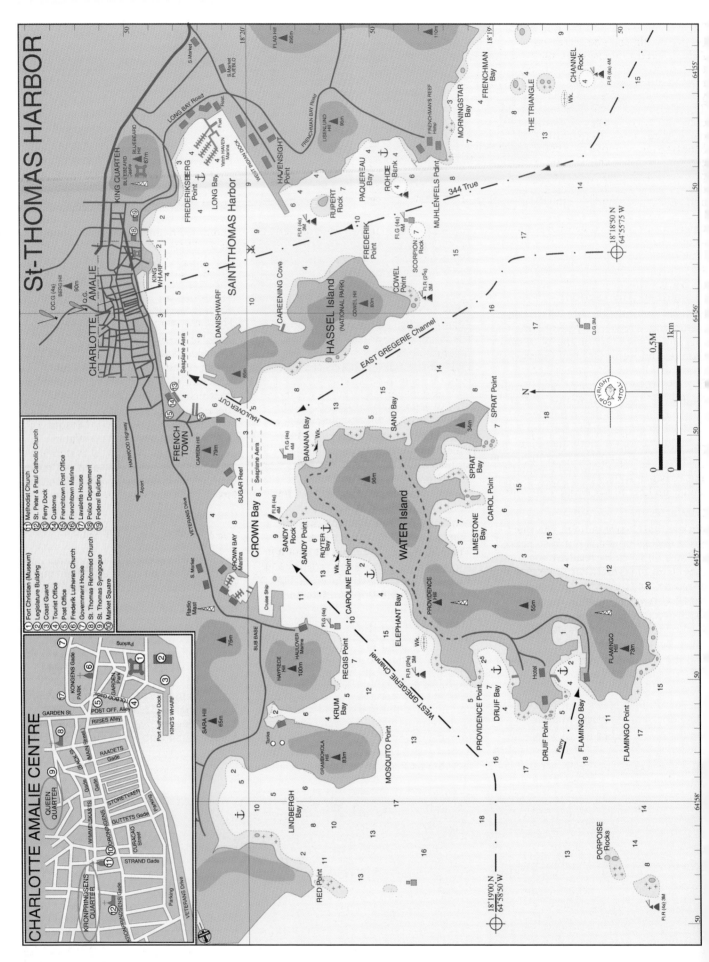

Thanks to renovations the number of berths should soon be increased. Ashore, on an extension on the S side of the marina you'll find the fuel dock, marina office, some shops, the offices of yacht service outfits and a chandlery. There's a restaurant-pub where yachties congregate. As a result of damage to the old Ramada Hotel from Hurricane Marilyn, the old hotel and commercial complex is out of commission but a new project is underway. The area around the marina is very busy. Supermarkets and all sorts of shops line the road leading from the E of St Thomas to Charlotte Amalie. Those attractions aside, this part of Charlotte Amalie has little of tourist interest.

S of the marina West Indian Dock is Charlotte Amalie's port. For many years it stayed a Danish concession. Today, however, its major focus is welcoming luxury cruise liners. St Thomas is a must for cruise liner itineraries around the West Indies. Just for the interest of it, it's worth watching one of these floating hotels come alongside and disgorge its thousands of tourists.

King's Wharf

This dock, right in the middle of Charlotte Amalie opposite Fort Christian, is restricted to shoal drafters and coastguard boats. You can tie your tender up here to get easily into town.

Charlotte Amalie Town

With its old Danish houses, the town has some charm, though it is so packed and busy it's a bit enervating. Everything is orientated to tourism, with duty-free shops, luxury shops, tourist restaurants and more. In the numerous shops, shopping malls and the large covered market in Market Square you

Above left Cruise liner at West Indian Dock
Above right West Indian Dock & Safehaven Marina

can buy everything you want as well as all your provisions. But given the innumerable traffic jams, there's little point in using a car or a taxi.

Frenchtown anchorage

Close to the area of Frenchtown (see Charlotte Amalie in Tourism above), this is the westernmost anchorage in St Thomas Harbor and close to Haulover Cut passage. Often choppy thanks to either a brisk trade wind or ferries, it isn't exactly peaceful. That said, there are some advantages to being close to Frenchtown and to the Immigration offices close to the ferry dock. On the Frenchtown dock, beside the fish market you'll find the two pontoons of Frenchtown Marina with some 20 berths with water and electricity, but not much else for yachts

Ashore There's the marina office and a charter company's office. There are some shops, but the main attraction is the number of restaurants that liven up this welcoming corner of town. Some of them even claim to serve French cuisine.

Careening Cove (Hassel Island)

There are numerous local boats moored in this bay on the E of Hassel Island. The anchorage is quiet enough but a long way from the town.

Below Frenchtown Marina
Bottom left Frenchtown Marina from N

Haulover Cut

This passage has been cut through the coral once joining Hassel Island to St Thomas. The line of the pass favours the St Thomas shore. It isn't buoyed, and though it's regularly dredged to 4m it's often silted to 2.5m on the W side.

Gregerie Channel

There are two parts to this channel:

East Gregerie Channel
This runs between Water Island and Hassel Island. It's of little interest except an anchorage W of Hassel Island often disturbed by ferry boat wash.

West Gregerie Channel
This channel runs from off Mosquito Pt up to Sandy Pt on the N of Water Island. Coming from the W watch out for the shoal ground that runs out more than 400m off Sandy Pt (lit). There are lots of boats anchored W of Sandy Pt

Druif & Flamingo Bays, Water Island

Water Island & E Gregerie Channel from S

though a few small cargo ships at anchor limit the available room.

Water Island

The island is government property and has been leased to a private company. That said, you can still anchor in the two obvious inlets if there's room.

Druif Bay (Honeymoon Bay)

Give a good berth to the reefs off Providence Pt and anchor, if you can, in the NE corner of the bay. Often very popular during the day, the buoy-cluttered anchorage can be rolly in SE winds. The beach, with its coconut palms, makes it a pleasant spot.

Flamingo Bay

This bay isn't much used by visiting yachts. It's full of live-aboard boats and the docks of the hotel. Swell often makes it uncomfortable in SE winds. It's all right for a day stop.

Bays N of Gregerie Channel

Sugar Reef

Just W of Haulover Cut there's a quay here with a fuel dock. Given the depths of around 6m, it's used mainly by deeper draft boats.

Ashore There are few specialist services for yachts, but there are some shops and restaurants with terraces looking out over Gregerie Channel.

Crown Bay

The W part of this area used to be a submarine base but all that's left these days is the name of the area–Subbase. The NW shore has been reclaimed to make extensive quays for cruise liners.

Crown Bay Marina

Part of this large port area, Crown Bay Marina (VHF 16/11) is splendidly equipped with some 100 berths (water & electricity) as well as a fuel dock.

Crown Bay Marina

Ashore The big elegant marina has the advantage of being open to the breezes as well as being near to an area that isn't too built-up, although the centre of Charlotte Amalie is still some distance away. To make up for this, several yacht services are based here, or are close by. There's a dry-stack hangar for secure stowing of small craft. On the dockside long low buildings are home to a well-equipped chandlery, several specialist services including a dive centre, and various shops. The marina office is on the first floor. On the main quay there's a lively bar-restaurant that's the yachties rendezvous. Close to the road (Veterans' Drive) there are other shops and restaurants as well as a supermarket and a big shopping mall for provisioning.

Haulover Marine

W of Crown Bay Marina towards Regis Pt, Haulover Marine Yachting Centre has brought together several highly specialist professional outfits. There's a crane and a dry dock that can lift very large vessels. The hard-standing is small and crowded. The arrivals dock is just a single rather dilapidated pontoon.

Lindbergh Bay

This anchorage is E of the airport. The head of the bay has a sandy beach. It's a pretty enough spot but the orientation means there's a risk now and then of a big swell rolling in.

Caution When leaving to the W, go S of the green buoy to stay clear of the reefs and shoals round Red Pt.

Ashore On the edge of the beach there's quite a luxurious hotel-restaurant with its bungalows and swimming pool, but no other shops.

Brewer's Bay

The seaward extension of the airport runway has formed a protective barrier for the SE part of the bay and therefore a sheltered anchorage. Anchor a good way off the rip-rap of the airstrip

reclamation in 4–5m, sand. The beach is almost deserted and only the noisy landing of aircraft will remind you that civilisation is nearby.

Islands S of St Thomas

Buck Island

This islet has a very useful light if you're making into St Thomas at night. An excellent dive site, there is a calm weather anchorage in the island's lee. There's the wreck of a cement carrier heeled over in about 10m. Anchoring is forbidden, but in theory there are mooring buoys available.

Little Saba (Turtle Dove Cay)

There's a lovely beach and anchorage on the leeward side for very calm weather. Good snorkelling and diving on the surrounding reefs.

Caution On your approach keep a sharp eye out for the numerous reefs and particularly for Dry Rock.

West coast

Savana Island

The island has a light to help a night approach to St Thomas, even though the island is never visited by yachts. The shoreline is fringed with reef and the anchorage on the leeward side is little protected from swell.

Salt Cay, West Cay and Big Current Hole

This is the passage between the W tip of St Thomas and West Cay. Called Big Current Hole, it is for shoal-drafters only, and only then in fair weather and calm seas. The pass is narrow and the least depth under 3m. The current through the pass can exceed 2kts. Bar a fair weather anchorage in Sandy Bay, there's no reliable shelter.

North coast

Caution Many anchorages along this coast are only practicable in fair weather when the trades are not blowing too strongly and the NE swell is slight.

Stumpy Bay

There's a day anchorage in the E of this bay if the swell isn't too ENE. It's a wild and lonely spot and not much visited.

Santa Maria Bay

Often disturbed by swell, especially in winter, this is a fair-weather day anchorage. Anchor close to the coconut palm-fringed beach staying clear of the shoals.

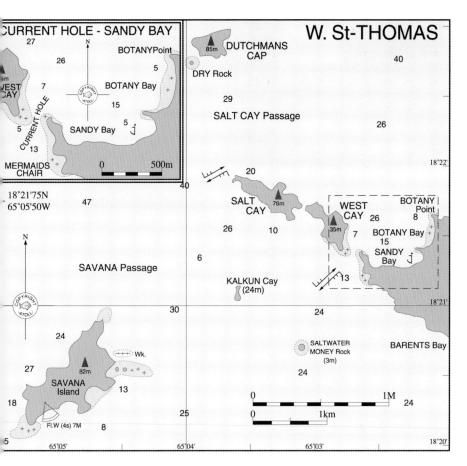

CURRENT HOLE - SANDY BAY

27

26

BOTANY Point

5

7

BOTANY Bay

EST CAY

15

SANDY Bay 5

13

MERMAIDS CHAIR

0   500m

18°21'75N
65°05'50W

47

N

SAVANA Passage

30

24

Wk.

27

82m

SAVANA Island 13

18

Fl.W (4s) 7M   8

25

5

65'05'

65'04'

W. St-THOMAS

85m DUTCHMANS CAP

40

DRY ROCK

29

SALT CAY Passage

26

20

SALT CAY 76m

WEST CAY 26

BOTANY Point

26   10

35m   7

BOTANY Bay
15

SANDY Bay

6

KALKUN Cay
(24m)

13

24

SALTWATER MONEY Rock
(3m)

BARENTS Bay

24

0   1M

0   1km

24

18°22'

18°21'

18°20'

65'03'

Outer and Inner Brass Islands

Outer Brass Island has no practicable anchorage. On the other hand it is possible to anchor in good weather off Inner Brass Island behind the small tongue of coral pushing out from the lee of the S point. Close to the beach are several bommies. Keep a fair way out and anchor in 3-4m. It's a deserted spot except at weekends.

Brass Channel/Hull Bay

To keep headed E be sure to give a clear berth to the reefs then either take the pass between Inner Brass I and Ruy Pt, or use Brass Channel. In good weather you can anchor W of Tropaco Pt close to Hull Bay beach.

Caution Between Inner Brass Island and Picara Pt there is an unmarked shoal, Ornen Rock, with less than 2m over it.

Magens Bay

Past Tropaco Pt you'll see this deeply indented bay opening up. Its E part ends in a magnificent beach – according to some – one of the finest in the Antilles. It's not overcrowded, but it is very touristy especially at the weekend.

Caution Be very careful of the shoal half way down the bay close to the SE shore.

In winter the anchorage can be made uncomfortable by swell.

Ashore On the fabulous beach there's a small snack-bar invaded regularly by

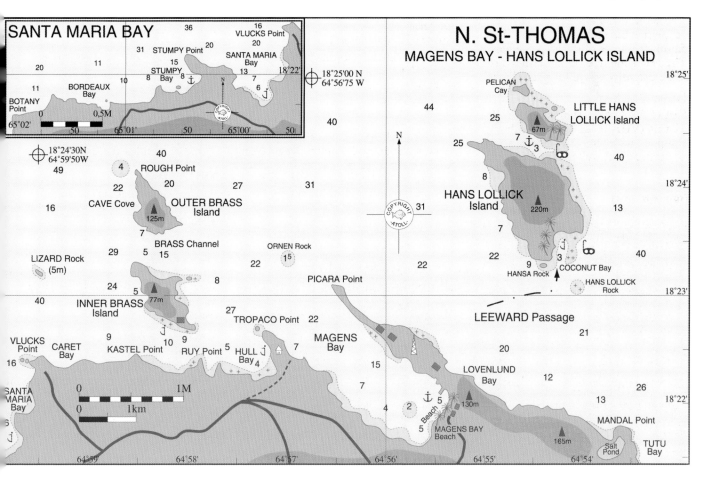

SANTA MARIA BAY

36

VLUCKS Point 16

31 STUMPY Point 20

SANTA MARIA Bay

20   11   15 STUMPY Bay   13   18°22'

BOTANY Point 11 BORDEAUX Bay 10 8 8 7

6

0   0,5M

65°02'   50   65'01'   50   65'00'   50

18°24'30N
64°59'50W   40

49   4   ROUGH Point

22   20   27   31

16 CAVE Cove OUTER BRASS Island

125m

7

BRASS Channel

ORNEN Rock

LIZARD Rock
(5m)   29   5 15   22   15

24   5   8

40 INNER BRASS Island 77m

VLUCKS Point   9

SANTA MARIA Bay CARET Bay KASTEL Point 10 RUY Point 5 HULL Bay 4

16

0   1M

0   1km

64'59'   64'58'   64'57'

PICARA Point

TROPACO Point 22

MAGENS Bay

7

15

4   2   5

Beach

5 MAGENS BAY Beach

64'56'

N. St-THOMAS
MAGENS BAY - HANS LOLLICK ISLAND

18°25'00 N
64°56'75 W

N

44

25

25

31

22

PELICAN Cay

LITTLE HANS LOLLICK Island

67m 7 3

HANS LOLLICK Island 220m

7

22   9   3

HANSA Rock COCONUT Bay

LEEWARD Passage

LOVENLUND Bay

130m

165m

18°25'

40

18°24'

13

40

HANS LOLLICK Rock   18°23'

21

20

12

26

13   18°22'

MANDAL Point

Salt Pond   TUTU Bay

64'55'   64'54'

Magens Bay

Anchorage between the two islands, Hans Lollick

streams of tourists from Charlotte Amalie.

Hans Lollick Island and Little Hans Lollick Island

These twin islands have two fair-weather anchorage possibilities. They are seldom visited.

- Hans Lollick SE Pt: tuck in behind the barrier reef, but only in good visibility and flat seas. The pass has about 4m, but from there on there are bommies coming up to less than 2m. This is for small yachts not drawing much water. In a big swell the anchorage is impracticable.

- between Hans Lollick & Little Hans Lollick: anchor behind the reef which almost completely links the two islands. Coming from the W make your approach with care and anchor near some bommies in 4–6m. The anchorage is also uncomfortable in a NE swell, but in good weather it gives access to the reef and two fine beaches on the windward coast. In the island's interior you can find the ruins of an old plantation.

Caution When leaving Hans Lollick headed E, keep a sharp eye out for unmarked, awash Hans Lollick Rock.

Useful Information for St Thomas

AIRLINE CONNECTIONS
International Airport: Cyril E King Airport
International long-haul flights direct flights to USA and Europe and other islands of the Lesser Antilles
Inter-island flights daily flights to neighbouring islands – seaplanes to St Croix & St John

FERRY CONNECTIONS
Daily ferries from St Thomas (Ch. Amalie and Red Hook) to St John (Caneel Bay Plantation and Cruz Bay) and the BVI

TELECOMMUNICATIONS
Calling from abroad: ☎ (1) 340 + 7 digits
Local call: 7 digits
Public call boxes: Caribbean Phone Card

TOURIST OFFICE
Charlotte Amalie, Emancipation Park, West India Company Dock
  ☎ 340 774 8784 *Fax* 340 777 9695
  Email info@usvi.net www.usvi.net
St Thomas Yacht Club, Cowpet Bay
  ☎ 340 775 6320 *Fax* 340 775 3600

GOLF
Mahogany Run Golf (designed by Tom Fazio)
  ☎ 800 2537103

FESTIVALS/FOLKLORE/YACHT RACES
Caribbean Ocean Triangle Tune-up Race: February
Rolex Cup Regatta (St Thomas Yacht Club): Easter
Carnival: end of April (see www.vicarnival.com)
Optimist Regatta: mid-June
Pigs in Winter (St Thomas Yacht Club): autumn
Women's Laser Regatta: November

PLACES TO SEE
Charlotte Amalie
Emancipation Park
Market Square
Fort Christian (1680): museum
Synagogue (Berecha V'Shalom 1883) – second oldest synagogue in USA
Frederik Lutheran Church (1820)
Government House (1865–1887, museum)
Government Hill (99 steps)
Paradise Point Tramway: Safehaven Marina
Elsewhere
Coral World Marine Park & Undersea Observatory: Coki Beach, Aquarium
Orchidarium – Crown Mountain

PUBLIC HOLIDAYS
New Year's Day (1 January), Three Kings Day (6 January), Martin Luther King Day (15 January), President's Day (19 February), Holy Thursday, Good Friday, Easter Monday, Transfer Day (31 March), Memorial Day (28 May), Organic Act Day (18 June), Emancipation Day (3 July), Independence Day (4 July), Hurricane Supplication Day (23 July), Labour Day (beginning September), Puerto Rico/Virgin Islands Friendship Day (mid-October), Hurricane Thanksgiving Day (mid-October), Liberty Day (1 November), Veterans' Day (11 November), Thanksgiving Day (mid-November), Christmas Day (25 December)

OFFICE HOURS
Government Offices, Mon–Thurs 0900–1700
Banks: Mon–Fri 0830–1500

ROAD TRANSPORT
Drive on the left
Local licence required
Hire car companies and taxis in main towns and at airport.

REGULATIONS
No underwater hunting, anchoring or taking of flora or fauna
For protected areas: (Buck Island, etc.) ask the authorities
Mooring buoy system: see St John

FORMALITIES
Arriving by air customs and immigration at the airport
Arriving by sea
  Charlotte Amalie, Wilmoth E Blyden Ferry Terminal, Veteran Drive.
  Hours: weekdays and Saturdays: 0800–1200, 1300–1700. Sundays and public holidays: 1000–1600 (variable) Overtime US$25 minimum charge.
  Waiting for clearance you must fly flag Q
  Short stay: Entry and exit clearance simultaneous
Fees and taxes Formalities free (you may have to pay for the forms)
  Cruising licence: Buying one of these (US$25) avoids having to complete formalities at every USVI island you visit.

Note A visa is obligatory, as is a passport, for everyone arriving in US territory unless they have a return ticket issued by an airline or shipping company. It follows that for yachtsmen other than Canadians a visa is obligatory. You must get one from a US Embassy or Consulate BEFORE you set out for the USVI.

Note The USVI authorities are extremely rigorous and vigilant with respect to both immigration control and suppression of all drug traffic (zero tolerance).

St Croix

Area 210sq km
Highest point Eagle Mount 350m
Population 55,000
Main town Christiansted
Language English
Currency US$
Politicalstatus Part of USVI
  Unincorporated Territory and a tax-free
  zone
Distances to nearby islands St Thomas
  35M, St-Martin 95M

Fort Christiansvaern, Christiansted

History

On 15 November 1494, before he turned N to find the other 'Virgins' two days later, Christopher Columbus discovered St Croix and baptised it Santa Cruz. From 1620 the Dutch and English tried to share the island by splitting it in two. But the two sides quickly came to blows, despite the regular attacks on both of them by the Spanish. The French Governor of St Christopher, the well-known Marquis de Poncy, enforced a peace in 1649 when he took possession of the island with a force of 200. It was a period scarred by incessant fighting and regular epidemics caused by the unhealthy climate. For some time before the French definitively ceded St Croix to the Danes in 1733 for 750,000 *livres l'or* (Gold Louis), the Knights Hospitaller of Malta had been helping the island recover. Once the land had been cleared and divided into estates, St Croix became more prosperous thanks to the high output from its plantations. It was the beginning of a prosperous era that peaked in 1800 and throughout which the majority of the colonists were not Danish but English, Dutch and even French.

Because of the massive use of slaves, the majority of the population was very soon African in origin. In 1848, following a violent slave uprising, the Danes abolished slavery. Yet despite that the ex-slave labour continued to be worked hard and to be underpaid. There was a new revolt in 1878 of which a black woman, Queen Mary, was the heroine.

Slowly St Croix's wealth declined whilst the island continued its semi-feudal way of life even after the USA bought it in 1917. Sugar cane growing didn't finally stop until 1966. Meanwhile, to counter the slow decline the authorities chose two strategies: the creation of a petro-chemicals storage and refinery zone on the S coast, and the development of tourism throughout the island.

Where the second of these was concerned St Croix had many advantages. As a complement to its fine, 18th century Danish architecture (the remains of its wealthy past) golf courses were created on the rolling slopes of the island. Luxury developments were built along the beaches and in the bosoms of old plantations. And a large airport allowed Americans easily to reach their exotic little island. Events, however, rather slowed this rush to growth. Suddenly, in the 1970s, the peaceable American tourists were put to flight by a climate of insecurity generated by outbreaks of criminal violence. And no sooner had calm been restored than in a succession of years terrible hurricanes struck the island, half wrecking its economy and infrastructure. Each time, St Croix bandaged its wounds and tried to re-launch the tourist industry necessary to its economic survival.

Tourism

Where to stay and what to see

At some distance from St Thomas and St John, St Croix (the largest of the three) lives rather to one side of the rest of the USVI. Some tourists, especially the sailors, more or less ignore it. However, those looking for attractions other than coconut palm lined beaches will like this different and surprising island for its singular character. If, looked at from afar, its rolling green hills seem entirely clothed with trees, one soon sees that in fact only the NE is forested. The remainder comprises grassy, relatively dry plateaux that are what's left of the old plantations. Grid pattern roads, some of them expressways, criss-cross the whole island, so you can visit everything quickly and easily. In fact, with the exception of a few specific spots, touring the island by land is a lot easier than by sea.

Christiansted

Sheltered behind its coral barrier, St Croix's main town, with its old Danish houses, seems to have emerged untouched from the 18th century. Its grid-pattern streets are line-ups of pastel coloured façades and arcades in which you'll find elegant shops and restaurants. Behind the crenellations of

Fort Christiansvaern (built 1749) batteries of cannon still pretend to play a part. From high in the battlements, within which there is a small museum, you get the most marvellous view over the town and the bay. Other buildings on the must-see list are: at the W end of the seafront, the Old Danish Customs House, which was used until the 19th century to check imported goods; and Government House in King Street, the old governor's residence dating from 1830.

And there are lots of other picturesque old buildings you'll come across by chance in the small streets, streets which still have their old Danish names as well as today's English versions. The other point of interest in the town is The Wharf where the day-charter boats are based. Every day they take tourists to visit Buck Island, an underwater reserve that has been made into a national monument.

Around the island

Queen Mary Highway (or Centerline Road) runs to the small town of Frederiksted in the island's far west. All along this arrow-straight road you'll see from time to time, forgotten in the middle of an abandoned plantation, a charming old house. Some have been restored, like Whim Great House with its charming little museum and pretty windmill. Close to the Botanical Gardens Mahogany Road runs off into the fine tropical forest which covers the NE part of the island. But St Croix has a second, industrial face on its S coast. By the side of an indigo sea, the Hess Oil Company (the world's third largest) and an aluminium smelter have sullied the countryside with their metallic structures and enormous storage tanks. Out in the offing vast tankers wait to offload their crude oil. You're reminded more of Detroit than a tropic island.

Frederiksted

Thanks to its huge jetty pushing out into deep water, St Croix's second town is accessible to cruise liners. Rebuilt in 1878 after a fire, the small town has kept all the charm of the Danish period

St CROIX

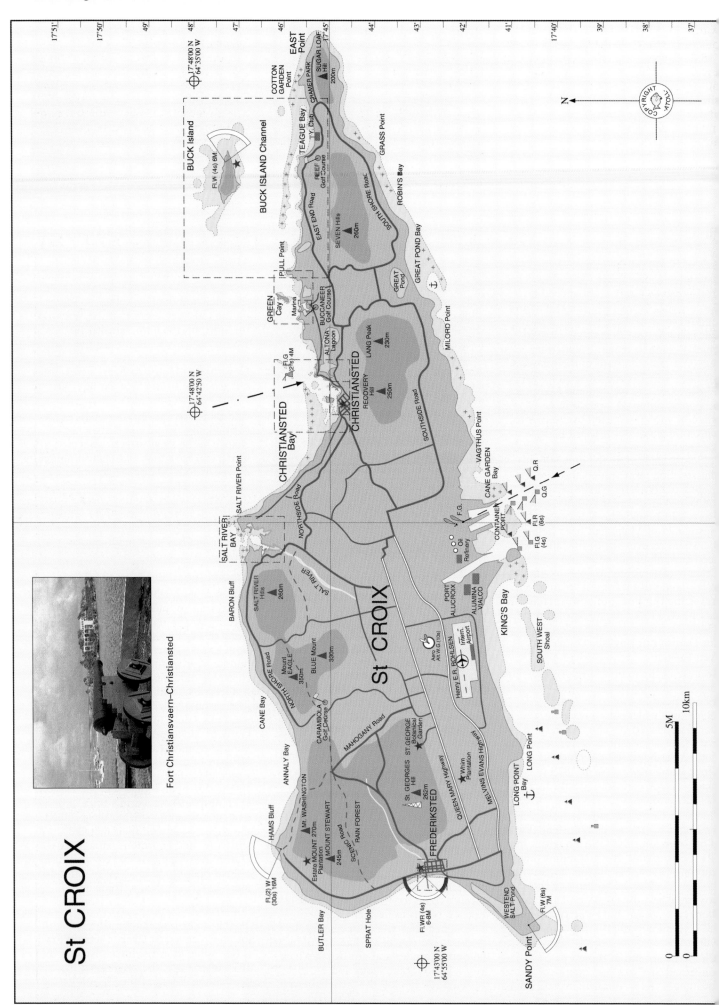

Fort Christiansvaern–Christiansted

St CROIX

BUCK Island

FI.W (4s) 6M

BUCK ISLAND Channel

EAST Point

COTTON GARDEN Point

SUGAR LOAF Hill 200m

CRAMER PARK

TEAGUE Bay

Y. Club

REEF Golf Course

GRASS Point

ROBIN'S Bay

EAST END Road

SEVEN Hills 260m

SOUTH SHORE Road

GREAT POND Bay

GREAT Pond

GREEN Cay

PULL Point

Marina

BUCCANEER Golf Course

ALTONA Lagoon

FI.G (2+s) 4M

CHRISTIANSTED Bay

CHRISTIANSTED

LANG Peak 230m

RECOVERY Hill 250m

MILORD Point

SALT RIVER Point

SOUTHSIDE Road

NORTHSIDE Road

VAGTHUS Point

17°48'00 N 64°42'50 W

SALT RIVER BAY

CANE GARDEN Bay

Q.R

Q.G

F.G.

Oil Refinery

CONTAINER PORT

FI.R (6s)

FI.G (4s)

BARON Bluff

SALT RIVER Hills 280m

SALT RIVER

PORT ALUCROIX

ALUMINA VIALCO

KING'S Bay

SOUTH WEST Shoal

CANE Bay

NORTH HILL Road

Mount EAGLE 350m

BLUE Mount 330m

CARAMBOLA Golf Course

MAHOGANY Road

Aero Alt.W.G.(10s)

Harry E.R. ROHLSEN Intern. Airport

ANNALY Bay

St. GEORGES Hill

ST. GEORGE Botanical Garden

QUEEN MARY Highway

Whim Plantation

MELVINS EVANS Highway

LONG POINT Bay

LONG Point

HAMS Bluff

Mt. WASHINGTON

MOUNT STEWART 245m

RAIN FOREST

SCENIC Road

Estate MOUNT 270m Plantation

FREDERIKSTED

LONG Point

BUTLER Bay

FI (2) W (30s) 16M

SPRAT Hole

FI.WR (4s) 6-8M

WESTEND SALT Pond

FI.W (6s) 7M

SANDY Point

17°43'00 N 64°55'00 W

5M

0   10km

N

with its old brick houses. The main buildings to see are the Customs House (18th century), Victoria House and Fort Frederik (1760). Between two shiploads of tourists, the town sleeps. You'll find shops existing to serve the tourist trade and charming restaurants tucked away in little painted houses or beneath the arcades of old residences.

Pilotage

Coast and anchorages

Cruising yachtsmen visiting the Virgins often disdain visiting St Croix both because of the 70M there-and-back detour involved and because the island doesn't have much of a reputation for good, easily accessible anchorages. All the same, the coast and especially all the charms of the interior certainly make the effort worthwhile for those who have

the time. Coming from St John or St Thomas you need to allow for the variable westerly current, usually about 0·5kt. It's hard to get your bearings on the coast, not least because Buck Island merges with it. Given the numerous shoals around St Croix, you must make your approach in good visibility. Although there is lit buoyage, avoid arriving in the dark.

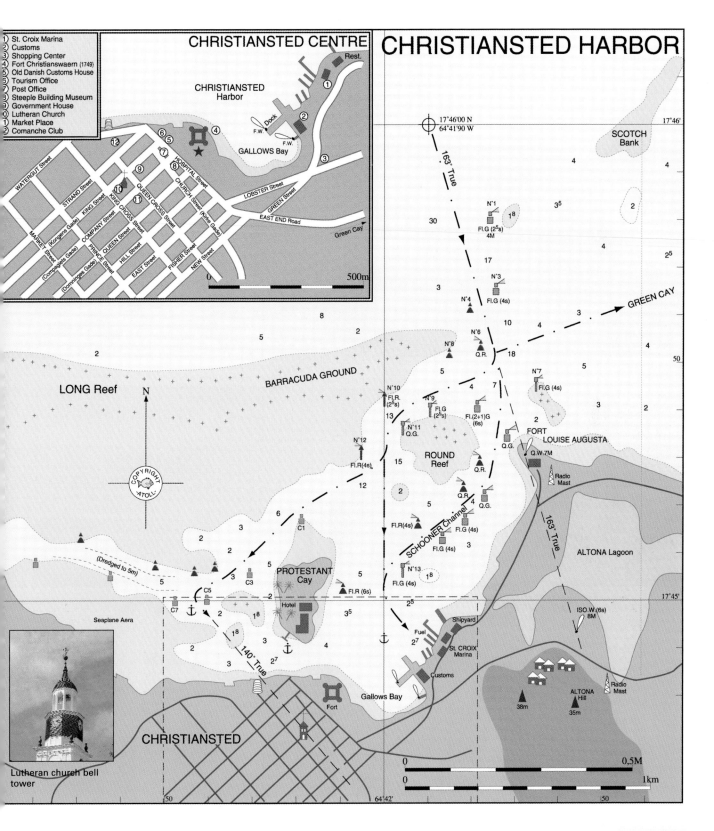

North coast

Christiansted Harbor

To get to the port the vital thing is to identify buoy No.1 and to stay clear of Scotch Bank to the E and then Barracuda Reef in the W. The approach line is on 163°T on the leading marks on Fort Louise Augusta peninsula. The radio mast on the hill is visible from a fair distance off. You can also use the conspicuous estate of houses on the flanks of Altona Hill behind for orientation. Once you've reached buoy No.6 you have two possible channels:

- to the S via Schooner Channel which leads directly to St Croix Marina
- to the SW towards Protestant Cay.

In each case follow the buoyed channels with care because some of the buoys can from time to time go missing.

Schooner Channel

This passage between Round Reef and the main island is narrow, but well marked by buoys, some lit. The channel has been dredged to around 5m.

St Croix Marina

Off the pontoons the bottom comes up here and there to less than 3m. There are about 40 berths with water and electricity and a fuel dock.

Ashore The office (VHF 16) is opposite the dock in a building combining a bar-restaurant and a small chandlery. The workshops and boatyard are to the left as you look inland. They've got good haul-out facilities with a railway slip (300 tonnes) and a travel lift (60 tonnes) as well as specialist services. St Croix Marine is the only specialist yacht repair and maintenance business in the island. One of its managers, Martin Oliver (truly polyglot) is happy to help visiting yachtsmen out and tell them about the island.

Customs and immigration are 100m S of the dock on the shore of the small basin called Gallows Bay. On the other side of the road from them there's the Chandlers Wharf shopping centre with various shops and restaurants.

Protestant Cay

Once you're through the buoyed channel between Barracuda Ground and Round Reef, you've two possible routes:

- to the S to reach the E side of Protestant Cay opposite Fort Christiansvaern, though the anchorage is a bit exposed. This is also the alternative way of getting to St Croix Marina.

Above Long Reef, Christiansted from S
Below Old Danish Customs House
Centre right Old windmill
Far right St Croix Marina
Bottom left Government House
Bottom right Old Scale House

op left Protestant Cay from E
op right Anchorage off Protestant Cay
bove Green Cay, Buck Island and Green Cay
Marina from W

- to the SW to keep going in the channel passing N of Protestant Cay. Once past the No.C5 port hand buoy alter SE on 140°T. On this heading you'll have a conspicuous clocktower in the town right ahead.

Caution Depths come up quickly to less than 2m all round you.

Only shoal drafters can keep going towards the Wharf where you can see the tower of an old windmill. The anchorage in the lee of Protestant Cay is always very crowded with moorings and local boats because it's the only sheltered, open anchorage in the port area. It's also bouncy because of boats going backwards and forwards and noisy from seaplanes landing and taking off. To get ashore, leave your tender in the small basin intended for them at The Wharf, at the base of the tower of the old windmill.

Ashore There are all the duty-free shops as well as the facilities of a medium sized town for provisioning. In the evenings the old part of town around The Wharf is full of life with bars and restaurants humming with crew from yachts and local people. Some of the establishments are delightfully placed in restored old buildings. A stop in Christiansted Harbor is also a good opportunity to make a tour of the island by car.

Green Cay Marina

Coming from Christiansted Harbor you've got two ways of getting to this marina:

- N of Scotch Bank

Once past buoy No. 1, head N for 1M before altering E towards Buck Island for 1·5M. From that point alter S towards the W side of Green Cay islet.

- through the pass S of Scotch Bank

This route is shorter but trickier. Once past the shoal ground off Fort Louise Augusta Pt, alter towards Green Island keeping clear of a few shoals with less than 2m over them S of Scotch Bank.

Green Cay Marina is S of Green Cay islet. You enter through a channel dredged to 3m, but allow for silting to have reduced this in places to 2·7m. It

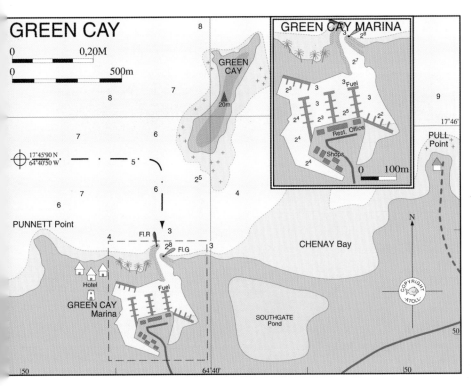

Geen Cay Marina

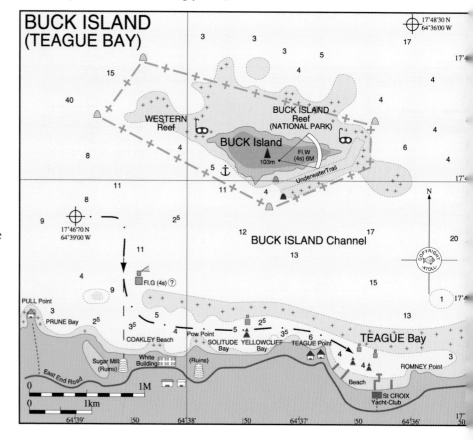

Top left Old sugar mill near Coakley Beach
Top centre Buck Island from W
Above Pontoons of the St Croix Yacht Club, Teague Bay
Right Teague Bay & East Pt from W

makes sense to call the office (VHF 16) to know if they have space and whether the fuel dock is occupied. Once inside there are 3 pontoons with about 150 berths with water and electricity, and a fuel dock.

Ashore Opposite the pontoons on the wide spaces of the waterfront you'll find the marina office and a restaurant, as well as some shops, though nothing specific for boats, in a single building. The marina is very well sheltered but mostly occupied by local residents.

Teague Bay

The St Croix Yacht Club, home to numerous local boats, is protected in this haven E of St Croix behind a long barrier reef. To get into it you must exercise care in good visibility, especially on your first visit.

Approach Once past Green Cay hold to approx. 080°T for about 1M until past Pull Pt. You'll see broad on the starboard bow on the shore the old tower of a one-time sugar mill. You take the pass by lining this mark up on 180°T, though naturally good visibility is essential. There's a small, almost submerged sandy cay to look for, which you leave to starboard. Once through the pass alter to port and head roughly E inside the barrier reef in depths of 2·5–3m.

Caution There are several bommies and reef patches S of the barrier reef pushing into the channel. Keep midway between the shore and the barrier and head carefully towards Teague Pt.

There are buoys marking the pass once you're level with Yellow Cliff Bay and again for the access towards the pontoons of the yacht club in Teague Bay. Don't go beyond Teague Bay because the area off Romney Pt is full of shoals. Close to the yacht club dock the bottom comes up to 2m. There are about 30 berths with water and electricity but no fuel dock.

Ashore are the offices of the Yacht Club and a welcoming restaurant and bar on a large terrace. However, there are no other shops or services. Visiting yachts,

though rare, are always made welcome by club members.

Buck Island

The island and the reefs around it have been made into a National Monument. Naturally it's pretty popular, but the beauty of the underwater world still makes a visit worth it. Yellow buoys mark the park limits. The usual anchorage is in the lee of the W of the island off the beach. Shoal drafters (<1·5m) can get into the mooring zone, with moorings near the park entrance.

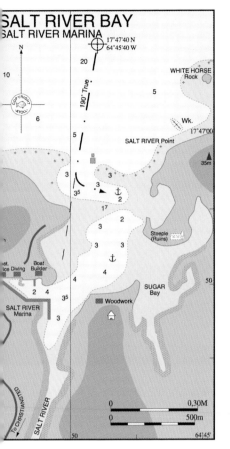

SALT RIVER BAY
SALT RIVER MARINA

Above right Salt River from S
Right Salt River Marina

The entrance itself is marked by two buoys. For others, the visit to the park proper must be made by tender. There's an underwater trail marked with arrows in the N of the lagoon. The coral is splendid and the fish remarkably fearless. You can admire but, of course, not touch.

Buck Island has a light helpful for a night approach to St Croix's coasts. *Caution* There's no light showing the island's E extremity.

Salt River

W of Christiansted, Salt River claims to have been where Columbus landed. The reefs almost closing this haven make both approach and entry difficult. You must have good visibility and a pretty calm sea. Once you've identified Salt River Point and the swell breaking on White Horse Reef, leave a green buoy to port whilst lining up the point on the W of the entrance of Salt River Bay on 190°T. These few marks should enable you to find the narrow channel which swings E between the shoals and the coral barrier with, ahead as a sort of leading mark, a sort of belfry on an old ruin. Yachts drawing much water should stop here because a sill with only 1.8m over it blocks the entry to the inner basin. Once over the sill depths return to around 4.5m.

To the W of the inner basin, dug out of the mangroves, Salt River Marina (VHF 16) has some 30 berths on docks with 1·8–2·5m alongside. There's no fuel dock, but you can probably get some delivered.

Ashore The surroundings are deep countryside and the ambience peaceful, but the services and installations have their limits. The office is above a bar-restaurant run by the same management. There's an active dive centre and a small chandlery next door. On the open space a bit further W there's a builder and repairer of catamarans. He's got a 10-tonne crane for shifting his boats into and out of the water.

Below left Cruise ship pier, Frederiksted
Below right Fort Frederik

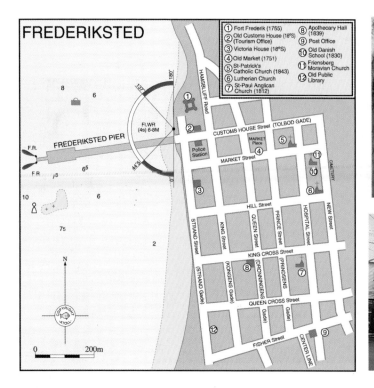

FREDERIKSTED

① Fort Frederik (1755)
② Old Customs House (18°S) (Tourism Office)
③ Victoria House (18°S)
④ Old Market (1751)
⑤ St-Patrick's Catholic Church (1843)
⑥ Lutheran Church
⑦ St-Paul Anglican Church (1812)
⑧ Apothecary Hall (1839)
⑨ Post Office
⑩ Old Danish School (1830)
⑪ Friensborg Moravian Church
⑫ Old Public Library

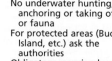

Top left and above Stone houses with arcades (Frederiksted)

Top right Whim Plantation mill

West coast

Frederiksted Harbor

From Christiansted it's an 18M down wind romp to Frederiksted, though you do have to make it back again! The normal anchorage is S of the big cruise liner jetty or, if there's room, you can moor to the jetty. The anchorage is completely open westwards and can be subject to swell.

Caution Watch out for the reefs between the jetty and the beach S of it.

Ashore There are no services for yachts. On the other hand, in the old buildings of the town there are several restaurants and, for general shopping and provisioning, a shopping mall and several other shops.

South coast

Great Pond Bay

For those who love solitude, St Croix Yacht Club members have told me of an excellent anchorage in the S of Great Pond Bay. It's not much visited and well protected by a coral barrier. You need good visibility to get into it and it's essential you know exactly where you are along the coast. Take the pass to the NE, giving a good berth to the reef to starboard. Once inside depths are 5·6m but quickly come up to less than 2m. The coral here is still well-preserved because it's less visited than on the N coast. All the same, from Buck Island a visit here requires coming and going round East Pt against the wind and the current for some 20 miles there and back!!

Useful Information for St Croix

AIRLINE CONNECTIONS
International airport: Henry E. Rohlsen Airport
International long-haul direct flights to N America
Inter-island daily flights to neighbouring islands and seaplanes to St John & St Thomas

TELECOMMUNICATIONS
Calling from abroad: ☎ (1) 340 + 7 digits
Local call: 7 digits
Public call boxes: Caribbean Phone Card

TOURIST OFFICE/ ASSOCIATIONS
Tourist Office, Christiansted, ☎ 340 773 0495
Fax 340 773 5074
Email caribquee@aol.com
Hotel & Tourism Association, Gallows Bay
☎ 340 773 7117
Fax 340 773 5883
St Croix Yacht Club: Teague Bay
☎ 340 773 9531
Fax 340 778 8350
Email stcroixyc@vitelcom.net

GOLF COURSES
Carambola Golf Club: course designed by Robert Trent Jones
The Buccaneer
The Reef (Teague Bay, 9 hole)

FESTIVALS/FOLKLORE
St Croix Festival: early December through 6th January
Carnival: end of December/beginning January
St Patrick's Day: 17th March
Christiansted's Jump-Up: Four times a year
Frederiksted: Harbour Night: Wednesdays every other week

PLACES TO SEE
Christiansted
Fort Christiansted (1749: museum
Steeple Building (1753): museum
Old Customs House (National Park Office)
Scale House (Visitors' Bureau)
Government House (1830)
Kingshill Lutheran Church (1753)
Frederiksted
Fort Frederik (1755)
Elsewhere
St George Botanical Garden
Whim Plantation Museum (18th century): restored plantation (on Route 70)
Cruzan Rum Distillery
St Croix Leap: rain forest road and wood carvers
Buck Island: buoyed Underwater Trail
Point Udall: viewpoint and the furthest point E in the USA

ROAD TRANSPORT
Drive on the left
Local licence required
Hire car companies and taxis in main towns and at the airport

REGULATIONS
No underwater hunting, anchoring or taking of flora or fauna
For protected areas (Buck Island, etc.) ask the authorities
Obligatory mooring buoy system: see St John

FORMALITIES
Arriving by air customs and immigration at the airport
Arriving by sea
Christiansted: Gallows Bay Dockyard close to St Croix Marina
Hours: weekdays 0800–1200, 1300–1700
No overtime
Note visas obligatory for all foreign yachtsmen (except Canadians)
See also Useful Information for St Thomas

Sailing in the Lesser Antilles

Top left Topsail schooner
Top right Traditional local sloops
Centre left Anchorage in Grenada
Centre right Anchorage at Marigot, St Lucia
Bottom left Marina du Marin, Le Marin, Martinique
Bottom right Captain Oliver's Marina, St-Martin

Table of Distances
(in nautical miles)

Distance between Islands or their main anchorages

See also: General Map, Routes & waypoints (opposite)

	WINDWARD ISLANDS							LEEWARD ISLANDS														VIRGIN ISLANDS				
	Martinique - Fort-de-France	St-Lucia - Castries	St-Vincent - Kingstown	Bequia	Union Island	Carriacou - Hillsborough	Grenada - St-George's	Dominica - Roseau	Dominica - Portsmouth	Les Saintes	Guadeloupe - Pointe-à-Pitre	Guadeloupe - Deshaies	Montserrat	Antigua - English Harbour	Barbuda	St-Kitts - Basseterre	Saba	St-Barth - Gustavia	St-Maarten - Philipsburg	St-Martin - Marigot	Anguilla - Road Bay	Virgin Gorda - Virgin Gorda Hb.	Tortola - Road Harbour	St-John - Cruz Bay	St-Thomas - St-Thomas Hb.	St-croix - Christiansted
Martinique - Fort-de-France		35	93	100	125	135	160	50	67	90	110	120	150	163	200	190	230	230	240	250	250	310	-	-	-	290
St-Lucia - Castries	35		53	62	85	102	125	-	-	125	150	150	-	200	-	-	-	-	-	-	-	-	-	-	-	-
St-Vincent - Kingstown	93	53		7	32	49	72	-	-	-	200	200	-	250	-	-	-	-	-	-	-	-	-	-	-	-
Bequia	100	62	7		25	35	65	-	-	180	214	215	-	260	-	-	-	-	-	-	-	-	-	-	-	-
Union Island	125	85	32	25		10	40	-	-	205	230	-	-	285	-	-	-	-	-	-	-	-	-	-	-	-
Carriacou - Hillsborough	135	102	49	35	10		30	-	-	-	-	-	-	295	-	-	-	-	-	-	-	-	-	-	-	-
Grenada - St-George's	160	125	72	65	40	30		200	-	235	260	260	-	305	-	-	345	-	-	-	380	420	-	-	410	385
Dominica - Roseau	50	-	-	-	-	-	200		17	37	60	67	97	109	-	144	-	-	-	-	-	-	-	-	-	-
Dominica - Portsmouth	67	-	-	-	-	-	-	17		20	42	50	80	92	-	127	-	-	-	-	-	245	-	-	-	232
Les Saintes	90	125	-	180	205	-	235	37	20		24	30	65	72	-	110	142	150	155	165	175	225	-	-	-	220
Guadeloupe - Pointe-à-Pitre	110	150	200	214	230	-	260	60	42	24		54	90	96	-	125	166	174	179	189	200	257	-	-	-	245
Guadeloupe - Deshaies	120	150	200	215	-	-	260	67	50	30	54		34	42	80	82	116	112	126	137	145	210	-	-	-	190
Montserrat	150	-	-	-	-	-	-	97	80	65	90	34		38	-	48	83	82	95	105	-	-	-	-	-	-
Antigua - English Harbour	163	200	250	260	285	295	305	109	92	72	96	42	38		42	60	85	83	95	100	120	183	-	-	205	180
Barbuda	200	-	-	-	-	-	-	-	-	-	-	80	-	42		60	80	65	80	90	100	165	-	-	-	165
St-Kitts - Basseterre	190	-	-	-	-	-	-	144	127	110	125	82	48	60	60		36	45	52	60	70	125	-	-	147	120
Saba	230	-	-	-	-	-	345	-	-	142	166	116	83	85	80	36		30	26	30	38	88	94	100	108	88
St-Barth - Gustavia	230	-	-	-	-	-	-	-	-	150	174	112	82	83	65	45	30		15	26	35	100	110	-	-	110
St-Maarten - Philipsburg	240	-	-	-	-	-	-	-	-	155	179	126	95	95	80	52	26	15		11	20	90	-	-	-	97
St-Martin - Marigot	250	-	-	-	-	-	-	-	-	165	189	137	105	100	90	60	30	26	11		12	82	-	-	-	95
Anguilla - Road Bay	250	-	-	-	-	-	380	-	-	175	200	145	-	120	100	70	38	35	20	12		80	-	-	111	97
Virgin Gorda - Virgin Gorda Hb.	310	-	-	-	-	-	420	-	245	225	257	210	-	183	165	125	88	100	90	82	80		13	25	35	45
Tortola - Road Harbour	-	-	-	-	-	-	-	-	-	-	-	-	-	-	-	-	94	110	-	-	-	13		14	22	40
St-John - Cruz Bay	-	-	-	-	-	-	-	-	-	-	-	-	-	-	-	-	100	-	-	-	-	25	14		13	35
St-Thomas - St-Thomas Hb.	-	-	-	-	-	-	410	-	-	-	-	-	-	205	-	147	108	-	-	-	111	35	22	13		37
St-croix - Christiansted	290	-	-	-	-	-	385	-	232	220	245	190	-	180	165	120	88	110	97	95	97	45	40	35	37	

Marinas, water, fuel, services, airports

(1) Unreliable or limited
(2) Subject to availability

Note
For all information and other relevant detail, see island entries and the services directory

	Barbados	Grenada	Carriacou	Petite Martinique PsV	Union/Palm Island	Bequia	St Vincent	St Lucia	Martinique	Dominica	Guadeloupe	Antigua	St-Kitts/Nevis	St-Barth	St-Martin/St Maarten	Anguilla	Tortola/Virgin Gorda	St-John	St Thomas	St-Croix
Marina	●(1)	●			●		●	●	●		●	●	●	●	●		●		●	●
Water	●	●	●(1)	●	●	●	●	●	●	●(2)	●	●	●	●	●	●	●	●(2)	●	●
Fuel	●	●		●	●(2)	●	●	●	●	●(2)	●	●	●	●	●	●	●	●(2)	●	●
Boatyard	●	●	●			●	●	●	●		●	●		●	●(1)		●	●(1)	●	●
Electrics and electronics	●(1)	●	●(1)		●(1)	●	●(1)	●	●		●	●	●	●	●		●	●	●	●
Mechanic	●	●	●(1)	●(1)	●(1)	●	●	●	●	●	●	●	●(1)	●	●	●(1)	●	●(1)	●	●
Sailmaker	●	●			●(1)		●	●	●		●	●	●	●	●		●	●	●	●
Chandlery	●	●	●	●			●(1)	●	●		●	●	●	●	●		●(1)	●	●	●
Dive bottle air	●	●	●		●	●	●	●	●	●	●	●	●	●	●	●	●	●	●	●
International airport	●	●						●	●		●		●(1)		●			●(1)	●	●
Inter-island flights	●	●	●		●	●	●	●	●	●	●	●	●	●	●	●	●	●	●	●

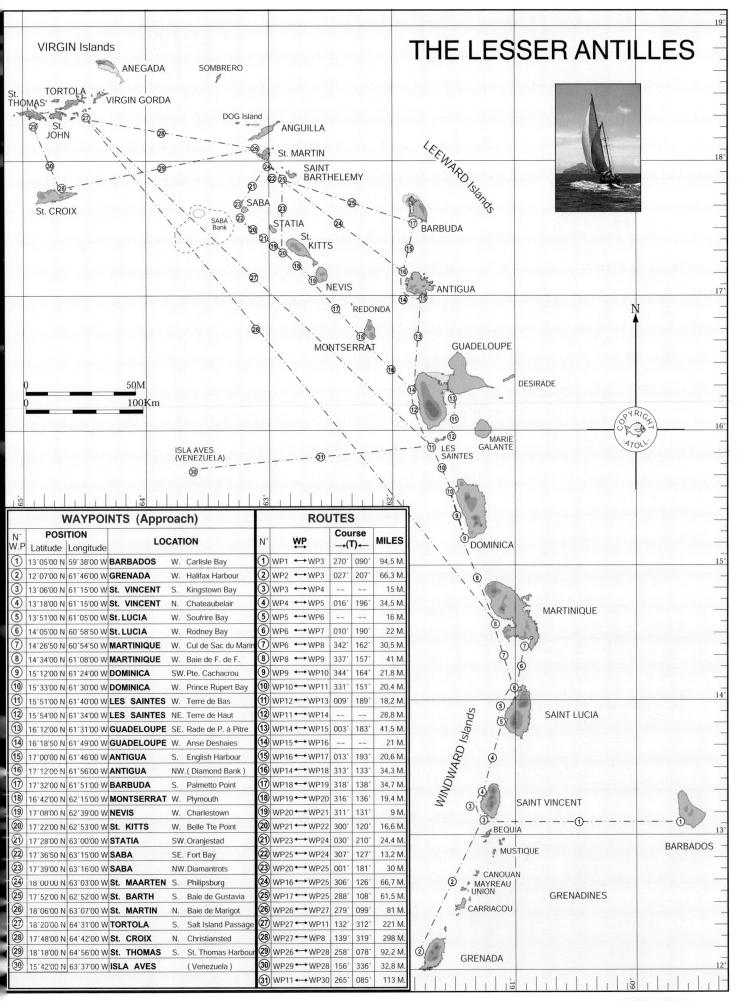

THE LESSER ANTILLES

VIRGIN Islands

ANEGADA

SOMBRERO

St. THOMAS

TORTOLA

VIRGIN GORDA

St. JOHN

DOG Island

ANGUILLA

St. MARTIN

St. CROIX

SAINT BARTHELEMY

SABA Bank

SABA

STATIA

St. KITTS

NEVIS

REDONDA

MONTSERRAT

BARBUDA

ANTIGUA

LEEWARD Islands

GUADELOUPE

DESIRADE

MARIE GALANTE

LES SAINTES

DOMINICA

ISLA AVES (VENEZUELA)

0 — 50M

0 — 100Km

N

COPYRIGHT ATOLL

MARTINIQUE

SAINT LUCIA

WINDWARD Islands

SAINT VINCENT

BEQUIA

MUSTIQUE

CANOUAN
MAYREAU
UNION

CARRIACOU

GRENADINES

BARBADOS

GRENADA

WAYPOINTS (Approach)				
N° W.P	**POSITION**		**LOCATION**	
	Latitude	Longitude		
①	13°05'00 N	59°38'00 W	**BARBADOS**	W. Carlisle Bay
②	12°07'00 N	61°46'00 W	**GRENADA**	W. Halifax Harbour
③	13°06'00 N	61°15'00 W	**St. VINCENT**	S. Kingstown Bay
④	13°18'00 N	61°15'00 W	**St. VINCENT**	N. Chateaubelair
⑤	13°51'00 N	61°05'00 W	**St. LUCIA**	W. Soufrire Bay
⑥	14°05'00 N	60°58'50 W	**St. LUCIA**	W. Rodney Bay
⑦	14°26'50 N	60°54'50 W	**MARTINIQUE**	W. Cul de Sac du Marin
⑧	14°34'00 N	61°08'00 W	**MARTINIQUE**	W. Baie de F. de F.
⑨	15°12'00 N	61°24'00 W	**DOMINICA**	SW.Pte. Cachacrou
⑩	15°33'00 N	61°30'00 W	**DOMINICA**	W. Prince Rupert Bay
⑪	15°51'00 N	61°40'00 W	**LES SAINTES**	W. Terre de Bas
⑫	15°54'00 N	61°34'00 W	**LES SAINTES**	NE. Terre de Haut
⑬	16°12'00 N	61°31'00 W	**GUADELOUPE**	SE. Rade de P. à Pitre
⑭	16°18'50 N	61°49'00 W	**GUADELOUPE**	W. Anse Deshaies
⑮	17°00'00 N	61°46'00 W	**ANTIGUA**	S. English Harbour
⑯	17°12'00 N	61°56'00 W	**ANTIGUA**	NW.(Diamond Bank)
⑰	17°32'00 N	61°51'00 W	**BARBUDA**	S. Palmetto Point
⑱	16°42'00 N	62°15'00 W	**MONTSERRAT**	W. Plymouth
⑲	17°08'00 N	62°39'00 W	**NEVIS**	W. Charlestown
⑳	17°22'00 N	62°53'00 W	**St. KITTS**	W. Belle Tte Point
㉑	17°28'00 N	63°00'00 W	**STATIA**	SW.Oranjestad
㉒	17°36'50 N	63°15'00 W	**SABA**	SE. Fort Bay
㉓	17°39'00 N	63°16'00 W	**SABA**	NW.Diamantrots
㉔	18°00'00 N	63°03'00 W	**St. MAARTEN**	S. Philipsburg
㉕	17°52'00 N	62°52'00 W	**St. BARTH**	S. Baie de Gustavia
㉖	18°06'00 N	63°07'00 W	**St. MARTIN**	N. Baie de Marigot
㉗	18°20'00 N	64°31'00 W	**TORTOLA**	S. Salt Island Passage
㉘	17°48'00 N	64°42'00 W	**St. CROIX**	N. Christiansted
㉙	18°18'00 N	64°56'00 W	**St. THOMAS**	S. St. Thomas Harbour
㉚	15°42'00 N	63°37'00 W	**ISLA AVES**	(Venezuela)

ROUTES				
N°	**WP**	**Course →(T)←**		**MILES**
①	WP1 ⟷ WP3	270°	090°	94,5 M.
②	WP2 ⟷ WP3	027°	207°	66,3 M.
③	WP3 ⟷ WP4	~~	~~	15 M.
④	WP4 ⟷ WP5	016°	196°	34,5 M.
⑤	WP5 ⟷ WP6	~~	~~	16 M.
⑥	WP6 ⟷ WP7	010°	190°	22 M.
⑦	WP6 ⟷ WP8	342°	162°	30,5 M.
⑧	WP8 ⟷ WP9	337°	157°	41 M.
⑨	WP9 ⟷ WP10	344°	164°	21,8 M.
⑩	WP10 ⟷ WP11	331°	151°	20,4 M.
⑪	WP12 ⟷ WP13	009°	189°	18,2 M.
⑫	WP11 ⟷ WP14	~~	~~	28,8 M.
⑬	WP14 ⟷ WP15	003°	183°	41,5 M.
⑭	WP15 ⟷ WP16	~~	~~	21 M.
⑮	WP16 ⟷ WP17	013°	193°	20,6 M.
⑯	WP14 ⟷ WP18	313°	133°	34,3 M.
⑰	WP18 ⟷ WP19	318°	138°	34,7 M.
⑱	WP19 ⟷ WP20	316°	136°	19,4 M.
⑲	WP20 ⟷ WP21	311°	131°	9 M.
⑳	WP21 ⟷ WP22	300°	120°	16,6 M.
㉑	WP23 ⟷ WP24	030°	210°	24,4 M.
㉒	WP25 ⟷ WP24	307°	127°	13,2 M.
㉓	WP20 ⟷ WP25	001°	181°	30 M.
㉔	WP16 ⟷ WP25	306°	126°	66,7 M.
㉕	WP17 ⟷ WP25	288°	108°	61,5 M.
㉖	WP26 ⟷ WP27	279°	099°	81 M.
㉗	WP27 ⟷ WP11	132°	312°	221 M.
㉘	WP27 ⟷ WP8	139°	319°	298 M.
㉙	WP26 ⟷ WP28	258°	078°	92,2 M.
㉚	WP29 ⟷ WP28	156°	336°	32,8 M.
㉛	WP11 ⟷ WP30	265°	085°	113 M.

The reputation of the Lesser Antilles as a 'sailing paradise' is no mere abstraction but the product of favourable conditions: climate, a wind regular in strength and direction and the short distances between islands. For all that, even these pluses remain subject to luck and all the rest of sailing's pitfalls. It's worth getting to know what these are so you can look out for and avoid them.

Wind, weather and sea

(See also the sections on Climate and Cyclones in the General Introduction)

Wind Regime

The Lesser Antilles are in the trade wind belt of generally regular winds, which seldom blow above force 6 except in squalls. The trades blow from the E quadrant, angling, depending on the season, anywhere from NE to SE. They are most regular and blow most freshly from December to May (also the season of least rain). From June to November they are more irregular and can even fall away to a calm. In the summer light to moderate breezes from the W quadrant can occasionally blow on what is normally the leeward (i.e. W) coast of the islands.

The regularity and steady direction of the winds, the almost total absence of gales save beneath the larger squalls or in the case of a tropical depression or cyclone (see introduction section on Cyclones), greatly simplifies one's sailing. This is most particularly the case between Grenada and Antigua where the islands lie across the line of the trades. On the other hand, headed W from Antigua or Guadeloupe to the Virgins you'll have the wind aft. But to come back eastwards, only if the wind is ENE or NE will you avoid having to make several tacks. In the same fashion you need to note, with the trades varying as they do from NE to SE, that more often than you'd expect, an upwind destination requires sailing hard on the wind. Under the higher islands (like Dominica, Guadeloupe, St Vincent, etc,) the wind shadow can be

either partial or total, requiring you to motor or motor-sail.

Squalls

The build up of massy cumulus before a squall hits warns you what's coming. They move down the line of the wind and usually carry rain, sometimes heavy. The increase in wind varies depending on the sort of squall in question. You can divide squalls as follows:

Black or dark squalls These darken the sky and usually have heavy rain. The gust cells are usually moderate and relatively short-lived.

White squalls Ahead of the arrival of one of these you can see the white curtain of water particles leaping up, caused by heavy rain and violent downbursts of wind. Under this sort of squall gusts can hit 35-40 kts for a short while.

Both phenomena suggest a prudent shortening of sail, above all for yachts that are a bit tender.

Sea state

On the Atlantic Ocean coasts the sea is usually moderate to rough depending on the strength of the trades. In the passages between the islands, it can be shortened and steepened by currents. On the leeward coast the sea is usually calm, sometimes with a low, gentle swell. In some periods of the year, most often when the trades are weak or have died away (usually in summer), the swell can cause a phenomenon locally known as a mini-tidal wave or strong surge caused by a big ground swell. Usually of small significance, this appears as long waves from the W usually causing an unduly high flood tide. Poorly anchored boats, or those too close to shore, can find themselves driven aground.

Currents

The current is generally westerly with a rate, on the Atlantic coast, of 0·5-1kt. It strengthens in the passages between the islands and in some of them can reach 2-3kts or more (for example in the Virgins and the Grenadines). The tides can produce counter-currents of a lesser rate felt closer to the coasts. These are a function of the time and the relative range of the tide.

Tides

They are diurnal or semi-diurnal depending on the time of year and place. The range is slight: from 0·2-0·3m, and exceptionally up to 0·9-1m in some places (for example the windward coast of Martinique).

Navigation

Important reminder
Lateral Buoyage: Zone B, red to starboard, green to port, (the opposite of the European Zone A).
Declination: Around +14° 10' (2002) rounded to 14°. Example: True course 310° = Magnetic course 324°

Dangers and precautions

The atmospheric conditions mentioned above make pilotage fairly simple but they do not remove all dangers, particularly the following:
- coral reefs
- conditions of poor visibility
- often inadequate (even non-existent) buoyage in some islands, with sometimes unreliable lights
- the strength of currents in some passages and channels that can set you to one side of your course
- the hurricane season (see introductory section on Cyclones)

It follows that in the Antilles (as elsewhere) you must:
- navigate carefully and precisely
- not rely only on GPS, nor use autopilot when close to coasts and hazards
- avoid night passages (or better, never make them) in some areas
- use passes only in good visibility (anyway subject to change from squalls or from having the sun ahead)
- have aboard all pilotage information, sufficient charts (see section on Charts) and all essential equipment as well as what is required by your country of registry
- have a properly maintained boat and motor
- keep abreast of the weather (especially in the hurricane season).

Buoyage and lights

(See also the section on Cartography and symbols)

It is essential not to forget that the Antilles are part of Zone B (the American continent) of the IALA system and therefore the opposite to the European Zone A.
Example
Entering a port or a channel with the lateral buoyage system:
Red buoy to Starboard
Green buoy to Port

As far as buoyage is concerned, the Lesser Antilles can be divided into two distinct parts:

The USVI and the French islands where, thanks to central government run administrations and large subsidies, buoys and lights are quite well maintained and generally conform to what you'll find on charts and official publications.

The ex-British, usually independent and relatively poor islands, where buoys are often inadequate or unreliable because ill maintained.

Buoys everywhere can be displaced or disappear (following a hurricane) and lighting can be unreliable.

Anchorages

The predominant E quadrant winds mean the majority of anchorages are to leeward of coasts. The few that are to windward are protected by barrier reefs and often tricky to get into. Natural harbours are numerous.

With the exception of the islands with a concentration of boats and services (Virgins, Antigua, Guadeloupe, Martinique, etc.) marinas are quite rare. Hence it's to the better provided islands that yachtsmen go for long stays, replenishment, repairs or a prolonged absence from their boats (see section on Marinas).

Open anchorages present few difficulties provided you take certain precautions:

- in some inlets the bottom drops off rapidly. It is recommended in such cases that you put a line ashore holding the stern off with an anchor
- when there is a risk of the current or wind changing direction by 180° (as sometimes happens during the night or in summer) it makes sense to use two anchors at an angle to each other or use a Bahamian moor (anchors 180° apart)
- finally you must note (in the context of conservation of the underwater world) the proliferation of mooring buoys (usually paying) in a number of anchorages, especially the Virgins. That you have paid for a mooring in no way guarantees its reliability, so if you can check things over, you should.

Note Welcoming committees or 'boat boys', often very obliging: these offer services (help with mooring, local products, etc.) for a few dollars. Be aware that some can be over-zealous to the point of being objectionable.

Remember In some islands you must take the usual precautions against theft.

Bearings, courses and variation

Even if your steering compass has no significant deviation, the Antillean area has a variation of around +14° (2002), a figure that you subtract from a magnetic bearing or course to get the TRUE bearing or course and vice versa:

Example
True course/bearing 310° =
Magnetic course/bearing 324°
Magnetic course/bearing 104° =
True course/bearing 090°

In the text and on the plans in this book, in order to avoid any confusion (see chapter on cartography) only TRUE courses and bearings are given.

Boat and equipment

Each yachtsman (charterer or owner) ought to be fully acquainted with the deck and rigging, the general equipment and the necessary safety gear on board his boat. Taking that as read, for sailing in the Lesser Antilles there are some points that are worth special attention:

Auxiliary engines

Simply put, your engine must be in good running order and sufficiently powerful to be able to leave an anchorage against the wind when the same manoeuvre is impossible under sail.

Sails

In the Antilles the basic principle, given the relative regularity of the winds and especially for sloops, is to avoid a complicated sail wardrobe. Roller furling sails are now increasingly ubiquitous. What they lose in performance (especially roller furling mains) is gained in the ease and speed of reducing sail. Save for full-on racing fanatics, the systems seem to satisfy most yachtsmen who are, after all, on holiday.

Tenders

Indispensable, especially in open anchorages. It should preferably be stable and have a sufficiently powerful motor. In the Antilles your tender is often your 'taxi' for doing the shopping, to go snorkelling or to make a trip ashore or to the beach.

Ground tackle

'It can never be too big.' Two anchors of adequate size are the absolute minimum. Have enough nylon warp, but you also need chain because the bottoms often have coral or bits of coral around.

Awnings and Biminis

An awning is a protection against the sun in an anchorage (and against squalls too) which you can't afford to ignore. Now, however, many prefer a bimini (an American invention taking its name from a island in the Bahamas) that,

thanks to the support of its frame, can be kept up when you're sailing. That said, the helmsman's view of the sails is sometimes impeded.

Electronics

Without going overboard with equipment for a full-on cruiser-racer, some modern instrumentation is a real boon to navigation.

- **Speed and distance log, windspeed and direction indicators**
  Sometimes nowadays these all work through a central processing unit to which you can also add an echosounder or even a chart plotter with an electronic charting package. But there is a drawback to such a system: if it breaks down, you lose everything. It seems wiser to keep your essential instruments, like the echosounder for example, separate or to have a back-up.
- **Autopilot** This piece of supplementary equipment, because it's so handy, is also becoming more and more widely used. However, if you use one you should observe the same rules of caution as with a GPS.
- **Radar** Although more accurate and more reliable for position finding when close to coasts than GPS (see next section), radar has tended to be replaced by GPS because it is more difficult to install and costs a lot more money.

To close this section, a reminder: the more computerised equipment you have aboard, the more things there are to go wrong.

Aids to navigation

Charts

(For symbols and abbreviations on the plans in this book, see introductory section on Cartography)

Note In order to allow exact plotting of satellite derived positions, recent editions of charts have either been reconciled to the WGS84 datum or have tabulated correction data for plotting GPS derived positions (see GPS below).

Below are noted the relevant charts published by Imray, the British Admiralty, SHOM (French Hydrographic Service) and NIMA (USA). Details are liable to change.

These charts are all available through Imray Laurie Norie & Wilson Ltd Wych House The Broadway St Ives Cambridgeshire PE27 5BT England
☎ +(0)1480 462114
Fax +(0)1480 496109
www.imray.com

There are several series of electronic charts on the market which are available from chart agents and chandlers. These include Maptech, C-Map, Navionics and Garmin.

IMRAY–IOLAIRE CHARTS FOR THE CARIBBEAN SEA

M – Metric edition

1   **Eastern Caribbean General chart** 1:1,824,000
Plan: Monjes del Sur

A   **Lesser Antilles – Puerto Rico to Martinique**
Passage Chart 1:930,000

A1   **Puerto Rico** Passage Chart 1:285,000
Plans: San Juan, Bahia de Ponce, Puerto Arecibo, Bahia de Mayaguez

A2   **Puerto Rico to St Christopher** Passage Chart 1:416,000
Plan: Sombrero I

A23   **Virgin Islands** 1:280,600 **and St Croix** 1:101,400
Plans: Christiansted, Port Alucroix & Limetree Bay, Frederiksted, Green Cay Marina

A231   **Virgin Islands – St Thomas to Virgin Gorda** 1:88,300
Plans: Charlotte Amalie, Virgin Gorda Yacht Harbour, Roadtown Harbour, Sea Cow Bay & Nanny Cay Marina, Cruz Bay

A232   **Virgin Islands – Tortola to Anegada** 1:87,550
Plans: Gorda Sound, South Sound, Roadtown Harbour and Approaches, Virgin Gorda Yacht Harbour

A233   **Virgin Islands.** A231 and A232 printed on a double sided sheet.

A234   **Northeast Coast of St Croix** 1:27,700
Plans: Salt River Bay, Christiansted Harbour, Green Cay Marina

A24   **Anguilla, St-Martin and St Barthélémy** 1:100,000
Plans: Road Bay, Oyster Pond, Gustavia, Prickly Pear Cays, Crocus Bay, Shoal Bay and Island Harbour, Groot Baai, Simsonbaai, Anse de Marigot

A241   **St Barthélémy** 1:33,800
Plan: Gustavia

A242   **St-Martin** 1:48,900

A25   **St Eustatius, St Christopher, Nevis, Montserrat and Saba** 1:103,600
Plans: Saba I (30,500) Montserrat I, (104,000) Fort Baai (Saba), Basseterre Bay (St Kitts), The Narrows, Plymouth (Montserrat), Oranjebaai (St Eustatius)

A26   **Barbuda** 1:44,500 **M**
Plan: Gravenor Bay

A27   **Antigua** 1:57,600
Plans: Nonsuch Bay, Mamora Bay, Falmouth and English Harbours

A271   **North Coast of Antigua** 1:29,600

A28   **Guadeloupe** 1:141,000
Plans: Pointe-à-Pitre, Anse Deshaies, Gozier, Port Louis, St François and Marina de la Gde Saline, Marina de Rivière Sens, Iles de la Petite Terre

A281   **Guadeloupe – Les Saintes** 1:20,150 **M Marie Galante** 1:67,500
Plans: St Anne & Anse Accul, Le Moule, Petit Havre Sainte Marie, N approaches to Pointe-à-Pitre, Grande

Anse (Desirade) Grand-Bourg

A29   **Dominica** 1:72,300 **M**
Plans: Prince Rupert Bay, Roseau Roads and Woodbridge Bay

A3   **Anguilla to Dominica** Passage Chart 1:397,000

A30   **Martinique** 1:92,000
Plans: Pointe du Bout, Rade de St Pierre, Cul-de-Sac Marin, Havre du Robert, Rade de Fort de France, Havre de la Trinite, Mouillage du François

A301   **Martinique – South & East Coasts** 1:60,000
Pointe du Diamant to Havre de la Trinité

A4   **Guadeloupe to St Lucia** Passage Chart 1:388,000

B   **Lesser Antilles – Martinique to Trinidad** Passage Chart 1:745,000

B1   **St Lucia** 1:72,000
Plans: Port Castries, Grand Cul-de-Sac Bay, Marigot Harbour, Rodney Bay & Yacht Harbour, Laborie Bay, Vieux Fort Bay & Point Sable Bay

B2   **Barbados** 1:56,900
Plans: Bridgetown, Speightstown, Port St Charles

B3   **The Grenadines – St Vincent to Grenada** 1:162,000 **M**

B30   **Grenadines – North Sheet** 1:86,000 **M St Vincent to Mustique**
Plans: Kingstown Bay (St Vincent), Calliaqua Bay and Blue Lagoon (St Vincent), Admiralty Bay (Bequia), West Coast of Mustique, Baliceaux and Battowia, Friendship Bay (Bequia), Chateaubelair Bay (St Vincent)

B31   **Grenadines – Middle Sheet** 1:86,000 **M Bequia to Carriacou**
Plans: Hillsborough Bay (Carriacou), Clifton and Ashton Harbours (Union I), Charlestown Bay (Canouan), Tobago Cays

B32   **Grenadines – South Sheet** 1:86,000 **M Grenada**
Plans: St George's Harbour (Grenada), Tyrrel Bay (Carriacou), Grenville Harbour (Grenada), South Coast of Grenada, Grenada Bay

B311   **Middle Grenadines** 1:25,000 **M Canouan to Carriacou**

B4   **Tobago** 1:63,600
Plans: King's Bay, Scarborough, Man of War Bay, Tyrrel's Bay, Plymouth

B5   **Martinique to Tobago and Barbados** Passage Chart 1:510,700

B6   **Grenada to Tobago and Trinidad** Passage Chart 1:378,000 **M**
Plan: Chaguaramas

BRITISH ADMIRALTY CHARTS

130	Anguilla to Puerto Rico showing approaches to the Virgin Islands	282,600
197	Northwest approaches to St Lucia	25,000
	Rodney Bay lagoon	5,000
254	Montserrat and Barbuda	
	Little Bay	7,500
	Montserrat	50,000
	Barbuda	60,000
371	Northern Martinique Fort-de-France	15,000
	Baie de Fort-de-France; Havre de la Trinité	25,000
	Pointe Caracoli to Fort-de-France	75,000
485	St Croix	60,000
	Frederiksted Pier	5,000
	Krause Lagoon channel and Limetree Bay	20,000
	Christiansted harbour	10,000
487	St Kitts, Sint Eustatius and Saba	
	Sint Eustatius to St Kitts	50,000
	Fort Baai	2,500
	Saba	50,000
	Oranje Baai	15,000
	Basseterre Bay	25,000
489	Approaches to Nevis	50,000
491	Harbours and anchorages in Guadeloupe	
	Basse-Terre; Petit Havre Saint-Anne and Anse	15,000
	Accul; Le Moule;	10,000
	Grand Anse; Saint-Francois; Grand-Bourg Les Saintes	17,500
494	Baie de Saint-Louis	25,000
	Southern Martinique	
	Baie du François	12,500
	Cul-de-Sac du Marin	22,500
	Havre du Robert and approaches	25,000
	Fort-de-France to Pointe Caracoli	75,000
499	Harbours in St Lucia	
	Port Castries	5,000
	Marigot harbour	5,000
	Grand Cul de Sac bay	10,000
	Vieux Fort	20,000
502	Harbours and anchorages in Barbados	
	Bridgetown harbour and approaches	12,500
	Speightstown including Arawak jetty; Oistins Bay	15,000
583	Sombrero Island to St Kitts	175,000
584	St Barthélémy to Antigua	175,000
585	Nevis and Antigua to northern Guadeloupe	175,000
593	Approaches to Guadeloupe	175,000
594	Southern Guadeloupe to northern Martinique	175,000
596	Southern Martinique to St Vincent	175,000
597	St Vincent to Grenada	175,000
618	Southern Guadeloupe including Marie-Galante and Les Saintes	75,000
697	Dominica	60,000
	Woodbridge Bay and Roseau Roads	12,500
	Prince Rupert and Douglas bays	30,000
791	St Vincent to Bequia	60,000
793	The Grenadines – Northern part	
	Charlestown Bay	12,500
	Mustique	25,000
	Bequia to Canouan	60,000
794	The Grenadines – Central part	
	Clifton harbour	20,000
	Tobago Cays	25,000
	Canouan to Carriacou	60,000
795	The Grenadines – Southern part	
	Watering Bay and approaches; Hillsborough Bay	25,000
	Carriacou to Grenada	60,000
797	Grenada	60,000
	Grenville harbour	12,500
	Grenada Bay and approaches; St David's harbour to Prickly Bay	25,000

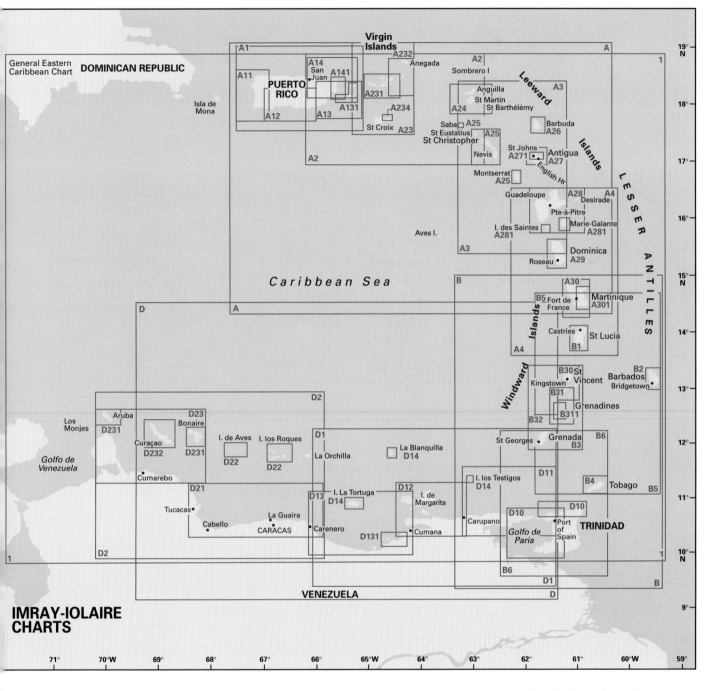

General Eastern
Caribbean Chart **DOMINICAN REPUBLIC**

Virgin Islands

PUERTO RICO

Caribbean Sea

Aves I.

Golfo de Venezuela

Los Monjes

Aruba

Bonaire

Curaçao

Cumarebo

Tucacas

La Guaira

CARACAS

Cabello

I. de Aves

I. los Roques

La Orchilla

La Blanquilla

I. La Tortuga

I. de Margarita

Carenero

Cumana

Carupano

I. los Testigos

St Georges

Grenada

Tobago

TRINIDAD

Golfo de Paria

Port of Spain

VENEZUELA

IMRAY-IOLAIRE CHARTS

Leeward Islands

Windward Islands

LESSER ANTILLES

Anegada
Sombrero I
Anguilla
St Martin
St Barthélémy
Saba
St Eustatius
St Christopher
Nevis
Barbuda
St Johns
Antigua
English Hr
Montserrat
Guadeloupe
Desirade
Pte-à-Pitre
Marie-Galante
I. des Saintes
Dominica
Roseau
Fort de France
Martinique
Castries
St Lucia
Kingstown
St Vincent
Barbados
Bridgetown
Grenadines
St Croix
San Juan
Isla de Mona

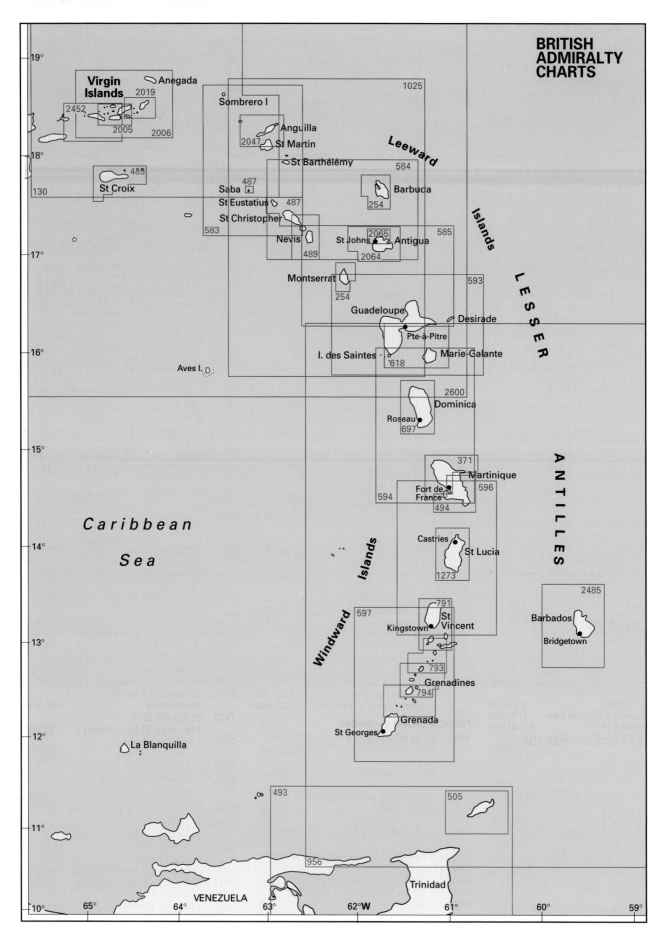

BRITISH
ADMIRALTY
CHARTS

19°

Virgin
Islands

Anegada

2019

2452

2005

2006

Sombrero I

Anguilla

2047

St Martin

130

485

St Croix

Saba

487

St Eustatius

487

St Barthélémy

584

Barbuda

254

St Christopher

583

Nevis

489

St Johns

2065

Antigua

2064

585

Montserrat

254

593

Guadeloupe

Desirade

Pte-à-Pitre

I. des Saintes

618

Marie-Galante

Aves I.

2600

Dominica

Roseau

697

371

Martinique

594

Fort de
France

596

494

Caribbean

Sea

Castries

St Lucia

1273

2485

Barbados

Bridgetown

597

791

St
Vincent

Kingstown

793

Grenadines

794

Grenada

St Georges

La Blanquilla

493

505

956

VENEZUELA

Trinidad

Leeward

Islands

LESSER

ANTILLES

Windward

Islands

18°

17°

16°

15°

14°

13°

12°

11°

10°

65°

64°

63°

62°W

61°

60°

59°

	Continuation to Dog Island	1:50,000
	Road Bay	1:15,000
5641.6	Montserrat	1:50,000
	Anguilla Channel	1:50,000
	Little Bay	1:7,500
5641.7	Baie de Marigot	1:15,000
	Oyster Pond	1:10,000
	Groot Baai	1:15,000
	Simson Baai	1:30,000
5641.8	St Kitts	1:50,000
	Basseterre Bay	1:25,000
5641.9	Nevis and The Narrows	1:50,000
5641.10	Antigua	1:60,000
	Mamora Bay	1:10,000
5641.11	Saint John's Harbour	1:25,000
	Parham Harbour	1:25,000
5641.12	Barbuda	1:60,000

SC5642 ANTIGUA TO MARTINIQUE AND BARBADOS

5642:1	Antigua to Guadeloupe	1:175,000
5642.2	Guadeloupe to Les Saintes	1:175,000
5642.3	Les Saints to Dominica	1:175,000
5642.4	Dominica to Martinique	1:175,000
5642.5	Guadeloupe – Saint Anne and Anse Accul	1:10,000
	Guadeloupe – Saint-François	1:10,000
	Guadeloupe – Basse-Terre	1:15,000
	Guadeloupe – Petit Havre	1:15,000
	Marie Galante – Baie de Saint-Louis	1:25,000
5642.6	Les Saintes	1:17,500
5642.7	Pointe-à-Pitre and Approaches	1:17,500
	Continuation to Pont de la Gabarre	1:17,500
5642.8	Dominica – Southwest Coast	1:60,000
	Prince Rupert and Douglas Roads	1:30,000
	Woodbridge Bay and Roseau Roads	1:12,500
5642.9	Martinique – Pointe du Prêcheur to Pointe des Nègres	1:75,000
	Martinique-Pointe des Nègres to Pointe des Salines	1:75,000
5642.10	Baie de Fort-de-France	1:25,000
	Fort-de-France	1:15,000
5642.11	Martinique – Cul-de-sac du Marin	1:22,500
	Barbados – Port Saint Charles	1:15,000
	Barbados – Bridgetown and Approaches	1:12,500
	Barbados – Oistins Bay	1:15,000
5642.12	Barbados	1:100,000

SC5643 SAINT LUCIA TO GRENADA

5643.1	Martinique to Saint Lucia	1:175,000
5643.2	Saint Lucia to Bequia	1:175,000
5643.3	Bequia to Ronde Island	1:175,000
5643.4	Ronde Island to Grenada	1:175,000
5643.5	Port Castries	1:5,000
	Rodney Bay Lagoon	1:5,000
	Rodney Bay	1:25,000
5643.6	Soufrière Bay, Anse de Pitons and Approaches	1:60,000
	Marigot Harbour	1:5,000
	Vieux Fort Bay	1:20,000
5643.7	Kingstown Harbour and Approaches	1:10,000
	Saint Vincent Southwest Coast	1:60,000
5643.8	Mustique	1:25,000
	Charlestown Bay	1:12,500
	Admiralty Bay	1:12,000
5643.9	Plans in The Grenadines	
	Clifton Harbour	1:20,000

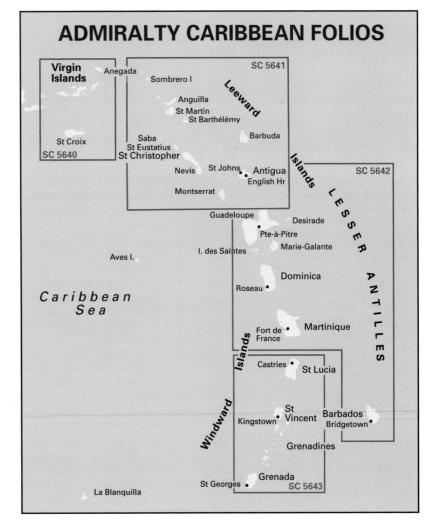

ADMIRALTY CARIBBEAN FOLIOS

	Tobago Cays	1:25,000
	Petit Saint Vincent Anchorages	1:25,000
5643.10	The Grenadines	1:60,000
	Continuation to Bonaparte Rocks	1:60,000
	Hillsborough Bay	1:25,000
5643.11	Grenada (Northern Part)	1:60,000
	Grenada (Southern Part)	1:60,000
5643.12	Saint George's and Approaches	1:10,000
	Prickly Bay to Westerhall Bay	1:25,000
	Saint David's Harbour	1:25,000

FRENCH CHARTS – SHOM

1003	De la Martinique à Saint Kitts	418,000
3127	Abords Basse Terre – Rivière des Peres à Pte du Vieux Fort	12,500
3418	De la Pointe du Vieux Fort à la Pointe Allegre	55,400
6738	La Martinique – Partie sud	60,000
6892	Baie de Fort de France	15,000
6948	Guadeloupe – Pointe-à-Pitre à Marie Galante – Canal Saintes	60,000
7041	La Martinique – Partie Nord	60,000
7087	Havre de la Trinité et Baie du Galion	125,000
7088	Havre du Robert et Baie du François	20,000
7089	St Pierre, Case Piilote, Cul-de-Sac du marin, Vauclin	15,000
7100	Guadeloupe – Abords de Pointe-à-Pitre, Ste-Marie	15,000
7101	Les Saintes	15,000

7102	Ports, mouillages Grande Terre, Marie Galante, Desirade	10,000
7208	De Marie Galante à la Desirade	60,000
7302	De la Pointe des Chateaux à l'Ilet à Kahouanne	59,900
7324	Grand Cuyl-de-Sac Marin – Du Lamentin à Port Louis	20,000
7345	Guadeloupe – De Montserrat à Marie Galante	149,000
7470	D'Anguilla à Nevis	148,000
7471	D'Anguilla à Saint Barthélémy	60,000
7472	St-Martin (Sint Maarten), St Barthélémy	15,000
7610	The Grenadines de Carriacou à Grenada	60,000
7611	The Grenadines de Canouan à Carriacou	60,000
7612	The Grenadines de Bequia à Canouan	59,9000
7613	Saint Vincent & Bequia	60,000
7614	St Lucia	60,000
7615	Barbados	100,000
7616	Dominica	60,000
	Prince Rupert Bay, Woodbridge Bay	30,000
7617	Montserrat & Barbuda	60,000
	Little Bay	7,500
7618	Antigua	60,000
	Falmouth & English harbours	20,000
	Mamora Bay	10,000
7619	Approches de Nevis	50,000
7620	Approches d'Anguilla	50,000
	Sombrero island	15,000
7621	Ports, mouillages Iles Vent du Bequia	12,500

	St Vincent	15,000
	Grenada	10,000
7622	Ports de St Lucia	
	Castries	5,000
	Vieux Fort	20,000
	Gran Cul-de-Sac	10,000
	Marigot	5,000
7623	Approches N St Lucia	25,000
	Rodney Bay	5,000
7624	Cote Nord d'Antigua	25,000
	St John's Harbour	12,500
7626	Saint Kitts, Sint Eustatius et Saba	
	Saba – Fort Baai	2,500
	Saba	50,000
	Sint Eustatius – Oranje Baai	15,000
	Saint Kitts – Basseterre Bay	25,000
7627	Grenada	60,000
	David's Harbour to Prickly Bay,	
	Grenvillage Harbour	25,000
7628	Ports et mouillages de Barbados	
	Bridgetown Harbour	12,500
	Oistins Bay, Speightstown	
	et Arawak Jetty	15,000
7630	De Anguilla à la	
	Guadeloupe	300,000

USA CHARTS – NIMA (National Imagery & Mapping Agency)

25480	St George's Harbour	
	(Grenada)	10,000
24581	Grenada	60,000
24582	Carriacou to Bequia	75,000
	Tobago Cays	24,000
25483	St Vincent Kingstown,	
	Calliaqua	15,400
	Bequia	12,500
25484	St Vincent	72,000
25485	Approaches to Barbados	100,000
	Bridgetown and Oistins Bay	25,000
	Speightstown	20,000
25487	Barbados Bridgetown Harbour	10,000
25521	St Lucia	75,000
25524	Martinique South &	
	East Coasts	60-,000
	Le Marin	15,000
25525	Baie du Francois to	
	Havre de la Trinité	15,000
25526	Martinique North &	
	West Coasts	60,000
	St Pierre	15,000
25527	Baie de Fort de France	
	Martinique)	12,500
25528	St Lucia Port of Castries,	
	Marigot Harbour	60,000
25550	Saint Barthelemy to	
	Guadeloupe	250,000
25561	Dominica	60,000
25563	Guadeloupe	130,000
25564	Les Saintes (Guadeloupe)	15,000
25565	Saint Louis to Grand Bourg	15,00
25566	Approaches to Pointe-à-Pitre	15,000
	Ste Marie	15,000
25567	Guadeloupe	
	Basse Terre, Le Moule,	
	Port Louis	15,000
25570	Approach to Antigua	75,000
25575	Northern Antigua	25,000
	Saint John's Harbour	12,500
25600	Anegada Passage with	
	Adjacent Islands	
25601	Approaches to St Kitts,	
	Nevis, Montserrat,	
	Redonda	55,000
25607	Saba, Statis and St Kitts	75,000
	Saba, Sint Eustatius	15,000
25608	Plans in the Leeward Islands	
	Baie du Marigot	14,912
	Port de Gustavia	14,936
	Plymouth	15,052
	Basseterre	14,987
	Approach to Barbuda	75,000

25609	St Thomas to Anegada	
	(Virgin Isands)	80,000
25610	Approaches to Gorda	
	Sound	12,5000
	Gorda Sound	7,500
25611	Approaches to Road	
	Harbour	30,000
	Road Harbour	15,000
25613	Approaches Anguilla,	
	St Martin &	
	St Barthélémy	30,000
	Philipsburg	15,000

Satellite positioning

(GPS – Global Positioning System)
(see also section on Cartography in the Introduction)

Although, thanks to the short distances involved, navigation in the Antilles is most often by eye and seldom at night, the use of GPS is spreading due to its ease of use and low price. That said, you should never forget that even if GPS signals are no longer degraded by the US authorities, GPS is not absolutely precise. This is for various reasons whose effects, whether minimal or temporary, can nonetheless be cumulative:

- poor, more or less intermittent, receiver signal reception
- default datum setting to WGS84. For all that WGS84 is a global geoid, there are local errors in some zones
- you must be certain the chart you are using has been accurately reconciled to WGS84
- be sure to apply any position correction factors for your chart to your receiver's WGS84 position before plotting it
- older, pre-WGS84 charts have no correction factors, so you cannot correct your GPS position before plotting it

Remember In light of the very relative precision of GPS positions with respect to the charting, all GPS waypoints shown on the plans in the guide have been placed well clear of the coast and all dangers. A GPS position close to coasts should always be checked against positions derived by other means (soundings, bearings, lights, radar, etc.) *This is for obvious safety reasons.*

Radio stations and weather forecasts

The weather is generally benign, but during the hurricane season you must follow the daily weather forecasts carefully. They are of two kinds:

- marine weather reports broadcast on VHF or SSB by marine radio stations and amateur networks (see Table I)
- weather forecasts broadcast on local FM and AM radio usually with the news (see Table II)

Some harbours and marinas also post weather forecasts on notice boards, especially in the hurricane season.

Note that large areas of the Antilles are not covered by VHF stations. When that is the case you must listen for the forecasts on local radio during the day, especially in the hurricane season.

Telecommunications

SSB

Given the rapid reduction, either in process or planned, of HF radio stations, the presence of an SSB transceiver aboard is increasingly rare. The sole survivors tend to be radio receivers (sometimes called 'marine') that, in addition to standard wavebands, can monitor marine SSB frequencies. All of these frequencies, given their range, remain extremely valuable for listening to forecasts, especially during the hurricane season.

VHF

This allows short range communication, monitoring weather reports, calling ports and marinas, etc. Don't forget too that in many of the islands (mainly the English speaking ones) yacht services and even restaurants listen out on VHF frequencies. On the other hand, except in the Virgins, the base stations no longer offer radio-telephone links to land lines.

Mobile phones (Cellphones)

Mobile phones can be useful, but only out to a few miles from the coast and only in zones covered by one's own provider's service network.

All networks have coverage, but check with your service provider before you leave for The Antilles and when you get there. Charter companies usually offer cellphones for hire during a cruise.

Conclusion

This is a fast changing but temporary period in telecommunications, so the cruising yachtsman in some areas of the Antilles occasionally finds establishing communications difficult because of range limits or partial coverage. These problems will only be resolved when satellite services offer perfect coverage and their prices become affordable.

I. MARINE WEATHER FORECAST STATIONS, FREQUENCIES & BULLETINS

Zone/Station	Frequency/Channel	Local time (GMT +4) (1)	Special Bulletins (in French & English)
CROSSAG (ex COSMA)	Coastal forecasts (in French) (2)		
Sea area: Martinique (Anguilla to Guyana)	VHF 16 & 79	0720, 0740, 1050, 1110 (3) 1820, 1840, 2020, 2040 (3)	Ch 16 & 79(4)
	VHF 16 & 80	0730, 0750, 1100, 1120 (3) 1830, 1850, 2030, 2050 (3)	Ch 16 & 80 (4)
Sea area: Guadeloupe	VHF 16 & 79/64	0800, 0820, 1130, 1150 (3) 1900, 1920, 2100, 2120 (3)	Ch 16 & 79/64 (4)
	VHF 16 & 80	0810, 0830, 1140, 1200 (4) 1910, 1930, 2110, 2130 (4)	Ch 16 & 80 (4)
Sea area: St-Martin	VHF 16 & 64	0900, 1230, 2000, 2200 (offshore forecast in French)	
Offshore forecasts (in French)	Every even hour		
Sea area: Antilles	2545 kHz (SSB) (announced on 2182 kHz)	0933, 1815, 2003 (in French) (2)	
Sea area: Atlantic	13640 kHz 15515 kHz 21645kHz 14118 kHz (Ham network)	0740 (in French) (2) 0700 (in English)	
Antigua	VHF 6 (call on 68)	0900 (in English)	
St-Martin & St Maarten	VHF 12 & 20	Variable & 0730 (in English)	
BVI (Tortola) Caribbean SSB Net (Ham)	USB 4003 kHz USB 8104 kHz	0815– 0845 (in English) 0830–0900 (in English)	
USVI (St Thomas) VI Radio (VAH) NOAA forecast	VHF 16 & 28/85 VHX WX3 & WX4	0600, 1000, 1400 (in English) Continuous (in English)	

(1) as a general guide–subject to change
(2) planned also to be in English
(3) VHF Channels and times vary with areas
(4) Every H +30

Atlantic crossing (Herb):	12359kHz	(SSB), 1600–1700
US Ham net (East Coast):	6224kHz	(SSB), 0800, 1815
Albatross Marine Weather:	4045kHz 5104kHz 8155kHz	USB, 0700 LMT USB, 0745 LMT
NMN Offshore Forecast:	4426kHz 6501kHz 8764kHz	USB, 0530, 1200, 2230 LMT

II. MAIN LOCAL BROADCAST RADIO WITH WEATHER FORECASTS

Island & Radio Station	Language	Frequency	Local time
Barbados: CBC Radio	English	900kHz AM	0700 (News)
Radio Grenada	English	535kHz AM	0700 (News)
St Vincent Radio	English	705kHz AM	(1)
St Lucia Radio	English	660kHz AM	0705
St Lucia (GEM)	English	93·7–94·5MHz FM	0730–0930
Radio Caraïbes	French	89·9MHz FM	(1)
Radio Martinique	French	92–94·5MHz FM	(1)
RFO Martinique	French	1310kHz AM	1025–2245 & 0645–1845
Dominica (GEM)	English	93·3MHz FM	0730–1630
Antigua (GEM)	English	93·9MHz FM	0730–1630
Antigua Broadcasting	English	620kHz AM	0650
Montserrat (GEM)	English	95·5–99·1MHz FM	(1)
St Kitts (GEM)	English	92·7–93·2MHz FM	0730 & 1630
Radio St-Barth	French	98·7MHz FM	0730, 1230, 1630
St-Martin (GEM)	English & French	88·9MHz FM	(1)
Voice of St Maarten PJD3	English	102·7MHz FM	(1) & 0900 (Sundays)
Tortola ZBVI	English	780kHz AM	0805 (weekdays); 0745 & 0945 (weekends)
St Thomas WVWI	English	1000kHz AM	Every hour
St Thomas WIVI	English	99·5MHz FM	0730, 0830, 1530, 1630
St Croixj279 WSTX	English	970kHz AM	

(1) weather bulletins H +30 after local news
Note Some radio stations give special bulletins during cyclone alerts

The following additional stations may give cyclone bulletins during an alert:

Barbados	Starcom Gospel, 790kHz AM BBS, 90·7MHz FM;Love FM; 104·1MHz FM; Radio Liberty, 98·1MHz FM; Faith, 102MHz FM
Grenada	Voice of Grenada, 95.7MHz & 106·3MHz FM; 1440 kHz AM and stations on 89·5, 90·1, 96·3, 98·5, 101·7, 105·5, & 106·3MHz FM
St Vincent	Nice FM, 96·3MHz FM; Hitz FM; 107·3MHz FM; WEFM, 99·9MHz FM
St Lucia	Reportedly has two stations (RCI and RSL) each with an AM channel and 2 FM channels, GEM is apparently now called The Wave and has 2 FM channels.
Dominica	DBS on 595kHz as well as 88·1, 88·6, 89·5, 103·2 & 103·6MHz FM; Kairi FM on 93·1, 107·9MHz FM; Vol on 1060 KHz AM & 90·6 & 102·1MHz FM. Two religious radio stations. A repeater for Radio Caribbean International from St Lucia on 98·1MHz FM
St Maarten	This may be PJD2 and may also broadcast on 1030 kHz AM
Montserrat	Also has ZJB with news at 0700
Anguilla	Has two stations: Radio Anguilla, 1505 kHz AM; ZJF, 105 MHz FM
St Kitts & Nevis	St Kitts: ZIZ broadcasts on 555 kHz AM and 96 MHz FM; Choice, 105 MHz FM Nevis: VON, 895 kHz AM; Radio Paradise, 825 kHz AM
Tortola (BVI)	ZBVI is reported to give weather reports hourly 0730–1830. There are four other stations Reggae, 97·3 MHz FM; Country, 94·3 MHz FM; Gold, 91·7 MHz FM; ZROD, 103·7 MHz FM

Chartering

For those who don't have a boat in the Antilles, chartering is a good formula and certainly not the most expensive of the two options. More to the point, the choice is huge and the prices competitive thanks to the growth of large charter fleets in the Antilles, particularly in the French islands and Virgin Islands. It's certainly one of the biggest concentrations of yachts in the world.

Types of charter

There are two ways of going about chartering a boat and each has its variations:

- chartering a whole, fully-equipped boat without crew for your exclusive use (usually called bareboat chartering).
- going either as an individual or as a group, and generally paying by cabin, on a large, fully crewed charter boat.

Individual bareboat

This offers free choice of:

- the model and size of boat according to how many people there are in the party
- the itinerary to be pursued (depending on limits set out in the charter contract)

When an agreement is made, the charterer (you) then assure the company:

- that you assume entire responsibility for navigation and safety
- that you and your party will handle all manoeuvres of the vessel and keep it clean and in good order.

Some companies offer, for additional payment, skippers and hostesses who can assume some of the usual duties of the charterer. This course of action may be unavoidable if the skills of the charterers are not up to handling the size of boat they have chartered or the itinerary they wish to follow.

Because bareboat chartering is a more and more popular solution to sailing in the Caribbean when you do not have your own boat, tough competition has developed between at least some companies.

One-way charters

This sort of chartering allows you to take a boat from one charter base and, if the company has more than one base, leave it in another. Alternatively you can have the boat brought back to base from where you want to go by the charter company's delivery skippers. The latter usually incurs a supplement to which you need to add the cost of getting yourself back on an inter-island flight. Averaging out the costs, the advantage of a one-way charter is that it enlarges your cruising radius by removing the need to return to your starting point.

Chartering a berth or a cabin

Taking this option frees you from any responsibility for keeping watch or navigation because these are entirely the duty of the skipper and his professional crew (see box). In some cases, given the size, on-board equipment and quality of service aboard offered on some high-prestige vessels, this can be equivalent to setting sail in a first class floating hotel. But here, as before, there are several categories of chartering and so various different rates.

Typical cruise itineraries

Port of departure	Route	Duration (in days)	Approx distance (in miles)
FROM MARTINIQUE			
Le Marin	St Lucia–Rodney Bay, Deux Pitons)–Le Marin	1–7	80
Le Marin	St Lucia–Bequia–Union (Grenadines)–Le Marin	6–12	250
FROM ST LUCIA			
Rodney Bay	St Vincent, Grenadines, Grenada, Rodney Bay	15–30	430
Marigot Bay	St Vincent, Grenadines, Marigot Bay	6–12	200
GRENADINES CRUISE			
St Vincent (Blue Lagoon or Union)	Bequia–Carriacou	6–15	60–90
FROM GUADELOUPE			
Pointe-à-Pitre	The Saintes–Dominica (Portsmouth)–Marie Galante–Pointe-à-Pitre	4–7	90
Pointe-à-Pitre	The Saintes–Deshaies–Antigua (English Harbour, North Sound, Green Island)–The Saintes–Pointe-à-Pitre *Note* returning via the Rivière Salée deduct 90M and 2 days	8–15	200–250
Pointe-à-Pitre	The Saintes–Nevis–St Kitts–St-Barth–St-Martin–St Kitts–The Saintes–Pointe-à-Pitre	15–20	380
FROM ANTIGUA			
English Harbour	W and NW coasts of Antigua, Barbuda, English Harbour	5–10	90
English Harbour	St Barts, St-Martin, Saba, Nevis, Guadeloupe, English Harbour	10–15	280
FROM St-Martin			
Marigot	St Barts–St Kitts–Statia–Saba–Marigot	7–10	150
Marigot	Anguilla–Prickly Pear–Marigot	4–7	50
Marigot	Anguilla–Tortola–Anegada–Virgin Gorda–Marigot	12–20	250[1]
BRITISH VIRGIN ISLANDS CRUISE			
Road Harbour (Tortola)	Soper's Hole–Jost Van Dyke–NE Tortola–Anegada–Virgin Gorda–Peter & Norman Islands–Road Harbour	7–15	80

1 Night passages possible.

Notes
1. The examples can be varied innumerable ways depending on your preferences.
2. The departure ports in Martinique, Guadeloupe & St-Martin were chosen because they have international airports and lots of charter companies.
3. The duration takes stops of one or two days in the main anchorages into account to allow for provisioning, tourism and a rest. The first figure is the minimum, the second for a more relaxed cruise. The assumption has been of an average speed of 5–7 knots. If you want to wander about a bit more, you'll need to add more days. One could also head off on a sort of 'race cruise' and 'tick off the islands'. And of course how long any cruise takes in the end comes down to the boat's average speed.
4. You must take into account you'll be on the wind returning from some of the northern islands in the Leewards, especially the Virgins. Sometimes you'll even have to put in a few tacks.

The downside maybe, unless you and a group of friends take the whole boat to yourself, is that you must fit in with other charter clients in a pre-organised programme. Going off cruising on this sort of charter is currently called 'long chartering' to distinguish it from 'day chartering'. The latter are simple outings lasting a day, often organised by travel agents, hotels or underwater dive clubs as part of, or supplementary to, their package of leisure activities. It follows that a day charter allows a tourist to enjoy for a short while the delights of sailing or the discovery of some otherwise inaccessible spot.

Don't confuse chartering a berth or a cabin with paying to sign on as participant crew. This system, followed by some boat owners and by some clubs or other associations, comes at a much lower cost to you. But that's because you, as well as paying your share of the costs of the cruise, also do your share of the work aboard.

Choosing

Once you've decided on what sort of chartering you prefer, you need to decide on:
- the kind of boat and its cost
- the charter company or agent to use
- the season you would like to sail in
- the itinerary of your cruise

Boat and price

As a general rule in the Antilles, charter companies or specialist agents offer new or fairly new and well-maintained boats (though there are naturally exceptions proving the rule!)

Whatever the size or model of boat, they fall into two quite distinct categories:
- monohulls
- multihulls

The boats in the first category have the devotion of their numerous besotted fans. For them sailing is still linked to certain mythic ingredients: the heel of a boat, the siren calls of a ballast keel, the tapering hull and a hard beat to windward.

Multihull enthusiasts, on their side, guarantee their privileged clientele the huge acreage of deck and vast interior, to which they add the virtually level ride.

And there are also other polemical and fanciful arguments in defence of each type, about speed, closeness to the wind, stability, etc.

In the end, and provided we're well enough informed about both, each of us will find in one or other type of boat pluses or minuses depending on our own chosen criteria.

And finally, when a choice must be made, there is the crucial relationship of quality and price – one of the most important considerations because when it comes down to it, although some rates seem very attractive, they don't always turn out to be the cheapest!

So you have to bear in mind:
- what supplies and services are included in the price and what's an optional extra
- what model of boat is it and when was it first commissioned (recently or some time back)
- what insurance is included and what is the deductible or excess
- what are the condition and quality of the boat's fittings
- whether the whole boat and all that comes with it have been well maintained.

And you need also to remember:
- that an older boat can be in excellent condition if it has been regularly and well-maintained.
- that a fairly new boat can have problems if it is over-used and its maintenance intervals are too far apart

Charterers and agents

To get your bearings you must first of all distinguish between:
- Management companies (normally called charter companies) who manage a fleet and whose principle job, once the company is established, is to maintain the boats and welcome clients.

The role of these people is fundamental because it is they who guarantee the supply and maintenance of the boats.
- Agents, who sell the services, whether bareboat or charter.

These too have their uses because most of the time they package together the charter price with the costs of flights and other relevant services (for example overnight accommodation), so the whole business has become associated with the idea of a 'package', which often comes competitively priced.

That said, the main function of agents is to make the best selection for their potential clients, in terms of quality versus price, from the range of charter fleets or 'long charter' yachts on the market.

Seasons

(see also section on Climate above)
The Antillean climate is at its best in the winter, especially in comparison to storms and freezing temperatures in northern European regions. It is also from November to May that the trade winds are at their most constant, squalls less frequent and, bar the odd

exception, hurricanes non-existent. That said, it's worth remembering that in winter the trades can blow pretty freshly (20-30kts) and that squalls still occur.

In summer, although the trades are weaker and more irregular, that's still not a flat calm.

As for hurricanes, despite a perceptible increase in frequency over the last few years (see section on Hurricanes), not every island is hit by one every year. And it's also worth remembering that the nature of the season is reflected in charter prices.

The best prices are on offer in low season (outside the peak winter period, festivals and school holidays). This period also goes together with anchorages being less crowded, which is no small point.

Cruising itineraries

Given the number of island and their variety, the choice is vast. Your choice will depend on your skills and the time at your disposal.

To help you choose a route depending on your other criteria, the table above gives some basic indications of the times and distances involved.

As a general rule you should remember:
- that in the Antilles the generally benign climate in no way guarantees permanent soldier's breezes!
- that the sea state in the passages between islands is often very rough, especially in winter
- that a crew that sails infrequently doesn't always have its sea-legs
- that, to the general demands of sailing, if you've come from Europe you must add possible jet-lag

What works with a cruise is finding the right balance between what you'd like to achieve and what your crew can manage.

Chartering and the law

You should note that chartering is now considered by the governments of many islands as a commercial activity. That being so, in some areas it falls under pretty strict regulations. These cover safety aboard, legal obligations and tax liability. This is particularly so in the French islands where all chartering is subject to merchant shipping regulations. In other islands (especially the ex-British ones) the regulations are laxer, even extremely liberal on condition certain taxes are paid.

MARINAS	No. of berths	Depths m	Water	Electricity	Fuel	BOATYARDS	Travel lift	Slip	Floating Dock	Crane	Depth limit m	NOTES
MARTINIQUE (+33)												
BAIE DE FORT DE FRANCE												
Marina de la Pointe du Bout: VHF 9 ☎ 05 96 66 07 74 *Fax* 05 96 66 00 50	100	3	•	•								Narrow entrance. Quite small.
						SIGBR: Bassin Radoub ☎ 05 96 72 69 40 *Fax* 05 96 63 17 69						Graving dock for large commercial ships
						Carénantilles: **Baie des Tourelles** ☎ 05 96 63 76 74 *Fax* 05 96 71 66 83	45 t				3	Many professional services nearby
Anse Mitan Ponton du Bakoua: VHF 68 ☎ 05 96 66 05 45 *Fax* 05 96 66 15 46	20	4–5	•	•	•							Dock for big ships often damaged by swell
LE MARIN												
Port de Plaisance du Marin: SAEPP VH/9 ☎ 05 96 74 83 83 *Fax* 05 96 74 92 20	600	2–4	•	•	•							The largest yachting. centre in Martinique Numerous services
						Carénantilles: Le Marin ☎ 05 96 74 77 70 *Fax* 05 96 74 78 22	55 t		700 t		4	All kinds of work and repairs. Numerous services nearby
LE FRANÇOIS												
Club Nautique du François: ☎ 05 96 54 29 54 *Fax* 05 96 54 14 77	20	2·5–3	•	•	•							No technical services, but good shelter. Managed by the Mairie. Many berths occupied by residents
LE HAVRE DU ROBERT												
Marin'Ehra: ☎ 05 96 65 38 74 *Fax* 05 96 65 46 42	5	1·5–1·9	•	•								Shallow. Mostly for residents power boats
ST LUCIA (+ 758)												
RODNEY BAY												
Rodney Bay Marina: VHF 16 ☎ 452 0324 *Fax* 452 0185	230	2·7–3	•	•	•	Rodney Bay Marina Yard: ☎ 452 8215	50 t			•	3	Good shelter, well equipped, numerous technical services
					•	CASTRIES **Castries Yacht Center:** ☎ 452 6234 *Fax* 453 2653	35 t		35 t		2·7	Fenced and guarded hard-standing. Some technical services nearby
ST VINCENT (+ 784)												
OTTLEY HALL												
Ottley Hall Marina: ☎ 457 2178 *Fax* 456 1302	20	4–5	•	•	•	CCYY: ☎ 456 2640 *Fax* 456 1302	40 t		500 t	35 t	4	Basin can suffer badly from slop. Big ship haulout facilities. Some services attached
BLUE LAGOON												
Marina The Lagoon: VHF 68 ☎/Fax 458 4308	50	1·7–1·8	•	•	•							Good shelter, limited draft in usual entrance; alternative pass dangerous
BLUE LAGOON												
Barefoot Yacht Charter: VHF 68 ☎ 456 9334 *Fax* 456 9238		1·8–2	•	•	•							As above. Few berths on dock
GRENADINES (+ 784/473)												
BEQUIA												
Bequia Marina: VHF 68 - ☎/Fax 458 3272		3	•		•	Bequia Slip: ☎/Fax 458 3272		25 t			2·5	Simple dock. Hard-standing limited
UNION												
Bougainvilla: VHF 16/68 ☎ 458 8678 *Fax* 458 8569	15	3–4	•	•	(1)							Dock and small technical and commercial centre Various services (1) Occasional.
Anchorage Yacht Club (AYC): VHF 16/68 ☎ 458 8221 *Fax* 458 8365	15	3–4	•									Hotel and dock services
CARRIACOU						Tyrell Bay Yacht Haulout : ☎/Fax 443 8175	50 t			(1)	3	(1) 5t crane and fuel dock to be installed. Some services
					(1)							
GRENADA (+ 473)												
St-GEORGE'S												
Grenada Yacht Club (Ex. GYC): VHF 16 ☎ 440 3050 *Fax* 440 6826	15	2–3	•	•	•							Well kept and secure
Blue Lagoon Real Estate Corp. (Ex. GYS): ☎ 440 6893 *Fax* 440 6891	30/40	3–5	•	•	•							Facilities run down, few services
PRICKLY BAY												
Spice Island Marine Services: VHF 16 ☎ 444 4257 *Fax* 444 2090	30	3	•	•	•	Spice Island Marine Serv. ☎ 444 4257 *Fax* 444 2816	35 t			•	3	Many additional professional services at the yard
TRUE BLUE BAY												
True Blue Bay Resort & Marina: ☎ 439 1000 *Fax* 439 1001	10	3	•	•								A few visitors berths. Partly occupied by a charter company. Being extended

MARINAS	No. of berths	Depths m	Water	Electricity	Fuel	BOATYARDS	Travel lift	Slip	Floating Dock	Crane	Depth limit m	NOTES
MT HARTMAN BAY **Secret Harbour Marina:** ☎ 444 4449 *Fax* 444 4819	40	3–4	•	•	•							Part of hotel complex
CLARKE'S COURT BAY **Clarke's Court Bay Marina** VHF 16/74 ☎ 439 2593 *Fax* 439 3603	26					Island Dreams Yacht Services VHF 74 islandreams@caribsurf.com						
			• (1)	•	• (2)	**ST DAVID'S HARBOUR** **Grenada Marine** ☎ 443 1667 *Fax* 443 1668	70 t				12	Very isolated. Some yacht services nearby (1) Water in emergencies (2) Fuel by arrangement
BARBADOS (+ 246)												
SIXMAN BAY **Port St Charles:** ☎ 419 1000 *Fax* 422 4646	10	3	•	•	•							Residents' marina. A few other berths in the outer basin behind the sea wall
BRIDGETOWN HARBOUR **Fishing Harbour**			•		•	**Willie's Marine Services** ☎ 424 1808 *Fax* 425 1060	45 t			5 t	5	Various on-site sub contractors
GUADELOUPE												
POINTE A PITRE **Marina du Bas du Fort:** VHF 16/9 ☎ 05 90 93 66 20 *Fax* 05 90 90 81 53	1000	2–4	•	•	•	**Marina Boatyard** ☎ 05 90 93 66 20	14 t			1 t	3·5	The biggest marina in the Lesser Antilles. Hugh technical yachting complex
						CARENAGE **Lemaire Marine Service:** ☎ 05 90 90 34 47 *Fax* 05 90 91 77 88		80 t 100 t		3 t	3	Multihull specialist. Several methods of haulout. Services nearby
						Top Gun Marine ☎ 05 90 91 10 11 *Fax* 05 90 91 96 52		800 t		15 t	5	Services nearby. Not always operating. Large capacity haulout
						Chantier (Boatyard) Forbin: ☎ 05 90 83 21 34 *Fax* 05 90 90 05 01	20 t	80 t		18 t	3	Services nearby
ST FRANCOIS **Marina de Saint-François:** ☎ 05 90 88 47 28 *Fax* 05 90 88 53 48	120	2·5	•	•	• (1)							Few services. Tricky entrance. Limited raft (frequently silts up). (1) Refuel by jerries in emergencies
BASSE-TERRE **Marina de Rivière Sens:** VHF 16 ☎ 05 90 81 77 61 *Fax* 05 90 99 00 41	350	(1) 2–3·5	•	•	•							Few yacht services in the area. (1) Depth in approach channel, max draft 2m
						LES SAINTES **Baie de Marigot, A.M.M.S** ☎ 05 90 92 20 49 *Fax* 05 90 92 21 05		100 t		•	2–3	Reopened recently, services still uncertain. Very isolated
ANTIGUA (+ 268)												
ENGLISH HARBOUR **Nelson's Dockyard:** VHF 16/68 ☎ 460 1053 *Fax* 460 1516	30/40	3–4	•	•	•	**Antigua Slipway** ☎ 460 1056 *Fax* 460 1566	35 t	120 t			2–4	Major haul-out facilities. Specialist services
FALMOUTH HARBOUR **The Catamaran Marina:** VHF 16/68 ☎ 460 1503 *Fax* 460 1506	40	2–3	•	•	•							Mega-yacht berths. On-site subcontractors. Many professional services nearby
Antigua Yacht Club Marina: VHF 68 ☎ 460 1544 *Fax* 460 1444	60	3–5	•	•	•							Mega-yacht berths. On-site subcontractors
Falmouth Harbour Marina: VHF 68 ☎ 460 6054 *Fax* 460 6055	40	3–5	•	•	•							Mega-yacht berths
MAMORA BAY **Saint-James Club Hôtel:** VHF 68 ☎ 460 8001 *Fax* 460 3015	20	3–4	•	•	•							Few vacancies in high season. Many motor-yachts. Difficult entrance
MOSQUITO COVE **Jolly Harbour Marina:** VHF 16/68 ☎ 462 6042 *Fax* 462 7703	150	3·5 –4	•	•	•	**Jolly Harbour Shipyard:** ☎ 462 6042 *Fax* 462 7703	70 t	20 t		2 t		Entry via a buoyed channel. Many specialist services in yard. Isolated
ST KITTS (+ 869)												
Port Zante: VHF 16 ☎ 466 5021 *Fax* 466 5020	60	3	•	•	•							Slop can be a major problem. Few services
ST-BARTHELEMY												
GUSTAVIA **Port de Plaisance:** VHF 16 ☎ 05 90 27 66 97 *Fax* 05 90 27 81 54	60	3–5	•	•	• (1)							Controlled anchoring zones inside & outside the basin. Beware of swell condition (1)Fuel in the commercial port

MARINAS	No. of berths	Depths m	Water	Electricity	Fuel	BOATYARDS	Travel lift	Slip	Floating Dock	Crane	Depth limit m	NOTES
St-Martin												
MARIGOT Marina Port la Royale: VHF 16/12/17 ☎ 05 90 87 20 43 *Fax* 05 90 87 55 95	80	2	•	•	• (1)							(1) Access via a shallow 2m channel with a lifting bridge to rather cramped basin in town centre
						SANDY GROUND Geminga: VHF 71 ☎ 05 90 29 35 52 *Fax* 05 90 29 65 36	22 t	50 t				Some services. Crane
SANDY GROUND Time Out: ☎ 05 90 52 02 88 *Fax* 05 90 52 02 89	15		•	•	•	**Time Out:** ☎/*Fax* as marina				15 t	2·5	Services in yard
ANSE MARCEL Port Lonvilliers: VHF 16/11 ☎ 05 90 87 31 94 *Fax* 05 90 87 33 96	140	2·8	•	•	•							Narrow entrance. Well sheltered & organised marina. Very isolated
OYSTER POND Captain Oliver's Marina: VHF 16/67 ☎/*Fax* 05 90 87 33 47	150	3	•	•	•							Tricky entrance. Good shelter. Marina part of an hotel. Services nearby but little for yachts
SINT MAARTEN (+ 5995)												
GREAT BAY Bobby's Marina: VHF 16 ☎ 422366 *Fax* 425442	30	1·5– 3	•	•	•	**PHILIPSBURG/ SIMPSON BAY** Bobby's Boatyard: VHF 69 ☎ Marina or ☎ 452890	80 t 25 t			27 t	3 4	Often full. Lots of specialist services nearby. Renovation planned
Great Bay Marina: ☎ 425705 *Fax* 424940	30	3	•	•								As above
COLE BAY Island Water World: ☎ 445310 *Fax* 43299 VHF 74	50	3	•	•						30 t		Haulout by crane. Many specialist services
Princess Yacht Club: VHF 16/78 ☎ 442953 *Fax* 444333	85	4	•	•	•							Deluxe atmosphere. Many specialist services nearby
SIMPSON BAY Simpson Bay Yacht Club Marina VHF 16/79 ☎ 442309 *Fax* 443378	120	3– 4	•	•	•							In Simpson Bay. Well sheltered. Many specialist services nearby
La Palapa: VHF 68 ☎ 452735 *Fax* 452510	20	6	•	•	•							In Simpson Bay. Well sheltered Many specialist services nearby
TORTOLA (+ 284)												
ROAD HARBOUR Prospect Reef Marina: ☎ 494 3311 *Fax* 494 5595	20	1·7	•	•	•							Tricky entry. Limited depths. Mainly reservices for motor boats and authorised hotel boats
Fort Burt Marina: VHF 12 ☎ 494 4200 *Fax* 494 2547	40	2– 2·5	•	•	•							Some yacht services and several shops nearby
Road Reef Marina: VHF 12 ☎ 494 2751 *Fax* 494 5166	20	2– 2·5	•	•								Often full. Some yacht services on site
PORT PURCELL Baughers Bay Marina: VHF 16 ☎ 494 2393 *Fax* 494 1183	30	3– 4	•	•	•	**Baughers Bay Shipyard:** ☎/*Fax*: as marina		(1)			2 (2)	Dock very close to ferry pier. Limited yacht services. (1) Slip only for small boats (2) To be dredged
WICKHAMS CAY I Village Cay Marina: VHF 16 ☎ 494 2771 *Fax* 494 2773	100	2– 3	•	•	•							Well sheltered. Lots of shops and yacht services nearby
Inner Harbour Marina: VHF 16 ☎ 494 4289 *Fax* 494 6552	20	2	•	•	• (1)							Often full. Charter boat base (1) Limited depths on fuel dock
WICKHAMS CAY II **The Moorings Marina** VHF 12 ☎ 494 2331 *Fax* 494 2226 Affiliated marina on same dock: **Mariner Inn and Treasure Isle Dock**	150	2·5– 3	•	•	•							Well equipped and well sheltered. Berths part taken up by bareboats of The Moorings fleet. Enquire from the office before arriving to see if there's space
						Wickhams Cay II **Tortola Yacht Services:** ☎ 494 2124 *Fax* 494 4707	37 t 70 t				3	One of the most specialist boat yards in the Virgin Islands
NANNY CAY Nanny Cay Marina Centre: VHF 16 ☎ 494 2512 *Fax* 494 3288	180	3	•	•	•	**Nanny Cay Marine Yard:** ☎/*Fax*: as marina	50 t			•	3	Entry requires care. Lots of specilist yacht services. A long way from any town
WEST END Soper's Hole Marina: ☎ 495 4740 *Fax* 495 4301	30	3– 4	•	•	•							Pleasant surroundings. Close to the Frenchman's Cay boatyard
Frenchman's Cay Marina: VHF 16 ☎ 495 4050 *Fax* 495 4678	20		•	•		**Frenchman's Cay Shipyard** ☎ 495 4350 *Fax* 495 4678	40 t	200 t				Berthing for mega-yachts. Slip can take very large vessels. Some specialist yacht services on site

MARINAS	No. of berths	Depths m	Water	Electricity	Fuel	BOATYARDS	Travel lift	Slip	Floating Dock	Crane	Depth limit m	NOTES
EAST END Harbour View Marina:: VHF 16 ☎ 495 1775	14	2–3	•	•	•							Managed by Tradewind Yachts
Penn's Landing Marina: VHF 16 ☎ 495 1134 Fax 495 1352	10	2–2·5	•	•								Available berths limited. Depths in berths restricted. Some maintenance services on site
MARINA CAY/MAYA COVE Pusser's Marina Cay: VHF 16 ☎ 494 2174 Fax 494 4775		4	•	•	•							A dock for going alongside to fuel and water. Hotel and restaurant
Hodges Creek Marina: VHF 16 ☎ 494 5538 Fax 494 6958	40	2–2·5	•	•	•							Tricky entry. Quite tight inside. Usually almost full. A charterboat base
VIRGIN GORDA (+ 284)												
GORDA SOUND Leverick Bay Marina VHF 16 ☎ 495 7421 Fax 495 7367	20	2–4	•	•	•							Large dock with access to hotel facilities
Biras Creek Marina: VHF 16 ☎ 494 3556/494 3555 Fax 494 3557		3	•	•	(1) •							Dock part of the hotel (1) On the next door dock
Bitter End Yacht Club Marina: VHF 16 ☎ 494 2746 Fax 494 4756	20	4–5	•	•	•					• (1)		Berths managed by the hotel (1) Haul out only for very small boats
Saba Rock: VHF 16 ☎ 495 7711 Fax 495 7373	5	4–5	•									Very few berths
YACHT HARBOUR Virgin Gorda Yacht Harbour: VHF 16/11 ☎ 495 5500 Fax 495 5706	120	3	•	•	•	**YACHT HARBOUR** Virgin Gorda Yacht Serv.: ☎ 495 5318 Fax 495 5685	70 t				4	Good shelter in pleasant surroundings. Shops on site. Boatyard and yacht services on site
PETER ISLAND (+ 284) Peter Island Yacht Harbour: VHF 16 ☎ 495 2000 Fax 495 2500	20	2–3	•	•	•							Docks and berths part of the hotel. Good shelter
ST JOHN (+ 340)			•		•	Caneel Bay Shipyard: ☎ 693 8771	30 t				3	Very limited space. In operation irregularly. Primarily reserved for work on local vessels
ST THOMAS (+ 340)												
CHARLOTTE AMALIE Safehaven Marina: VHF 16/68 ☎ 774 6050 Fax 774 5935	150	3–5	•	•	•							Marina being refitted after hurricane damage. Some yacht services available
Frenchtown Marina: ☎ 777 9690 Fax 777 9750	30	2–4	•	•								In the town centre. Most berths taken by a charter company fleet
CROWN BAY Crown Bay Marina: VHF 16 ☎ 774 2255 Fax 776 2760	100	4·5	•	•	•							Very well equipped and sheltered. Big shopping and business centre nearby
						Haulover Marine Center: ☎ 776 2078 Fax 779 8426		350 t	50 t		3–4	Not much room. Some yacht service specialists on site
COMPASS POINT/BENNER BAY Compass Point Marina: VHF 16 ☎ 775 6144 Fax 779 1547	<80	2	•	•								Few visitors' berths. Draught limits
						Independent Boatyard: ☎ 776 0466 Fax 775 6576	50 t			10 t	2–4	Professional services nearby. Many specialists on site
La Vida Marina: ☎ 779 2799 Fax 779 1937	20	2	•	•	•							Pretty full with local live-aboards
Saga Haven Marina: ☎ 775 0520	50	2	•	•	•							Full. Draught limit
Fish Hawk Marina: ☎ 775 9058 Fax 775 9701	5	2			•							Full. Draught limit
RED HOOK American Yacht Harbour: VHF 16/11 ☎ 775 6454 Fax 776 5970	85	2–3	•	•	•							Many berths taken by residents and charter boats. Some yacht services. Huge area of business and technical services locally
Vessup Point Marina: ☎ 779 2495	20	3–6	•	•								Opposite American Yacht Harbour
Sapphire Beach Marina: VHF 16 ☎ 775 6100 Fax 775 4024	65	2–3	•	•	•							Full of local boats. No yacht services on site
ST CROIX (+ 340)												
St Croix Marine: VHF 16 ☎ 773 0289 Fax 778 8974	40	3	•	•	•	St Croix Marine Boatyard: ☎ 773 0289	60 t	200 t		15 t	3	Lots of specialist yacht services. The island's only boat yard
Green Cay Marina: VHF 16/68 ☎ 773 1453 Fax 773 9651	150	3	•	•	•							Well protected marina. No yacht services
Salt River Marina: VHF 16 ☎ 778 9650 Fax 778 0706	30	1·8–2·5	•	•	(1)					10 t		Very tricky entry with draught limits. No yacht services on site. (1) Fuel has to be delivered

GLOSSARY

Accra	Spicy fish cake
Arawaks	Amerindian people originally from Venezuela. First inhabitants of the Antilles, with peaceful and artistic ways
Bakoua	Straw hat woven from the leaves of a plant called 'bakoua' (Martinique)
BBQ	Barbecue
Békés	Descendents of first white colonists (a plausible etymology is the English name 'Baker' because of a baker's floury face)
Biguine	A popular Antillean dance and related melody
Bilharzia	Illness caused by a parasite
Blaff	Spicy fish stock
Blanc-Pays	The descendants of the old white settlers in Guadeloupe (q.v. Békés)
Calypso	Antillean dance and song form (esp. Carnival in Trinidad)
Caribs	Amerindian people. Warlike and possibly cannibal. (Origin of the name Kalinas = fierce people.) Chased the Arawaks from the entire Lesser Antilles
Carbet	A Carib Chief's large hut and gathering place
Carême	The dry season (winter). The French word means Lent
Case	Hut – a small, lightly built home
Caye (English 'Cay' or 'Key')	A submerged coral reef (from Spanish 'cayo', reef). The word is also sometimes used to refer to the small, often impermanent sand islands you find above the surface on the cays
Ciguatera	Poisoning from the ciguaterine poison accumulated in some fish
Cinq pou cent	Five per cent – popular term for the second glass of ti-punch (half the first)
Creole	Anything of Antillean origin – people, architecture, art, cuisine, etc. Also a semi-technical term for a language one up from a pidgin, originally mixing Spanish or French, English and various African languages, variants of which are spoken in many places in the Caribbean.In St Lucia, for example, Kweyol is the local patois version of 'Creole' and the name of a Creole!
EC$	The currency of the ex-British Caribbean islands (East Caribbean Dollar)
Fonds Blancs	Sandy shoals behind a coral barrier covered at half-tide on Martinique's windward coast

Gommier	A kind of gum tree. The dugout canoes made from them are also called gommiers
Hivernage	The wet season (summer); curiously the French term actually means 'wintering-over time' – i.e. the close season for sailors
Jump-up	Very lively night-time street festival of local dancing and music.
Lambi	Edible shellfish
Lolo	Simple local restaurant (fixed in location or moveable) with typical local food. The word comes from a slang French word for 'tit' or 'boob' – the original fast food for kids
Madras	Hat of coloured fabric that sends a love message according to the number of points it has
Manchineel	Also called the 'poison guava'. The tree, a spurge of the family *Euphorbaciae*, has very poisonous yellow-to-red, sweet scented, apple-like fruit, a sap that irritates the skin and the smoke of which, if it's used for fuel, irritates the eye. On the other hand, it's good wood for making furniture and polishes up well!
Maroon	A rebel slave
Merenguée	Usually spelled 'mérengue'. An Antillean folk dance in four time originating in Haiti or the Dominican Republic. It usually has three parts, paseo, merengue, and jaleo
Metro	A mainland Frenchman working in the French Antilles
Morne	Hill or hillock
Octroi de Mer	Import tax in the French Antilles
Ouassou	River (freshwater) crayfish of Guadeloupe
Pitt	Cock pit for cock fighting
Quimboiseur	Healer and caster of spells (connected with Voodoo beliefs and ritual)
	The roots of the word come from the Creole contraction of "Y a qu'a boire" (and possibly derived from the Christian Mass, ". . .Drink this. . .")
Raccoon	The local term in Guadeloupe, of which this almost extinct mammal is the National Park emblem, is 'raton laveur'. In French that literally means 'washing rat', from the raccoon's habit of washing its food before eating if there's water around for the purpose
Ravet	Antillean cockroach

Reggae	Music developed in the late 1960s & early 1970s from Jamaican 'ska', with powerful 4-beat music originally accompanying emotional songs often expressing rejection of established white-man culture. The best known exponents were Bob Marley & The Wailers, Jimmy Cliff and Toots and the Maytals
Saintoise	Local craft built in the Saintes Islands
Salako	Traditional Saintes islander's hat
Steel band	A band of 4 to 100 performers playing steel drums made from specially treated, cut off steel shipping drums for liquids. The drums originated in Trinidad and are now found throughout the Caribbean. They come in four sizes from bass to treble, called boom, cellopan, guitar pan, and ping pong. The music is foot-tappingly compulsive
Ti-punch	The Antillean drink of drinks; rum with cane sugar and green lime
Trace	French term for a footpath, used in Guadeloupe
Trigonocéphale	*Fer-de-lance* snake. The French word, meaning 'triangular headed', describes the shape of the snake's head. This snake is endemic in Martinique and its bite is dangerous and possibly fatal
Yen-yen	Small, very aggressive mosquito that appears around sundown
Yole	Local Martiniquan sailing boat, perhaps from the English word 'yawl', a common term for small, lugsail fishing craft, though Martiniquan yoles are spritsail schooner rigged
Z'habitant	River (freshwater) crayfish of Martinique
Z'oreilles	Pejorative term in the French Antilles for people from mainland France.
Zouk	Popular music of the Lesser Antilles

Services Directory

To help save you time hunting out information during your cruise or tour, we've listed here as many specialist businesses for the marine and tourist industry as possible. Under each island you'll find their names listed by business alphabetically, with addresses, phone and fax numbers and email contacts.

Nature of business

Airlines
Travel agents
Ferry companies
Marinas & docks
Hotels & restaurants
Car hire companies/
Taxi companies
Tour operators

Yacht Services

Boatyards, haul-out, hard standing
Chandlers and marine equipment stockists
Tenders, liferafts and outboards (sale and service)
Sailmakers, canvas and awning makers, riggers
Mechanics and diesel maintenance
Electrical, electronic and refrigeration engineers
Boatbuilders and GRP laminate specialists
Maintenance and repair services
Joinery
Surveyors
Dive shops and clubs
Charterers and brokers

Listing order for each island

For sailing
Marinas, docking, boatyards and professional yacht services

For tourism
- A selection of restaurants and hotels whose reputation, value for money, proximity to an interesting site or anchorage, or simply the local colour seems to us worth a passing tourist's or yachtsman's notice (see also the notes on restaurants and hotels below).
- Car hire companies close to airports, in the main towns or in marinas
- Main airline and shipping companies with inter-continental or inter-island services.

All this information is subject to rapid change that affects its accuracy. Readers are advised to use the list with caution.

Restaurants

The approximate prices are given in four categories A to D and calculated according to the following currency conversion rate:

EURO ZONE	US$ ZONE (US$1 = EC$ 2·60)
A = €12–18	US$12–18
B = €18–25	US$18–25
C = €25–32	US$25–32
D = >€32	>US$32

These prices do not include drinks and in no way guarantee the quality of the food.

Note for the ex-British or the US islands, expect an additional charge of 15–17% for sales tax and service.

Hotels

Simple Simple with adequate bathroom and toilet facilities
Comfortable Comfortable with bathroom or shower
Luxury Very comfortable, all facilities
Very luxurious Top of the range, very full facilities
The quality of each category can vary between islands according to the level of tourist infrastructure development.

Martinique

Note when calling numbers in French islands from non-French islands, omit the 0 after the country code

AIRLINES
CTA Air Martinique
☎ 33 (0)5 96 42 16 40
Fax 33 (0)5 96 42 16 52
Air Calypso
☎ 33 (0)5 96 42 12 72
Fax 33 (0)5 96 42 18 68
Air Caraïbes
☎ 33 (0)5 06 42 14 36
Fax 33 (0)5 96 51 11 06
Air France
☎ 33 (0)5 96 55 33 00
Fax 33 (0)5 96 71 75 77
Corsair
☎ 33 (0)5 96 42 16 40
Fax 33 (0)5 96 42 16 39
Liat
☎ 33 (0)5 96 42 16 03
Fax 33 (0)5 96 57 07 60

FERRY COMPANIES
Brudey Frères Quai Ouest, Fort de France
Inter island routes
☎ 33 (0)5 96 70 08 50
Fax 33 (0)5 96 70 53 75
Vedettes Madinina Quai Ouest, Fort de France
Routes
Fort de France to La Pointe du Bout; Fort de France to Anse à l'Ane/Anse Mitan
☎ 33 (0)5 96 63 06 46
Fax 33 (0)5 96 63 80 68
Contact@vedettesmadinina.com
L'Express des Iles Quai Ouest, Fort de France
☎ 33 (0)5 96 63 12 11
Fax 33 (0)5 96 63 34 47
Vedettes Somatour *Fort de France to Pointe du Bout*
☎ 33 (0)5 96 73 (0)5 53
Societé Saintanaise *Ste Anne to Fort de France*
☎ 33 (0)5 96 76 83 23
Fax 33 (0)5 96 74 65 58

MARINAS/DOCKS (WATER/FUEL)
FORT DE FRANCE
CBS Baie des Tourelles
☎ 33 (0)5 96 71 73 91
Fax 33 (0)5 96 71 73 96
CBS@sasi.fr
Fuelling possible
Marina Pointe du Bout
☎ 33 (0)5 96 66 07 74
Fax 33 (0)5 96 66 00 50 VHF 9
marina3ilets@wanadoo.fr
Ponton du Bakoua Anse Mitan
☎ 33 (0)5 96 66 05 45 *Fax* 33 (0)5 96 66 15 46 VHF 68
Fuel (Total service station)
CUL-DE-SAC DU MARIN
Port de Plaisance du Marin (S.A.E.P.P.) ☎ 05 96 74 83 83
Fax 05 96 74 92 20 VHF Ch 9
port.marin@wanadoo.fr
Water and fuel

BAIE DU FRANCOIS
Club Nautique du François
☎ 33 (0)5 96 54 29 54
Fax 33 (0)5 96 54 14 77
VilleFRANCOIS@wanadoo.fr
Fuel on the dock

LE HAVRE DU ROBERT
Marin'Erha (Marina Ernest Hayot)
☎ 33 (0)5 96 65 38 74
Fax 33 (0)5 96 65 46 42
jennifer.evasion@wanadoo.fr
Fuel on the dock

PROFESSIONAL YACHT SERVICES
Boatyards/Haulout/Antifouling
FORT DE FRANCE
Multicap Caraïbes Bassin Radoub, Fort de France
☎ 33 (0)5 96 71 41 81
Fax 33 (0)5 96 71 41 83
MCM@multicapcaraibes.com
Carenantilles Baie des Tourelles
☎ 05 96 63 76 74
Fax 05 96 71 66 83
carenfdf@sasi.fr
SIGBR Bassin du Radoub
☎ 06 96 72 69 40
Fax 05 96 63 17 69
LE MARIN
Nautic Services Le Marin
☎ 33 (0)5 96 74 70 45
Fax 33 (0)5 96 74 70 52
nautic.services@wanadoo.fr
Carenantilles Ancienne Usine
☎ 05 96 74 77 70
Fax 05 96 74 78 22
carenmarin@sasi.fr

Chandleries/Watersports/Diving equipment
Carene Shop Le Marin
☎ 33 (0)5 96 74 74 80
Fax 33 (0)5 96 74 79 16
carene.shop@wanadoo.fr
Plus Nautique
Fort de France
☎ 33 (0)5 96 60 58 48
Fax 33 (0)5 96 63 73 31
plusnaut@wanadoo.fr
Le Marin
☎ 33 (0)5 96 74 62 12
Fax 33 (0)5 96 74 62 22
info@mer-et-sport.com
Caraïbe Gréement Le Marin
☎ 05 96 74 80 33
Fax 05 96 74 66 98
Le Ship
Pointe du Bout – Trois Ilets
☎ 05 96 66 05 40
Fax 05 96 66 04 08
Le Marin – Port de Plaisance
☎ 05 96 74 87 55
Fax 05 96 74 85 39
le-ship-martinique@wanadoo.fr
Multicap Caraïbes
Bassin Radoub, Fort de France
☎ 05 96 71 41 81
Fax 05 96 60 10 97
MCM@multicapcaraibes.com
Polymar Baie des Tourelles, Fort de France
☎ 33 (0)5 96 70 62 88
Fax 33 (0)5 96 60 10 97
polymar@sasi.fr
Coopemar SA Baie des Tourelles, Fort de France
☎ 33 (0)5 96 63 68 49
Fax 33 (0)5 96 63 76 63
coopemar@sasi.fr
Sea Services Fort de France
☎ 33 (0)5 96 70 26 69
Fax 33 (0)5 96 71 60 53
Scuba' Tech Fort de France
☎ 33 (0)5 96 72 86 84
Fax 33 (0)5 96 66 13 36
Sub Evasion Trois Islets
☎ 33 (0)5 96 66 11 25
Fax 33 (0)5 96 66 13 36
Sea Shop Le Marin
☎ 33 (0)5 96 74 63 65
Fax 33 (0)5 96 66 13 36
Wind Rivière Salée
☎ 33 (0)5 96 68 21 28
Fax 33 (0)5 96 68 21 38

Yacht Services
Caribizz on Line Le Marin VHF 12
☎ 33 (0)5 96 74 16 82
Fax 33 (0)5 96 74 16 83
info@caribbizz.com
Cyber Carene Carenantilles, Le Marin
☎ 33 (0)5 96 74 77 70
carenmarin@sasi.fr

Dinghies/liferafts/outboards (sale and repair)
La Survy
Fort de France
☎ 33 (0)5 96 79 70 66
Fax 33 (0)5 96 79 35 69
Le Marin
☎ 33 (0)5 96 74 63 63
Fax 33 (0)5 96 74 63 00
lasurvy@wanadoo.fr
Coopemar SA Baie des Tourelles, Fort de France
☎ 33 (0)5 96 63 68 49
Fax 33 (0)5 96 63 76 63
ooopomar@oooi.fr
CBS
Baie des Tourelles, Fort de France
☎ 33 (0)5 96 71 73 91
Fax 33 (0)5 96 71 73 96
CBS@sasi.fr
Ancienne Usine, Le Marin
☎ 33 (0)5 96 74 70 30
Fax 33 (0)5 96 74 70 31
Camaco Bassin Radoub, Fort de France
☎ 33 (0)5 96 73 70 45
Fax 33 (0)5 96 60 28 03
Crocquet Fort de France
☎ 33 (0)5 96 60 54 54
Fax 33 (0)5 96 63 66 08
OMC Cours Plissonneau, Fort de France
☎ 33 (0)5 96 60 03 58
Fax 33 (0)5 96 63 70 91
CMCI Le Lamentin
☎ 33 (0)5 96 51 11 57
Fax 33 (0)5 96 51 13 26
Yave Marine/Madia Nautic
Le Lamentin
☎ 33 (0)5 96 45 68 55
Fax 33 (0)5 96 57 22 53
yavemarine@wanadoo.fr
Jennifer Evasion Marin'Erha
☎ 33 (0)5 96 65 78 34
Fax 33 (0)5 96 65 46 42
jennifer.evasion@wanadoo.fr

Sailmakers/awnings/riggers
Incidences Martinique/Voiles Caraïbes
La Pointe du Bout
☎ 33 (0)5 96 66 07 24
Fax 33 (0)5 96 66 09 98
incidences.marin@wanadoo.fr
Le Marin
☎ 33 (0)5 96 74 88 09
Fax 33 (0)5 96 74 87 94
North Sails Caraïbes Fort de France
☎ 33 (0)5 96 68 03 34
Fax 33 (0)5 96 63 65 23
northmartinique@wanadoo.fr
Manu Voiles Baie des Tourelles
☎ 33 (0)5 96 63 10 61
Fax 33 (0)5 96 68 50 69
Caraïbe Gréement Le Marin
☎ 33 (0)5 96 74 80 33
Fax 33 (0)5 96 74 66 98
Voilerie Assistance Le Marin
☎ 33 (0)5 96 74 88 32
Fax 33 (0)5 96 45 40 48

Mechanics/diesel engines
AMS Le Marin
☎ 33 (0)5 96 74 70 78
Fax 33 (0)5 96 74 63 71
antillesmarine@sasi.fr
IDS (Inboard Diesel Service)
Case Pilote
☎ 33 (0)5 96 78 71 96
Fax 33 (0)5 96 78 80 75
Madia Boat
Baie des Tourelles, Fort de France
☎ 33 (0)5 96 63 10 61
Fax 33 (0)5 96 63 48 70
Croisières Assistance
Marina Pointe du Bout
☎ 33 (0)5 96 66 17 82
Fax 33 (0)5 96 66 13 80
croisièresetassistance@wanadoo.fr

Mecanique Plaisance
Pointe du Bout – Trois Ilets
☎ 05 96 66 05 40
Fax 05 96 66 04 08
Le Marin – Port de Plaisance
☎ 05 96 74 68 74
Le Marin – Carenage
☎ 05 96 74 72 72
mecaplai@sasi.fr
Yave Marine/Madia Nautic
Le Lamentin
☎ 33 (0)5 96 45 68 55
Fax 33 (0)5 96 57 22 56
yavemarine@wanadoo.fr
Jennifer Evasion
Marin'Erha
☎ 33 (0)5 96 65 78 34
Fax 33 (0)5 96 65 46 42
jennifer.evasion@wanadoo.fr

Electrics/electronics/refrigeration
Madia Boat Baie des Tourelles, Fort de France
☎ 33 (0)5 96 63 10 61
Fax 33 (0)5 96 63 48 70
Julian Cadet Petit Baie des Tourelles, Fort de France
☎/*Fax* 33 (0)5 96 23 67 75
AMS Le Marin
☎ 33 (0)5 96 74 70 78
Fax 33 (0)5 96 74 63 71
CS Services Le Marin
☎ 33 (0)5 96 74 91 13
Fax 33 (0)5 96 74 91 74
Cs.services@wanadoo.fr
Diginav Le Marin
☎ 33 (0)5 96 74 76 62
Fax 33 (0)5 96 74 76 63
Magic Froid Le Marin
☎ 33 (0)5 96 68 39 09
Sud Marine Electronique
Le Marin
☎ 33 (0)5 96 74 65 56
Fax 33 (0)5 96 74 69 54
Sudme@wanadoo.fr
Tilikum Le Marin
☎ 33 (0)5 96 74 67 03
Fax 33 (0)5 96 74 66 63
Croisières Assistance
Marina Pointe du Bout
☎ 33 (0)5 96 66 17 82
Fax 33 (0)5 96 66 13 80
croisièresetassistance@wanadoo.fr

Boatbuilders/laminates/woodwork
Latitude 14·28°
Le Marin
☎ 33 (0)5 96 74 78 58
Les As Teck
Le Marin
☎/*Fax* 33 (0)5 96 74 72 85
Multicap Caraïbes
Bassin du Radoub, Fort de France
☎ 33 (0)5 96 71 41 81
Fax 33 (0)5 96 71 41 83
MCM@multicapcaraibes.com
Plastik Services Le Marin
☎ 33 (0)5 96 74 70 37
Fax 33 (0)5 96 74 70 43
Polymar
Baie des Tourelles Fort de France
☎ 33 (0)5 96 70 62 88
Fax 33 (0)5 96 60 10 97
polymar@sasi.fr
Nautic Bois
Baie des Tourelles, Fort de France
☎ 33 (0)5 96 71 82 33
Fax 33 (0)5 96 71 95 74

Maintenance/welding
Ets Chalmessin,
Quai Ouest Fort de France
☎ 33 (0)5 96 60 03 75
Fax 33 (0)5 96 63 49 67
INFO.chalmessin@wanadoo.fr
Rolland Jean Michel
Fort de France
☎ 33 (0)5 96 71 49 28
Fax 33 (0)5 96 71 95 74
Crater Tony
Le Marin
☎ 33 (0)5 96 74 66 60

Martinique Sud Sablage
Le Marin
☎ 33 (0)5 96 74 70 45
Fax 33 (0)5 96 74 70 52
Nauticservices@wanadoo.fr
Entretien Multiservices
Le Marin
☎ 33 (0)5 96 74 80 00
Fax 33 (0)5 96 74 78 77
Tour de Fraise
Le Marin
☎ 33 (0)5 96 74 85 65
louismargiotta@voila.fr
Jennifer Evasion
Marin'Erha
☎ 33 (0)5 96 65 78 34
Fax 33 (0)5 96 65 46 42
jennifer.evasion@wanadoo.fr
PBS Helices
St Pierre
(Propellers) ☎ 33 (0)5 96 78 18 00
Fax 33 (0)5 96 78 17 07
Provisioning
Caribizz
☎ 33 (0)5 96 74 16 82
Fax 33 (0)5 96 74 16 83
info@caribizz.com
Online yacht provisioning
Marine surveyors
F Morel ☎ 33 (0)5 96 25 20 88
H Schwaratt
☎ 33 (0)5 96 27 29 61
SAE
Fort de France
☎ 33 (0)5 96 63 85 85
Fax 33 (0)5 96 73 55 26
Le Marin
☎ 33 (0)5 96 74 02 14
Fax 33 (0)5 96 74 02 15
sae@wanadoo.fr
DIVING
(Dives/air/equipment)
Espace Plongée Martinique
Marina Pte du Bout
☎/Fax 33 (0)5 96 66 01 79
Okéanos Club (Pierre & Vacances)
Ste Luce
☎ 33 (0)5 96 62 52 36 *Fax* 33 (0)5 96 62 24 64
Planète Bleue
Marina Pte du Bout
☎ 33 (0)5 96 66 08 79
Fax 33 (0)5 96 66 10 01
Planbleu@ais.mq
Plongée Passion
Grande Anse d'Arlet
☎ 33 (0)5 96 68 71 78
Fax 33 (0)5 96 68 72 52
Tropicasub Diving
St Pierre
☎ 33 (0)5 96 78 38 03
Fax 33 (0)5 96 52 46 82
Sub Evasion
Le Marin
☎/Fax 33 (0)5 96 74 63 65
subevasion@wanadoo.fr
Marina Pte du Bout
☎ 33 (0)5 96 66 11 25
Fax 33 (0)5 96 66 13 36
Comptoir des Iles et des Planètes
Ile Bleue/Ile Verte Marina Pte du Bout
☎/Fax 33 (0)5 96 66 10 13
club@ilebleue.com
Les Amis de Neptune
Marina Pte du Bout
☎ 33 (0)5 96 66 18 02
Fax 33 (0)5 96 27 06 80
neptune@wanadoo.fr
YACHT AND BOAT SALE & CHARTER
Petit Breton Antilles
Le Marin
☎ 33 (0)5 96 74 74 37
Fax 33 (0)5 96 74 74 43
pba@outremer.com
VPM Antilles
Le Marin
☎ 33 (0)5 96 74 70 10
Fax 33 (0)5 96 74 70 20
Chimere.yachting@wanadoo.fr

vpmmartinique@cgit.com
Bambou Yachting
Le Marin
☎ 33 (0)5 96 74 78 05
Fax 33 (0)5 96 74 82 77
Bamboumart@wanadoo.fr
Chimère Yachting
Le Marin
☎ 33 (0)5 96 74 78 56
Fax 33 (0)5 96 74 78 57
Chimere.yachting@wanadoo.fr
Corail Caraïbes
Le Marin
☎ 33 (0)5 96 74 10 76
Fax 33 (0)5 96 74 67 91
Corail.mart@wanadoo.fr
Kiriacoulis Antilles
Le Marin
☎ 33 (0)5 96 74 86 51
Fax 33 (0)5 96 74 73 41
Kiriacoulisantilles@wanadoo.fr
The Moorings Le Marin
☎ 05 96 74 75 39
Fax 05 96 74 76 44
moorings@moorings.fr
www.moorings.com
Star Voyage Le Marin
☎ 05 96 74 70 92
Fax 05 96 74 70 93
Star.voyage.marin@wanadoo.fr
Sunsail/Stardust Le Marin
☎ 05 96 74 77 61
Fax 05 96 74 77 80
www.sunsail.com
Tropical Yacht Service Le Marin
☎ 05 96 74 82 22
Fax 05 96 74 78 19
tys@tropical-yacht-service.com
www.vcomvoile.com
Internet charter bookings
RESTAURANTS/HOTELS
FORT DE FRANCE
La Cave à Vins
118 rue Victor Hugo
☎ 33 (0)5 96 70 33 02
Traditional food, choice of wines, price B
Le Marie Sainte
160 rue Victor Hugo
☎ 33 (0)5 96 63 82 24
Fax 33 (0)5 96 70 57 66
Simple Créole specialities, price A–B
Le Vieux Milan
Ave des Caraïbes
☎ 33 (0)5 96 60 35 31
Fax 33 (0)5 96 63 38 82
Italian food, pizzas, price B
Aux Pâtes Fraîches
Rue Victor Hugo
☎ 33 (0)5 96 63 21 34
Fax 33 (0)5 96 63 38 82
Italian food, price B
La Belle Epoque
Route de Didier
☎ 33 (0)5 96 64 41 19
Fax 33 (0)5 96 64 32 61
Gourmet French food, price D+

SCHOELCHER
Le Coté Sud
Patio de Cluny
☎ 33 (0)5 96 60 47 70
French food, price B
Le Citron Vert
Route de Cluny
☎ 33 (0)5 96 73 09 39
Fax 33 (0)5 96 70 42 75
Créole & French food, price B
Le Jardin de Jade
Anse Collat (ex Lido)
☎ 33 (0)5 96 61 15 50
*Chinese & Thai food, price B–C
Lovely view over the sea.*

POINTE DU BOUT/TROIS ILETS
Hôtel Le Méridien
Trois Ilets
☎ 33 (0)5 96 66 00 00
Fax 33 (0)5 96 66 00 74
MeridienFDF@compuserve.com
Theme menus, music, price C–D

Hotel: luxury
Bakoua Sofitel
Pointe du Bout
☎ 33 (0)5 96 66 02 02
Fax 33 (0)5 96 66 00 41
HO968@accorhotels.com
*Le Chateaubriand Restaurant
French gourmet food, price D+
Hotel: Luxury*
Novotel Carayou
Pointe du Bout
☎ 33 (0)5 96 66 04 04
Fax 33 (0)5 96 66 00 57
H1500@accorhotels.com
Surrounded by palms, near the beach. Hotel: luxury
Hôtel la Pagerie
Pointe du Bout
☎ 33 (0)5 96 66 33 05 30
Fax 33 (0)5 96 9666 00 99
Hpagerie@cgit.com
Hotel: luxury
Le Village Créole
Pointe du Bout
☎ 33 (0)5 96 66 03 19
Fax 33 (0)5 96 66 07 06
Infos@villagecreole.com
Hotel: very luxurious
Sapori d'Italia
Village Créole
☎/Fax 33 (0)5 96 66 15 85
Italian food, price B–D
L'Amphore
Anse Mitan
☎ 33 (0)5 96 66 03 09
International menu, musical entertainment, price B–C
La Villa Créole
Anse Mitan
☎ 33 (0)5 96 66 (0)5 53
Fax 33 (0)5 96 66 08 56
Créole & French food, price B–C
Le Nid Tropical
Anse à l'Ane
☎ 33 (0)5 96 68 38 36
Fax 33 (0)5 96 68 47 43
*Snacks & grills, price A
Hotel: simple, rooms & bungalows*
Pignon sur Mer
Anse à l'Ane
☎ 33 (0)5 96 68 38 37
Fax 33 (0)5 96 68 25 39
Créole & French food, price B–C
Chez Jojo
Anse à l'Ane
☎ 33 (0)5 96 68 36 89
Fax 33 (0)5 96 68 47 72
jojo.beach@wanadoo.fr
Créole food, price A–B, beach restaurant
Domaine de Robinson
Anse Noire
☎ 33 (0)5 96 68 62 82
Fax 33 (0)5 96 68 76 07
ansenoir@sasi.fr
*Créole food, price B–C
Hotel: comfortable, bungalows*

ANSES D'ARLET/ANSE DUFOUR
Chez Gaby Grande Anse
☎ 33 (0)5 96 68 65 04
Fax 33 (0)5 96 68 75 72
Créole food, price B
Ti-Sable Grande Anse
☎ 33 (0)5 96 68 62 44
Fax 33 (0)5 96 68 70 29
*Créole food, seafood, price B–C
On the beach*
Le Bout Dehors, Petit Anse
☎ 05 96 98 68 74 38
French, price B-C
Chez MarieJo, Anse Dufour
☎ 05 96 68 61 52
Creole, price A

STE LUCE
Hotel: Caribia
☎ 33 (0)5 96 62 20 62
Fax 33 (0)5 96 62 59 52
Hcaribia@cgit.com
Hotel: luxury

LE MARIN
Auberge du Marin in the town
☎ 0 96 74 83 88
Fax 33 (0)5 96 74 76 47
*Créole & French food, price A–B
simple, family atmosphere
Hotel: simple*
La Carêne on the terrace at the boatyard
☎ 33 (0)5 96 29 22 64
Simple menu, price A
Calebasse Café on the waterfront
☎ 33 (0)5 96 74 69 27
Fax 33 (0)5 96 74 84 20
calebasse@wanadoo.fr
*Events, exhibitions, cybercafe.
Créole food, fish, price B–C*
Habitation la Fontaine
on the hill above the bay
☎ 33 (0)5 96 74 82 49
Fax 33 (0)5 96 74 96 09
Hotel: comfortable, bungalows & studios
La Girafe
☎ 33 (0)5 96 74 82 83
Fax 33 (0)5 96 74 90 51
*Hotel: comfortable, studios & apartments
Restored 17th century residence*
Marin Mouillage
☎ 33 (0)5 96 74 65 54
Local food, price A–B
Mango Bay at the marina
☎ 33 (0)5 96 74 60 89
Fax 33 (0)5 96 42 18 56
Mangobay@wanadoo.fr
International menu, BBQ, price B–C

STE ANNE
Pol et Virginie
☎ 33 (0)5 96 76 77 22
Fax 33 (0)5 96 76 76 86
Créole & French food, fish, price B–C
Chez Gratieuse Route Cap Chevalier
☎ 33 (0)5 96 76 93 10
*Local & fish
Créole food, crayfish, price B*
Le Man Soufran
Rte Cap Chevalier
☎ 05 96 74 04 48
Creole food, crayfish, price A-B
La Dunette
☎ 33 (0)5 96 76 73 90
Fax 33 (0)5 96 76 76 05
infos@ladunette.com
*Créole food, crayfish, price B–C
Lovely terrace overlooking the sea
Hotel: comfortable*
Le Touloulou, Pointe Marin
☎ 33 (0)5 96 76 73 27
Fax 33 (0)5 96 76 94 97
Crayfish & fish, price B–C
Le Coco Neg' behind the church
☎ 33 (0)5 96 27 93 18
Fax 33 (0)5 96 76 94 82
*Traditional Créole food, price B
Very warm welcome, worth a detour*
Les Tamariniers Place de l'Eglise
☎ 33 (0)5 96 76 75 62
Fax 33 (0)5 96 76 78 33
Créole food, price B–C
L'Endroit Pointe Marin
☎ 33 (0)5 96 76 76 74
Beach restaurant with grills, price A–C

LE DIAMANT
Diamant les Bains Diamant town
☎ 33 (0)5 96 76 40 14
Fax 33 (0)5 96 76 27 00
*Near the beach among coconut palms
L'Assiette Créole Restaurant
seafood, price B–C
Hotel: luxury, rooms & bungalows*
Le Diam's Place de l'Eglise
☎ 33 (0)5 96 76 44 46
Fax 33 (0)5 96 76 28 56

Créole food, price B–C
Le Poisson Rouge
Quai Taupinière
☎ 33 (0)5 96 76 43 74
Fax 33 (0)5 96 76 25 51
Créole food, price A–B
Novotel Diamant Coralia Pointe
de la Cherry
☎ 33 (0)5 96 76 42 42
Fax 33 (0)5 96 76 22 87
HO461@accorhotels.com
La Cabane du Pecheur
Restaurant, *Créole, fish, price C–D*
Le Flamboyant, buffet, price C
Hotel: luxury
Relais Caraïbe 'La Cherry'
☎ 33 (0)5 96 76 44 65
Fax 33 (0)5 96 76 21 20
Créole & French food, price B–D
Hotel: luxury

LE FRANCOIS/ILET OSCAR
La Maison de l'Ilet Oscar
Le Francois
Colonial House
☎ 05 96 65 82 30
ilet.oscar@cgit.com
Frégate Bleue (Relais du Silence)
☎ 33 (0)5 96 54 54 66
Fax 33 (0)5 96 54 78 48
Fregatebleue@cgit.com
Hotel: luxury

LA TRINITE
La Caravelle,
Route du Chateau Dubuc
☎ 33 (0)5 96 58 07 32
Fax 33 (0)5 96 58 07 90
Caravelle@sasi.fr
Créole & French food, price B–C
Open evenings only, reservations
recommended
Hotel: very luxurious
Le Madras Tartane
☎ 33 (0)5 96 58 33 95
Fax 33 (0)5 96 58 33 63
Créole food, fish, price B–C

STE MARIE
Le Colibri Mornes des Esses
☎ 33 (0)5 96 69 91 95
Fax 33 (0)5 96 69 61 40
Créole family food, price B–D
Primerêve
Anse Azero
☎ 05 96 69 40 40
Fax 05 96 60 09 37
Primereve@sasi.fr
Le Balisier
Restaurant, *Créole, price B-D*
Hotel: comfortable

LE CARBET
La Datcha Plage du Coin
☎ 33 (0)5 96 78 04 45
Local food & crayfish, price B–C
L'Imprévu Grande Anse
☎ 33 (0)5 96 78 01 02
Fax 33 (0)5 96 78 08 66
Créole food, price A–B
Le Marouba Club Quartier Choisy
☎ 33 (0)5 96 78 00 21
Fax 33 (0)5 96 78 05 65
Créole & French food, price B–C

LE PRECHEUR
Habitation Céron Anse Céron
☎ 33 (0)5 96 52 94 53
Fax 33 (0)5 96 52 96 02
Créole food, freshwater crayfish,
price B–C
Chez Ginette Abymes, Precheur
☎ 33 (0)5 96 52 90 28 (lunchtime)
Local food, price A–B

MACOUBA
Pointe Nord Route de Grand
Rivière
☎ 33 (0)5 96 78 56 56 (lunchtime)
Freshwater crayfish, price A–B

GRAND RIVIERE
Yva chez Vava Le Bourg
☎/*Fax* 33 (0)5 96 55 72 72
Créole food, price A–C
Chez Tante Arlette
☎ 33 (0)5 96 55 75 75
Fax 33 (0)5 96 55 74 77
carinetantearlette@wanadoo.fr
Gourmet Créole food, price B–D
Hotel: simple

ST PIERRE
Le Fromager Route Fonds St
Denis
☎ 33 (0)5 96 78 19 07
Fax 33 (0)5 96 70 77 64
Créole food, price A–C
La Vague
☎ 33 (0)5 96 78 19 54
Local food, price A
Le Tamaya
☎ 33 (0)5 96 78 29 09
Local food, crayfish, price A–B
La Tartine
☎ 33 (0)5 96 29 46 39
Local food, price A
Habitation Josephine St Pierre
Local food, crayfish, price A
At the proprietor's home

ELSEWHERE
Hotel: Plantation de Leyritz Basse
Pointe
☎ 33 (0)5 96 78 53 92
Fax 33 (0)5 96 78 92 44
Hleyritz@cgit.com
Le Ruisseau Restaurant
Créole food, price B–D
Hotel: luxury, an old plantation
house
Havre du Voyageur Morne Rouge,
Fond Marie Reine
☎ 33 (0)5 96 52 40 00
(Reservations required)
Fixed daily menu, Créole food,
price B
Auberge de la Montagne Pelée
Morne Rouge, Route de l'Aileron
☎ 33 (0)5 96 52 32 09
Fax 33 (0)5 96 52 54 03
Créole food, price B–C
A mountain hut accessible
without any effort
Jennifer Evasion Havre du Robert
☎ 33 (0)5 96 65 78 34
Fax 33 (0)5 96 65 46 42
jennifer.evasion@wanadoo.fr
Local food, price B
La Plantation Pays Mêlé, Le
Lamentin
☎ 33 (0)5 96 50 16 08
Fax 33 (0)5 96 50 26 83
Créole & French food, price D+

CAR RENTAL
Budget Central reservations
☎ 33 (0)5 96 63 69 00
Fax 33 (0)5 96 51 36 48
Hertz Central reservations
☎ 33 (0)5 96 51 01 01
Fax 33 (0)5 96 51 26 46
Europcar Central reservations
☎ 33 (0)5 96 42 42 42
Fax 33 (0)5 96 42 42 44
Madin-Loc Le Marin
☎/*Fax* 33 (0)5 96 74 05 54
madinloc@wanadoo.com
Funny Rent Fort de France
☎ 33 (0)5 96 63 33 05
Fax 33 (0)5 96 63 45 78
Jumbo Car
Central reservations
☎ 05 96 42 22
Fax 05 96 42 22 32
Marina Pointe du Bout
☎ 05 96 66 11 55
Fax 05 96 66 09 00
Marina du Marin
☎ 05 96 74 71 77
Fax 05 96 74 79 77
resamar@jumbocar.com

St Lucia
AIRLINES
Air Caraïbes
☎ 758 452 2463 *Fax* 758 453 6868
American Airlines
☎ 758 454 6777 *Fax* 758 454 6358
British Airways (BWIA)
☎ 758 452 3778 *Fax* 758 454 5223
Liat ☎ 758 452 3051
Fax 758 453 6583
Helen Air Caribbean
☎ 758 453 2777 *Fax* 758 451 7360
Eagle Air (air taxi service)
☎ 758 452 1900 *Fax* 758 452 9683
FERRY COMPANIES
L'Express des Iles Castries
☎ 758 452 2211 (high speed ferry)
Windward Lines Castries
☎ 758 452 1364 *Fax* 758 453 1654
MARINAS/DOCKS (WATER/FUEL)
The Moorings Marigot
☎ 758 451 4357 *Fax* 758 451 4353
VHF 16
moorings@candw.lc
Water and fuel at the dock
Rodney Bay Marina Rodney Bay
☎ 758 452 0324 *Fax* 758 452 0185
VHF 16
rbmarina@candw.lc
Water and fuel at the boatyard
dock
St Lucia Yacht Services Vigie
Cove
☎ 758 451 9164
Fax 758 452 6787 VHF 16
slys@candw.lc
Fuel & other services
PROFESSIONAL YACHT
SERVICES
Boatbuilding/Haulout
Castries Yacht Center Castries
☎ 758 452 6234 *Fax* 758 453 2653
Water and fuel at the dock
Rodney Bay Marina Yard Rodney
Bay
☎ 758 452 8215
Water and fuel at the boatyard
dock
Chandlery/dinghies
Johnson Hardware Ltd
Rodney Bay (Johnson Marine
Centre)
☎ 758 452 0299 *Fax* 758 452 0311
Castries ☎ 758 452 2392
Rodney Bay Ship Services
☎ 758 452 9973 *Fax* 758 452 9974
Liferaft & Inflatable Center
Rodney Bay Marina
☎ 758 452 8306 *Fax* 758 458 0679
lifeafinflatable@candw.lc
OMC Marines Vieux Fort
☎ 758 454 6681 *Fax* 758 454 5024
Sailmaker/awnings
The Sail Loft, Rodney Bay Marina
☎ 758 452 8648 *Fax* 758 452 0839
syacht@candw.lc
Mechanics/diesel
repairs/outboards
International Diesel and Marine
Services Castries Yacht Center
☎ 58 453 2287 *Fax* 758 453 2523
idams@candw.lc
OMC Marines Vieux Fort
☎ 758 454 6681 *Fax* 758 454 5024
AF Valmont & Co Ltd Castries
☎ 758 452 3817 *Fax* 758 452 4225
afvalmont@candw.lc
Electronics/refrigeration
Regis Electronics Rodney Bay
Marina
☎ 758 452 0205 *Fax* 758 452 0206
stlucia@regiselectronics.com
Amtec Rodney Bay Marina
☎ 758 452 0498 VHF 72
YACHT CHARTER
Sparkling Charter Rodney Bay
Marina
☎ 758 452 8531 *Fax* 758 452 0183

sparklingcharter@free.fr
The Moorings
Marigot Bay Marina
☎ 758 451 4357
Fax 758 451 4230
moorings@moorings.fr
www.moorings.com
Destination St Lucia (DSL
Yachting) Rodney Bay
☎ 758 452 8531 *Fax* 758 452 0183
info@dslyachting.com
Kiriacoulis Rodney Bay
☎ 758 452 0932 *Fax* 758 452 0401
DIVING
Buddies Scuba
Rodney Bay Marina
☎/*Fax* 758 452 9086
Gros Ilet ☎ 758 450 8406
buddies@candw.lc
Scuba St Lucia
Anse Chastenet
☎ 758 459 7000 *Fax* 758 459 7700
Rodney Bay St Lucian Hotel
☎ 758 452 8009
Rosemond's Trench Divers
Marigot Bay
☎ 758 451 4761 *Fax* 758 453 7605
Marigot Beach Dive Marigot
☎ 758 451 4974 *Fax* 758 451 9311
mbc@candw.lc
Dive Fair Helen Vigie Cove
☎ 758 451 7716 *Fax* 758 451 9311
Frogs Windjammer Landing
Villa Beach Resort
☎ 75 450 0913 *Fax* 758 450 8831
RESTAURANTS/HOTELS
RODNEY BAY AREA
Bay Gardens Hotel
☎ 758 452 8060 *Fax* 758 452 8059
Hotel: comfortable
Key Largo
☎ 758 452 0282 *Fax* 758 452 9933
Pizzas from wood fired oven,
price B
Pizza! Pizza!
☎ 758 452 8282, *price A–B*
The Lime Restaurant
☎ 758 452 0761 *Fax* 758 452 9446
Local food & seafood, price B–C
Charthouse West shore of the
lagoon
☎ 758 452 8115 *Fax* 758 450 8252
BBQ, fish, price B–C
The Nouveau Bistro SE shore of
the lagoon
☎ 758 452 9494 *Fax* 758 452 0758
Seafood & fresh pasta, price C
(evenings only)
Razmataz Tandoori SE shore of
the lagoon
☎/*Fax* 758 452 9800
Indian cuisine, price C–D

CASTRIES AREA
Bon Appétit Morne Fortune
☎ 758 452 2757
International menu, price C–D
San Antoine's
☎ 758 452 4660 *Fax* 758 450 9434
International menu, price D
Well restored old building
international cuisine

VIGIE COVE AREA
The Coal Pot Restaurant
☎ 758 452 5566 *Fax* 758 453 6776
Local dishes in nouvelle cuisine
style, price B–C
French management
Froggie Jack's
☎ 758 458 1900 *Fax* 758 458 2911
Local food, price A–B
Windjammer Landing Resort
Labrelotte Bay
☎ 758 452 0913 *Fax* 758 452 9454
4 restaurants, lovely setting in
greenery, price A–C

MARIGOT BAY AREA
The Shack
☎ 758 451 4145 VHF 16
mratteray@candw.lc

BBQ, salads, price A–B
Chateau Mygo (ex Mama Sheila's)
☎/Fax 758 451 4772
Indian and Créole food, price A–B
Marigot Beach Club Hotel (ex Doolittle's) on the lagoon
☎ 758 451 4974 Fax 758 451 4973
mbc@candw.lc
Local food, price B–C
Hotel: comfortable, bungalows
Moorings Bay Hotel on the lagoon
☎ 758 451 4357 Fax 758 451 4353
International & local food, price D
Hotel: luxury cottages
J.J's Paradise, Marigot Harbour
☎ 758 451 4076
Fax 758 451 4146
VHF 16/14 Free ferry
Local food, Price B–C
Luxury bungalows

SOUFRIÈRE/DEUX PITONS/MALGRETOUTE AREA
Villa de la Gracia
Marigot Harbour
☎/Fax 758 458 3119
info@villadelagratia.com
Hotel: luxury
Anse Chastanet Resort Anse Chastanet
☎ 758 459 7000 Fax 758459 7700
ansechastanet@candw.lc
Shops, mountain bike expedition company
Hotel: very luxurious
The Old Courthouse 1898
Soufrière Waterfront
☎/Fax 758 459 5002 VHF 16
theoldcourthouse@yahoo.com
Local food, price B
Batiks for sale in the arcade
Camilla's Soufrière
☎ 758 459 5379 Fax 758 459 5684
Local food, price A–B
Hotel: simple, guesthouse
The Still Plantation Beach Resort NE Soufrière Bay
☎ 758 459 7224 Fax 758 459 7301
duboulayd@candw.lc
Créole food, seafood, price C
Hotel: comfortable studios, set amongst greenery
Hummingbird Beach NE Soufrière Bay
☎ 758 459 7232 Fax 758 459 7033
hbr@candw.lc
Local & French food, price B–C
Hotel: very luxurious, studios set amongst greenery
Batiks for sale in the arcade
Ladera Resort up the hill in Soufrière
☎ 758 459 7323 Fax 758 459 5156
ladera@candw.lc
Lovely view & setting
Dasheene Restaurant Local & international food, price C–D
Hotel: luxury, bungalows
Jalousie Hilton Mouillage des Pitons
☎ 758 459 7666 Fax 758 459 7667
domingues@jalousiehilton.com
4 restaurants, international food & seafood, price D
Hotel: very luxurious, cottages
Bang Beau Estate
☎ 758 459 7864
Local cuisine & seafood
Shady terrace
Harmony Beach Restaurant/Benny's Bar Malgretoute
☎ 758 459 5050 Fax 758 459 5033
VHF 16
Local seafood, price B
Anse Mitan Malgretoute
☎ 758 459 5174 VHF 16
Local food & snacks, price A–B

VIEUX FORT
Il Pirata Ristorante outside the town
☎ 758 454 6610
Italian food, price A–B
Kimatrai overlooking the anchorage
☎ 758 454 6328
Seafood, price A–B
Hotel: simple
CAR RENTAL/TAXIS/TOUR OPERATORS
CTL Rent-a-Car Rodney Bay Marina
☎ 758 452 0732 Fax 758 452 0401
ctlslu@candw.lc
TJ's Car Rental Rodney Bay Marina
☎ 758 452 0116 Fax 758 452 0466
Cool Breeze Jeep Car Rental Soufrière ☎ 758 459 7729
Fax 758 459 5309
Rodney Bay ☎ 758 458 0824
Toucan Travel Rodney Bay Marina
☎ 758 452 0896 Fax 758 452 9806
toucantravel@candw.lc
Travel World Vide Bouteile
☎ 758 451 7443 Fax 758 451 7445
travelworld@candw.lc
CJ Taxi Service Rodney Bay Marina
☎ 758 452 9957 Fax 758 452 0185
Ben's Taxi Service, Soufrière
☎ 758 459 5457 Fax 758 459 5719

St Vincent

AIRLINES
Liat
Kingstown ☎ 784 457 1821
Fax 784 457 2000
Airport ☎ 784 458 4841
Mustique Airways Ltd
☎ 784 458 4380 Fax 784 456 4586
SVG Air
☎ 784 457 5124 Fax 784 457 5077
svgair@caribsurf.com
Helen Air
☎ 784 458 4528 Fax 784 4586
FERRY COMPANIES
MV Bequia Express
☎/Fax 784 458 3472
bequiaexpress@caribsurf.com
MV Baracuda
☎ 784 456 5180
Admiralty Transport
☎ 784 458 3348 Fax 784 457 3577
MARINAS/DOCKS (WATER/FUEL)
KINGSTOWN
Fishing Dock North part
Water & fuel
WALLILABOU
Wallilabou Anchorage
Water

OTTLEY HALL
Ottley Hall Marina
☎ 784 457 2178 Fax 784 456 1302
ottleyhall@caribsurf.com
Water & fuel on the dock

BLUE LAGOON
The Lagoon Marina
☎/Fax 784 458 4308 VHF 68
info@lagoonmarina.com
Water & fuel on the dock
Barefoot Yacht Charter
☎ 784 456 9334/9526
Fax 784 456 9238
barebum@caribsurf.com
Water & fuel on the dock

VILLA VILLAGE
Aquatic Club
☎ 784 458 4205 Fax 784 457 5289
VHF 68
aquaticclub@vincysurf.com
Water on the dock

PROFESSIONAL YACHT SERVICES
Boatyards/haulout
Ottley Hall Marina
☎ 784 456 2640 Fax 784 456 1302
ottleyhall@caribsurf.com
Chandleries
Howard's Marine Calliaqua Bay
☎ 784 457 4328 Fax 784 457 4268
VHF 68
hml@caribsurf.com
St Vincent Sales & Services Kingstown
☎ 784 457 1820 Fax 784 456 2620
Mechanics/outboards/workshops
Howard's Marine Calliaqua Bay
☎ 784 457 4328 Fax 784 457 4268
VHF 68
hml@caribsurf.com
Oscar's Machine Shop Belair
☎/Fax 784 456 4390
KP Marine Ltd Kingstown
☎ 784 457 1806 Fax 784 456 1364
St Vincent Sales & Services Kingstown
☎ 784 457 1820 Fax 784 456 2620
kpmarine@caribsurf.com
Electrics
Nichol's Marine Belair
☎ 784 456 4118 Fax 784 456 5884
VHF 68
Boatbuilders
Bulhers Yachts Ltd Calliaqua
☎/Fax 784 458 4639
DIVING
Dive St Vincent Villa Village
☎ 784 457 4714 Fax 784 457 4948
VHF 68
bill2s@DiveStVincent.com
Dive Fantasea Villa Village
☎ 784 457 5560 Fax 784 457 5577
divefantasea@vincysurf.com
Wallilabou Dive Experience Wallilabou
VHF 68 ☎ 784 456 0355
walldivexp@caribsurf.com
Petit Byahaut
☎/Fax 784 457 7008 VHF 68
petitbyahaut@caribsurf.com
YACHT CHARTER
Barefoot Yacht Charters Blue Lagoon
☎ 784 456 9334 Fax 784 456 9238
Sunsail/Stardust Blue Lagoon
☎ 784 458 4308
Fax 784 458 4308
www.sunsail.com
TMM Blue Lagoon
☎ 784 456 9608 Fax 784 456 9917
VHF 68
sailtmm@caribsurf.com
Blue Lagoon Marine Blue Lagoon
☎ 784 456 8433 Fax 784 456 8378
cruising@vincysurf.com
Power boat rentals.
RESTAURANTS/HOTELS
CHATEAUBELAIR AREA
Beach Front Restaurant
☎ 784 458 2853 Fax 784 456 9238
VHF 16/68
Local food, price A–B cuisine

CUMBERLAND AREA
Stephens Hideout
☎ 784 458 2209 VHF 68
Local food & seafood, price A–B
Bennett
VHF 68
Local food, price A
Tours organised

WALLILABOU AREA
Wallilabou Anchorage
☎ 784 458 7270 Fax 784 457 9917
VHF 68/86
wallanch@caribsurf.com
Local food & fish, price A–B
Hotel: simple
Port of entry, mooring buoys, water & yacht services

PETIT BYAHAUT AREA
Petit Byahaut
☎/Fax 784 457 7008 VHF 68
petitbyahaut@caribsurf.com
Seafood, vegetarian food, price C–D+
Hotel: comfortable, lodges
Mooring buoys available (fee added to the bill), tours & watersports

KINGSTOWN AREA
Basil's (Cobblestone Inn)
☎ 784 457 2713 Fax 784 456 2597
Local food and callaloo soup, price C

YOUNG ISLAND/VILLA VILLAGE AREA
Slick's Restaurant
☎ 784 457 5783 VHF 68
International menu, seafood, price B–C
Aquatic Club
☎ 784 458 4205 Fax 784 457 5289
aquaticclub@vincysurf.com
Local food, price B
Various services, live entertainment Friday evening
Lime Pub Restaurant
☎ 784 458 4227 Fax 784 456 9333
VHF 68/13
Fish, BBQ, price B–C
Shady terrace with agreeable setting
Mariners Hotel
☎/Fax 84 457 5261
marinershotel@caribsurf.com
Royal Harbour Restaurant Local food, price C–D
Hotel: comfortable
Pleasant setting with swimming pool
Sunset Shores
☎ 784 458 4411 Fax 784 457 4800
sunshore@caribsurf.com
Seafood, price C–D
Hotel: luxury
Pleasant setting with swimming pool.
Young Island Resort
☎ 784 458 4826 Fax 784 457 4567
VHF 68
yisalnd@caribsurf.com
International menu, buffet, price D+
Hotel: very luxurious, rooms & bungalows
Elegant setting, luxurious ambiance

BLUE LAGOON AREA
Barefoot Bistro
☎ 784 456 9526 Fax 784 456 9238
barebum@caribsurf.com
Local & international food, price A–B
Sunsail Lagoon Marina Hotel
☎ 784 458 4308
sunsailsvg@caribsurf.com
International & local food, price B–C
Hotel: very luxurious

CAR RENTAL/TAXIS/TRAVEL AGENTS
Avis Rent a Car
Airport ☎ 784 456 4389
Kingstown ☎ 784 456 2929
Fax 784 456 2777
humps@caribsurf.com
Kim's Rentals Arnos Vale
☎ 784 456 1884 Fax 784 456 1681
mail@kimsrentals.com
Baleine Tours Villa Village
☎ 784 457 4089 Fax 784 457 2432
VHF 68
prosec@caribsurf.com
Sam Taxi & Tours Cane Garden
☎ 784 456 4338 Fax 784 456 4233
VHF 16/68
samtaxitours@caribsurf.com
Fantasea Tours Villa Beach
☎ 784 457 4477 Fax 784 457 5577

fantasea@caribsurf.com
Jeffrey's Taxi & Rentals
☎ 784 458 4308/458 4944 VHF 68

Grenadines

AIRLINES
Air Caraïbes
Union ☎ 784 458 8826
St Vincent ☎ 784 458 4528
Fax 784 458 4187
Liat St Vincent
☎ 784 458 45841
Fax 784 457 2000
Helen Air
☎ 784 452 1958
SVG Air
St Vincent ☎ 784 457 5124
Fax 784 457 5077
Union ☎ 784 458 8882
The Mustique Airways St Vincent
☎ 784 458 4380 *Fax 784 456 4586*

FERRY COMPANIES
BEQUIA
Bequia Ferry to St Vincent
☎ 784 458 3348 *Fax 784 457 3577*
admiraltrans@caribsurf.com
CARRIACOU
Osprey Express Ltd Hillsborough
Daily to Grenada & Petite
Martinique (except Wednesday)
☎ 473 444 8126 (Carenage
Grenda)

DOCKS (WATER/FUEL)
BEQUIA
Bequia Marina Admiralty Bay
☎ 784 458 3272 VHF 68
Fuel & water on the dock
Daffodil Marine Taxis Admiralty
Bay
☎ 784 458 3942 VHF 68
Fuel delivered to the dock
MUSTIQUE
The Mustique Company
☎ 784 458 4621 *Fax 784 456 4565*
mustique@mustique-island.com
*Mooring buoys for rent (private
area)*
UNION
AYC (Anchorage Yacht Club)
Clifton
☎ 784 458 8221 *Fax 784 458 8365*
VHF 16/68
aycunion@caribsurf.com
Water
Eillon Gas & Diesel Clifton
☎ 784 458 8869 *Fax 784 458 8163*
VHF 16
Fuel
**Bougainvilla Anchorage Yacht
Club**
VHF 16
☎ 784 458 8678
Fax 784 458 8569
bougainvilla@caribsurf.com
Water, Fuel

PETIT ST VINCENT (PSV)
PSV Resort
☎ 784 458 8801 *Fax 784 458 8428*
Water & fuel on the dock.

PETITE MARTINIQUE
B&C Fuels Enterprise
☎ 473 443 9110 *Fax 473 443 9075*
Fuel, Water on pontoon

PROFESSIONAL YACHT SERVICES
*Note In principle all services listen
out on VHF 68*

Boatyards/haul-out
BEQUIA
Bequia Slip Admiralty Bay
☎/Fax 784 458 3272
neilsan@vincysurf.com

CARRIACOU
Tyrell Bay Yacht Haulout Tyrell
Bay
☎/Fax 784 443 8175
☎ 473 443 6940
tbyh@usa.net

Chandleries/dinghies
BEQUIA
Grenadines Yacht & Equipment
Admiralty Bay
☎ 784 458 3347 *Fax 458 3696*
VHF 16
gyebequia@caribsurf.com
Bequia Marine Supply Admiralty
Bay
☎/Fax 784 457 3157
☎ 784 457 3951
Budget Marine (Bo'Sun's Locker)
Admiralty Bay
☎ 784 458 3426 *Fax 784 458 3925*
budmarbequia@vincysurf.com
Wallace & Co Admiralty Bay
☎/Fax 784 458 3360
wallco@caribsurf.com
Bequia Venture Admiralty Bay
☎ 784 458 3925 *Fax 784 458 3000*

CARRIACOU
Windward Marine (Mike's Marine)
☎ 473 443 8500 *Fax 473 443 8092*
windwardmarine@hotmail.com

Miscellaneous services
Carriacou Yacht Club Tyrell Bay
☎/Fax 473 443 6292 VHF 16
carriyacht@caribsurf.com
Various services, warm welcome.

Outboards/mechanics/electrics
BEQUIA
Grenadines Yacht & Equipment
Admiralty Bay
☎ 784 458 3347 *Fax 784 458 3696*
VHF 16
gyebequia@caribsurf.com
Max Marine (Bequia Marine
Supply) Admiralty Bay
☎/Fax 784 457 3157
Fax 784 457 3951
Caribbean Diesel Admiralty Bay
☎/Fax 784 457 3114
Fixam Engineering
☎/Fax 784 457 3406

UNION
Unitech Marine Bougainvilla
☎/Fax 784 458 8913 VHF 16
unitech@caribsurf.com
Island Marine Special Clifton
☎ 784 458 8039 VHF 68

Maintenance/Welding
CARRIACOU
Ateliers G & D Weber Tyrell Bay
☎/Fax 473 407 1151 VHF 16 *Sea
Rose*
dominiqueweber@hotmail.com
Floating workshop

Sailmakers/awnings
BEQUIA
Bequia Canvas Admiralty Bay
☎ 784 457 3291 *Fax 784 457 3523*
Turbulence Sails Admiralty Bay
☎/Fax 784 457 3297 VHF 16
turbsail@caribsurf.com
Grenadines Sails on Bequia
Marina Admiralty Bay
☎ 784 457 3507 VHF 16/68
gsails@caribsurf.com

CARRIACOU
Ateliers G & D Weber Tyrell Bay
☎/Fax 473 407 1151 VHF 16 *Sea
Rose*
dominiqueweber@hotmail.com

YACHT AND BOAT CHARTER
CANOUAN
The Moorings Tamarind Beach &
Yacht Club
☎ 784 482 0655 *Fax 784 482 0654*
rbrown@vincysurf.com
www.moorings.com

UNION
Overseas Sailing Bougainvilla
☎ 784 458 8647
Scaramouche Clifton
☎/Fax 784 458 8418
Captain Yannis Clifton
☎ 784 458 8513 *Fax 784 458 8976*
yannis@caribsurf.com

DIVING (DIVES/AIR/EQUIPMENT)
BEQUIA
Dive Bequia Admiralty Bay,
Gingerbread Complex
☎ 784 458 3504 *Fax 784 458 3886*
VHF 16/68
bobsax@caribsurf.com
Bequia Dive Adventures
Admiralty Bay
☎ 784 458 3826 *Fax 784 458 3247*
VHF 16/68
adventures@caribsurf.com

CANOUAN
Glossy Diving Club Canouan
Beach Hotel
☎ 784 458 8888 *Fax 784 458 8875*
Blue Way International Tamarind
Beach Hotel
☎ 784 458 8044 *Fax 784 458 8851*
VHF 16

MUSTIQUE
Mustique Watersports
☎ 784 456 3486 VHF 16/68

UNION
Grenadines Dive Clifton
☎ 784 458 8138 *Fax 784 457 8122*
GDive@GrenadinesDive.com
The Dive Shack Clifton
☎ 784 458 8508

CARRIACOU
Tanki's Watersports Paradise
L'Esterre
☎ 473 443 8406 *Fax 473 443 8391*
paradise@cacounet.com
Lumbadive Ltd Centre Beuchat
☎/Fax 473 443 8566
lumbadive@lumbadive.com
Arawak Divers Tyrell Bay
☎ 473 443 6906 *Fax 473 443 8312*
VHF 16
Carriacou Silver Diving
☎/Fax 473 443 7882 VHF 16
scubamax@caribsurf.com
Silver Beach Resort Silver Beach
☎ 473 443 7337 *Fax 473 443 7165*
silverbeach@caribsurf.com

RESTAURANTS/HOTELS
BEQUIA
*Most of the establishments on
Bequia listen out on VHF 68.*

PORT ELIZABETH
Le Frangipani
☎ 784 458 3255 *Fax 784 458 3824*
frangi@caribsurf.com
*Regular crew meeting place,
steelband*
Hotel: comfortable
Local food, BBQ, price B–D
Whaleboner Inn
☎/Fax 784 458 3233
English food, curries, price B–C
Gingerbread
☎ 784 458 3800 *Fax 784 458 3907*
Local food, price B–C
Mac's Pizzeria
☎ 784 458 3474 *Fax 784 458 3417*
VHF 68
Pizzas and lasagnes, price C–D
L'Auberge des Grenadines
☎/Fax 784 458 3201 VHF 68
frenchella@caribsurf.com
*French & West Indian food,
crayfish, price C–D*
*French manager ex the French
Restaurant on Y. Island*
The Plantation House
☎ 784 458 3425 *Fax 784 458 3612*
info@hotel-plantation.com
*Lovely building in a coconut
plantation. Steelband twice*

weekly in season.
*International menu, BBQ price
C–D*
*Hotel: very luxurious, rooms &
cottages*
The Port Hole
☎ 784 458 345
Local food, price A
Le Petit Jardin Back Street
☎ 784 458 3318
Fax 784 457 3134
VHF 16/68
petitjardin_bequia@hotmail.com
French cuisine, seafoods
Timberhouse
☎ 784 457 3495 *Fax 784 457 3418*
VHF 68
*Local cuisine & seafood, price
C–D*
Lion Heart Café
☎ 784 457 3917
*Local & vegetarian food, price B
Rasta atmosphere*
Columbus Place near Bequia
Marina
☎ 784 452 3881
columbusplace@caribsurf.com
*Italian food, seafood, sushi, price
B–C*
De Bistro
☎ 784 457 3482
mitchbistro@vincysurf.com
Local food, price A–B

ELSEWHERE
Coco's Place Lower Bay
☎ 784 458 3463 *Fax 784 458 3797*
Local food & seafood, price A–B
Old Fort Country Inn Mt Pleasant
☎ 784 458 3440 *Fax 784 458 3340*
*Old restored fort with superb
view*
*Local and international food, price
C–D*
Hotel: comfortable, quaint rooms
Spring on Bequia Spring Bay
☎ 784 458 3414 *Fax 784 457 3305*
*Local food with curry specialty,
price C*
Bequia Beach Club Friendship Bay
☎ 784 458 3248 *Fax 784 458 3689*
Local food, price B
Friendship Bay Resort Friendship
Bay
☎ 784 458 3222 *Fax 784 458 3840*
labamdas@caribsurf.com
*International menu, seafood, price
B–C*
Hotel: luxury rooms

MUSTIQUE
Basil's Bar Grand Bay
☎ 784 456 3350 *Fax 784 456 5825*
VHF 68
basils@caribsurf.com
*Local food, BBQ, steelband, price
C–D*
The Cotton House
☎ 784 4564777 *Fax 784 456 5887*
cottonhouse@caribsurf.com
*Hotel: very luxurious, cottages
and rooms*
The Firefly Britannia Bay (on the
hill)
☎ 784 456 3414 *Fax 784 456 3415*
VHF 10
International menu, price C–D
Hotel: luxury, rooms & bungalow

CANOUAN
Canouan Beach Hotel South
Glossy Beach
☎ 784 458 8888 *Fax 784 458 8875*
VHF 16
infocanouan@grenadines.net
*International, French & local food,
BBQ, steelband, price C–D*
Hotel: luxury, bungalows
Tamarind Beach Hotel
☎ 784 458 8044 *Fax 784 458 8851*
International menu, price C–D+

MAYREAU
Dennis Hideaway Saline Bay
☎/Fax 784 458 8594 VHF 68
denhide@vincysurf.com
Local food, BBQ, price A–B
Hotel: simple
Island Paradise Saline Bay
☎ 784 458 8941 VHF 68
Local food, price B live music
Robert Righteous Saline Bay
☎ 784 458 8203 VHF 68
Local food & seafood, price B
Rasta atmosphere, reggae
Salt Whistle Bay Club Salt
Whistle Bay
☎ 784 458 8444 Fax 784 458 4944
VHF 16/68
swbreserve@yahoo.com
(credit cards not accepted)
International menu, price C–D
Hotel: comfortable, bungalows

PALM ISLAND
Palm Island Resort
☎ 784 458 8824 Fax 784 458 8804
jgrae@yahoo.com
Local food, seafood, BBQ, price
B–C
Hotel: very luxurious, bungalows.

UNION
Anchorage Yacht Club
☎ 784 458 8221
Fax 784 458 8365
aycunion@caribsurf.com
ayc-hotel-grenadines.com
Water at the dock
Live music
International menu, seafood, price
C–D
Hotel: luxury bungalows
The West Indies Restaurant
Bougainvilla
☎ 784 458 8311 Fax 784 458 8569
VHF 16
noelle@caribsurf.com
French & local food, crayfish,
BBQ, live music, price B–C
Sydney's near the airport
☎/Fax 784 458 8320 VHF 16
Local food, price A–B
Sunny Grenadines Clifton
☎ 784 458 8327 Fax 784 458 8398
Local food, price B
Hotel: simple
Captain Gourmet Clifton
☎/Fax 784 458 8918
capgourmet@caribsurf.com
Takeaways & provisioning
Clifton Beach Hotel Clifton
☎/Fax 784 458 8235
cliftonbeachhotel@caribsurf.com
Local food, price B
Hotel: comfortable
Lambi's Clifton
☎ 784 458 8549 Fax 784 458 8395
Local food, price B

PETIT ST VINCENT
PSV Resort
☎ 784 458 8801 Fax 784 458 8428
psv@fuse.net
International menu, price D+
Hotel: very luxurious, exclusive
cottages

PETITE MARTINIQUE
Palm Beach Restaurant and Bar
VHF 16 ☎ 784 443 9103 VHF 16
Local food, price B–C
Free water taxi between PSV &
Pte Martinique

CARRIACOU
Callaloo by the Sea Hillsborough
☎ 473 443 8004
Local food, seafood, price B
Seawave Restaurant Hillsborough
(under renovation)
☎ 473 443 7380
Local food, price A–B
Ade's Dream Guest House
Hillsborough

☎ 473 443 7317 Fax 473 443 8435
adesedea@caribsurf.com
Hotel: simple, guesthouse
Silver Beach Resort Silver Beach
☎ 473 443 7337
Fax 473 443 7165 VHF 16
Local food, price B–C
Hotel: comfortable, bungalows
John's Silver Beach
☎ 473 443 8345 Fax 473 443 8348
junique@caribsurf.com
Local food, price A–B
Hotel: simple
The Cassada Bay Resort Belmont
☎ 473 443 7494 Fax 443 7672
Hotel: comfortable
Le Poivre et Sel Tyrell Bay
☎/Fax 473 443 8390 VHF 16
poivreetsel@usa.net
Local & French food, price A–B
Hotel: simple, guesthouse
Twilight Restaurant Tyrell Bay
☎ 473 443 8350 VHF 16
Local food, seafood, price A–B
Saraca Carriacou Yacht Club
Tyrell Bay
☎/Fax 473 443 6292
Local food, price A
Seablast Tyrell Bay, Cybercafé
☎ 473 443 8625 VHF 14
seablast@caribsurf.com
Local food, price A–B
Scraper's Restaurant Tyrell Bay
☎ 473 443 7403,
Local food, price A–B
Hotel: simple, guesthouse
After 'Ours Tyrell Bay
☎ 473 443 6159
Local food, price A–B, music
Friday evenings
Turtle Dove Restaurant Tyrell Bay
☎ 473 443 8322 VHF 16
turtledove@caribsurf.com
Pizzeria, price A–B, small dinghy
pontoon

CAR RENTAL/TAXIS
BEQUIA
Handy Andy Rental Port Elizabeth
☎ 784 458 3722 Fax 784 457 3402
VHF 68
Sam Taxi Tours Port Elizabeth
☎ 784 458 3686 Fax 784 458 3427
VHF 16/68
sam-taxi-tours@caribsurf.com
Various services

MUSTIQUE
**MMS (Mustique Mechanical
Services)**
☎ 784 456 3555 VHF 68
UNION
Erika's Marine Bougainvilla
☎ 784 485 8335 Fax 784 485 8336
VHF 68
erika@caribsurf.com
Bicycle hire, Internet and other
services
Wind & Sea Ltd
Agent, Tour operator, Charter
☎ 784 45 88 878
windandsea@vincysurf.com
www.grenadines.net/union/
windandsea/htm

CARRIACOU
Quality Jeep Rental L'Esterre
☎/Fax 473 443 7454
Barba's Auto Rentals Tyrell Bay
☎/Fax 473 443 7454
☎ 473 443 8167
Ade's Dream Hillsborough
☎ 473 443 7317 Fax 473 443 8435
adesdea@caribsurf.com

Grenada
AIRLINES
American Eagle
☎ 473 442 2222
British Airways
☎ 473 444 4121 Fax 473 444 1672
BWIA
☎ 473 444 1221
Liat: St George's
☎ 473 440 2796 Fax 473 440 4166
Air Jamaica
☎ 473 444 5975 Fax 473 444 5976
Monarch
Customer.services@monarch-
airlines.com
Charter flights from London
FERRY COMPANIES
Osprey Express Ltd Carenage
☎ 473 444 8126
Daily connections between
Carriacou & Petite Martinique
(except Wednesdays)
Ferry service: Carenage (daily)
MARINAS/DOCKS (WATER/FUEL)
Grenada Yacht Club (ex GYC) St
George's
☎ 473 440 3050 Fax 473 440 6826
VHF 16
gyc@caribsurf.com
Water & fuel
**Blue Lagoon Real Estate Corp
(GYS)**
☎ 473 440 6893
Fax 473 440 6891
Water
True Blue Bay Resort & Marina
☎ 473 439 1000
Fax 473 439 1001
horizonsyachts@caribsurf.com
Water
**Secret Harbour Marina (The
Moorings)** Hartman Bay
☎ 473 444 4449
Fax 473 444 2090
moorgrn@caribsurf.com
Water & fuel at the dock
Spice Island Marine Services
Prickly Bay
☎ 473 444 4257 Fax 473 444 2816
VHF 16
simsco@caribsurf.com
water & fuel at the dock
Grenada Marine St David's
Harbour
☎ 473 443 1667 Fax 473 443 1668
info@grenadamarine.com
water & fuel
PROFESSIONAL YACHT
SERVICES
Boatyards/haul-out
Spice Island Marine Boatyard
Prickly Bay
☎ 473 444 4257 Fax 473 444 2816
VHF 16
simsco@caribsurf.com
Grenada Marine St David's
Harbour
☎ 473 443 1667 Fax 473 443 1668
info@grenadamarine.com
Chandleries/dinghies
Marine World Ltd Melville
St George's
☎ 473 440 1748
Budget Marine St George's
☎ 473 439 1983
salesbudmarGD@caribsurf.com
Outfitter's International Lagoon
Road St George's
☎ 473 440 7949 Fax 473 440 6680
VHF 16
footloos@caribsurf.com
Island Water World
Lagoon Road St George's
☎ 473 435 2150 Fax 473 435 2152
iww@caribsurf.com
St David's Harbour:
☎ 473 443 1028 Fax 473 443 1038
Anro Agencies Grand Anse
☎ 473 444 2220 Fax 473 444 2822

Spice Island Marine Services:
Prickly Bay
☎ 473 444 4257 Fax 473 444 2816
VHF 16
steveo42@hotmail.com
agent for Budget Marine
*Mechanics/electrics/outboards/
workshops*
Anro Agencies Ltd Grand Anse
☎ 473 444 2220
Fax 473 444 2822
Mc Intyre Bros Ltd True Blue
☎ 473 444 3944/1555 Fax 473 444
2899
macford@caribsurf.com
Outfitters International
St George's
☎ 473 440 7949 Fax 473 440 6680
VHF 16
footloos@caribsurf.com
Ross & Sons Lagoon
☎ 473 440 3018 Fax 473 440 9800
Spice Island Marine Services
Prickly Bay
☎ 473 444 4257 Fax 473 444 2816
VHF 16
simsco@caribsurf.com
Sailmakers, awning makers
Johnny Sails & Canvas Grand
Anse
☎/Fax 473 444 1108
Outfitters International
St George's
☎ 473 440 7949 Fax 473 440 6680
VHF 16
footloos@caribsurf.com
Carpentry
Cottle Boatworks Grand Anse
☎ 743 444 1070
DIVING (DIVES/AIR/EQUIPMENT)
Dive Grenada Grand Anse,
Allamanda Beach Hotel
☎ 473 444 1092, Fax 473 444 5875
diveg'da@caribsurf.com
1st Spice Divers Grenada Secret
Harbour Hotel & The Moorings
☎ 473 444 1126, Fax 473 444 1127
VHF 16
aquanaut@caribsurf.com
Eco Dive (Grand Anse Aquatics)
Coyoba Beach Resort
☎ 473 444 2133 Fax 473 444 1046
True Blue (Scuba Express)
☎ 473 444 7777 Fax 473 444 1046
ecotravel@caribsurf.com
Spice Island Diving Grand Anse
Spice Island Beach Resort
☎ 473 444 3483 Fax 473 444 3473
ddresser@caribsurf.com
YACHT CHARTER
Moorings Secret Harbour
☎ 473 444 4439
Fax 473 444 2090
moorings@moorings.fr
www.moorings.com
Island Yacht Charters Calivigny
Harbour
☎ 473 443 5624
Horizon Yacht Charters True Blue
Bay Resort & Marina
☎ 473 439 1000 Fax 473 439 1001
horizonyachts@caribsurf.com
Trade Wind Yacht Charters Prickly
Bay
☎ 473 444 4924 Fax 473 444 5497
sark@caribsurf.com
RESTAURANTS/HOTELS
ST GEORGE'S
The Nutmeg Carenage
☎ 473 440 2539 Fax 473 440 4160
The yachties' favourite
local food & fish, price A
Mamma's Lagoon Rd
☎ 473 440 1459
Typical local food, price D+
Tout Bagay Carenage
☎ 473 440 1500/440 3000
Local food and fish, price B–C
Rudolf's Restaurant Carenage
☎ 473 440 2241

Jazz Wednesdays & Fridays
seafood, local & international
food, price B
Tropicana Inn Lagoon Rd
☎ 473 440 1586 *Fax* 473 440 9797
Local & Chinese food, price B–C
Chopstix Chinese Restaurant
Belmont
☎ 473 440 7849
Chinese food, price B

GRAND ANSE/MORNE ROUGE/ PT SALINES
Aquarium Restaurant Pt Salines
La Source
☎ 473 444 1410
Fish, BBQ, seafood, price C–D
La Dolce Vita Morne Range
☎ 444 4301/444 3456
Italian
Brown Sugar Grand Anse
☎ 473 444 2374 *Fax* 473 443 0660
brownsugarrest@caribsurf.com
Music, local food, price B–C
Cinnamon Hill Morne Rouge
☎ 473 444 4301
Fax 473 444 2874
cinnamonhill@grenadaexplorer.
com
Hotel: luxury bungalows, good
view
Laluna Morne Rouge
☎ 473 439 0001 *Fax* 473 439 0600
Music & dancing
International menu, seafood, price
B–C
Hotel: luxury, bungalows
Mariposa Beach Resort Morne
Rouge
☎ 473 444 3171
mariposa@caribsurf.com
French bakery, good selection
Coconut Beach Grand Anse
☎ 473 444 4644
Créole & French food, seafood,
BBQ, price C–D
Blue Horizons Grand Anse
☎ 473 444 4316 *Fax* 473 444 2815
blue@caribsurf.com
La Belle Créole Restaurant, local
food, price C–D
Hotel: comfortable, studios
Pirates' Cove Grand View Inn,
Morne Rouge
☎ 473 444 2342
gvinn@caribsurf.com
International & French food, price
B–C
La Boulangerie Marquis Hall
Grand Anse
☎ 473 444 1131
French bakery, takeaways
Allamanda Beach Resort Grand
Anse
☎ 473 444 0095 *Fax* 473 444 0126
allamanda@caribsurf.com
Hotel: luxury
Siesta Hotel Grand Anse
☎ 473 444 4646 *Fax* 473 444 4647
siesta@caribsurf.com
Hotel: very luxurious
The Flamboyant Hotel Grand
Anse
☎ 473 444 4247 *Fax* 473 444 1234
flambo@caribsurf.com
Hotel: very luxurious, rooms and
cottages

TRUE BLUE
True Blue Bay Restaurant
☎ 473 443 8783 *Fax* 473 444 5929
mail@truebluebay.com
Indigo Restaurant
Local & Mexican food, price C–D
Hotel: very luxurious

PRICKLY BAY/MT HARTMAN BAY
The Calabash Hotel Prickly Bay
☎ 473 444 4234 *Fax* 473 444 5050
calabash@caribsurf.com
Hotel: very luxurious
The Boatyard Restaurant Prickly

Bay
☎ 473 444 4662 *Fax* 473 444 4677
Crew rendezvous, steelband at
weekends, local, Mexican &
Italian food, price B
The Red Crab Anse aux Epines
☎ 473 444 4424
Local & international food,
price C–D
Secret Harbour Resort
Mt Hartman Bay
☎ 473 444 4439 *Fax* 473 444 4819
secret@caribsurf.com
International & local food, price
D+
Hotel: very luxurious, rooms and
cottages

ST DAVID'S
Petit Bacaye Cottage Hotel
☎/*Fax* 473 443 2902
hideaways@wellowmead.u-
net.com
Hotel: simple, bungalows

GRENVILLE
Ebony Restaurant Victoria
☎ 473 442 8558
Local food, price A–B

CAR RENTAL/TAXIS/TRAVEL AGENTS
Outfitters International Lagoon
Road, St George's
☎ 473 440 7949 *Fax* 473 440 6680
VHF 16
footloos@caribsurf.com
Dollar Rent a Car Pt Salines
Airport
☎ 473 444 4786 *Fax* 473 444 4788
Y & R Car Rental Ltd L'anse aux
Epines
☎ 473 444 4448 *Fax* 473 444 3639
y&r@caribsurf.com
McIntyre Bros Ltd True Blue
☎ 473 444 3944 *Fax* 473 444 2899
mcintyre@travelgrenada.com
Eco Dive & Trek
True Blue ☎ 473 444 7777
Fax 473 444 1046
Grand Anse ☎ 473 444 2133
ecotravel@caribsurf.com
Spice Island Trekking & Cycling
Grand Anse
☎ 473 444 5985 *Fax* 473 444 0385
spicetreks@hotmail.com
Henry's Safari Taxis/Tours
☎ 473 444 5313 *Fax* 473 444 4460
VHF 68
safari@travelgrenada.com
David's Car Rental David's
Harbour
☎ 473 444 3399 *Fax* 473 444 5777
cdavid@caribsurf.com

Barbados

AIRLINES
Air Canada
☎ 246 428 5177
American Airlines
☎ 246 428 4170
British Airways
☎ 246 436 6413
BWIA
☎ 246 426 2111
Liat
☎ 246 434 5428
MARINAS/DOCKS (WATER/FUEL)
Port St Charles St Peter VHF 16
☎ 246 419 1000 *Fax* 246 422 7447
dockmaster@portstcharles.com.
bb
Dock only for clearance
Water, fuel

PROFESSIONAL YACHT SERVICES
Boatyards/Assistance
The Boatyard Carlisle Bay VHF 16
☎ 246 436 2622 *Fax* 246 228 7720
boatyards@sunbeach.net
Mooring buoys
Barbados Yacht Club Carlisle Bay
☎ 246 427 7318 *Fax* 246 435 7590
byc@inaccs.com.bb
Various services including
clearance
Maintenance/mechanics/ outboards
Willie's Diving & Marine Services
Shallow draft area
☎ 246 424 1808 *Fax* 246 425 1060
mikie@caribsurf.com
Krowles Marine Mechanic
☎ 246 435 3068
McEncarney's Wildey – outboards
☎ 246 467 2400 *Fax* 246 427 0764
Marine Management Services
Bridgetown Harbour
☎ 246 234 4733
mms@sunbeach.net
Pelican Marine
Shallow draft area
☎ 246 424 1808 *Fax* 246 425 1060
Chandleries/riggers
Carter's Fishermans Corner
☎ 246 436 6049 *Fax* 246 431 0799
VHF 06
boatyard@sunbeach.net
Marine Management Services
Bridgetown Harbour
☎ 246 234 4733
mms@sunbeach.net
Sailmakers/awnings
Doyle Offshore Sails Ltd
St Philips
☎ 246 423 4600 *Fax* 246423 4499
doyle@caribnet.net
Roger Edgehill Sails Christ Church
☎ 246 429 5800

DIVING
Hazell's Water World The
Boatyard
☎ 246 426 9423 *Fax* 246 436 5726
hwwdivers@sunbeach.net
The Dive Shop Y. Club Carlisle
Bay
☎ 246 427 9947 *Fax* 246 426 0655
Underwater Barbados
☎/*Fax* 246 426 0655 VHF 08
myoung@underwaterbarbados.
com

RESTAURANTS/HOTELS
BRIDGETOWN
Mustor's Harbour Restaurant
McGregor Street
☎ 246 426 5157
Local food, price A–B
The Boatyard Beach Club Carlisle
Bay
☎ 246 436 2622 *Fax* 246 228 7720
boatyard@sunbeach net
Beach restaurant, entertainment
International menu, price B–C
Waterfront Café The Careenage
☎ 246 427 0093
Local food, seafood, live music,
price B–C
Rusty Pelican The Careenage
☎ 246 436 7778
rustypelicanbds@hotmail.com
Local food, seafood, price B–C

PORT ST CHARLES
La Mer
☎ 246 419 2000
hans@portstcharles.com.bb
Local food, seafood, price B–C
CAR RENTAL
Coconut Car Rentals Ltd
☎ 246 437 1297 *Fax* 246 228 9820
coconut@caribsurf.com

Dominica

AIRLINES
Air Caraïbes
☎ 767 448 2181
Fax 767 448 5787
American Eagle/American Airlines
☎ 767 448 0628
Fax 767 445 7477
Liat
☎ 767 448 2421
Cardinal Airlines
☎ 767 449 432 8923
Caribbean Star Airlines
☎ 767 445 8936
Fax 767 449 1060
FERRY COMPANIES
L'Express des Iles Roseau
☎ 767 448 2181
Fax 767 448 5787
whitship@cwdom.dm
PROFESSIONAL YACHT SERVICES
Anchorage Yacht Services
Anchorage Hotel
☎ 767 448 2638
Fax 767 448 5680 VHF16
anchorage@hotmail.com
Moorings, water, fuel (jerry
jugged), security
Pancho's Services Roseau
☎/*Fax* 767 448 1698 VHF 16
panchoservices@yahoo.com
Water, provisioning, security
(French spoken)
Qualified guide, walks organised
DIVING
Anchorage Dive Center
Anchorage Hotel
☎ 767 448 2639
Fax 767 448 5680
anchoragedive@hotmail.com
Cabrits Dive Center
S of Portsmouth
☎ 767 445 3010
Fax 767 445 3011
cabritsdive@cwdom.dm
Dive Castaways Roseau
Castaways Hotel
☎ 767 449 6244
Fax 767 449 6246 VHF 19
castaways@cwdom.dm
Dive Dominica Roseau
Castle Comfort Lodge/Fort Young
Hotel
☎ 767 448 2188
Fax 767 448 6088
dive@cwdom.dm
East Carib Dive Salisbury
☎/*Fax* 767 449 6575
ecd@cwdom.dm
Nature Island Dive
Soufrière St Mark
☎ 767 449 8181 *Fax* 767 449 8182
natureidive@cwdom.dm
RESTAURANTS/HOTELS
Roseau
Anchorage Hotel
☎ 767 448 2638 *Fax* 767 449 5680
anchorage@cwdom.dm
Ocean Terrace Restaurant
Local food & international menu
BBQ buffet (Thurs. evening),
steelband, price C–D
Hotel: luxury
Castaways Beach Hotel
☎ 767 449 6244 *Fax* 767 449 6246
castaways@cwdpm.dm
Local food, BBQ, price B–C
Hotel: comfortable, rooms &
bungalows. Not always operating
La Robe Créole waterfront
☎ 767 448 2896 *Fax* 767 448 5212
larobecreole@marpin.dm
Local food & international menu,
BBQ, price B–C
Ticaz Café waterfront
☎ 767 449 8686 *Fax* 767 449 9774
Salads, fresh fruit. Price A

Cocorico
Boat provisioning, French produce, French manager (also of Ticaz Café) offers warm welcome
cocorico@cwdom.dm
Pearl's Cuisine
☎ 767 448 8707
Chinese & West Indian food, price B
The Laughing Lobster waterfront
☎ 767 449 9372
Seafood, shellfish, price B
Fort Young Hotel
☎ 767 448 5000 *Fax* 767 448 8065
fortyoung@cwdom.dm
Marquis de Bouille Restaurant
International & creole menu, price C–D
Hotel: luxury
Callaloo
☎ 767 448 3386
Local food, price A–B

North Dominica
Coconut Beach Hotel Portsmouth
☎ 767 445 5393 *Fax* 767 445 5693
cocobeach@netscape.net
Local food, price B–C
Hotel: comfortable, bungalows
Blue Bay Portsmouth Lagoon
☎/*Fax* 767 445 4985
Local food, price A–B
Mango's Portsmouth Bay Street
☎ 767 445 3099
Local food & seafood, price A–B
Hotel: Comfortable, rooms
Purple Turtle Beach Club
Portsmouth
☎ 767 468 5296
Local & fast food, price A–B
La Guinguette de Calibishie
Calibishie
☎ 767 445 7783 *Fax* 767 445 8495
Local & French food, price B–C

South Dominica
The Sundowner's Cafe/Herche's Place (ex Gachette Sea Side)
Scott's Head
☎ 767 448 7749
herches@cwdom.dm
Seafood & local food, price A–B
Hotel: simple
Riverbank Farm Grand Bay
☎ 767 446 4141
vronick@caramail.com
Hotel: camping

Centre of the island
Papillote Rainforest Restaurant
near Trafalgar Falls
☎ 767 448 2287 *Fax* 767 448 2285
papillote@cwdom.dm
Surrounded by greenery
Creole food & BBQ (Weds), price B–C
Hotel: simple
Fallsview Guest House
Trafalgar Village
☎/*Fax* 767 448 0064
fallsview@c&w.dm
Local food, price B–C
Hotel: simple rooms

CAR RENTAL/TAXIS/TRAVEL AGENTS
Avis Roseau/airport
☎ 767 448 0413
Valley Rent a Car
Roseau ☎ 767 448 3233
Fax 767 448 6009
Portsmouth ☎ 767 445 5252
valley@cwdom.dm
Garraway Rent a Car Roseau
☎ 767 448 2891 *Fax* 766 448 0541
garraway@cwdom.dm
Mally's Taxi & Tours Service
Roseau
☎ 767 448 3114/448 3689
Dominica Tours Anchorage Hotel
☎ 767 448 0990 *Fax* 767 448 0989
Pancho's Services Roseau
☎/*Fax* 767 449 8181

panchoservices@yahoo.com
Nature Island Dive Soufrière St Mark
☎ 767 449 8181
Fax 767 449 8182
natureidive@cwdom.dm

Guadeloupe
Note when calling numbers in French islands from non-French islands, omit the 0 after the country code
AIRLINES
Air Caraïbes Pôle Caraïbes
☎ 33 (0)5 90 82 47 00
Fax 33 (0)5 90 82 47 48
Air Canada
☎ 33 (0)5 90 21 12 77
Fax 33 (0)5 90 21 12 76
Air France
☎ 0820 820 820
Air St-Martin
☎ 33 (0)5 90 21 12 89
Fax 33 (0)5 90 21 12 87
American Airlines
☎ 33 (0)5 90 21 11 80
Fax 33 (0)5 90 20 88 45
Corsair ☎ 33 (0)5 90 21 11 21
Fax 33 (0)5 90 21 14 40
Liat ☎ 33 (0)5 90 21 13 93
Fax 33 (0)5 90 21 13 94
FERRY COMPANIES
L'Express des Iles Quai Gatine
Pointe-à-Pitre
☎ 33 (0)5 90 91 13 43
Fax 33 (0)5 90 91 11 33 05
info@express-des-iles.com
Brudey, Frères Quai Gatine
Pointe-à-Pitre
☎ 33 (0)5 90 90 04 48
Fax 33 (0)5 90 93 00 79
St François
☎ 33 (0)5 90 88 66 67
St François/La Désirade
Trois Rivières
☎ 33 (0)5 90 92 69 74
Trois Rivières/Les Saintes
TMC Archipel Quai Gatine
Pointe-à-Pitre
☎ 33 (0)5 90 83 19 89
Fax 33 (0)5 90 83 66 68
Deher CTM Quai Gatine
Pointe-à-Pitre
☎ 33 (0)5 90 21 69 51
Fax 33 (0)5 90 82 25 80
Les Saintes
☎ 33 (0)5 90 99 50 68
Trois Rivières/Les Saintes
Colobri St François
☎ 33 (0)5 90 21 23 73
St François/La Désirade
Iguana Beach Ste Anne
☎ 33 (0)5 90 50 05 09

MARINAS/DOCKS (WATER/FUEL)
Marina du Bas du Fort
☎ 33 (0)5 90 93 66 20
Fax 33 (0)5 90 90 81 53
marina@marina-pap.com
www.marina-pap·com
Water, Fuel

GRANDE TERRE
Marina de St François St François
☎ 33 (0)5 90 88 47 28
Fax 33 (0)5 90 88 53 48
Water & fuel (south dock)

BASSE TERRE
Malendure Yacht Service
☎ 33 (0)5 90 98 83 65
malendure-yacht@wanadoo.fr
Water & emergency fuel supplies; mooring buoys
Marina Rivière Sens Gourbeyre
☎ 33 (0)5 90 81 77 61
Fax 33 (0)5 90 99 00 41 VHF 16
Hours 8am–4pm

Monday–Saturday
Water & fuel (southwest dock)

LES SAINTES TERRE DE HAUT
Fuel Baie de Marigot, shipyard dock
Yacht Services d'Iles en Iles
Le Bourg
☎/*Fax* 33 (0)5 90 99 57 82 VHF 68
PROFESSIONAL YACHT SERVICES
Boatyards/haulout
Zone Technique Marina Bas du Fort Pointe-à-Pitre
☎ 33 (0)5 90 93 66 20
Fax 33 (0)5 90 90 81 53
marina@marina-pap.com
Multicap Caraibes Marina Bas du Fort Zone Technique
☎ 33 (0)5 90 91 377 10
Fax 33 (0)5 90 91 37 65
MCM@multicapcaraibes.com
Chantier Forbin Carénage Pointe-à-Pitre
☎ 33 (0)5 90 83 21 34
Fax 33 (0)5 90 90 05 01
Lemaire Marine Service Carénage Pointe-à-Pitre
☎ 33 (0)5 90 90 34 47
Fax 33 (0)5 90 91 77 88
Top Gun Marine Carénage Pointe-à-Pitre
☎ 33 (0)5 90 91 10 11
Fax 33 (0)5 90 91 96 52
A.M.M.S. (Anse Morel Marine Services) Les Saintes-Terre de Haut
☎ 33 (0)5 90 92 20 49
Fax 33 (0)5 90 92 21 05
michelirurzun@aol.com
Chandlery/diving equipment
Electro-Nautic P.à.P
☎ 33 (0)5 90 21 36 70
Fax 33 (0)5 90 90 24 01
Société Nouvelle Karukera Marine
Marina Bas du Fort
☎ 33 (0)5 90 90 90 96
Fax 33 (0)5 90 90 97 49
karukera.marine@wanadoo.fr
Tropic Marine Jarry Industrial Zone
☎ 33 (0)5 90 38 00 25
Fax 33 (0)5 90 26 84 59
tropic_marine@mediaserv.net
Yacht Services/assistance
L'Amer Deshaies
☎ 33 (0)5 90 28 50 43
Yacht Club des Saintes Terre de Haut
☎/*Fax* 33 (0)5 90 99 57 82 VHF 68
Water, on board delivery service, internet
Restaurant le Génois Terre de Haut
☎ 33 (0)5 90 99 53 01
Fax 33 (0)5 90 99 59 45
legenois@hotmail.com
Water, on board delivery service, technical assistance (Sunsail)
Bagage Plus Marina du Bas Fort
☎ 33 (0)5 90 93 60 91
Fax 33 (0)5 90 93 61 05
bagageplus@wanadoo.fr
Airport baggage service, other assistance
Sailmakers/awnings/riggers
Atelier Voilerie Incidences Marina Bas du Fort
☎ 33 (0)5 90 90 87 65
Fax 33 (0)5 90 90 82 76
Caraïbes Covering Marina Bas du Fort
☎ 33 (0)5 90 90 94 75
Fax 33 (0)5 90 90 94 22
caraïbes.covering@wanadoo.fr
Marina Confection Marina Bas du Fort
☎ 33 (0)5 90 90 85 04
Fax 33 (0)5 90 90 77 64
North Sails Caraïbes Marina Bas du Fort

☎ 33 (0)5 90 90 80 44
Fax 33 (0)5 90 90 89 76
andrew@sales.northsails.com
CTA Gréeur Impasse Dessout, Jarry Industrial Zone
☎/*Fax* 33 (0)5 90 90 38 78 98
Phil à Voile Terre de Haut
☎ 33 (0)5 90 99 55 03
Fax 33 (0)5 90 99 58 69
Diesel mechanics/electrics
Ateliers Philis Marina Bas du Fort
☎ 33 (0)5 90 35 32 47
Fax 33 (0)5 90 83 79
Ets Aiguadel Top Performance
Carénage Pointe-à-Pitre
☎ 33 (0)5 90 91 68 15
Fax 33 (0)5 90 91 75 71
Général Mécanique Marine Inboard Marina Bas du Fort
☎/*Fax* 33 (0)5 90 90 70 51
GEN-MEC-Yves.HECQ@wanadoo.fr
GMD Volvo Marina Bas du Fort
☎ 33 (0)5 90 90 94 03
Fax 33 (0)5 90 90 96 23
gmdvolvopenta@wanadoo.fr
Fred Marine Yanmar Marina Bas du Fort
☎ 33 (0)5 90 90 71 37
Fax 33 (0)5 90 90 86 51
fredmarine@wanadoo.fr
Nautil's Service Le Moule
☎/*Fax* 33 (0)5 90 23 47 02
nautil.services@wanadoo.fr
Dinghies/liferafts/outboards (sale & repair)
Espace Océan Marina Bas du Fort
☎ 33 (0)5 90 90 75 48
Fax 33 (0)5 90 90 31 88
espace-ocean@wanadoo.fr
Fred Marine Yanmar Marina Bas du Fort
☎ 33 (0)5 90 90 71 37
Fax 33 (0)5 90 90 86 51
fredmarine@wanadoo.fr
EuroSurvie Petit Bourg
☎ 33 (0)5 90 32 24 51
Fax 33 (0)5 90 32 24 52
eurosurvie@wanadoo.fr
Electro-Nautic Suzuki Antilles
Pointe-à-Pitre
☎ 33 (0)5 90 21 36 70
Fax 33 (0)5 90 90 24 01
Soguamar Yamaha Jarry Industrial Zone
☎ 33 (0)5 90 25 20 55
Fax 33 (0)5 90 25 20 13
Winston's Motors
Marina Bas du Fort
☎ 33 (0)5 90 90 82 73
winston.motors@wanadoo.fr
Ateliers Philis Marina Bas du Fort
☎ 33 (0)5 90 35 32 47
Fax 33 (0)5 90 83 79
Electronics/electrics
Pochon Electricité Marina Bas du Fort
☎ 33 (0)5 90 90 73 99
Fax 33 (0)5 90 90 90 51
stephane.poguad@wanadoo.fr
Way Point Marina Bas du Fort
☎ 33 (0)5 90 90 94 81
Fax 33 (0)5 90 90 42 63
waypoint@outremer.com
Refrigeration
Richard Dupuis
Marina Bas du Fort
☎ 33 (0)5 90 61 48 00
Maintenance/welding
AMF Chantier Marina Bas du Fort
☎ 33 (0)5 90 58 24 14/33 (0)5 90 90 01 88
Chantier A Foy Les Saintes
☎ 33 (0)5 90 99 50 75
CTA Impasse Dessout ZI Jarry (Industrial Zone)
☎/*Fax* 33 (0)5 90 91 85 30
Marine surveyors
Socarex (Ch. Mir) Porte de la Marina

☎ 33 (0)5 90 90 89 30
Fax 33 (0)5 90 90 89 21
UCE (Union Caraïbéenne d'Expertise)
☎ 33 (0)5 90 93 05 35
Fax 33 (0)5 90 92 92 43
Martial Barriel
☎/Fax 33 (0)5 90 28 14 41
Expert.maritime.barriel@
wanadoo.fr
YACHT AND BOAT CHARTER/SALES
ZONE DE POINTE A PITRE
Tropical Yacht Service
Marina Bas du Fort
☎ 33 (0)5 90 90 84 52
Fax 33 (0)5 99 90 82 83
tys@tropical-yacht-service.com
Corail Caraïbes Marina Bas du Fort
☎ 33 (0)5 90 90 91 13
Fax 33 (0)5 90 90 90 58
VPM Antilles Marina Bas du Fort
☎ 33 (0)5 90 90 74 98
Fax 33 (0)5 90 90 83 10
vpmguadeloupe@cgit.com
Sunsail-Stardust Place Créole, Lagon Bleu
☎ 33 (0)5 90 90 92 02
Fax 33 (0)5 90 97 99
www.sunsail.com
Star Voyage Marina Bas du Fort
☎ 33 (0)5 90 90 86 26
Fax 33 (0)5 90 90 85 73
www.vcomvoile.com
Charter hire on the internet
DIVING/TANK FILLING
Nitrogen Marina Bas du Fort
☎ 33 (0)5 90 90 78 26
nitrogensarl@wanadoo.fr
Ecole de plongeé St François
Galerie du port
☎ 33 (0)5 90 85 81 18
bescales2@wanadoo.fr
ACP (Anse Caraïbes Plongée)
Pointe Noire
☎ 33 (0)5 90 99 90 95
jasor.rene@wanadoo.fr
Chez Guy et Christian Pigeon
☎ 33 (0)5 90 98 82 43
Fax 33 (0)5 90 98 82 84
Les Heures Saines
Bouillante ☎ 33 (0)5 90 98 86 63
Fax 33 (0)5 90 98 77 76
Petite Anse ☎ 33 (0)5 90 98 70 29
heusaine@outremer.com
CIP Bouillante
☎ 33 (0)5 90 98 81 72
Fax 33 (0)5 90 98 16 23
cip.bouillante@wanadoo.fr
Archipel Plongée Bouillante
☎ 33 (0)5 90 98 93 93
Fax 33 (0)5 90 98 99 28
plongée@archipel-plongée.fr
Tropical Sub Deshaies Le Bourg
☎ 33 (0)5 90 28 52 67
Fax 33 (0)5 90 28 53 48
tropisub@outremer.com
Le Banc des Vaisseaux Ste Anne
☎ 33 (0)5 90 55 11 28
Pisquettes Les Saintes Terre de Haut
☎ 33 (0)5 90 99 88 80
Fax 33 (0)5 90 99 88 20
plongée@pisquettes.com
La Dive Bouteille Les Saintes
☎ 33 (0)5 90 99 54 25
Fax 33 (0)5 90 99 50 96
mail@divebouteille.com
Scubaguad Marie Galante
Capesterre
☎/Fax 33 (0)5 90 97 20 59
paul.villevieille@wanadoo.fr
RESTAURANTS/HOTELS
MARINA DU BAS DU FORT
Côté Jardin
☎ 33 (0)5 90 90 91 28
Fax 33 (0)5 90 90 79 57
French & Créole food, price C–D
Le Bar Ouf Restaurant de l'Aquarium

☎ 33 (0)5 90 93 63 02
French food & Tex Mex, price B–C
La Route du Rhum
VHF 72
☎ 33 (0)5 90 90 90 00
Fax 33 (0)5 90 90 77 97
French & Créole food, price B–C
Le Plaisancier
☎ 33 (0)5 90 90 71 53
Fax 33 (0)5 90 91 26 43
French & Caribbean food, price B–D
Le Sextant
☎ 33 (0)6 00 00 02 22
Fax 33 (0)5 90 90 70 43
Daily menus, salads, price B–C
Le Chang 12 rue Belair
☎ 33 (0)5 90 84 20 17
Vietnamese food, price C–D
Village Soleil
☎ 33 (0)5 90 90 85 76
Fax 33 (0)5 90 90 93 65
Hotel.village.soleilhotel@
wanadoo.fr
Hotel: comfortable, studios with kitchenette
GOSIER
Auberge de la Vieille Tour
☎ 33 (0)5 90 84 23 23
Fax 33 (0)5 90 83 43 43
H1345@accor-hotels.com
Gourmet menu, price D+
Hotel: very luxurious
Le Salako
☎ 33 (0)5 90 82 64 64
Fax 33 (0)5 90 84 22 22
hotel.salako@wanadoo.fr
Le Saintois Restaurant
French food, price C–D
Hotel: luxury
La Mandarine in the town
☎/Fax 33 (0)5 90 84 30 28
Gourmet menu, French & Créole food, price C
Le Négresco View over Ilet Gosier
☎ 33 (0)5 90 84 29 41
Local specialities, price C–D
Créole Beach Hotel
☎ 33 (0)5 90 90 46 46
Fax 33 (0)5 90 90 46 66
creolebeach@leaderhotels.gp
Le Zawag Restaurant
Créole food, price B–C
Hotel: luxury
Résidence Canella Beach
☎ 33 (0)5 90 90 44 00
Fax 33 (0)5 90 90 44 44
canellabeach@wanadoo.fr
Hotel: luxury studios

LE PETIT HAVRE
Restaurant les 2 Oursins
☎ 33 (0)5 90 85 20 20
Fax 33 (0)5 90 85 83 08
Créole food, price B–C
Big palm thatch hut on the beach

STE ANNE
La Mionette Rte de l'hôtel de Rotabas
☎ 33 (0)5 90 88 02 83
Créole food, price A, (lunch only)
La Toubana Baie de La Caravelle
☎ 33 (0)5 90 88 25 57
Fax 33 (0)5 90 88 38 90
toubana@leaderhotels.gp
Le Baobab Restaurant
Créole food, fish, price C–D
Hotel: luxury, bungalows
Kouleur Kréol Route de la Plage
☎ 33 (0)5 90 85 21 38
Créole food, price B–C
Les Pieds dans le sable 'Chez Louisette'
Plage des Galbas
☎ 33 (0)5 90 88 37 13
Local food, price A–B

ST FRANCOIS
Côté Cour Port de pêche
☎ 33 (0)5 90 85 50 47
sebastien.guerey@wanadoo.fr

Fish, price B–D
Iguane Cafe Rte Pte des Châteaux
☎ 33 (0)5 90 88 61 37
Fax 33 (0)5 90 85 03 09
Créole & French food, price C–D
La Plantation Ste Marthe Hauts de St François
☎ 33 (0)5 90 93 11 11
Créole food, price B–C
Hotel: luxury, studios
Le Mareyeur Haut du Bourg
☎ 33 (0)5 90 88 44 24
Créole food, price B–C
Le Méridien beside the lagoon & golf course
☎ 33 (0)5 90 48 05 10
Fax 33 (0)5 90 88 50 28
Créole food, fish, price C–D
Hotel: very luxurious
Le Zagaya on the seafront
☎ 33 (0)5 90 88 67 21
Fax 33 (0)5 90 88 41 84
Fish & crayfish, price B–C
Le Vieux Port Port de pêche
☎ 33 (0)5 90 88 46 60
Fax 33 (0)5 90 88 71 15
Gourmet menu, price B–C

LE MOULE
Chez Mimi
☎ 33 (0)5 90 23 64 87
Créole food, price A–B
Le Petit Jardin chez Lucille
☎ 33 (0)5 90 23 51 63
Fish, seafood, price B
ANSE BERTRAND
Folie Plage Chez Prudence
☎ 33 (0)5 90 22 11 17
Créole food, price A–B
Le Château de Feuilles Campêche
☎ 33 (0)5 90 22 30 30
Fax 33 (0)5 90 22 30 46
Créole food, price D+
STE ROSE
La Pomme Cannelle
☎ 33 (0)5 90 28 61 08
Créole & French food, price B–C
Chez Clara
☎ 33 (0)5 90 28 72 99
Créole specialties, price B–C

DESHAIES/GRANDE ANSE
Fleurs des Iles
☎ 33 (0)5 90 28 54 44
Fax 33 (0)5 90 28 54 45
Hotel: comfortable, bungalows
L'Amer terrace over the water
☎ 33 (0)5 90 28 50 43
Local food, price B–C
Le Coin des Pêcheurs
☎ 33 (0)5 90 28 47 75
Fish, price C
Le Mouillage 'Chez Racine'
☎ 33 (0)5 90 28 49 56/
33 (0)5 90 28 41 12
Créole specialties, punch price B–C
Le Karacoli south of Deshaies
☎ 33 (0)5 90 28 41 17
Créole food, price B

POINTE NOIRE
Caféière Beauséjour
☎ 33 (0)5 90 98 10 09
Fax 33 (0)5 90 98 12 49
contact@cafeierebeausejour
Old plantation with museum of the environment
Gourmet food, lunch only, price C–D
Hotel: luxury, bungalows

ROUTE DE LA TRAVERSEE — POINTE NOIRE
Restaurant des 2 Mamelles
☎ 33 (0)5 90 26 16 75
Créole specialties, price B
Couleur Caraïbes
☎/Fax 33 (0)5 90 98 89 59
Créole & French food, lunch only, price A–C
Hotel: comfortable, studios
Chez Jackye

☎ 33 (0)5 90 98 06 98
Créole & French food, price B

BOUILLANTE/MALENDURE/PIGEON
Chez Loulouse
☎ 33 (0)5 90 98 70 34
Fax 33 (0)5 90 98 97 05
Big 'lolo' on Malendure beach
Créole specialties, price A–B
Domaine de la Malendure
☎ 33 (0)5 90 98 92 12
malendure@leaderhotels.gp
Creole and international, price B–C. Hotel: comfortable, studios
La Touna on the waterfront, Galet Pigeon
☎ 33 (0)5 90 98 70 10
Fax 33 (0)5 90 98 92 28
Créole & French food, price B–D
Le Paradis Créole Pigeon Bouillante
☎ 33 (0)5 90 98 71 62
Fax 33 (0)5 90 98 77 76
heusaine@outremer.com
International & gourmet food, price C–D
Hotel: comfortable
Chez Margo Bouillante
☎/Fax 33 (0)5 90 98 95 39
Créole food, price A– B
Hôtel du Domaine de Pte Anse Bouillante
☎ 33 (0)5 90 98 78 78
Fax 33 (0)5 90 98 80 28
philippe.sangiorgio@wanadoo.fr
Hotel: comfortable, rooms & studios
Le Rocher de Malendure opposite Ilet Pigeon
☎ 33 (0)5 90 98 70 84
Fax 33 (0)5 90 98 89 92
lerocher@outremer.com
Créole & French food, price B–D
Hotel: simple, bungalows
Habitation Massieux Hauts de Malendure
☎ 33 (0)5 90 98 89 80
International & Créole food, price B–C
Les Tortues Plage des Tortues
☎ 33 (0)5 90 98 82 83
Créole & French food, price B–C

VIEUX HABITANTS
Le Relais du Pêcheur Plage Simaho
☎ 33 (0)5 90 98 58 57
Home Créole cooking, price A–B
Le Rocroy Plage du Rocroy
☎ 33 (0)5 90 98 42 25
Fax 33 (0)5 90 98 47 00
Créole & French food, price A–B
Hotel: comfortable

PETIT BOURG VERNOU
Restaurant Saut de la Lézarde
☎ 33 (0)5 90 94 84 63
Créole & French food, price B–C

BASSE TERRE
Le Phoënix Rue Schoelcher
☎ 33 (0)5 90 81 50 56
Créole & French food, price A–B
Le Filao Rue Victor Hugues
☎ 33 (0)5 90 81 98 26
Fax 33 (0)5 90 81 96 59
Créole & French food, price B

TROIS RIVIERES
Blue Caraïb
☎ 33 (0)5 90 92 76 21
Fax 33 (0)5 90 92 68 09
Pizzeria, price A

LES SAINTES (TERRE DE HAUT)
Auberge aux Anacardiers
Terre de Haut
☎ 33 (0)5 90 99 59 99
Fax 33 (0)5 90 99 54 51
petitssaints@yahoo.fr
Art gallery/antiques/pool
Gourmet food, table d'hôte

'dinner), price C–D
Hotel: luxury, personalised rooms
Yacht Club des Saintes
☎/Fax 33 (0)5 90 99 57 82 VHF 68
Local food, price A–B
Café de la Marine
☎ 33 (0)5 90 99 53 78
Fax 33 (0)5 90 99 52 41
Local food, price A–B
L'Anse Mouillage
☎ 33 (0)5 90 99 50 57
Fax 33 (0)5 90 99 88 30
Local food, price A–B
Le Kanoa Terre de Haut
☎ 33 (0)5 90 99 51 36
Fax 33 (0)5 90 99 55 04
KANOA@wanadoo.fr
Local food, price B–C
Hotel: comfortable
Mikazia Débarcadère
☎ 33 (0)5 90 99 57 63
Local food, price B–C
El Dorado Place de la Mairie
☎ 33 (0)5 90 99 54 31
Créole food & pizzas, price B–C
Le Triangle Fond du Curé
☎ 33 (0)5 90 99 50 50
Fish, salads, price A–B
Le Génois Quartier du Mouillage
☎ 33 (0)5 90 99 53 01
Pleasant ambiance at the 'Havane
Club des Saintes'
Créole food, wine cellar, price B–C
La Saladerie Anse Mire
☎ 33 (0)5 90 99 53 43
Local food, price A–B
La Paillotte Terre de Haut
☎ 33 (0)5 90 99 50 77
Fax 33 (0)5 90 99 54 30
Créole food, price A
Gîte rural Jacques Boone
☎ 33 (0)5 90 99 52 31
Fax 33 (0)5 90 99 55 98
boone.jacques@wanadoo.fr
Lovely view across the bay
Hotel: comfortable, rooms &
bungalows
Hotel le Bois Joli
☎ 33 (0)5 90 99 50 38
Fax 33 (0)5 90 99 55 05
boisjoli@ifrance.com
Créole & French food, price B–C
Hotel: comfortable

LES SAINTES (TERRE DE BAS)
Chez Eugénette Plage de Grande
Anse
☎ 33 (0)5 90 99 81 83
Créole & local food, price A
Best 'accras' in the Caribbean
A la Belle Etoile Plage de Grande
Anse
☎ 33 (0)5 90 99 83 69
Créole & local food, price A

MARIE GALANTE
Le Touloulou Petit Anse
Capesterre
☎ 33 (0)5 90 97 32 63
Fax 33 (0)5 90 97 33 59
contact@letouloulou.com
Local food, price B–C
Hotel: simple, studios
Les 100 Moulins Grand Bourg
☎ 33 (0)5 90 97 88 01
Fax 33 (0)5 90 97 56 54
Créole & French food, price A–B
L'Assiette de Iles St Louis
☎ 33 (0)5 90 97 10 93
Local food, price A–B
L'Oasis Grand Bourg
☎ 33 (0)5 90 97 59 55
Hotel: comfortable, rooms &
bungalows
La Cohoba Hôtel Folle Anse
Grand Bourg
☎ 33 (0)5 90 97 50 50
Fax 33 (0)5 90 97 97 96
Hotel: luxury

LA DESIRADE
La Payotte Plage de Fifi
Beauséjour
☎ 33 (0)5 90 20 01 29
Local food, fish, price A
La Providence/Chez Nounoune
Baie Mahault
☎ 33 (0)5 90 20 03 59
Local food, price A–B
Hôtel le Mirage Grande Anse
☎ 33 (0)5 90 20 01 08
Hotel: simple rooms

CAR RENTAL
Jumbo Car Centrale de
resérvation
☎ 33 (0)5 90 91 55 66
Fax 33 (0)5 90 91 22 88
Aéroport Pôle Caraïbes
☎ 33 (0)5 90 21 13 50
Fax 33 (0)5 90 21 13 53
resagua@jumbocar.com
Marina du Marin
☎ 33 (0)5 90 90 86 32
Fax 33 (0)5 90 90 93 64
Cap Caraïbes Marina Marina du
Bas du Fort
☎ 33 (0)5 90 93 61 68
Fax 33 (0)5 90 93 62 86
cap-caraibes@caramail.com
Europcar Airport
☎ 33 (0)5 90 21 13 52
Fax 33 (0)5 90 21 13 53
Pop's Car Central reservations
☎ 33 (0)5 90 21 13 56
Fax 33 (0)5 90 21 13 57
popscar.pe@wanadoo.fr
Stella Auto Basse Terre
☎ 33 (0)5 90 81 75 62
Avis St François Av. de l'Europe
☎ 33 (0)5 90 85 00 11
Easy Rent St François Galerie du
Port
☎ 33 (0)5 90 88 76 27
Location+ Grand Savane, Marie
Galante
☎ 33 (0)5 90 61 96 14
Fax 33 (0)5 90 97 56 54
Ets Defaut Marie Galante Pier
☎/Fax 33 (0)5 90 97 56 63
Locasun Le Désirade
☎ 33 (0)5 90 20 07 81 *scooters &*
pushbikes

Antigua

AIRLINES
Air Canada
☎ 268 462 1147 *Fax 268 462 2679*
American Airlines
☎ 268 462 0952 *Fax 268 462 2067*
British Airways
☎ 268 462 0876 *Fax 268 462 3218*
BWIA
☎ 268 480 2925 *Fax 268 480 2940*
Liat
☎ 268 480 5600 *Fax 268 480 5625*
Carib Aviation Charter
☎ 268 462 3147 *Fax 268 462 3125*
MARINAS/DOCKS (FUEL AND
WATER)
ENGLISH HARBOUR
Nelson's Dockyard
☎ 268 460 7976/1379
Fax 268 460 1516
Managed by the National Park
Authority
Antigua Slipway
☎ 268 460 1056 *Fax 268 460 1566*
antslipway@candw.ag
Water and fuel on the pontoon
FALMOUTH HARBOUR
The Catamaran Marina
☎ 260 460 1503 *Fax 268 460 1506*
VHF 16/68
CATAMARANmarina@hotmail.
com
Water and fuel on the pontoon
Antigua Yacht Club Marina
☎ 268 460 1544 *Fax 268 460 1444*
VHF 68
falconec@candw.ag
Water on the pontoon

Falmouth Harbour Marina
☎ 268 460 6054 *Fax 268 460 6055*
falmar@candw.ag
Water on the pontoon
MAMORA BAY
St James Club Hotel dock
☎ 268 460 8001 *Fax 268 460 3015*
VHF 68
Water and fuel on the pontoon
ST JOHN'S
Joe's Cafe Redcliffe Quay
VHF 16
Water on the dock
MOSQUITO COVE (JOLLY
HARBOUR)
Jolly Harbour Marina
☎ 268 460 6041/6042
Fax 268 460 7703
VHF 68
jollymarina@candw.ag
Water and fuel on the pontoon
PROFESSIONAL YACHT
SERVICES
Note: all services listen out on
VHF 68
Boatyards/haulout
ENGLISH HARBOUR
Antigua Slipway
☎ 268 460 1056 *Fax 268 460 1566*
antslip@candw.ag
MOSQUITO COVE (JOLLY
HARBOUR)
Jolly Harbour Shipyard
☎ 268 462 6042 *Fax 268 462 7703*
jollymarina@candw.ag
Chandlers
ENGLISH HARBOUR
Antigua Slipway
☎ 268 460 1056 *Fax 268 460 1566*
antslip@candw.ag
Lord Jim's Locker
☎ 268 460 1093 *Fax 460 1524*
lordjim@candw.ag
ST JOHNS
Aqua Sports Heritage Quay
☎ 268 462 5620 *Fax 268 480 3076*
Island Motor Ltd
☎ 268 462 2199 *Fax 268 462 2138*
VHF 82
ismo78@yahoo.com
(Offices also at Nelson's Dockyard
& Jolly Harbour)
Redcliffe Water Sports
☎ 268 462 9785/460 6355 *Fax 268*
462 9790

FALMOUTH HARBOUR
Falmouth Harbour Marine
Services
☎ 268 463 8081 *Fax 268 463 8082*
Catamaran Marina
☎ 268 460 1503 *Fax 268 460 1506*
CATAMARANmarina@
hotmail.com
Lord Jim's Locker AYC Marina
☎ 268 460 1147 *Fax 460 4093*
lordjim@candw.ag
Seagull Inflatables Catamaran
Marina
☎ 268 460 1020 *Fax 268 460 1135*
flatgull@candw.ag

MOSQUITO COVE JOLLY
HARBOUR
Budget Marine
☎ 268 462 8753
☎/Fax 268 462 7727
sales@budmar.ag
Sailmakers/awnings/riggers
ENGLISH HARBOUR
A&F Sails Ltd
☎ 268 460 1522 *Fax 268 460 1152*
afsails@candw.ag
Antigua Sails
☎ 268 460 1527 *Fax 268 460 1526*
antsails@candw.ag

Nicholson's Caribbean Yacht
Sales
☎ 268 460 1093 *Fax 268 460 1524*
nicholsoncy@candw.ag
Tend Aloft Rigging Company
☎/Fax 268 460 1151
trigging@candw.ag

FALMOUTH HARBOUR
Antigua Rigging
☎ 268 460 8575 *Fax 268 460 1123*
antrig@candw.ag
Seagull Services
☎ 26 460 3050 *Fax 268 460 1767*
seagull@candw.ag
Electrics/electronics/refrigeration
ENGLISH HARBOUR
The Signal Locker
☎ 268 460 1528 *Fax 268 460 1148*
lockers@candw.ag
Antigua Yachts
☎ 268 460 7670 *Fax 268 460 7671*
anuyot@candw.ag
Caribbean Current
☎ 268 460 7670 *Fax 268 460 7671*
VHF 68
current@candw.ag

FALMOUTH HARBOUR
Marionics
☎ 268 460 1780 *Fax 268 460 1135*
marionic@candw.ag
Cays Electronics
☎ 268 460 1040 *Fax 268 460 1227*
cayelec@candw.ag
Aboard Refrigeration
☎ 268 460 1690 *Fax 268 858 0544*
aboardrf@candw.ag

MOSQUITO COVE (JOLLY
HARBOUR)
Star Electronics
☎ 268 464 3510
Shipwrights/joiners/GRP
ENGLISH HARBOUR
Awl Grip2 Antigua Antigua
Slipway
☎ 268 460 8184

FALMOUTH HARBOUR
Chippy/Seaward sales
☎ 268 460 1832 *Fax 268 460 1491*
VHF 68
Woodstock Boat Builders
☎ 268 463 6354 *Fax 268 562 6359*
refit@woodstockboats.com

MOSQUITO COVE (JOLLY
HARBOUR)
Harbour Woodworks
☎ 268 462 7715
Harris Boat Works
☎ 268 462 5333 *Fax 268 462 5332*
harrisja@candw.ag
Mechanics/workshops/diesel
FALMOUTH HARBOUR
Marine Power Services
☎ 268 460 1850 *Fax 268 460 1851*
mps@candw.ag
Seagull Services
☎ 268 460 3050 *Fax 268 460 1767*
seagull@candw.ag
A1 Marine Services
☎/Fax 268 462 7755
YACHT CHARTER
ENGLISH HARBOUR
Sunsail-Stardust
Nelson's Dockyard
☎ 268 460 2615
Fax 268 460 2616
www.sunsail.com
Antigua Charters Services
☎ 268 562 2893 *Fax 268 562 2894*
charterservices@candw.ag
Nicholson Yacht Charters
☎ 268 460 1530 *Fax 268 460 1531*
Nicholson's Caribbean Yacht
Sales
☎ 268 460 1093 *Fax 268 460 1524*
nicholsoncy@candw.ag

DIVING

ENGLISH HARBOUR
Dockyard Divers English &
Falmouth Harbours
☎ 268 460 1178 Fax 268 460 1179
dockyard_divers@candw.ag
Octopus Divers English Harbour
☎ 268 460 6286 Fax 268 463 8528
octopusdivers@candw.ag
Jolly Dive Jolly Harbour
☎/Fax 268 462 8305
Aquanaut St James' Club
☎ 268 460 5000 Fax 268 460 3015

RESTAURANTS/HOTELS

*Note: Most restaurants are only
open evenings*
ENGLISH HARBOUR
Admiral's Inn
☎ 268 460 1027 Fax 460 1534
admirals@candw.ag
*Beautifully set in an old restored
building, terrace on the lagoon,
steelband at weekends.
Traditional food, price C–D
Hotel: historic charm, luxury*
Catherine's Cafe E.H. Slipway
(French manager) ☎ 268 460 5050
*International menu, fish, price
B–D*
Abracadabra
☎ 268 460 1732
abra@candw.ag
Italian food, price B–C
The Copper and Lumber Store
☎ 268 460 1058 Fax 268 460 1529
c/hotel@candw.ag
*Splendidly & luxuriously restored
18th century building
The Wardroom restaurant 2
menus, local & international,
elegant, price D.
Hotel: luxury, studios & suites*
Famous Mauro
☎ 268 460 1318 VHF 68
Pizzeria & bakery
Shirley Heights Lookout
☎ 268 460 1785 Fax 268 460 3490
VHF 68
*BBQ, steelband (Thursday &
Sunday), price A–B*

FALMOUTH HARBOUR
Playbach Terrace
☎ 268 460 6575
playbach@hotmail.com
Pub food, music, price B–C
The Catamaran Hotel
☎ 268460 1036 Fax 268 460 1339
catclub@candw.ag
Hotel: comfortable, on the beach

MORRIS BAY
Curtain Bluff Resort
☎ 268 462 8400 Fax 268 462 8409
curtainbluff@candw.ag
*International cuisine, price D+
Hotel: very luxurious, on the
beach*

JOLLY HARBOUR
Dogwatch Tavern
☎/Fax 268 462 6550
Fish, BBQ, price B–C
Jolly Harbour Beach Resort
☎ 268 462 6166 Fax 268 462 6167
Hotel: luxury
Al Porto Restaurant
☎ 268 462 7695
Pizzeria, fresh pasta, price A–B

GALLEY BAY
Chez Pascal Galley Bay Hill
☎ 268 462 3232 Fax 268 460 5730
chez@candw.ag
*Beautiful view over Galley Bay
French proprietors, French food &
wine, price B–C
Hotel: luxury*

ST JOHNS
Big Banana Redcliffe Quay
☎ 268 480 6985 Fax 268 460 6989
Pizzas, salad, price B

The Commissioner Grill Redcliffe
Road
☎ 268 762 1883
ezra@candw.ag
Crayfish, seafood, price B–C
The Redcliffe Tavern Redcliffe
Quay
☎ 268 461 4557 Fax 268 462 1450
keyproperties@candw.ag
Local food, price B–C
La Baguette Redcliffe Quay
☎ 268 562 1820
Sandwich bar
Joe Mike's Hotel Plaza Nevis
Road
☎ 268 462 1142 Fax 268 462 6056
joemikes@candw.ag
Hotel: simple
Millers by the Sea Fort James
☎ 268 462 9414 Fax 268 462 9591
Seafood, live music, price C–D

HODGES BAY
The Bistro
☎ 268 462 3881 Fax 268 461 2996
pgbistro@candw.ag
*French food, price C–D, evenings
only*

BROWN'S BAY
☎ 268 460 4120 Fax 268 460 4406
harmony@candw.ag website
www.harmonyhall.com
*Italian & Caribbean cuisine, price
C–D*

WILLOUGHBY BAY
Alberto's Willoughby Bay
☎ 268 460 3007 VHF 68
alberto@candw.ag
*Italian food, price B–C, evenings
only*

MAMORA BAY
St James' Yacht Club
☎ 268 460 5000 Fax 268 460 3015
*Local and international menus,
price C–D
Hotel: very luxurious, cottages &
rooms*

CAR RENTAL/TAXIS/TRAVEL AGENTS

Hyatt's
English Harbour ☎ 268 460 6551
St Johns ☎ 268 463 2012
Hertz Jolly Harbour
☎ 268 462 4114 Fax 268 462 1048
hertz@candw.ag
Lion Car Rental
English Harbour
☎ 268 460 1400 Fax 268 460 2707
Airport Road
☎ 268 562 2708
allison@candw.ag
ATS Archibald Taxi Service
☎ 268 4610441 Fax 268 461 5700
ats@candw.ag
Caribbean Helicopters Jolly
Harbour
☎ 268 460 5900 Fax 268 460 5901
helicopters@candw.ag
*Tours over the island, trips to
Montserrat*

Barbuda

RESTAURANTS/HOTELS

K-Club
☎ 268 460 0300 Fax 268 460 0305
kclub@candw.ag
*International menu, price D+
Hotel: very luxurious, bungalows*
Park Terrace Codrington
☎ 268 460 0092
Local food, price A
Palm Tree Restaurant Codrington
☎ 268 460 0517
Local food, price A

Palmetto Beach Hotel
☎ 268 460 0442 Fax 268 460 0440
palmetto@candw.ag
*Italian food, price C & D,
Hotel: luxury*

CAR RENTAL/TAXIS/TRAVEL AGENTS

George Jeffrey
☎ 268 460 0143
VHF 16/68 'Garden of Eden'
Taxis Burton/Jonas
VHF 16/68

Montserrat

AIRLINES

Helicopter service (except
Wednesdays)
☎ 664 491 2533 Fax 664 491 7186
helicopters@candw.ag

MARINAS/DOCKS

Port Little Bay
☎ 664 491 2791 Fax 664 492 8063
Water

DIVING

Sea Wolf Diving School
☎/Fax 664 491 7807
krebs@candw.ag

RESTAURANTS/HOTELS

Bitter End Beach Bar Little Bay
Seafood & snacks, price A–B
Tina's Restaurant Brades Main
Road
☎ 664 491 3538
Local food, price A
The Attic Restaurant Olveston
☎ 664 491 2008
Local food, price A–B
Grand View Baker Hill
☎ 664 491 2284 Fax 664 491 6876
grand@candw.ag
*Local food, price A–B
Hotel: simple*

CAR RENTAL

KC Car rental
☎ 664 491 5756 Fax 664 491 6085
kccarrental@hotmail.com
Jenny's Tours
☎/Fax 664 461 9361
burkeb@candw.ag
*Many taxis operate on the island
see Tourist Office*

Nevis

AIRLINES

Nevis Express (air taxis)
☎ 869 469 9755 Fax 869 469 9751
Winair ☎ 869 469 9583

FERRY COMPANIES

Carib Breeze/MV Caribe Queen
Shuttle between Nevis & St Kitts

PROFESSIONAL YACHT SERVICES

Mechanic
Albert Myers Main Street
☎ 869 469 5739

DIVING

Dive Nevis Newcastle
☎ 869 469 9395 Fax 869 469 9375
Scuba Safaris Oualie Beach
☎ 869 469 9518 Fax 869 469 9619

RESTAURANTS/HOTELS

Cafe des Arts Main Street
☎/Fax 869 469 7098
Local & international food, price B
Courtyard Cafe Main Street
☎ 869 469 1854
Local food, price B
Eddy's Restaurant Main Street
☎ 869 469 5958 Fax 869 469 0129
Local food, price B–C
Unella's by the Sea waterfront
☎ 869 469 5574
Local food & seafood, price A–B
The Four Season's Resort
Pinney's Beach
☎ 869 469 1111 Fax 869 469 1085
Hotel: super luxury, suites &

cottages, tennis, golf
Under the Sea Cades Point
☎ 869 469 1291 Fax 869 469 3937
terramar@caribsurf.com
*Local food & snacks, price B–C
Boutique & aquarium*
Oualie Beach Hotel Oualie Bay
☎ 869 469 9735 Fax 869 469 9176
oualie @caribsurf.com
Hotel: comfortable, cottages
Inland
Golden Rock Plantation Inn
☎ 869 469 3346 Fax 869 469 2113
gdhobson@caribsurf.com
Hotel: luxury, cottages
Montpelier Plantation Inn
☎ 869 469 3462 Fax 869 469 2932
montpinn@caribsurf.com
*Local & international food,
price D+
Hotel: luxury, bungalows with fine
décot*

CAR RENTAL/TAXIS/TOUR OPERATORS

Nevis Car Rental Newcastle
☎ 869 469 9837
Noel's Car Rental Farm Estate
☎/Fax 869 469 5199
TDC Rentals/Thrifty Rentals
Charlestown
☎ 869 469 1005 Fax 869 469 1329
Taxi Service Charlestown
☎ 869 469 1140 Fax 869 469 5399
Top the Bottom
☎ 869 469 9080
walknevis@caribsurf.com

St Kitts

AIRLINES

American Airlines
☎ 869 465 5000
Winair
☎ 869 465 8010 Fax 869 465 9583
BWIA/Liat
☎ 869 465 8613

FERRY COMPANIES

MV Caribe Queen
operates between Nevis & St Kitts

MARINAS/DOCKS (WATER/FUEL)

Port Zante
☎ 869 466 5021 Fax 869 466 5020
VHF 68
udccorp@caribsurf.com
Shell Station Prince William
Street
☎ 869 469 5397 Fax 869 469 0401
Fuel deliveries

PROFESSIONAL YACHT SERVICES

Chandlery/charts
Leeward Island Charters The
Circus
☎ 268 465 7474 Fax 268 465 7070
Sail repair/awnings
Caribbean Canvas
☎ 869 466 9636 Fax 869 466 9635
canvasup@caribsurf.com
Boatbuilders
Carib Yachts Ltd
☎ 869 465 8411 Fax 869 465 6177
caribyachts@visto.com

DIVING

Pro Divers Turtle Beach
☎/Fax 869 466 3483
prodivers@caribsurf.com
Kenneth's Dive Center Basseterre
☎/Fax 869 465 2670 VHF 16
Blue Water Safaris Ltd Basseterre
☎ 869 466 4933 Fax 869 466 6740
waterfun@caribsurf.com
Dive St Kitts Bird Rock Beach
Hotel
☎ 869 465 1189 Fax 869 465 1675
brbh@caribsurf.com
OTI Basseterre
☎ 869 465 2754 Fax 869 465 1057
otiskitts@caribsurf.com

RESTAURANTS/HOTELS
Circus Grill Basseterre
☎ 869 465 0143
Fish, price B
Lovely terrace
The Ballahoo Basseterre
☎ 869 465 4197 Fax 869 465 7627
Local food & seafood, price
B–terrace on The Circus.
Bayembi Cafe Basseterre
☎ 869 466 5280
bayembi@aol.com
Local food, price A–B
Mango's Independence Square
☎ 869 465 4049 Fax 869 465 1335
man0209@caribsurf.com
Créole & international food, price
B
Ocean Terrace Inn Fine view over
Basseterre Bay
☎ 869 465 2754 Fax 869 465 1057
oti@stkitts.com
Fisherman's Wharf Restaurant
seafood, BBQ, price B–C
Hotel: luxury
Turtle Beach
☎ 869 469 9086 Fax 869 466 7771
VHF 16
gary@caribsurf.com
Local food, BBQ, price A–B
The Golden Lemon Dieppe Bay
Town
☎ 869 465 7260 Fax 869 465 4019
artmrt@caribsurf.com
Créole & international food, price
B–C
Hotel: luxury, rooms & cottages
The Garden Room Frigate Bay
Resort
☎ 869 465 8935 Fax 869 465 7050
frigbay@caribsurf.com
Local & international food, price C
CAR RENTAL/TAXIS/TOUR
OPERATORS
Caines Auto Services Basseterre
☎ 869 465 2366 Fax 869 465 6172
TDC/Thrifty Rentals Basseterre
☎ 869 465 2991 Fax 869 465 8855
tdcrent@caribsurf.com
Scooter Rentals Basseterre
☎ 869 466 7841
Fax 869 466 8487
midasscooter@caribsurf.com
Liamuiga Taxi Association
☎ 869 465 3006/465 4128
(evenings only)

Statia

AIRLINES
Winair
☎ 599 318 2381
Golden Rock Charters,
☎ 599 318 2786
DIVING
Dive Statia Lower Town
☎ 599 318 2435 Fax 599 318 2539
divestatia@megatropic.com
Golden Rock Diving Center Lower
Town
☎/Fax 599 318 2964
goldenrockdive@megatropic.com
Scubaqua Dive Center Lower
Town
☎/Fax 599 318 2160
scubaqua@goldenrock.net
RESTAURANTS/HOTELS
Ocean View Terrace Oranjestad
☎ 599 318 2934 Fax 599 318 2433
Local & international, price B–C
Sonny's & Cantonese Upper
Town
☎/Fax 599 318 2929
Chinese, price A–B
Golden Era Hotel Lower Town
☎ 599 318 2345 Fax 599 318 2445
Créole & international food,
price B
Hotel: comfortable

The Old Gin House Lower Town
☎ 599 318 2319 Fax 599 318 2135
reservation@oldginhouse.com
In a restored warehouse
International and local, price D
Hotel: luxury
King's Well Resort Bay Road
☎/Fax 599 318 2538
International and local, price C–D
Smoke Alley Bar
VHF 69
☎/Fax 599 318 2002
Mexican, price A–C
Free ferry if you call on VHF
Chocolate Restaurant Golden
Rock
☎ 599 318 2830
BBQ, price A–B
Free ferry if you call on the phone
CAR RENTAL & TAXIS
Co-Rentals Oranjestad
☎ 599 318 2941 Fax 599 318 2940
Brown's Car Rental
☎ 599 318 2266 Fax 599 318 2454
**Rainbow Car Rental/Rosies Lopes
Taxi**
☎ 599 318 2811 Fax 599 318 2586

Saba

AIRLINES
Winair
☎ 599 416 2255
FERRY COMPANIES
The Edge Sint Maarten
☎ 599 54 2640 Fax 599 54 2476
Voyager St-Martin
☎ 33 (0)5 90 87 10 68
**PROFESSIONAL YACHT
SERVICES**
Chandlery
Sea Saba Fort Bay
☎ 599 416 2246 Fax 599 416 2362
seasaba@aol.com
DIVING
Saba Deep Fort Bay
☎ 599 416 3347 Fax 599 416 3397
diving@sabadeep.com
Sea Saba Fort Bay
☎ 599 416 2246 Fax 599 416 2362
seasaba@aol.com
Saba Divers Windwardside
☎ 599 416 2740 Fax 599 416 2741
sabadivers@unspoiledqueen.com
RESTAURANTS/HOTELS
Note: reservations are
recommended as are prior
arrangements for transport.
Lollipop's The Bottom Road
☎ 599 416 3330
Local food & fish, price A–B
lovely view
Cranston's Inn The Bottom
☎ 599 416 3203 Fax 599 416 3469
Local food, seafood, price B–C
Hotel: simple
In Two Deep Fort Bay
☎ 599 416 3438
Local food, price A–B
Brigadoon Windwardside
☎ 599 416 2380
Local & international food, price B
Divers' meeting place
Juliana's Windwardside
☎ 599 416 2269 Fax 599 416 2389
juliana's@unspoiledqueen.com
Local & American food, price B
Hotel: comfortable
Tropics Cafe Windwardside
☎ 599 416 2429
International & seafood, price A–B
Scout's Place Windwardside
☎ 599 416 2205 Fax 599 416 2741
sabadivers@unspoiledqueen.com
American food, price B
Hotel: comfortable (dive
packages)

CAR RENTAL/TAXIS
Johnson's
☎ 599 416 2269
Mike's & Son Car Rental The
Bottom
☎/Fax 599 416 3259
Taxis Call via the Customs post
(Gloria VHF 16)

St-Barthélémy

Note: when calling numbers in
French islands from non-French
islands, omit the 0 after the
country code
AIRLINES
St-Barth Commuter
☎ 33 (0)5 90 27 54 54
Fax 33 (0)5 90 27 54 58
Air Caraïbes
☎ 33 (0)5 90 27 61 90
Fax 33 (0)5 90 27 67 03
Winair
☎ 33 (0)5 90 27 61 01
Air St Thomas
☎/Fax 33 (0)5 90 27 71 76
FERRY COMPANIES
Voyager I and II Colombier
☎ 33 (0)5 90 27 54 10
Fax 33 (0)5 90 27 77 23
Gustavia Express (from Anse
Marcel, St-Martin)
☎ 33 (0)5 90 27 54 65
Fax 33 (0)5 90 27 19 83
St-Barth Jet Ferry
☎ 33 (0)5 90 87 89 38
MARINAS (WATER/FUEL)
Port de Plaisance de Gustavia
☎ 33 (0)5 90 27 66 97
Fax 33 (0)5 90 27 81 54 VHF 16
port.de.gustavia@wanadoo.fr
St-Barth Marine Commercial port
☎ 33 (0)5 90 27 75 75
Fax 33 (0)5 90 27 91 11 VHF 16
Fuel & water
**PROFESSIONAL YACHT
SERVICES**
Chandlery
Le Shipchandler du Port Franc
☎ 33 (0)5 90 27 86 29
Fax 33 (0)5 90 27 85 73
mariesully@wanadoo.fr
Sailmakers/awnings
La Voilerie du Port France
☎/Fax 33 (0)5 90 27 56 58
Mechanic/diesel
engines/outboards
Hughes Marine
☎ 33 (0)5 90 27 50 70
Fax 33 (0)5 90 52 33 05 04
hughesportier@wanadoo.fr
JML/Boatinox
☎/Fax 33 (0)5 90 27 99 14
Haulout/boatbuilders
JML/Boatinox
☎/Fax 33 (0)5 90 27 99 14
Electrical/workshops/welding
JML/Boatinox
☎/Fax 33 (0)5 90 27 99 14
Hughes Marine
☎ 33 (0)5 90 27 50 70
Fax 33 (0)5 90 52 33 05 04
hughesportier@wanadoo.fr
DIVING (DIVES/AIR/EQUIPMENT)
La Bulle Océan Must
☎ 33 (0)5 90 27 62 25
Fax 33 (0)5 90 27 95 17
oceanmust@wanadoo.fr
St-Barth Plongée
☎/Fax 33 (0)5 90 27 54 44
Fax 33 (0)5 90 27 75 57
BIRDY.Dive@wanadoo.fr
West Indies Dive
☎ 33 (0)5 90 27 70 34
Fax 33 (0)5 90 27 91 80 VHF 74
marine.service.stbarth@
wanadoo.fr
Yannis Marine
☎/Fax 33 (0)5 90 29 89 12
yannis.marine@wanadoo.fr

Scuba Diving Center
☎/Fax 33 (0)5 90 27 55 94
Le Shipchandler du Port Franc
☎ 33 (0)5 90 27 86 29
Fax 33 (0)5 90 27 85 73
mariesully@wanadoo.fr
YACHT CHARTER
Nautica FWI Rue de la Republique
☎ 33 (0)5 90 27 56 50
Fax 33 (0)5 90 27 56 52
nfyachts@compuserve.com
Marine Service Quai du Yacht
Club
☎ 33 (0)5 90 27 70 34
Fax 33 (0)5 90 27 70 36
marine.service.stbarth@wanadoo.
fr
Océan Must La Pointe
☎ 33 (0)5 90 27 62 25
Fax 33 (0)5 90 27 95 17
oceanmust@wanadoo.fr
RESTAURANTS/HOTELS
GUSTAVIA
La Marine
☎ 33 (0)5 90 27 68 91
Fax 33 (0)5 90 27 10 13
Fish and seafood, price C–D
L'Escale
☎ 33 (0)5 90 27 81 06 '
Fax 33 (0)5 90 27 67 64
lescale.saintbarth@wanadoo.fr
Pizzas & fish, price B–C, evenings
only
Pleasant terrace on the Quai Sud
Le Select Bar
☎ 33 (0)5 90 27 86 87
Yachties' watering hole
L'Entracte
☎ 33 (0)5 90 27 70 11
Pizzas & BBQ, price A–B
Le Route des Boucaniers
☎ 33 (0)5 90 27 73 00
Fax 33 (0)5 90 27 73 05
boucaniers@wanadoo.fr
French & Créole food, price B–C
Le Repaire below the chandlery
☎ 33 (0)5 90 27 72 48
Fax 33 (0)5 90 27 73 28
International menu, price B–C

BAIE DES FLAMANDS
Hotel St-Barth Isle de France on
the beach
☎ 33 (0)5 90 27 61 81
Fax 33 (0)5 90 27 86 83
isledefr@saint-baths.com
La Case de l'Isle Restaurant
French food, price C–D
Hotel: luxury, bungalows

ST JEAN/LORIENT
Eden Rock a legendary spot in St
Barts
☎ 33 (0)5 90 29 79 99
Fax 33 (0)5 90 27 88 37
info@denrockhotel.com
Gourmet food, price D+
Hotel: very luxurious
Le Tom Beach Hotel Plage de St
Jean
☎ 33 (0)5 90 27 53 13
Fax 33 (0)5 90 27 53 15
tombeach@wanadoo.fr
La Plage Restaurant fish & BBQ,
price D
Hotel: luxury

GRAND CUL-DE-SAC
Hotel Guanahani
☎ 33 (0)5 90 27 66 60
Fax 33 (0)5 90 27 70 70
guanahani@st-barths.com
Le Bartolomeo Restaurant
international menu, price D+
Hotel: very luxurious
Le Rivage
☎ 33 (0)5 90 27 82 42
Fax 33 (0)5 90 27 70 75
Créole food, fish & salads, price
B–C

ANSE GRANDE SALINE
L'Esprit Salines
☎ 33 (0)5 90 54 46 10
Fax 33 (0)5 90 52 46 01
Guillaume.hennequia@
wanadoo.fr
BBQ, salads, price A–B
Le Grain de Sel
☎ 33 (0)5 90 52 46 05
Fax 33 (0)5 90 27 71 03
*Snacks & salads, price A–B,
(lunch only)*

SHELL BEACH
Dô Brazil
☎ 33 (0)5 90 29 06 66
Brazilian food, fish, price D+

CAR RENTAL
Budget *Gustavia*
☎ 33 (0)5 90 27 67 43
Fax 33 (0)5 90 27 83 93
budgetsaintbarth@wanadoo.fr
Thrifty
☎ 33 (0)5 90 27 75 25
Fax 33 (0)5 90 27 73 05
satfranclocation@yahoo.fr
Chez Béranger *Gustavia/Airport*
☎ 33 (0)5 90 27 89 00
Fax 33 (0)5 90 27 80 28
alamonation@wanadoo.fr
Mega Moto *Gustavia*
☎ 33 (0)5 90 52 92 49
Fax 33 (0)5 90 29 85 33

TAXIS
Port taxi rank
☎ 33 (0)5 90 27 66 31
Airport taxi rank
☎ 33 (0)5 90 27 75 81

St-Martin

*Note: when calling numbers in
French islands from non-French
islands, omit the 0 after the
country code*

AIRLINES/AGENTS
St-Barth Commuter Grand Case
☎ 33 (0)5 90 87 80 73
Fax 33 (0)5 90 87 97 53
Air Calypso Grand Case
☎ 33 (0)5 90 29 46 00
Fax 33 (0)5 90 29 46 02
Air St-Martin Grand Case
☎ 33 (0)5 90 87 10 36
Fax 33 (0)5 90 87 10 80
Air France Marigot
☎ 33 (0)5 90 87 02 02
Fax 33 (0)5 90 51 03 68
Corsair/Nouvelles Frontières
Marigot
☎ 33 (0)5 90 87 27 79
Fax 33 (0)5 90 87 27 80
Héli Inter Caraïbes Anse Marcel
☎ 33 (0)5 90 87 35 88
Fax 33 (0)5 90 87 34 47

FERRY COMPANIES
Voyager I and II Baie Nettlé
to St-Barth, Saba
☎ 33 (0)5 90 87 10 68
Fax 33 (0)5 90 29 34 79
CGM Interline
connections with Guadeloupe, St
Lucia, Saba, San Juan
☎ 33 (0)5 90 87 37 10
Fax 33 (0)5 90 87 87 32
cgminterline@powerantilles.com
Gustavia Express (from Anse
Marcel, St-Martin)
☎ 33 (0)5 90 27 54 65/33 (0)5 90
27 19 83

MARINAS/DOCKS WATER/FUEL
MARIGOT/SANDY GROUND
Marina Port la Royale
☎ 33 (0)5 90 87 20 43
Fax 33 (0)5 90 87 55 95 VHF 16
Regine-Hee@wanadoo.fr
Water
Cadisco Sandy Ground/Lagoon
☎ 33 (0)5 90 66 18 98
Fax 33 (0)5 90 87 33 05 59 VHF 22

Fuel & water
Marine Time Marigot waterfront
☎ 33 (0)5 90 87 20 28
Fax 33 (0)5 90 87 20 78 VHF 10
marinetime@wanadoo.fr
Fuel delivered to Port Galisbay
Time Out Sandy Ground/Lagoon
☎ 33 (0)5 90 52 02 88
Fax 33 (0)5 90 52 02 89
timeoutboat@hotmail.com
Water
Boats Services Sandy Ground
☎ 33 (0)5 90 87 11 84
Fuel
St-Martin Marine Center Sandy
Ground Bridge
☎ 33 (0)5 90 87 86 32
Fax 33 (0)5 90 87 04 28
st-martin-marine-
center@wanadoo.fr
Fuel & water

ANSE MARCEL
Port Lonvilliers
☎ 33 (0)5 90 87 31 94
Fax 33 (0)5 90 87 33 96 VHF 16/11
Fuel & water

OYSTER POND
Captain Oliver's Marina
☎/*Fax 33 (0)5 90 87 33 47 VHF 16*
captoli@wanadoo.fr
Fuel & water

PROFESSIONAL YACHT SERVICES
Boatyards/haulout
Polypat Caraïbes Sandy Ground
Bridge
☎ 33 (0)5 90 87 12 01
Fax 33 (0)5 90 87 92 13
polypatcaraibes@wanadoo.fr
Chantiers Geminga Sandy
Ground Road
☎ 33 (0)5 90 29 35 52
Fax 33 (0)5 90 29 65 36 VHF 71
geminga2@wanadoo.fr
Time Out Sandy Ground/Lagoon
☎ 33 (0)5 90 52 02 88
Fax 33 (0)5 90 52 02 89
timeoutboat@hotmail.com
Chandleries
Madco Discount Bellevue
☎ 33 (0)5 90 51 05 40
Fax 33 (0)5 90 29 43 70
madco.sxm@wanadoo.fr
Team Number One Marigot
☎ 33 (0)5 90 87 58 27
 Fax 33 (0)5 90 87 95 75
L'Ile Marine Sandy Ground
☎ 33 (0)5 90 29 08 60
Fax 33 (0)5 90 29 08 96
l.ile.marine@wanadoo.fr
Budget Marine agent
Yachting Maintenance Anse
Marcel
☎ 33 (0)5 90 87 43 48
Fax 33 (0)5 90 87 43 84
francois.chevalier2@wanadoo.fr
Budget Marine agent
Profil Océan Sandy Ground
Bridge
☎ 33 (0)5 90 29 00 66
Fax 33 (0)5 90 20 00 67
profil@profil-ocean.com
Captain Oliver's Ship Oyster Pond
☎/*Fax 33 (0)5 90 87 48 01*
captoli@wanadoo.fr
*Dinghies/liferafts/outboards (sale
& repair)*
Egreteau Marine Services Sandy
Ground Bridge
☎ 33 (0)5 90 87 23 92
Fax 33 (0)5 90 87 23 96
alain.egreteau@wanadoo.fr
Madco Discount Bellevue
☎ 33 (0)5 90 51 05 40
Fax 33 (0)5 90 29 43 70
madco.sxm@wanadoo.fr
Profil Océan Sandy Ground
Bridge
☎ 33 (0)5 90 29 00 66

Fax 33 (0)5 90 20 00 67
profil@profil-ocean.com
Motorsports Marine Sandy
Ground/Lagoon
☎ 33 (0)5 90 29 00 41
Fax 33 (0)5 90 29 01 22
motsport@outremer.com
St-Martin Marine Center Sandy
Ground Bridge
☎ 33 (0)5 90 87 86 32
Fax 33 (0)5 90 87 04 28
st-martin-marine-
center@wanadoo.fr
Mechanics/diesel engines
Diesel Marine Services Port
Sandy Ground
☎ 33 (0)5 90 87 53 45
Fax 33 (0)5 90 87 20 14 VHF 71
dmssxm@powerantilles.com
Mécanique Yachting Caraïbes
Time Out Boatyard/Sandy Ground
☎ 33 (0)5 90 29 06 55
Fax 33 (0)5 90 51 08 12
Mendol Sandy Ground
☎ 33 (0)5 90 87 05 94
Fax 33 (0)5 90 87 07 78 VHF 16
mendol@wanadoo.fr
Bookay Marine Bellevue
☎/*Fax 33 (0)5 90 29 69 34*
bookay@wanadoo.fr
Electrics/hydraulics
JMC Time Out Boatyard/Sandy
Ground
☎ 33 (0)5 90 62 15 21
Fax 33 (0)5 90 29 09 79
jmcstmartin@wanadoo.fr
Workshops/welding
Mendol Sandy Ground
☎ 33 (0)5 90 87 05 94
Fax 33 (0)5 90 87 07 78 VHF 16
mendol@wanadoo.fr
MCJ Fabrication Aire de
Cadisco/Sandy Ground
☎ 33 (0)5 90 53 74 89
Fax 33 (0)5 90 87 33 91
mcjtemp@wanadoo.fr
Sailmakers/awnings/leatherwork
Incidences Sandy Ground Bridge
☎ 33 (0)5 90 87 06 04
Fax 33 (0)5 90 29 41 68
Sailen Sandy Ground
☎ 33 (0)5 90 87 53 72
Fax 33 (0)5 90 87 53 54 VHF 12
Arc en Ciel Time Out Boatyard
☎/*Fax 33 (0)5 90 29 53 39*
Sellerie Caraïbes St James
☎ 33 (0)5 90 87 77 29
Fax 33 (0)5 90 87 80 77
Voilerie Grenadine Auberge de la
Mer
☎ 33 (0)5 90 87 41 35
Fax 33 (0)5 90 87 00 99
grenadine3@wanadoo.fr
DIVING
Blue Océan Baie Nettlé
☎ 33 (0)5 90 87 89 73
Fax 33 (0)5 90 87 26 36
Sea Horse Diving Hotel Mercure
Baie Nettlé
☎ 33 (0)5 90 87 84 15
shd@wanadoo.fr
Scuba Fun Anse Marcel/Port la
Royale
☎ 33 (0)5 90 87 36 13
Fax 33 (0)5 90 87 36 52 VHF 12
contact@scubafun.com
The Scuba Shop Oyster Pond
☎/*Fax 33 (0)5 90 87 48 01*
info@thescubashop.net
Octoplus Grand'Case
☎ 33 (0)5 90 87 20 62
Fax 33 (0)5 90 87 20 63
octoplus@octoplus.fr
YACHT CHARTER
MARIGOT – PORT LA ROYALE
Anyway Marine
☎ 33 (0)5 90 87 91 41
Fax 33 (0)5 90 29 34 76
anyway@wanadoo.fr

Boat Rental Company
☎ 33 (0)5 90 87 91 74
Fax 33 (0)5 90 87 55 95

**OYSTER POND/CAPTAIN
OLIVER'S MARINA**
Moorings
☎ 33 (0)5 90 87 32 55
Fax 33 (0)5 90 87 32 54
moorings@moorings.fr
www.moorings.com
**Captain Oliver's Marina
Sunsail-Stardust**
☎ 33 (0)5 90 29 50 50
Fax 33 (0)5 90 87 31 58
sunsail.com
Sun Yacht Charters
☎ 33 (0)5 90 87 30 49
Fax 33 (0)5 90 87 31 58 VHF 74
Activités Desk
☎ 05 90 87 46 13
Fax 05 90 87 31 16
captoli@wanadoo.fr
Day and longer term charters

**ANSE MARCEL/PORT
LONVILLIERS**
VPM Antilles
☎ 33 (0)5 90 29 41 35
Fax 33 (0)5 90 29 42 75
vpmsaint-martin@cgit.com
Nautor's Swan Charters
☎ 33 (0)5 90 87 35 48
Fax 33 (0)5 90 87 35 50
nautor.swan@wanadoo.fr

Marine surveyors
Pujol Concordia
☎ 33 (0)5 90 87 94 00
Fax 33 (0)5 90 87 88 64
RESTAURANTS/HOTELS
MARIGOT
Le France (ex Bouchon) Marina
☎ 33 (0)5 90 29 20 90
*French food, crew meeting place,
price A–C*
Petite Auberge des Iles Marina
☎ 33 (0)5 90 87 56 31
French & Créole food, price A–C
La Belle Epoque Marina
☎ 33 (0)5 90 87 87 70
Fax 33 (0)5 90 52 09 15
Pizzas & French food, price B
Le Point G Marina
☎ 33 (0)5 90 66 10 33 05
Sushi bar & French food, price B
La Main à la Pâte Marina
☎/*Fax 33 (0)5 90 87 71 19*
*(Open Sunday lunchtime)
Italian & Mediterranean food,
price A–B*
Hotel Marina Royale Marina
☎ 33 (0)5 90 87 52 46
Fax 33 (0)5 90 87 92 88
Hotel: luxury
Durêche seafront
☎ 33 (0)5 90 87 84 21
*Fast food, price A–C
Frequented by local people*
Hotel Beach Plaza Baie de
Marigot
☎ 33 (0)5 90 87 00 70
Fax 33 (0)5 90 87 18 87
beachplaza@powerantilles.com
*Le Corsaire Restaurant French
food, price B–C
Hotel: luxury*
Ô Plongeoir near Semsamar
☎ 33 (0)5 90 87 94 71
Unusual food & decor,price B–C
Chili's Café Sandy Ground
☎ 33 (0)5 90 29 38 08
Tex Mex, price B–C

BAIE NETTLE
Layla's Beach
☎ 33 (0)5 90 51 00 93
Beach restaurant, price B

ORIENT BAY
Bikini Beach
☎ 33 (0)5 90 87 43 25
bikinibeach@wanadoo.fr
Beach restaurant, price B–C

OYSTER POND
Captain Oliver's Resort at the marina
☎ 33 (0)5 90 87 30 00
Fax 33 (0)5 90 87 40 84
captoli@wanadoo.fr
www.captainolivers.com
Buffet, french food, price D+
Hotel: very luxurious
Nice décor
Le Planteur on the hill
☎ 33 (0)5 90 29 53 21
Fax 33 (0)5 90 87 46 79
French food, price C–D

GRAND'CASE
L'Escapade
☎/*Fax* 33 (0)5 90 87 75 04
escapade@top-saint-martin.com
French food, price C–D, evenings only
Le Cottage
☎ 33 (0)5 90 29 03 30
Fax 33 (0)5 90 29 51 88
French food, good cellar, price C evenings only)
Il Nettuno
☎ 33 (0)5 90 87 77 38
Italian food, price B–C
La Case à Rhums on the beach
☎ 33 (0)5 90 53 30 62
Local food, crayfish, price B–C
Lolotte et Jojo on the beach
☎ 33 (0)5 90 87 05 65
Local food, price A–B
Calmos Café on the beach
☎ 33 (0)5 90 29 01 85
Local food & BBQ, price B–C

ANSE MARCEL/PORT LONVILLIERS
Hotel Méridien at the marina
'Habitation et Domaine de Lonvilliers'
☎ 33 (0)5 90 87 67 00
Fax 33 (0)5 90 87 30 38
esasxm@powerantilles.com
La Veranda Restaurant
☎ 33 (0)5 90 87 67 99
Buffet, French food, price D+
Hotel: very luxurious
Upmarket but rather kitsch Créole décor.
Le Privilège at the marina
☎ 33 (0)5 90 87 37 37
Fax 33 (0)5 90 87 33 75
hotel.privilege@wanadoo.fr
www.hotelprivilege.free.fr
French food, price C–D
Hotel: very luxurious
La Louisiane at the marina
☎ 33 (0)5 90 87 88 38
Fax 33 (0)5 90 87 44 12
privilege@wanadoo.fr
Traditional French food & pizzas, price A–C
Calypso at the marina
☎ 33 (0)5 90 29 41 60
Fax 33 (0)5 90 87 09 46
Fast food, salads, price A–B

CAR RENTAL
Island Trans Rent-A-Car Marigot, rue de Lowtown
☎ 33 (0)5 90 87 91 32
Fax 33 (0)5 90 87 70 87
Adventure Car Rental Auberge de la Mer
☎ 33 (0)5 90 29 23 74
Fax 33 (0)5 90 87 53 51
Just Rent a Car Baie Nettlé
☎ 33 (0)5 90 29 28 26
Fax 33 (0)5 90 29 28 80
Thrifty/Jumbo Car Central reservations
☎ 33 (0)5 90 29 24 24
Fax 33 (0)5 90 29 24 79

Sint Maarten

AIRLINES
Air France & Air Caraïbes
☎ 599 545 4212 *Fax* 599 545 3650
Air Canada
☎ 599 542 3316
KLM
☎ 599 545 4747 *Fax* 599 545 4748
American Airlines
☎ 599 545 2040 *Fax* 599 545 3461
Liat
☎ 599 545 4203 *Fax* 599 545 2402
Winair
☎ 599 545 2568 *Fax* 599 545 4229

FERRY COMPANIES
Voyager Bobby's Marina (to St Barts, Saba)
☎ 599 542 4096 *Fax* 599 542 2858
The Edge Pelican Marine (to Saba)
☎ 599 544 2640 *Fax* 599 544 2476
Link Ferry near Juliana Airport (to Anguilla)
☎ 264 497 2231 *Fax* 264 497 3290
fbconnon@anguillanet.com

MARINAS/DOCKS (FUEL AND WATER)
PHILIPSBURG/GREAT BAY MARINA
Bobby's Boatyard
☎ 599 542 2366 *Fax* 599 542 5442
VHF 16
bobmar@sintmaarten.net
Water & fuel
Great Bay Marina
☎ 599 542 5705 *Fax* 599 542 4940
gbmarina@sintmaarten.net
Water & fuel (at the end of the Old Pier)

SIMPSON BAY LAGOON/COLE BAY
Island Water World
☎ 599 544 5310 *Fax* 599 544 3299
VHF 16/74
service@islandwaterworld.com
Water & fuel
Princess Yacht Club
☎ 599 544 2953 *Fax* 599 544 4333
VHF 16/78 USA
princessyc@yahoo.com
Water & fuel
Simpson Bay Yacht Club Marina
☎ 599 544 2309 *Fax* 599 544 3378
VHF 16/79 USA
marina@SintMaarten.net
Water/Fuel
Palapa Marina
☎ 599 545 2735
Fax 599 545 2510 VHF 68
palapamarina@megatropic.com
Water & fuel

PROFESSIONAL YACHT SERVICES
Boatyards/haulout
SIMPSON BAY LAGOON/COLE BAY
Bobby's Boatyard Airport Road
☎ 599 545 2890 *Fax* 599 549 2889
VHF 16/69
at Great Bay Marina same ☎/*Fax* as marina
bobmar@sintmaarten.net
Island Water World
☎ 599 544 5310
Fax 599 544 3299 VHF 74
service@islandwaterworld.com
Chandleries/Dinghies
PHILIPSBURG/GREAT BAY MARINA
Island Water World Bobby's Marina
☎/*Fax* 599 542 2675
sales@islandwaterworld.com

COLE BAY
Budget Marine
☎ 599 544 3134
sales@budmar.an
Island Water World IWW Building

☎ 599 544 5310 *Fax* 599 544 3299
sales@islandwaterworld.com

SIMPSON BAY LAGOON
Budget Marine Simpson Bay Yacht Club
☎ 599 544 2866 *Fax* 599 544 4847
nau@budmar.an/sus@budmar.an
Sailmakers/awnings/riggers
SIMPSON BAY LAGOON/COLE BAY
Tropical Sail Loft BM Building Cole Bay
☎ 599 544 5472 *Fax* 599 544 5676
tsl@sintmaarten.net
Sint Maarten Sails opposite IWW Cole Bay
☎ 599 544 5231 *Fax* 599 544 5044
sxmsails@sintmaarten.net
FKG Rigging Cole Bay
☎ 599 544 4733
☎/*Fax* 599 544 2171
VHF 71 *Squarerigger*
fkg@megatropic.com
Mechanics/outboards
SIMPSON BAY LAGOON/COLE BAY
Momec/Diesel Outfitters warehouse 3B
☎/*Fax* 599 544 2320
Simpson Bay Diesel Services NV IWW Building
☎ 599 544 5397 *Fax* 599 544 5747
VHF 74
sbdiesel@sintmaarten.net
Allard Benjamin Palapa Marine Center
☎ 599 517 5055 *Fax* 599 544 2220
Simpson Bay Marine Yamaha Building
☎ 599 544 3249 *Fax* 599 544 2370
yamaha@friendlyisland.net
Joinery/GRP
PHILIPSBURG/GREAT BAY MARINA
SMX Woodworkers Philipsburg
☎/*Fax* 599 542 2851

SIMPSON BAY LAGOON
MSC Full Marine Services Palapa Marina
☎ 599 556 4479 *Fax* 599 545 2510
mscmarine@hotmail.com
Electrics/electronics/refrigeration
PHILIPSBURG
Radio Shack
☎ 599 542 3310 *Fax* 599 542 2497

SIMPSON BAY LAGOON/COLE BAY
Electec BM Building Cole Bay
☎ 599 544 2051 *Fax* 599 544 3641
electec@sintmaarten.net
Perma Frost Palapa Marina
☎ 599 522 5705 *Fax* 599 545 5599
permafrost@pocketmail.com
Necol S of Palapa Marina
☎ 599 545 2230 *Fax* 599 545 2349
necol@sintmaarten.net

DIVING
Scuba Shop Dive Safaris Bobby's Marina
☎ 599 542 9001 *Fax* 599 542 8983
Palapa Marina
☎ 599 545 3213 *Fax* 599 545 3209
keough@sintmaarten.net
Tradewinds Dive Great Bay Marina
☎ 599 547 5176 *Fax* 599 542 3605
Ocean Explorers Dive Center Simpson Bay Beach
☎ 599 544 5252 *Fax* 599 544 4357
Pelican Watersports/Aqua Mania
☎ 599 544 2640 *Fax* 599 544 2476

YACHT CHARTER
Sunsail Bobby's Marina
☎/*Fax* 599 542 2966
RESTAURANTS/HOTELS
Sea Food Galley Bobby's Marina
☎ 599 542 3253

Fish specialties, price C–D
Chesterfield's Great Bay Marina
☎/*Fax* 599 542 3484
Fish, price C–D
Barefoot Terrace Philipsburg
☎/*Fax* 599 542 0360
Créole food, price B
Reggae Cafe Philipsburg
☎ 599 542 1281 *Fax* 599 544 4984
reggaecafe@megatropic.com
American food, very lively, price A–B
Le Bec Fin Philipsburg
☎ 599 542 2976 *Fax* 599 544 4508
lebecfin@sintmaarten.net
French food, price C–D
L'Escargot Philipsburg
☎/*Fax* 599 542 2483
Seafood & French food, price C–D

MAHO BAY
Rosa Too
☎ 599 545 3470
Italian food, price B–C
Cherri's Cafe on the beach
☎ 599 545 3361
American food, price B

SIMPSON BAY/COLE BAY
Le Charolais Simpson Bay Marina
☎ 599 544 5531 *Fax* 599 544 4437
Grills, price B
Felix Restaurant
☎ 599 544 2797
Local and seafood, price B–C
Top Carrot Simpson Bay Yacht Club
☎ 599 544 3381
Vegetarian food, price B
Rancho Argentinian Grill Palapa Center
☎ 599 545 2495 *Fax* 599 545 2498
BBQ, price B–C
Dario's Princess Yacht Club
☎ 599 544 2201 *Fax* 599 544 5222
Italian food, price C–D

CAR RENTAL
Adventure Car Rental Airport Rd
☎ 599 544 3688
Cannegie Car Rental Philipsburg
☎ 599 542 2397 *Fax* 599 542 2497
Thrifty Car Rental Juliana Airport
☎ 599 545 2393
Fax 599 545 4231
Hertz Juliana Airport
☎ 599 545 4541 *Fax* 599 545 4540

Anguilla

AIRLINES
Tyden Air
☎ 264 497 2719 *Fax* 264 497 3079
tydenair@anguillanet.com
Air Anguilla
☎ 264 497 2643 *Fax* 264 497 2982
American Eagle
☎ 264 497 3131 *Fax* 264 497 3502
Liat/Winair
☎ 264 497 2238/5000
TAA (Trans Anguilla Airways)
☎ 264 497 8690 *Fax* 264 497 8689
transang@anguillanet.com
FERRY COMPANIES
The Link Ferry
☎ 264 497 2231 *Fax* 264 497 3290
fbconnor@anguillanet.com
PROFESSIONAL YACHT SERVICES
Chandlery
Ian's Chandlery Sandy Ground
☎ 264 497 5907 264 497 2914
Mechanic/outboards
Anguilla Techni-Sales/Rebel Marine Road Bay
☎ 264 497 2419 *Fax* 264 497 3319
DIVING
Anguillian Divers Ltd Meads Bay
☎ 264 497 4750 *Fax* 264 497 4632
axadiver@anguillanet.com

Anguillian Diving Adventures
Road Bay
☎ 264 235 8438
dcarty@anguillanet.com
Shoal Bay Scuba Hotel Allamanda
☎ 264 497 4371
sbsscuba@anguillanet.com

RESTAURANTS/HOTELS
Johnno's Sandy Ground
☎ 264 497 2728 Fax 264 497 8406
Live music at weekends
Local cuisine, price A–B
Ship's Galley, Sandy Ground
☎ 264 497 2040
Music at weekends
Fish & shellfish, price B
Bits & Bites Cyber Cafe
Sandy Ground
☎ 264 497 8364 (weather forecast
and Fax service)
bitsandbites@anguillanet.com
Breakfast, snacks, price A–B
Barrel Stay Sandy Ground
☎ 264 497 2831, on the beach
michelart@anguillanet.com
Creole & fish, price B–C
La Terrasse South Hill Plaza
☎ 264 497 6502 Fax 264 497 8899
Pizza & seafood, price B
Malliouhana Hotel Mead's Bay
☎ 264 497 6111 Fax 264 497 6011
International menu, price D+
Hotel: very luxurious
Mango's Barnes Bay
☎ 264 497 6479, Fax 264 497 6492
mangos@anguillanet
BBQ & local cuisine, price B–C
Roy's Place Crocus Bay
VHF 16
☎ 264 497 2470, Fax 264 497 5428
royboss1@anguillanet.com
Creole, fish, crayfish, price C–D
The Gorgeous Scilly Cay
Scilly Cay
☎ 264 497 5123, Fax 264 497 5981
gorgeous@anguillanet.com
Wonderful setting on a sandy islet
Fish BBQ, crayfish lunchtimes,
price C–D
Cap Juluca Maunday's Bay
☎ 264 497 6666 Fax 264 497 6617
Superb Moorish architecture
George's Restaurant
Mediterranean & Spanish
Price C+
Hotel: very luxurious
Cuisinart Resort & Spa
Rendez-Vous Bay
☎ 264 498 2000 Fax 264 498 2010
International menu with organic
food, price D+
Hotel: very luxurious
Rendez-Vous Bay Hotel
Rendez-Vous Bay
☎ 264 497 6549 Fax 264 497 6026
Cedar Grove Cafe West Indian
seafood, price B–C
Hotel: luxury
The Dune Preserve
Rendez-Vous Bay
☎ 264 497 7910 Fax 264 497 2660
Local food, fish, price A–B
Live music worth going to hear

CAR RENTAL
Island Car Rental airport
☎ 264 497 2723 Fax 264 497 3723
islandcar@anguillanet.com
High-Way Rent a Car George Hill
☎ 264 497 2183 Fax 264 497 2306
highway@anguillanet.com
Connor's Taxi & Car Rental
The Valley
☎ 264 497 6894 Fax 264 497 8305
VHF 16
Taxis Airport/Blowing Point

British Virgin Islands
AIRLINES
Air St Thomas Virgin Gorda
☎ 284 495 5935
To Puerto Rico, USVI
Cape Air Tortola
☎ 284 495 2100
To Puerto Rico, USVI, Anegada
Liat Tortola
☎ 284 495 1187
To Puerto Rico, Sint Maarten,
Antigua, St Vincent etc
Winair Tortola
☎ 284 495 2347
To Sint Maarten
Fly BVI Tortola
☎ 284 495 1747 Fax 284 495 1973
info@fly-bvi.com

FERRY COMPANIES
Inter-Island Boat Services
☎ 284 495 4166
Tortola (West End)/ St John's
(Cruz Bay)
Smith's Ferry Services
☎ 284 495 4495 Fax 284 494 2355
Tortola/St Thomas/Virgin Gorda
Speedy's Virgin Gorda
☎ 284 495 5240 Fax 284 495 5755
Tortola ☎ 284 495 6154 VHF 16
capsteve@surfbvi.com
Peter Island Ferry
☎ 284 494 2000
Tortola (Road Town)/Peter Island
Yacht Harbour
Jost van Dyke Ferry Service
☎ 284 494 2997
Pusser's Marina Cay Ferry
☎ 284 494 2174 –free
Saba Rock Resort Ferry Service
☎ 284 495 7111 in North Sound.

**MARINAS/DOCKS (WATER &
FUEL)**
TORTOLA
ROAD HARBOUR AREA
Fort Burt Marina Burt Point
☎ 284 494 4200 Fax 284 494 2547
Water & fuel (at the end of the
dock, unreliable)
Prospect Reef Marina Burt Point
☎ 284 494 3311 Fax 284 494 5595
resort@prospectreef.com
(no visiting yachts)
Water & fuel
Road Reef Marina Burt Point
☎ 284 494 2751 Fax 284 494 5166
tmm@candwbvi.net
Managed by TMM
Baugher's Bay Marina (ex CSY)
BVI Marine Services Ltd
☎ 284 494 2393 Fax 282 494 1183
VHF 16
fkrouwel@caribsurf.com
Water & fuel (easy approach)
Village Cay Marina Wickhams
Cay I
☎ 284 494 2771 Fax 284 494 2773
villcay@caribsurf.com
Water & fuel (Dock A)
Inner Harbour Marina Wickhams
Cay I
☎ 284 494 4289 Fax 284 494 6552
sailbvi@surfbvi.com
Managed by BVI Yacht Charters
Water & fuel
The Moorings Marina Wickhams
Cay II
☎ 284 494 2331 Fax 284 494 2226
moormm@candbvi.net
Managed by Footloose Sailing
Charters
Part of the same marina complex
Mariner Inn & Treasure Island
VHF 12 Dock
Water & fuel (West Quay)

NANNY CAY AREA
Nanny Cay Resort & Marina
☎ 284 494 2512 Fax 284 494 3288
VHF 16
nannycay@surfbvi.com

Water & fuel (at the quay near the
boatyard)
WEST END AREA
Soper's Hole Marina
☎ 284 495 4740 Fax 284 495 4301
VHF 16
sopershole@surfbvi.com
Water & fuel
Frenchman's Cay Shipyard
☎ 284 495 4050 Fax 284 495 4678
f.m.cshipyard@surfbvi.com

MAYA COVE ZONE
Hodge's Creek Marina
☎ 284 494 5538 Fax 284 494 6958
sunyacht@candwbvi.net
Managed by Sun Yacht
Charters/Stardust
Water & fuel

FAT HOG'S BAY/EAST END
Harbour View Marina
☎ 284 494 6892
twytort@surfbvi.com
Managed by Tradewind Yachts.
Penn's Landing Marina
☎ 284 495 1134 Fax 284 495 1352
VHF 12/16
penns@mmsbvi.com
Managed by Marine Management
Services.
Water on the dock

MARINA CAY AREA
Pusser's Marina Cay
☎ 284 494 2174 Fax 284 494 4775
marinacay@pussers.com
Water & fuel

VIRGIN GORDA
GORDA SOUND AREA
Biras Creek Marina North Sound
☎ 284 494 3555 Fax 284 494 3557
biras@biras.com
Water & fuel (dock on south bank)
Private dock
Bitter End Yacht Club Marina
North Sound
☎ 284 494 2746 Fax 284 494 4756
VHF 16
quarterdeck@bitterendbvi.com
Water & fuel
Saba Rock Resort North Sound
☎ 284 495 7711 Fax 284 495 7373
sabarock@caribsurf.com
Water
Leverick Bay Marina
☎ 284 495 7421 Fax 284 495 7367
VHF 16
leverick@surfbvi.com
Water & fuel (at the end of the
pontoon)

ST THOMAS BAY AREA
Virgin Gorda Yacht Harbour
☎ 284 495 5500 Fax 284 495 6390
VHF 16/11
vgyh@surfbvi.com
Managed by Little Dix Bay Hotel
Corporation
Water & fuel (South Quay)

PETER ISLAND
Peter Island Yacht Harbour
☎ 284 495 2000 Fax 284 495 2500
VHF 16
jroterberg@peterisland.net
Water & fuel (east quay)

ANEGADA
Kenneth's Station Service
Emergency fuel available, by jerry
can

**PROFESSIONAL YACHT
SERVICES**
TORTOLA
ROAD HARBOUR AREA
Boatyards/haulout
BVI Marine Services (ex CSY)
Baugher's Bay Marina
☎ 284 494 2393 Fax 282 494 1183
VHF 16
fkrouwel@caribsurf.com

Tortola Yacht Services Wickhams
Cay II
☎ 284 494 2124 Fax 284 494 4707
tys@tysbvi.com
Chandleries
Clarence Thomas Ltd Wickhams
Cay II
☎ 284 494 2359 Fax 284 494 2959
hispeed10k@hotmail.com
Golden Hind Chandlery
Tortola Yacht Center Wickhams
Cay II
☎ 284 494 2756 Fax 284 494 4707
chandlery@tysbvi.com
Island Marine Outfitters
Road Reef Plaza
☎ 284 494 2251 Fax 284 494 2290
ims@stcroixmarine.com
Paint Factory Port Purcell
☎ 284 494 1800 Fax 284 494 1803
serenity@surfbvi.com
Maintenance
Caribbean Refinishing Co
Tortola Yacht Center Wickhams
Cay II
☎ 284 494 3353
tobacco@surfbvi.com
Sailmakers/riggers
Doyle Sailmakers Road Reef
Marina
☎ 284 494 2569 Fax 284 494 2034
VHF 10
junior@doylecaribbean.com
ELM Sailmakers Ltd Road Town
☎/Fax 284 494 6455
Phillips Sail & Canvas Road Town
☎ 284 494 4982 Fax 284 494 8996
Richardson's Rigging Services
Road Town
☎ 284 494 2739 Fax 284 494 5436
Wickhams Cay II Rigging
Tortola Yacht Center Wickhams
Cay II
☎ 284 494 3979 Fax 284 494 4417
wickrigging@surfbvi.com
Island Marine Outfitters Road
Reef Plaza
☎ 284 494 2251 Fax 284 494 2290
ims@stcroixmarine.com
Mechanics/welding/workshops
Marine Power Services Ltd
Tortola Yacht Center Wickhams
Cay II
☎ 284 494 2738 Fax 284 494 2944
wycpower@surfbvi.com
Nautool Machine Ltd Wickhams
Cay II
☎ 284 494 3187 Fax 284 494 5629
nautool@surfbvi.com
Parts & Power Tortola Yacht
Center Wickhams Cay II
☎ 284 494 2830 Fax 284 494 6972
partspwr@candwbvi.net
T&W Machine Shop Baugher's
Bay
☎ 284 494 3342 Fax 284 494 1382
Outboards (sale/repair)
Tradewind Yachting Services Ltd
Fort Burt
☎ 284 494 3154 Fax 284 494 5892
tradewind@surfbvi.com
Electrics/electronics/refrigeration
Cay Electronics
☎ 284 494 2400
Fax 284 494 5389
caybvi@candwbvi.net
www.cayelectronics.com
Al's Marine Ltd Wickhams Cay II
☎ 284 494 4529 Fax 284 495 1833
alsmarine@surfbvi.com
Parts & Power Tortola Yacht
Center Wickhams Cay II
☎ 284 494 2830 Fax 284 494 6972
partspwr@candwbvi.net
Island Care Electronics Road Reef
Marina
☎ 284 494 3998 Fax 284 494 6761
CCT (Boatphone company)
Wickhams Cay II

☎ 284 494 3825 *Fax 284 494 4933*
info@bvicellular.com
Caribbean Technology Ltd
Wickhams Cay II
☎ 284 494 3150 *Fax 284 494 5389*
cabtech@caribsurf.com
Joiners
The Carpenter's Shop
Frenchman's Cay Shipyard
☎ 284 495 4353 *Fax 284 495 468*
The Woodshop
Baugher's Bay Marina
☎ 284 494 2393 *Fax 284 494 1183*
fkrouwel@surfbvi.com
Omega Caribbean Ltd
Wickhams Cay II
☎ 284 494 2943 *Fax 284 494 6119*

NANNY CAY AREA
Boatyard/haulout
Nanny Cay Resort & Marina Boatyard
☎ 284 494 2512 Fax 284 494 3288
nanycay@surfbvi.com
Chandleries
Island Marine Outfitters Nanny Cay
☎/Fax 284 494 0329
ims@stcroixmarina.com
Mechanic/welding/workshop
BVI Marine Management
☎ 284 494 2938 *Fax 284 494 5006*
VHF 16 (Rescuer 1)
rescuer1@surfbvi.com
Electronics
Island Care Electronics
☎ 284 494 6183 *Fax 284 494 6761*
Maintenance
BVI Painters Nanny Cay
☎ 284 494 4365/284 494 5960
BVI Marine Management
☎ 284 494 2938 *Fax 284 494 5006*
VHF 16 (Rescuer 1)
rescuer1@surfbvi.com
Virgin Islands Refinishing
Nanny Cay Boatyard
☎ 284 494 2512 *Fax 284 494 4548*

WEST END AREA
Boatyard/haulout
Frenchman's Cay Shipyard
☎ 284 495 4353 *Fax 284 495 4678*
f.m.cshipyard@surfbvi.com

FAT HOG/EAST END AREA
Chandleries
Marine Depot Inc Harbour View Marina
☎ 284 494 0098 *Fax 284 494 0099*
Maintenance
Wood's Marine Service Penn's Landing Marina
☎/Fax 284 494 0002
woodsjg@surfbvi.com
VI Shipwrights East End
☎ 284 495 4696 *Fax 284 495 4977*

VIRGIN GORDA YACHT HARBOUR AREA
Boatyard/haulout
Virgin Gorda Yacht Services
Virgin Gorda Yacht Harbour
☎ 284 495 5318 *Fax 284 495 5685*
vgyh@surfbvi.com
Chandleries/outboards
The Chandlery VGYH Shipyard
☎ 284 495 5628 *Fax 284 495 5677*
vgyh@surfbvi.com
Clarence Thomas Ltd The Valley
☎ 284 495 5091/284 495 5900
tlplumb@candwbvi.net
Bitter End OMC Bitter End Yacht Club
☎ 284 494 2745 *Fax 284 494 4756*
nikedowling@surfbvi.com
Sailmakers/awnings
Next Wave Sail & Canvas VGYH
☎/Fax 284 495 5623
nextwavebvi@hotmail.com

Maintenance
Caribbean Refinishing VGYH
☎ 284 495 5810 *Fax 284 495 5328*
tobacco@surfbvi.com
Joiners
The Workbench VGYH
☎ 284 495 5310 *Fax 284 495 5352*
wrkbench@surfbvi.com

DIVING (TRIPS/AIR/EQUIPMENT)
TORTOLA
Underwater Safaris
Wickhams Cay II, Moorings, Mariner Inn
☎ 284 494 3235 *Fax 284 494 5322*
info@underwatersafaris.com
Aquaventure Scuba Services
Village Cay Marina
☎ 284 494 4320 *Fax 284 494 5608*
aquavent@surfbvi.com
Blue Water Divers Nanny Cay
☎ 294 494 2847 *Fax 284 494 0198*
bwdbvi@surfbvi.com
UBS Dive Center Harbour View Marina
☎ 284 494 0024 *Fax 284 494 0623*
VHF 16
ubs@scubabvi.com
Baskin in the Sun
Prospect Reef ☎ 284 494 2858
Fax 284 494 4304
Soper's Hole ☎ 284 495 4582
reservations@baskininthe sun.com

VIRGIN GORDA
Dive BVI
Virgin Gorda Yacht Harbour
☎ 284 495 5513 *Fax 284 495 5347*
VHF 16
Leverick Bay Resort
☎ 284 495 7328
Marina Cay ☎ 284 495 9363
info@divebvi.com
Kilbride's Under Water Tours
Bitter End Yacht Club
☎ 284 495 9638 *Fax 284 495 7549*
sunscuba@surfbvi.com
Leverick Bay Watersports
Leverick Bay Resort
☎ 284 495 7376 *Fax 284 495 7014*
VHF 16

YACHT CHARTER
TORTOLA
Tortola Marine Management
Road Reef
☎ 284 494 2751 *Fax 284 494 5166*
tmm@surfbvi.com
Conch Boats Fort Burt Marina
☎ 284 494 4868 *Fax 284 494 5793*
conch@surfbvi.com
Footloose Sailing Charters
Wickhams Cay II
☎ 284 494 0528 *Fax 284 494 0529*
BVI Yacht Charters Village Cay Marina
☎ 284 494 4289 *Fax 284 494 6552*
sailbvi@surfbvi.com
Sunsail-Stardust Hodges Creek Marina, Road Town
☎ 284 495 1178
Fax 284 494 1111
www.sunsail.com
Moorings Road Town
☎ 284 494 2332
Fax 284 494 7940
moorings@moorings.fr
www.moorings.com
VPM Village Cay Marina
☎ 284 494 8998 *Fax 284 494 7277*
nlutyens@vpm.fr
Barecat Charters Fat Hog's Bay
☎/Fax 284 495 1979
barecat@candwbvi.net
Catamaran Charters Nanny Cay Marina
☎ 284 494 6661 *Fax 284 494 6698*
VHF 12
mdlp@surfbvi.com
Horizon Yacht Charters Nanny Cay Marina
☎ 284 494 8787 *Fax 284 494 8989*
info@horizonyachtcharters.com

North South Yacht Vacations
Nanny Cay Marina
☎ 284 494 0096 *Fax 284 495 7543*
ntsth@caribsurf.com
Virgin Traders Tortola Nanny Cay Marina
☎ 284 495 2526 *Fax 284 495 2678*
trudy@virgin-traders.com
Power boats

RESTAURANTS/HOTELS
Note: Most restaurants listen out on VHF 16 or 68

TORTOLA
ROAD HARBOUR AREA
Brandywine Restaurant
Brandywine Bay
☎ 284 495 2301 *Fax 284 495 1203*
brandywn@surfbvi.com
Italian specialities, fish, price D+
(Same proprietor as the Capriccio and the Calamaya)
Le Cabanon Road Town
☎ 284 494 8660 *Fax 284 494 0186*
lecabanonbvi@netscape.net
Elegant French food, good winelist, price C–D
Meeting place for Tortola's French community
Capriccio di Mare Road Town
☎ 284 494 5369 *Fax 284 495 1203*
Italian food & pizzas, price A–B
The Pusser's Co-Store & Pub
Road Town
☎ 284 494 3897 *Fax 284 494 2376*
Pub, pizzeria, boutique, price B–C
The Pub Fort Burt Marina
☎ 284 494 2608
Seafood & grills, price A–B
Music, yachtie rendezvous
Fort Burt Hotel & Restaurant
☎ 284 494 2587 284 494 2002
fortburt@surfbvi.com
International & local food, price C–D
Pleasant setting
Hotel: very luxurious
Prospect Reef Resort
☎ 284 494 3311 *Fax 284 494 5595*
resort@prospectreef.com
Callaloo Restaurant
Local food, price C–D
Overlooking the marina
Hotel: very luxurious
C&F Restaurant (Carol & Franck)
Purcell Estate, near Rite Way supermarket
☎ 284 494 4941 *Fax 284 494 1088*
Elegant local food, BBQ, price B–C
Spaghetti Junction Inner Harbour
☎ 284 494 4880
Italian food, price B–C
Village Cay Marina & Hotel
☎ 284 494 2771 *Fax 284 494 2773*
villcay@candwbvi.net
Local & continental food, pizzas, price B
Hotel: comfortable
Virgin Queen Pub Baugher's Bay
☎ 284 494 2310
Local and pizzeria, price B

NANNY CAY AREA
Nanny Cay Resort
☎ 284 494 4895 *Fax 284 494 0555*
nannycay@surfbvi.com
Peg Leg's Restaurant
☎ 284 494 0028 *Fax 284 494 3288*
International menu & pizzas, price C–D
Hotel: luxury
Plaza Cafe
☎ 284 494 2512
Fast food & snacks, price A–B

WEST END AREA
Club House Restaurant
☎ 284 495 4844 *Fax 284 495 4056*
BBQ, fish, price B–C
Hotel: comfortable
The Jolly Roger Inn
☎ 284 495 4559 *Fax 284 495 4184*
louis@candwbvi.net

Terrace dining with pleasant ambiance
Local food, price C
Hotel: comfortable
The Pusser's Landing
Frenchman's Cay
☎ 284 495 4554 *Fax 284 494 4976*
Seafood, BBQ, price B–C
Live music on Fridays
Frenchman's Cay Hotel
☎ 284 495 4844 *Fax 284 495 4056*
fmchotel@candwbvi.net
Terrace dining with pleasant ambiance
Hotel: comfortable
Kelly's get there by dinghy through the creek
☎ 284 495 4304 *Fax 284 495 4453*
Local food, price A
Emergency provisioning.

CANE GARDEN AREA
Myett's Garden & Grill Cane Garden Bay
☎ 284 495 9649 *Fax 284 495 9579*
myettent@surfbvi.com
Local food, BBQ, price B
live music at weekends
Sugar Mill Apple Bay
☎ 284 495 4355 *Fax 284 495 4696*
sugmill@candwbvi.net
International & local food, price C–D
Hotel: luxury
Restored mill

TRELLIS BAY/MARINA CAY AREA
The Last Resort Trellis Bay
☎ 284 495 2520
American food, price C
Music
De Loose Mongoose Trellis Bay
☎ 284 495 2303 *Fax 284 495 1611*
mongoose@surfbvi.com
American grills, price B
Hotel: Beef Island Guest House comfortable
Trellis Bay Cyber Cafe Trellis Bay
☎ 284 495 2447 *Fax 284 495 1626*
jwright@surfbvi.com
Marina Cay Resort on the islet
☎ 284 494 2174 *Fax 284 494 4775*
marinacay@pussers.com
Local food, BBQ, price D
Hotel: luxury, rooms & cottages
Free ferry from Beef Island

FAT HOG'S BAY/EAST END
Harbour View restaurant
Harbour View Marina
☎ 284 495 2797 VHF 16
mickdoro@surfbvi.com
Terrace above the chandlery
American & continental food, price B
Eclipse Restaurant Penn's Landing Marina
☎/Fax 284 495 1646
Local food & seafood, price A–B
Fat Hog's Bob's
☎ 284 495 1010 VHF 16
Local food, BBQ, price A–B
Terrace beside the reef

MAYA COVE AREA
Calamaya Hodges Creek Marina
☎ 284 495 2126 *Fax 284 495 1203*
Mediterranean & Italian food, price B–C
Music at weekends
Pelican's Cafe Hodges Creek Marina
☎ 284 495 1515 *Fax 284 495 1111*
wodgercox@hotmail.com
Snack, pizzas, price B

CARROT BAY AREA
Mrs Scatliffe's
☎ 284 495 4556
Local food, homecooked, price A–B
Book in advance.
Clem's By the Sea
☎ 284 495 4350

Local food, BBQ, price A–B
Live music Mondays

VIRGIN GORDA
ST THOMAS BAY AREA
Bath & Turtle Pub in the arcade
☎ 284 495 5239 *Fax* 284 495 5963
bathturtle@surfbvi.com
Snacks & salads, price A–B
Same proprietor as the Bamboo
Chez Bamboo
☎ 284 495 5752
Evenings only
Seafood & Créole food, price B–C
Jazz on Fridays

LITTLE DIX BAY AREA
Little Dix Bay Resort VGYH
☎ 284 495 5555 *Fax* 284 495 5661
ldbhotel@surfbvi.com
Le Pavilion French food
Dinner & dancing with buffet at
weekends, very dressy, price D+
The Sugar Mill lunch, price D

SAVANNA & MAHOE BAY AREA
Giorgio's Table Mahoe Bay
☎/*Fax* 284 495 5684 VHF 16
giorgiostable@surfbvi.com
Italian food, price D+
Accessible by dinghy, depending
on sea state
Mango Bay Resort Mahoe Bay
☎ 284 495 5672 *Fax* 284 495 5674
mangobay@surfbvi.com
Hotel: luxury cottages

GORDA SOUND AREA
Drake's Anchorage Inn Resort
Mosquito Island
☎ 284 495 5871 *Fax* 284 495 7045
'French' food, price D+
Hotel: luxury bungalows
Leverick Bay Resort Leverick Bay
☎ 284 495 7421
Fax 284 495 7367
info@leverickbay.com
Hotel: luxury
(Spa at Leverick Bay
☎ 284 495 7367)
The Lighthouse Leverick Bay
☎ 284 495 7154 *Fax* 284 495 7329
lighthouse@surfbvi.com
International, seafood &grills,
price B–C
The Biras Creek Resort North
Sound
☎ 284 494 3555 *Fax* 284 494 3557
caribisles@aol.com
International, seafood &grills,
price D+
Hotel: very luxurious cottages
The Bitter End Club House North
Sound
☎ 284 494 2746 *Fax* 284 494 4756
The Club House Restaurant buffet
& international menu, price C–D
Hotel: very luxurious cottages
Saba Rock Resort North Sound
☎ 284 495 7711 *Fax* 284 495 7373
sabarock@caribsurf.com
Entertainment, mooring buoys,
provisioning, water, ferry
International & seafood, price C–D
Hotel: comfortable
Sand Box Beach Prickly Pear
Island
☎ 284 495 9123 *Fax* 284 495 9127
sandbox@surfbvi.com
Local food, seafood, price A–B

JOST VAN DYKE
GREAT HARBOUR AREA
Ali Baba's
☎ 284 495 9280 VHF 16
Local food, seafood, BBQ, price C
Band during the season,
Friday/Monday
Club Paradise
☎ 284 495 9267 *Fax* 284 495 9633
VHF 16
Seafood, BBQ, price C
Foxy's Tamarind Restaurant

☎ 284 495 9258 *Fax* 284 495 9892
info@foxysbar.com
Local food, price B–C
Musical entertainment
Rudy's Mariner's
☎ 284 495 9282
Local food, seafood, price B–C
Buffet, live music Thursdays,
minimarket
Hotel: simple rooms
Sandcastle White Bay
☎ 284 495 9888 *Fax* 284 495 9999
relax@sandcastle-bvi.com
Local & American food, price B–C
Hotel: simple rooms

LITTLE HARBOUR AREA
Harris's Place
☎ 284 495 9295 *Fax* 284 495 9296
VHF 16
BBQ, seafood, price B–C
Live music Thursdays
Abe's
☎ 284 495 9329 *Fax* 284 495 9529
VHF 16
Local food, price B, emergency
stores

PETER ISLAND
Peter Island Resort
☎ 284 495 2000 *Fax* 284 495 2500
peterisd@candwbvi.net
Tradewinds Restaurant
international food, price C–D
Hotel: very luxurious rooms &
cottages

ANEGADA
Anegada Reef Hotel
☎ 284 495 8002 *Fax* 284 495 9362
aneghtl@surfbvi.com
Seafood, price C–D
Hotel: very luxurious
The Big Bamboo Loblolly Bay
☎ 284 495 2019 VHF 16
Local food, seafood, price B–C
The Neptune's Treasure
☎/*Fax* 294 495 9439
neptunetreasure@surfbvi.com
Seafood, price C–D
Hotel: very luxurious cottages
The Pomato Point Beach Resort
The Lobster Trap Restaurant
☎ 284 495 9466
Seafood, price D+
Whistling Pines
☎ 284 495 9521 VHF 16
whistpines@surfbvi.com
Seafood, BBQ, price B–C

COOPER ISLAND
Cooper Island Beach Club
Manchioneel Bay
☎ 284 494 3721 *Fax* 284 495 9180
CIBC@surfbvi.com
Local fast food, price C
Hotel: luxury studios

NORMAN ISLAND
Billy Bones
VHF 16 (dinghy dock)
pirates@surfbvi.com
Seafood, grills, price B–C
William Thornton floating
restaurant
☎ 284 494 0183 *Fax* 284 494 6543
Fast food, price B–C
CAR RENTAL
TORTOLA
Hertz Village Cay Marina
☎ 284 494 6228/284 494 6060
hertzbvi@hotmail.com
Dollar Rent a Car
Prospect Reef/Long Bay Beach
☎ 284 494 6093 *Fax* 284 494 7837
dollar@surfbvi.com
Waterfront Taxi Association Road
Town
☎ 284 494 3456/284 494 6456

Taxi Dinghy Dock West End
☎ 284 495 4934/284 495 4881
VIRGIN GORDA
Mahogany Car Rentals South
Valley
☎ 284 495 5469 *Fax* 284 495 5072
Hertz The Valley
☎ 284 495 5803
Speedy's Car Rental The Valley
☎ 284 495 5240 *Fax* 284 495 5755
capsteve@surfbvi.com
ANEGADA
ABC Jeep Rentals
☎ 284 495 8018/284 495 9466
Tony's Taxi & Bike Rentals
☎ 284 495 8027

St John USVI

FERRY COMPANIES
Inter Boat Services Cruz Bay
☎ 340 776 6597
Varlack Ventures Inc Cruz Bay
☎ 340 776 6412
DOCK
Caneel Bay Shipyard
☎ 340 693 8771
Water & fuel
**PROFESSIONAL YACHT
SERVICES**
Boatyard/Haulout
Caneel Bay Shipyard
☎ 340 693 8771
Mechanics/chandleries
Budget Marine
☎ 340 774 2667 *Fax* 340 774 9292
budmar@islands.vi
Barry's Small Engine Repair
☎ 340 776 7464
Coral Bay Marine Service
☎ 340 6665 *Fax* 340 776 6859
VHF 16
In a truck near the landing stage
Dr Knight & Co
☎ 340 776 7958
Sailmakers/awnings
The Canvas Factory Cruz Bay
☎ 340 776 6196
Coral Bay Sails
☎ 340 776 6665 *Fax* 340 776 6859
VHF 16
DIVING
**Cinnamon Bay Water Sports
Center**
☎ 340 776 6330
Coral Bay Water Sports
☎ 340 776 6850
Cruz Bay Water Sports
☎ 340 776 6234
Low Key Cruz Bay
☎ 340 693 8999 *Fax* 340 693 8987
lowkey@viaccess.net
Saint John Water Sports
☎ 340 776 6256
**Natural Park Guided Snorkeling
Trip**
☎ 340 776 6201
RESTAURANTS/HOTELS
Skinny Legs Coral Bay
☎ 340 779 4982
Salads, burgers, price A–B
Just Pepe's Coral Bay
☎/*Fax* 340 776 6800
American food & salads, price
A–B
Lovely airy terrace with unusual
decor
Asolare Caneel Hill on the hill
☎ 340 779 4747
European & Asian food, price C–D
Paradiso Restaurant Cruz Bay
Mongoose Junction complex
☎ 340 693 8899
Modern American cuisine, price
C–D
Diner with André Cruz Bay
☎ 340 693 7399

purplefrog777@hotmail.com
French, price B–C
Café Wahoo Cruz Bay
☎ 340 776 6600
Wharfside Village complex
International food & seafood,
price C–D
Gorgeous terrace
Banana Deck Cruz Bay
☎ 340 776 5055
Wharfside Village complex
American food, seafood, price B
Divers' rendezvous
The Fish Trap Raintree Court Cruz
Bay
☎ 340 693 8590
raintree@island.vi
Seafood, price B–C
Caneel Bay Plantation Resort
Caneel Bay
☎ 340 776 6111 *Fax* 340 693 8280
Equator Restaurant International
food, price D+
Hotel: luxury, rooms & cottages
Old 18th century plantation
Ellington's Gallows Point
☎ 340 693 8490
International food, price B–C
Wonderful view
Château de Bordeaux Carolina
☎ 340 776 6611
International food, price C–D
**CAR RENTAL/TAXI
COMPANIES/ISLAND TOURS**
Delbert Hill's Jeep Rental Cruz
Bay for taxis & tours
☎ 340 776 6637
St John Car Rental
☎/*Fax* 340 776 6103
Spencer's Jeep & Taxi Service
Cruz Bay
☎ 340 693 8784 *Fax* 340 693 8399

St Thomas USVI

AIRLINES
American Airlines/Eagle
☎ 1 800 474 4884
Air St Thomas
☎ 340 776 2992
Cape Air ☎ 340 774 3700
Liat ☎ 340 774 2313
FERRY COMPANIES
Inter Island Boat Services
☎ 340 776 6597
Smith's Ferry Services Ltd
Veteran's Drive
☎ 340 775 7292 *Fax* 340 774 5532
The Native Sun Charlotte Amalie
☎ 340 774 8685
MARINAS/DOCKS (WATER/FUEL)
CHARLOTTE AMALIE AREA
Safehaven Marina
☎ 340 774 6050 *Fax* 340 774 5935
VHF 16
Water & fuel
Frenchtown Marina
☎ 340 777 9690 *Fax* 340 777 9750
VHF 16
john@cyoacharters.com
Water, no fuel

CROWN BAY AREA
Crown Bay Marina
☎ 340 774 2255 *Fax* 340 776 2760
VHF 16
info@crownbay.com
Water & fuel

BENNER BAY AREA
Compass Point Marina
☎ 340 775 6144 *Fax* 340 779 1547
davesdiesel@islands.vi
Water & fuel
La Vida Marina
☎ 340 779 2799 *Fax* 340 779 1937
lavidamarina@vitelcom.net
Water & fuel
Saga Haven Marina
☎ 340 775 0520

Fish Hawk Marina
☎ 340 775 9058 *Fax* 340 775 9701
Water & fuel

RED HOOK AREA
American Yacht Harbor
☎ 340 775 6454 *Fax* 340 776 5970
VHF 11
cgroce@americanyachtharbor.
com
Water & fuel
Vessup Point Marina
☎ 340 779 2495
alaunt53@hotmail.com
Sapphire Beach Marina
☎ 340 775 6100 *Fax* 340 775 4024
VHF 16
sbmsales@islands.vi
Water & fuel

**PROFESSIONAL YACHT
SERVICES**
CHARLOTTE AMALIE AREA
Chandlers
Island Marine Outfitters
Safehaven Marina
☎ 340 776 0088 *Fax* 340 776 8123
im.outfitters@att.net
Lighthouse Vitraco Park
☎ 340 774 4379 *Fax* 340 774 1840
lighthouse@islands.vi
Budget Marine Vitraco Park
☎ 340 774 2667 *Fax* 340 774 9292
budmars@islands.vi
Sailmaker/awnings
Virgin Islands Canvas Safehaven
Marina
☎ 340 774 3229
Mechanics/diesel repair
Gary's Marine Services La Vida
Marina
☎ 340 779 2717
VI Techno Diesel West Indian
Quay
☎ 340 776 3080 *Fax* 340 774 9292
Electronics/refrigeration
Electronic Unlimited
☎ 340 777 7000 *Fax* 340 777 7007
Reefco Marine Refrigeration
Safehaven Marina
☎/*Fax* 340 776 0038
dennyreefco.vi@worldnett.att.net
Joiners/welding
Monty's Hassel Island
☎ 340 774 4538
Custom Welding & Repairs
Frenchtown
☎ 340 774 3879

CROWN BAY AREA
Boatyard/haulout
Haulover Marine Yachting Center
Sub Base
☎ 340 776 2078 *Fax* 340 779 8426
haulover@viaccess.net
Chandlers
Island Marine Outfitters
Sub Base
☎ 340 714 0788/340 774 8877
Crown Bay Marina
☎ 340 776 0753
Fax 340 776 8123
Sailmaker/awnings/riggers
Bayside Canvas Gregerie East
☎/*Fax* 340 775 4422
Shadows Sail Loft Haulover
Complex
☎ 340 777 5638 *Fax* 340 777 5632
shadows@islands.vi
Island Rigging & Hydraulics Sub
Base
☎ 340 774 6833 *Fax* 340 5024
islrig@viaccess.net
Mechanics/electrics/outboards
A & J Power System Haulover
Complex
☎ 340 774 5590
Crown Bay Maritime Crown Bay
Marina
☎ 340 774 6085 *Fax* 340 774 9372
crownbaymar@vitelcom.net

Offshore Marine Sub Base
☎ 340 776 5432 *Fax* 340 775 4507
stan@offshorevi.com
Power Distributors Inc Crown Bay
Marina
☎ 340 774 6085
pdi@islands.vi

BENNER BAY AREA
Boatyard/haulout
Independent Boatyard
☎ 340 776 0466 *Fax* 340 775 6576
independance44@hotmail.com
*Chandlers/watersports
equipment/dinghies*
Budget Marine Independent Boat
Yard
☎ 340 778 2219 *Fax* 340 714 0466
budmarby@islands.vi
Caribbean Inflatable East End
Boat Park
☎ 340 775 6159 *Fax* 340 775 2014
cisco@viaccess.net
Sailmaker/awnings/riggers
Compass Point Canvas Compass
Point Marina
☎ 340 779 2788
Skip's Rigging Compass Point
Marina
☎ 340 779 1651 *Fax* 340 779 3590
Island Rigging & Hydraulics
Independent Boatyard
☎ 340 779 2960
Mechanics/outboards
Garry's Marine Services La Vida
Marina
☎ 340 779 2712
T & J Outboard Repairs Compass
Point Marina
☎ 340 775 5505 *Fax* 340 775 0585
riverside10@worldnet.att.net
Dave's Diesel Service Compass
Point Marina
☎ 340 775 9912 *Fax* 340 779 1547
davesdiesel@islands.vi
Benner Bay Marine Independent
Boatyard
☎ 340 779 2631
*Subsidiary of Offshore Marine at
Sub Base*
Electrics/electronics/refrigeration
Tropicom Associates La Vida
Marina
☎ 340 775 4107
Nautelec Inc Compass Point
Marina
☎ 340 775 1863
nautelec@viaccess.net
Dave Gott
☎ 340 775 4540
Joiners
Yacht Carpentry Plus Independent
Boatyard
☎ 340 775 9255 *Fax* 340 775 6576
Sailmark Designs La Vida Marina
☎ 340 779 2060
Wood Shop Compass Point
Marina
☎ 340 775 4940
reddoy@islands.vi

RED HOOK AREA
*Chandlers/watersports
equipment/outboards*
Island Marine Outfitters AYH
☎ 340 775 6789 *Fax* 340 775 6789
Island Yachts
☎ 340 775 6666 *Fax* 340 714 4194
sailing@iyc.vi
Bruce Merced
☎ 340 775 7075
Sailmaker/awnings
Sail Loft/Doyle Sailmakers
American Yacht Harbor
☎ 340 775 1712 *Fax* 340 714 4286
sailloft@islands.vi
Workshop/welding
All Island Machine Shop
☎ 340 775 7676

Surveyors
Howe Marine Surveys East End
Boat Park
☎/*Fax* 340 775 6081
whowe@iname.com
Davis Marine Compass Point
Marina
☎ 340 776 0284 *Fax* 340 776 0276
tdavis@viaccess.net
DIVING
Chris Sawyer Diving Center
Compass Point ☎ 340 775 7320
Fax 340 775 9495
American YH ☎ 340 777 7804
sawyerdive@islands.vi
Blue Island Divers Crown Bay
Marina
☎ 340 774 2001 *Fax* 340 777 9600
diveusvi@islands.vi
St Thomas Diving Club Charlotte
Amalie
☎ 340 776 2381 *Fax* 340 777 3232
Underwater Safaris Safehaven
Marina
☎ 340 774 1350 *Fax* 340 777 8733
VHF 7
vws@diveusvi.com
Caribbean Divers East End Boat
Park
☎ 340 775 6384 *Fax* 340 775 0822
cardiv1@aol.com
Coki Beach & Dive Club Coki
Beach
☎ 340 775 4220
pete@cokidive.com
Dive in Sapphire Marina Sapphire
Marina
☎ 340 775 6100 *Fax* 340 777 9029
diveinusvi@worldnet.att.net
YACHT CHARTER
VIP Yacht Charters Compass
point
☎ 340 776 1510 *Fax* 340 779 2543
millarg@compuserve.com
CYOA Frenchmen Marina
☎ 340 777 9690
Fax 340 777 9750
john@cyoacharters.com
Island Yachts American Yacht
Harbor
☎ 340 775 6666 *Fax* 340 714 4194
sailing@iyc.vi
Limnos Charter American Yacht
Harbor
☎ 340 775 3203 *Fax* 340 775 3790
limnos@att.net
RESTAURANTS/HOTELS
CHARLOTTE AMALIE AREA
Alexander's Frenchtown
☎ 340 774 4349
*Local & international food, price
B–C*
Lovely setting
Chickie's Place Frenchtown
☎ 340 714 2204
*International & French food, price
C–D*
Hook, Line & Sinker Frenchtown
☎ 340 776 9708
Local & seafood, price A–B
At the fishing harbour
Craig & Sally Frenchtown
☎ 340 777 9949
International menu, price B–C
The Pointe Frenchtown
☎ 340 774 4262
Buffet, French food, price C–D
Lovely house in a park (Villa Olga)
Hervé Government Hill
☎ 340 777 9703
French & Créole food, price C–D
Lovely view & pleasant setting
Hotel 1829 on Government Hill
☎ 340 776 1829 *Fax* 340 776 4313
Seafood, price D
Hotel: luxury
Mafolie Hotel on the hills above
Charlotte Amalie
☎ 340 774 2790 *Fax* 340 774 4091
Lindy's Restaurant local food,

price C
Hotel: comfortable
Lovely view
Gladys Café Charlotte Amalie
Music on Fridays
☎ 340 774 6604
Local food, price B

CROWN BAY AREA
Carib Beach Resort Lindbergh Bay
☎ 340 774 2525 *Fax* 340 777 4131
Hotel: luxury
The Isalnd Beachcomber Hotel
Lindbergh Bay
☎ 340 774 5250
ibh.vi@worldnet.att.net
Hotel: luxury
Tickles Dockside Pub Sub Base
☎ 340 7766 1595
Seafood, snacks, price A–B
On the terrace above the marina
Victor's New Hideout Sub Base
☎ 340 776 9379
Local food, fish, seafood, price B

BENNER BAY AREA
Bottoms Up Independent
Boatyard
☎ 340 775 *Fax* 340 715
Local food, BBQ, price A–B
Raffles Restaurant Compass Point
☎ 340 775 6004 *Fax* 340 715 1035
*International, West Indian food &
seafood, price B–C*

RED HOOK AREA
Café Wahoo American Yacht
Harbor
☎ 340 775 6350
*International menu & seafood,
price B–C*
Terrace at the marina
**A Whale of a Tale & Molly
Malones** American Yacht Harbor
☎ 340 775 1270 *Fax* 340 714 4234
*International menu & seafood,
price B–C*
At the marina
Latitude 18 Vessup Marina
☎ 340 779 2495
Salads & BBQ, price A–B
Agave Restaurant East end
☎ 340 775 1270 *Fax* 340 714 4234
International menu, price B–C
Lovely setting & view
Sapphire Beach Resort Sapphire
Beach
☎ 340 775 6100 *Fax* 340 775 2403
sbrsales@isalnds.vi
Hotel: luxury, rooms & bungalows

ELSEWHERE
The Old Stone Farmhouse
Mayen's Bay
☎ 340 777 6277
International menu, price D
Old plantation, near golf course
CAR RENTAL/ISLAND TOURS
Budget Rent a Car
Crown Bay ☎ 340 776 4324
Sapphire Beach ☎ 340 775 0637
Charlotte Amalie ☎ 340 776 5340
John's Auto Center Crown Bay
☎ 340 774 8740 *Fax* 340 774 8720
johnsauto@viaccess.net
Tri Island Car Rental
Havensight ☎ 340 776 2879
Red Hook ☎ 340 775 1200
Taxi Association
☎ 340 774 4550
East End Taxi Service
☎ 340 775 6974

St Croix

AIRLINES

American Airlines/Eagle
☎ 340 778 1140
Dolphin Airlines
☎ 340 778 7650
Liat ☎ 340 778 9930
Fax 340 778 9634

MARINAS/DOCKS (WATER/FUEL)

St Croix Marina Gallows Bay
☎ 340 773 0289
Fax 340 778 8974 VHF 16
stcroixmarinacopr@worldnet.
att.net
Water & fuel
Green Cay Marina
☎ 340 773 1453 *Fax* 340 773 9651
VHF 16/68
gcmarina@islands.vi
john@cyoacharters.com
Water & fuel
Salt River Marina
☎ 340 778 9650 *Fax* 340 778 0706
VHF 16
info@crownbay.com
Water, fuel deliveries
St Croix Yacht Club
☎ 340 773 9531 *Fax* 340 778 8350
stcroixyc@vitelcom.net

PROFESSIONAL YACHT SERVICES

Boatyard/haulout
St Croix Marine Boatyard Gallows
Bay
☎ 340 773 0289 *Fax* 340 778 8974
VHF 16
stcroixmarinacopr@worldnet.att.
net

Chandleries/watersports equipment
Island Marine Outfitters St Croix
Marina
☎ 340 773 0289 *Fax* 340 778 8974
The New Paint Locker
Christiansted
☎ 340 773 0105 *Fax* 340 773 0887

Sailmakers/awnings/riggers
Canvas Loft Christiansted
☎ 340 773 3044 *Fax* 340 774 9292
shadows@islands.vi
Wesco Awning & Marine Canvas
☎ 340 778 9446

Mechanic/outboards
Outboards Only Frederiksted
☎ 340 772 0300

Electrics/electronics
Al's Marine Christiansted
☎ 340 773 5611
Glentonics
☎ 340 778 6505
Robert Electronics
☎ 340 778 6640

Boatbuilder
Gold Coast Yacht Salt River
Marina
☎ 340 778 1004 *Fax* 340 778 2859

DIVING

Anchor Dive Center Salt River
Marina
☎ 0 800 532 3483
Fax 340 778 1522
anchordivecenter@juno.com
Big Beard's Christiansted
☎ 340 773 4482 *Fax* 340 773 7977
bigbeards@unitedstates.vi
Dive Experience Club Comanche
☎ 340 773 3307 *Fax* 340 7030
Mile Mark Watersports
Christiansted
☎ 340 773 7400 *Fax* 340 773 2628
Cane Bay Dive Shop Cane Bay
☎ 340 773 9913 *Fax* 340 778 5442
canebay@viaccess.net
Scubawest Frederiksted
☎ 340 772 3701 *Fax* 340 713 1459
adventure@divescubawest.com

RESTAURANTS/HOTELS

CHRISTIANSTED AREA

Cormorant Beach Club
☎ 340 778 8920 *Fax* 340 778 9218
Local food, price C–D
Hotel: luxury
Swimming pool, tennis courts
Royal Garden near St Croix
Marina
☎ 340 773 3424 *Fax* 340 773
92220
*Thai & Vietnamese food, price
C–D*
King Christian Hotel
☎ 340 773 6330 *Fax* 340 773 9411
kchotel@viaccess.net
Hotel: comfortable
Harbour view
STIXX at the harbour
☎ 340 773 5157
Pizzas, seafood, BBQ, price B–C
Yachtie rendezvous, very lively
Fort Christian Brew Pub at the
harbour
☎ 340 713 9820 *Fax* 340 778 1486
golfnsand@worldnet.att.net
New Orleans food, price C

GREEN CAY MARINA

Tamarind Reef Hotel
☎ 340 773 4455 *Fax* 340 773 3989
tamarind@usvi.net
*The Deep End Bar, international
menu, price, D*
Hotel: luxury
The Galleon
☎ 340 774 9949
thegalleon@virginislands.net
*French & International food, price
D*
Piano bar

CANE BAY & NORTH

The Waves
☎ 340 778 1805 *Fax* 340 778 4945
Local food, price B–C
Hotel: comfortable, studios
Hibiscus Hotel
☎ 340 773 4042
Fax 340 773 7668
Hotel: comfortable studios

SALT RIVER MARINA AREA

Columbus Cove
☎ 340 778 5771
Very simple local food, price A–B

FREDERIKSTED

Café du Soleil
☎ 340 772 5400
*Seafood & continental food, price
C–D*
Le St Tropez
☎ 340 772 3000 *Fax* 340 772 9775
ducsxt@viaccess.net
French & local food, price C–D
French owned
Pier 69 Strand Square
☎ 340 772 0069 *Fax* 340 772 1441
Salads, snacks, price A–B
Sunset Grill Sprat Hall
☎ 340 772 5855
Local food, BBQ, price B
Good for glorious sunsets

CAR RENTAL/ISLAND TOURS

Budget Airport
☎ 340 778 9636 *Fax* 340 778 7201
Olympic Car Rental
Christiansted ☎ 340 773 6997 *Fax*
340 773 6870
Frederiksted ☎ 340 772 1617
olympic@viaccess.net
St Croix Heritage Tours
Christiansted
☎ 340 773 6997 *Fax* 340 719 9079

Index